PIONEERS OF THE BLUES REVIVAL

Music in American Life

A list of books in the series appears at the end of this book.

The folk whose blues
inhabit wilderness, renew a truth.
Figure Foundation

PIONEERS
OF THE
BLUES REVIVAL

Expanded Second Edition

STEVE CUSHING

•

INTRODUCTION BY BARRY LEE PEARSON

UNIVERSITY OF ILLINOIS PRESS
Urbana, Chicago, and Springfield

P 5 4 3 2 1
∞ This book is printed on acid-free paper.

Frontispiece: Tampa Red at Sacred Heart Home, Chicago, 1977. Photo Robert Fogt.

Library of Congress Cataloging-in-Publication Data
Names: Cushing, Steve, author. | Pearson, Barry Lee, writer of introduction.
Title: Pioneers of the blues revival / Steve Cushing ; introduction by Barry Lee Pearson.
Description: Expanded second edition. | Urbana : University of Illinois Press, 2018. |
Series: Music in American life | Includes index.
Identifiers: LCCN 2017042832 | ISBN 9780252083617 (pbk. : alk. paper)
Subjects: LCSH: Blues (Music)—History and criticism. | Ethnomusicologists—Interviews. | Sound recording executives and producers—Interviews. | Musicologists—Interviews. | Sound recordings—Collectors and collecting—United States—History—20th century.
Classification: LCC ML3521 .C87 2018 | DDC 781.643092/273 [B]—dc23
LC record available at https://lccn.loc.gov/2017042832

CONTENTS

Acknowledgments ix
Introduction by Barry Lee Pearson xi
Preface by Steve Cushing xxiii

Paul Oliver 1
Sam Charters 22
Pete Whelan 49
Dick Waterman 69
Gayle Dean Wardlow 85
Robert M. W. Dixon 121
Bob Koester 135
John Broven 166
Mike Rowe 179
Ray Flerlage 188
Jim O'Neal 207
Richard K. Spottswood 227
Jacques Demêtre 242
Phil Spiro 253
Chris Barber 270
David Evans 292
Chris Strachwitz 323
Paul Garon 345
Mack McCormick 374

List of Interviews 421
Index 423

ACKNOWLEDGMENTS

Special thanks to the interviewees who sat patiently and shared generously. Thanks also to the friends who made their many photos available in support of the stories. And thanks as well to the staff at the University of Illinois Press, including Laurie Matheson.

INTRODUCTION

Barry Lee Pearson

Pioneers of the Blues Revival brings together interviews with nineteen notable blues researchers/collectors in a single accessible volume. Their commentary, which covers the second half of the twentieth century and the first decade of the twenty-first century, comes primarily from Steve Cushing's long-running radio show, *Blues Before Sunrise*. An experienced interviewer, Cushing knows what questions to ask his subjects, and they, in turn, are more than capable of telling their own stories in their own words, even when they have a particular axe to grind. My role in writing this introduction is to provide a general context for their observations, and to that end I consider the interviews collectively rather than individually, presenting an overview of blues history and the impact of the blues revival on the blues tradition. Within this framework I look to two connected stories, each combining multiple backstories and subplots. The first involves the process by which a group of record collectors documented the blues, recasting a community-based oral tradition into the print medium. The second describes a parallel process by which blues shifted from a black vernacular tradition to global popular music.

Blues date back to the turn of the twentieth century, forged in the black experience in the Southern United States. Vaudeville blues star Ma Rainey and composer W. C. Handy, the so-called Mother and Father of the Blues, recall encountering the form in 1902 and 1903, respectively. Rainey is credited with introducing blues into her stage show and consequently into black popular culture. Handy wrote of meeting an itinerant slide guitar player singing blues in a Mississippi train station and later began to interpret folk blues into his own compositions, scoring several major hits that crossed over to white consumers and initiating broader popular interest in blues.

Earlier still, observers tell of blues-like songs coming in a wide variety of forms, usually with the caveat that although they sounded like blues, they were not called blues at that time. More likely they were termed "reels," a black folk term referring generically to secular dance music. Blues, however, soon replaced reels as favored dance music in the black community and even had a brief moment as a popular culture song fad. But for the most part they remained an evolving form of black expression reflecting African American experience and shaped by a distinct black aesthetic.

By the time blues were recorded and actually disseminated in phonograph record format, they had been around for more than twenty years and carried the stamp of that time frame. These two decades witnessed intense repression against blacks in the rural South. The combination of poverty and anxiety, the inability to speak one's mind without fear of swift retribution, and the unpredictability of violence are all embedded in blues and blues culture. At the same time, blues music and songs as performed at small functions provided relief from the constant pressure of daily life. This duality, blues as synonymous with feelings of stress and oppression and blues as social dance music or a relief from such feelings, is exemplified in the proverbial phrase "laughing to keep from crying" and the general ambivalence that is endemic to the form. Although blues recordings were considered a form of entertainment, the debate over the degree of protest in recorded blues in both overt and encoded form rages even to the present day.

Beyond the broader historical perspective already put forward, the roots of the blues revival tie directly to the phonograph recording industry and the dissemination of black blues and blues-like music in this medium. On August 10, 1920, Perry Bradford and Mamie Smith recorded a smash hit on the OKeh label titled "Crazy Blues." Although other blues had been recorded before it, "Crazy Blues" is generally conceded to be the first major recording by black artists in black style purchased by black consumers, ushering in what producer Ralph Peer allegedly designated "race records." The unexpected sales of "Crazy Blues" demonstrated both that black consumers had the purchasing power to support black recording artists and that blues as a genre was a viable commercial product. Recordings provided a new medium for black expression beyond the more ephemeral "juke" or street-corner performances. Like sheet music, they also provided artifacts that were collectible.

Over the next forty years their first audience, the black consumers who purchased blues recordings, bought them for personal listening or to enliven social occasions, and they kept up with changing musical trends by sharing a preference for major stars like Lonnie Johnson, Leroy Carr, or Bessie Smith. Prior to the Depression a wide variety of blues artists had the opportunity to record and met with varied success. Some, like Blind Lemon Jefferson, Blind Blake, Big Bill Broonzy, Jim Jackson, or Memphis Minnie, did quite well as far as record sales, while others remained almost totally obscure.

The second half of the 1920s proved to be a "golden age" of recordings. Hundreds of regional artists recorded music, but with the stock market crash of 1929 and the onset of the Depression, it was as if these artists fell off the face of the earth. Not just individual artists, but record companies disappeared as well. In the hard times that followed, only the reliable hit makers were called on to record. By the time the Depression ended and by the end of World War II, many of the early wave of recording artists and their songs had gone decidedly out of fashion and were largely forgotten. But their recordings survived in the hands of junk shop dealers, or in the attics and basements of the black families who bought them in the first place, and, ultimately in the possession of blues record collectors who initiated what has come to be known as the blues revival.

There is no single agreed upon definition for the term "blues revival," or if there was a revival in the first place, or if "revival" is an appropriate term for whatever happened. The term remains politically and racially charged, dating back to its heyday in the turbulent 1960s. Nevertheless, the cooling effects of some fifty years have allowed scholars and participants to look back in a more objective manner, often with an eye toward their own personal involvement, bringing a more self-reflexive awareness to the issues. I offer some commentary edging toward definition, but it falls far from being inclusive. Nor can it satisfy all the contesting parties who have wrestled with the term for so many years.

Whether one views the term "blues revival" and what it stands for positively or negatively, most agree that it refers to one or more chapters in blues history during which a fundamental change occurred involving blues audiences and aesthetics. What had been perceived as African American lower-class art was later viewed as a less racialized form of global popular music. The process involved a complex sequence of events that took place on both sides of the Atlantic, covering half a century, culminating in the decade of the 1960s.

Like the term "folk revival," "blues revival" remains in common usage despite its troublesome history. For our purpose the parent term "folk revival" was first created in an attempt to distinguish nontraditional artists from traditional artists, as in the case of latter-day white New Yorkers singing 1930s black Delta blues. But it also described traditional artists playing for nontraditional audiences as in the case of Leadbelly or Josh White performing for New York cabaret audiences. A misguided conception of purity or authenticity partially guided these distinctions, attaching value to those who were perceived as the more authentic artists at the expense of newcomers to whatever traditional forms were being scrutinized.

"Folk" or "blues revival" also refers to bringing back older styles of music that have generally faded from memory but, once reintroduced, attract a substantial following and enjoy a second go-around in public consciousness. For example, there can be an actual revival, as in the case of the current black string band revival, which involves black artists reclaiming the fiddle and banjo dance tunes that blacks and whites shared during the first several decades of the twentieth century. Similarly, certain older blues forms that remained acoustic—Piedmont or Appalachian blues, for example—have also been reintroduced by black musicians, many of whom grew up with an appreciation for their own regional styles. Conscious of their music as part of their cultural heritage, they sought to pass it on to younger musicians to keep it alive or in the public eye. Several examples of these cultural caretakers would be the late John Cephas, the late John Jackson, and the late Archie Edwards, who taught several generations of musicians in the Washington, D.C., area. Role models like Cephas and his partner, Phil Wiggins, also drew an older black audience who, while they never quite gave up on blues, considered the music old-fashioned. But once it was back as a musical option, they re-embraced the form, joining blues societies and attending blues festivals, concerts, and clubs.

But there are still problems with the term. First, blues were never lost, and they did not need to be revived. They simply evolved as traditional music tends to: by keeping up with the changing needs of the communities that maintain them. Within the various black communities these changes followed the path of the great migration, morphing through such forms as rhythm and blues, rock, soul, soul blues, or even hip-hop, or through regional sub-styles like zydeco. Second, if "blues revival" refers to the variety of ways that white artists and audiences adopted black music, it has been commonplace throughout the course of American history. Interest in black music is by no means exceptional. In fact, white interest in, appreciation for, and emulation of black musical forms has been a recurring phenomenon for generations in both the United States and Britain. Dating back to the nineteenth century, black touring groups performed and popularized spirituals. The minstrel stage show, with its assortment of alleged plantation melodies and dance, was enormously popular worldwide. In the first decades of the twentieth century, one could look to white vaudeville artists like Sophie Tucker or Gilda Gray or, more commonly, white country artists such as Uncle Dave Macon, Jimmie Rodgers, the Carter Family, or Frank Hutchison as representative white performers working blues in a style that was somewhat like that used by black performers. Similar white participation followed each evolutionary shift through Bill Haley, Elvis Presley, and the Rolling Stones to the blue-eyed soul generation and on to Eminem. So what sets the blues revival apart? To a certain degree it is the sense of blues as something that was lost but then found, coupled with a misguided notion that blacks no longer supported blues, thus making it fair game for white appropriation.

There is no agreed upon time frame for the blues revival, nor is there agreement as to whether there was one or many, but most researchers look to the 1960s as a pivotal decade in blues history. While there is considerable debate over exactly what happened to bring about this revival, there is a shared sense that a confluence of events occurred, including the emergence of significant long-playing reissue albums; the rediscovery of a number of older black artists who initially made 78 rpm recordings; the development of blues-related literature, including discographies, books, and periodicals to document the recordings and the artists; the emergence of festivals and tours; and the proliferation of white blues performers in both solo acoustic and electric band formats.

As for the blues revival pioneers in this book, the single most dominant thread running through their lives remains phonograph recordings. The process of collecting, buying, selling, trading, documenting, reissuing, and, finally, producing sound recordings of blues represents the alpha and omega of the blues revivalist story. Recordings are the documents and artifacts that initially drew the majority of the interviewees to blues, and a number of them—Jim O'Neal, Sam Charters, Chris Strachwitz, Paul Oliver, Dick Spottswood, Bob Koester—wound up producing them at some point in their lives.

As collectors they speak of "the game"—that is, the art and science—of record collecting. These accounts, while hardly altruistic, offer advice on the techniques of canvassing black neighborhoods, the poker-faced negotiation skills required for deals in used record shops. Part economics, part fetishism, the game did little to revive blues or illuminate blues culture. But it did illuminate who arbitrated orthodoxy and how a system of what was "pure" or what was "authentic" was determined. One thing was certain: what guided blues production in the first place had very little to do with an African American aesthetic. Rather it was a secondary system developed in part by white collectors who then shared their opinions with white critics and white consumers.

The terms "blues revival" and "folk revival" also refer to the rediscovery of America's roots music heritage in the 1960s, in which blues and other forms of music from the 1920s and 1930s captured on 78 rpm records were reissued to a new audience on 33 ⅓ rpm records and, later, CDs. Compilations by Harry Smith, Sam Charters, and others allowed a new access to an American musical heritage that previously had been in the hands of a limited number of collectors. To a degree it democratized these earlier recordings. And because the artists they featured were from the pre-electric blues era, they conformed to the folk revival ban on electric instruments.

While the reissue projects spawned countless popularized imitations of traditional music, including blues, it also initiated a broader debate over what was to be considered authentic as record collectors and revival performers sparred over who was the most genuine. As early as 1937 critics argued about authenticity; in one example John Hammond Jr. was so taken by a recording of Robert Johnson that he wrote that Johnson made Leadbelly sound like an accomplished poseur. Although Johnson died in 1938, he would become one of the darlings of the folk revival, blues revival, and record collectors and provides a powerful example of how the revival's participants were inclined to rewrite blues history according to their own values.

These interviews flesh out such backstories as the discovery and progressive lionization of country blues by tracing a pattern in which relatively obscure regional artists, particularly those from the Mississippi Delta, were considered the most authentic and their recordings the most valuable, even though these perceptions did not conform to the values of the black consumer.

After Columbia reissued *King of the Delta Blues Singers* in 1961, Johnson's work was democratized and taken up by the literary elite and the blues mafia alike. This album, on the heels of Sam Charters's *The Country Blues*, elevated Johnson to blues sainthood. It also furthered the process that determined orthodoxy with regard to the idea that country blues was the most authentic mode of blues expression. Later, Charley Patton would usurp Johnson's place as the most authentic. After the release of the 1970 *King of the Delta Blues Singers, Vol. 2*, not only was Johnson no longer obscure enough, but he also was marketed in relation to the roots of rock 'n' roll, an association that older folkies and country blues advocates deemed unacceptable.

Although researchers and collectors claimed they used recordings to learn more about black culture, they consistently ignored the first audience's preferences. If a particular recording sold well, it did not increase its value as a cultural document, but rather worked against its value as a collectors' item, even to the point of discrediting the artists who produced it as being too sophisticated and commercial for the collectors' palate. The collectors group showed little interest in black aesthetics as they competed among themselves. In the case of Charley Patton, for example, we can track his elevation through New York collectors Jim McKune and Bernie Klatzko, who, with the help of Southern fieldworker Gayle Dean Wardlow, initiated a process leading to his deification. The same situation occurred as with

Robert Johnson, whose researchers and biographers included Wardlow, Charters, Oliver, McCormick, and many others. These artists and their work became valuable economic properties whose reissue projects garnered Grammy Awards, popular culture notice, and a great deal of money.

The reissue projects and the publication of Sam Charters's 1959 book, *The Country Blues*, also led to a new fascination with the artists who made these early recordings, initiating a subsequent search not just for recordings but for the artists themselves. John Estes, Son House, John Hurt, Skip James, Furry Lewis, Bukka White, Robert Wilkins, Big Joe Williams, Yank Rachell, and Arthur Crudup were found and entered secondary musical careers for white audiences in coffee shops, bars, and festivals throughout the country. Other, more contemporary blues artists who had continued working for black audiences also took a turn on the festival circuit. These included two of the most prolific black artists of all time, Lightning Hopkins and John Lee Hooker, who, although they were among the greatest electric guitar players ever, were forced to go unplugged for an audience still dominated by folk revival orthodoxy. The folk revival's prejudice against modern electric blues stemmed in part from an attempt to compartmentalize blues and keep it in the past, as well as an elitist anti–rhythm and blues, rock 'n' roll, or anti-popular music bias. Fortunately, this bias would not last through the 1960s, but for some critics the focus on so-called folk blues and the eventual acceptance of more contemporary electric stylings separate the blues revival into at least two stages.

Despite the assertions of Sam Charters, Ralph Gleason, and others who argued that what was then currently on black radio was the folk music of the day, confusion persisted. Moreover, the insistence that acoustic was folk and electric was not represented an imposition of an arbitrary set of rules coming from outside the black community, a trait typical of the blues revival. The blues revival of the 1960s also involved an explosion of blues literature, much of it coming from overseas, including the monumental discography by Robert M. W. Dixon and collaborators John Godrich and Howard W. Rye, *Blues and Gospel Records, 1890–1960*. Pioneer British researcher Paul Oliver published *Blues Fell That Morning* in 1960, *Conversations with the Blues* in 1967, and *The Story of the Blues* in 1969. In the United States, Sam Charters followed up the admittedly romantic *The Country Blues* with *The Bluesman* in 1969. Charles Keil began to challenge the old guard with his *Urban Blues* in 1966, and in 1964 Big Bill Broonzy's *Big Bill Blues* was published, the first book by a traditional Mississippi-born blues artist. In 1970 *Living Blues*, America's foremost blues periodical, first appeared, with its focus on blues as a living, dynamic black art form.

Throughout its duration the blues revival was a transatlantic venture. Just after World War II the U.S. military presence in Britain reintroduced black American music through Armed Forces Radio, recordings left behind by American servicemen, and, in some cases, encounters with black troops stationed nearby. Paul Oliver, the dean of British blues scholars, recalled listening to radio and recordings but also hearing black soldiers singing in local pubs and while on work details. The popular music of the postwar years held little interest for British youth who wanted something different from the music heard on the

BBC and from their parents' generation. Several forms of black American–based niche music provided such options, including skiffle, a hybrid form of traditional jazz, blues, and other forms of American roots music.

Fans of these American forms scoured used record shops to snatch up American records and British reissue albums and, later on, American imports issued on the London labels. For example, British discographer John Broven, who came to blues via 1950s rock, noted he would hit the local record shops every Saturday morning along with countless other youth who, although they didn't know each other at the time, were engaged in the same pursuit. Eventually fan clubs, newsletters, and record trade magazines served to connect and inform these likeminded fans and collectors, culminating in the publication of the major British magazine *Blues Unlimited*.

The 1960s also saw an increase in blues artists visiting Europe. Prior to the 1960s the number of blues artists visiting Europe was limited. During the war years the International Sweethearts of Rhythm went there to entertain black servicemen; Leadbelly visited briefly in 1949, the year he died; and Big Bill Broonzy, Sonny Terry, and Brownie McGhee visited in the 1950s. Primarily acoustic practitioners, they set the tone for what the British and French thought blues ought to sound like. When later 1960s electric acts went over, they initially shocked the older British fans with their volume and dynamic stage presence, which was so unlike the acoustic blues acts. But they did catch the attention of aspiring young musicians who found models and mentors first via phonograph recordings and now supplemented by in-person tours. Between 1962 and 1970, Horst Lippmann and Fritz Rau and their American partner, Willie Dixon, sponsored American Folk Blues Festival tours. Dixon later wound up as a facilitator, hooking up British blues rock acts with their American idols.

British researchers also took the lead in the documentation of blues. John Broven noted, "It's interesting that all the discographies on American music have been done by foreigners and in their spare time." The reference to "spare time" reinforces the notion that record collecting at this time was a hobby. Moreover, the scarcity of American recordings reduced the sheer numbers of items available to work with. In the United States there was greater access to recordings as well as a stronger sense of blues as a tradition and the release of blues recordings as an ongoing, unending process. In addition, for the British collectors, black music was exciting, conjuring up exotic images of a distant world. Where American jazz historians placed blues in the past as one of the roots of jazz, the British distancing was not only temporal but geographic as well. This sense of distance initially allowed British collectors to ignore living manifestations of the blues tradition, permitting them free use of their imagination without the interference of living contemporary artists. The centrality of phonograph records can also be seen in early British publications that often featured photographs of recordings as opposed to people and places. While this may simply reflect the unavailability of more lively images at that time, it also suggests a vision of blues driven by artifacts rather than a living culture or artists. In the United States, discographical journals like *78 Quarterly* also showed recordings, particularly those most sought after.

Moreover, as blues evolved it became closer to rock or other forms that purists disdained. But the purists, who accepted only older forms of jazz and blues, slowly lost ground to critics who argued for the inclusion of more modern styles, in effect arguing for a greater acceptance of black musical preferences and a more progressive approach to black music. Over the years, more and more black blues artists visited Europe, drawing European writers to do fieldwork in the United States. This shift in blues politics demanded participatory fieldwork that British fieldworkers Paul Oliver and John Broven readily undertook. They hooked up with American fieldworkers Sam Charters, Mack McCormick, David Evans, Chris Strachwitz, and Jim O'Neal, each helping the others with their projects.

In return from the British side, the initial blues-like export to the United States was the 1956 hit "Rock Island Line" by Lonnie Donegan, a member of Chris Barber's band. Done in skiffle style, the song was initially based on a field-recorded piece collected from black prisoners by John and Alan Lomax. It became part of the repertoire of Huddie Ledbetter, or Leadbelly, who visited England in 1949. This would not be the first time an American song was sent to Great Britain and then sent back as an international hit.

Inspired in part by the visits of Muddy Waters and other American Folk Blues Festival artists, England erupted with blues bands in the 1960s. The list includes, but isn't limited to, Blues Incorporated, formed in 1961 by Alexis Korner and Cyril Davies; the Rolling Stones and the Animals in 1962; the Yardbirds and John Mayall and the Bluesbreakers in 1963; Cream in 1966; Fleetwood Mac in 1967; and Led Zeppelin in 1968. While most did not remain hard-core blues bands, they started off as such. Moreover, they were part of what has been termed the "British Invasion," bringing their brand of blues rock to America and achieving remarkable success. Groups like the Rolling Stones, Cream, and Led Zeppelin achieved superstar status, introducing American youth to rock blues and sometimes to the black blues artists these groups patterned themselves after.

In the United States a similar shift occurred in which an initial folk blues revival eventually gave way to an acceptance of electric blues and the subsequent proliferation of white or mixed electric blues bands. The acoustic scene developed in New York City and Cambridge, Massachusetts, while the electric bands, modeled as they were on Chicago artists, were initially a Chicago-based phenomenon. But even in Chicago the roots of the blues revival was an offshoot of the folk revival. For example, in Chicago, North Side clubs began to book blues acts, beginning with Big John's on Wells Street. As Charlie Musselwhite recalls:

> There was the folk revival going on, and there were some folk clubs around, and me and Big Joe [Williams] were living together behind a record store up on Wells Street. There was a little bar down the street called Big John's and at that time it just a little neighborhood bar. They asked Joe to come down and play, and they thought Joe was kind of like a folksinger. They didn't know what they were getting into. Acoustic guitar, you know. So it was a holiday, Fourth of July or something, and that's why they decided to have this folk music. So we played there. Joe asked me to play with him and the place was just packed. The crowd loved it, and the owners thought it was so good that they just wanted Joe to keep on playing there, and by this point [Mike] Bloomfield had joined in playing piano, and I was playing harp [harmonica]. So when Joe finally left, we just stayed on and kept the gig going

> and Mike started playing guitar. We got a drummer and a bass player, and then we started telling the owners about other blues bands. You know, "Why don't you book Muddy Waters or Howlin' Wolf?" So they started booking them and eventually it was seven nights a week, live blues, live electric blues from the South Side. And then other clubs started having blues and that caused a shift to the North Side, because you couldn't make any money on the South Side. So I think this was really where it started, that whole shift, when they hired Big Joe for that little holiday weekend. A lot of people don't remember Big John's. You don't see it in any books or anything.

These new venues signaled a significant shift for blues artists in the city who had played in black taverns on the South and West Sides. But, bolstered by their success and lured by bigger money and new respect, the city's blues artists were drawn farther and farther from their home stomping grounds. Soon college towns throughout the Midwest, like Ann Arbor, Michigan, and Madison, Wisconsin, were featuring blues at parties, clubs, and festivals.

In New York City a blues revival began even earlier in the 1930s and '40s with the arrival of Josh White, Leadbelly, Sonny Terry and Brownie McGhee, and the Reverend Gary Davis. These artists found work in clubs like Café Society or found parts in plays like *Cat on a Hot Tin Roof* for white or mixed audiences. Besides cabaret work some artists continued to score with black R & B hits such as White's "Jelly, Jelly, Jelly" or Terry and McGhee's "New Baseball Boogie." But for the most part they became enmeshed in the New York folk revival scene of the late 1950s and early 1960s. Here, a cadre of white blues players, singers, and songwriters like Woody Guthrie, Cisco Houston, Jack Elliot, and Dave Van Ronk performed a wide variety of black music forms. Some, like Van Ronk, came from trad jazz, jug, and skiffle bands.

A shift to the electric blues rock band format soon followed. Bolstered by the proven sales of the British bands, American labels gained the confidence to sign white or mixed blues bands. Several had initially played folk festivals and were signed by labels associated with folk acts. Perhaps the most notable, the Paul Butterfield Band was formed in 1963 and, after adding Mike Bloomfield, recorded in 1965. Memphis-to-Chicago harp blower Charlie Musselwhite recorded his first album in 1966, and the Siegal-Schwall Band's [Corky Siegel and Jim Schwall] first album appeared in the mid-1960s. Other groups included Jessie Colin Young and the Youngbloods, the Blues Project, the Allman Brothers, and Electric Flag. Record companies invested a good deal of money in electric blues, culminating in a 1969 bidding war for the services of Texan Johnny Winter. As with the British groups, these bands were cited for drawing consumer attention to the blues form and, hopefully, raised the profile of the black artists they emulated, initiating an economic trickledown effect.

While Chicago blues stalwarts like Muddy Waters and Howling Wolf benefited from the greater exposure, there was a sense of ambivalence among the musician mentors who watched their protégés outsell them. In 1969 West Side guitarist Jimmy Dawkins noted how the changes in Chicago helped the blues profile: "Muddy Waters taught Paul Butterfield, but since him and Mike Bloomfield got in it, this has been the greatest thing for the blacks. Blacks are making more money, there's jobs, there's more customers, more of everything because of those guys."

But the specter of racial inequity was never far behind, as Dawkins continued: "I can play as good as any guitar player I have seen on television that's trying to copy B. B. [King] or copy Muddy. If he got white skin then he's on TV making ten or twelve thousand a night. But I make ten or eight dollars a night, and color is the difference. And that's why I say, well, this is wrong."

The stories of Cushing's interview subjects also touch on economics and the creation of value related to the collection, evaluation, and reissuing of historical recordings; the careers of the artists who made those recordings; and the production and marketing of new recordings of both black artists and the white artists who have adapted and performed their own version of blues.

Repackaging blues or retooling the art for a broader audience, even a global audience, constitutes one component of the blues revival. But the shift to a new cultural fan base involves aesthetic alterations balancing the older set of values with the preferences of the new. While most artists welcome an expanded audience, questions of authenticity, ownership, and economic return complicate the picture. Reactions to the blues revival and what it represents vary. From one perspective, it is the inevitable result of acculturation and a sharing of great music along with a positive contribution to America's musical gumbo. From another, it is primarily cultural theft.

Pioneers of the Blues Revival presents a vision of blues as seen through the prism of the white collector. While not entirely shifting away from blues as a black tradition, emphasis on a white perspective is inevitable, considering the fact that the subjects here came to blues from outside the blues tradition. All the interviewees are older white males, six of whom are European. Most were born in the North, Northeast, or Midwest, and their birth dates range from 1915 to 1942. The majority had little early contact with black culture, coming to the blues as outsiders through the medium of phonograph recordings.

Several were, or are, professional musicians—most prominently, Chris Barber, who was a major player in the British skiffle craze and backed touring American blues artists. David Evans has also worked on and off as a performer but has been a folklorist, ethnomusicologist, teacher, and producer as well. Sam Charters played clarinet in a traditional jazz band, moving to New Orleans to learn more, but wound up becoming a historian, writer, and eventually a record producer of various forms of music. But the group is also quite diverse. Paul Oliver, David Evans, and Robert Dixon held academic appointments in architecture, ethnomusicology, and linguistics, respectively. John Broven became a corporate banker. Photographer Ray Flerlage, Dick Waterman, and Jim O'Neal were journalists, as was Pete Whelan, and Bob Koester was, and is, a record store owner and record producer.

Where does this collection fit within the history of blues scholarship? For almost a hundred years white scholars, critics, journalists, and the general public have expressed curiosity about African American blues. During the first half of the twentieth century, fieldworkers and interpreters Howard Odum and Guy Johnson, Newman Ivey White, John and Alan Lomax, Abbe Niles, Carl Sandburg, Dorothy Scarborough, John Work, and W. C.

Handy, the first black musician spokesperson for the blues, attempted to answer questions about blues origins, meaning, and what clues it held about black culture. In turn, during the latter part of the twentieth and the first decade of the twenty-first century, another wave of researchers, including David Evans, Benjamin Filene, Robert Gordon, Marybeth Hamilton, Bruce Nemerov, John Szwed, Jeff Titon, and Elijah Wald, looked back at the work of these pioneering scholars, critiquing their methods, interpretive abilities, and conclusions. *Pioneers of the Blues Revival* allows us to continue the process of investigating blues investigators by providing a new set of revealing self-presentations, shedding new light on another cadre of blues interpreters.

Coupled with prior investigations of the ways blues have been represented and repackaged, Cushing's work marks new sophistication in blues scholarship in which researchers have moved beyond their traditional subjects—blues history, blues artists, the record industry, blues and African American studies—and are pausing to reflect on how earlier researchers collectively shaped representations of blues and its role in American culture. Moreover, by moving into the second half of the twentieth century, this book supplies further data for scholarly introspection. By bringing us more or less up to date, we can look back over almost the entire century to piece together why we think what we do about blues, who shaped our perceptions, what their biases and credentials were, and what media they depended on.

The interviews provide insight into a secondary chapter of blues history that encompasses the origin stories of the media used to document blues, including, but not confined to, newsletters; fan clubs; discographies; reissue labels such as Folkways, R.B.F., Origin Jazz Library, Piedmont, and Blues Classics; magazines like *Blues Unlimited, Living Blues, 78 Quarterly, Blues Revue Quarterly,* and *Juke Blues*; and new record labels such as Delmark, Rooster, Alligator, and Vanguard, not to mention the hundreds of books detailing blues history and meaning. They also help document the rise of blues festivals and eventually blues tourism in which cities like Chicago, Helena, Memphis, and Clarksdale, among others, have become sites of interest for touring blues fans.

Pioneers of the Blues Revival documents the efforts of a quirky set of researchers who slowly pieced together a version of blues history and meaning. This dedicated cohort, despite their widely different backgrounds, somehow brought together the skill sets necessary to create a literature based on blues research. Some would say that in the process they reinvented blues in their own image. Regardless, their work affected mass culture perception of blues. For many, this may not be viewed as such a benign project. It could also be seen as the story of how a group of record collectors and researchers codified and appropriated a living African American art form, removing its vitality for the sake of organizing and then selling its products.

PREFACE

Steve Cushing

Whatever transgressions academia may ascribe to the pioneers of the blues revival, my purpose in compiling this book is to acknowledge and honor the work of this select group of early blues enthusiasts from the late 1950s and 1960s and to profile them as they tell their own stories in their own words. I selected these particular individuals because I was influenced by their work during the earliest days of my exploration into blues—by their books, their magazines, their reissued vintage recordings, and newly produced recordings by vintage artists.

In recent years it has become stylish to disparage their efforts and the era, but I regard their efforts as selfless, honorable, and positive. And talking with the nineteen interviewees found in this manuscript has served only to reinforce that opinion. Their efforts resulted in financial comfort and renewed artistic acclaim for a number of prewar blues artists and provided a new audience for postwar blues that had been eclipsed as a commercial enterprise by doo-wop, rock 'n' roll, and soul music. And viewed through a much wider lens, I believe the blues revival served as a second front in the 1960s civil rights movement, a benign alternative to the clashes in Alabama and Mississippi, an alternative where there was communication between the races, regardless of how awkward the early conversations may have been, as at least this small contingent of the two races began to learn how to talk to each other—no small accomplishment in a world of segregation. It's been more than fifty years since they initiated the decade of blues activism we refer to as the "blues revival," and most of the interviewees included here are about seventy years old or older. I hope this book will serve to help document these pioneers and their work.

PAUL OLIVER INTERVIEW

Well, I was born in Nottingham, England, but my family actually came from the west of England near Wales. So that was in 1927.

If you were born in 1927, that would make you about twelve years old when the war broke out. Do you have any home-front experiences that you can relate?

Well, I was in the London suburbs during much of the war, so I was there at the time of the bombing, but it wasn't as heavy in the suburban areas as it was in the East End of London and Central London. We did have incendiary bombs fall on our house, but we all put them out, and other than that we had no serious problems. Later in the war—from that time on, actually—I was working in harvest camps and later in the war in forestry and ran forestry camps for felling trees and logging. But that was my kind of war effort, because I was still too young to serve, and when I was called up right at the end of the war, I had asthma very badly and they didn't accept me.

Paul Oliver, Cheltenham, UK, July 2006. Photo Cilla Huggins.

I know that you're an expert in a couple of different fields. Which came first—the music or the architecture?

Well, I think probably by a year or so the music came first in the sense that I was already excited by boogie-woogie in the 1930s when I was about ten or eleven. In fact, the rhythm of the trains was so like boogie that I used to travel on the steam trains just to enjoy that—and put my mind in that kind of field. So really I started quite young in that respect. I didn't understand that to be blues or anything; I just knew it by the popular name of the day, boogie-woogie. So that was really up until about '42 . . . And around about that time I had to help my father, who was an architect, but he had been seconded to the war office to help with drawing up and planning the situation from the very heavy bombing in places like Plymouth and Exeter, which destroyed the cities and caused tremendous problems. That involved me to quite an extent in housing of the poor and difficulties in relating that to other architecture around the world. So within a year or so both of them were my obsessions and have been so all my life.

Let's follow the music trail. How was it that you were exposed to boogie-woogie?

It started from about 1938 through to the early war years—I suppose off and on for about three or four years, really. After that I got interested in other things, but, you see, the boogie recordings of people like Pete Johnson and Meade "Lux" Lewis and so forth were all entering Britain at that time. And people don't always realize how many blues records were available in Britain in the 1930s. So it was fairly accessible. Of course we weren't actually hearing the musicians themselves, but I did eventually in one or two of the areas where the American military settled in.

It was records, not radio broadcasts, that you heard?

We heard radio too as the years went by, but Alan Lomax came to England and he brought with him a number of Library of Congress recordings, and those were played on the radio as well. But very early on we started having our own bands and groups, and I was interested in documenting the subject as far as I could, but really it was recordings that were the primary source at that time.

How did you make the jump from boogie-woogie to the rest of the blues world? Over what time did that happen, and what events led you to expand your enthusiasm?

Well, the basic thing was that on one of the trips that I had made to work during the summer vacation—I was still in school, I was working in harvest camps, and one was in the East Anglia area of England—that's in Suffolk—the American army was just digging in at that time—the American air force, in other words. So it happened to be that their camp was next door to the camp where I was working. And a friend of mine said he wanted me to hear something and took me off to hear the most extraordinary sounds. I just never heard anything in my life like it. Even now it gives me quite a shiver when I think about it. These people were on fatigue essentially, but these were black Americans who had been digging in but for some reason or other had defaulted, and they were singing. My friend said, "You're listening to blues." Actually I think they were work songs really, but at that time, anyway, that turned me on enough to get me interested in it. His name was Stan Higham and he was killed in the war later. But Stan had quite a good collection of jazz records and some blues records and he got me started.

Can you remember the names of the artists that Stan introduced you to?

Well, there were quite a few that were being issued. I mean often the circulation was very, very small because there were limitations of up to ninety-nine copies, so to speak, and because they couldn't afford to consume much material. But even so, I managed to get recordings of "Pinetop" Smith and certainly of the pianists who accompanied blues singers, Big Joe Turner and so on. They were among the earliest ones I collected. And of course some of the classic singers. But particularly Bessie Smith was available, because though it's not generally known in the United States, her last session was, in fact, commissioned and paid for from England.

I was just going to ask you a foolish question—if you were interested at this time in postwar blues—but it hadn't yet happened, had it?

No, it certainly hadn't. I was interested in there being one day perhaps a postwar period, but we didn't know whether the war was going to last for three years or ten years or what. You know, there was no indication really. It was a pretty difficult time. So much so that we didn't talk too much about what things would be like after the war in case "after the war" didn't come. Well, my interest continued to develop actually during the war years, because, as I say, there were quite a few records that had been issued, and I was very interested in going around junk shops and just finding early recordings, and I was gradually getting an idea of who was worth listening to and who wasn't. Fortunately, just at the end of the war, as the American servicemen were going back to the States, they left quite a lot of 78 records with the junk shops, so I bought quite a few at that time. "Kokomo" Arnold, I think, was the first one.

By the end of the war I was busy getting a collection together, and in the immediate postwar years we formed a small jazz society which we called the Jazz Purists Society, which was both jazz and blues, so to speak, because jazz was becoming very popular. Jazz was, for a number of years, really the dominant popular music in Britain. So I was just as interested in the blues after that and continued with my own researches. I obviously had difficulty getting the information, but slowly it came together, and at that time it was still possible, after the war, to order 78s like Bukka White and so forth directly from the United States. And we traded also. We traded English dance bands such as Harry Roy and Ambrose, many of whom had jazz musicians from the States playing with them. We traded those records and got a lot of blues records that way. So gradually the collections were building up, and I got very interested. You see, most people were saying, "Don't bother listening to the words." You know, they were concentrating on the music. I got very interested in the words. So one way or another it gradually got me started, but not with any particular objective at that time beyond just wanting to know more about it.

In what capacity did black American GIs serve in England?

Well, in very poor capacity. In theory the army was not segregated, but in practice it was. So that most of them were doing the digging in, the fairly menial work on the locations. But you see, while we were actually working on the farms, we often used to go down to the local pub for a drink in the evening, and generally one or two of the black Americans would be there, and they got very excited by the fact that we welcomed them and wanted to hear them play. Plenty of them played piano and so forth. Interestingly, in 1960, when

I was doing my fieldwork in the United States, I met several blues singers who had visited Britain during the war, and all of them had the most warm memories of it, which was very helpful in the sense that they were very positive to me.

Were you lucky enough to run into people who could actually play?

Yes, we did! These were people like ourselves—sort of amateurs—so that, in a sense, they weren't likely to have any kind of career. But it was *their* music, and that's what they played when they sat down in the saloons, see. Most of them were pianists that we heard, so we—I say *we* because there were several of us who were interested—as we had already got these boogie records and so on, it wasn't difficult to encourage them to play some.

Did you have any curiosity about the actual persons who made this music—what their lives might be like, if they were still alive, any notions of that sort?

That's why I did the fieldwork, when I was able to do it in the States, to find that out. That was the motivation behind my fieldwork—to try and find out what the lives of the singers and musicians were, especially in the South, when they weren't, at that stage, really wrapped up in the business, so to speak, where their music wasn't any kind of club or show music, but when they largely played for each other or themselves. So I was personally interested in the background. But already, you see, I had some indication or intimation to that just by talking with people. It just seemed to me that the research had to be done in the South.

After you had the Jazz Purists Society, where did your interest go from there? How did it manifest?

First and foremost it manifested by what I listened to most and what I liked to collect most, which tended to be the blues records. And then immediately after the war—surprisingly rapidly after the war—quite a few collectors like ourselves began to start small record companies, so the repertoire was expanding. And knowledge also rose in the process, see. One or two people got me interested in discography, so we began to try and work out how certain singers came to be working in the company of others. We were piecing together all this information. So it was a piecemeal business, but it was actually coming together and taking shape . . . so that finally in 1951 I wrote and sent an article, which in fact was about gospel music, because I felt that people weren't taking any notice of it. That was published by *Jazz Journal*. In those days blues was always thought of as being an influence on jazz. It still wasn't thought of as being an idiom of its own. One of the things I was intent on doing was trying to get blues recognized as a genre; that was one of the things that motivated me. So I started writing for various jazz magazines, but always about blues.

Did you have any particular favorite artist at this point?

In 1951 Big Bill Broonzy came over to France, where he was playing. We had difficulty getting very close to him because of the big crowds, but we were at least getting an idea of what he sounded like. In '52 he came to England, and when he came over to England my wife and I got to know him well. I eventually did some illustrations for his autobiography. We got to know Big Bill well, and I think he was probably the most inspired. He had the greatest contact with the audiences. Josh White came over, but he was very much playing in the kind of Greenwich Village club idiom. And Lonnie Johnson came over, but Lonnie—brilliant though he was—completely misjudged the audience and thought it was a kind of American club audience and played things which were of no interest. [*laughs*] He did come again later. I got to know him and realized how great he was, but he was very disappointing when he first came over to England. Big Bill was a real surprise, so I think he largely shaped my interest and taste in terms of live performance.

Jazz News magazine featuring Paul Oliver article on Howling Wolf. Courtesy Alan Balfour.

Had he been your favorite before you met him in person?

I can't say favorite, because there were a number of people that I had on record, but Big Bill was certainly one of them. I had people like Barbecue Bob, who had in fact died, though I didn't know that at that time. So there were all sorts of names that appeared on record. Quite often I chose the people with the strangest names, like Peetie Wheatstraw or whatever, because they often turned out to be very interesting people. I might have missed a few in the process, but nevertheless that was a way of sorting the blues singers from the jazz singers.

Were you at any point categorizing the different genres of music? Were you detecting genres just among the blues records themselves?

Yes, that's what I was trying to do, yes, certainly! And that's where the discography came in. I eventually realized on the wax there would be *D-A-L* or something, and I began to realize that these were clues as to where the recordings were made. So I got interested in collecting recordings including singers who had been recorded in Texas and in Atlanta. These compared with the ones we had previously, which all seemed to be recorded in New York. And then we found out that there had been field units that eventually worked in the South that recorded the kind of folksingers in the South. It began to make sense. What would seem to be a series of puzzles began to take shape.

I know that you talked about the fact that there were people who were bringing these records in. Did you have any contacts in the States in terms of procuring records?

Yes, there were one or two people who dealt in the States. I can't even remember their names offhand, but there were a few. And the magazines like *Record Changer* and so forth, which were—I mean, they were just duplicated magazines in those days, but they at least gave us contacts, people we could actually write to and contact and see if they were

Record Changer magazine. Author's collection.

interested in trading records and so forth. So that's a good idea how that happened.

And then from about 1953 or '54, I started doing a series of articles in a magazine called *Music Mirror* which I called "Sources of African American Music." So by that time I'd really already sorted it out. And I'd got enough to be able to write about different traditions and the different veins of the development of music. I did that for a few years until I'd written these first articles. That also was very useful, because by doing so we made contact with various other people who were interested and had other records. By the mid-fifties I was beginning to think I'd like to do a book on the content of blues, you see. So I made friends with various people. In those days if you wanted to hear somebody's records, there was no tape recording even or any of the technologies available now. So one had to get on the train and visit them just to hear a record. [*laughs*] We did that! We went to Paris to hear records Jacques Demêtre had, and so on. Those of us who were really excited about the music and wanted to know more about it were prepared to do it.

Were there any particular artists who when you heard them for the first time seemed like a revelation?

Well, yes, I think Blind Lemon Jefferson was the first person whose records really were a revelation to me. I think that not only the very fact that he was a blind musician but that his recordings were extremely early and just the quality of his blues poetry and so forth fascinated me. So I think he was the first person. I heard a couple of records of Robert Johnson, but they were very difficult to get ahold of. A friend of mine, Derrick Stewart-Baxter, used to write a blues column in one of the jazz magazines, *Jazz Journal*—he had a couple. I thought he was very impressive, but I didn't have the kind of fanatic admiration for him that seems to be the case nowadays. So I found him very interesting, but there were a whole lot of other people who were interesting as well. We were never short of new discoveries.

So I started work on writing this book, which was a book I wanted to do which was on the themes of the blues. So that there were blues that I collected, and I contacted friends who drew my attention to items, and so I went to hear them—blues about prison, blues about traveling and migrating, blues about disasters, and so forth. I was trying to sort these out and to try to see what was the connection between them. I was very fortunate at this time because I was teaching, teaching art, and I took classes to France.

Although I wasn't teaching languages, but to help members of the staff who were teaching languages, we took groups to France to settle in for Easter. And during that time I was in Paris, and I met up with Richard Wright, the black writer. And although he was twenty years older than me, we hit it off extraordinarily well. He helped me greatly in introducing me to a number of black expatriate writers and so forth living in Paris. So when I had problems with what certain verses would mean, what a subject or word or phrase might mean—"eleven twenty-nine"—what did "eleven twenty-nine" mean? Was it the name of a train? I was quite surprised to find out that it was just short of a one-year sentence but had a legal implication—if you got eleven twenty-nine and not a one-year sentence or two months. So all this was explained to me. So I was able to solve the problems about meaning. Really, from boyhood I had been a passionate collector of books on the background of blues. I was just collecting every kind of book that I could find that would throw light on black culture in the United States. So all of this was being very helpful to me in putting together this book.

I find it surprising that black expatriate writers would be in touch with black culture. Was it the black dialect that they could help with?

Well, no. These were black Americans, expatriate writers! Richard Wright, for example, was a member of the Communist Party, and he'd been threatened during the McCarthy years, so he came to live in Paris. We met many writers and so forth—again, black Americans who were expatriates; this included dancers and singers as well. They were tremendously helpful, and I think they were just as excited by the very fact that people were interested in Europe, where they couldn't get much interest in the States, not from the white community at that time.

Were there any reference books on blues at that time?

Well, no, there weren't. There was just one booklet, which was called *The Background of the Blues,* which actually wasn't that at all. He should have called it *The Background of Jazz,* because his argument was that blues was a part of jazz and it was the origins of jazz. But it was only a booklet—about thirty-six pages long, something like that, and cost a few cents. But that was the only thing that was published. There was an article written by Max Jones which was round about 1953 or '54 called "On Blues." But otherwise there was nothing until I wrote the first full-length book on it in Europe. It was called *Blues Fell This Morning.* It was published with "The Meaning of the Blues" as its subtitle. In point of fact I wanted to call it "Meaning *in* the Blues," but they thought "Meaning of the Blues" was a better title. It was also published in the States and has not really been out of print ever since.

With all this research done in your own country and in Europe, when was the first time you actually came to the States, and how did that come about?

As I say, I wrote *Blues Fell This Morning* and it was published in England in 1959 and 1960. The American embassy, who'd had been a tremendous help anyway and had always been helpful in getting books that I was looking for and so on—in those days they were very, very active. It's not like that now, but they were tremendously good. The embassy said to me, or at least the cultural affairs officer said, that they would support me if I wanted to make an application to visit in the States, now that I got the book published and people could see that

Paul Oliver, Clifton Chenier, Cleveland Chenier, and Valerie Oliver, American Folk Blues Festival, Royal Albert Hall, London, October 1969. Photo Val Wilmer.

I knew a lot about the subject and needed to know more. They felt that I would stand a good chance and they would back it. Well, they did, and I did get a grant. I mean it was quite a big grant in those days—a thousand dollars plus the travel. It sounds ridiculous now, perhaps, but in 1960 it was a lot of money and made a lot of difference for me. So putting savings together, my wife and I made the field trip in 1960. But that was actually after doing the first book. It wouldn't have been possible probably otherwise.

And I'll bet you had a very active and extensive agenda when you came here the first time. Can you tell me what it was you had in mind?

[*laughs*] Well, what I had in mind was to interview blues singers but also to understand the environment from which they came and also to interview people that may have worked with them or ran clubs or whatever! I had only a kind of loose frame, and I wanted to keep it that way, because I wanted to leave room for the people I might discover who I didn't know anything about. So that was the idea, and I went to Washington, D.C., first, because that was a requirement of the grant, but rapidly on to New York, where I met up with Sammy Price and one or two others, then to Detroit. John Lee Hooker had come to England, and he had given me a few contacts in Detroit. I looked them up and that was helpful, and then on to Chicago. And in Chicago—I'd already met Muddy Waters, of course, in England. He'd been over to my house, and he invited me and my wife to stay with him in Chicago, so we did. That was obviously a tremendous experience, going to various clubs with Muddy and so forth—extraordinary! Then we went south—flew down to Memphis, Tennessee, and I met up with Chris Strachwitz, who runs the Arhoolie record label, but he didn't have it at that time. He was planning on doing a tour recording in the South, and we'd arranged to meet up and work together—me to be recording for the BBC and interviewing people, and he would do recordings with a possible view to issuing them. And that worked out very well. So we worked slowly through Mississippi, Louisiana, and Texas, and on the West

Coast. After that I came back to St. Louis and so forth. It was several months obviously, but it was a fantastic experience.

What type of recording equipment did you bring with you?

[*laughs*] It's quite amusing really, because it was impossible to purchase a portable recording machine right up until about a month before I left. But the army did already have a portable piece of equipment, and the BBC had actually obtained one of the army's portable recording machines. So I had that; they let me have that and they gave me a couple of days' instruction on it. So I carried it with me to the States. It weighed a tremendous amount. It was portable, yes, but only just. [*laughs*] So I made it with that. In fact, I had to hide it, because it was all covered with army signs; otherwise they would think I was doing a military event. Anyway, that's what I took with me, and the quality was surprisingly good! It also had a very interesting feature: you could not delete on it.

Of course there were times I'd recorded something and I was furious because I didn't think the quality was good enough, and I should have cleaned it and made another recording, and everything I recorded was there. But I was so glad afterward, because background noises like trains going through and crops growing actually gave a marvelous depth to many of the records. They were so very clearly field recordings. It's a good thing that the machine didn't allow me to wipe that off.

Were the electrical systems in the States and the UK compatible?

It was run by batteries. You had to stuff a lot of batteries into it in order to get it to work, but I took a box load of batteries with me to replace. The main problem, most curiously, was that while we were in Mississippi it was very hot and very humid, and the dial melted—at least the adhesive holding it—and it dropped down into the machine and disappeared. So I, when we went down to Texas, I took it to be repaired. He said, "Leave it with me for a couple of days." So we did. After a couple of days we came back to collect it and he hadn't done anything. And I asked him why, and he said he couldn't get it to work—he couldn't get any point where he could plug it in. So I said, "Really, it's run by batteries." This is an electrician [*laughs*], and he hadn't even discovered it was run by batteries. Eventually we got that sorted out, and at least we heard people like Lightning Hopkins and so forth, working in their clubs, so it was really quite a useful pause in the recording.

Did this recorder use quarter-inch tape?

Yes. Well, actually it was a little bit wider than quarter-inch, but you could call it that, yes. And it was on five-inch spools, not seven-inch.

Who were some of the people, and who were the memorable folks you spoke to and recorded during this trip?

I actually recorded about seventy people, so it's quite difficult to answer that immediately in the sense that they were—so many of them—extraordinarily interesting for so many different reasons. For example, Whistling Alex Moore played with such vigor, and he had this incredible kind of folk poetry and was so spontaneous a person. He was a very outstanding character, although I mistook him for a pile of old rags when I first found him outside a saloon in Texas. Then, on the other hand, one or two people were obviously pretty well known, like Little Walter and so forth. Also John Lee Hooker. John Lee Hooker was always a very taciturn man, and I was surprised how good the interview was with him. I didn't think I'd really get very far with it, but he relaxed and he was extraordinarily good. Chris Strachwitz—who I was with, and Mack McCormick—he'd discovered Mance Lipscomb, who termed himself a "songster." He insisted he wasn't a blues singer—he was a songster. It was the first time we'd actually heard the word used by a singer. He was a very good interviewee as well, very spontaneous. This was in a tiny little place called Navasota on the Brazos River in Texas. In Memphis I interviewed Will Shade and Gus Cannon from the old Memphis Jug Band—Gus Cannon and His Jug Stompers—and so forth. You see, so many of these people were still around. In St. Louis I was recording people like Stump Johnson and Walter Davis, and women singers like Edith Johnson and Mary Johnson—not related to her, but it's a popular name among blues singers. And in New York I interviewed Victoria Spivey. So there were just so many people. Sometimes it was people who had never recorded that you might find the most interesting—for example, Buster Pickens. He was really the last, I think, of the barrelhouse pianists that worked in the lumber camps in Texas and Louisiana. He told me a lot about the other singers like Black Boy Shine and others he had known. He was quite remarkable and a very good pianist himself. He told me about the rough life that it was, and unfortunately two years later he was shot and killed.

Are you responsible for the Buster Pickens sessions?

Yes, of course! Most of those recording are mine, but some had been recorded by McCormick.

Where did you find Jasper Love?

Now, he was in Clarksdale. He had actually been interviewed by an American writer, and [the writer] gave me an indication of where he thought Jasper Love would be. He was actually a relative of Willie Love, who was a very interesting recorded blues singer from further south in Greenville, Mississippi. He wasn't around when we got there. I think he had probably died, but Jasper certainly was there. There were just so many. Wade Walton in Clarksdale, Mississippi, was a great help to us. He was a barber, and as had been the tradition amongst barbers in those days in the black community, he always had a guitar in the corner so that somebody waiting to have their hair done could just sit and play guitar until they were ready. And that very thing happened. A chap parked his tractor outside the barbershop [*laughs*] and came in to have his hair done. Wade was already cutting the hair of somebody else, so he sat down to play guitar, and this turned out to be Robert Curtis Smith, who's now a religious singer, I understand, but he's still around anyway. So we recorded Smith and we recorded Wade. Wade got me in touch with a number of other people. So that's how it all fitted together.

Paul Oliver watches Johnny Shines perform at the Ann Arbor Blues Festival. Photo Jim O'Neal.

Did I hear you say that you had interviewed Little Walter?

Yes, I did. But unfortunately my interviews with both Little Walter and Muddy Waters were accidentally wiped clean. It made me absolutely furious about it, but they were, and it was absolutely too late for me to be able to do anything about it. This was when I got back to Washington. A chap wanted me to play some items on the radio, and somehow they'd got something in reverse or whatever. I don't know exactly quite what happened, but anyway the tapes were useless. Fortunately, I quickly realized what had happened, so I didn't lose any more, but I lost those. It would *have* to be them, but that's just what happened. Because obviously I was choosing the best-known names to play for the radio audience. In fact, that was the last I heard of those. Fortunately, what I had done for the whole trip, I was gradually, when I had the spare time, transcribing some of them. So there were transcribed bits of the text. They were able to use those fragments and that's why they're short.

Can you tell me the time frame of your trip?

I can't tell you exactly, because I can't quite remember. It was the end of June and—certainly to the end of September, early October that I was back here anyway . . .

What did you do with all the fruits of your trip—the tapes and photos?

Before I left for the States I'd been asked by the American embassy if I'd be prepared to do an exhibition about blues. Well, they knew that I was going, and that gave them further impetus. So I went to the States, and when I came back, obviously they wanted to know how I got on, but also, interestingly, the new embassy had just been completed and was ready for opening. So they invited me to give the first lecture at the new American embassy, which was quite an extraordinary honor and experience but, from their point of view, something people wouldn't expect. Certainly they'd have an amazingly large audience out of sheer curiosity, so that was good. So they then firmed up their request that I put together an exhibition. Well, obviously I'd got a lot of photographs that I'd taken—hundreds of them—but even so, I could only cover those people I'd seen. But whenever I could I collected photographs, so I got a fair collection.

I went to other people that had collections also and helped me out with items. So gradually I put together this exhibition, which was called "The Story of the Blues." It didn't open until 1964, because it took quite a long time preparing it and trying to decide what the panels would have on them. But anyway, the exhibition was visited by the members of the American Folk Blues Festival, so people like Little Walter and Lightning Hopkins and the Zero Renaissance writers, as they called them—Langston Hughes and others—all came to see the exhibition. So it was a great success from the American embassy's point of view as well. Having done all that, the exhibition was up for many months, but when we finally took it down it then traveled around a few places in England. I didn't want it to get too damaged, but we had to do Exeter and a few other places. Then I thought, "Well, I really ought to try to work on this in the form of a book." So that's how *The Story of the Blues* book started, you see.

Had the outline for the various blues genre, their locations, and a timeline been clear in your mind?

It was "becoming clearer" would be a better way of putting it. It was confusing and difficult to sort out at first, but there were various clues. What I mean by that is that as a result of my interviews with people, I could work out that the percentage of black American musicians who moved to the North—to Chicago and Detroit—was pretty large. I'd already written about that migration in *Blues Fell This Morning*. But I wasn't quite sure if the singers had done that as well, which they hadn't, many of them. It was a case of finding out where they came from—those who came from Georgia, and those who came from Louisiana, and those who came from Mississippi, and Texas, and so forth, and from the Carolinas. And of course Brownie McGhee and Sonny Terry were very good friends. Brownie was teaching my wife to play guitar, and Sonny was happily accompanying on the harmonica. We had them over many times—they stayed with us. They were a tremendous help. It was a case of gradually filling in the answers to the questions that were bothering me by just interviewing the singers and knowing what I wanted to find out. If I knew what they were talking about and knew the records and could reach over and get a record and put it on for them, all of this gave them a kind of assurance, and they were very relaxed and helping. So it was "gradually fitting together" was the way I would put it. It wasn't just a simple process; it had to evolve—partly from research and partly experiment—in a sense.

Were you having any trouble understanding black dialect at this point?

No, I never did have any trouble. I had no trouble understanding black dialect right from the very start, but I think that's probably because I was introduced to it when I was very young. It was rather curious in a way, because, you see, because we had a lot of people from the Caribbean coming in during the early 1950s, and I actually found them far harder to understand than the black Americans. Then again, writers like John Williams and Sterling Brown and Langston Hughes and Richard Wright were all very helpful.

So how did you transform the successful blues exhibition into the book that became *The Story of the Blues*?

Well, the exhibition was the start of it. Obviously I didn't want to do the book as an exhibition, but the point about the exhibition was that it provided me with a very large number of photographs and ephemera which I could use. I was strictly interested in obtaining those which were contextual, that gave an indication of what the levees looked like, or what a lumber camp looked like, and all that kind of thing, you see. I was gradually able to work those in, and then while I'd been in the States I'd spent much of my time when I was in Washington at the Library of Congress collection, going through the photographs there, and they were very helpful. They made all sorts of things available to me, provided I could find them, which I did. So it was all pieced together. After the exhibition had closed down, I just felt all this stuff was really too good to waste. That's why I really embarked on the book.

When was it actually published?

It was first published in July 1969 by Barrie and Rockliffe. The Crescent Press, in the States and in England, and a firm named Chilton—I think they were in Philadelphia—published it in the States.

Let's talk about the broadcasts for the BBC.

Okay. I obviously had all these recordings and wanted to know how to use them on the BBC. With the producer, Anthony Smith, we worked out a way in which the singers would tell the whole narrative; there would be no interviews or speech from me at all. And that worked very well. We had these two programs, and it was quite interesting what the public's reaction was. There were some people who were furious because there was no connecting link, and others were congratulating us for a new approach to interviews, and so forth. At least it stirred up a lot of interest. In subsequent programs I used the interviews in the context of the recordings made by the various singers. I did that also with the records that I had collected, because from the mid-1950s on I was also doing broadcasts. So by the time of the field trip, 1960, I had already been broadcasting on blues for quite a few years. I just wrote a book called *Broadcasting the Blues*, which was a collection of the scripts—those scripts, at least, which have survived—from about 1956 through to 2000.

So that was *Broadcasting the Blues*?

Yes, it's called *Broadcasting the Blues*. It's published by that title in France under the Routledge name.

With these programs, since you'd already been doing a blues broadcast, were these special programs for the BBC or just within the context of your own program?

No, they were broadcasts for the BBC; I was contracted with the BBC. In 1964 I went to West Africa to live for a while, and while I was there I did about twelve programs for

Radio Ghana. That was also a very important phase for me. But it was one of the reasons why the exhibition "The Story of the Blues" was somewhat delayed, because I was actually in Africa until I got back for the opening. It was a good period; there were lots of things happening from my point of view.

How long were these programs?

They would vary from half an hour to an hour. I reckoned I could play six records in a half-hour program playing half the item in each case. In an hour program I could probably play a dozen, sometimes up to fifteen. But I found that half an hour was normally enough. It was better to do a series of half-hour programs than two or three one-hour programs.

Pardon me, but I don't know where Ghana is. Is that on the west coast?

Yes, it's on the west coast. It's adjacent to Togo and Dahomey, and they are adjacent to the west side of Nigeria. And on the other side of Ghana is Côte d'Ivoire, the Ivory Coast.

Did this trip to Africa have anything to do with your research on music?

It was the background to it as far as my interest in the African connection. It was a piece of luck, really. I had gone there because I was working in architectural education and also writing about architecture, so that in Africa I'd gone to lectures on the history of architecture at the University of Kumasi [Kwame Nkrumah University of Science and Technology] in Ghana, which is a couple hundred miles north of the coast. And then a project was being introduced which was going to result in the damming of the Volta River, and this would have meant huge areas being flooded where many black villages and communities lived, you see. So I was asked to go up and investigate this and also to devise a means whereby our students from the Ashanti region could talk to these others and find out what they wanted in the way of housing to replace what was going to be lost. I did this, but in the process of doing so a couple of men, Kunaal and Sosira their names were, started playing and they were griots, and I never heard of those before. These were a kind of local singers who would have to learn the whole history of the family that employed them, but they would also sing in the markets a kind of song division referred to—very witty! I was so struck by certain characteristics that were so close to blues that got me excited about that, I started doing research on their music. Fortunately, Kwabena Nketia, who now lives in California, was then running the Department of American Studies for the university in Accra, and he invited me to come and lecture about black American music, which I did on jazz and blues. That's why I was invited to do these programs for Radio Ghana, but also it gave me an opportunity to widen my resources and back up further my research.

And this resulted in the book *Savannah Syncopators*?

That's right. That resulted in *Savannah Syncopators*. If you look in *Savannah Syncopators*, a photograph I took—not a terribly good one because of conditions—but a photograph of Kunaal and Sosira starts the book, the couple I had first recorded there. Fortunately, I'd taken the BBC recorder with me just in case I did hear music, so I was able to record them

1980 University of Memphis Blues Conference, August 1980. *L to R*: Gayle Dean Wardlow, Bruce Bastin, Cheryl Thurber, David Evans, Bob Vinisky, Jim O'Neal, Kip Lornell, Doug Seroff, and Paul Oliver. Courtesy David Evans.

and record the country dancers and some of the large bands. I did quite a lot of recording and did programs on African music there for the BBC as well.

Speaking of books, didn't you have a hand in some fashion in the publishing of the blues discographies, both prewar and postwar?

Yes, I did have a hand in it. The thing was, I used to write for a magazine called *Jazz Monthly*. The editor was then Albert McCarthy. McCarthy and another writer named Dave Carey, they were doing a kind of serialized discography of jazz called "Jazz Directory." They were trying to cover all blues records in it as well. I didn't think that was a very good idea, but at least it did reveal already an amazing amount of material, because they'd been collecting their data and getting it from record companies and so forth. A couple of friends at the time, R. W. Dixon and his friend John Godrich, were already putting together listings of various record companies who'd issued blues records. They were beginning to distribute, particularly among collectors and those interested. At the same time a chap named Brian Rust, who worked for the BBC, had done a big jazz discography. So I said to them I thought it would be a good idea if they published this as a blues discography. That's a very rare volume now, and tremendously heavy, but at least it got it published and we managed to get a publisher to publish it in a more manageable format. So that's really how it happened.

Of the two who worked on the prewar discography, isn't Dixon still around?

Yes, he's a professor of linguistics in Melbourne, Australia.

And John Godrich was the other author on that volume?

John, yes, John Godrich. He was very nice. He was very different. It's interesting. Just to give you an idea of the span of interests of blues collectors at that time. Bob, as we said, was a professor of linguistics, and John Godrich was kind of a clerk, and both of them were passionate about discography. [*laughs*] That's what I liked about collecting in those days—people came from all sorts of backgrounds. It kind of brought us all together!

And what about the postwar discography? Is there anyone left from that project?

Neil Slaven is still around, certainly. Mike Leadbitter died many years ago. He was active, really, only for a few years, unfortunately. And Simon Napier, who'd worked with him, continued. But then Simon also died many years ago. It was very sad, really. I don't quite know why it happened like it did, but tragically that was the case.

You must have taken a bit of pride in seeing these discographies published.

I don't think I felt any pride about it. I just felt very delighted that it was happening. It was a relief and satisfaction. I can't say that I felt any credit for it.

It seems that there would be a world of difference in doing a prewar discography as compared to the postwar discography. Much of the prewar material is still owned and cataloged by major companies while the postwar material came from thousands of independent small enterprises offering no documentation of dates, location, or sidemen. What an impossible job the latter would be . . .

[*laughs*] There's a lot of truth in that! There were one or two people in these record magazines in the States who would do research on particular labels, and one or two in England—well, quite a lot, really! There were two magazines here, one called *Discophile* and one called *Matrix*. Both of them were really collections of discographies, sometimes labels and sometimes the individual artists. But these were generally coming out quarterly, if not monthly. There were lots of collectors who, because they had the records, could provide information when it was missing. So this also tended to bring people together and support each other. That was one of the nice things about the whole field, really. There was remarkably little in the way of any disagreements of any profound nature, no kind of backbiting and so forth—just amazingly supportive of each other.

Would you talk more about the bluesmen that visited the UK before your trip to the States in 1960? Did we talk about Blind John Davis?

Well, Blind John Davis was playing in France, but he didn't come over to England. The fact that he was blind and didn't quite know where he was—he didn't return when Big Bill returned. In the main, the singers were largely booked in as intermission artists, because there was a dispute between the English Musicians Union and the American Federation of Musicians. They didn't want any European bands going over to the States, because it would take the bread from the American musicians, and the British acted in a similar fashion.

That sounded very ridiculous, but there was an exception, and that was for intermission artists, or variety artists. So they would bring someone like Big Bill or Josh White and then later on Roosevelt Sykes or Little Brother Montgomery, and they'd bring them over as intermission artists to play in the breaks between two performances of a band—particularly Chris Barber with his jazz band. They booked in blues artists as intermission artists, so that means we were able to hear the blues singers.

Who else came over? Aren't there recordings by Muddy and Otis Spann in 1958?

Yes, that's right! I believe that's the correct year, because Big Bill had just died. I first heard about Muddy from Big Bill. That was 1958, just shortly before I went to the States. And as I said, we'd made good friends with Muddy. There were various other people, but not generally so well known—like Curtis Jones, who also came over and played over here ... Eddie Boyd. And some of them actually decided to stay in England or in Europe. But then there was also the series of folk blues festivals put on by a German team and toured in Germany, France, Switzerland, and, of course, Britain—and the Netherlands and Scandinavia. These were Horst Lippmann and Fritz Rau. They put together, generally with the help of Willie Dixon in Chicago, a whole group of singers who would come over and play on these festival tours. So that introduced us to a lot of other singers, and major names—like Son House, for example—were among them, and Big Joe Williams. So that was quite remarkable. And because I did a lot of writing I always had backstage access, so I was able to interview the singers—people like Howling Wolf in England. Especially before going to the States myself, this was very helpful in establishing contacts.

Were you given to any degree of romanticizing of these bluesmen and their lives?

I think—if you're asking me about my own point of view or whether I find this in others, the point is—what I've always been concerned about is trying to get to the truth of the matter, whatever it was. Whether it was pleasant or unpleasant, whether it was strange and bizarre or very mundane, whatever it was, I really wanted to know what the situation was, so that in that sense I personally wasn't romanticizing. I was just extremely inquisitive and interested to try to get to the truth of the matter. Obviously many singers didn't have a romantic following. Someone like Jack Dupree, for example, who really rather traded on it, but he was very witty all the same and an amazing character. And he stayed over in Europe. Quite a few of these people, like Jack Dupree and Curtis Jones and Eddie Boyd, they decided to stay here and lived in Europe. Some of them got married and most died in Europe as well. And of course that was following a path that was also designed among the jazz musicians, the most remarkable of those being Sidney Bechet.

Did you have any personal favorites among the musicians, not necessarily as musicians but as personalities?

This might be a surprise, but the person I got along most easily with was J. B. Lenoir. That was because we were the same age, virtually. I think he was about six months older than me [*laughs*], so we were really buddies. He got me to all sorts of clubs and joints and got me to meet up with various odd reverends in churches and so forth, as well as taking me to the clubs. J. B. was a tremendous friend. But there were a number of other people. Living with Muddy was quite an experience in itself because, you see, a number of singers lived in the basement of Muddy's house. One of these was "St. Louis Jimmy," James Oden. I got along with him very well too. He was a very nice friend and he wrote blues for a lot of blues singers. We corresponded for several years afterward. Quite often it was not necessarily the big names but often the very interesting people, who are probably passed over by collectors these days, who were the most amenable and easy to get on with.

At the other end of the spectrum, was there anyone who was particularly difficult to get along with?

I think Howling Wolf was the most difficult to get on with—for me. He seemed to be pretty irritable most of the time; whenever I saw him he seemed to be irritable. So I think the singer I least had a relationship with was Howling Wolf. For the most, I didn't really have much difficulty. I thought it would be very difficult in the South, and certainly Chris Strachwitz and I and my wife, we had to use various devices for means of avoiding the white population, because we were persona non grata, really. That we did, very successfully. So I didn't have too many difficulties. Occasional brushes here and there, but not normally with the blues singers, more with the white people.

Is there anything I'm passing over you feel we need to discuss here?

Probably we could discuss a little bit the other kind of genre. I'm personally very interested in the idioms that preceded the blues to the degree to which they could be traced or explained. Some try to fit in the songsters—the kind of generation of pre-blues singers who also must have put blues in their repertoire. These are people who must have inherited much of the music of the nineteenth century. What is very, very difficult in any of this to sort—and I still find it difficult in all these years—is getting much in the way of indication of the music and song between the end of the Civil War and the beginning of segregation. That period is peculiarly badly documented except for the Reconstruction era. This, I think, was the formative period when blues was taking shape. What is interesting is that there were a number of singers, like Frank Stokes, who did record songs which had been collected in the early years of the twentieth century and had been written up by early writers—not writing about blues, but before blues, as far as they were concerned.

I'm very interested in trying to trace what had been written about and collected in the teens of the twentieth century and was actually on record. I did a book called *Songsters and Saints*, which was really about this, about songsters—people who sang these pre-blues songs—and also the "saints" from the various churches, because there was a parallel kind of tradition prior to the popularization of gospel. That's an aspect which I'm still very interested in. Of course, there are many other aspects of the blues which I think have gotten overlooked over time. So I've been working on a book, "Blues the World Forgot," using a provisional title—a working title, anyway—which is really about the aspects which have not been totally undocumented but have been rather neglected in much of the writing of the last twenty years or so. That's one of the things I'm working on at the present time—I'm really writing this out of curiosity—and that is the difficult question—of exactly where the blues began and how it did.

Were you able to meet Tampa Red?

No, I didn't meet Tampa Red, unfortunately. He was quite ill in a hospital. I didn't really want to disturb him there. Jacques Demêtre of Paris, though he only went to Chicago and didn't go south—but he did go the year before, 1959—he met up with Tampa Red. But Tampa, as I say, got very ill so I didn't see him.

Paul Oliver at Buddy Guy's Legends, Chicago, 1999. Photo Robert Barclay.

How about Thomas Dorsey?

I was introduced to Tom Dorsey through J. B. Lenoir. He was not only a pianist, but he was also a preacher. J. B. took me to the church where he used to preach. He was on his best behavior. I did try to interview him informally, but he was a little bit uncomfortable being asked about blues when he was wearing his religious gear. I don't think it was a particularly successful interview, but it was interesting to meet up with him.

When you were with Chris Strachwitz, did you say that Mack McCormick was with him?

Yes, in Texas; we met up with Mack. Before I met up with Chris, he had done so previously, on the same trip, but coming to meet me, he'd met up with Mack. And Mack had taken him to hear Mance Lipscomb, who he had just discovered. So they were saying to me, "We've got somebody you've just got to hear!" Then they took me and we recorded Mance. Personally I was very interested in trying to find Black Ace. We did find him in Fort Worth. Also I was interested in trying to find Buddy Woods, who Black Ace had worked with. Unfortunately, it turned out he'd died. We did meet up with the pianist, who'd been his pallbearer. I mean, all sorts of curious things happen—I can't go into all the details of those things—but, yes, Mack and I were going to do a book on Texas blues, but it became eventually rather unmanageable.

This trip led Chris Strachwitz to many of the people he recorded and issued on his Arhoolie label, didn't it?

Yes, yes, it did, certainly! That was certainly the case. And it also gave Chris a lot of experience in recording people, so that when he got back to California he was able to pick up on one or two of the blues singers who were there. These days he still makes a trip to the South every year. And he's also very into Mexican and Tex-Mex music as well.

Did you meet any label owners on your trip?

I did meet one or two of the people who recorded. They were the talent scouts rather than the recording company people. The companies were there for commercial purposes, and I was more interested with meeting the people who were doing the field recording, or just trying to find artists.

In your travels to St. Louis I know you interviewed both Signifyin' Mary Johnson and Edith North Johnson. Do you have any reminiscence or anecdotes of them?

Mary Johnson—"Signifyin' Mary." She was a Johnson because she was married to Lonnie Johnson for a while. I met her and her mother. She lived very close to Biddle Street and much of the black quarters of St. Louis. A very quiet and rather pleasant person, but shy in a way. Edith Johnson was very different. Her husband had run the Deluxe Music Shop and at one time, the Booker T. Washington Theatre, I think it was, in St. Louis. She was very much more somewhat brash and outgoing in the way that Victoria Spivey was—more of a classic blues singer—where Mary Johnson was a kind of folk blues singer. That was kind of fascinating in itself but not my plan. It simply turned out that way. It was interesting listening to the two and the way they talked, the things they talked about, the way in which Mary would continually refer back to her mother. Whereas Edith Johnson would push her mother out, who was also there. [*laughs*] But it was kind of a different outlook and behavior pattern. I found that interesting because it revealed something about why one was in professional show business and the other one wasn't.

I stayed in touch with many of the people I talked to for several years afterwards, because the agreement I had with the BBC was that every person who I interviewed and who recorded for me would be paid. And BBC are very good about that and they agreed to do so. I found that it was better not to tell the people straightaway, so that they weren't just saying yes because they were going to get some money out of it. I wanted them to say yes because they were prepared to talk to me, and then I'd tell them afterward they were going to get paid and it was a real "whoopee" for them. The BBC did follow this up, so I did stay in touch with them to let them know it was coming and get them to send me back a little signed document that confirmed that they received it. They would correspond if they could or get someone else to write the letter if they couldn't write.

In your opinion, has the blues stopped, or does it continue today?

In my view I feel that it's followed a path similar to jazz in the sense that it was essentially a music of an ethnic minority and had its own identity, but then at a certain stage it becomes popularized or changed. Also, regrettably, it becomes picked up by white musicians, who were probably easier to book and to a large extent have taken over. I think that happened with jazz, too, to quite an extent. It was a major change in the nature of jazz, and I think blues followed a rather similar path, so that these days there are blues musicians and guitarists—some of them are very good—in just about every European country. They play well, but they're not blues musicians as far as I'm concerned. They'd probably be offended by that, but I'm interested in it as a music of a particular people rather than just anybody who picks it up and cares to play it. My writing, therefore, tends to concentrate on the period up to the 1960s but not much after that.

Well, that's very honest of you! I guess if blues is defined as a black folk music, then by definition nobody else can play it.

Well, if you put it that way 'round—in the sense because of the race, but more because, I think, of the culture. In other words, the music played a role—blues in earlier years—in the black community. I don't think it plays quite the same role now and hasn't done so for a long time. Probably soul music took over, and certainly gospel did for quite a while. Rap probably has now, but for me it has no music. It has poetry and writing, but I don't get any musical satisfaction out of it at all.

SAM CHARTERS INTERVIEW

I was born in Pittsburgh, Pennsylvania, in 1929. My family moved to California in the fall of 1945. I began traveling a few years later. I spent a year in Europe when I was eighteen. I first went to New Orleans and began the research in December of 1950 when I was twenty-one. I went into the army in the spring of 1951 and spent two years in Alaska. I got out of the army two years later and spent six months in northern Alaska, then to San Francisco for six months and back to New Orleans. I was twenty-four when I returned to New Orleans. I returned to live there and write the book after my discharge. I spent a lot of the next eight years working on that first book, *Jazz: New Orleans, 1885–1957*. I stayed that first month in New Orleans on Bourbon Street in a raggedy old house with Dick Allen, who, like me, was totally obsessed with New Orleans jazz.

You began with your focus on jazz. When did that focus shift over to blues?

Well, this is that thing that many blues fans don't understand, and that is that the blues first began for everyone like myself as classic blues. So that in the 1930s, when I was a kid seven or eight years old, I grew up in a family that loved jazz, so I was already hearing Bessie Smith and Ma Rainey and these people. Blues at that time was something we all knew about if for no other reason than that Louis Armstrong was playing all those accompaniments. Blues with a guitar—that was all right, but it had none of the excitement of the classic blues, which had the greatest jazz musicians accompanying some very great singers.

Samuel Charters, 2011. Photo Henry Denander/Kamini Press.

So they went hand-in-hand—the blues singers and the jazz players?

Well, there was a wonderful dichotomy that happened in the studios, Steve. When it all began, the first blues recordings actually were by the white singers, who began recording in 1916. The first queen of the blues was Marion Harris with "The St. Louis Blues" that in the spring of 1920 was a huge hit. Six months later when the first African American performed a blues song, they were pretty much following in a well-worn path. The recording companies began bringing these stately voiced women singers into the studio, who sang at very slow tempos, not danceable. And then they began bringing in jazz musicians like Armstrong to accompany them. What happened was this wonderful osmosis between the two: the jazz musicians taught the singers how to swing, and the singers taught the musicians how to vocalize on their horns. And the result by around 1924 or 1925 was that you had essentially a jazz vocal.

In your personal work, which came first—the blues reissue packages or the field trips?

The field trips came much first. In 1950 I went to New Orleans to learn to play the clarinet better, and I spent my time taking lessons from clarinetist George Lewis. There was this moment—I had read the four books on black jazz, and I thought I understood the history. Then one day I came early. George usually took a nap. He worked as a stevedore and was taking his nap. And he woke up and he was lying there on the bed. I had seen him the day before with Jim Robinson, his trombone player, walking in the French Quarter, and they were well dressed in their suits and hats. And I said, "Where've you been?" They said they'd been to a funeral, and I said, "Who was it?" And they said, "'Big Bama,' a trumpet player." And I had read every jazz book—all four of them—and I had never heard of Big Bama. So that next day, Monday, I said to George, "Tell me about other people I've never heard of." And he began talking, and he talked and talked and talked. And I realized a world was there and that world was disappearing. So I felt that I had to do what I could to preserve what was there. It soon became very obvious.

What I did was I went to junk shops and old furniture stores and began just buying junk 78s. Dick Allen was doing the same thing. We piled them up beside our cheap phonographs, and the rule was that you had to play everything in the pile—in order—both sides. I very quickly became aware that there were a lot of blues records. It was through these I became aware that there was something really there. In 1948, before I went to Europe even, I was playing in a band. We used to end our rehearsals with one of two 78s: one was Blind Willie Johnson's "Dark Was the Night, Cold Was the Ground," and the other was an acetate copy of something called "Stones in My Passway" by Robert Johnson. So already in 1948 I was aware that there was this other voice within the world of African American musical expression. Certainly I had so much to do writing this book on New Orleans jazz, but I was already collecting, already gathering, and I did my first country blues recordings in the summer of 1954.

What initiated the first of your field trips?

Well, I went to New Orleans to learn to play the clarinet better. And then I discovered a number of things. I discovered the richness and the complexity of the African American community. I also walked into institutionalized racism, which I had not understood. Certainly Pittsburgh was not liberal, but my classes were at least token integrated. And my family having always been interested in jazz, I had never been conscious of the pervasiveness of Southern racism. It extended to the North, but it was more hidden. In the South it was open, it was naked, and it was terrifying. So this became a great deal of the emotional spur that pushed me into doing the work.

What initiated the various trips throughout the South after your stint in New Orleans?

I was aware that throughout the whole Southern area there was a rich vernacular music, which was being lost. So I couldn't limit myself totally to New Orleans jazz. The book that I published, *Jazz: New Orleans*, was a biographical dictionary of every black musician I could find information about who played in the city from 1885 to 1957, when the book was published. At the same time I was aware that there was this *other* world out there. So the first country blues I did was with the Mobile Strugglers in Alabama in 1954, but through my interest in jazz I had already discovered the jug bands. One of the first great releases by Jelly Roll Morton, "Dr. Jazz," on 78 in 1926, actually has the Dixieland Jug Blowers on the other side. So I knew about the Memphis Jug Band and I knew about Cannon's Jug Stompers. So in 1956 I took my tapes of what I had been recording up to New York to Moe Asch to ask him if he would begin putting out my material, and on the way back I stopped in Memphis. And that was my first time in Memphis, and I found Will Shade of the old Memphis Jug Band. I walked into his little rented room the next day, and there was Will Shade and Charlie Burse, who'd been with the Memphis Jug Band in later days, *and* Gus Cannon of Cannon's Jug Stompers. So I recorded them, and actually the first recordings of all this material came out on an album called *American Skiffle Bands* that Folkways released in 1956.

At the same time, I had been going back and forth between New Orleans and California for the G.I. Bill. I was technically in school at Berkeley, so I'd travel back and forth. And I began trying to find Blind Willie Johnson. And I went all over Texas, simply asking people who knew him. And I was sent from one person to another and they would sing me his songs. And then my first wife, Mary, and I found his widow in Beaumont, Texas. The first real documentation that I did was an album by Blind Willie Johnson on Folkways. The first side of it was a kind of narration/collage of voices I recorded in the search for him, and then the other side was a series of reissues. So that record had both things happening at the same time, reissues and documentation.

I should say that I never intended to do anything that I did. I had a dream that I would do four albums and that would be the end of that. One was of the Eureka Brass Band, one was Blind Willie Johnson. The third one was the Six and Seven-Eights String Band, a New Orleans group that had been together since 1913. And the fourth would be a Scott Joplin album, a Joplin bouquet—and those were the four I was going to do, and then I was going to become the great American novelist. [*laughs*]

This was very early on in the relations between black musicians and white public audience. What were communications like between the Memphis musicians and yourself?

Well, there's a difference between my approach and someone like Harold Courlander or Alan Lomax. As musicologists they essentially worked with nonprofessionals, and I decided there's no use of us all working the same side of the street, because there was *so much* to be done, and the clock was against us. So I essentially worked with musicians who had recorded. These people were used to the very specific circumstances of someone coming in and "wanting to make a record." So, yes, for their neighbors or people around them, the fact that I was sitting there was very difficult, because they were probably going to get in trouble—or was music really all I wanted?—because the old man next door, he'd never done anything that they thought was special. But Furry Lewis, Will Shade, and these people—they had recorded, worked within the idea of a recording session with people like me. So I didn't have that other situation. Occasionally out in the country I *did* record musicians that hadn't recorded. These were people for whom the whole concept was new. But otherwise I was working with older pros.

Did you ask them to do biographic profiles? To recount their lives in addition to recording musical performances?

Well, if you remember those old albums [*laughs*], every one of those old albums I did for Folkways includes at least one track where they simply talk, about their lives and about their backgrounds. I remember the first time I met Taj Mahal in Boston, when he was still a student up there in Cambridge. [*laughs*] He sang and recited for me the whole first side of the Furry Lewis LP, including the interview—doing both our voices! It was wonderful!

As I was going through the books, I ran across profiles of various musicians and wondered what/who were the specific sources. For instance, did you actually meet and interview Blind Willie McTell?

McTell had died. Many people contacted me after *The Country Blues* came out. There was wonderful response to the book, other people who understood that there was work to be done. A man named Ed Rhodes wrote me from Atlanta. He had done the last session with Blind Willie. He came up and brought the tapes. I remember sitting in a darkened room. My cousin was sleeping in the room, so we couldn't turn on the lights. So we sat in the dark and listened to McTell's last session that I put out on Prestige Records. That session was actually Ed Rhodes.

What was the nature of the stir that centered around your book *The Country Blues*?

There was a consciousness among many people; people don't remember today that the initial excitement about blues came from folkies. So it was the folk blues. For one thing we were intensely fascinated with the guitar playing. So here was Mississippi John Hurt with that alternate thumb guitar picking, and the folk world almost fainted. [*laughs*] They just couldn't believe how exciting it was with the acoustic guitar styles that came from every part of the South. *The Country Blues* made people aware—for the first time—of what was there. No one had any idea about it, or that you could set it in a place. I think *The Country Blues*, by setting the blues in a place—not recording studios, not folk clubs, but in its country environment, its country setting—I think that's what made the big difference.

It's one thing to interview a living musician; it's quite another task to reconstruct the events in the life and career of a dead musician. What was the source for the Blind Lemon Jefferson profile?

What was absolutely central to my growth in this field was the book *Jazzmen*, which was published in 1939. That was essentially what the editors who'd written different chapters in the book had done; they had simply interviewed elderly people and created a portrait from the various bits of material that they got—reminiscences—and with some shrewdness had tied it to what we could see of the scene. And also the sense, if these musicians had recorded, could we have the record? We had no discography; this was an incredible problem. Each record we found in those days was like finding another bit of the coastline of a very mysterious continent, because we had no idea who had recorded, who they were, how much they recorded, anything! We just didn't know anything. But with *Jazzmen* they went back to New Orleans in the pre-recording era and created vivid portraits of people whose music we had never heard, whose lives we knew very little about. They made a legend out of Buddy Bolden, and we know less about Buddy Bolden than we do about Shakespeare. So I was very used to this, and this had shaped me very much. I still write like Charles Edward Smith, who wrote the romantic interludes in *Jazzmen*. And I was very close, finally, to Fred Ramsey, the main man behind the book; when he came to New Orleans in 1954, he became as much of a mentor as I ever had.

Interesting. Can you expound on this point? How did the two of you work together?

I had bought a tape recorder before I left Alaska, and I was simply recording, street singers, everything! But I had no sense of the mechanics; I had no idea of the kind of documentation you should do of your recordings. So Fred was there for a few weeks in New Orleans on a Guggenheim. He'd gotten the first Guggenheim for African American musical studies. So he had gone back to Livingston County, Alabama, and then to Mississippi doing *in depth* an attempt to capture the music of these areas. So he hung out in New Orleans to listen to what he had and make notes. His wife and son couldn't stand the heat, so they went back and he rented a raggedy room over on Coliseum Avenue. And he simply told me how you handle the documentation, the kind of notes you were supposed to take. He also had some very useful tips!

Frederick Ramsey Jr. Historic New Orleans Collection.

We were dealing with tape recorders, which were new to us, and he told me that if I recorded at too high a level I'd get print-through. And if I recorded on a stereo machine, to use only one channel and kill the other channel when I play it back to avoid the hiss. So when I go back to listen to some of those tapes I did in the early 1950s, there's no print-through, and one can still get a very decent clean signal from them. And just the sense of documentation—the sense of tying the recordings to the place, to who was there, what was there, what were the circumstances, since the circumstances influence the recording you get. And then he told me about Moses Asch and told me to go to Moe and take the tapes I had. So Fred and I stayed close friends until I moved to Europe fifteen years later.

That sounded like some valuable advice all the way around.

Absolutely, absolutely! I think that at some stage or other, since what we're doing is complex, I know that some people use my books as a template for what they did. But at that point there were no books like mine, but I had Fred Ramsey!

Can you describe the tape recorder that you were using?

It was a Pentron. God, it was a big bulky thing. It was big and square, and it had a little green eye that showed me the volume, and essentially that was it. I only used one speed—seven and a half inches. I could record on two sides, but, as I said, I never did. I carried it all over. God, I carried it to Mexico. I must have recorded about thirty albums on that thing. I never was able to afford anything better until I got the contract to do *The Country Blues* in 1958. Then I was able to buy an Ampex, which also was big and bulky. I wasn't able to get a Uher until I went to Africa in 1974. Fred was using one of those wind-up machines, and you go crazy . . .

What was the source for the information on Rabbit Brown?

Actually there was a review of Rabbit Brown in *Bookman* magazine back in the 1920s by a very important, influential white writer, Abbe Niles. He at least gave me some sense that Rabbit Brown was known outside of this world of the record collector. And in New Orleans, I don't know which one of the hundreds of musicians I talked to told me a little bit about Rabbit Brown. But the little bit I knew about him was what I was told in New Orleans.

And would you talk a little bit about James Alley?

Well . . . I know it's complicated whether it's Jane Alley or James Alley. In the 1950s when I was there, it was still there with the sign on it—Louis Armstrong was born in James Alley—people there would show you any one of the two or three rooms they were certain he'd been born in. I photographed it, and there's a photo in the book I have coming out this week, *A Trumpet around the Corner: The Story of New Orleans Jazz.* There are some of the old photos I took in James Alley. It's two blocks long near Conti Street. It's in the Uptown—the Baptist African American neighborhood—as distinguished from the Creole neighborhood on the other side of Canal Street.

And there were activities that went on there?

Well, not in itself . . . it led to the honky-tonks on Perdido Street. Storyville was on the French Quarter side of Canal Street, and the black version of Storyville was on the western side, which was around Uptown. The whole area was later taken away for the Superdome—that was the center. But you see these old jazz recordings with those street names, "Perdido Street Blues," "Gravier Street Blues"—there were honky-tonks on every corner—a very informal, very lively music scene. Never documented as much as Storyville was, nor was it indeed so organized. It seems to have been just a lot of drop-in musical sessions of people playing whatever they felt like. A lot of street beggars, a lot of street music—very lively, a richly creative neighborhood. Louis Armstrong wrote about it beautifully in his memoirs. One has the sense that, yes, there was really something there.

And what about the source for the profile of Lonnie Johnson?

People didn't realize when I wrote *The Country Blues* that I was really trying to be conscious of the African American audience for the music, and Lonnie was a *major* figure. We didn't know, unfortunately, much of anything about him, as we didn't in those days. But I had a great deal of music to write about, so I could simply extrapolate from the recordings. I was also very aware that Johnson was a very complex figure, because in my record collecting I was buying all his King label records, where he sang beautiful versions of popular ballads, like "My Mother's Eyes." And I also knew, from my jazz days, that he had played those blistering solos on "Hot and Bothered," with the Duke Ellington Orchestra, and he'd also performed with Armstrong's Hot Five as guitar soloist. So he was a richly complex musical artist. At this point none of us had any idea of the kind of romanticization that would follow *The Country Blues* after the publication of the book. I assumed that people loved Lonnie Johnson and so they would continue to love Lonnie Johnson, which wasn't the case at all!

Please explain.

Johnson's appeal was to an African American audience; his confidence, his stance as a successful performer was not the kind of profile we were looking for. The poète maudit, the Baudelaire, the starving poet—this was the white image of what we wanted blues singers to be. And we certainly didn't want them to be successful and have long careers singing in lounges. Lonnie did a wonderful thing—I couldn't believe it—in a Carnegie Hall concert. He came out and faced all his blues fans and sang "Red Sails in the Sunset," because that's what he sang in black clubs, and the audience looked at him like he'd lost his mind. I edited those two volumes of the tapes that Lonnie had done for Moe Asch. He said, "You know, people get the wrong idea about me. They think I've had a hard life—I've had a wonderful life!" [*laughs*] He fit none of the clichés of raggedy Mississippi!

Will you talk about one of my favorites, Edith North Johnson?

[*laughs*] That was so much fun! As I guess you know from reading the liner notes, there was absolutely *no way* to fit this wonderfully confident, well-dressed businesswoman into the life of the very young woman who'd made these lovely recordings in the 1920s because she'd happened to be married to the guy who was a talent scout for the record company. And the contrast between Edith and Henry, the accompanist; Henry was really ragged and down-and-out. There was Edith all through the warm-ups—Henry kept playing the piano—and Edith was sitting over across the room with three or four of the businesswomen, very well dressed, who were just simply chatting. She'd be interrupted during the recording because she had to take a business call. She was charming, sensible, and she had a wonderful feeling about the recordings she had done. She was proud of them. But it was not something she had elected to do, so the fact that she hadn't become a star wasn't important. The fact that people still remembered that she'd done these couple of records, *that was nice*—she enjoyed that. I thought she had a wonderful balance to what she had done.

In your latest book you do a profile of Mamie Smith without having met Mamie Smith. Am I correct?

That's right, Mamie had died. But as I *did* say in the book, Dan Burley—the young, at that time, African American writer for the *Amsterdam News*, the big Harlem newspaper—had done incredible, in-depth work with interviews with Mamie and Perry Bradford, who worked with her. And also, when I wrote the history of jazz in New York City [*Jazz: A History of the New York Scene*] with Len Kunstadt, every morning Len would wake us up with a riff on his kazoo, playing a Johnny Dunn lick outside our basement apartment window, and then deliver piles of material so that I could move on to the next chapter of the book. He had interviewed everyone else and actually been close with everyone else still alive—Lucille Hegamin, Victoria Spivey—so that he had a consciousness and a sense of the Harlem background that had been Mamie Smith's milieu. And if you were in New York, you were very aware that the picture of the blues in New York was totally different than the picture of the blues outside New York. When I went to New York in 1958 after I left New Orleans, I spent a lot of time with Len, and he introduced me to this side which was Mamie Smith—the mansions and the big clothes, and the stage shows, the stage presentations. I met a lot of the musicians who worked with Mamie Smith. I had no feeling that I was having to make up anything with Mamie Smith; I really thought that's who she was.

Just off the top of your head, is it possible to tell how many field trips you went on all totaled?

No, I really couldn't tell and it gets rather complicated. [*laughs*] You could say when I did the album series *Chicago: The Blues Today*, that was one field trip. [*laughs*] A New York record company sent me out to Chicago. I did a lot of recordings that were never released. And also understand that after *The Country Blues*, my wife and I spent a year living in Scotland and I did four albums there. Wonderful field trips to the west coast of Ireland, to the Orangemen of Northern Ireland, to the Scottish/English borders. I just had a wonderful time! And in 1958 Annie and I did the three albums in the Bahamas, where we found Joseph Spence. And then, let's see, all the field trips to Africa and all that recording. [*laughs*] No one's ever asked me how many. I've never thought of it. It just seems for a while that's all I did. I carried my tape recorder on buses all over Mexico hoping I could find something to record, and the only recordings that I made were in northern Mexico, in Sonora. I lived there while I wrote *Jazz: New Orleans*. It turns out the recordings I made there got royalty statements from Folkways, since these recordings were the only ones made of the Yaqui

Indian musicians at this moment. Some years these sell more than anything else. [*laughs*] Totally bewildering! I can't even pretend I know what goes on.

How did you travel when you made the trips in the continental US?

Well . . . I was always starving. If I made three thousand dollars a year I was wide-eyed. I worked as a picture framer, part-time. . . . I rode buses as a checker for the New Orleans bus company—anything—anything to get by. So when I did *The Country Blues* research—I did a lot of recording with Furry Lewis and Lightning Hopkins, just a whole lot of recording—I had borrowed the little green coupe that Ann, who became my wife, owned. She had driven it from California to join me in New York, then we went to the Bahamas and came back with it, and then she let me take the car to the South. When I got the money to do the Eureka Brass Band from Moe Asch—I'd been trying to record the Eureka Brass Band to finish one of my four albums so I could move on—he sent me $358. It was union scale. I was in Sacramento, California, so that's what Moe sent me; he sent me $358. [*laughs*] So for that field trip I traveled from Sacramento, California, to New Orleans on a Greyhound bus with my feet on top of the tape recorder, sleeping for three days to get there so that I could make the recording. It was always pretty scrappy, hand-to-mouth. [*laughs*]

Would you talk about your landmark summit meeting with Lightning Hopkins?

I had heard his recordings in New Orleans. I was managing a picture frame shop there for a time. The radio was on all the time and I heard a lot of Lightning Hopkins, who was recording a lot in the mid-1950s. I was aware that Lightning was something very special, but no one knew where he was or anything about him. We always ate at a place called the Bourbon House on the corner of Bourbon and St. Peter which was very raggedy—and cheap! One of the cooks heard us talking and said, "That's my cousin. He's in Houston." So at least we knew that Lightning was in Houston. I was in Houston a couple of times and couldn't find him. So then as part of *The Country Blues* trip I decided, "This time I'm gonna find him." From one of my New Orleans contacts I had gotten the name Mack McCormick. So I stayed with Mack McCormick, who had also been looking for Lightning. So with Mack I'm driving the little green coupe that my wife had, and we managed to find his guitar in pawn. We went to this big pawn shop and there was his guitar, but nobody knew where *he* was. At this point Lightning's life was very much on the edge—a lot of gambling, a lot of things he was involved in that weren't legal—so nobody wanted to tell us where he was. Who were these two white guys who obviously were some kind of police or something? Who were they, and what were they doing looking for Lightning?

Finally Mack had a job and he had to go back to work, so that next morning I set out by myself. The day before, we'd met an old girlfriend and we met Lightning's sister, who wouldn't tell us much of anything. So the next day I was driving down Dowling Street, a gray winter's day, and I stopped at a red light and a car stopped beside me with the window rolled down. There was a man with dark glasses and he looked at me. "You lookin' for Lightnin'?" [*laughs*] I said, "Yes, I am." He said, "That's me." Immediately

Lightning understood that I was someone wanting to make a record—it was something he was totally familiar with—and I would, of course, pay him money, which everybody did. He didn't have a guitar, and I made the decision then, which really irritated him, but for the audience at that moment, 1959, validated what we did. I went and rented him an acoustic guitar. And we were driving along, and I remember the broken string; it had only five strings. And we passed a bunch of schoolgirls going off, and Lightning, just on the five strings, began playing more guitar than I'd ever heard, singing his version of "Good Morning Little School Girl," and I realized that I really had something here. I had very little money, but I arranged to record him in his room. He had a really ragged room that he was renting from a lady on the back of Dowling Street. It was quiet—it was on a quiet street—that was the most important thing. And it was actually not a large room, but it had hanging drapes and things, so the acoustics were pretty good. And I had a decent microphone, so I said, "Lightning, let's go!" So he sat on a chair. I sat on the bed with the microphone in between us. I bought him a pint of gin—that's all I could afford—and then we started.

I hand-held the microphone so I could move it back and forth. When he was singing I could hold it closer to his lips but hold back so he couldn't lean too far forward and pop and give me distortion. And when he played a guitar solo I could then gently move the microphone down to the guitar. So for three hours I held my arm out straight making this recording. [*laughs*] He hadn't ever thought of an LP; he was entirely thinking in terms of a single. And I'd offered him all the money I had—two hundred dollars. And of course when he'd done two songs, as far as he was concerned he'd earned his two hundred dollars. [*laughs*] At this point he was wary; he was absolutely without a penny. He couldn't imagine that what I was doing had any reality, and the fact that it was going to be two hundred dollars was finally all that mattered. And then I began asking him for *old* songs, and that seemed truly to spur something in him. There was enough gin to draw him back into his memories, but not so much that he became the maudlin drunk I had to work with later on, when more money was involved. I think because it was brand-new what was happening to him; this was the first time he'd been asked any of these questions about the past, about Blind Lemon Jefferson. He *was* an artist. All the other things Lightning was, he was a consummate artist. Also, since I'd done a lot of field recording, I didn't hesitate to make him tune the damn guitar, so that it kept staying continually in tune. And because I had had a lot of experience at this point recording, I got a fairly decent recorded sound. I was very, very happy with the record. It's interesting. It was much more modern and contemporary than the kind of recording I'd been doing with the Memphis Jug Band or the Mobile Strugglers, which was genuinely in the 1920s country blues mode. This was Lightning, which was a timeless blues expression. When I brought the tapes back that evening and played them for Mack McCormick, he was appalled. He thought it was just rock, and rhythm and blues, and why did I bother with that? But of course six months later he was suing me as Lightning's manager, demanding to know where the royalties were. [*laughs*]

After Bill Quinn [Gold Star label] and Anne Cullom [Aladdin label], I'll bet Lightning was trying to figure out what kind of operation you were running—a raggedy white guy shows up and do it in his room . . .

And with a lousy car! The fact that it was a really old small car, that baffled everybody I recorded, the fact that I wasn't driving any status-symbol car.

Are there any other field sessions you'd like to discuss that I haven't brought up?

I had a marvelous contact with Henry Townsend in St. Louis. He was a fine artist, and for him the recording was very significant. He was not ragged and down-and-out. He was selling insurance, had a decent life. But he had been working steadily as a musician. The album we did, which was ultimately released on Prestige, was the first electric session I'd ever done, with an electric guitar and an electric bass, Tommy Bankhead. And Henry had been working with Henry Spaulding in the 1920s, and he sang that incredible version of "Cairo Blues," which for me was one of the high points of my field recording. "Daddy Hotcakes," that photo that Ann took that has been on books and records and has appeared over and over and over and has been exhibited in galleries—and Daddy Hotcakes, who made up the blues as he went along—he was just astonishing! Most of the St. Louis sessions came out late—on Folkways, some on Prestige. But the J. D. Short, Edith North Johnson, Daddy Hotcakes sessions came out together on Folkways in the 1980s.

Let's talk about some of the recordings you did. Let's start with the microgroove reissues of sides that were originally issued as 78s. You had that one landmark reissue package, *The Country Blues*.

Well, you understand that all of this had been preceded by jazz reissues; Fred Ramsey had done an eleven-volume set of jazz reissues. And of course in 1952 there was the Harry Smith set. The first thing that Annie and I did when we began living together was scrape together thirty-five dollars, somehow, and buy the complete set. This was 1952. Fred Ramsey's series began as soon as there were ten-inch LPs, so I was very used to the concept of reissues. Then there was the copyright problem; we all got in trouble, so we essentially backed off. But then for *The Country Blues*—I don't know if you remember the original notes, but the original notes are a long, spirited defense of the fact that we had to bootleg [*laughs*], since the major companies wouldn't release the material and there was no way we could get permission. And yet this was part of the American cultural heritage; we couldn't simply allow it to sit in some company's vaults because they didn't believe in it.

But there was already a lot going on. Victor, for example, had begun the X label series. Understand that this had been going on in the jazz world for a decade before the blues world picked it up. What we did in the blues world was absolutely just follow in the footsteps of where jazz had already gone. And working for Folkways, which already had the Harry Smith albums and had been reissuing jazz 78s for years, what I did with *The Country Blues* album I think confused people, because I attempted to make the album in part mirror what black society had been hearing and buying. That's why Lonnie Johnson was there, but also artists like Blind Willie McTell, who never sold very well but whom I really love.

And the one oddball of all, I reissued Robert Johnson, whom nobody had ever heard of, and I apologized for that since it was just a personal preference. Then I went on with the RBF series. Moe Asch denied this, but RBF was set up as a separate corporation—Record, Book, and Film—so that should there be lawsuits—Were there lawsuits? Of course there were lawsuits. We were endlessly fighting lawsuits. RBF was set up, as Moe said, "to be my window on the world." And I think at least those first three albums featured included that photo of me that was on the back of *The Country Blues*. I told Moe, "I'm beginning to feel like that Victor dog listening to the phonograph!" and I asked him to stop. [*laughs*] I did twenty-five or thirty albums of the issues of blues and jazz, and also ragtime, gospel, and calypso.

You read my mind. I was curious about the RBF label.

This is also interesting. Moe Asch asked me if I could do a record of blues poetry. I was doing a literature series at the same time for Folkways—Emerson, Stephen Crane, Walt Whitman, Herman Melville—for school use. That was the time when, to catch up with the Russians, the government was giving money to the schools to buy cultural things, and that was essentially what kept Folkways Records afloat. And Moe asked me to do an album of the poetry of the blues. So I put together a number of blues records which I thought had real poetic bite. And then I had to listen to the tape. And I have to say, Steve, I couldn't understand it myself. The dialects were really hard! And I would take it to African American friends, and they had as much trouble as I had with those Mississippi dialects. If you didn't grow up in Tunica County, you didn't know *what* they were singing, and on some old 78s we *still* don't. So I went to Moe and I said, "Look, Moe, I did this but it won't make any sense at all. Why don't I write it as a book?" He said, "Go ahead." It took me seventeen days. I turned what had been the recording and my notes into *The Poetry of the Blues*. And to our surprise it sold and sold and sold and sold.

When you did the reissues on RBF, what was the source for the vintage recordings?

I had a lot of them. I still *do* have a lot of them. I was in a friendly blood fight with Pete Whelan and his group, who in answer to me did the album *Really! The Country Blues*, which emphasized the Mississippi singers. I had not emphasized them, because within the black community those singers were not central. There were a lot of reasons why, mostly the fact that their recordings were done and issued locally in small areas in Mississippi and, except for [Charley] Patton, they sold very poorly. I would borrow records from Pete Whelan. I remember I was going to do something where I needed Blind Willie Johnson, and I remember just going over to Pete's. He had ones I didn't have, I had ones he didn't have, and I sat there with Ben Kaplan and Pete Whelan and listened to virtually every Blind Willie Johnson recording to choose the ones I needed. I did work with Pete on his own label. I actually put together a jug band record with him. And Moe Asch had a lot of records. What people hadn't understood was that of the Harry Smith recordings, half of them were Moe's. Moe had been collecting records. Fred

Ramsey had recordings; I borrowed from Fred too. It goes on today. England is where all the great reissue programs go on today, and everything is borrowed from collectors and borrowed from each other.

You said Fred Ramsey sent you to Moe Asch initially. What was that meeting like, and what was your arrangement with him?

I finally, sometime in the late 1980s, did for a period of some months actually work for Folkways, but I never was employed by Folkways in all those early years. Moe Asch had a vision of human creativity which was so large that it could contain all our other visions.

So there I was associated with people like Langston Hughes. Langston was also associated with Moe the same way I was—Fred Ramsey, Harold Courlander. He trusted us, and because his concept contained ours we would bring our work to him. I didn't know, really, how to edit tape. I actually got to record the Six and Seven-Eights String Band in the summer of 1954. Fred had returned to New Jersey at that point, so I sent him the tapes and said, "Fred, what do I do?" So he edited the tapes for me, and they came out on Folkways. It was the first production of mine that was actually released. He gave me an insight on how to do it. And with Folkways, of course, in 1952 I'd heard about the Harry Smith thing, I knew about the other Folkways records. Folkways was our goal at that point. I had all these recordings, and I was thinking I would do a musical portrait of the city of New Orleans, which I did. It's a five-volume set that came out on Folkways later in the 1950s, before the blues material. And Fred said, "Take the tapes up to Moe." I was working in a carwash at that point, and for $150 I bought the car that was at the carwash. It was three different colors, so I painted it a fourth different color [*laughs*] and set off. And it got me to New York with all the tapes in the back, a whole carton of them in the trunk that I took to Moe.

I met Moe, this really gruff guy, in a totally jammed office off of Times Square and Forty-sixth Street. I left him the box of tapes. I sort of explained what I was going to do, and he kind of looked at me and said, "Come back tomorrow." The next day I went back, and he looked at me and growled, "I'll put them out." And that essentially was our agreement. And each record was done individually. I'd bring him tapes, and ninety percent of the time he took them. There was never any censorship, never any editing, and the only consideration was whether this new material extended the horizon of human creativity, this documentation that Moe was attempting to create. I've even lost track of how many records I did with him, but there were a lot!

As an example, in 1958 Annie and I went down and did the Bahamas recordings. I had no idea of what we were going to get, but we drove down to Miami and we stayed on Andros Island and made these recordings. I had come to an area that was about five decades earlier in time than the American South; there were no radios or anything, so it was like going to the South would have been in 1870. And here I was in an out island of the Bahamas in 1958. I came back and I edited three albums out of the material, and I sold them to Moe for fifty dollars a piece with the proviso that he would put out the first of them as I edited it. I was kind of anxious about whether he would put them out. And that one was the Joseph

Spence solo guitar record, which sold and sold and became the key for everything else that was done in the Bahamas during that period.

How did you find electricity in the Bahamas?

Gasoline generators. Some of the guys hand-built these sloops, little fishing boats, thirty feet long, that they built out of lumber. They built them on the beach. And they had gotten to the point where there were electric tools which they brought over from Nassau, and they ran them from the little generators. The problem with generators is that they're very noisy, so I would have to borrow every extension cord I could find in the little settlements. And they had small earth cellars, so they could cool things, and I would take the generator and stick it down in the earth cellars and stretch out all these extension cords in the darkness, hoping that the land crabs wouldn't get them and they'd hold together long enough to do the recording. [*laughs*]

Did you ever pitch projects to Moe Asch where he would finance trips?

Never—never, never, never. I did the recording and I'd get one hundred or two hundred dollars against future royalties. But everything is a trade-off. What was I getting from Moe Asch? I was getting the opportunity to create something that I believed in, and created in my own way, since there was no consideration made for commercial potential—none! The other great, great temptation was that it would stay in print forever. For someone like myself who was concerned with documenting a culture that was being quickly lost, how could I say no? So of course I worked for him. It was difficult. In the spring of 1959 I wrote *The Country Blues*; in the summer of 1959 I wrote *Jazz: A History of the New York Scene*—those two books. And then we were going to move to Europe. We stopped in St. Louis and we did four albums, which I confidently expected Moe would pick up. Two hundred dollars each was what I paid the artists; we weren't talking about much money. Moe absolutely said, "No, sorry, sorry, I can't do it." I was absolutely distraught. So finally I called Ken Goldstein, who was gathering material for Prestige, and told Ken the situation. There was a long silence, and finally he said, "Don't ever do this to me again." But he took the albums, and at least I got my gas money out of it—nothing more than that. So with Moe you simply had to be prepared for the fact that you weren't going to make much money.

Dave Van Ronk and I lived together for a while in 1958 when we had a cold-water flat above the Folklore Center in New York. Dave had done some records for Folkways, and he had a Folkways outfit of total rags he had gotten from the Salvation Army, and he'd go up to Moe and say, "Oh, Moe, I need some royalties." And Moe would pick up whatever piece of paper he had on the desk and say, "I just did a royalty statement and I owe you seventy-five dollars." [*laughs*] Somehow that kept us going, but you can understand having that kind of creative freedom was worth the other things we had to do. And we believed in what Moe was doing. How could you *not* believe? Marion Distler was his partner. Actually it was very complicated. She was a complete Trotskyite. But Moe was not a Bolshevik; he was a Menshevik, and what people don't understand is that the whole scene was totally political. We were all intensely political in our attitudes and ideas, and anyone trying to understand Bob Dylan who doesn't understand this misses the whole point.

Moses Asch. Photo Diane Davies/Smithsonian Collection.

What was a press run on a typical Folkways release?

[*laughs*] Well, actually it was very easy to keep track of. Moe changed covers every thousand copies. He printed a thousand covers, and then the cover would be either redesigned or printed in slightly different colors. The printers could never match the colors. So the same album would appear over and over again, but every time a different color, another thousand.

I think it was a wonderful era just in terms of black stock jackets with the various particulars pasted on . . .

[*laughs*] Absolutely! And as I wrote at the end of the introduction to my book *Walking a Blues Road,* it was wonderful for me on one hand because I could write at length. This, of course, caused another problem for me when I had to adjust to writing those hundreds of liner notes I wrote for other albums. I had to adjust to the fact that I *only* had the space on the back of the album.

So the fact that Moe didn't have money for the St. Louis material you'd recorded did not spell the end of your relationship with him?

Oh, never—never, never! Moe didn't have the money. Moe was a very complicated man, but if he'd had the money, all of us who worked for him would have had it. He simply didn't have the money. He never had any money. I remember one time I had been doing some work for him; I also edited a lot of albums for him. I came down—my wife was teaching in New Hampshire and I came down. I was supposed to meet him in the office, but the record business, as you know, goes through its own cycles of depression and boom that doesn't have a thing to do with the rest of the economy. I saw Moe sort of shuffling along Sixth Avenue. He saw me coming along with my package of things for him, and he looked at me, shook his head, and said, "Go back to New Hampshire . . ." He just didn't have a penny. But he hid this.

His father was a very famous novelist, Sholem Asch; he made a lot of money. Moe would laugh and say, "My father collected Rembrandt and the Great Masters; I collect Picasso and Matisse." But of course he had no money at all. And the thing that was hanging over Folkways all the time was the fact that he couldn't pay copyright royalties. You can get away with not paying artist's royalties, but mechanical royalties are handled by the Harry Fox office, and they can shut you down—they can close you up overnight! So Moe lived in perpetual fear of this fact, that he paid no royalties for the song materials he used.

It's a very difficult, complex issue, but there was no way he could handle it. And then I discovered when I was there in the 1980s that the pledge he'd made that everything would stay in print killed him. You had to press a minimum of three hundred copies at that point, and these records sold maybe three a year, four a year? So you had to get three hundred copies and you were going to have a lifetime supply. The Folkways shelves were filled with these records, and the capital, what there was of it, was sitting there on the shelves.

Who owns the Folkways today?

The Smithsonian. I helped negotiate the sale. I did a huge survey of the label for the Smithsonian people and worked with Ralph Rinzler to make it possible. And there were a number of problems. I understood that Folkways at one time was "red channeled"—you know, [put on] that list of subversive organizations. All of us were investigated over and over and over again. Certainly Pete Seeger had his share of it; Langston Hughes was brought before the House of Un-American Activities [House Un-American Activities Committee]. I went through my thing. I had my political problems. Certainly Marion Distler, who looked like Moe's secretary but actually through an earlier bankruptcy owned Folkways, was a Trotskyite. And Trotskyites believed in continuing revolution, so it was a very complicated issue. Everything involved with Folkways was very complicated.

Let's jump to Prestige. How did you get involved over there?

I'm trying to remember how exactly everything went with Prestige. Kenneth Goldstein financed his PhD in folklore by working for a lot of record companies, doing a lot of recording—a lot of blues recordings, a lot of folk recordings. He could very quickly turn out a record and did a very credible job. He did lots of them. Any artists that came through New York and played the blues could be counted on to have recorded for Ken for some label or other. The longest and most prolific stretch of work I did for Prestige was when I returned from Europe. I wrote *The Country Blues*; then after it was published Ann and I left. I was living in Edinburgh, becoming the great American novelist, which, it turns out, if you don't have any talent, is not a good idea. But at the time it seemed like that was the way to go. I had written *The Country Blues*, as you know, as an incredible romantic adventure, describing looking for these forgotten artists, though I never used the first person. The pronoun "I" never appears in the book. I simply wanted to create a fantasy for someone like myself to go and find these artists, to try and find them and tell their story. Because as I was driving around the South in 1956, 1957, 1958, and 1959, I realized I couldn't do it alone; the South was too big, there was just too much.

Then in the year I was gone in Edinburgh, people read the book and these wonderful kids went out and they found *everybody*. It was one of the great research projects; it was done totally by amateurs for love and enthusiasm and excitement. If they relied on the academics to do it, they'd still be arguing over funding and grants and discussing the range and scope of the project. The kids just went out and did it! When I came back I never thought I'd be doing blues recording again [*laughs*], but two days after I got back I got a phone call! [*laughs*] Would I go to Memphis and record Furry Lewis?—and then would I go over to Spartanburg, South Carolina, and record Pink Anderson?—and anybody else I could think of and let them know. And this was all through Ken Goldstein, who at this point was finishing his PhD at the University of Pennsylvania.

What was Ken Goldstein's official position at Prestige?

He was a freelance producer. The owner of Prestige Records was Bob Weinstock, and he had been the most daring, most creative and innovative of the people recording the new jazz in the 1950s. He had made the crucial recordings of Thelonius Monk and of Miles Davis and Sonny Rollins—he was doing everybody. But already, after 1956, after Elvis's first recordings, jazz had suddenly lost direction, and new directions seemed to be things like the blues. So he set up a line called Bluesville, which Ken supervised. Ken was never an employee. My first recordings for Prestige were done on the same basis as the work I'd done for Folkways, except this time they paid expenses. So they paid for me to travel to Memphis. It certainly wasn't much. Also, I was able to use recording studios, so I did those first recordings in the Sun Studios with Elvis Presley's guitarist Scotty Moore as the engineer [*laughs*], which was incredibly complicated, because Scotty's a guitar player. And here I am paying for the studio, and he's sitting out there in the studio with Furry Lewis. Furry would start a new tune, and Scotty would say, "Ah, what tunin' have you got there? C'mon, let me come out there and you show me how you've got the guitar tuned." So here are the two of them exchanging guitar tunings while I'm paying Prestige's money to make the recording. [*laughs*]

Let's talk about Vanguard. Some of your most notable work—for postwar fans, anyway—was done for the Vanguard label. How did that happen?

After 1958 I was hanging out in New York as a part of the folk music world. I made a record playing with Dave Van Ronk in 1958. I was busking in the Village like everybody else, and Dave and I lived together. The Cadillac of the folk labels was Vanguard, because they had Joan Baez. At one point they had three LPs in the top ten. It was incredible.

I knew Maynard Solomon, who directed the company with his brother, Seymour, from a distance, but I was one of the scrubby rebels who did things for Folkways, so I was very, very suspicious of Vanguard. But then my *Country Blues* album caused a big stir, and nearly every song became popular somehow or another. "Walk Right In," by Cannon's Jug Stompers, became a number one single for the Rooftop Singers, and Eric Darling and the group claimed the copyright. So I went to Southern Music, who had done the original recording, and said, "Do you know that the number one single is a song of yours?" And they said, "Oh, no, we didn't. What's the name of that song?" I explained to them and they immediately turned around and sued Vanguard and Eric Darling. And then it turned out that they were suing on their own behalf, not on Gus Cannon's behalf. It turns out they had recorded it under something they called "work for hire," which is what Ralph Peer did with all his recordings in the South, which meant that he simply said that the artist was an employee of its company Southern Music and everything they did was sole property of Southern Music.

So then I went to Vanguard and said, "Well, look, I'm sorry that I managed to stir all this up, but I think you're going to have to sue Southern Music for Gus Cannon." They said, "Can you find him?" and I said, "Of course." So Maynard Solomon, who's a very decent guy, hired a really, really top Broadway showbiz copyright lawyer, and the three of us flew to Memphis—Maynard, myself, and this lawyer—to talk to Gus Cannon. It was wonderful walking through the back alleys behind Beale Street and the people looking at us and saying, "We know what you're here for. We know what you're here for!" Gus was there behind his door, looking out his window—"Why, hello!" And Gus, to be careful, always spoke to me as "White Folk"—"Hello, White Folk!" [*laughs*] He was absolutely delighted! We did get a deposition and worked out a deal so that Eric Darling only got half the copyright. [*laughs*] The other half went to Gus Cannon, and he had a very comfortable life for the rest of his years as a result, and I felt very good about that. Also I got closer to Maynard, and we understood each other *much better* after we made this trip.

Maynard was recording the Newport Folk Festival every year, and he had an enormous amount of tape. He understood that I was freelancing, and he asked if I would edit the tapes for the 1963 Folk Festival. Since we'd gotten to know each other, when I finished the tapes and brought them in, he looked at me and said, "What should we do now?" Without hesitation I simply said, "Chicago." I had tried to do Chicago recordings for Prestige, but there was no money, no belief, no consciousness that it was something important to do. They had a huge catalog of R & B, they had singers like Jimmy Witherspoon—they didn't need something from Chicago's South Side. But I felt it was something that *had* to be done. So I worked out an arrangement with Vanguard that I would go and record. It became the series *Chicago: The Blues Today*, which I did in 1965. I'm very proud of that set. I had a chance to document something that was vital and alive on the South Side, and musically it was incredibly exciting. The three albums were laid out as a total portrait. I went from older artists like Johnny Young to contemporary artists like Junior Wells. I went from guitarists like Buddy Guy and Otis Rush to pianists like Otis Spann. And I went from the older instruments like the mandolin, and I touched back into the blues history with Johnny Shines. When I was asked to reconsider reediting the series, it turned out there were actually no alternate takes, which I'm sure there are *somewhere*; we just couldn't find them. But I redid it for Vanguard on the twenty-fifth anniversary. For the first time in all these years I simply sat down and, starting with track one, disc one, listened to it from beginning to end. What I had dreamed of doing was there. I felt very good about it.

Let's talk more about *Chicago: The Blues Today*. For those unfamiliar with the work, there were originally three LPs featuring three different artists on each LP. Who picked the bands?

I did, and in every case that I could I tried to find working bands. Otis Rush was a working band. Junior Wells was leading his quartet, and they were working two or three nights a week. Johnny Young had been working with his group of musicians, so that I could trust them, whoever they would bring in. Hutto brought in a group—J. B. Hutto and the Hawks—that he had been working with them over at the Blue Flame. So I had no sense that there was going to be a problem. With Otis Spann and Jimmy Cotton, they had just come in off the road with Muddy, and I went down to Muddy's house and hung out. They agreed to be included. I had recorded the band before for Prestige.

There was a big concert at Carnegie Hall which was one of those "discovery of folk roots" kind of things. I was the emcee, and I'm sort of onstage delivering a story about all of this. I opened with Son House and was going on to the Muddy Waters band, and then it was to end up with Chuck Berry. It turns out that Muddy's band had been hired simply to accompany Chuck Berry. This was 1963–64 and Muddy hadn't had a hit since 1958, so as far as people like Chuck Berry were concerned, he [Muddy] wasn't even worth considering. And the audience at that point was still folkies, so Carnegie Hall was filled with people who wanted to hear an acoustic guitar. So Muddy Waters's band was *politely* received, but just politely. What was issued sounded like commercial R & B, which it was. But I enjoyed Muddy, and there was a big hassle with Chuck Berry over money, sitting there on this couch, saying, "Well, I do believe I have to have fifteen hundred dollars before I go out onstage." And there was all this shouting: "You already had a contract! You've already been paid!" "Well, I believe that I do have to have fifteen hundred dollars." "Well there's no way we can get the money!" And Chuck would say, "I'm sure if you were to go out to the box office, I'm sure . . ." And here's Muddy standing in the corner of the room watching all this go on—and silent, as Muddy could be, that incredible impassivity that Muddy could do.

So I got a phone call from him the next morning. He couldn't pay the hotel bill; he couldn't get back to Chicago. He didn't have any money. Could I organize a recording session? This was Saturday morning, and I *could* do it, because I was with Prestige. I *was* an employee; there *was* a studio I could get. So starting at ten o'clock in the morning I organized a recording session. The kicker was that I couldn't use Muddy's name, and he couldn't sing solo or play with a slide because of the Chess label connection. I nearly got fired for doing the record, because there was no sense in doing a record that featured Otis Spann and Jimmy Cotton. We recorded it in an afternoon, so I was able to help him out and get him back. Muddy and I always enjoyed each other, so when I was doing *Chicago: The Blues Today* the band had just come in off the road and I was down at the house there. And Spann and Cotton had been so pleased to do that first LP, since it was their first LP release, that they were absolutely delighted to come in the studio, even though, as you heard on the record, Spann had a terrible cold. But Cotton actually blew his ass off. Those four Cotton tracks are marvelous!

How did you get around using Muddy without listing his name?

Dirty Rivers! [*laughs*] That's what his name is on the record!

On the *Chicago: The Blues Today* series, did you have any bands that didn't make the cut, or tracks that were left over?

No. My recording budget from Vanguard was five thousand dollars, for the whole project, including notes and expenses. [*laughs*] And somehow I did it!

Doesn't the same cover photo appear on all three records?

Yeah, the picture of the El [Chicago's elevated train] platform that Annie took, it's on all three.

I've always thought that particular shot was the most romantic and representative shot of the Chicago blues scene ever!

She was roaming the South Side alone with her camera [*laughs*] while I was in the studio with the artists, and then she would come back, at times return to the studio to take portrait photographs of the artists. We did a book called *Blues Faces* that has a lot more of the photo material that she took in it.

Let's talk a bit about the blues scene in Chicago as you did *Chicago: The Blues Today*. Who were the bands and what were the clubs?

They were scattered throughout the ghetto. There was a little kind of alternative entertainment scene, but that was on Wells Street and they were only doing folk. I did a lot of folk recordings with folk artists there for Prestige. But the blues was South Side/West Side. Otis Rush was working at Curley's, a very upscale West Side black lounge with a large dance floor. Junior and Buddy were playing in Theresa's, which was simply two rooms in a cellar in a tenement there on the South Side. Muddy was playing at Johnny Pepper's; actually I did some live recording at Johnny Pepper's. The clubs were small. They were neighborhood clubs, and the scene was complicated. I remember that the Blue Flame, where Hutto was playing, Shakey Walter Horton had taken us there and we weren't welcome.

Generally we were the only white people in the places, and everyone was aware that a great deal of injustice had been committed, was being committed—and here we were. Once, we were attacked at Johnny Pepper's when a fellow was drunk and went after us, and Johnny Pepper and a couple of guys from the band had to pull him off. With the Hutto band, the first night got very out of hand; finally somebody stabbed Walter outside for having brought us in. I remember one time we came outside—it had been quieter that time at the Blue Flame than usual—and we went outside and there was a Chicago police car making sure we got out "safe." Working-class clubs, no money, very tough neighborhoods.

I remember I did an album with Mighty Joe Young in an industrial area in South Chicago, in the old mill area. He told me where to go, and I had a rented car at that point. This was for another record company. I had learned at this point some of the way to deal with the situation. Understand, the assumption was I was either looking for drugs, or I was a narc. I was a policeman looking for people selling drugs, or else, in some misguided way, I was looking for sex. People couldn't see any other legitimate reason for me to be there. I remember for this club I just suddenly realized this was going to be a little tricky. So I took along four or five of the LPs that I had produced. I came in and sat down and was looked over very, very carefully and sat at a side table—very, very dark, of course. The band began playing. Mighty Joe was a fine musician, but in the middle of his first set I could see that the controlling gang—they were sitting across from me—were really looking me over. Finally they dispatched a young guy to come over and check me out. I had the records spread out on the table in front of me. He came over, he looked at me, he looked down at the records, and he picked them up; they were all blues records. He looked at me and said, "You a record man?" I said, "Yeah." He said, "Okay." He turned around and went back and I had no trouble.

I remember doing the live album at Johnny Pepper's. That was Blackstone Ranger territory, a very tough gang. I remember the session went late, and we looked out the windows and we could see out on the street there were faces looking in at us, and it was two o'clock in the morning. These weren't friendly faces, and we still had to get the recording equipment out of there. It was simply a matter of finding enough people in the club who were willing to stand on the sidewalk, make a crowd, and let us get all the stuff out of there. And we got it all out safely.

Chicago was tough. It was tough for everybody. You did the best you could. Because of Chess Records many of the artists were tied up. I really wanted to record Little Walter and hung out with Little Walter and got an agreement with him, but he had gotten so many advances from Chess there was no way he dared go into the studio for us, because he'd be hearing from the *man* for having done this. If he was going to record for anybody, since he'd taken a lot of money from Chess, it was going to be for them. We did go on one job with him, and Annie got these wonderful photos of Walter playing with a band led by Lee Jackson. So at least we do have something permanent associated with Little Walter.

You've mentioned the Blue Flame Lounge. Was that the same place that became Turner's Lounge on Indiana Avenue?

You may be right. It was located under the El.

When you talked about recording live at Pepper's, who was it that you were recording?

Junior Wells. Part of the first solo album I did with Junior included the live recordings at the club. But that was not a part of *Chicago: The Blues Today*. Those sessions were all done in that big RCA studio that they'd used for their Bluebird blues line. There was a lot of history in those studios. It was marvelous to be there.

Do you remember a drummer that worked with Junior Wells—Levi Warren?

I can't remember. There were so many sidemen, and there were so many sessions that I worked with in Chicago over the years. I'd actually done two albums in Chicago before I did *Chicago: The Blues Today*. I did Homesick James and Billy Boy Arnold. So I'd had some previous experience. Thank goodness I had some experience with Chicago recording. I didn't really get it right until the first Buddy Guy session—*A Man and the Blues*. That's the finest Chicago blues recording I made. I look back at that and I'm very, very satisfied with it.

After you did *Chicago: The Blues Today*, you worked with both Junior Wells and Buddy Guy. . .

That's right! The way I was able to do *Chicago: The Blues Today* was that I didn't ask anyone for an exclusive contract. I made no restriction on the material that they wanted to do, and I only asked them for four tunes, just a standard union session. Nobody was recording—the scene was dead; there hadn't been any interest in their music for several years, though they all were still playing well! They were just fine, fine musicians at the height of their powers. I simply offered them this chance. They'd never heard of Vanguard—Vanguard didn't do singles; Vanguard wasn't in Chicago [*laughs*]—but here was this person offering them union scale. What I put in each one of the contracts was that we had the option to do a solo album within a year after the release of the set, not exclusive. Again, I wasn't tying anybody up, and they'd been through a lot. They all had dealings with record companies. I wasn't dealing with guys from the country, who'd never seen a record contract. These guys were all professionals. They understood that this could be a kick-start for their careers. As it turned out, it was. With Junior I took advantage. I said right away, "Let's go back and do it again!" and then asked him to agree to another one. So I had another option for a second album.

With Buddy I recognized that he could be somebody very special, so I actually signed Buddy as an exclusive artist and did the first two albums with him. It was not a happy relationship finally. After I left Vanguard, after I was fired, there was quite a bit of acrimony, and Buddy moved on into what was essentially limbo for the next twenty years. He hesitated a lot over signing with Vanguard. His wife simply did not want him to sign a contract. She didn't want him to be leaving town, because there would, of course, be other women. I so intensely believed in Buddy as an artist, but it was all very complicated.

I'd have followed up on the contracts with everybody. I did the follow up album with Otis Spann—not very good, not a good record at all. And I tried and tried and tried and tried with Otis Rush to get him back into the studio. [*laughs*] I finally did, but that was in Stockholm in 1977, after I'd moved to Europe. I finally got to do my solo album with Otis Rush. It came out originally on Sonet Records in Stockholm.

How much of a "hands on" record producer are/were you, and what—if any—kind of changes did you feel entitled to request?

I loved all those years in recording studios. The first one I walked into was on April 10, 1951. That's when I made my first record, and I looked around and I felt instantly at home. I was a musician myself, for many years playing and performing, so I had a very good idea of what a studio was for. The first record I made in 1951 I actually led a small band. I made a 78 for a small record company in California. So I knew about recording from that side, and I knew kind of what you had to do. I just instinctively responded to them as artists, and I did what the artists needed. If they didn't need anything, I simply sat back out of the way. If they needed encouragement, if they needed responsiveness, if I had to tune the instrument—fine.

With some of the bands, like Country Joe and the Fish, I was involved in the arrangements, the whole thing. Some sessions I would wind up playing two or three different instruments. Not on the blues sessions; these were rock sessions. But once I did a session with Big Joe Williams—he recorded for forty-five minutes—and I had the complete album plus three extra tracks. [*laughs*]

With many others you had to work and sweat to get them to be comfortable in the studio, to respond to work. I would approach each session saying, "Oh, my God. What do I do?" And I think this was good, because I never walked in thinking, "Oh, I know how to do this! You do this and you do this!" and we'd have an album. I walked in saying, "Who are you? What do you want to do, and how can we do it?" It worked out very well. I think I was effective. I'm not a commercial producer—I was never a Phil Spector—and I could never produce the hit single. I think that's the great goal of the record producer. I had some that did well, but I never had the dynamite "classic single."

With someone like Robert Pete Williams, I think we did a lovely album in Louisiana. I hung out with him, we talked, traded stories, had a lovely supper that his wife cooked. She came along with us to the studio, and then it was just a matter of getting the guitar in tune, shaping the session as to the kind of songs I wanted, to be an ear. Musicians need an ear. Some producers sit there all the time talking on the telephone [*laughs*] or reading a newspaper. You can't! You have to give them attention like they've always wanted in their lives. And they're musicians, proud of what they do. Nobody ever kisses you off in the studio. They're proud of what they do, and they want to do their best. And if they understand that you want this from them—this is what you want from them, what they are as a person doing the best they can—then they'll do it for you!

Do you recall any particularly difficult sessions?

Oh, sure. I did a whole series of jazz recordings, and I do recall a couple of sessions where there was a great deal of cocaine, and that makes things very difficult. And, as you know, I was a rock 'n' roll producer for many years, and that often was very difficult for other reasons. For seven years I was producer for Bill Haley and the Comets, and Bill was an alcoholic. He was a very difficult alcoholic. He would get very violent. We'd have to lock our doors at the motels at night, because Bill would begin roaming, and it got pretty heavy. So you never knew.

I did find, though, that over the years the alcoholics were more difficult to deal with than the druggies. Druggies were usually calm, whereas the alcoholics got very "vetchy." It was impossible at the end working with Lightning Hopkins—the kind of maudlin self-pity and sense of entitlement, and simply the laziness. He would get very drunk quickly and believe he'd done enough, and why were we torturing him to make him go on and do more—and da-da-da-da-da, and, yes, the guitar's out of tune. [*laughs*] Once you get in the studio, all reality stops and it's a different reality.

Will you tell me of your association with Country Joe and the Fish?

One of the blues fans, Eugene "ED" Denson, who with John Fahey discovered Bukka White and did that album with him, he'd been a friend. I'd known him through the folk blues days. He'd stayed in my raggedy apartment there on 109th Street in New York when Annie and I were gone. He called me from San Francisco and said, "I've got a rock band here and you're going to record them." It was Country Joe and the Fish. He managed them and I was the producer.

Do you want to go into the subject of your political dissatisfaction and exile?

For me it hasn't been exile at all. I've had a very rich, very full recording career in Europe. Some of my finest recordings, unfortunately, are all in Swedish. [*laughs*] And I've had a very full life. I still live there and now I have dual citizenship, Swedish and American. The Vietnam War was a little hard for all of us, as you know. I first went to Sweden with Country Joe and the Fish. You couldn't get mainstream radio in America to play their recording "Fixin' to Die Rag," but it was a number one hit in Northern Europe [*sings*]: *One, two, three, what are we fightin' for? Don't ask me, I don't give a damn. Next stop is Vietnam!*" So the band went on a tour. Being a number one single artist is life on a different planet, and I thought, "Well, I'll experience this one." So I went along with them. We went to Sweden, which I enjoyed a lot, enjoyed so much actually that I stayed after the band went on. We'd started in Denmark; we were going to go back to Denmark and then play Albert Hall in London. So I said, "Look, I'll meet you in Albert Hall." So I just rented a car and drove north. I couldn't speak a word of Swedish. I had no idea where to go, but the forests around the airport looked beautiful, so I just started driving north.

Then in May of the next year, 1970, there was a wave of demonstrations against the war. I'd been demonstrating for years against the war, but this was the one after the poor kids from Kent State College were killed, shot by the National Guard. So there was this huge demonstration. The first time I demonstrated at the White House in the early 1960s there were maybe fifty of us. The organizer said, "Just kneel at fifteen-foot intervals and look soulful." So we did. And of course the FBI took lovely photos of all of us. But this time, after the Kent State killings, we went back and there were one hundred thousand of us, and we were gonna burn the White House down. It got violent, real confrontational street fighting. My wife was with me in this one, and she kept saying, "How will I know the tear gas?"[*laughs*] and I said, "You'll know." Allen Ginsburg was chanting, and since this was just after the Kent State shootings we had no idea what was going to happen. I managed to fight my way through the barricades, carrying a mock coffin to the ring of buses that were lined around the White House. And I actually managed to get on the roof of the bus, and I could see that the lawn of the White House was filled with soldiers with bayonets on their rifles, and they're putting on their gas masks. And then the police threw me back into the crowd. Luckily I didn't land in the street; people caught me as I came down. We were determined to occupy that street if they killed us. We stayed there until six PM.

Then I realized that this had really gotten out of hand. I was forty years old, I had a wife, I had a new child. Friends of ours were taking care of our baby in Georgetown while I was across town trying to get into the White House. [*laughs*] So I thought, "I know Sweden is there, the record company is there. I can take a step back and try to find myself." I wrote to them. They were absolutely agreeable: "You must understand, this is a very small country, a very small market." I took a ninety percent pay cut, went back to Sweden, and became a part-time record producer for a very small record company in a very small market. I still sometimes kiss the sidewalk for what I found there, as a society and as a way to live. I've had a long career in Sweden with many, many friends.

My fourth book is coming out in Swedish in the fall, and I wrote the first book on Swedish folk fiddling; there had never been one before in Swedish. I had produced "Fixin' to Die Rag," a great protest song in the States. I had produced a hit with a protest song in Sweden, and it was a great song! [*laughs*] I have absolutely no regrets.

It was difficult for my wife, who couldn't find a teaching position on her university level. So, though she felt the same thing I did, in 1974 she went back to her career as a professor of modern American literature here. In 1971, though, my name could not be on the book; we had written the first biography of Jack Kerouac. My name could not be on it, because I was so known as a blues writer that the publishers felt it would take away the credibility of the book if a music writer was associated with it. I must say I got a little jealous when the book was a big success. She kept being invited to literary parties in London, and they didn't invite me.

How do you divide your time today? How much time here, how much time in Sweden?

I have two daughters that are here in New York, and my son's in New Orleans, so I still have deep ties here, and my wife, though she's now emeritus at the university, teaches the fall semester. So she's here in the United States from September through February and March. And I usually come back for Thanksgiving and Christmas and then hang out for a couple of months. My daughter just had her third child, so I'll be here longer. Also I'm organizing an exhibition of Swedish women's arts from our art collection for the university here. We have an apartment in New York and an apartment in Stockholm and a house here in Connecticut—they're all home. I travel a lot, but usually I'm in the United States maybe three months a year.

Have you read the book by Mary Beth Hamilton, *In Search of the Blues: Black Voices, White Visions*?

I'm about to pick it up when we hang up here. It's gotten two reviews—one very good and one very bad—and I'm totally confused.

If I understand it correctly, one of the things she is saying is that it was the small band of pioneering collectors—including Pete Whelan, Bernie Klatzko, and Ben Kaplan, among others—who decided that deep country blues was the thing to listen to. And that this was misleading because Delta blues/deep country blues was such a small slice of the overall pie.

And I said essentially the same thing. Robert Johnson's records sold maybe 275 copies, and he was of no importance in the black community at all. But now that we have redone the history of the blues, there he is. We say many times, "We can't change the past, but it's the future we can control." I keep saying it's the exact opposite: we have no control over the future, but we can do what we want with the past.

If we find the judgment of this small group of pioneering collectors faulty for selecting Delta/deep country blues as the center of the universe, can't we consider postwar Chicago as affirmation that these pioneering collectors weren't entirely off-base? Here's a second generation of bluesmen using these early artists and their records as the basis for their work?

Again, we come at it completely wrong. The South Side Chicago scene was very limited to the South Side. Those records sold in only limited quantities. By that point what was the black audience listening to? They were listening to the Ink Spots, to Nat Cole. What I said in my books all along was the pretense that the blues was the music of the black community. Nothing could have been further from the truth. The middle-class black community hated the blues, had nothing to do with it. I've been going to Harlem for fifty years, hearing music in Harlem. There are five hundred churches in Harlem. I haven't been to all five hundred churches, but every Sunday morning there is gospel music in Harlem, there are clubs in Harlem, there are lounges in Harlem. *In fifty years I have never heard one blues singer.*

The essence of the music that gave the black community its strength and its power to continue in spite of what they faced was gospel. That's the heart of black music in America. I made the conscious decision I made to work with the blues, because I was operating from a sociopolitical point of view. The judgments I made for the books I did were simply that although there was only a small blues audience in the black community, there was a potential blues audience in the white community. And, yes, the artists we found and the recordings we made were for these white listeners.

Can you list your most notable books? There were quite a few.

Actually if you add in the novels there are about forty all together. I wrote the blues books for this new audience. *Country Blues* was shamelessly romanticized as an attempt to open people's eyes as to the excitement and drama and to please come out and help, and it worked very well. *The Poetry of the Blues*—again, this was before the civil rights revolution—was saying, "If I can get one person who reads this book to hear a blues singer as a human being, they will see that across this racial barrier there are human beings. And we must reconsider the message of society from this point of view." And I felt I needed to correct the exaggerations and romanticizations in *The Country Blues,* so I wrote *Bluesmen.* The title, of course, was a tribute to jazzmen—*Bluesmen.* Fred Ramsey gave me permission to echo their title. So I fleshed out in greater detail the blues story and told it in terms of regions and also made the corrections for artists who weren't in *The Country Blues*. There was a huge section on Mississippi, analyzing the whole song style and everything related to it. I would have done a third volume, but Mike Rowe did a wonderful book on Chicago, so I didn't need to do Chicago. But I went on to do the Carolinas and the East Coast in *Sweet as the Showers of Rain.* Then I was asked to do something on Robert Johnson, so I wrote the Robert Johnson book. We had very little biographical material, but I did very good song transcriptions, plus I did an analysis of the sources of Robert Johnson songs in that. Then there are the two New Orleans jazz books, the New York jazz book.

And then in 1974 I decided I had been recording black music for twenty years, and I thought it was just nonsense that I hadn't been to Africa, so I made the first of my African trips. At that point there had not been Alex Haley's *Roots,* so I was able to work with griots in West Africa. Out of that came *Roots of the Blues,* which for me is the best of the blues books. I recently did a biography of the Cuban pianist Bebo Valdes, which came out in Swedish and then was translated into French. I was asked last fall to go to Seville, Spain, simply to introduce the book as one of three world music authors at a world music expo in Seville. I met a whole crowd there of the people who had had the same response to the *Roots of the Blues* that the earlier group had to *The Country Blues:* they had read the book and just set off to Africa. They looked for the griot artists and to the artist/singers that I recorded. I've always felt that the most important piece that I ever recorded in the whole field was the song which for me defines what I was looking for. It was a griot song I recorded in West Africa about the sale of slaves to the Europeans in the 1600s. And it was interesting for me; the other two speakers on the platform with me to talk about our new books simply wanted to talk to me about this song, which they agreed was the most important thing I had ever recorded. Please, could I tell them more about that! [*laughs*]

PETE WHELAN INTERVIEW

Pete Whelan. Courtesy Pete Whelan.

I was born in New York City, May 17th, 1929. My father was an ex-millionaire's son. They had lost their money in the crash of '29. My mother was a budding painter. She studied at the Sorbonne and fell in love with a Russian count who was a cab driver, and her parents dragged her away from Paris and brought her back to Lock Haven, Pennsylvania. My parents met at a Florida resort. It was sort of a golf resort for the well-to-do.

Where did you go to school?

Well, I got thrown out of a Catholic boarding school at the age of twelve. But then I went to a school in New Hope, Pennsylvania, called Solebury School, which was a great school. Among the former graduates of Solebury was the jazz biographer and critic Fred Ramsey Junior. He was the editor of the first American book on jazz, called *Jazzmen,* and it included people like Bill Russell, who was a specialist in New Orleans jazz—no blues! Blues was not considered legitimate when that book was published in 1939. There were jazz collectors, but there were no blues collectors.

Did you have any personal contact with Ramsey at all?

When I was fourteen or fifteen I used to see him bicycling down the streets of New Hope. He used to live in that area. But he was sort of formidable looking; he was about six foot three and sort of a giant in a way. So I never was able to approach him, but later on, in the 1990s I did an interview with him for *78 Quarterly.* At that point he was developing Alzheimer's disease. I think he was in his mid- to late seventies at the time. He was very angry but kind of fascinating. He did have some information on the first jazzman in New Orleans, Buddy

Frederick Ramsey Jr., William Russell, Charles Edward Smith. Courtesy Pete Whelan.

Bolden, that had never been published before. I put all that in the interview in *78 Quarterly*. He died shortly after that of Alzheimer's. He was writing a book about Buddy Bolden, but apparently he wasn't.

Did you have any reason to look up to him when you were a child at school?

Oh, yeah! When I was fourteen I was subscribing to the *Record Changer*; everything about jazz seemed to appear in the *Record Changer*. There were columnists and Fred Ramsey had an occasional article. There were reviews by semi-famous critics, who were very impressive. But they didn't review blues records; it was just jazz.

How did you first begin to take an interest in music?

Well, I began when I was eleven years old with the trumpet, and my way into blues came by way of jazz. I was basically interested in black New Orleans jazz and the later Chicago jazz of the 1920s, where it sort of reached its golden age under people like Johnny Dodds and Freddy Keppard and a bunch of others. But still, there was very little mention of blues; it wasn't collected. In fact, there was one jazz collector, long since dead, who came across three complete runs of Paramount—that's the great label. He wrote me and said that each big group of Paramounts he came across, he picked out all the jazz and left the blues behind. [*laughs*] The blues would have included people like Charley Patton, Son House, Skip James, Tommy Johnson, and all the great singers, most of them were on Paramount, so they were all left behind and probably dumped in the trash. And this went on for three different places! His name was Bill Love and he lived in Tennessee.

What notable jazz players were out on Paramount?

There was an earlier period. Now, the jazz run—I'm calling it a jazz run—was from around 1923 to about 1927, '28, at which point Paramount recorded blues singers and very little jazz. But it was the other way around from that 1923 to 1928 period. Any blues that existed were from vaudeville, so-called vaudeville blues singers such as Ma Rainey, Ida Cox, and so on.

So you might have trumpet players like Tommy Ladnier or Dewey Jackson?

Ladnier, yes! Of course, Johnny Dodds, a great clarinetist, was on an awful lot of those jazz Paramounts, usually led by a female piano player named Lovie Austin. There were really standouts like Freddy Keppard's Jazz Cardinals doing "Salty Dog" with Papa Charlie Jackson doing vocal and Johnny Dodds on clarinet.

None of these were microgroove, were they?

Oh, no! There were some experimental sessions done with microgroove in the 1930s, but microgroove didn't come in until the 1950s, beginning with 45s and 33s.

At this point your collection was essentially a jazz collection, right?

No, I started collecting blues. I stumbled onto it. I think I was twelve at the time. Somehow I had heard blues somewhere—I don't know where. So I went out looking for records, because at that time the only thing going was swing music—you know, Harry James, Benny Goodman. So I went into this record store in Asbury Park, New Jersey. The guy behind the counter was so typical of small-time record shop owners and dealers—very cynical and offhand—you know, take-it-or-leave-it kind. Invariably they were all bald for some reason. [*laughs*] I was trying to describe the kind of music I wanted, and I said, "It's kind of sweet sounding," which actually it is. He said to me, "Like this?" talking about swing records. I said, "No, no, that's not it." And I kept trying to describe it, and I said, "Maybe it's kind of bluesy." And he said, "Oh, you mean race records." And he went under the counter and brought out this stack of blue-label Vocalions. At that time you could play the records and hear them in these little sort of recording booths. So I brought a bunch of them in, and I bought two or three. That was all the money I had. I think they were like forty-nine cents each or something. And they included really nothing terrific. It was the "Yas Yas Girl"—Merline Johnson—and a couple of others. One was a New Orleans group that recorded on Vocalion. I can't remember their name.

But that was it. That set me off. I would haunt these various places in Philadelphia, and in Newark also when I lived there or the Oranges. In Newark there was always the Savoy Records shop that had used blues records—nothing rare at all—ninety percent of it was Leroy Carr. I picked up what I could along with records that I got from thrift shops and Salvation Army stores. And in Philadelphia it was even better. There was one store—I can never remember the name of it—it was another guy that was bald with the same kind of cynical attitude. He would mark the labels in black crayon with the prices. I wish I could remember the name of that record store. It later became the Walnut Street Music Shop, but that wasn't the name of it at the time. Nobody else I know in Philadelphia can remember the place. You'd meet an occasional collector there, and they were all old-time collectors. One guy said he had thirty thousand jazz and blues 78s in his collection. I remember what he looked like, but I never found out his name. Now, I used to go there at least once a week, and I'd pick up mostly blues, nothing really rare except for a couple of original tests. Very little in the way of Paramounts in Philadelphia. No Gennetts, no Champions, but lots of Victors and OKehs.

There was a collector named Charlie Huber who lived in Philadelphia for a while. He found a Ma Rainey in a garbage can once, but it was broken. He also found whole bunches of Paramount sleeves, but no Paramounts. But he was fearless. He was the premier door-to-door collector, knocking on doors in African American neighborhoods. He was sort of a short, pugnacious guy that had the courage to do all that. He was strictly a jazz collector.

As far as I know he's still alive, living in Connecticut. He became the CEO of an insurance company, but he retired and has been living in Connecticut for a long time. He invented something called "bullet canvassing," which was to ride in an open car—he'd do this in Southern towns and cities. He'd ride in a convertible with the top open, holding out 78s up in the air and shouting, "Do you have any old blues records?" This is the sort of fanaticism that existed then.

Big Joe Klauberg. Courtesy Pete Whelan.

In 1954 I was getting out of the navy, and I was bidding in the *Record Changer*. I was very interested in a label called Gennett on their Electrobeam series beginning in 1926. They started recording blues singers, country blues singers that accompanied themselves on guitar. I was very taken at the time with this guy that recorded on Gennett named Sam Collins. He made this one great session, his first session at Gennett. Later on I talked to Sam Collins's original manager, who wandered into the Jazz Record Center in New York on West Forty-seventh Street off Sixth Avenue. The guy's name was Harrison Smith. He was what they call a Maroni type; he had tan skin, brownish hair. But anyway, he was a talent scout for Gennett. I asked him if he had ever heard Sam Collins, and he said, "What a great player he was!" and "What a nice guy he was!" Now very little is known about Sam Collins. Unfortunately, I was curious but not curious enough to go on asking, "What was he like? Where was he from? What did he look like?" There is sort of a photo of him and there's some dispute about his age. One account has him being born in the 1870s, and the other, there's now a belief that it was much later. From his emotional, Mississippi-like singing, it seems he must have been born a lot later—maybe in the late 1890s or early 1900s.

You've mentioned the Jazz Record Center and some other people. Can you tell me about them?

"Big Joe" Klauberg—he was a full-blooded Indian or half. A great big guy—he must have weighed three hundred pounds, six two, six three. But he never said anything. He was very quiet. He slept a lot, but he kept one eye opened for thieves. [*laughs*] He was very nice and the prices were good, very reasonable, of course. It was at a time when most collectors that collected 78s were poor.

In contrast was Jake Schneider, who I did an article about in the first issue of *78 Quarterly*. He was a worldly wise man, very much out of shape. He ate awful meals like corned beef sandwiches with a lot of fat in the sandwich. He was born in Russia. One of his first memories was being saved in a town that he was in when Cossacks ran through and killed everybody on the street, and he was pulled in just in time by a woman. He had the world's largest collection of records, most of which were pop things that really were of no value and very little musical interest. But he did have a tremendous collection of jazz—and, unbeknownst to a lot of people, of rare blues too. I started out buying jazz and wound up buying blues. He sort of treated me like a son. He said, "If I were your age, I'd give away my record collection just to be young again." He was always on the lookout to buy complete collections, and he was the first to do that. He bought out store stocks, also. There was a famous one at 125th Street and Lenox Avenue in Harlem. He bought out their store stock. He said he was charged fifty cents apiece for records—Victor, Vocalion, OKeh—except for Paramounts, which were seventy-five cents for some reason, maybe because the label looked interesting.

Jake Schneider had what he called "the vault." It was a big closet full of rare jazz—some of the rarest. He had four copies of certain things, like Gennetts and Paramounts—but no blues. With blues you looked through his list, and you saw something that caught your eye, you immediately, surreptitiously expressed a slight desire to get it. If you were overwhelmed with desire, it would cost maybe ten dollars. If you were modestly interested, it might be three or four dollars. [*laughs*] So it was always this cat-and-mouse, but it was fun! We all enjoyed playing that game.

Was this a bona fide record store?

No, Jake Schneider had law offices. What he would do is rent spaces. Like the last place he was in was on Eighty-first Street, I think. And it was the basement of a large New York hotel, but the hotel didn't exist anymore. So he would hire these movers, and they'd move five hundred thousand records from one place to another. From 1950 to 1970 he moved

L to R: Tiny Tim, Jake Schneider, Max Vreede. Courtesy Pete Whelan.

to three different places carrying hundreds of thousands of records. But he kept them all cataloged and he spent most of his time there, most of Wednesdays and Saturdays, which was when he was open. This was separate from his law offices. He was a divorce lawyer, and in fact I got my divorce through Jake. It involved a trip to Mexico on the part of the ex-wife. [*laughs*]

What was the biggest record you ever snared from Big Joe's?

I never really snared that much from Big Joe's; it was mostly Jake Schneider. The biggest records I got from Big Joe were two Champions by a guy named Scarecrow—Willie Owens—accompanied by a great trumpet player who sounded like Punch Miller but wasn't. An obscure unknown trumpet player; somebody came up with a name once, but I forgot it.

What was the biggest record you ever snared from Jake Schneider?

Probably a new copy of [Charley] Patton's "Runnin' Wild" on Paramount, which came out of the Henry Renard collection. Either that or the Long Cleve Reed "France Blues" on Electrobeam Gennett, under the name of Sonny Boy and His Pals. At that time the Patton would cost fifteen dollars, and that was high. The Electrobeam Gennett was around thirty dollars, which was a lot, and it was only because in New York City there were very few Electrobeam Gennetts, and there were very few in his collection. He always said, "If I have less than two copies, you know it's rare!" He always claimed that he had just about everything.

Would you tell the story of Jim McKune?

Well, it's a long story. He was brought up in New Jersey. I first met McKune in 1954 at the Jazz Record Center in Manhattan on West Forty-seventh Street off Sixth Avenue. A lot of musicians used to go into the Jazz Record Center. That's where I first met McKune. He asked me who my favorite blues singer was. As I mentioned earlier, I was a fan of Sam Collins, who recorded for Gennett and Champion. McKune says, "No, he's good, but the greatest is Patton." Charley Patton—that was the first I'd heard of him, never heard anything by him. At that time I was mostly collecting New Orleans to Chicago jazz. My familiarity with blues singers—the only one I really liked was Sam Collins. And I had never heard any of the other ones, like Son House or Skip James. McKune was interested in getting converts to the great Paramount blues singers; number one on the list was Charley Patton. So McKune asked me if I'd be interested in hearing some Patton records, and I said, "Yeah!" At that time he was living at the YMCA in Brooklyn on 179 Marcy Avenue, which was kind of a tough white section of Brooklyn off of the Manhattan Bridge; when you go up the Manhattan Bridge you run right into it. He kept all of his records under his bed in boxes. And he had a portable, primitive turntable. And I heard Patton and really liked him, of course.

McKune was around fifty at the time, when I was in my early twenties. He was like primarily a priest of the blues. He was quite brilliant and a terrific writer. He had worked as a reporter for the *Long Island Star*, but now he was working for the post office, on his way to a sort of descent in life. At that time he didn't drink, till after a couple of years he told me he would drink a pint of whiskey to put himself to sleep. So that began another decline into alcoholism. McKune visited Bernie Klatzko, who was an accountant and a great friend of mine. He visited Bernie in his office, and there was this New Yorker that Klatzko was taking care of. Bernie described him as a typical, cynical New Yorker. This guy took one look at McKune, and after McKune left he said, "Now, there's a man on his way down."

Jim McKune. Courtesy Pete Whelan.

McKune was about six feet tall but weighed about 125 pounds. He was scarecrow thin; in fact, he looked a little bit like a scarecrow. He was very pale. You could see the veins in his neck and his arms. His arms were rail thin. He gesticulated with stiff arms when he got excited. You'd find yourself moving backwards; he was getting more and more excited and be talking. He used his hands a lot, almost like a judo performer [*laughs*]—you know, the slice with the back of the hands. His clothes were really super-nondescript. He always wore a white shirt, a long-sleeve shirt with the sleeves rolled up past the elbow. The pants he wore were usually that blackish color with a slight shine, which were the kind of clothes worn by the working people of the lower middle class of New York, and they always had black shoes! The epitome of the nondescript dress. His hair was straight, slight brown going gray, slicked back—sharp-pointed nose. He didn't wear glasses; in fact, I think his eyes were really good. His handwriting was microscopic. He did complain about one magazine called *Record Research,* where the print kept getting smaller and smaller, going down to about five-and-a-half-point type. He complained about that. He said he needed a magnifying glass for all the issues. There's an early photo of him in *78 Quarterly,* issue number three. Bernie Klatzko got it from McKune's sister, who lived in New Jersey.

How many records did McKune have?

My guess is around fifty, somewhere between fifty and a hundred. They were in boxes. You can get maybe twenty-five records in a box, and the question is how many boxes can you fit under the bed.

In addition to Patton, who else was McKune promoting to you?

Well, he wasn't familiar with Son House at that time, because those records were so rare. He liked a lot of offbeat people, like Walter Roland, just about any of the good blues singers. Skip James, Robert Wilkins, Mississippi John Hurt.

I don't know how McKune originally came to be a blues fan. He also liked several jazz pieces. Like Frenchy's String Band, which he had three new copies of. It's a great record which features a New Orleans trumpet player ["Polite Frenchy" Christian]. It's not that rare; it was on the Columbia 14000 series. It was Frank Driggs that found out his name. Apparently Frenchy went to Texas like Bunk Johnson, who he sounded like. He had a very Creole-sounding name. He doesn't seem to be mentioned much in the history of New Orleans jazz. It's one of the great trumpet solos—probably the best—and McKune spotted it right away! Another one he had three copies of was Buster Johnson "Undertaker Blues." He had three Varsity label tests of it, which came from Big Joe at the Jazz Record Center via Eli Oberstein. This is another one that McKune turned me on to. One side only—one half of a record! One of the great blues records! He liked all the great stuff. A favorite of his was the Reverend F. W. McGee, especially the ones where there was singing, like "Fifty Miles of Elbow Room." And Reverend D. C. Rice was another. And, of course, Bessie Johnson!—and [Lonnie] McIntorsch and Edwards—all those great sanctified singers!

McKune wrote a very interesting article about Patton in *VJM* magazine, but nobody seems to be able to find it. But I remember McKune's first words in the article: "I like Charley Patton because he's pure!" He was talking about Patton's artistry being undiluted, non-compromised by urban thinking. Now I can't find the article, but it was the first in a series that appeared in *VJM* around 1962. McKune would show me letters he had written. They were incredible, very simply written. Like perhaps Hemingway or Elmore Leonard [*laughs*]—verbs and nouns, very few adverbs and no adjectives. He had it all down. He could have been a terrific writer if he had been published, but it never happened.

McKune was in touch with two pioneer collectors. One was a blues collector out on the West Coast, I think in Washington State, or Oregon, named Wally Umphrey. The other was one in New York State, named Jack Whistance. McKune would show me their letters. They were pretty interesting. They admired the blues singers, but I think McKune was telling them which ones to listen to. I never met Jack Whistance—or Wally Umphrey, who died. The closest to McKune at that time, when I first met him, was Henry Renard, who lived in New Jersey and worked for Jake Schneider. He had a blues collection that he sold to Jake when he got married around 1956. When that happened I was able to buy a lot of great blues records, for not very much. I didn't know Renard well at the time. I got to know Henry a lot better later on. I don't know if he's still alive at this point. He had a collection of McKune's letters, as did Jack Whistance.

McKune was not in touch with the other collectors who were picking up blues at the time—the two Ertegun brothers and Harry Smith, who put out Folkways. Henry Renard was going to do an article about Harry Smith for *78 Quarterly*. Harry put out different blues singers along with country and western. He started out in 1929 with the Victor label as a recording engineer. He then worked for Eli Oberstein in a building in the upper East Fifties. Eli Oberstein put out Varsity label reissues of Gennett/Champion material, which he must have had the masters for. Some of the originals never showed up, they were so rare. But they all came out under pseudonyms. Eli Oberstein also put out the Crown label, which reissued a lot of Paramounts. Now, the guy that owned Folkways, Moe Asch, worked in the same building, in the same group of rooms, and took it over from Eli Oberstein. So Harry Smith continued to make records for Moe Asch. Harry Smith left his collection, which was quite valuable, to the New York Public Library. I never met Harry Smith. I never talked to him over the phone or anything, but I had heard somewhere that he was over in Africa, and he was a man with a great big beard! We were primarily jazz collectors, but we started collecting blues about the same time.

Would you say that Gayle Dean Wardlow was another of McKune's converts to Charley Patton?

No, they only met once! Wardlow came up to New York in 1965, maybe. And McKune at this point was staying at the YMCA on Eighth Avenue in Manhattan. Wardlow was staying there at the same time. I met both of them separately at around the same time. I was surprised because I came over to see Wardlow, and I was surprised to see McKune there. I don't know if they actually even met. I remember telling Wardlow that McKune was also living there, and I'd just finished talking to him. No, Wardlow was on his own and he liked the music. I think both Bernie and myself influenced him.

I'd read that by the time he died, McKune no longer had a record collection. Is this true?

It didn't really disappear. He may have sold part; another part went to Ben Kaplan. I think he was preparing himself for the end. He wound up in a skid-row hotel as an alcoholic and died a bizarre death. He was found murdered. Police said he was found naked, tied to a chair and gagged, and he suffocated to death. It turns out McKune was a closeted gay. Bill Givens noticed this right away; neither Bernie nor I ever had an inkling. But homicide detectives said that they thought it was a homosexual serial killer who had killed several other people in that same area. Apparently this killer must have lured people to their deaths. Police found a letter from Bernie in McKune's pocket, and they contacted Bernie to find out what they could about McKune. I got a letter from Bernie. I was down in Key West, Florida.

You mentioned Bernie Klatzko. Weren't you and he pals?

Oh, yeah! We were very close, and our tastes were almost identical. We both loved the great blues and the great jazz. Except that Bernie liked sanctified singing a little better than I did. Of course that was then; now I like sanctified singing just as much as blues, by the great black religious singers which began in the 1840s and is still around today, unlike blues or jazz. Jazz had a very short golden age, from maybe 1915 to 1928. Blues lasted longer, from 1900 to maybe 1940. I'm talking about the golden age.

Bernie Klatzko and Pete Whelan. Courtesy Pete Whelan.

Bernie was very matter-of-fact, very easy to be with, completely unpretentious, and had a way of cutting through to the truth in about two seconds and had an instinct for that.

And he did describe his blues collecting when he first started as "compares to the sex drive of a teenager!" [*laughs*]

Were you close to the same age?

Yes, Bernie was three or four years older and he died; he had lymphoma discovered in the early 1960s. He had x-ray treatments and they really didn't know how to handle it. They cured the lymphoma, but the scar tissue from the x-ray kept increasing and increasing, and that's what finally killed him, five or six years ago.

It occurs to me that your name and his name were the names we often saw on the Yazoo label reissues. Did you guys loan records to Nick Perls?

Oh, yeah! Yeah! Actually Bernie had his own record company. He started Yazoo with Nick Perls, but he was cut out. So then he reissued jazz and blues on another label, called Herwin, which was named after another 1920s label. He also put out some 78s on Herwin—of Skip James, Son House, and Willie Brown.

It seems there is no serious record collector who has managed a successful marriage. What are your thoughts on this subject?

It's like a seesaw. As the love interest in a woman increases, the interest in collecting 78s decreases. And when people get divorced—and I know a lot of people who've had this experience—they start collecting again. Very often when they first get married they sell their collections. There's a sexual thing about record collecting. I've never delved into it, but it's fascinating! It's one of those great truths in life. [*laughs*]

I always thought that it was financial irresponsibility. Most collectors are not financially responsible.

Right! But they couldn't have made a better investment than in rare blues, and maybe rare jazz too. I've bought records for a dollar or two dollars that are worth a thousand dollars today—or more! It's if you bought the right records and held on to them. It's like a Warren Buffet investment.

Which speaks louder to you in collecting records—is it the actual music, or is it the romance of the record as a collectible item?

There's three things involved in collecting 78s. Number one, the music has to be seventy percent of it. The next is the label; if it's really interesting and the record company has an interesting history, like Paramount and Gennett both do, that adds to the interest. And a label like Black Patti, which has a fascinating history and is exciting visually, that adds a great deal. The other thing, of course, is possession; if you have the only copy, you have the only copy and you're a star! [*laughs*]

Most collectors are familiar with the big-name blues singers on Paramount. Who were the heavy hitters on the Gennett label?

William Harris, number one—a great singer, the equal of any on the Paramount label. He was intense, and he had his less intense moments, but he's right up there. And I'd rate Sam Collins—the first Gennett session—as right up there, though price-wise he's not up there with William Harris. Then there's Jaybird Coleman, the second greatest harmonica player and blues singer. It's a combination of the two, unaccompanied harmonica with blues singing. He was a master at that. There's only one other harmonica player I think is greater; that's a wild man on Paramount named George "Bullet" Williams. Then you run through the Gennett catalog and there are all sorts of obscure blues singers that were really interesting. The same with Paramount.

With Gennett it was only a sideline throughout its history. They ran out of money and had this cheaper label called Champion, and they continued issuing blues on Champion and a side label called Superior. When Champion ran out of red paper, they had some orange paper left over, so they issued records on orange paper. And then they ran out of orange paper and they had some black paper left over from the Electrobeam/Gennett label. But at that time they were issuing maybe only fifty copies per record, sometimes eighteen copies, other times maybe two hundred at the most. So needless to say, those records are sought after along with the Paramounts from the same years, which also had short runs.

Can you address the phenomenon exclusive to the Paramount label in which a mint, perfectly clean copy will split from center hole to edge?

Well, there still can be a lot of surface on a clean Paramount pressing. The odd thing about the material that they used—and they used really strange material, including gravel—like a record that's in really bad shape. Like let's say it's G plus, where the surface noise is a little bit louder than the singing. Now, on Victor if you look at a G plus Victor, it's not very pleasant, but a G plus Paramount that looks [like] G plus, plays better. Something about the composition material was a lot harder, so it held up better. I don't know if that was deliberate. I suspect it wasn't; they were just probably looking for the cheap thing.

Any theories on what caused those records to split?

I'm not sure what you mean by split?

From the center hole to the rim . . .

Oh, the cracks! Well, they all cracked. The thinner the pressing, the more likely it was to crack. Like a lot of Electrobeam/Gennetts and Black Pattis were thin pressings, and they cracked easily and get hairline cracks, which sometimes you hear and sometimes you don't. Columbias had a tendency to get what they called "lam cracks," which was only on the surface. Underneath the surface there was a thing that looked like paper and that somehow absorbed the cracks. But all 78s crack—unless there're flexible—very easily. So when shipping, beware!

In issue number twelve of *78 Quarterly* you published a series of pictures from the Paramount pressing plant. You have a picture with a wagon filled with wooden crates of records being shipped. How were they packed?

Oh, yeah! They shipped them in wooden crates. I don't know how they packed them, but my guess is there was a lot of breakage. But they did send them railway express, which in those days—I don't know if that still exists anymore—but they were very careful. When I was a child I bought a lot of reptiles by way of railway express. In one case the box was open and this giant head of an alligator came out. [*laughs*] The police were called and it was a really big deal!

At some point didn't you have to sell your first collection?

Yes! That was when I was really pressed for money. I was supporting two women at the time, in two different apartments. One was an ex-wife. I was working, but I wasn't making enough to cover expenses, so . . . But then I was in love, so it was easy to sell.

Where did the collection go?

Most of it wound up with Rich Nevins, who didn't buy it at the time, but I sold a bunch to Bernie Klatzko and to Nick Perls—that's where they went. Of course, both are dead. And Bernie sold his collection eventually to Nick Perls, and Nick Perls died and Rich Nevins managed to buy the collection.

Didn't Gayle Dean buy somebody's collection?

He bought a lot of rare blues Paramounts from Bill Russell, who had found a mint stock of Paramounts in Bloomingdale's basement in New York City, oddly enough. [*laughs*] Bill Russell was a pioneer jazz collector and he didn't care much about the blues, but he picked them up anyway. This was in the mid or late 1930s he picked them up. Included were some really rare Pattons and other things. Gayle traded piano rolls to Bill Russell. And he bought a lot of Paramounts from John Steiner—who, in effect, bought out Paramount in around 1943 or thereabouts. Paramount hadn't been producing records for over ten years. There

William Russell at the Caledonia in New Orleans. Historic New Orleans Collection.

were still a few floating around. John Steiner wanted to reissue Paramounts, mostly jazz, so he bought the company out for practically nothing.

Did he get metal parts?

As it turned out I think there was one metal part; he just wanted to get the rights to reissue Paramounts, in a legitimate way, from the company itself. But that's another story as it turns out. At that time you could reissue things, but major record companies like Columbia would sue, knowing that if it ever went to trial they couldn't really stop you from reissuing, because sound was not copyrightable then; sheet music was. The songs were copyrightable, but the sound on 78s wasn't. It was strange.

What kind of a turntable do you use at home for your personal listening?

I use a pretty cheap one [*laughs*] called a Newmark. The best turntable is one that's portable, but you can't do anything with it. As it is now I can make CDs through the amplifier. Sony has a pretty good CD burner through the turntable without having to do it through a computer.

I have a few collector friends that use a set of styli for better sound quality. Do you use a set of styli?

I don't bother with it, but I should. Many collectors, like Rich Nevins, are really experts at that. They usually have three or four different styli. I always figured wrong on the size of the styli. [*laughs*] I figured Paramounts would take a great big wide stylus, but they don't, because you can see the grooves look wide. But it's a matter of what's inside the groove. Does the needle fit inside, or does it sit on top of just one groove? It's tricky! The guy who really is the best at that is Rich Nevins.

Were Paramounts recorded acoustically or electronically?

They were acoustically recorded until 1925. And that's another story. A lot of the records that sound acoustic were made by Orlando Marsh, who invented electric recording. His electric recording was actually inferior to acoustic recording. By 1926 all the Paramounts were electric—even by 1925! Nineteen twenty-five was sort of the cutoff date between acoustic and electrical recordings, and the earliest electrical recordings sometimes were not as good as the best acoustics. Now, OKeh and Columbia probably had the best sound. And, of course, as electrical recording got better, it got terrific. Probably Columbia, including the surface—they had a laminated surface. There was much less surface noise on Columbia and their subsidiary at the time, OKeh, than just about any other label.

Didn't record companies standardize playback speed at this same time?

They did, but they didn't! It was supposed to be 78, but it depends. That's one of the ways you can tell a reissued dub from the original is the speed. I discovered there's a record called "Hastings Street" by Charlie Spand and Blind Blake. On the Paramount it has this mellow deep sound, and on the Columbia reissue it has this shallow sound because it was recorded at a faster speed. It was dubbed at a faster speed for some unknown reason. But they vary; usually they can run from 74 rpm to 80 rpm. Now, I have a record of a female singer, Tillie Johnson, accompanied by a good pianist named Buddy Burton. And she sounds like this quivering child on the record because the speed is so sped up. Just to make it fit in that ten-inch distance, they had to speed it up. I don't know why they even issued it—the vocal is very strange.

Do you have a pitch control?

Yes, I do! It starts at 78 rpm and will play up to ten percent faster or ten percent slower. There's a range in there, and there's some records that sound a lot better when they're faster. In fact, most—if there's any question about it—sound better when they're faster, except for "Hastings Street"! [*laughs*]

Have you paid any attention to the popular school of thought that maintains the Robert Johnson masters were somehow sped up during mastering?

No, I never heard that.

Certain enthusiasts theorize the Johnsons acquire this dynamic quality because they are sped up, and have slowed them for purposes of comparison. It would be interesting to get your reaction to the altered-sound versions.

You know, I sold all my Robert Johnson records quite awhile ago. He was never my number one—or number ten, for that matter. I think he's a little too sophisticated for me. I much prefer his mentor, who was Son House. But that's just me . . .

I saw a name and I wondered if you can shed some light on who this was—Bob Travis?

Oh, yeah, Bob Travis! He collected jazz, and in fact I got probably my most prized blues record from him. I met him when Dick Spottswood told me there was a Washington, D.C., collector that found a new copy of Son House "My Black Mama" on Paramount. Travis had moved to New York, Manhattan, in the East Thirties. I called him up and went over and asked him if he would be at all interested in selling his Son House. He said, "No, but if you let me tape some of your records from your collection, I'll give it to you." [*laughs*] So I went over once a week dutifully bringing boxes of blues records over, which he would tape. He had this terrific recording equipment; he should have been a recording engineer instead of a technical writer. In fact, after the first OJL [Original Jazz Library] label issue on Charley Patton—from then on up through OJL number 5 or 6—he was our recording engineer. He told me he found the Son House in a stock of Deccas—the only Paramount in three hundred Deccas. Rich Nevins now has it. These great rarities go through a lot of hands and a lot of travels.

Let's talk about the OJL label. How did that happen?

I started the Origin Jazz Library label with Bill Givens in 1960. Bill Givens and I did OJL. I first thought of doing it with Bernie [Klatzko] because he and I had exactly the same taste on just about everything. But, unfortunately, we were competing for rare 78s at the time, and I foresaw that there would be some slight difficulty, maybe even resentment, about who got what record. Putting out OJL was a great entrée into people that had records. They would write and tell me they had certain blues records, so that was a plus. I was inspired at the time. I thought that Robert Johnson would be the perfect one to reissue, because he was good, and I could see that he would become popular. But then I got a phone call from a friend of mine, Frank Driggs, who was working for Columbia at the time. And he said, "Stop, because Columbia is doing a Robert Johnson reissue!" So we stopped, and that's when we put out Patton, who was much more—I hate to use this trite expression—"down-to-earth," but much more interesting and varied in different ways, the "great master," probably. So I had a bunch of his Paramounts in decent enough shape. Bernie Klatzko had some Paramounts and Vocalions, and on that we issued the Charley Patton. It was done at a place called Sanders Recording Studio in Times Square, New York. He used to make home recordings for people, so we used him. He was sort of a colorful character. Then the records were pressed up in the Bronx. Little did we know, but the guy that was pressing them pressed a bunch of extras and was selling them on the side. [*laughs*]

What was a press run for an OJL release?

If I remember it was usually two or three thousand. Sometimes we went into second pressings, like on, for some reason, the jug band OJL number four was the most popular, and they still are. But, for example, less popular was Henry Thomas, the great Texas blues singer—and country singer too.

So OJL did a Henry Thomas reissue?

Oh, yeah, that was OJL number three. He was quite old when he recorded in the 1920s. He appeared at the Chicago Exposition—I believe it was 1893?—and he was performing there. So I believe he was at least in his sixties when he recorded, or maybe older.

I'm familiar with a Herwin label reissue. Was that Bernie's?

Yeah, that was Bernie's. That was much later; that was in the mid-1960s. But we put out the best sides by Henry Thomas; it didn't sell well.

I think the quills may be an acquired taste.

Yeah, but Canned Heat made a big seller out of one of the Henry Thomas records ["Bull Doze Blues"], but it's very similar to the Henry Thomas original.

At what point in the catalog did you finally leave the label?

Well, I was working full-time, and Bill Givens was not working. He was handling all the distribution and he wanted the company. He wanted to move to Washington, D.C., and then California, so I gave it to him. That was at OJL number fourteen, the last of the two sanctified albums.

That's about halfway through the catalog, isn't it?

Yeah! The rest of the catalog fell down because the records weren't there. Bernie and Nick Perls started putting out their labels. They had the records, and Bill Givens didn't.

Was anybody else doing microgroove reissues at that point?

Folkways. Sam Charters did a record called *The Country Blues*, which came out a year before OJL. But he didn't have the records to put out a really great album. There were some interesting things on it, but it was complementary to his book *The Country Blues*.

And for some reason a lot of people disliked what he wrote, but I thought he was really fascinating—and good! I thought, last I heard, that he was teaching at the University of Connecticut.

Didn't I read in the Slotnikoff [Joel Slotnikoff, publisher of *Blues World*] interview that you started OJL in response to Charters's Folkway album?

The response was the second album, which was—Bill Givens came up with this title; I didn't like it, because it was too competitive. It was called *Really! The Country Blues*. It was because it had Son House and Skip James, all the great ones.

Who did Sam include on his album? It seems as though people took offense at what he reissued on his album.

McKune certainly did, and the few hard-core country blues collectors did. It was sort of urbanized blues, and I think it was only because he didn't have access to the original records. Now, earlier—I think around 1950, maybe later, maybe 1952—Folkways had put out a lot of great country blues along with some white country stuff; they were all mixed in together. They were put out by a pioneer collector who's shrouded in mystery. This was Harry Smith! His collection did go to the New York Public Library. But he put out a whole bunch of reissues of great stuff, not that rare. Richard "Rabbit" Brown, Sleepy John Estes—mostly Victor, some Vocalions, a few Paramounts—there was a Patton in there! But when you look over the entire list of country blues records, you're talking about one hundred to two hundred rather than fifteen or twenty. And he didn't have a lot of the stuff either. It turns out that a lot depends on what you have in your collection to be able to reissue the great stuff. At that time, if you didn't have it, you couldn't reissue it, unless you had a friend who had it.

78 Quarterly magazine. Courtesy *78 Quarterly*.

Wasn't Charters reissuing on a label called RBF, for Records, Books, and Film?

That rings a bell . . . I don't know.

You've portrayed McKune as one of your mentors. Is there anyone you'd like to claim as a disciple?

Well, Dick Spottswood always claimed that I was his mentor. You never know. It could be done accidentally. A lot of English collectors bought OJL records. Later on a lot of people read *78 Quarterly*, but who knows?

How did you decide to start *78 Quarterly*?

Initially I did it in response to not being with OJL anymore. I was still collecting, and

I thought it would be interesting to have a magazine primarily for blues collectors, who actually collected 78s—also jazz collectors! It started in 1967. I put out two issues and then everything stopped. I left New York, went to Key West, and then at some point I decided I'd start up again with issue number three. I think that was about twenty years later. [*laughs*]

What was a run for *78 Quarterly?* How many copies per issue?

That varied. Usually two thousand to three thousand. A couple were sold out. The Robert Johnson issue—that was sold out, and that was reprinted again. So that totaled maybe six thousand or seven thousand. The combined reissue of numbers one and two—that sold out but wasn't reprinted again. There are still issues around and I'm boxing some up. There's one distributor, City Hall Records, and I'm just shipping by the box-load. Key West Printers are kind of primitive. They didn't put enough dryer in the ink [*laughs*], so the back cover of one issue and the front cover of the other, when they were stacked up, stuck together. [*laughs*] So when you pull them apart, there's always these little imperfections.

You've said that you don't have a regular time scheduled for publication. How do you know when you have enough material and that the issue is complete, ready to publish?

Well, sometimes the amount of pages varied from 70-something all the way up to 140. A lot depended on what material I got, things people sent in. If it was a lot of material, it became a bigger issue. [*laughs*]

Did you solicit for articles, or did people solicit you?

They solicited me, actually.

Who are some of the authors that have written articles for *78 Quarterly* over the years? Isn't there a core group of perhaps eight or ten writers?

Steve Calt, who is a brilliant writer and has health problems, emphysema. And Gayle Dean Wardlow.

What editing techniques do you use to publish the magazine, and have they changed over the years?

Yeah! I love to do paste-ups and half-tones with a Daylighter stat camera. And I would paste it up and give to the printer. But there came this electronic revolution in printing about three years ago. Printers now will not accept paste-ups. I used to able to make what's called a Velox; it's a line shot half-tone [on Velox photographic paper]. But they won't accept that anymore. You leave it now to the discretion of the printers, which I don't like. On issue twelve they burned it onto a CD and it was fine, except for some of the captions under the photos were missing. I don't see any way around it. Half of the fun of doing the magazine was doing the artwork. Electronic artwork, to me, isn't as much fun as manual art work or as interesting. Computer artwork is not my métier. [*laughs*]

Did you ever do any firsthand, door-to-door blues research?

No, no, I never did any. I'm not sure why. Maybe because it was nerve-wracking. [*laughs*] I've done it by phone—asked questions, got answers, used a tape recorder that backed into the phone. But in person I never really traveled that much. I enjoyed Steve Calt's interviews with Skip James. I also knew Skip James and talked a lot with him! We even played the piano together, and Skip James would say, "Well, I do it a little different." Very modestly he would say it, but of course he was much better.

Did you take any interest when all the prewar bluesmen were being rediscovered during the 1960s folk boom?

Yeah! Oh, yeah! Well, that would be Skip James and Mississippi John Hurt, who was very popular. Skip James—there's a great movie out, but try and find it, try and get ahold of it. When Skip James was first discovered—it was 1964 at the Newport Folk Festival—he was cinematized with sound. And he made this great performance of "If You Haven't Any Hay, Get on Down the Road," and he did it on the guitar and he wiggled at the same time. It was the most stunning thing. There's a guy who's holding on to this and won't let anybody see it! It was just one of the great blues items. Also, there's some terrific Son House on there. But ultimately, after that year, Skip James's health went into decline, and he declined musically along with his bad health. Mississippi John Hurt played terrifically up until the day he died. Of course, Spottswood would be the guy to interview about John Hurt. He was John's co-manager.

How about Robert Wilkins? Did you see him?

No, I didn't, unfortunately . . .

How about Bukka White?

No!

Reverend Gary Davis?

No! [*laughs*] No, I guess Skip James and Mississippi John Hurt, and that's about it.

How did you guys decide that Paramount and Gennett—and the deep country blues guys that were issued on those labels—how did you decide that those were the guys to listen to?

Just because we were moved emotionally and musically. It was a flash of recognition. And it amazes me why jazz collectors thought of it as trash. I'm dumbfounded, because jazz—golden age black jazz was great! But maybe greatest were the great country blues singers, but I never understood the divide. The blues struck not only me but a lot of blues collectors the same way, so there's something there! I know that sounds vague.

There are some revisionist writers, who, if I understand correctly, say there was a small group of guys—you would be included—who decided many years ago, fifty years ago, that the heart and soul of black music was country blues—Delta blues. That this music attained mythological status because you early collectors both collected and promoted this specific genre. They maintain that this music didn't sell very well, and it was very small slice of the black music pie. If I correctly understand what they are saying, they maintain that we've been misled all these years by thinking this was the taproot, the heart and soul, of black music.

I don't think it's the heart and soul of black music. I think the heart and soul of black music is religious singing, but I think that country blues was a peak in artistry, as was certain jazz a peak in artistry. The whole picture of black music would be eighty percent religious, with a special thing in sanctified singing. I think country blues was a pinnacle in black music.

As a radio host with a large black listening audience, I can attest to the notion that there is wide variety in their tastes in music—jazz, R & B, soul. But what speaks to the artistry of country blues is not that a small trailblazing group of white record collectors were enthralled with it, but that a second generation of black musicians—the postwar generation of bluesmen—were so deeply influenced by it. The fact that your generation of collectors, who listened without benefit of any knowledge of the artists, their personalities and careers, is further affirmation of the artistry of country blues.

It was black music for a black audience. There was always the occasional white person that liked the blues especially black ragtime, which has been ignored. Big Bill and Blind Blake had some tremendous ragtime pieces. Those aren't mentioned much, but I would rank them almost with the country blues, because it's emotionally moving also.

There was so much country blues recorded in the 1920s, starting around 1926 and going into, say, 1932, a tremendous amount of country blues recorded—at least as much as jazz. For me, people dismiss Ellington as too sophisticated; the same with Louis Jordan. But I personally [*laughs*] dislike that music. It's a different kind of music.

You've published countless articles on the Paramount and Gennett labels. Were you ever able to meet any of the company execs from either company?

As far as I know the last execs from the Gennett Company died in the mid-1950s. At Paramount they were dead in the late 1940s. I never had a chance to meet any of them. But my impression of them was that they were not very interested in the music. It was just a business. Sometimes it was an inherited family business. They were kind of amateurish about it. They weren't very good businessmen like the executives of the Victor and Columbia labels.

Being in New York City, did you ever meet any of the classic blues singers?

The only one I met—and it was a physical meeting—was Billie Holiday. I was sixteen and on my way into a club called the Famous Door. This rather beautiful, exotic woman came running out, angrily shouting at somebody behind her—and smashed right into me! [*laughs*] That was the only one! There was another one I did hear in the mid-1950s: Chippie Hill, Bertha "Chippie" Hill! She recorded with Louis Armstrong on OKeh—"Trouble in Mind." She was good. She was terrific in person! She was rediscovered before Alberta Hunter. I always wanted to hear Ida Cox in person, because I always liked her singing. My favorite, though, was the New Orleans singer Ann Cook. She was accompanied by Louis Dumaine and His Orchestra, recorded in New Orleans. She was great.

Did you participate in the Document label project conducted by Johnny Parth? And if so, what records did you make available?

Yes! I provided a lot of rare stuff that hadn't been reissued. Such as Herve Duerson on Gennett; William Harris—I think all the William Harris stuff—and a bunch of other stuff

. . . I've always been curious to know if there was great black music in the 1890s and what it sounded like—nobody knows. I wish recording had come in earlier, like around 1860, that there had been some cylinders or something recorded of black music from 1860 to 1915. It would have been fascinating and illuminating. It would have made a great difference in everybody's perspective. I know as far as blues goes, the Spanish guitar was a big element, and it was introduced around the turn of the century. That made all the difference in the style of singing, because if there was self-accompaniment before that, it was on banjo, which didn't really lend itself to blues singing.

Isn't it Wardlow's contention that blues all began around 1900?

Yeah, that sounds right. At least blues did. Sanctified singing, from descriptions, go[es] back to 1840, which is a long time ago, and continues through today. I think of that as the predominant black American music. Right now I'm involved in writing a book—a book on jazz trumpeter Freddy Keppard in 1907–1908 New Orleans—so I'm trying to figure out what the music sounded like.

Wasn't Keppard the guy who would never play his best licks on record because he didn't want anybody else to steal them?

Right, that's the rumor! I don't think it's true. I think he was insulted by some Victor label executive in 1916. He was turned off and said he wouldn't record for them. I think that is the real story; it may have been a racial slur. He was a wonderful trumpet player.

In fact, I met Perry Bradford. He came into Big Joe's one time. He wore this camel-hair overcoat that came down below his ankles and sort of dragged along the floor. [*laughs*] He was probably in his eighties at that time. He was talking to Joe Klauberg, who was just mumbling along, "Yes, yes." Perry Bradford said, "Buddy Bolden—he was nothin'! I was in New Orleans in 1905, and he was nothin'! The guy there was Freddy Keppard. He was the greatest trumpet player of all! You could hear him from here (Forty-seventh Street) all the way to 125th Street and Lenox Avenue. He was so loud! When he played in auditoriums, people would move out of the first five rows 'cause they got blasted away!"

He made a few records where you can hear that. They must have put him way in the back. By the way, I think maybe the first or second greatest cornet playing I've ever heard is on Bessie Smith's "Young Woman Blues," accompanied by Joe Smith on coronet. Unfortunately, Joe Smith disappeared into the Fletcher Henderson Orchestra and was never heard from again! [*laughs*] He was heard from, but it was one of the great tragedies. Fletcher Henderson swallowed up a whole bunch of great coronet players, including Tommy Ladnier—and Shirley Clay, another great one.

DICK WATERMAN INTERVIEW

I was born in Plymouth, Massachusetts, which is, of course, home of Plymouth Rock and which has the nickname of "America's Hometown." I was born in 1935 and went to school there. I graduated in '53 and then went to college for several years. Then I was in the army for three years. I was a cryptographer, which sort of accounts for my ability to remember numbers over the years. I have a very bad memory for names and faces, but if I ever called you, I remember your phone number or your area code or your zip code or something like that. I have a good memory for numbers. After I got out of school, I was a newspaperman in Connecticut, in Miami, and then I moved back to the Cambridge area in '63. I fell into the Cambridge folk music scene, which was Joan Baez, Bob Dylan, Tim Harden, Phil Ochs, New Lost City Ramblers, Eric Anderson—people like that. And at that point I had seen Reverend Gary Davis, of course. I had seen Brownie [McGhee]

Dick Waterman at Ground Zero blues club, June 2012. Photo courtesy of Madge Marley Howell.

and Sonny [Terry], and a San Francisco folk bluesman named Jesse Fuller. And he had a song called "San Francisco Bay Blues," which Peter, Paul, and Mary covered for a big hit. Then I had the opportunity to promote a concert with the newly rediscovered Mississippi John Hurt in early '64. And I did a week of shows with John Hurt at a little club called the Café Yana.

Then a few months later I promoted Bukka White. While Bukka was in town he stayed with Alan Wilson and Phil Spiro, who roomed together. Phil did a radio show at the MIT radio station. Alan and David Evans were interviewing Bukka, and they were running through a list of other prewar bluesmen they thought Bukka may have known. When David mentioned Son House, Bukka said, "Oh, I just saw him coming out of a movie theater." So this was really an electrifying move, because Son House had recorded once in 1930 and then for Alan Lomax in the early forties. So having had somebody say they had just seen Son House at a movie theater was pretty exciting stuff.

Had there been much clamor among the white enthusiasts about the possibility that Son House was still alive? Had anybody heard about that? Or was this the first evidence that anybody had come up with?

Well, really, there was nothing. There was a label called Origin Jazz Library which had an album, and I think it was called *Really! The Country Blues,* and there was some Son House on there. And then they had taken his Lomax recordings and issued half an album on Folkways. It was called *The Son House/J. D. Short Album*—Son House on one side of an LP and J. D. Short on the other. This was music that was recorded by Lomax by the Library of Congress and was never supposed to be commercially released. So the only Son House available was on Origin Jazz Library and on half an album on Folkways. But, no, there had been no rumors of sightings or anything like that.

So Phil Spiro, who was a computer programmer, and Nick Perls, who was a college dropout who would later go on to found Yazoo Records—the three of us got in a red Volkswagen Bug and we drove from Cambridge through New York down to the Mississippi Delta. And June of '64 was the summer of "Mississippi Burning," and it was not a very hospitable time to be down there. So we were there about three or four weeks in June, and it's really a long, complicated story. We met an old man whose son had once been married to Son House's stepdaughter. So we spoke to the son and we said, "You were once married to a woman and Son House was her stepfather." And he said yes. So then we got her phone number in Detroit and called her. And we said, "Your mother was married to the blues singer Son House." And she said yes. We knew his first name started with *E.* So we had mistakenly thought it was Eugene. Actually it was Eddie. So on June 21 of 1964, we spoke to a man who went and got Son House and brought him back to the phone. Son didn't have a phone. So we spoke to him and we said, "Are you the Son House that knew Charley Patton? Are you the Son House that made Paramount records? Are you the Son House that recorded for Alan Lomax?" And there was a pause and he said, "Hey, who is this anyway?" So we said, "Is that you?" and he said, "Yeah, that's me. I've done them things." And we said, "Okay. Hold on. We're on our way." And he was in Rochester, New York, and we were in Mississippi. So we drove straight through to Rochester, New York, and found him on June 25th.

Now, Phil Spiro went back to being a computer programmer and Nick Perls basically wasn't doing much of anything, so it fell to me to find work for our newly rediscovered bluesman. And I had been a pretty good sportswriter and I was very happy in my career as a journalist, and I had no intentions of leaving sportswriting to end up in this folk music business. I don't know how it happened. It just—weeks became months became years became decades. And at some point I knew I wasn't going to be a sportswriter anymore.

Did the three of you take any kind of precautions to let it be known that you weren't there necessarily as civil rights protesters?

Well, that's an interesting point. And the fact is we didn't. We just felt that since we weren't there for voter registration—we were there for the music—we were going to have some protective bubble over us. And my point is that when we were up on dirt roads and guys in pickup trucks with shotguns up on the racks, they would say, "What you doing down here?" And we would say, "Well, we're looking for blues music." And they would look at the three of us—and I mean, I'm five eleven, and Spiro's over six feet and, you know, Nick's average size . . . and they would look at that little yellow Volkswagen and they would say, "You three guys come all the way from New York in that little bitty car just to hear blues music?" And we'd say, "Well, yeah." And they were more bemused by this than anything. They would shake their heads and they would say, "Well, we've got it here and you're welcome to it." And they said, "There ain't a porch down here ain't got some kind of nigger sittin' on it, playin' away on that music. You're welcome to it. We've got plenty of it down here." So we avoided any racial flap; we never had any. It was just that they were totally bemused by the fact that three grown men would get into a Volkswagen Bug and drive from New York to Mississippi just for the music!

Did they help you find anybody?

No, since we did no more than ask for driving directions, because it was a segregated society. What I would interject here is that, if we had known then, in '64, that Robert Johnson would become the cultural icon that he became, we really could have become Robert Johnson experts. At that point, if Robert had been alive, he would have only been in his early fifties. So we met lots of people who knew Robert, had Robert stories, had seen Robert play, knew things about Robert—lots of people in their forties and fifties who had their memories and recollections and their Robert Johnson stories. So we actually could have mined that area really well and come away with a tremendous amount of Robert Johnson factual information, artifacts, whatever. At that point he had one Columbia LP out, and the Robert Johnson theme "Lift Up" didn't come until some years later. We ascertained that he was dead—and long dead. But once we had the Son House trail, we just abandoned all the Robert Johnson stuff.

You discovered Son House. Where did it go from there? How did you handle this discovery?

Well, in the 1960s the folk umbrella covered all sorts of traditional music. If you went to a folk festival, you heard gospel, blues, Cajun, zydeco, topical folksingers, French Canadian, and South African musicians. The folk music umbrella covered everything. The Newport festivals from '63, '64, '65 were just marvelous. They were very eclectic. There was a lot of bluegrass and old-timey, and we did that. "Mother" Maybelle Carter and Bob Dylan and Mississippi John Hurt and Cesar Chavez and the grape pickers in California—it was really a whole mixed bag. Then the music fragmented so there were bluegrass festivals and mandolin festivals and things like that. The first blues festivals were not until much later, but at that point it was all under the folk umbrella.

You have to realize that in that pre-Internet, pre-email, pre-fax kind of thing, we wrote letters. I had a manual Underwood typewriter, an old open-top Underwood. And I sat and wrote letters for Folk Song Society, one after the other after the other, and tried to get Son House hired. And I did that from '64 to '65. Then in '65 I was at Newport and some of the other bluesmen came to me, and they said, "We see that Son House got a record out on Columbia and he's playing festivals." So I nodded that yes, that was so. And they said, "Well, will you work for me? Can I come and be with you?" Skip James did, Fred McDowell, Elizabeth Cotton, Babe Stovall, you know, Mance Lipscomb, Lightning Hopkins—people like that.

Did you handle John Hurt?

Yes, in the last year of his life. He recorded a song called "Avalon's My Hometown" after his hometown in Mississippi, and he was found in Avalon, Mississippi. So I named my business Avalon Productions after John.

How about two others—Gary Davis and Robert Wilkins. Did you handle them at all?

Wilkins I knew well because Wilkins had performed at Newport. I don't remember whether it was '64 or '65. And he had made an album for the same label that had recorded Mississippi John Hurt. It's a really, really very, very nice album. He was a marvelous instrumentalist with a very distinct style. He wrote or was holding the copyright on "And That's No Way to Get Along," which is also called "Prodigal Son," which the Rolling Stones did. And after some confusion at the beginning, he did get his Rolling Stones royalty on it.

My friend Manny Greenhill, who was known in Ann Arbor, worked for and in the music business. Manny represented Gary Davis, John Hammond, Kweskin Jug Band, and Jesse Fuller. So I knew Reverend Davis well. You know, it was just sort of like a really odd sort of thing. There was no competition and jealousy. That Manny had Reverend Davis, and Jesse Fuller, and Brownie and Sonny, and John Hammond and people like that. And I had Son and Skip and Joanne, and if I was going to the Mariposa Folk Festival in Canada, and Reverend Davis is going to be there, Manny would give me a call and ask me to keep an eye out on the Reverend—make sure he made his set list okay and things like that. And so you would say, "But he's the competition—why would you do it?" But there was so little money in those days that there was more of a bond, more of a friendship, and we took care of each other.

Who actually had the Son House bug? Among the three of you—you, Nick, and Phil—who was it that had the real driving force to find Son House?

I think Phil Spiro, because Spiro actually played music. I did not and neither did Nick. Spiro, a retired computer programmer in California, played. He actually played as a duo with Al Wilson, who, under the nickname of "Blind Owl," moved to California and was the founding member of Canned Heat. Al was from Cambridge, and Al and Spiro actually were a performing duo. I really can't say enough good things about Al Wilson. He had the ability to drop into a supporting role either on a wooden guitar or a steel guitar or harmonica. In other words, not to be heard himself, but to augment whoever he was playing with, be it Son House, John Estes, or Lightning. The musicians loved to have a backup musician, and Al had no ego. Al was all about just making the other guys sound better, and he was an incredibly gifted musician who died way too soon.

How many of the records—and I know that the output at that point of prewar recordings was sort of limited—but how familiar were you, were the three of you, with all of the artists before the war? Were you fans, or did that come as you became acquainted with these people through the folk revival?

Well, I was a sportswriter. In other words, I had met John Hurt and just fell under his spell. So that when people said "Son House," he was just a guy off of scratchy 78s. So I was really not that familiar with him, nor did I have any anticipation of this world that I was getting into.

So you didn't sit and go through the list, the roster of the prewar recordings and say, "Wow! I wonder if he's alive, or if he's still alive, where could we find this guy?"

In that time period, let's remember, there was a Robert Johnson LP out and a Charley Patton LP. So that made them big. But on a lot of the others, there just wasn't enough material available. Rubin Lacey, Ishman Bracey, Garfield Akers—these were just, you know, names. And of course you had the incredibly wonderful Willie Brown, who had only done two solos, "M & O" and "Future Blues." So there's a whole legend on a guy who only did two songs!

Back in the 1960s Stefan Grossman played "Future Blues." So his nickname was "Kid Future." And his girlfriend at the time, I guess was fourteen or fifteen years old, was Rory Block. And Rory would sit next to Stefan, and she'd play that big guitar that Reverend Davis played. Stefan was like seventeen and Rory was fourteen or fifteen, and the two of them were really good. If something like that came along now, it would be hard to believe, but in Greenwich Village in those years it just seemed to be a kind of natural thing.

And then there were guys like John Sebastian, who just worshiped Mississippi John Hurt. You just have to realize the magic of John Hurt. He had wisdom. He had a sense of peace and calm. He was your favorite grandfather and he knew all the secrets. So people like Dave Van Ronk or Rory or Stefan or whoever—if you mentioned John Hurt to them, they'd just break into a smile. John Sebastian named his group from a line in a John Hurt song that said, *"I got to go to Memphis, from there to New York. I got to see my baby about a lovin' spoonful."*

How did John Hurt reemerge? Who handled that?

The point that I would make on John Hurt or Son House or so many of the others is they just played it the way they played it before rediscovery, no matter where they were. There's an interesting story. George Weir, who was the promoter of the Newport festival, who is still in his seventies, probably the greatest folk music impresario, and I was showing him some photos and we were talking. I said to him, "Out of all of the artists that you did over the years, what's the biggest surprise you ever had?" And he looked at me and he said, "Mississippi John." And I said, "Really?" He said, "You know, those night concerts drew seventeen or eighteen thousand people. And if they didn't like you, they didn't hesitate to let you know." He said, "I was standing on one side of the stage, and I looked at the crowd and I looked across the stage in the wings, waiting to be introduced, and there was this small black man with work clothes and a bowler hat. And he was soon come on stage with a wooden guitar, and I said, 'This is going to get ugly. They're going to kill him! They're going to eat him alive.' And they introduced John and he came out, and it was like he was on his porch. He was like in a rocking chair. And the first song, he had them quiet. And after two songs, he had them in his hand. And they just fell in love. And when he finished, they came to their feet and they would not let him go. They would not let him go. It was the most amazing thing I ever saw. He took seventeen thousand people, and he made every one of them fall in love with him. And I was there!"

And that's just the way John Hurt was. In other words, with all of those guys—Son, Skip, and the others—you never had the feeling that "This is a paid entertainer. He has come to your town to play music, to play music for money. And the next night, he will do it somewhere else, and somewhere else." They just came in and they did it the way they had always done it. They did it with a real authenticity. They did it straight from the heart. But when you saw Son House, whether it was ten people or a hundred or fifteen thousand, he just closed his eyes and the sweat broke out on his forehead and he just went someplace else. He went to 1928. He went to 1936. He went to Banks. He went to Walls. He went to Lula. He went to Tunica. He went to Greenville. He just transported himself back to another place in time, and the songs would go for six minutes, or ten minutes, or twelve minutes, whatever. And then, when he finished, he'd like blinked his eyes, blinked his eyes, and he came back to you. He came back to the present. But it was just absolutely miraculous to watch those guys. They did it the only way they knew how. They did it with a real authenticity. If you liked it, okay. If you didn't like it, they weren't going to put on a faux performance. Now, there were professionals in those days. Brownie and Sonny did a real slick professional show. But Son or Skip or John, or Mance or people like that, they did not.

Can you tell me a couple of Son House anecdotes? A couple of stories about Son House?

I tell you that the greatness of Son House was not in watching Son House. The greatness of Son House was to look at the face of Muddy Waters or Howling Wolf or Jimmy Reed or whatever when he played. Because you saw the majesty of Son House written on their faces. There's this great quote from Buddy Guy. Buddy's still being very active, of course.

When Buddy used to watch Son House and they did a lot of shows together, Buddy would just shake his head and say, "That old man's playing a different kind of music than the rest of us." He was just on a whole other level, you know?

He was a lifelong alcoholic, as far as I knew. He had a major drinking problem when I found him in '64, and I did my best, I did my real best, to hide this: that I carried bourbon and he drank before a performance. But we couldn't let him have all he wanted, or else there would be no show. So he was in Rochester, living at home, and had way too much to drink in a January. And he passed out in a snowdrift and they found him in the morning. And he had frostbitten fingers, and they saved his fingers. He was able to play guitar after that, but never as well as he had.

But the thing of it was Bill Graham, a promoter, was bringing in Bonnie and Delaney Bramlett. And on rhythm guitar was going to be Eric Clapton. It was going to be Delaney and Bonnie and Friends. Remember that group? "Never Ending Song of Love"—that was their single. Delaney and Bonnie and Friends with Clapton. And Bill called me and he said, "Listen, I understand that Delaney Bramlett and Eric Clapton worship Son House." And I said, "I can't speak for Delaney, but I know it's true that Eric worships Son." So he said, "Listen, I got them coming in to Fillmore East, and we're selling out everything the minute I put it on sale. Can Son House come in and play in front of them? Be the opening act?" So I said, "Well, I don't think he's capable of doing, you know, forty minutes." So Bill said, "No, no, no. I just want him to do about fifteen. Just do twelve or fifteen minutes. I know if Delaney Bramlett and Eric Clapton stand on the edge of the stage and they watch Son House play fifteen minutes, it's a win-win situation. They're going to rise up to the occasion and they're going to put on a show that will be just incredible!" And we lost that when Son had his hands frostbitten in a Rochester winter. But that offer did come from Bill Graham for Son House to open for Delaney and Bonnie and Clapton.

How about Skip James? What was Skip like to be around and to handle?

Well, he was very aloof. He was aloof, conceited, but there's an expression that says, "It ain't bragging if you can do it." And Skip James could do it. So it really wasn't bragging, you know?

I know he thought very highly of himself and if you thought very highly of him, he agreed with you. He wasn't much of a mixer. When he performed, he would look out at someplace over the head of the audience, whether he was in a club or a big outdoor stage. And he would play music *at* people, not *to* people. John Hurt, who wore a hat when he performed, would tip his head forward until his hat brim shaded his eyes. And then he would pick out a face, or faces, in the front row, and he would play right to those people. And Son would kind of look around and spot people and play to people. But Skip did not. Skip played *at* people.

I had Son House and Skip James going to Europe in October of '67, and Clapton was in New York with Cream. So I don't remember how I did it, but I called Clapton at his hotel. And we were leaving that night and he was opening his tour that night. So we agreed to meet in the office of Vanguard Records in Manhattan. So there were three chairs in the lobby. And Son

House, Skip James, and I were sitting there and the door opened—and it was a very small lobby—and Clapton came striding off the elevator and he came face-to-face with Son House and Skip James. Now, Cream had recorded Skip's "I'm So Glad." So I did the introductions. "This is my friend, Eric. Eric, this is Son House. Eric, this is Skip James. Skip, this is a young man from that English group that recorded your song 'I'm So Glad.'" So they shook hands all around and then a guitar came out. I think it was Skip's. And Skip, who was not about to lose the show to some young kid from England, proceeded to play "I'm So Glad." And just a dazzling version of it! And then Son played a song. And then the guitar went to Eric. And Skip basically said—and Skip would talk about himself in the third person—he said, "Now, Skip has played a song for you. Now you must play a song for Skip." And Eric, no fool, was having no part of this. He demurred and said, no, he appreciated the invitation but he was honored to listen and was not going to play in their presence.

Would you run through the history of how you got these guys on record?

There was the assumption that I would go to Delmark or go to Arhoolie, but my point was, why not shoot for the biggest and the best? In other words, if I succeed, I'd try the next one and the next one. The worst that happens is that I end up at Delmark and Arhoolie. I knew that John Hammond, who was a developer of talent acquisition at Columbia, had been responsible for the Robert Johnson album. And he had done his famous [From] Spirituals to Swing concert in Carnegie Hall in 1938, in which he tried to bring Robert Johnson up to New York City only to find out that Robert was dead. And I think he put Big Bill Broonzy on the show instead. So, with John Hammond, a huge Robert Johnson fan, I had my "in" there. So I made the connection and asked him if he would be interested in Son House on Columbia. And in my book, I mention—there's a chapter in there about Son House and how I got Son House to Columbia Records in New York City. And we sat in the office and John came in, and he just couldn't stop talking: "Oh, Son, I'm so happy to have you. Do you know I'm a big fan of Robert Johnson, and I released a Robert Johnson album, and Robert Johnson and 'Terraplane Blues' and 'Come On in My Kitchen,' and Robert this and Robert that."

Now, you have to realize that Son was Robert's mentor. But Son, significantly older, only knew Robert as being a real pain in the ass, who, as a kid, would borrow his guitar, break strings, unreliable, wouldn't make gigs—whatever. So now fast-forward forty years or so, and he's sitting in the office of a record executive who had put out a Robert Johnson LP and cannot stop talking about Robert Johnson and how great he was, and it just went on and on.

So Son lit a cigarette and looked out the window. And at that point I knew that John Hammond had totally lost Son House's focus on this thing, because if there's anything that Son didn't want to hear, it was about the successes of some *kid* who had just not been very good, you know, many years ago. So I let John go on for a while, and then I kind of waved my hand, and I said, "With all due respect, Mr. Hammond, you have to realize that Son's appreciation of Robert might not beam as brightly as yours, because Son was the teacher and Robert was the student." And John just stopped, flabbergasted. And then you could see the light go on over his head. And he said, "Well, of course! Well, of course! In other words, you were making records long before him." And then he came around the desk and he said, "I'm honored. Columbia Records is honored to have you. And I know we're going to make a great record together." And here's an interesting thing. I just found out from the Blues Foundation that Son House's "Death Letter [Blues]" from those 1965 sessions is being inducted into the Blues Hall of Fame as the single of the year, 2007, and will be inducted into the Hall of Fame at the Handy's.

Did Son regard that as any kind of a challenge at all?

No, no. We're now in 1965 and Robert Johnson had just vanished off of the radar at some point in the mid-1930s. Robert Johnson was thirty years gone. He wasn't anybody that Son ever thought about, you know. If we were someplace and the Robert Johnson LP was being played, you know, then Son would recognize it. But, I mean, no, no. The musician that Son respected above all was Charley Patton—Charley Patton and Willie Brown. And although he never met him, he was very fond of Blind Lemon Jefferson.

How about the Skip James? Did Skip go to Vanguard?

Yeah. What happened was Skip had been found in '64 by two guys who were not very good at what they did. They were inept in business. And so what happened was that when Skip came back to play at Newport in '64, he only knew three or four songs. And he just captivated Newport. He stopped the show—absolutely stopped the show! He did these three or four songs at the blues workshop in the afternoon, and he just knocked people out. And they found ten minutes on the night concert so he could perform at the night concert. And he did those songs again. And the word just swept around. "Some rediscovered Negro guy just did three or four songs and it's incredible!" It was so charismatic that it was just lightning! It was amazing. He had it all! He had the voice. He had the material. He could play. There was a great human interest story. It was fabulous!

What happened is that the people taking care of him lost a year. Nothing happened with Skip from Newport '64 to Newport '65. He made no recordings. He didn't play any major festivals. And he lost a year. The buzz was gone. The buzz from Skip at Newport '64 was just electric! He just absolutely had people who were not blues fans just talking about him. But he lost a year through inept management. So he came to me at Newport '65 and asked me to take over his booking and management. But at that point we had lost whatever leverage we had; he was now just a guy who was a year away from his great rediscovery.

And you're saying that Skip in '64 knew three or four songs. Had Skip quit playing before he was discovered? Rediscovered?

I don't know. The only book on the subject is a Stephen Calt biography that I sued for libel. It's just a terrible book. And it was libelous. I don't know what Skip was doing. He recorded in '31 and was found thirty-three years later in '64. I don't know if he worked on a railroad or if he was a preacher or ran a grocery store. I have no idea. But when he came back, his playing was frail but very assertive and very melodic. He was just an incredible instrumentalist. If you looked into Skip's recording from '31 to his rediscovery stuff in '64, his fingering and progression is exactly the same. You could say the same thing for John Hurt. In other words, these guys have their playing down.

So how did you make the connection for him with the recording then?

Well, there really wasn't a whole lot of fighting for Skip's services. Vanguard, Elektra—they were the major folk labels of their day. Maynard Solomon wrote—not a major blues fan, but he had an ear for that which he felt he wanted to have in the Vanguard family. And he recorded a lot of stuff that were not commercial sellers. So he thought that Skip would be a good fit. I'm trying to remember where we recorded. It was a hotel ballroom on the New York's Upper West Side. I don't remember the name of the hotel, but the ballroom had good acoustics. So we went in there at night and did our recording there.

What was Skip's attitude towards the idea of going back in and making more records some thirty years later?

I don't think any of these guys really spent a lot of time introspectively looking inward. It was a gig. It was what they did. It was the way they earned their living. In other words, I never looked at it from a sociological point of view. These guys were sitting and playing for young, wealthy white kids between the ages of eighteen and twenty-three, who were all going to Harvard and Yale and Brandeis and Trinity and Wesleyan and were, you know, privileged kids. What did these old Negroes think about playing for them? I never went into that. I never asked them. My plate was full. My job was to find work for them, not to start doing sociological papers on the great racial divide.

There was a black writer by the name of Julius Lester. And I think Julius was the only one who interviewed them at any length and wrote about it. So I think that Julius Lester's writings, possibly in *Sing Out*, might be able to be found. As far as people to whom they would confide their thoughts, I would say there really were not a lot. There was a guy in Philadelphia, a young black musician named Jerry Ricks, "Philadelphia" Jerry Ricks. And whenever they came through Philadelphia, Jerry would play second guitar behind them and they would be very friendly with Jerry. The other one was Taj Mahal, of course, who was already on the scene by the mid-60s. And Taj had a great personal interest as a young black man in making sure that these guys were well taken care of and were being fairly treated. So if you get a chance to interview Taj, you can ask Taj about Mississippi John or Son or Bukka or those guys, because he was a confidant of them.

Did you handle Bukka White?

I did. And he's probably one of the few that I had an unhappy and unsuccessful experience with. I found him to be disloyal and through my, whatever, forty-five years in the music business I'm loyal. If I have any quality at all, it's that. I'm fair and I'm loyal. You give me your loyalty, I give you mine. I shook hands with people—Junior Wells, Buddy Guy, "Magic Sam" [Samuel Gene Maghett]. I never had to have a piece of paper. All loyal people. And I put Bukka out on tour, and it was a very good tour and a very lucrative tour.

And I got no callbacks. Nothing. No callbacks. And it turned out that he had told people that he didn't like giving Dick Waterman ten percent of his money, so here's his number in Memphis; call him directly and he will come back and play for them directly. So there was that example. And then there's another one and another one. And finally I found that I couldn't have disloyalty on my artists roster. And if you have a little bit of it, it's only going to poison the well. So I ended my relationship with Bukka and never spoke to him again.

Just in terms of the prewar bluesmen that were rediscovered, who was in your stable? Who was in the roster of bluesmen when you had the most artists working?

Who were the artists that I had?

Yes.

Well, see, I formed Avalon Productions in '65, and John [Hurt] died in '66. And by '67 Skip's cancer had advanced and . . . Then it was Son, Skip, John, and Mance Lipscomb, Lightning Hopkins, Fred McDowell, and Elizabeth Cotton. And then my first act out of Chicago was Junior Wells. I added Junior Wells in '66, Buddy Guy in '67, Magic Sam in '68, Luther Allison in '69, J. B. Hutto in '70.

Would you explain how that all came about, when you made the changeover from the acoustic artists, the prewar artists, to the modern Chicago bluesmen?

Well, what happened was that Bob Koester at Delmark was releasing an album called *Hoodoo Man*. And he and I had been talking and John had died, so I then was giving serious thought to going back to be a sportswriter. I had done this music thing for a few years. And Bob said to me, "You know, there's a whole generation of younger blues musicians—Muddy is out there and known. And Wolf, although he's not out there, he's making records and he's known. And Little Walter and Sonny Boy [Rice Miller]. But there's a whole lot of these guys that are *really* good. You know, guys born in the mid-1940s. And they're just aching to get out." So I said, "Okay. You find me one who's loyal, hardworking, wants to travel, and somebody that I can really trust." And he said, "I'm coming out with an album called *Hoodoo Man* by Junior Wells, used to be in Muddy's band and has a lot of local Chicago, regional hip." So I said, "Okay." So I became Junior's manager and booked a bunch of dates for him before I ever met him! I met him on the grounds of the Philadelphia Folk Festival. And there I was.

I just only have great things to say about Junior Wells. Juniors Wells's level of ethical conduct and loyalty is probably unsurpassed. That Junior Wells was your guy. If he shook your hand and looked you in the eye, Junior Wells was locked with you. The level of integrity that I had from Junior Wells was unsurpassed. He was one of the most profoundly important human beings I ever met. He was just a great guy. I only have good things to say about Junior. In his last years he could become very difficult, but I put Buddy and Junior together in the same band for a Rolling Stones tour in 1970. And they stayed together for some years after that. Maybe it would have been better off to leave them with separate shows, because Buddy and Junior together was inconsistent. It had high nights and low nights.

Did you have any anything to do with Junior going to Vanguard?

Yes. Sam Charters had done an absolutely essential three-record set on *Vanguard* called *Chicago: The Blues Today*. Three LPs and it presented all of Chicago blues. It's over forty years old and it's still the best Otis Rush. It's the best Homesick James. It's the best James Cotton. It's just incredibly, incredibly wonderful stuff. And the drummers are great and the bass players are great, whatever. Vanguard was already working with these guys and had the material out there. It was the easiest way to go. So they went from *Chicago: The Blues Today* to being featured artists with their own LPs. And when Buddy got off of Chess, Buddy recorded for Vanguard also.

Was it easy to find them work at that point? And where did they work?

Well, in '66, '67, '68, '69, the psychedelic bar rooms were happening. They played the Kinetic Playground in Chicago or they played Fillmore East, Fillmore West, Electric Factory, Boston Tea Party. In other words, there was really, really very good money there, and they were like large, big audiences. And they were on three- or four-act shows, so they only had to do forty or fifty minutes. That was really the way to go.

Tell me about Magic Sam and how you got caught up with Sam.

I think over the years that he's been gone—and Sam died in November of '69—that I think there's a few artists who we say, "I miss that body of work." One would be [Jimi] Hendrix. One would be Otis Redding. One would be a guy named Tim Harden, folksinger, who died young. And I would put Magic Sam right up with them. In other words, the quality of his albums—I cannot tell you how many copies of *West Side Soul* on Delmark I have given away. You play it for somebody, and they love it so much that you give it to them. It's so great—you give them your copy and get another one. And then you give it away and get another one. And if you're making a desert island list of ten LPs or five LPs, then I think Magic Sam's *West Side Soul* is there. He could do it all. He could sing, he could play, he just *lit* up the stage.

I'll tell you a Magic Sam story. He was at the '69 Ann Arbor Blues Festival in August. And little did he know he would die three months later. In August of '69, and Sam's in the dressing room, and he's due to play that night. And he's sitting there without a band. And he said, "Whose drum kit is onstage?" And they said, "Sam. Sam Lay's," who I think was drumming with Cotton. So Sam turned to Sam Lay, and he said, "You want to go up with me?" and Sam nodded his head. And then he nodded to a white face—to Bruce Barlow, who was with a band called Commander Cody and His New Lost Planet Airmen. And Bruce was just a long-haired blond guy, good bass player. And Sam said, "Hey, man, you want to go up?" And Bruce said, "Sure. Okay." And right then and there, the great Magic Sam performance of '69 Ann Arbor just came together. "You want to go on?" "Sure." "You want to go on?" "Sure." "Okay." "[*chuckles*] And that was the way Sam was; he was spontaneous. And this set at Ann Arbor '69 was brilliant—just brilliant!

The mark of Sam was just untouchable. When you looked back over a year—they were all born around 1934, '35, '36, '37. Buddy, Junior, Lee, Cotton, Luther Allison, Magic Sam,

Freddie King were all born about the same time. So that particular wave of young musicians that was ready to come out of Chicago in the mid-sixties. Magic Sam just defined charisma! And when you figure that the loss of body of work that we lost with him over the decades is probably right up with "what if"? What if Hendrix had lived another forty years? What if Otis Redding or something like that? Jackie Wilson and Sam Cooke. Just that terrible sense of loss of the art. In other words, the arts lost decades of work. I would put Sam right up there with them—Sam Cooke and Jackie Wilson and Otis Redding and people like that.

What's your understanding of what happened when Sam died?

He died at the end of November. I don't know exactly, November 29th, 30th, something like that, of '69. My understanding was he got out of bed, came into the kitchen. His wife was there. And he was talking to her and he said, "I have a terrible headache." And he went back and laid across the bed and died, but it was something like a cerebral hemorrhage. But I never heard anything else other than it was just natural causes. That he just got up, had a headache, went back, laid down on the bed, and died. I was at his funeral, by the way, and in those days we had no money. And I was living in Cambridge. And I put my dollars together and rode the bus just to see Sam.

You also handled, and I think were instrumental in the beginning, of the career of Bonnie Raitt.

Right. She was at Radcliffe, which is actually Harvard. Or in those days, Harvard had a women's division, Radcliffe. But now it's folded into Harvard. And she was a white blues singer. When she lived in Southern California, I think she had seen Lightning or seen Brownie and Sonny or whatever. And she had gotten a *Blues at Newport* LP from the 1960s. It had John Hammond Junior, and Gary Davis, John Lee Hooker. And she had learned everything. So by the time I met her in '67, she was a skilled guitarist. She was a really, really fine guitarist. So she was in school and I brought her to some blues shows. So she met Skip James and Son, and she did not meet John Hurt. John had died in '66. And she met Fred McDowell, and the two of them really, really hit it off in some sort of the odd-couple friendship in that Fred being old and black and illiterate and Bonnie being young and white and literate and very well educated.

Now, once you realize that Bonnie's father, John Raitt, was a famous—and I mean a really famous—Broadway leading man, from *Oklahoma!*, *Carousel*, *Pajama Game*. He was the top-of-the-line leading-man baritone of Broadway of his era. So she came from top-of-the-line music heritage stock. So she knew what music fame was all about, which made it much easier, much, much easier to work with her, because she knew all about how fame—fame was a magnet that attracts both the bad and the good. And it's a good thing to be a little cynical when people crowd around you when you're hot, when you've got that fame thing going. So those people aren't going to be here when you're . . . when that flame goes out.

So working with somebody in that environment is really good. It's much better. I asked her if she wanted to do it professionally, because she was good enough. And she said, "No." And that was okay. And then I asked her again and she said, "Well, maybe she'll try it." So she played a folk club in Philadelphia called the Second Fret, and it went well. It was successful. And she played other places in the Philadelphia area and ultimately the Philadelphia Folk Festival, and then her career went on from there. Capitol Records came looking and then Warner Brothers came looking. And as it turned out through fate, she had a number of albums on Warner Brothers and then made her big commercial breakthrough after she switched to Capitol around '89 or '90.

Who else haven't we talked about that you handled?

Well, I had long friendships with people that I never worked with. In other words, I'm very, very proud of my long friendship with Muddy, with Wolf. And I, of course, have known B. B. since the mid-sixties. I just wrote B. B.'s biography in '05 for when he turned eighty years old. So my long friendship with B. B. is invaluable to me, you know. Robert Lockwood. I'm a friend of Robert Lockwood and Ruth Brown, and the last year or so I'm just losing friends here—Sarah [Vaughan], Miles [Davis] and Henry Townsend, Homesick [James].

By the way, what is the name of your B. B. King book?

It's called *B. B. King Treasures*. I interviewed people who have known him. I interviewed Pervis Spann from Chicago and Evelyn Johnson, his first manager. I had a wonderful interview with Little Milton [James Milton Campbell Jr.], who's a good friend. And then B. B.'s first manager, Sid Sidenberg, and whatever. So B. B.'s a good guy. There are certain people that you sit in the audience and you say, "I bet if I met him, I'd really like him. I bet he's a genuine guy and I'd really like him." And it's true with B. B. He emotionally is an insecure person and he wants to be liked. So that B. B. knows one of the great truths of live music: somebody, somewhere, every night is going to see you for the only time they'll ever see you. So the impression that they get this night is their only impression. And B. B. wants to be liked. And B. B. wants to be on the top of his form every night. He doesn't want anybody to ever leave him saying, "I saw him and you know what? He didn't show me much. He must have been having an off night." B. B. plays for that person and that person that will never see him again.

There's also another book. Let's talk about that one.

Well, I was really not a photographer; I had my camera with me. It was a good camera. It was a Leica. And I started shooting about '62, '63, shooting Son and Skip and John. And then at folk festivals, Doc Watson, Mother Maybelle Carter, the New Lost City Ramblers, John Hammond, Roy Acuff, and Eddie Arnold. People like that. So I got to into the 1990s and thought about a book and people like that. And a disc jockey and record reviewer in New York named Bob Porter said to me, "You know, you don't owe a book to me, because I knew Muddy and I knew Wolf and some of the others, but, you know, there's a lot of blues fans out there now that are young—in their forties or thirties or twenties—and they never knew Muddy or they never knew Magic Sam or they never knew Mississippi John. And there's a lot of misinformation out there. You have the stories, you have the photographs of them, and you can carry it forward. You can give the anecdotes and humor and the personalities of these people, show your photographs and bring it to a whole new generation. It's the young people who weren't around in the sixties—you owe *them* the book!"

So I thought it over, and really the book came out in November of '03, which was the Year of the Blues [by congressional proclamation]. But there's really no reason that the book couldn't have come out earlier. There were a few photos in it that were recent like the Pinetop Perkins and some others. I needed a working title for the book while it was being written, so I loved the Son House line that said, *"I woke up this morning between midnight and day; I was hugging the pillow where my baby used to lay."* So I just called it *Between Midnight and Day*. So then when the book was finished, I said, "What's the title?" And they said, "Oh, no, no, no! We're locked in *Between Midnight and Day*. Everybody loves it!" Oh, that's it. *Between Midnight and Day*. Now, it came out in softcover. There was also a hardcover version. I wanted a hardcover version of it. And the difference in price between softcover and hard was not much: hardcover was going to be forty-five dollars; the softcover, thirty dollars—only fifteen dollars' difference. So they printed two thousand hardcovers; fifteen hundred in North America, five hundred in England. The fifteen hundred in North America sold out really quickly, within six or eight months. But it has taken me about two and a half *years* to get the unsold hardcovers back from England. So I'm the only one who has the hardcover of my book. It's not available in stores. I have the hardcover version. So if anybody wants to go to my website—fortunately, no one was using my name and I got dickwaterman.com—so, you know, you can get a copy of the B. B. book or a soft or hardcover of *Between Midnight and Day*. I'll be happy to sign it, inscribe it.

What do you do today? Do you handle any talent today?

No. No. No, no, no. They asked me if I would handle Precious Bryant, who was a woman from Georgia who records for Terminus. And I said I would list her name if it would help her, and then I would pass the stuff along to the record label and, you know. But, no. I do photography exhibits. I do photo lectures. And have my own line of blues T-shirts made up of my photographs, which are also available off of my website. So you can get a Son House T-shirt or Mississippi John Hurt T-shirt or something like that. John Lee Hooker.

You're located in Oxford now, aren't you? Oxford, Mississippi.

I grew up in Plymouth, which had a population of twelve to thirteen thousand. Oxford is just about the same—twelve to thirteen thousand. Plus, the University of Mississippi is another ten or twelve thousand. So it's about twenty-two to twenty-three thousand. I'm a little under an hour from the Memphis airport, which hubs Northwest Airlines. I can go Miami, Seattle, San Diego, Boston. I can fly anywhere nonstop. So there's a really nice small-town feel. It's a very literate town. It's a good town for writers, poets, potters—you know, painters, whatever. The appreciation of art, music, dance is really very high here. The mayor of the town owns the bookstore, which I think speaks very well for the town. It's a really lovely town and I like it. I moved here from California in '86, so I've been here a little over twenty years.

Dick Waterman, Portland, Oregon, 2006. © 2006 Michael "Hawkeye" Herman. www.Hawkeye Herman.com.

Do you have any official affiliation with the archive there?

Nothing. No. No, no, no. In other words, it's sort of unfortunate. In other words, the Blues Archive [at the University of Mississippi] knows I'm here. The paradox is that every February they do a blues seminar and I've never been invited to participate.

Do you have any ambitions or plans for the future?

I think I'll probably do a book of folk photography. I, like, had lots of access to Dylan in '62, '3, '4. I have a lot of photographs of Dylan, Phil Ochs, Eric Anderson, Tim Harden, Mother Maybelle Carter, Judy Collins, and Buffy St. Marie. So I don't know if there's a market for a coffee-table book, but, you know, but the work is good and it's unpublished.

GAYLE DEAN WARDLOW INTERVIEW

I was born August 31, 1940, in a little town called Freer, Texas, which is down in South Texas. My daddy worked as an oil man; he worked in the oil fields, and we were moving around so much, Steve. My granddaddy lived down in Louisiana, you know, so my mom built a house down there next to my granddaddy. We lived in a little town in Louisiana called Castor. And that was close to Minden; Minden was the county seat. Later on when I found King Solomon Hill, he was from Minden, or Sibley, right below Minden. I used to go through those towns as a little boy!

Wasn't Percy Mayfield from Minden?

Yes, and it's close to Arcadia, where Bonnie and Clyde got killed. I didn't live out there long. My father died when I was seven years old, 1948. And when my daddy died we moved to Mississippi. So I grew up in Mississippi, in Meridian, the home of Jimmie Rodgers! I started collecting records when I was about twelve years old. Roy Acuff was my daddy figure and my hero, and I was going to jukebox companies collecting records throughout the 1950s, buying Roy Acuff, and I'd also buy Bob Wills. I'd go to jukebox companies and pick up western swing records. That western swing piano is what fascinated me. Twenty years later I found out that the western swing piano players were taught by black piano players

Gayle Dean Wardlow. Courtesy Gayle Dean Wardlow.

in Texas. And some of the first records I ever found "junking" were by Peetie Wheatstraw and Leroy Carr, so I could get into the piano real quick.

I graduated high school in 1958. Believe it or not, a black radio station went on the air in my hometown about 1958, and I was listening to WLAC in Nashville, Hoss Allen Show, Ernie's Record Shop. It was all rhythm and blues and rock 'n' roll. That's all they played. That's what the white kids listened to in the South, WLAC Nashville. Hoss Allen, Gene Nobles, and John R. [Richbourg]. They all played rhythm and blues records. I was listening to Jimmy Reed in 1958. That's before "Big Boss Man" came out. But he was the first guy to cross over to the white kids. I'd hear a little bit of Howling Wolf and Muddy Waters, but it was too heavy for me. But I liked the Jimmy Reed stuff. As a matter of fact, I went to see Jimmy Reed in 1961. I went to an all-black college, Jackson State, to see Jimmy Reed. Me and a friend of mine—we were the only white kids there, sitting in the front row at Jackson State University!

By 1961 I had a full collection of Acuff records. I think I had about a thousand 78s. I had western swing and hillbilly. A guy out in California who was a record dealer told me that if I would find him jazz records, he'd swap all the Acuff records I wanted. I decided one day—I was about twenty-one—right below my house was the black neighborhood. We called it the "colored section" at that time. So I just decided to walk down and maybe I could find some records. And I walked down and I went to a couple of houses—and found nothing. I said, "I buy old records. You got any blues records?" And they said, "Whatdya mean, blues records? No, I don't have any." I'd go up to another place. "No, I don't have any." I worked about two blocks of houses and found an old lady in her eighties. She said, "I believe I still got some of those old records." So she went in looking for them, and I believe she must have waited five minutes before she found them. She came back out and there were two records. One of them was Bertha Chippie Hill with Louis Armstrong—Armstrong playing coronet behind her and Richard M. Jones on the other side—and a rare Champion, 16000. I took them back to the house and I put them on and played them. I said to myself, "Wait a minute. That don't sound bad. Maybe I ought to keep some of these. I'll have to see." That's how I got started collecting blues records.

For two years before I went to college I was working for a pest company, Orkin. I was twenty-one or twenty-two and working as a fumigator, working out of Jackson, running a pest route forty or fifty miles out. In the early 1960s I moved to Jackson, Mississippi, and starting in 1962 I got a degree in history from Belhaven College in Jackson; that was 1965. All the time I was in college I was working for a newspaper, the *Jackson Daily News*, covering sports. They'd send me to cover one of the football teams that would play in places like Clarksdale, Greenwood, and Greenville. They'd send me out on Friday and cover my expenses. I was in college until 1965, and then 1966 and '67 I worked part-time at the newspaper. In 1968 I worked full-time as a newspaper reporter in Meridian. Then I got a job as a college PR [public relations] man at a little university in Alabama. So I became a college PR man for five years, doing all the college's news and sports publicity. I was based on campus, but I traveled with all the sports team too. I lived in east Mississippi; the university was forty miles away in west Alabama. If you've ever heard of Alabama football,

I worked for them as a graduate assistant in athletic publicity. In 1975 I got my master's degree in journalism, and I taught in colleges up until 1990. After 1990 I got kicked out of my teaching job. Then I worked part-time for a newspaper. I went back to college and got my master's degree in library science, but I was in my fifties, and I only had one brief job as a librarian, that was it.

All those years I was door-knocking, searching for records. I bought and sold records. All through the 1960s on weekends I would go out and door-knock. And on days while I was out there spraying, I would go out there door-knocking for records at dinnertime. A record collector in New York City, Bernie Klatzko, heard through a record collector in Birmingham that I was in Mississippi and that I had some records by Charley Patton. Bernie wrote to me and said, "We know nothing about these guys. All we know are their names on record labels." So I decided I'd be a blues detective. I was a record collector first and a researcher second. Most of my research was done from 1961 to 1969. Between 1961 and 1962 I worked on Patton. That was the first guy I was working on, because nobody knew anything about Patton, except that he was dead. As early as 1963 Bernie Klatzko came down and we went to Dockery's farm and traced Patton's career. By 1963 we pretty much knew about his life.

So I was always out there trying to find more information on the Delta bluesmen that no one knew anything about. I was trying to be a journalist, trying to do it newspaper style, trying to document my facts. Death certificates helped me to document. I got the death certificates on Charley Patton, Tommy Johnson, and Willie Brown in 1965. I came up with the death certificate angle because I was working at the Jackson newspaper part-time, and I asked one of the reporters, "How do you get a death certificate?" He said, "You just go out to the State Bureau of Health." So I trotted out to the State Bureau of Health and put in for death certificates on Charley Patton, Tommy Johnson, Willie Brown, and Robert Johnson for a dollar apiece. Charley, Tommy, and Willie all came back, but nothing on Robert.

Let me tell you what happened. In late 1967 Sam Charters published an article with Johnny Shines that said Robert had died near Greenwood, so I immediately filed for a certificate under Leflore County and Greenwood and they found it. The first time [1965] I listed Robinsonville in Tunica County as the location for Johnson's death, and they missed it. So I went back and put in Greenwood in Leflore County. *Bingo*—they found it! So it came from information from that interview by Charters. But he didn't know how to file for a death certificate or didn't try to file. But that's how I found it. I believe it was dated January 11, 1968. And I

Gayle Dean Wardlow business card. Courtesy Gayle Dean Wardlow.

was one of the first guys to use city directories in the big cities. I never found anybody after the early 1970s; they were starting to die. Everything was done by that time.

How did you start writing for *78 Quarterly*?

The publisher, Pete Whelan, was very close friends with Bernie Klatzko, so he knew I was out there doing research back in the 1960s. Pete and his partner, Bill Givens, owned the OJL [Origin Jazz Library] record label. Pete wrote to me about 1964 or 1965 asking me to write liner notes for their album called *Really! The Country Blues*. That's how I got to know Pete. And we were both record collectors, so we stayed in touch afterward, buying and selling records. When he started the magazine, he wrote to me and said, "If you have any articles you want to write for me, please send them." So when he came out with the first issue of *78 Quarterly*, I'd found the relatives of King Solomon Hill over in Louisiana. So the lead article in *78 Quarterly* number one was on King Solomon Hill. And I wrote one on the Blackbirds of Paradise, a jazz band. I found former members of the band in Montgomery, Alabama. I also did an article on LeDell Johnson, Tommy Johnson's brother.

I was contributing to Pete and the magazine all the time if I had something. He would pay forty or fifty dollars for an article. It wasn't much money, but I got my name out there. And I was also saving things for a book with Steve Calt, who I had met in 1964 when he and Nick Perls came down to see me to go canvassing for records. And at the same time I was sending articles over to *Blues Unlimited* in England; in fact, that's where I did most of my articles, because Pete had gone out of publishing after a few issues . . . I did articles on Willie Brown and Blind Joe Reynolds. I remember that Mike Leadbitter and Simon Napier stopped by and visited me in Mississippi. They were on their way to Texas. This had to be 1968 or 1969.

Tell me how your books came about.

Chasin' That Devil Music was published in 1998. By the way, that book has now sold over twenty-two thousand copies—and is still selling. That's probably more than any blues book has ever sold. After I got the back side of the Robert Johnson death certificate [in 1996], I sent it to a friend, Jas Obrecht, at *Guitar Player* magazine. And they published it. They paid me to publish the back side of the death certificate. Jas said, "Why don't you do a book? Collect all your articles and do a book? I know the guy down at Miller-Freeman." Miller-Freeman at that time owned *Guitar Player* magazine. Jas said, "Why don't you send a proposal to the editor at Miller-Freeman? I know him and I'll give him a call." So Ed Komara wrote a proposal for me. We sent it to the editor, and within six weeks' time the editor called me and said, "We'll take it!" So it was on the market in November of 1998.

Weren't you involved in another book as well?

Steve Calt and I did one on Charley Patton. That was a fifteen-year odyssey because Steve took forever! I met him in 1964, he and Nick Perls. I taught Perls how to canvass for records, believe it or not. He came from New York and wanted to learn how to find records, so I took him out canvassing. I met Steve Calt at the same time. We started writing back and forth and talked about doing a book on Mississippi bluesmen. Eventually it evolved into a book on Charley Patton. It took him forever to finish the manuscript, but he took it to a number of New York publishers, and nobody was interested. So somewhere around the late 1980s, when Nick Perls died, he was going to publish it himself. And when he died, his label, Yazoo, was sold to Rich Nevins. Rich gave his word to Nick that he would publish our manuscript, so he printed three thousand copies of the Charley Patton book. It sold out, but that's all there were. But it was all written by Calt. He had the final say-so. It was mostly my historical research, but he had the final say-so on contents, and his writing style is totally different than mine. But that's what happened. We couldn't get a publisher, so three thousand copies were printed by Shanachie Records.

How much of the information in the books first appeared in *78 Quarterly*?

On Charley Patton very little, because there were only three or four issues of *78 Quarterly,* and then it went out of business. The only duplication I can recall is a long article on the cause of Charley Patton's death. It was just the basic information on Charley's death certificate in 1967 in *78 Quarterly.* It was all new information. And *78 Quarterly* stopped publishing in the late 1960s. When he started back in the 1990s, I wrote articles for him again. I wrote an article on Henry Simms, William Harris, and people like that.

You've done tremendous research over the years. Do you think being from the South helped you?

Of course it helped me! Being from Mississippi helped me. I could walk up and talk to black people. Here's a young white guy wants to talk to them about people they heard twenty, thirty, and forty years ago. They were amazed! And if they'd seen somebody like Patton, they'd talk to me. Also I was a record collector and could talk to them about the old records. And often if you played records for the people you were talking to, it helped them remember. Also nobody in Mississippi was really out hunting anything in those days, and I saw the value of it. I thought it was very valuable to find out as much as I could before all the people were dead. By 1965, '66 I started carrying a portable tape recorder. I always turned on the battery-operated portable tape recorder when I interviewed people. I have about forty or fifty hours of tapes. Ole Miss has a copy of them now and so does Middle Tennessee State. [MTSU has now made the interviews available online for listening.]

Would you speak about your collection?

Quite honestly, I built one of the two best collections of Delta blues and Mississippi blues in the world. At one time I had eighteen Charley Patton records; I had six Skip James; I had Willie Brown; I had two Son House records. It was right up there with Nick Perls's collection, which is owned by Rich Nevins at Shanachie Records now. He bought the Perls collection after Perls died. I eventually sold quite a few records—I bought myself a nice house with the proceeds—and I've still got a lot of great records! You know, it's tough to sell your records, but I saw a lot of old record collectors with a lot of great records. They died and the records were still there. It didn't do them a bit of good. One of them was Bill Russell, the

Gayle Dean Wardlow visits his record collection at a safety deposit box. Photo Joel Slotnikoff.

pioneer jazz collector. I used to visit him in New Orleans, and he lived in a little old apartment. He had great records—tons of them. They never did him much good. He never wanted them to go to a university. Guess what—when he died, a museum bought them from his brother. So I decided to sell off enough of my great records to buy a nice house, and there are still a lot of great records here. But mine was one of best record collections in the world. One time I figured that I had traded records with forty-nine different record collectors over a period of forty years—jazz collectors, blues collectors, a little bit of everybody!

Let's talk about some of the amazing things your research has turned up over the years.

Well, I've told you how I started finding records by door-knocking in the early 1960s. I would go door-knocking when I worked my job, at dinnertime and on weekends in small towns in around Jackson, Mississippi. I'd go over to Louisiana and began to find some pretty good records like that. In a year's time I'd found three Robert Johnsons in Meridian in 1961. They sold quite well in the South. Believe it or not, I found two Charley Patton Paramounts in Edwards, Mississippi, one day at noontime. The old guy told me that day, "I think that Charley Patton used to come to Jackson." Later I found out that Charley was born in Edwards. I began to find rare records that the New York collectors didn't have. I was contacted by Bernie Klatzko. Bernie was from New York City, and he was with Pete Whelan, and they were into country blues. They scooped up as much as they could from jazz collectors. He heard I had some Charley Pattons, and he tried every way to buy them. Finally he wrote me and said, "We don't know anything about Charley. Since you're in Mississippi, maybe you can find some information about Charley." It was Bernie who put me onto Charley Patton and the great Delta blues at that time.

You didn't know anything about the artists and their careers. It seems everybody was more or less working in the dark at that point.

Absolutely!

Were these the records that were moving you?

Yeah! After I began to listen to them. Charley was pretty hard to grasp at first with his diction, but I liked what he was doing with his guitar. Johnson didn't move me that much—I know, it's heresy to some people. But I liked "Sweet Home Chicago," which I found by him, and "Last Fair Deal Gone Down." But like Bernie Klatzko said at that time, most people can't get beyond Johnson, back to the 1920s and the great Delta men like Son House. You listen to Son House and you see where Johnson got a lot of his style from. At that time we knew nothing about House, Willie Brown, Patton, and Skip James. All they knew about Robert Johnson was that he was dead, and there was not a lot of interest in Johnson at that time. Columbia put out the one album about 1961, and they reissued that. It probably didn't sell that good. But it went to England and caused a stir among English rock musicians.

In addition to Johnson and Patton, who were some of the names that you had collected during your door-knocking?

Garfield Akers, Ishman Bracey, Tommy Johnson. The first record I ever found in Jackson was a Tommy Johnson, a Victor by Tommy Johnson—"Big Road Blues." In a white neighborhood, of all places. So white people sometimes bought some of these great blues records too! So those were the names, and I would get some of the Origin Jazz Library records when they came out. One came out, *Really! The Country Blues.* They had the greatest of the greatest. They had Henry Thomas, George "Bullet" Williams, Skip James, Ishman Bracey, Tommy Johnson, Son House––on one album! Just dynamite stuff—"My Black Mama" and "Woman Blues" by Bracey. All great classics!

Were you providing any of the material for these reissues?

Not at that time I wasn't. Later on I would send some records up for use on reissues. They had most of the records at that time. I'm happy to say I've still got two or three copies of the sides that were used on the first Patton reissue. There's a great record called "Bird Nest Bound" and "Dry Well Blues" by Patton—very rare. There's only three copies that have ever been found of that record. I got the original copy back somehow that was used on that first OJL reissue. The rarity of some of those records is quite extremely rare. Some people don't realize that the great Mississippi records, most of them came out in 1930, 1931, and 1932, when there was *no* money, especially in Mississippi. And some of those records may have sold less than a hundred copies. Patton recorded in 1929 before the Depression hit. Starting in about January of 1930, record sales really go down. Patton had a few records out. He sold in 1930, but by the beginning of 1931 and '32 nobody had any money. Who had seventy-five cents to go buy a record when that amount of money would buy you enough food to last you all week?

Did you ever wonder if any of the artists on the blues records were still alive?

Yeah! It occurred to me that there could be quite a few of them alive, and actually I went to Jackson in March of 1962, and I was already looking for information on Charley Patton. And about 1963 we knew that Charley was dead, and about August of 1963 Bernie Klatzko came to Mississippi, over forty years ago. We went and found Dockery's Plantation. I'd found out that Charley used to live on Dockery's, and he had died near Indianola. So we went up there and found where Charley was buried [at Holly Ridge] and went to Dockery's and found one of Charley Patton's sisters.

How did you find that he was at Dockery's?

Well, I had found one of his wayward girlfriends somewhere near Vicksburg. I don't remember how; somebody had told me he had an ex-wife in a little town called Bovina. And so I went to find her—I think her name was Minnie Franklin. She had run off with his pistol and some cash money, they said. I went there asking if she had ever known Charley Patton, and at first she didn't want to say much. She had another man she lived with, but she finally admitted she'd been his girlfriend at one time. I asked what happened to Charley—"Where did Charley die?" She said he died up near Holly Ridge. I said, "Where's Holly Ridge?" She said, "That's just out of Indianola." She was right about that. I asked where he came from and she said Dockery's. I asked, "Where's Dockery's?" She said, "Up there around Cleveland."

So we came from Jackson to Yazoo City, drove into the Delta, drove up to Indianola, Indianola up to Cleveland. And we found one of Charley's earlier wives, his first wife—a woman named Minnie Toy. She had a daughter named China Lu. We tried to talk to her, but she was kind of senile and she didn't say much about Charley. But Bernie went back and wrote this up, notes on our trip. It was 1963 and this came out in 1964 on the next Charley Patton album [on OJL]. But that was the first information. Many people have been to Dockery's now and take the photo of Dockery's farm. I'm proud to say I was first—me and Bernie.

Steve Cushing visits Dockery's Plantation, 1988. Photo Jim O'Neal.

Has that painted grain tower always been there?

Yeah! It was there in 1963! I went back there in 1967 with Steve Calt. We co-authored the book called *King of the Delta Blues Singers: The Life and Music of Charley Patton*. I went back there and got an original photo of Will Dockery from his son and some coins and paper money from Dockery's. It's hard to believe it's forty years ago.

Share with us some of the amazing trivia about Charley Patton.

Well, his daddy owned some land. He share-cropped on Dockery, and he was respectable and went to church. And he wanted Charley to be respectable, but Charley wanted to play music. Now, what's interesting is that in 1968 I found someone who knew him personally. I found Reverend Booker Miller while door-knocking in Greenwood. It was divine intervention. I was walking down the street with a record under my hand, and I saw this guy coming down the street. So I said, "I buy old Victrola records. Do you know anybody who's got any of them? I buy old records like Charley Patton." He said, "Charley Patton?" I said, "Yeah, Charley Patton." He said, "Well, I used to play with Charley Patton." "What!" He said, "Oh, yeah, I used to play with Charley Patton when I was a boy. I used to know him real well." I said, "Well, where do you live?" He said, "Just up the street here." So I walked up the street with him. I sat down and started talking with him and realized he really *did* know Charley Patton! He knew some of his songs and he knew a lot about his life. That's how I met Reverend Booker Miller. I just walked into him on the streets in Greenwood.

He had met Patton in Ruleville when he was nineteen years old. And Charley took a liking to him and he played and traveled with him for four years. He told a lot of stories about Charley. He said Charley was the first professional bluesman in the Mississippi Delta, and he was proud of it! After he made the records in 1929, he was a big name, but he'd been playing in the Delta in little juke houses and parties since 1910. He said Charley told him this: that Charley had woman problems when he was about eighteen years old, and he went and got a guitar and sat down on the porch and started trying to play one song. And he ended up before the night was over being able to play a song called "Maggie." That same melody was used in a number of Patton songs, and it was later used by Tommy Johnson.

Bernie Klatzko and I would listen to Patton, and Bernie would say, "Charley Patton must be at least six foot three and weigh 250 pounds," because he had such a powerful voice. No, he weighed about 140 pounds and stood five foot six. He had a giant of a voice, and no one knew anything about him when they first heard the records. When you heard Patton, didn't you think he was a large man? He just had a powerful voice! Miller said he was with Charley one time over in Ruleville, and this man walked up to him and said, "You're Charley Patton? You can't be Charley Patton!" He said, "I is Charley Patton." He said, "Why, to hear you on records I thought you was at least six foot two and 225 pounds!" Charley said to him. "I'm five foot six and 140 pounds." He had a giant of a voice, but he was small! There were a lot of little stories like that you know.

Here's one that's interesting and it's in my book *Chasin' That Devil's Music*. When he went to a party or juke, Charley would always order some fat pork meat. See, the thing about a musician, he'd get supplied with whiskey and food before he'd get paid. Now, the thing about Charley, he would always ask for the fattest pork meat he could get. I asked the Reverend, "Why would he want the fattest pork meat?" He said, "Because he eats that first and then he could drink more. That fat works on the whiskey, absorbs that whiskey. You don't get drunk!" He said Charley would start playing at five in the afternoon and still be playing at three o'clock in the morning. Stomping them feet and singing and clowning! He did like to put that guitar behind his head. Charley Patton was an entertainer, besides being a great musician too. He couldn't drive, but he'd get somebody to drive or take the train. Reverend Miller told me that Charley said he made sixty dollars one night when he played, and that was the most he ever made! In those days, if you made three hundred dollars, that was a lot of money, almost a year's salary. He ran with Willie Brown some, and he had a lot of different wives. I believe they've found eight different marriage certificates now! I don't think he ever got a divorce; he just went and married another one and got another marriage license. He was a tremendous guitar player, and you can't tell that by listening to the Paramount recordings, because the quality of that company was so poor, as you know.

How did Charley come to record?

In 1963 I found Ishman Bracey alive in Jackson. I went over to see Ishman and he was in the church, and we talked awhile about his recording. I said, "How did you get on record, Reverend?" He said, "Mr. Speir got me on record." I said, "Who's Mr. Speir?" He said, "He used to have a music store here on Ferris Street in Jackson." I said, "What ever happened to him?" He said, "He's selling real estate. I saw an ad for him one time in the paper not long ago." I go look in the phone book—H. C. Speir. So I headed across the river over into Rankin Country and go find H. C. Speir. And he'd gotten Charley on record. He got Skip James, Tommy Johnson, Ishman Bracey, Mississippi Sheiks—and everybody! Robert Johnson came to his store. So I went over to see him [Speir] and I wanted to know about Charley first—and Tommy Johnson and those guys. He said, "Charley wrote me a letter. He couldn't really read or write; somebody must have written the letter for him." He thought he was good enough to make a record. "I'd heard about him." He said he'd heard about him from Bo Carter. Bo was kind of a scout for Speir. Bo had recorded and recorded with the Sheiks. He was also part of that group. And he had recorded earlier as part of the Jackson Blue Boys. As a matter of fact, Speir was responsible for that.

But Speir went to Dockery's. He told the plantation owner, Dockery, that he wanted to see Charley. He wanted to see about putting him on record. Dockery said, "Go on over to see him." You didn't just go on somebody's plantation looking for a laborer at that time without letting them know what you're there for. That was just the way you did things. But he went out there and he said Charley got a guitar out in the old wagon. He stood back there and started playing for him. Speir said, "I heard him play and I knew he'd go. He had five or six or seven songs, all different songs." So he gave him money to come to Jackson. He wired Paramount in Grafton, Wisconsin, and said, "I'm sending Charley up." Speir put him on the train. He went to Richmond, Indiana. He was met at the Gennett studios at that time. That's how Charley got on record.

But Speir was adamant on one thing a lot of people don't understand. They say there must have been a lot of guys down there that were really good that didn't get recorded. No, not really! They may have been good on guitar, but every record company was looking for new songs. He said, "There were guys out there that played really good, but they didn't have any original songs." If you didn't have any original songs, you couldn't get recorded. They didn't want you singing somebody else's songs, even in those days. And Speir said, "The record companies want you to have four songs, at least." The reason for that, see, is that Patton puts out his first record, "Pony Blues," and it sells real good. Then they can issue the next two sides. So that's why they want at least four sides. He said, "Charley could do a number of songs." Charley recorded fourteen songs at his first session—he was that good. He had so many songs. That's why some guys didn't get recorded—they couldn't write original songs. They could play somebody else's song, but they weren't creative. The record companies didn't want a song already done by somebody else!

Do we know whether Charley Patton wrote those tunes, or did he borrow them from other artists that were unknown, never recorded?

Charley didn't learn from other people. There are some people who claim that a man named Henry Sloan was the first bluesman who influenced Charley Patton. That is incorrect. We talked to different people. I went back to the plantation. Henry Sloan "frailed"; in other words, he just chorded. Henry Sloan was *not* a bluesman. Blues didn't come along until the early 1900s in the Delta. Charley Patton started playing blues around 1909 or 1910. Charley was one of the first bluesmen in the Delta. He was playing bottleneck too at that time. Charley learned his *own* style and his *own* way, and there's no one else who picks like Charley Patton who recorded even before him. That's why he's often called the Founder of the Delta Blues, or King of the Delta Blues, which they put on Robert Johnson—to sell records, of course.

Charley had his own original style—in fact, a number of styles. He plays in the different tunings. There's an often repeated story that in 1903 W. C. Handy heard a bottleneck player at Tutwiler playing "Where the Southern Cross the Yellow Dog." It's said he went back and was influenced by this to write songs. In Handy's original biography—I've looked at it before—he didn't give a precise year, but he didn't write a song until 1909 and didn't publish the song until 1912, which was the original "Memphis Blues"! And he wrote "Yellow Dog Blues," but it didn't come out until 1914—and "The St. Louis Blues" in 1914 also. Why would he wait ten years to write "The Yellow Dog Blues"? So I think he heard the bottleneck player in a different year than 1903, but nobody ever asked him about the gap of about ten years before he died in 1959. I think perhaps there's a typo or mistake somewhere. No one has ever challenged this story, but I'm challenging it on that basis. I may be going out on a limb, but I really do believe the date should be different than 1903. If he heard the bottleneck player at the Tutwiler depot in 1903, why did he wait until 1914 to write "Yellow Dog Blues"? That had the verse in it about *"Goin' where the Southern cross the Dog."*

And are you making the point that this kind of blues wasn't around that early?

It may have been going on—it's possible. It was started in the early 1900s. I'm not saying he didn't hear somebody in 1903. Bernie Klatzko used to think it might have been Charley sitting there in the depot playing that bottleneck. But there were a number of guys that played bottleneck in the Delta. The Hawaiian influence is what started that basically as a way of playing Hawaiian music. You can put the bottleneck on instead of a bar and putting the guitar on your lap. Charley could play on his lap, by the way.

You know, the Mexicans brought the guitar to the Delta. They came in to work on the railroads and clear the swamps in the early 1890s and 1900s. The Delta was very primitive at that time; it was all swamps until they cleared land for the railroads and they cleared land for the plantations. They brought the guitars to the Delta. The black men saw it, learned how to play it—and got more attention from the women! Originally in the 1830s and 1840s there was Greenville, and Natchez, and Vicksburg; they were all river ports. They had plantations close to the river, but in the inner Delta it was all forest.

So you challenge the notion that there ever was an earlier generation of bluesmen who were out there playing but were too early to get on record, that this earlier generation never existed?

No! Charley was born in 1887, and in talking to Reverend Booker Miller he said his granddaddy started playing blues around the early 1900s. Handy really brings blues songs to the surface, to the American public, but it's 1912 to 1914. But the guitar was coming into the Delta, so they learned how to play it. That's why you have so many regional styles in Mississippi. Before records influenced people, they picked up the guitar and tried to learn how to play it. It's how all the styles came about; the Mexicans brought the "Spanish G" tuning into the Delta. But there is no one playing before Charley Patton. There are some other people playing about the same time as Charley Patton. One man was named Tee Nincy Wade. "Tee Nincy" means very small. There was man named Tee Nincy Wade who played about the same time as Charley Patton, who clowned like Patton.

But the blues didn't start until the early 1900s, and I don't believe that Charley Patton learned from anybody. All he learned from Henry Sloan was basically some chords. They've made Henry Sloan into an older bluesman, but there's no evidence to back it up, based upon the different people I've talked to at Dockery's--even his sister, Viola Cannon. She was Charley's older sister, about ninety years old. When we got there in 1963, she was still alive. She said he would follow Henry Sloan some, but he was a chord player. Before the blues, blacks were playing the guitar and singing songs like "Careless Love," "Late Last Night," "Willie Come Home"—songs that made it through, but they weren't really playing blues on the guitar.

What about Patton disciples? Who did Charley teach the blues?

Howling Wolf was one. Wolf come and looked at him and was impressed with what he saw in Charley. If you sort through the discography in the 1930s, there is nobody that records in Patton's guitar style. It's too difficult. Now, you talk about regional styles. Son House was playing a different style than Charley Patton. Willie Brown played a style very similar to Charley Patton and, from what we were told, learned most of his guitar from Charley Patton. Willie was a slightly younger man. He was born around 1900. But there's not a lot of people that follow and record using Charley's guitar style in the 1930s. It was almost too hard to play.

I talked to an elderly woman, and she knew Robert Johnson when he was a young man, and she'd seen Charley Patton play. Her name was Elizabeth Moore. Robert told her and her husband that Charley made too much noise when he played and stomped when he played, and what Charley played on the guitar he couldn't play. So he didn't want to play like Charley, but he sure listened to Son House on things like "Walking the Blues" and "Preaching the Blues" and things like that.

But I've always been amazed—nobody plays like Charley. He was a great bottleneck player, but he just had so many different styles. And I don't think he taught too many people. He showed Booker Miller how he played, but Booker Miller never played with a bottleneck. I asked if he played Charley's songs, and he said, "I'd play with him." "But did you play them by yourself?" "I might play them off somewhere else. But I wouldn't try to play them in front of Charley!" He said, "I never heard a man could play a guitar like he could. He could play on one string! He'd just make one string talk. I saw guys try to go up against Charley and he'd cut 'em! They couldn't stand him. He'd just run them off. He was so good at what he did!"

What have you been able to find out about Charley, personality-wise?

One guy, Hayes McMullen, called him a "squabbling scuttlebutt." He was always squabbling, always arguing. He got in a lot of arguments. He was boisterous at times. Miller said Charley would go into a place where he didn't know anybody, and he'd try to tell jokes. He said, "You look so mean, death can't claim you!" He said he'd say something like that sometimes to see what effect it had on the people and watch how they'd react. If he went into a place where he didn't know anybody, he'd want to feel out the audience. He was always getting into fights. He'd argue a lot. Son House told how they argued back and forth on their way up to Grafton, Wisconsin, to record. He was a squabbler. He drank real heavy. Charley got his throat cut one time. Supposedly the story was a woman sat down on his lap, and her jealous man slashed Charley's throat and it left a wicked scar. It didn't get the jugular vein, didn't kill him. He got shot in the foot one time. He would take time with someone like Miller, but if somebody was trying to outplay him, he'd just run them off with his music.

Were there any major points that you and Steve Calt disagreed about when it came to Charley Patton?

We didn't disagree on a lot of things. Steve can be negative about a lot of things, but we didn't disagree about Charley Patton. It was primarily my research, and he talked to people in the North. He interviewed Honeyboy [David Edwards] and he interviewed Son House, who was always really negative toward Patton. I think it was from jealousy probably. He said he didn't sound as good in person as he did on records. Calt did a lot of musical analysis. We just made the point that he was the first Delta bluesman, and he became the first real professional bluesman in Mississippi and the Delta. He made his living that way. And he became a hero to the black people. Patton was a hero to Howling Wolf. Wolf went to find him and watched how he played on the streets. Bukka White talked about how Patton was a hero to the younger bluesmen coming along. He was a guy who'd made it. He was making money. He was famous. He didn't have very good luck with women, however.

How did Patton die?

Charley probably had rheumatic fever when he was young. They had stories that he was struck down by lightning, by the wrath of God. There were other tales—he'd been shot or he'd been poisoned, all the different stories. By the way, you have to remember that in those days, if someone died, how did you hear about it? TV—no! Radio—no! By word of mouth . . . and by the time it made its way through the community, it got turned around: he died this way; he died that way. No! He died from the effects of rheumatic fever. He had a mitral valve to the heart and it was leaking—probably damaged by rheumatic fever—and eventually his heart just stopped on him. He couldn't breathe anymore. He was about forty-four years old; he was born in about 1887. The census records show 1891. There's some dispute between 1887 and 1891, but 1891 is the date the census shows.

In that era would a black man go to a hospital for treatment?

Actually Charley went to see a doctor. As a matter of fact, on the death certificate, which I found in the early 1960s, he was going to a doctor in nearby Indianola, and the doctor recognized that he couldn't do anything for the heart at that time. They didn't have anything for heart valve damage. You'd get short of breath and have massive sweats. The death certificate said a doctor had seen him about a week before he died in Indianola. Charley had enough money to go see a doctor.

You read about musicians who picked cotton and played in their off time. But the more likely story, it seems to me, is that most musicians were determined not to do physical labor.

That's true. Charley didn't want any part of physical labor. His daddy wanted him to work in the cotton fields. His daddy was a sharecropper at Dockery's and wanted Charley to work in the cotton fields and be an honorable man. But Charley didn't want to. He wanted to play music. Once he got to be about eighteen or nineteen, he realized he could make a little money playing music, on a weekend, on a Saturday. The guys who became bluesmen, they hated work. Working in the cotton field and planting cotton, and hoeing cotton and picking cotton is not the easiest life. I picked some when I was a little boy in Louisiana—just a little bit—my grandfather had some. But I can tell you it's not easy. And when you can go and play a juke house, and get free whiskey and all the food you can eat, and make five dollars for playing for a party, it's a good life . . .

And a juke, by the way, is where you go dancing. A lot of people don't know that term. It means to dance. Here's what a lot of people don't understand: blues has always been dance music. Let's go back, the first thing they had they started by having house parties, and Hayes McMullen told me about this. He was an old bluesman that never made records, but I got to know him in the 1960s, and he played a lot in the Delta in the 1920s. He played some with Willie Brown. They had house parties, or "frolics." It was where people made food to sell, so they had a little party. And if you have a party, you want to be able to dance. So they say, "'Hey, Hayes has a guitar. Let's invite him!" So he comes and he starts playing at the little house parties. Then they say, "We've got a party and a good musician so people can dance. Let's sell a little whiskey, a little moonshine."

So the bluesmen found that they could play for people to dance, and the people would buy food and drink too—if they can dance. And if a bluesman made five dollars on a Saturday night, that was more money than a laborer could make in an entire month. He might start at just a couple of dollars, but once he got popular—once Charley's records came out, he could play wherever he wanted to. Everybody tried to get him to play. But that's the whole idea of the juke, where you come to dance and drink. But it started out as little house parties on the plantation, or frolics. It went from there to the juke and bringing the moonshine in. You're making money off the whiskey, so you got the bootleggers, and you get a little gambling going on. You get to the bigger cities like Chicago or Memphis, and you got prostitution going on. But you wouldn't necessarily have that in the Delta.

Did Patton have a set price?

I don't remember any particular set price, but once he got big he would ask twenty or twenty-five dollars at least, and he got tips. He told Booker Miller he made sixty dollars—it was the most he ever made in one night. Sixty dollars in 1929 or 1930, that was a lot of money. You could buy a new car for three hundred dollars in those days. And you didn't pay taxes back then. Money went a long way in those days. And Charley got fifty dollars per song for every song he made. He brought back over six hundred dollars from the first recording session he made for Paramount.

Let's talk about the sessions. Let's take them in order, starting with the first session.

Well, he wrote to Speir and Speir went up to Dockery's Plantation. Speir said once he heard Charley, he knew he'd go. And the reason Speir knew he'd go was because Charley had different guitar styles—and so many songs. He said the same thing about Skip James when he heard Skip James in his store. Speir said he had so many different songs that he knew Skip would go, because the record companies wanted people who would do original songs. Generally, Speir was one of the most honest of all the record men. He ran a music store, and the record companies in those days would go to the different towns and tell music store owners, "If you've got any talent, let us know." And Speir was turning up some good talent.

How much later was the next Patton session?

The first session was in June of 1929. He cut fourteen sides. He went back about six months later—in December of that same year or January 1930. His records were selling so well that Paramount wanted him back immediately. He went to Grafton, Wisconsin, and Paramount had put in a little recording studio in Grafton. That's right out of Port Washington. Grafton is five or six miles away. They'd been recording down here in Chicago in Marsh Studios, but they put in better equipment in Grafton, and he recorded fourteen more songs at the second session. Of course Paramount would take every song he would record. He was so good. He was making good money. He was making fifty dollars a song, Speir told me.

When he did these sessions, did he go alone?

On the first session he went by himself, to Richmond, Indiana, which was the Gennett Studios. They were farming out, doing masters for Paramount. And the second session he did for Paramount he took Henry Sims, the fiddler. Later on Muddy Waters played in the Henry Sims band, a string band. And the third session was in May. The discography by Godrich and Dixon says May, but I think it's much later into summer, as late as the last of August. When he went back that time he took Son House, Willie Brown, and Louise Johnson up with him . . .

Tell us about that session.

Well, here's the situation. About April of 1930 Paramount was beginning to see the record business go down. The company owner—his name was Moser—wrote to Speir. They wanted him to come up and they would talk about selling the company to him. He would have moved it to Jackson, Mississippi. He had found a black quartet in Lula, which was where Patton was staying at that time. That's right up near Helena in Arkansas. And he carried the Delta Big Four [Wheeler Ford, Pecan Allen, Will Mosely, Archie Smith] up to record. They said, "We want to record Patton again." They had a year's contract ending in June, and they wanted to get Patton on record again as soon as they could and make sure some other company didn't grab him. Speir went back and tried to raise the money--thirty thousand dollars—and he couldn't do it, but he told Art Laibly, the recording director at Paramount, where Patton was at.

So Laibly took the train down to see Patton. He got a man named Wheeler Ford, who was a member of the Delta Big Four, to drive that group to Grafton to record. And somebody once mentioned to me that he wished he could have been a gas station attendant to go out and clean their windshield, just to hear what they were saying inside that car. But that had to be the greatest recording session in Delta blues history. There's no doubt about it! You had Patton, Son House, Willie Brown, and Louise Johnson, who I'm sure they were all hitting on. She was in her early twenties.

I wonder what kind of behavior Son House displayed in Charley Patton's presence?

I think they squabbled a lot and I think they cussed each other. I suspect it was back and forth. I think there was jealousy between them. Son House was a very strong individual, but Charley was a name at that time. If it wasn't for Charley, Son House would never have been recorded.

How so?

It was very simple. Laibly said, "If you can, bring me some more people." And he gave Patton a little extra money for bringing them, a finder's fee. Laibly said, "You bring anybody that you think can make good records!" Charley didn't bring them out of the kindness of his heart. He might have carried Willie Brown. He was just making a little more money, picking it up for bringing them. He'd heard House. Willie Brown at that time was playing with House, and he had played many years with Charley Patton.

Did Patton regard Son House—or anybody, for that matter—as bona fide competition?

I think Patton thought he was the best, and he usually proved it! He could take the audience away from anybody else. So I don't think he had any fear of Son House. House played a little different style, but you have to realize that House had to look up to Charley to go where Charley was playing. He was introduced to House through Willie Brown. Son House told the story that he took Louise Johnson away from Charley Patton. She was Patton's girlfriend going up, and he took her away from Charley. They squabbled and bragged a little bit, but the fact is they were so competitive that they never played together after that. Patton played his own places. He wouldn't invite House, because House would want money too; you'd be splitting the take! He'd bring Willie Brown along to play second guitar, but Willie Brown was teaming with House at that time, so they weren't going to play at the same place. They made the records, they went back, and they went their separate ways. And it wasn't long before Patton left that part of the north Delta and went back down to Sunflower County in the lower Delta.

Let me tell you some other things I heard from Booker Miller: Patton had gray hair by the time he was in his forties and looked older than he was. He never had gold teeth, never put any gold in his mouth. He bought a fancy Stella guitar with pearloid on the headstock and the fret board. That was a way of showing off. He didn't flash his money around. He'd carry a gold coin occasionally. He knew how big he was, though.

Were there any other Patton disciples?

I don't know of anybody else. I know Honeyboy Edwards heard him a little bit. I was in a hotel room with Honeyboy. We'd been making a documentary in 1991 on "The Search for Robert Johnson," and he started playing a little bit of Charley Patton. I said, "Honeyboy, play that a little more." I didn't know he could do it, but he said he learned from Charley. But he never carried on and played like Charley. It's really interesting. I think he just had so many different styles, and the way he sang and projected and stomped his feet. It was just hard to play his style. You know one thing about Charley? He never hits bad notes. He's not out of tune. He didn't hit bad notes like other musicians did sometime. That man was always in tune. He seemed to know what he was doing always.

You were talking about tunings earlier today, and you hear the records and you're never quite sure, because there are several different ways of tuning to arrive at the same key. Could another musician sit in the audience and understand by Patton's fingering where he had tuned?

Sure, if you could see the fingering. The fingering is how you do it. Everybody in the Delta knew open G tuning, which is "Spanish"; they call it "Spanish G." There's "natural." They call that standard tuning. There's something they call "Sevastopol," which is an open E or an open D tuning, but they knew the different tunings. They would show each other different tunings, but it's what you do with the tunings. Now, Patton did one thing that was very interesting. Some of his greatest blues were in the key of B. He would take his guitar—normally you'd take a standard tuning and tune the E down to a D and you get Spanish G. Patton would keep the E note and tune the rest of the strings up, where he'd be tuned to an open A chord. Then on his twelve-fret guitar he'd capo on the second fret and play in the key of B, and he'd get a great Delta sound! Howling Wolf did that in the 1950s. He'd capo up and sing in the key of B. So B is the hidden key for the real Delta blues.

I know you pick some guitar, but how do you know this? Where does this information come from?

It came from talking to some of the old musicians, and it came from Steve Calt, who got the pitches on all the Patton songs. I knew they tuned in open A. I'd heard that, so I finally just decided to try it one night. I put the capo on the second position, or on a fourteen-fret guitar you can put it on the fourth fret and you get the same effect. But they only had twelve-fret necks in those days, not fourteen, and that sound is there. That's where it is! So if anybody's listening out there early in the morning, coming home from playing, go home, put your guitar in open G tuning and capo up four frets, put your bottleneck on it, and you'll hear the real Delta sound right there!

Do you want to talk about the Patton songs?

There's so many! "Down the Dirt Road" is a great, great song. "High Water Blues, Part One," about the Mississippi River flood. "When Your Way Gets Dark," a great bottleneck piece! "Dry Well Blues," that last session. That last session is where he did "Moon Goin' Down" and "Bird Nest Bound." There's so many Patton songs. "The Bo Weevil Blues" is about as primitive if you wanted to hear what early blues might have sounded like. It's almost not even a blues. It's like a field holler with one chord. "Spoonful," the bottleneck is *so* good! He had one song where the last line of the song was *"My baby got a heart like a piece of railroad steel."* He took the next song and called it that! He just picked it up from there. He could make songs up like that. "The Moon Goin' Down" is Delta dance music. "Down the Dirt Road" is Delta dance music. It drives and drives—just *boom*!—just drives! For just one guitar it was amazing what the man could do.

Let's do some thumbnail portraits of some of the bigger names in country blues. Let's start with Son House.

He's been interviewed many times, but I never interviewed him. He was found in Rochester, New York, and carried to the coffeehouses about 1964. I was out there trying to find Son House. I'd been looking for him for a year, but I couldn't find him. I went to Robinsonville one time looking for Son House. I was in college. I had ten dollars to my name and I drove up there. I drove all day up there and all night back; I didn't have any money to stay in a motel. All they told me was that Son House had moved to St. Louis. So how are you going to find a man named Son in St. Louis? It's a totally different style of playing from Charley Patton. He says he learned the bottleneck from an older guy down near Matson, Mississippi, playing bottleneck with a pocketknife, and he liked it. So he tried to learn how to play like that. But what's amazing, if I remember correctly, is that Son House didn't pick up a guitar until 1928! His style is totally different from Patton. Again, it's those regional styles!

House was a sharecropper and he played music on weekends. He was never really the professional musician that Charley was, where he traveled a lot. He stayed in his home territory, right there in Tunica County, around Robinsonville, and Lake Cormorant. They call it Lake Carmen, but it's actually Lake Cormorant. House didn't travel a lot, but he played with Willie Brown. Willie Brown and Patton used to fight a lot and Willie just got tired of it, and so he teamed up with Son House. Son's one of the greatest. There's no doubt about it. The sad part is that he didn't record any more than he did. His first record came out in the fall of 1930, "Dry Spell Blues." It was followed by "Preaching the Blues." Only one copy of that record has ever been found. It was found in the late 1950s in Virginia. It's been reissued over and over again, but it came out in January or February 1931 and nobody had any money. In fact, with each of his three records, less than ten copies of each record are known to exist. "My Black Mama," there are four copies. But there is only one known copy of the last Charley Patton record, "Joe Kirby Blues." Of most of the Pattons from 1931 and 1932 there are only two or three copies of each—that's all!

What can you tell us about Willie Brown?

Charley Patton taught him. Willie was born in 1900. I found a death certificate on him. In 1965 I was in college and I'd learned about death certificates. So I went down to the Mississippi Bureau of Vital Statistics, and I put in for death certificates at a dollar a piece: Charley Patton, Tommy Johnson, Willie Brown, and Robert Johnson. They found everything but Robert Johnson. Willie Brown's certificate said he was born in 1900; he died in 1952. He never played the harmonica as the Willie Brown in the movie *Crossroads* did. But Willie Brown was a lazy guy. He liked to play behind Charley Patton. He didn't like to sing very much. He had a fairly weak voice. He just liked to play, and he liked to play second guitar, not lead. He didn't have an outgoing personality like Patton. He learned from Charley and he followed Charley around. Charley was the superior of the two musicians.

What can you tell me about Tommy Johnson?

Tommy was up in the Delta around 1913 or 1914. He was playing up around Drew [Mississippi], and he *did* play around Charley Patton. One of his first songs is a melody that Charley Patton used. I don't have any doubt that he learned some of his guitar from Patton. I found his older brother, LeDell Johnson, in Jackson in 1967. He told me a story that when Tommy was fifteen or sixteen years old, an older woman ran off to the Delta with him to Rolling Fork, which is above Vicksburg, and when Tommy came back he was playing "Big Road Blues." "Big Road Blues" is up-tempo, and if you listen to Tommy, he doesn't play up-tempo very much. Tommy was a great bluesman, but a lazy bluesman if you think about it. He sings "Cool Drink of Water" and "Big Fat Mama"—great guitar and great voice! Speir said, "Nobody could sound as good as Tommy Johnson. He would throw his voice up, yodel!"

Very few people know this today, but Johnson stuttered. Speir told me he stuttered. Ishman Bracey told me he stuttered. When I found Ishman Bracey, I asked him about Tommy. He said that Tommy would stutter until he started playing, but then he could sing without the stutter. He always carried a chaw of tobacco in his jaw. Johnny Temple told me that after Tommy came back from Memphis after his first recording session, he came back with about two hundred dollars. He said Tommy went up to Mill Street at Knotty George's, a little old dive café. He gave a boy some money and told him to bring him a gallon of moonshine. He brought back the gallon of moonshine, and before the weekend was over all the money was gone! He spent his money, bought drinks for people, and just sat there and played his guitar!

What's amazing is that he lived quite late—sixty years old. He was born in 1896, and in 1928 he was singing "Canned Heat Blues." Drinking antiseptic or taking canned heat—for people who don't know, it's Sterno. You heat it and boil it, and you take a handkerchief and you let the alcohol drip through the handkerchief. Then you drink the alcohol. You drink antiseptics and get a little buzz. But what's amazing is that he lived to be sixty years old drinking that canned heat. You'd think his liver would have killed him many years before that, because he was a hard drinker since his teenage years! People don't realize they were drinking moonshine. They weren't drinking bonded whiskey. Mississippi was a totally dry state in those days. Bracey told a story. They got to Wisconsin to record for Paramount and they had some Old Charter [whiskey] up there. Tommy had never had any bonded whiskey in his life and he got drunk. And they were finally going to run him off [from recording] because he kept ruining so many masters! Old Charter was the whiskey they had. Tommy just went wild. He'd never had any bonded whiskey!

That's something else. I want to make this point. You talk about somebody being poisoned. These guys were drinking moonshine made by people, and sometimes they were made out of old car radiators, and the possibility of getting high lead content in that moonshine was very high. If you drink enough of that moonshine over a period of years, it's going to do something to you. It wasn't bonded whiskey these bluesmen were drinking. They couldn't get it. If they did get it somebody brought it back from Memphis or somewhere where it was legal. You have to remember we were in Prohibition from 1918 to 1933.

When did Tommy Johnson quit playing? We know that he drank to the end of his life. Did he ever do any other sessions?

He did two sessions for Victor and one for Paramount. In. February of 1928 Speir sent him and Ishman Bracey up to record in Memphis and then sent them back in August. Victor wrote and got them back, because the records were selling. Then he sent Bracey and Tommy to Wisconsin in 1930. Paramount would take anyone he sent, that he thought was good enough. They trusted him with anyone he thought was good enough to record. When they were out of their contract with Victor, Speir just took them and sent them to Paramount to record. In early 1930 the Paramounts didn't sell at all; they were very poorly received at that time. The Depression was having its effect on record sales.

Gee, I wonder why with that clarinet in there . . .

Tommy made two sides or three sides—maybe four—with just the guitar. I asked Bracey, "Reverend, why is it you wanted to put that clarinet in there?" He said, "Well, they [Paramount] wanted to try something new, and we thought it might sound different." But Bracey made "Woman Woman" with the guitar, which was really good, and Tommy made a couple of records, and there's only been one or two known copies that have ever been found of Tommy just with the guitar. There's two known copies of "Sliding Delta." And as far as I know, there's only one copy of "Alcohol and Jake," which is a remake of "Canned Heat." It's just so rare . . .

Were you able to discern at what point he quit playing? Did they ever want him back again?

There was a story told—and I don't know where it came from—that he auditioned for Mrs. Lillian McMurry at the Trumpet label in Jackson in the early 1950s and she turned him down. He was an old man by that time and he probably wasn't playing very good. I found one of his nephews and interviewed him in the 1960s and again right before he died. He said that Tommy was playing the night he died. He was playing guitar in a little house in 1956 and he went back in the room and sat down. They came back to check on him and he had died of a heart attack. He was playing guitar the same night he died, so he was still trying to play a little bit for friends and family. He was playing at one of his relatives' houses. He was down near Crystal Springs.

It seems as though there was a Crystal Springs school of blues—Tommy Johnson, Houston Stackhouse, and then Robert Nighthawk.

He taught them. Tommy taught them! They learned from him, either in the Delta or down in Crystal Springs. He was a guy who would freely show people how to play his songs and his style of guitar. And they took it and began to play his music. There were more people playing like Tommy Johnson than there were like Patton. Very few people played like Patton. You had the Mississippi Sheiks. They played "Stop and Listen," which was their version of "Big Road Blues." They made it for OKeh and later for Paramount as "The New Stop and Listen Blues." Tommy Johnson's style was easier to pick up and play than Patton's style. And Charley wasn't necessarily going to sit down and show you his style, but Tommy would show you how he played it. That's pretty well what happened with Tommy.

Let me tell you something about Tommy Johnson. Bracey told Speir where Tommy Johnson was. He was living up on the Pearl River, north of Jackson. He went up there to see him. Speir told me that at that time Tommy had only one good song. Speir told him, "Now, Tommy if you want to record, you've got to get four songs together." So Tommy started working up songs, and Speir had him come and play for him and made sure Tommy had four original songs before he sent him to record for Victor. And what happened was that Speir made tests of both Tommy and Bracey on his little recording machine. He sent the tests to Victor and never heard anything from them. Three months later Ralph Peer telegrammed him and said, "Have these guys in Memphis on such and such a date to record."

Speir always loved Tommy's falsetto, how Tommy threw his voice up. That was the most impressive thing about Tommy. And he always felt sorry for him. Tommy was always getting thrown in jail for vagrancy or drunkenness, things like that.

Didn't you tell me a story about the end of his career?

In the early 1930s—1930 or '31—Tommy got picked up by the Jackson police on charges of drunkenness or more serious charges of fighting. Anyway, Tommy called Speir and asked if Speir would bail him out, because Speir had done this before. He told me that sometimes the guys would get in trouble, and the sergeant would call Speir and say, "We got one of your boys down here!" He asked them what the bail might be, and he'd say. "Keep them until tomorrow morning and I'll take care of the fine." And he'd come by and pay the fine. Or he might say, "Keep him until tomorrow and just make sure he's sober." But he told me—and it was an astronomical amount—he put up a bond of $150 for Tommy, and that meant it was a pretty serious charge. And Tommy jumped bond and ran off and he went to Louisiana. Speir had to go and get his money back.

It was Depression time, and he had never put money like that up before. He put it up for Tommy, and Tommy was supposed to show up [in court]. Speir went to Crystal Springs looking for him. He wasn't there. He went down towards Louisiana to Tylertown. He wasn't there. He finally found him in a little town called Angie, Louisiana, across the state line from Tylertown. He said he walked up to him in a field. He said, "You gotta go back with me." He put handcuffs on him. Tommy said, "Please don't take me back." He was begging and begging. "Please don't take me back!" Speir said, "I got to take you back. I'll lose $150!" And Speir took him back and he had to stand trial.

Who was Ishman Bracey and how did you find him?

Ishman Bracey recorded in 1928. He ran a lot with Tommy Johnson in the 1920s. He and Tommy first met up at a party down there in Jackson and then again in a place near Crystal Springs. They were playing around Jackson, little parties on the weekends. Here's an interesting thing: Bracey was playing up on Farish Street in Jackson one Saturday morning, playing for nickels and dimes, and a man in a blue suit walked up to him. The man stopped and listened to him and said, "Play me some more." Bracey said he thought it was a detective, and he'd been drinking. It was H. C. Speir, and he said, "Come on down to my music store." Speir took him down to his store and listened to him and made an acetate recording of him. He talked to him, figured he had enough songs and was good enough to record. Then Bracey lead Speir to Tommy Johnson at the fish camp up on the Pearl River where he was living. Bracey did three 78s for Victor, or six songs.

Bracey had a very big hit at that time with "Saturday Blues." He learned that up in the Delta. He used to go up there like Tommy did. It was his biggest up-tempo song, probably his best song, "Saturday Blues." *"My special woman [tote] my pocket change, and my sometime woman, Lord, she does the same. Better not let my special catch you here."* He talks about buying his woman "high-brown powder, Palmer's Skin Success." It's a real good song. He

Hawkeye Herman and Gayle Dean Wardlow. Photo © 2006 Michael "Hawkeye" Herman. www.HawkeyeHerman.com.

had another called "Leaving Town Blues." It was not quite as popular in Jackson among the people, but his first record sold better than Tommy Johnson's. He said Victor told him he sold six thousand copies of his first record.

But here's an interesting point: H. C. Spier got Tommy on record, and Speir told me if they sold five hundred copies of a record, the record company broke even. Once they sold more than five hundred copies, they started making money. So if Bracey had a record that sold six thousand copies they made money. Once they made money on somebody and he had more songs, then they'd get him back in the studio. Bracey went back a second time with Johnson in August 1928, and later he went to Grafton, Wisconsin, to record for Paramount. He never recorded after that. When I found him he had become a minister. He'd gotten out of the music business. He had terrible guilt about his blues days. He said, "I've been the devil. I've done everything you can do wrong against the Lord."

How did you find him? And did you know who he was when you found him?

Yeah! Because he was on the reissue that the OJL label sent me. Ishman Bracey. They said, "We think this guy is from Mississippi." So I started asking around in Jackson, and I was working at the Jackson airport at night, refueling airplanes, and going to college in the daytime. I asked a guy who was working with me, "Did you ever hear of Ishman Bracey?" "Oh, yeah!" he said. "I know Bracey. He lives over on such and such street." "He's still alive?" I asked. "Yeah, he's still alive. He's preaching now." So I went from that. I believe he was actually in the Jackson phone book. I didn't know it. I went and looked in the phone book and found him. I called and found him! I went over to the little place where he was living and helped him get on social security and get on welfare too.

At that time he was living in a little room and he wasn't preaching on a regular basis. He was sixty-three or sixty-four, and he wasn't in good health and he was still painting. He was having a hard time. He lived to be seventy. But he didn't want to listen to blues. He had so much guilt, and his wife wouldn't even let him play the blues. He played church songs for me. But I finally got him to one night. I paid him a little money and sat him down and got him to listen to records by him and Tommy Johnson, Robert Johnson, Patton. And I got him to talk about some of the musicians he knew. He'd met Patton in Jackson. He talked about his falling out with Tommy Johnson. He was a great bluesman for what he was doing. They always called him a Delta bluesman, but he was never a Delta bluesman. It's ironic. He was a Jackson bluesman and just visited the Delta during the fall of the year when cotton money was plentiful.

Bracey played a song he learned in the Delta, but his guitar style was mostly from central Mississippi. Tommy Johnson played "Big Road Blues" and stuff he learned in the Delta, from Charley Patton and other people, in his own little style. But he was living in Crystal Springs, down below Jackson. So he didn't really live in the Delta that long. But people were saying that Bracey and Johnson were Delta bluesmen. They weren't really Delta bluesmen. They'd go up and play in the Delta and they'd come back to Jackson. Now, Tommy learned more guitar in the Delta than had Bracey. It's interesting. Now they call Skip James a Delta bluesman. He never was. Bentonia [where James was born] is in the hill country on the way to Yazoo City. It's not in the Delta.

Did these bluesmen—talk about the country suppers and the juke joints; it would lead me to think that there weren't any white listeners—at any point did white folks listen to this music?

Yeah, they listened to it some. And the thing was, you didn't have it in the Delta as much, but if you could, you always wanted to play for the white man, because he paid more money. Bracey told me he'd rather play for a party for white people to dance to and listen than he would for blacks, because they paid more money. But they also came up and listened on the streets, but understand the bluesmen were playing on the black streets. They weren't playing in the white neighborhoods.

But this brings back a great memory. Tommy Johnson and Bracey were playing in front of the King Edward Hotel. That's the biggest hotel in Jackson. One night a white man walked up to them on the streets. He said, "You boys sound pretty good. Play me some more." And they played him another tune. And he said, "You boys are pretty good. You're good enough to make records." He asked them if they made any records. And Bracey says, "Yeah, we recorded for the Victory label." It was "Victor," but Bracey always called it the "Victory" label. This white guy said, "I'm Jimmie Rodgers!" So Jimmie Rodgers, the blues yodeler, took Tommy Johnson and Bracey upstairs on the roof of the King Edward Hotel to play for the white people, up there at night where Jimmie Rodgers was playing. He also gave them a bottle of whiskey—and a five-dollar bill! So they thought he was the greatest guy in the world. But Jimmie Rodgers was always around black workers singing on the railroad.

How did you approach Bracey about his blues history when he was so reluctant to relive that part of his life?

I'd give him a few dollars and he'd talk about it. He just wouldn't play it! He was proud that he made records, but he wasn't proud of the lifestyle he lived. He met a woman who got him out of that lifestyle and into the church. That saved him. And by 1940 nobody was listening to his kind of music. He pretty much stopped playing by the 1940s.Tommy kept on playing, but Bracey would take other jobs, as a house painter. That's how he was making his living. But he would talk about it if his wife wasn't there. We'd walk down the street and I'd ask him about Tommy Johnson and I'd ask him about Charley Patton and he'd talk about them. I had a friend I carried over there and paid him to try and teach him guitar. I'd start to leave and he'd always say, "You got a dollar or two now for the preacher, haven't you?" I didn't have much money. I'd give him a couple of dollars.

When I first found him, I went over there one night and brought him a copy of his record "Saturday Blues" and "Left Alone Blues" and showed it to him. His wife didn't want him back in the lifestyle, and he had so much guilt. He grew up in the church and left the church. Reverend Rube Lacey and Son House had that same conflict: they grew up in the church, and the blues was the devil's music. Where the blues was played, that's where everything wrong happened—gambling, drinking, fighting, fornication, adultery. Everything happened where the blues was played. It was kind of an attraction for all evils that the church said were wrong. You either lived with the Lord or you lived with the devil. Bracey said, "I lived with the devil for a long time!" Remember Robert Wilkins? It was the same thing. He left blues playing, got totally out of it and never went back. He got in the Church of God in Christ in Memphis.

How did Bracey and Tommy Johnson fall out?

Tommy wanted more money. He thought he was the bigger of the two. He would ask for more money. Bracey said he and Tommy would be playing together, and Tommy would get so drunk he couldn't even play. And he wanted more money and Bracey didn't want to hire him. Bracey said, "We had an argument over it and I just wouldn't play anymore. We stopped playing together for years and years." In an interview in my book Bracey told me a story that in 1956 he was painting houses, and Tommy came over and said, "I want to change and be a preacher just like you." Bracey told him, "You got to pray and God will help you." Bracey said, "Tommy went away crying, and I was crying, and my wife was crying. And the next thing we heard, Tommy had died!" Bracey said it really struck a note with him. It hurt him so bad.

How did Bracey die?

He died of natural causes, a stroke and heart attack in 1970. He led me to H. C. Speir, because I asked Bracey how he got on record. He said, "H. C. Speir got me on record. He had Speir's Music Store." So I checked the phone book and there was "H. C. Speir." I called him. He found the greatest of the Mississippi bluesmen who ever recorded. You can just go down through the list. He gets Patton on record, he gets Tommy Johnson, Skip James, Ishman Bracey, the Mississippi Sheiks, Bo Carter, and Robert Johnson. He got obscure people like Blind Joe Reynolds on record.

He told me that people actually would come to his store. Musicians would write to the record companies and they'd tell the musicians to go to Jackson, to his store and audition. So he'd let people come in, and he'd take them in the back room and audition them. Skip James told a story that Speir's Music Store had people line up to audition on a certain date and that he was the only person accepted out of that line of people. But that's not true. Skip went down there and Speir listened to him, but there wasn't anyone else there. He was good enough to record, but he kind of embellished it a little bit. Speir didn't hold regular auditions. He just let them come in when they came in, and he listened to them.

How did you meet Speir, and what was his story?

I called him on the phone after Bracey told me about him . . .

Did you know who he was?

Well, I knew he got Tommy and Bracey on record. Other than that I didn't know who he was.

You didn't know that he'd gotten all these other bluesmen to record?

No! Nobody did! But I went out there and I also asked him about Charley Patton, and he said, "I got ole Charley on record, sure!" And so I'd go out there every time I could and pick his brain. He remembered Charley Patton. He remembered Bracey. He remembered Tommy Johnson and Skip James. Those stood out in his mind. But I would talk to him about Paramount Records and who else he might have gotten on record and where they might have been from, because I was going to go out and find those guys. But anyway, Speir had Bo Carter scouting for him. But Speir told me he received a set sum. He told me he got $150 for sending Charley Patton to Paramount. He took a lump sum plus expenses. A hundred and fifty dollars was a lot of money in 1929, so he was making good money. Also he never wanted to take royalties. So he never made a lot of money, but he put the money back into his music store.

He opened the music store in Jackson in 1926 in the black neighborhood, because he saw there wasn't anybody marketing black records. There were other record stores in white neighborhoods, but they didn't want to sell race records and they didn't want black people coming in their stores. But he got in the race record business in 1926, and by late 1927 he began sending people, sending talent to Birmingham for the Gennett record company. He picked up Jim Jackson, who recorded "Kansas City Blues." He said that Jim Jackson used to play in Jackson, Mississippi, in the streets. He was a cokehead, a cocaine addict. And he said he didn't want to handle him, and he went up to Memphis and picked him up in Memphis playing on Beale Street. He had heard him in Jackson before, and he listened to him and said he got a little concerned that he might have some dope on him. So he turned around and sold him to a guy named Loren Watson, who was another talent scout in Memphis, and Watson turned around and took him to Vocalion. And he recorded "Kansas City Blues"—a massive hit! But Speir said he didn't want to handle him because, number one, it was slow, and he didn't think it would sell. It was a real slow song. And, number two, he said, "I just didn't want to take any chance." So he sold him to the other talent scout.

For the folks who don't know prewar blues, that was one of the massive hits. "How Long How Long" by Leroy Carr, "Black Snake Moan" by Blind Lemon Jefferson, and "Kansas City Blues"—that was a monster seller! But that's how Speir got into it. He got the store first and then he got a little recording machine, and you could go in there and have your own little personal record made for five dollars. He got into it more and could make money from it. He came to Chicago to record. He went to a lot of places. He went to Memphis, Dallas, Birmingham, and Atlanta for different sessions, including two times carrying people up to Chicago. He went to Grafton, Wisconsin, at least once.

Didn't you do a description of what Speir's store was like?

There was a picture in there and you could actually see it. You could walk in there. He had Victrolas for sale on one side and radios for sale on the other side. He had listening booths, three listening booths. You see, you pulled a 78 record out, and you take it in the booth to listen to it and then decide which one you want to buy. And he told me that he sold as many as six hundred records on a good weekend! Six hundred 78s! He'd open at eight in the morning and stay open until ten at night on Saturdays. You walk in and he's got these record advertisements in back near these listening booths. He had his picture taken in the store in 1929, and it's in my book.

One of the points you made in the book—and perhaps you can elaborate—most record players were not electric, were they?

Gayle Dean Wardlow interviews a lead. Photo Joel Slotnikoff.

No, they were wind-up Victrolas. They sold wind-up Victrolas. Now, in a city like Jackson, once they came in with Victrolas that *would* play with electricity, Speir later put some of those in his listening stalls. But originally, before they began making the electric Victrola—and Victor started about 1928 with an electric motor you could plug in—but you had the wind-up machines, because that's all people had at their houses. They didn't have electric Victrolas. When they started making Victrolas in the early 1900s, they were for people who didn't have electricity. People who lived in the country and people who lived in the small towns, they didn't have electricity. You wind them up! As a matter of fact, I've never seen an electric Victrola in any black home I ever went in all my life! You always saw the wind-up machines. If you were living out in the country in the Deep South, in the small towns, they didn't have rural electric until Rural Electric Association came through with power lines after World War II.

Up in the mountains in East Tennessee in the 1930s they had those Tennessee Valley Authority plants, but when I lived in rural Louisiana we didn't have electricity until after World War II, when they came in and put power lines in. So in rural Mississippi you bought the wind-up Victrolas, and those electric Victrolas cost so much, how were you going to buy them? You could buy a little suitcase model you wind-up for about $9.95. In those days you'd pay over a hundred dollars when you bought a good Victrola. You might pay a couple of hundred for the top-of-the-line player. It was always the black woman who worked for the white man as a cook, or whatever she did—she had the money to buy a Victrola. Speir told me ninety percent of the records were bought by women in those days. And they sold for seventy-five cents for a 78 rpm two-sided record.

Didn't you have a breakdown of what it cost the record company to manufacture records?

Twenty-seven and one-half cents! It costs the majors like Columbia and Victor twenty-seven and one-half cents to make a record. They wholesaled it for forty-five cents. Then they marked it up to seventy-five cents. So the company made seventeen and one-half cents for every record they sold, and the dealer made thirty cents. But there were no returns in those days. As a retailer, if you bought the record you were stuck with it if it didn't sell. Eventually you'd mark it down to fifty cents, forty-five cents, or a quarter to move the records and get some of your money back.

Let me explain something to record collectors. The reason in 1930, 1931, and 1932 that you find so many records by only the big artists like Memphis Minnie, Peetie Wheatstraw, or Leroy Carr is because they had a track record of selling records. Why would you spend forty-five cents on a record in 1931 or 1932 that's not going to sell and you can't return it? They didn't start the returns policy, where you could actually return the record and get credit for it, until the late 1930s. Charley Patton records were selling good in 1929 and 1930, so dealers were buying them. But they only bought the artists who were going to sell. You didn't try that with a new singer.

How did retailers receive records? Where did they ship from?

They got them from their "jobbers," wholesalers. OKeh, Paramount, and Vocalion shipped out of St. Louis from the St. Louis Music Company. It was a big wholesaler! Columbia shipped out of New Orleans; Victor shipped out of New Orleans; OKehs came out of Atlanta or St. Louis. Speir did a lot of business with the St. Louis Music Company, and they also had the Herwin label in those days for mail-order customers.

Where were they pressed?

Paramounts were pressed in Grafton, Wisconsin. Back in the 1920s the Columbias were pressed in Bridgeport, Connecticut. They also had a pressing plant on the West Coast, in Oakland. OKeh was out there, and Victor's main pressing plant was in Camden, New Jersey.

I know that you're a 78 collector. Has it been your experience that any one label is more susceptible to splits?

Oh, yeah! Paramount. Paramount used very little shellac, and they used clay they got in Wisconsin, and they used just a little shellac to cut down on the cost. They pressed twelve hundred records. Most companies in those days would make a metal part. They made metal parts, a metal master and a stamper. Columbia and Victor would stamp nine hundred copies per stamper. Paramount would push it to twelve hundred, and they didn't have much shellac. And Paramounts are notoriously bad for breaking. I'd say half the Paramounts I've seen from 1926 on, they spread. Crack. The cold and the heat would cause the Paramounts to start splitting. There are so many Paramounts I've seen with cracks in them.

It would seem to me that with our modern technology somebody could find a process to correct the splits.

There's one guy out in California named Jim Cooprider. He has a way of taking the Paramounts and heating them and bringing the splits back together. He can repair 78 cracks better than anyone in the world. He's known as the man who can repair split Paramounts. He saved a Willie Brown Paramount for me. It had been dropped and broken in half, and he saved it and it plays. It clicks, but it plays. But somehow he's able to heat them and bring that crack back together. Jim Cooprider, he's well known among 78 collectors for being able to repair Paramounts. Paramount's the worst label. Victors and Columbias don't spread like that. Vocalions, Victors, Columbias—you don't see those kinds of hair cracks like that as you do on the Paramount label.

Didn't Speir also sell instruments?

He sold a few guitars. He told me he sold the National guitars for thirty-two dollars, the old metal-bodies. He sold those in the 1930s. He didn't sell a lot of guitars, primarily records and radios. He sold Stellas for $9.95. As a matter of fact, he was always selling Stellas to Charley Patton. Charley would come down and buy a new guitar. If I recall, he *gave* new Stellas to Tommy Johnson and Bracey to take and play at their recording sessions. I don't think he'd do that for everybody; they'd buy them. They sold for $9.95. They were made out of birch. Absolute best blues guitar at that time!

Was it an advantage to have a new guitar as opposed to a guitar that you were used to?

Oh, yeah! Because the old one was probably worn out. They wear out real easy. Speir sold Nationals for up in the thirties, and Stellas. He stayed in business until 1942 but ended up in the furniture store business in the late 1930s and got out of the music store business. Then he got out of the record business. He thought the record business was dead. The record ban came along in 1942 and he thought it was all dead, so he got out and went into the furniture business.

Had he been scouting and producing up until that time?

He pretty much stopped scouting and producing around 1937 or 1938. He said the style was changing and moving to Chicago and they were coming up with a "city sound." They really didn't want to come down South as much. And he was getting older. He was in his late thirties. He was born in 1897, so he got to the point he didn't want to travel. Robert Johnson came into his store, and he sent Johnson's name to the ARC [American Record Company] salesman Ernie Oertle down in New Orleans. Oertle came and picked Johnson up and carried him to San Antonio to record. By that time Speir wasn't really scouting, but talent would still come to see him.

Did you stay in touch with Speir up until his death?

Yes, I stayed in touch with him and would go to see him from 1964 up until the early 1970s, when he died of a heart attack. I hadn't seen him for six months when he died.

You have tape on him?

Yeah, I finally got him to let me put him on tape. What was amazing is that Speir never saw the value of what he did. He just said it was a business and he liked the music. You know he also recorded some of the greatest "hillbilly" music. He got Uncle Dave Macon on record; he came from Nashville to Jackson to record at an OKeh session. He got the Leake County Revelers on record for Columbia. He came out of the hill country and he liked fiddle music, but he loved blues too. When I first used to go see him, I hoped he had Charley Patton and Skip James records, but he didn't have any. He had hillbilly fiddle records. He didn't have any of the records, but he remembered those guys. He remembered Skip. He said, "You catch Charley Patton. Charley was the best you ever heard on guitar! You catch Skippy James on the right day, and he was 'bout as good as Charley on that guitar." He said there was nobody better than Patton. Skippy was next, and Tommy

Johnson had the best voice; the way he sang and moaned was the most mournful sound you'd ever hear.

Did you do much research on Skip James? And did you have anything to do with finding him?

Most every bona fide blues fan knows that during the early years of the folk boom/blues revival one of the seminal events of that era was the rediscovery of a handful of prewar bluesmen and that John Fahey was responsible for rediscovering two of the more prominent prewar bluesmen, Bukka White and then Skip James. In the case of Bukka White, the story is legend. Fahey sent a postcard to Bukka White addressed to "General Delivery" in Aberdeen, Mississippi, requesting that Bukka call him collect. Bukka had relatives in Aberdeen, who forwarded the postcard to Bukka in Memphis—try that today! John Fahey is also given credit for rediscovering Skip, and he did. But what isn't so widely known is that I was busy trying to find Skip myself, and Fahey ultimately located Skip by using one of the leads I had turned up. Here's how it happened.

The first time I met John Fahey I was in Washington, D.C., in 1960. I had gone up there to stay with my brother for a few months. He was in the air force as a jet pilot, stationed at Andrews Air Force Base. He was transferred to Spain, but I decided to stay in Washington and try to get a job for a few months. It was the summer of 1960. I heard about a coffeehouse there in D.C. where folk music was big at that time. I played Dobro guitar, and I went down there one Saturday night where people were sitting-in, and that was the first time I met Fahey. I'd say he was about eighteen or twenty years old. He had just played, and I walked up and told him I played. He asked me where I was from. I told him I was from Mississippi and that the guitarist I liked was Roy Acuff.

He asked if I had ever heard Charley Patton. I told him I hadn't. He told me that Patton was a great bluesman from the Mississippi Delta. He invited me to come back to his room and listen to Charley Patton. It was about ten o'clock and the club was breaking up. So he took me over to his room and put on a tape of Charley Patton. He played me a bottleneck piece—you know, slide guitar. As I listened I kind of liked the guitar, but when he began to sing, I thought, "Yee-gads—what is that?" [*laughs*] I couldn't understand a word Patton said. Listening to him was just like listening to the Wildman of Borneo. It was so primitive, I'd never heard anything like him. I was only there ten or fifteen minutes and he played me two or three songs. I said, "Whoa, that's kind of tough to understand." [*laughs*] Two years later I'm out looking for Patton records. That's the irony of the whole situation! Well, anyway, that was my first contact with John Fahey.

In the case of Skip James, as I mentioned earlier, Bernie Klatzko wrote to me and sent a list of names of people that I should look for, people he thought were from Mississippi. After Charley Patton, Son House, and Willie Brown, he mentioned Skip James. It was the fall of 1963 and I had found Ishman Bracey living in Jackson. I asked him about Skip James, but he didn't remember anything about him. Later that fall I heard that Johnny Temple had moved back from Chicago and was living in north Jackson. So I went over to see Johnny.

We were just sitting and talking; he was telling me about Elmore James living with him. I asked him if he had ever heard about Skip James, and he said, "Oh, you mean Skippy! That's what we called him, Skippy. Yeah, I used to play with him. He'd come down here and we'd go out and play in west Jackson." "Where was Skippy from?" "Bentonia." I'd never heard of Bentonia, and he told me it was about thirty miles north, up by Yazoo City. I asked if he knew what had happened to him, and Johnny told me he never had heard that Skip had died. He told me to go up and look for Henry Son Stuckey, that Henry Stuckey and Skippy used to play together. "Stuckey was a fine guitar player. He used to back Skippy up." So I headed immediately for Bentonia looking for Henry Stuckey, and I finally found him living west of Bentonia about seven or eight miles out on the Big Black River. I talked to him, and he said "Yeah, Skippy was here up until two or three years ago. He owed a man some money for a crop, and he left in the middle of the night." I asked if he knew where Skippy went. "He went to Tunica County somewhere—that's all I know." Stuckey was the man who taught Skip James the E-minor tuning. Stuckey learned it in Europe in France during World War I from a group of black soldiers from somewhere in the Caribbean, like Trinidad. So he shows it to Skippy and Skippy adopts it and makes it his own.

I was still in college and working football games on Friday night, so I couldn't go immediately. I finally got some money in the spring of '64, and I headed to Tunica County to look for Skip James. I stopped in Tunica and talked to an old gambler, who said, "That guy you're talking about used to come up here and play piano. But he moved to West Memphis." So I headed to West Memphis. I went into a club and asked around, and they said, "Yeah, there was a guy up here, but he got run out of town by the police, either for moonshining or illegal gambling—or something. We heard he went back to Tunica County." They called him "Curley" and said he played a great piano. I went back to Tunica, but I couldn't find him, so I went back home.

In looking back I can see that I made a couple of tragic mistakes. When I first found Ishman Bracey, I called Dick Spottswood at the Piedmont label to let him know I had located Bracey and to see if Piedmont might be interested in issuing sides by him. Bracey wouldn't sing blues, but I thought we might be able to record him singing religious tunes. They weren't interested, because they'd just found Robert Wilkins. I also let Spottswood know that I had started looking for Skip James. I said, "I'm on the trail of Skip James. If I find him, I'd like to work an agreement out with you where I can make some money for college tuition. I'll keep you posted and let you know if I find him. He *is* alive." Another mistake I made, I went back to Bracey and told him I was on the track of Skip James and that his trail led to Bentonia. Then it all came back to him--"Yeah, I remember that guy now. He used to come down here to play. That's right, Bentonia"--which kind of surprised me. I was in Jackson for summer school, and I didn't know it, but Dick Spottswood was in touch with John Fahey, who by that time was out on the West Coast.

That summer John Fahey, Henry Vestine--later of Canned Heat—and a guy named Bill Barth came looking for Skip James. They came by to see Bracey, and Bracey sold me out for thirty pieces of silver. [*laughs*] I believe I read somewhere that thirty dollars was all they had between them. They paid Bracey thirty dollars for the information on Skip, and when he told them, they headed for Bentonia. They were fortunate. They found somebody in Bentonia that had an address where Skip James was living in Tunica County. They went there—it was the little town of Hollywood—and found out he was in the hospital. So they found him alive in the Tunica County hospital.

That's how Skip James was found. I was the guy who did all the legwork behind Skip. I found out where he came from. No one knew anything about Skip James. He left no memories in Mississippi; he was just a local musician. He played in Bentonia, he played up in Yazoo City, and he played down in Jackson with Johnny Temple. Somehow Fahey and his friends paid Skip's hospital bills and took him to Memphis. He first performed at a coffeehouse called the Bitter Lemon in Memphis. Then they took him straight to Washington, D.C., and he appeared at Newport. So I missed Skip James. I guess the sad part of it was I opened *Newsweek* magazine and there was a picture of Skip James and Son House; they'd just discovered both of them. I'd been looking for a year and nobody picked up the phone to tell me, "We found Skip James." It was hurtful.

Who found Robert Wilkins?

He first recorded for Victor in 1928, so he probably showed up and auditioned for Victor in Memphis. They came there every year starting in 1927. He would have heard the company was in town. The word would be out on the street. He first recorded for Victor—one record--and then he recorded for Brunswick, and they were much better. I don't recall who found him in the early sixties when he was rediscovered.

How about Papa Freddie Spruell?

Papa Freddie was living in Chicago when he recorded. I actually talked to his wife about 1981; she talked to me on the phone. He called himself Mr. Freddie, but they all called him Papa Freddie Spruell. In those days they would call a man Papa because he was a man of distinction—and he had money. Papa Freddie Spruell was from Lake Providence, Louisiana, and he moved to Chicago when he was a teenager, about 1917 or 1918. He was playing guitar like he learned to play in Mississippi, but he was from Louisiana. He first recorded in Chicago in 1926, for OKeh, and some people think it's Richard M. Jones talking to him on a song called "Milk Cow Blues." The other side is called "Way Back Down Home Blues." What was interesting was he played a twelve-string guitar, the first record with a twelve-string. Twelve-strings were sold in Atlanta—all the blues singers there recorded playing twelve-strings.

But if he recorded in 1926, doesn't he predate all the eastern seaboard artists?

He would have. You're right! He recorded in 1926, and McTell's Victors aren't recorded until 1927. You're right. That's a very good point! He was also the first Delta-sounding musician to record also.

Twelve-string wasn't common in the Delta, was it?

No, not common at all! Nobody played twelve-string in the Delta. It was totally unusual. He came out of Lake Providence. Probably what happened was he got up here, and twelve-strings were sold in the stores in Chicago. So if you've got a twelve-string, your guitar is a little louder and you might attract a little more attention. So first he records for OKeh and then for Paramount. They probably found him on the streets, or he went down and auditioned for Mayo Williams, who was running Paramount's operation at that time. Then he recorded again for Bluebird in 1935, but that was the same thing: he was in Chicago, and Bluebird was recording in Chicago.

Would you tell the story of one of your earliest discoveries—finding the real name of the artist who recorded as King Solomon Hill?

Back in those days Stephen Calt was listening to lyrics and I was listening to lyrics. And on the tune "Gone Dead Train," Calt thought he heard him say, "*I'm goin' windin'*" or "*I'm goin' to Minden*"—windin' or Minden. I listened to it, and I thought it was Minden instead of windin'. And lo and behold, that was about thirty miles from where I grew up as a little boy, Minden, Louisiana. So when I went to visit my granddaddy in Louisiana, I stopped in Minden and I started asking about anybody who made records and they said, "'No, they didn't know anybody." And I talked about the songs, and they said, "Oh, I remember somebody named Joe Holmes. He was down in Sibley, and he used to sing those songs about the 'Gone Dead Train' and like that." And I thought I was on to something. So I went down to Sibley and asked around a little bit and located his wife. And from his wife it led to one of the guys he'd played with and ran around with. I interviewed him and I came back and wrote the story.

A year later I found a man named John Willis, and I asked him about Joe and he said, "Joe told me that he made some records and I didn't believe him, because he'd lie a lot. I never saw none of his records, so I didn't believe he made no records." I played the "Gone Dead Train" and "Tell Me Baby" for him, and he said, "That's Joe, all right. That's naturally him! That's his voice and that's his guitar." So I wrote this in the first *78 Quarterly* in 1967. I went back to Louisiana a few years later and found the King Solomon Hill Baptist Church

Gayle Dean Wardlow interviews another lead. Photo Joel Slotnikoff.

as identified by John Willis, one of Joe Holmes's friends. It sits on King Solomon Hill community. King Solomon Hill was just a little community in between two towns. But the way I was able to prove it without a doubt was I found the mailman who had delivered mail through there for the U.S. government, and he wrote me a letter and said, "Yeah, I used to deliver mail on the King Solomon Hill community."

I published that letter in *Blues Unlimited* under a title, "One Last Walk up King Solomon Hill." I've got a copy of "Gone Dead Train," and there are no composer credits—just "Gone Dead Train" and "King Solomon Hill." I believe what happened was that they always took your name and the place where you lived so they could find you again—if your record started selling good and they wanted to get you back to record. They looked under "Joe Holmes" and saw the "King Solomon Hill," Louisiana, address and thought, "That sounds better than 'Joe Holmes.'" So they put it out under "King Solomon Hill."

The guy who was harder to find was Blind Joe Reynolds. Speir told me he found Blind Joe Reynolds outside of Lake Providence, Louisiana, at a lumber camp. I went to Lake Providence looking for Blind Joe Reynolds in 1965. He'd been gone from there for fifteen or twenty years. They remembered a blind man playing on the streets. Again, I used to carry that little portable tape recorder that operated on batteries. So I played them the records by Blind Joe Reynolds, and they said, "Yeah, that's him." It took me three years to track Blind Joe Reynolds, and I finally tracked him to Monroe. I was just asking around on the street, and they said, "There's a Blind Joe that plays here on the street." And he was playing on the streets of Monroe in 1965 and '66 and died in 1967 or '68. I found out where this Blind Joe lived and I went to the house, but the house was locked up. Nobody was there. I came back about nine months later and he had died. But he was still alive at the time that Cream put out their first album and put out one of his songs, "Outside Woman Blues." But I tracked him for three years before I found him. That was the longest I ever tracked anybody.

He recorded under the name Blind Joe Reynolds, but that was his alias. According to his nephew and a good friend, his real name was Joe Sheppard and he was on the run from the law. He'd spent some time in prison in Arkansas. He was supposed to have carried a loaded pistol with him all the time. He was blinded when he was a youth. He was in a crap game with another guy, and they argued about who shot what. They both went for their weapons and they both had shotguns. Joe peered out from behind a tree, and the guy shot him in the face with a shotgun. He was blinded. It was most likely birdshot. If you see pictures of him, he had little pellet marks, scars on his face. But he was on the run from the law, so even if I had found him he probably would have denied that he ever made the records. It turns out that he reportedly died from pneumonia around 1968. By that time he was using an electric guitar.

Wasn't he the Nehi guy?

Yeah, he did "Nehi Blues" and "Outside Woman Blues"—"*When you lose your money, great God, don't you lose your mind.*" And Clapton put it on the first album. That original record by Blind Joe was found about 1966, and once it was reissued in 1967 it was heard in England and Clapton immediately put it on that first Cream album.

You've also done some research on Robert Johnson?

Two years ago I found out where Robert Johnson was really buried. I had found Robert Johnson's death certificate back in 1968; I was the first person to ever find it. And I published it in 1971, and a lot of the research was done by Mack McCormick—and also done by Steve LaVere based on the death certificate information: he was born in Hazlehurst and so forth . . . The death certificate said no doctor was present. The only thing it gave on the death certificate, it said burial was at a Zion Church, but it didn't say which Zion Church. About 1991 Skip Henderson formed the Mount Zion Fund to put grave markers on unknown graves. And the first monument he decided to place was Robert Johnson's, based on what Honeyboy Edwards had said: that Johnson was buried at the Mount Zion Baptist Church. They found a Three Forks store which was very close to the Mount Zion Baptist Church. The death certificate said place of burial was Zion Church. It didn't say *Mount* Zion! And so they determined to put a monument there. Well, there was always some doubt. A lot of things didn't make sense. For instance, I had talked to Honeyboy about it too. He said Robert was poisoned out at Three Forks, out in the country, and brought back into the city. But it made no sense. Mount Zion Baptist Church is some ten miles below Greenwood. If Robert Johnson had died in Greenwood itself, they'd have taken him out to a pauper's grave and buried him right there in Greenwood; they wouldn't have carried him down to the Mount Zion Baptist Church. So I always had doubts. The informant was Jim Moore, but nobody could find Jim Moore.

Later on a woman told the story that Robert Johnson was actually buried in Payne Chapel, which is one hundred or two hundred yards down the highway from Mount Zion. But it never made sense why he died in town. Honeyboy said he died in town in Baptist Town. What I discovered was that Johnson used to stay up in the black section called Baptist Town of Greenwood. He'd get a room up there when he came to play music in the area. About two years ago I discovered this woman and I went to talk to her. Earlier she had been found by LaVere also. Her name was Rosie Eskridge. She lived on the Luther Wade Plantation, which is about two or three miles out of Greenwood on the Money Road, the same road that goes to Avalon, where John Hurt lived. She never knew Robert Johnson, but she knew a blues singer had died on the plantation.

She said Mr. Wade came up and knocked on her door during the day and told her husband to go up and dig a grave at Little Zion Baptist Church. That was the church for the plantation. Her husband dug the grave. She said they went down to the county barn and picked up a little old pine box, brought it out to where he died on the plantation, put his body in the pine box, sealed it up there, and put it in the grave. She never saw the man, didn't know him. But she knew Jim Moore, personally, for many, many years, and she knew that they went and got a coffin from the county—a homemade coffin—and put him in there. So she verified what was said on the back side of the death certificate, which

I discovered in 1996. I didn't discover the back side until 1996. Don't ask me why! There was a front side *and* a back side, and I finally went back and got the back side, and on the back side was the fact that he was buried in a homemade coffin supplied by the county.

So she took us up to the grave—me and Ace Atkins, who was with me—and we went up there with her. Later I put up a temporary monument up there, and now a benefactor has put a thirty-seven-hundred-dollar monument out there on Johnson's real grave. There's no doubt he's buried there, because the Three Forks store where he was supposedly playing that night, it's only about two miles from there out to Luther Wade's Plantation. So they brought him back to Luther Wade's Plantation and he died in a house on the plantation. She had no idea who Robert Johnson was. Later on she heard he was a famous blues player. Robert Johnson is buried at Little Zion Baptist Church on Money Road. He's not buried at Mount Zion, which is down Highway 8 towards Morgan City, or at Payne Chapel. We went up there to see the real grave. She [Eskridge] took me and Ace to see the grave. And right there was a big old water oak—it was *right* over the grave where she said Robert Johnson was buried.

I think it's ironic that all the graffiti and half bottles of whiskey are constantly found around Johnson's grave, but nobody ever does that at Dockery's for Patton.

No, of course not! Robert Johnson's a hero. They want to play like him. Robert Johnson's greatness is in his guitar. It's in his lyrics, but it's his Delta guitar. He put it all together—he really did. He put the "walking boogie" together with great bottleneck. He was the first person to do that on record. That's really his claim. And he wrote some great lyrics! He knew that the more songs he wrote, the more money he got paid. He probably only made about ten dollars per side. That's all he would have been paid. Roy Acuff went to Chicago in 1936 to record for ARC Vocalion. He was paid $250 for twenty songs. That's $12.50 per side. You better believe Robert didn't make that much. And they weren't paying any royalties. But it helped him make that "name" so he could go back home and play and make more money, *and* you were a professional musician! Back in those days there were only five record companies and only three making blues records: Vocalion and its ARC labels, Bluebird, and Decca. If you made a record in those days, you were really something. You had to really be good to get on record! You had to be original and have original songs.

ROBERT M. W. DIXON INTERVIEW

I was born in Gloucester—in the UK, of course—on the 25th of January 1939. I was brought up for the first few years in Stroud, a little town in the Cotswolds. At the age of eight we moved to Nottingham, and I spent my formative years in Nottingham.

How I got interested in all of this, there was a trad [traditional] jazz boom in the 1950s in England, bands like Ken Colyer and Chris Barber and Mick Mulligan. Chris Barber had Ottilie Patterson as a singer with his band. I remember she sang "Weeping Willow Blues" and "Nobody Knows You When You're Down and Out" by Bessie Smith. I had that version of the record before I had Bessie Smith. Mick Mulligan had a man named George Melly who sang with him. So I originally got interested in jazz. I didn't know very much about the blues. In the late 1940s and early 1950s before there were many LPs, microgroove records, a number of small companies were reissuing 78 rpm records in England—a company called Tempo, another called Jazz Collector—and I was buying these, and I started making lists of all the Jazz Collectors. I mean, I bought Jazz Collector L20: Ma Rainey, "See See Rider Blues" and "Jealous Hearted Blues." And then there was a very exciting piano record by Jabo Williams, "Jab Blues" and "Pratt City Blues" on L51. And so I was making these lists.

Now, there wasn't a full discography of all the original recordings of blues. There was this thing called *Jazz Discography* by Albert McCarthy and Dave Carey, which got as far as *L* and then it sort of petered out. By then, of course, I got interested in looking at the original records—the original issues—and doing discographies on the original issues. Then I was interested in buying records that hadn't been reissued. There was a wonderful magazine called *Vintage Jazz Mart* produced by Trevor Benwell, who was an air traffic controller at London airport and a wonderful jazz collector. And he put out this magazine that came out the fifth of every month. And they had a

Robert Dixon, 1996. Courtesy Robert M. W. Dixon.

series of lists of records, and normally the lists of records were auctions, so you put in a bid. The prices were not great at that stage. You could get a Sleepy John Estes for about fifteen shillings, which is about two dollars. So I started buying records. I then went up to Oxford to study mathematics, and I didn't have much money, of course. So what I was doing was buying records, often from the States, and I bought an early tape recorder, a Telefunken tape recorder—this was about 1958 or so—so I'd record the records and then sell them. I'd sometimes make a slight profit, but the main thing was that I had the music.

I've always had the kind of mind that likes to catalog everything and know where everything is. The details of the records of the American companies, some of them were available. This was an important thing in my getting together with John Godrich, because we formed a very important team. There was one lady called Helen Chmura at Columbia Records, and she had mimeographed out the complete matrix listings and the complete issued listings of all the records on Columbia and OKeh in the 1920s and 1930s. These had come in before my time, but they'd gone to a couple of English collectors called Bill Wyatt and Derek Coller.

The Decca Record company's interesting. In 1934, just as America was coming out of the Depression, the English record company called Decca formed an American branch, and they were putting out records for thirty-five cents. You had to do that to sell. Back in the twenties seventy-five cents would be the normal price, although there were also dime store records pressed on very poor quality shellac for thirty-five cents and things like that. And they started a series for, I believe it was called then, the "Negro market," which were put out in a special series. They were called "race series." And Decca started a race series in 1934 with the number 7000. It got to 7910 by the time it finished in the early forties. And I was trying to make a complete list of these.

John Godrich. Courtesy Godrich Family.

There were no company files we could get to there, so I advertised in *Vintage Jazz Mart* for information, and at the same time John Godrich had advertised for the same thing. So we got together and we pooled our resources. John was interesting. He was born about 1927. His mother was a doctor in Swansea, South Wales. He ran away to sea when he was about fifteen, joined the Merchant Navy towards the end of the Second World War. Then when he left the navy he worked as a docker—what you would call a longshoreman—on the Swansea docks. Naturally, he injured his back on the docks, and then he was working in the office then. It was about 1959 we got together. I was about twenty and he was about thirty-two, and we just pooled all our resources.

We borrowed from Bert Wyatt and Derek Coller the information which Helen Chmura had circulated.

John typed out some of it and I typed out some of it—we made copies for each other. I was studying mathematics, and you don't have to work very hard, you don't tend to work many hours in mathematics. If you work in science you have to go to the lab; if you're working on English or history you have to write an essay every week. In mathematics you just solve a few problems, do a few sums. I had plenty of time. I used to go out on the river at Oxford as students do there, but I had plenty of time for typing out all these lists.

John and I, in fact, didn't meet for some time. We started working together in 1959; we didn't meet until two or three years later. We actually met in Dobell's Record Shop at 77 Charing Cross Road, the center of record buying in England. I think it was 1961. By that time I had moved to Edinburgh; when I finished my time in Oxford I moved to Edinburgh. I was employed as a research fellow in statistical linguistics, trying to apply statistical methods to linguistics. The interesting thing was when we first started working together, he made a list—a rough guide to blues discographies appearing in jazz magazines—and he sent it to me. John didn't have a typewriter but I did. So I typed it up and put at the top "by John Godrich" to be sent to Trevor Benwell for *Vintage Jazz Mart*—they had a few little tiny articles at the beginning. And then John wrote on [it] "and Bob Dixon" as well. All I did was type it up at that stage. Then we started working together and we had twenty of these "Margin Notes" articles appear. We had an index to labels which appeared in jazz magazines. We had indexes to traditional, swing, and modern jazz articles appearing in jazz magazines. We had an interesting index to items on blues singers which appeared in jazz magazines. And Paul Oliver—an amazing man and a hero of mine but also a good friend—we did a complete listing of the articles by Paul Oliver which had appeared in magazines from 1954 until 1958. We also had articles by Bob Koester on the bottom of the same page.

Paul Oliver played a very important role. I was writing to him about discography, and he said, "Come up and spend the weekend with us." At that time he was just an art teacher at a high school in London, a drawing master. I went and spent the weekend with him. That was in January, just before his first book, *Blues Fell This Morning*, came out; the book came out in April 1960. In the summer of 1960 he got some kind of fellowship so he could go to the United States and go to Chicago and the Southern states and find some of the old blues singers and the new blues singers. But he had no money to do any recording. So I started a thing called a "blues recording fund," and people sent in three pounds, which is about six dollars, as sort of a loan. We got a few hundred dollars in order to record people like Wade Walton and Little Brother Montgomery. These were issued on LP records, small specialized labels in England. And we did pay the money back. People lent three pounds and they got back three and a half pounds about three years later.

But all the time we were building up our files. In those days photocopying barely existed, but everything was typed out with carbon paper. And if you made a mistake you had to rub it off on each of the four copies, so you didn't make mistakes as you were typing data out. So I had a copy and John had a copy and we'd circulate other copies. In 1961 Brian Rust published the first edition of his jazz discography from 1897 to 1931 [*Jazz Records, A–Z, 1897–1931*]. Later on he did a second volume, 1932 to 1942, and later he combined them,

Brian Rust with trumpeter Sylvester Ahola. Originally from *VJM* magazine and courtesy of Mark Berresford Collection.

and there have since been many editions of it, but this was the first one. He had included some blues singers that had jazz accompaniments. And in September 1961 I had moved to Edinburgh, and I came down to London to do a course on some crazy programming system, Fortran, that they had at the time at IBM. John and I were doing all this discography just for our own benefit. We each had other things to do. It was just sort of a hobby. Paul Oliver was very helpful and very close to us. And Paul said, "Why don't you two get together and do a blues discography, like the Brian Rust discography?" So we went around to see Brian, and he said yes, he would publish it. The publishing consisted of typing out the material on paper masters and then printing them. They did just over a thousand copies and then they were worn out.

What we did when we were compiling *Blues and Gospel Records,* starting in 1961 we produced nine files—one for each of Columbia, OKeh, Vocation/Brunswick, Paramount, and Gennett in the twenties and early thirties; one for RCA [Victor and Bluebird labels]; one for the American Record Corporation [later Vocalion/OKeh and other labels, such as Perfect and Melotone]; one for Decca, of course; and a final file for all the small labels which flourished in the twenties. Then we circulated those to seven collectors. And each of them went through the whole of every file. We were trying to be absolutely systematic. If you want to get all the records by someone like Big Bill Broonzy, how do you know when you've got them all? They recorded all over the place, on so many different labels. So we decided that the only thing we could do was make a complete listing of all the records on every one of the appropriate labels or series.

For Columbia and OKeh there was this wonderful woman named Helen Chmura, who worked in some documentary department of the Columbia record company—before they were all bought up by the Japanese. She had typed out a complete list of all the recordings by matrix number, including all the issues in the race series, and circulated these in the early 1950s. So there was no difficulty at all with Columbia and OKeh. We added the matrix and take numbers, but the accompaniments had to be worked out; it wasn't all done. All of these companies had special race series, and all you had to do was get everything in the Columbia 13000/14000 series.

Victor and Bluebird, which was a major label, didn't have a special series. Well, they had a couple of very short special series, but most of the time the records were issued in the general series. So what you had to do was make an overall listing of everything in the general series, which was quite a big thing—all the pop, and jazz, and hillbilly, and blues. There would be four or five jazz and then four or five blues, then four or five country and western, and then ten pop—something like that—but the blues were issued in batches. So you'd get something like five a month and then home in on those blocks. You'd identify the batches of blues records and get more information in detail on those. We hadn't got a lot of information on matrix numbers and recording dates on Victor and Bluebird.

And these were in the files of the HMV company in Hayes, Middlesex—quite close to where Brian Rust lived. Brian had an eidetic memory, so he could just look at a page and memorize it, go home, and write it all down. So I sent Brian a list of all the information we needed. A number of discographies had been published on individual artists in the various magazines, and of course we were using everything that we could possibly find. So he went around to Hayes, got the actual information, put it in his head, and came home and wrote it down. So we were able to get a pretty complete listing. So we got everything on Victor and Bluebird, the Radio Corporation of America labels from when they started recording blues in 1927 up to 1942.

And for Paramount there were quite a few people that worked on that. Michael Wyler had a series of articles in *Jazz Monthly* in the late fifties, going through something like eleven hundred issues on Paramount. No company files have survived there. And then Max Vreede worked on it later.

The Brunswick 7000 series and the Vocalion 1000 series—the companies started out separately but later merged—there was a card file for that, and this was lent to me, as I remember, about January 1960. I spent about six hours a day just typing out the whole of that. And there were also comments; for instance, I'm looking at Vocalion 1217 by Reverend A. W. Nix and His Congregation. The matrix numbers given in the file are 2479 and 2480—"Begin a New Life on Christmas Day, Part One" and "Begin a New Life on Christmas Day, Part Two." But it's obscure as to what the dates are—281101—which would be the first of November 1928. That, I think, was when the information was typed up in the head office, which may have been a couple of weeks later than it was recorded. The next entry is "Midnight Rounders," "Bull Fiddle Rag," and "Barrel House Dance," which is canceled. Then the next one says "Midnight Rounders," "Shake Your Shimmy," and "Bull Fiddle Rag"—they changed one of the titles. There's no advice on the cards, so apparently it wasn't used. Then it says 1218, "Midnight Rounders," "Shake Your Shimmy." The other side says Albert Wynn's Gut Bucket Five, "Crying My Blues Away." So they had three goes at what they were going to put on 1218—either the "Midnight Rounders," " Bull Fiddle Rag," and "Barrel House Dance," or "The Midnight Rounders" "Shake Your Shimmy," and "Bull Fiddle Rag." Eventually that number came out with only one side by the "Midnight Rounders," "Shake Your Shimmy," and the other side was "Crying My Blues Away" by Albert Wynn's Gut Bucket Five. So you can see exactly the mechanism of what they were doing back in 1928.

In the twenties there were quite a number of small labels. There was a label called Meritt, which was put out by a Kansas City music store, a beautiful colored label—six issues, something like that. And we had to cover those as well.

We had a page for every artist. For the big discography you give the date of recording, you give the artist's name, of course, and they would always be the singer for blues, and whether they accompanied themselves on anything—or the other accompaniments, the date and the place. We also put the day of the week in. People said, "That's irrelevant." I don't think that's irrelevant at all! It's interesting to know if something was recorded on a weekday or a Saturday or Sunday. A lot of artists would have commitments at various times. It doesn't take up any extra space; there was room on the line. And then of course you have to have the matrix number, which is the consecutive number allocated by the record company for all their recordings.

Some companies would have special series for different cities; the regular series would be for New York but would have a "C" prefix for Chicago. And then a lot of the companies went down South; they'd spend a couple of months, they'd go to Atlanta, and they'd go to Memphis, and then they'd go to New Orleans, and then somewhere like Dallas. And they'd put "MEM" in front of the Memphis sides, and "ATL" in front of the Atlanta sides, and "NO" in front of the New Orleans ones. Then you have to have a take number, because in the 1920s they would normally make two or three takes of each title. Then they'd take them back to New York and try to work out which was the best one. Sometimes one take would be issued on one label and another take on another label or on a reissue. And then you had to have issue numbers. Sometimes things were issued on a number of different labels.

The Gennett company, based in Richmond, Indiana, was some sort of furniture company which started doing records, and they did some of the finest records by black artists. But it was a very racist place; you could hardly stay the night in Richmond. You'd come in from Chicago and record and take the next train back. Sam Collins, for instance, was issued on Gennett under his real name. But one of the things that really blew my mind—nowadays everything's available on CD or LP, but in those days the only way you could get Sam Collins was to buy a 78 record of his. But I remember this one I bought—I sent away to the States for it; it was about 1960. It was Gennett 6167, "The Jailhouse Blues" and "Riverside Blues" by Sam Collins, recorded in Richmond, Indiana, on Monday, 25th of April 1927. This was completely different from anything I'd ever heard before, and it was the most beautiful thing I'd heard. He recorded for Gennett, but it was reissued on different, cheaper labels sold in chain stores. So Sam Collins was called "Big Boy Woods" on the Bell label; "Jim Foster" on Champion, Silvertone, and Superior; and "Jelly Roll Hunter" on Supertone. We had to sort out all this duplication. Normally they didn't change the names of the tunes, but still that was quite a big thing to do.

How *did* you sort out all these pseudonyms? You had all these different names on the budget labels. When did you figure out that they were the same artist?

Well, we weren't the first. People had been working on this for years before us. It was known that this happened; it was just a matter of sorting them out. Some of these chain stores' labels were pressed on inferior shellac, and they were sold into homes where they were not so well treated as the seventy-five-cent records, so that copies of them were pretty rare. We had an incredible network of correspondents in England, Europe, and the States, and we just put together all the information that we had, sometimes working out what the pseudonyms were, to a certain extent, just by listening to them.

In gospel there were essentially three types of recordings. There were guitar evangelists like the Reverend Clayborn, there were down-home preachers like the Reverend J. M. Gates and the Reverend F. W. McGhee, and there were the quartets. And the African Americans down South who were religious would only buy religious records. They wouldn't buy any blues records; they would say it was the work of the devil. But quite a number of quartets would record gospel records and then record secular records as well, but they would use a different name. One of my favorites were the Birmingham Jubilee Singers. They would record tunes like "Every Time I Feel the Spirit" and "Walking to Jerusalem—Just Like John." But then they'd record things like "How Come You Do Me Like You Do" and "Toot Toot Tootsie Bound," and then they'd used the pseudonym "Birmingham Quartet" or the "Mobile Four," but one only has to listen to the records to realize that it's the same group. Once you started looking at the discography, "Every Time I Feel the Spirit" and "How Come You Do Me Like You Do" were recorded on the same day—Friday, November 6th, 1926, in the same place, Atlanta, Georgia, by the Columbia Phonograph Company. So you can see they recorded a couple of religious ones and a couple of secular ones at the same session.

One of the things that I think I was the first person to work out—Blind Lemon Jefferson was an itinerant blues singer. He'd do some guitar picking on a street corner in Dallas, and then he'd go up north and record for Paramount. Most of his records were secular, highly secular. But there were a couple of his records put out as Deacon L. J. Bates. I listened to these and I thought, "These are Blind Lemon Jefferson." And then there was the "L. J." for Lemon Jefferson—Deacon L. J. Bates. But then I looked at the discographical details for "Black Snake Dream Blues" and "Hot Dogs" by Blind Lemon Jefferson, given matrix numbers 4577 and 4578. Then the next matrix number is "He Arose from the Dead" by Deacon L. J. Bates, and the matrix number is actually on the record. In many cases they weren't for all labels, but for Paramount they were. So, discographically, obviously they were the same person coming from the same session. You have to be very careful about having aural identifications. There are a lot of people saying, "I'm certain that the pianist on this is the same as the pianist on that." But someone else will say the exact opposite, you know. So you have to be careful; you really do need to have the proper checking for things like this.

John Godrich with Francis Wilford-Smith. Courtesy Robert M. W. Dixon.

For Columbia and OKeh—and early Vocalion and Brunswick—these various series sort of finished at the Depression. There was virtually no recording in '32 and '33, and then in '34 things started up again. We had some useful information, but we still had to work out all the accompaniments. "Lovin' Sam from Down in 'Bam," Sam Theard accompanied by piano. Was it his own piano or was it "Cow Cow" Davenport on piano? It gives you the composer credits as well: Brunswick 7090, "Lovin' Sam from Down in 'Bam," Sam Theard accompanied by piano; "Get Your Mind On It," composed by Theard and Davenport. The other side was "Doodle It Back," composed by Davenport. So you say, "Ah-ha! Maybe it *was* Cow Cow Davenport on piano. Let me just look up in the book and see what was decided upon." What we say is, "Probably Cow Cow Davenport on piano and Tampa Red on guitar." I don't think Sam Theard played anything—just a singer.

Again, when we were compiling *Blues and Gospel Records,* starting in 1961 we produced files for each of the major companies and the minor companies—nine files—and then we circulated those to seven collectors. We sent them to Paul Oliver, Bert Wyatt, Derek Coller—also a wonderful friend, Francis Smith, who later became Francis Wilford-Smith, who was really quite a character and a very enthusiastic collector. He's also a very well known cartoonist under the name Smilby. He would draw cartoons for *Playboy* every month. It kept him in money to buy a lot of records.

Another important thing is that from 1960 onwards a lot of these blues singers were being rediscovered in America. Some of them were living in obscurity. Mississippi John Hurt was living in Avalon. He'd written a song called "Avalon Blues," and Dick Waterman went and found him. But others were just playing in the juke joints in Chicago and they were brought across to England. And Francis Smith used to have this wonderful manor house, about an hour south of London—a 1560 house, something like that—and he used to invite them down for the weekends. We had Speckled Red, and Roosevelt Sykes, and Little Brother Montgomery. And Little Brother came up to Nottingham. I was still at Oxford but I came home for vacations. An impresario there, Bill Kinnell, asked me if I would meet him at the station and take him to the gig and then take him back and put him on a train back to London afterwards.

I was growing up in a very middle-class white English household, not too different, I imagine, from a middle-class white American household of the time. My father was principal of [a] technical college, and I said to Mother, 'I'm picking up Little Brother Montgomery. Can I bring him home for an hour or two?' She said, "Well, better not. I don't think your father would like it." So I took him off elsewhere.

I remember taking around Speckled Red. In fact, there was a photographer named Valerie Wilmer who made quite a name for herself taking photographs of jazz artists, and Valerie Wilmer and I both called on Speckled Red at the same time. We took him out one afternoon. We took him to the Tower of London, where he could see the Crown Jewels and where all the people had their heads chopped off. Henry the Eighth said, "I won't touch my lunch until that man's head rolls." Outside there was a Houdini-type person—you know, tie himself all up in a sack and someone would tie him up in chains, and he would get out of it. Speckled Red was tickled pink by this, and I had to stop him from giving all his money away—you know, "Five pounds is quite enough, no need to give him twenty pounds." It was fun getting to know these people. We played them some of their old records and asked about accompanying artists and filled in quite a few gaps in the discography.

I went to Edinburgh in September. I'd been studying mathematics towards a PhD at Oxford. The mathematics was too arbitrary; you made up your own axioms and you worked from those. But in linguistics you take the material in real languages. You can't change that; you have to analyze that. So I was a research fellow over there in statistical linguistics. What I was doing was applying statistical methods to the linguistic data. I was doing that all day, and in the evenings I'd be typing up the discography. First of all, I did a complete file for RCA-Victor. Then I did a complete file for the American Record Corporation, and I was halfway through the Decca one by December. John and several people were looking at them and giving us comments and so on.

And then linguistics suddenly gripped me so much I embarked on an incredible love affair with it, which has lasted all my life. I said to John, "I haven't got time to do this anymore." He said, 'Okay, I'll take over." So John did about seventy percent of the first edition. It was all based upon our joint work over the years. Then after we'd got the individual files—one for each label—if an artist occurred in several, then they had to be collated. So I said to John, "Big Bill was in about four different labels, so you'd have to collate those." Then we sent them down to Brian Rust in 1963, I think, and he typed the whole lot up—there were no computers in those days—on these paper matrixes, and the book came out in 1964. And it was a reasonably good listing. Obviously there were many more things that would come up and a lot of people we hadn't been in touch with. A huge number of collectors read it. They were wonderful in sending us in corrections and comments and further information. So John had a regular column called "I Believe I'll Make a Change," which is a record by Peetie Wheatstraw, and about four or five other people in the middle thirties. Then we had a second edition in 1969. That was published by Storyville Publications—again, a very small company. Brian Rust was just Brian Rust, but Storyville put out a regular magazine called *Storyville*.

And then after Edinburgh I went to Australia and did some fieldwork up on disappearing aboriginal languages of northeast Queensland. Then I went back to teach linguistics at University College London. Then I spent a year in America at Harvard, 1968 to 1969. Then in 1970 I moved to Australia for good, at the Australian National University at Canberra. I was the first professor and chair of the linguistics department there. John Godrich had a very bad back and his health was pretty poor. He said, "I can't carry on with this. Who shall we get to do it?" I said, "I'll do it. I'll take over." He said, "I thought you were going to a new job in Australia and wouldn't want to spend time on discography." "No, no, I'll be happy to do that." So from 1970 onward I took over.

The first edition in 1964 was actually by Dixon and Godrich, but that was by alphabetical order. Then the second in 1969 was by Godrich and Dixon, because he did most of it. We brought another one about 1982—that was also done by Storyville—and that was by Dixon and Godrich. You see, people were sending in information all the time, but you have to be careful, because some people can't read labels properly. They think it's a take number, but it's not a take number; it's some other sort of number. But we would know from experience with the records. And aural identifications always are a bit iffy; it's very good to have this information, but you have to put it with other things as well. Plus we added information on the Library of Congress records made by John Lomax and people like that, going around the South. These were not for commercial issue. Of course many of them have been issued since.

And we also extended the coverage in the third edition to 1943. It started in 1902, because the first genuine recording by an African American group in the African American style that we knew of was then the Dinwiddie Colored Quartet. Then we stopped in 1942, because there was a recording ban. The music styles and the methods of recording changed completely after the war, so we stopped in 1942. But in fact there were some recordings made during the war by nonunion musicians for small companies—gospel singers and things like that—and so we added the stuff in 1943. For the fourth edition we were able to go back to 1890, including details of early cylinders by African American artists.

We were always hoping we'd get it published by a proper commercial publisher. University of Illinois Press approached me when I was there in '69. I said, "Well, we've just got an edition coming out with Storyville Publications in England now. We'll keep you in mind for later on." So when we were planning the third edition a few years later, I wrote but it was very hard to get a reply out of them. I think the person who had talked to me had moved on. We never got an answer out of Illinois. So Storyville published the third edition.

And then for the fourth edition we got Oxford University Press to do it, which was obviously much better from our point of view. By this point John wasn't playing a very active role, but I was still talking to him about everything and showing him everything, and he was giving me ideas and so on. Howard Rye, who's a bit younger than us—John was twelve years older than I, and Howard's about twelve years younger than me. Howard Rye was working for Storyville, and he typed out the whole of the third edition. He's a tremendous jazz expert and he was sort of a co-author, so we invited him to join us as an official co-author for the fourth edition. And then John Godrich died just as it was being planned. He'd approved some changes we were making, but he died in about 1991. He was only about sixty-four.

What we did for the fourth edition—up until then we'd only listed records by black artists for a black audience. We'd missed out on the Tuskegee Institute Singers and the Pace Jubilee Singers and things like that. Doug Seroff, a collector from Nashville, Tennessee, kept on writing and saying, "You've got to put these people in." Doug was persuasive in the extreme and so it seemed a reasonable thing. John wasn't at all happy about it, but he approved of it, and Howard wasn't very happy either. It's just not the sort of music we particularly like ourselves, I suppose, but we got happier about it as time went on. So that was the big addition for the fourth edition.

With the fourth edition you added cross-reference sections in the back of the book. Who was responsible for that?

Do you mean the indexes? Howard Rye was responsible for all of that. We'd always wanted the indexes, but it was Howard's idea and he was prepared to do the work. One criticism people have given me is that we don't give composers for the tunes. Well, if we wanted to do that, we should have done it when we started, I suppose. We do have the composer information for some but not for others. But to do it now would be such a huge job. It would also make the book a lot bigger, but I agree in principle it should be done.

How many copies—all four editions totaled—has the book sold to this point?

I can tell you because obviously we like to document ourselves. If you look in the introduction to the fourth edition, page xiii, it says it ran to three printings of the first edition, spring and autumn 1964 and then spring 1965. Brian Rust did 500, then he did another 250, and then he did 350, and then the paper masters wouldn't print any more. So the first edition we had 1,100 copies. The second edition was published in the summer of '69, and there were 2,000 copies altogether. The third edition was published in 1982 with an initial printing of 1,500 copies, then another 500 copies. So we had 1,100 for the first edition; 2,000 for the second edition; and 2,000 for the third. And Oxford University Press for the fourth edition, they did 1,334 copies in 1997, and then they did a reprint of another 400 two years later. Altogether they did less than 2,000.

The music books editor of Oxford University Press, Bruce Phillips, agreed with us that the book should be kept in print forever. It doesn't sell a huge number, but it does have a steady sale. But Oxford University Press [OUP], a few years ago, wrote and said, "Your book sold quite well, but it's going to be out of print now." Now, this was just the same time that Tony Russell's *Country Music Discography* was being published by OUP New York. It seemed funny; his is sort of based upon ours in some way, the whole way of doing it with cross-references.

By this time Bruce Phillips had retired and all music books were being done through OUP in New York, not through the home office in Oxford. But the New York office agreed they would reprint it, so now it comes from them. Howard Rye gets very annoyed about this. It's almost impossible to buy a copy. People often try to buy it and are told it's not available. They sell about thirty copies a year, so it's available *somehow* from OUP New York.

There's one very important difference between Brian Rust's *Jazz Records* and our *Blues and Gospel Records:* Brian Rust lists everything which he identifies as being a jazz performance, whether by a black performer or a white performer. Whereas in *Blues and Gospel Records* we only include records made by African Americans. There were a few records issued by white performers in the race series. One of the things we've done over the years is to try and establish whether these performers were black or white. There were quite a few black performers with records issued in the hillbilly series as well. We've tried to identify any record in the race series which was by a white person and eliminate those. And it's interesting how I only thought this through a couple of years ago: we were absolutely color conscience, whereas Brian Rust wasn't—he was just a connoisseur of music.

If we have a fifth edition—and we'd like to do that, though it's difficult to know how to do that now—it might have to be electronic, the way the world is going. I've suggested to Howard Rye that we should actually include all the details for all the records that were marketed as if they were by African American artists though they weren't by African American artists.

All the copies of *Blues and Gospel Records* seem to be hardcover. Were there ever any paperback copies printed?

One interesting thing which I wanted to mention: there used to be a thing called *Books in Print* published by Bowkers in New York. I was looking through it once. I've written quite a number of books on linguistics. You can get a bit depressed. You look and see that only half your books are still in print. I suddenly saw there was a *Blues and Gospel Records* published by somebody called Scholarly. It was obviously a pirated issue. This was seventy-five dollars, and at the time we were selling the third edition for thirty-five dollars, something like that. When I looked in the index for *Books in Print* there were four companies whose name began with Scholarly. I wrote to all four of them. Three wrote back saying, "No, it wasn't ours." It was obviously the fourth one, and they had pirated the first edition—Brian Rust forgot to put a copyright notice on the first edition.

So I wrote to *Books in Print* and said, "Do you realize you're including something on a book that while not officially illegal is completely immoral?" And it was the first edition, which was way out of date. Seventy-five dollars for the first edition when you could buy the third edition for thirty-five dollars. The people were actually called Scholarly Press, Saint [Claire] Shores, Michigan, USA. Bowkers wrote to them and they said, "Well, we haven't actually done anything that's wrong—we haven't broken any laws." But it was withdrawn very soon after that.

But it never has been in paperback. It's interesting that Oxford University Press are going to be issuing a paperback edition of Tony Russell's *Country Music,* because there's a lot of demand from universities for courses on country music. These books are so big that a paperback edition would hardly be wieldy. You really need proper binding for it. But nobody's ever talked about a paperback edition of ours.

It's interesting that all the discographies on American music have all been done entirely by foreigners—and in their spare time. For the first great discography of jazz in the thirties was by a Frenchman named Charles Delaunay, and then there was *The Jazz Discography* [*Directory*] by Albert McCarthy and Dave Carey—and Tony Russell, who's from Oxford like Harold Rye and myself. And quite a lot of people in American universities. They have big grants to do this sort of thing, and university salaries, and produce very little, while we do it in our spare time.

Didn't you and John collaborate on another book, *Recording the Blues*?

We certainly did. Paul Oliver organized a series of twelve blues paperbacks, published by Studio Vista in English. Stein and Day in New York also published the first four, then said they wouldn't do any more. Ours was number four, in 1970. It tells of how the recording companies operated and the artists whose work they captured for posterity.

I wrote the first draft of all of this except for the few pages on Gennett, which John did. But we shared the meager fee equally, as we always did no matter how much each of us had done. Paul read the draft and said it was a bit wooden. So I went through and souped the whole thing up, quoted some song verses, and rewrote bits, so that Paul said it now spun along. There were fifty-four illustrations—of singers, record labels, contemporary advertisements, extracts from catalogs, and the like.

In 2001 Paul got Cambridge University Press to reissue three of the blues paperbacks in one volume, called *Yonder Come the Blues*. He wanted them republished without change, each author just adding an updating postscript—Howard Rye did one for us. Only twenty of the original illustrations were used, and some of these were put in the wrong place. I said that I'd like to rewrite some bits, improve them, I can write better now than I did then. But it wasn't allowed. Still it's good to have it back in print.

Robert Dixon and Rosie Runaway. Courtesy Robert M. W. Dixon.

Besides discography my main job is as a professor of linguistics. I've worked on the languages from northeast Queensland in Australia. Those languages I was working on in the sixties, seventies, and eighties—I was working on five languages—four of them are extinct, the last speakers are gone, and the other just has two or three speakers. But the people are very interested to revive the languages from the materials which I got from their fathers and grandfathers. I mean they weren't at all interested then. I also lived in a monolingual village in Fiji in the eighties and worked in language and grammar there. I've also had about seven field trips to Brazil, working on a language from the middle of the Amazonian jungle, Jarawara. I've also published quite a lot of books on linguistic theory. I'm just about to complete a scholarly autobiography called *I Am a Linguist*, by Brill in the Netherlands. [It was published in 2011.] Chapter 4 of that is on discography, about the principles of discography, and a lot more besides. I also point out how it ties in to my other interests as well. My life is not just separate compartments. Some of the things I've done in linguistics I've used some of the principles that I developed in discography and applied them to other fields as well. They all interrelate.

How many linguistic books have you authored at this point?

I've probably written about twenty books, I think. I've got a three-volume book called *Basic Linguistic Theory*, the first two volumes of which have just been published; I'm now writing the third volume [published in 2012 by Oxford University Press]. This is described by the publisher John Davey of Oxford University Press as "The triumphant outcome of a lifetime's thinking about every aspect and manifestation of language and immersion in linguistic fieldwork." Earlier I wrote a book called *Searching for Aboriginal Languages: Memoirs of a Fieldworker*, published in Australia in 1984 and then put out by the University of Chicago Press in 1989. And also in the eighties I had two novels published under the nom de plume of Hosanna Brown, called *I Spy, You Die* and *Death upon a Spear*.

I'm surprised that you still have a hands-on involvement with the discography, considering all the linguistic activity you have going on.

The discography has always been one of the loves of my life, something to be proud of. I'll never turn my back on it. In the seventies, and eighties, and nineties lots of people sent in corrections and additions on a regular basis. I put all these letters in a file, and about every five or six months I deal with them all. I'd write and say, "Thank you very much!" People know they'll get a reply from me, but in about six months' time. I'd spend the evenings for a few weeks doing it, and then wait another six months and do it again. We have far fewer of these additions since the fourth edition. It's never complete, but with the fourth edition we got quite close. Really the corrections are mostly minor now—punctuations on the labels and things like that.

BOB KOESTER INTERVIEW

When and where were you born?

October 30th, 1932, in Wichita, Kansas. There was my mom and dad, and I was one of five brothers.

Was there music in your family background?

We bought—sometime prior to December 7th, 1941; everybody remembers where they were on December seventh—we bought a house from my grandmother on Douglas Avenue, a big house! Grandpa Koester had died back in the mid-1930s and had left behind—aside from a lot of wine-making apparatus, which I didn't appreciate at the time—a stack of old 78s. There was one by the Georgians—a pretty mediocre white jazz group—and one by the O.D.J.B. [Original Dixieland Jazz Band]; and those kind of spoke to me. Later, in sixth grade I had polio. I was in a polio ward, and I didn't get to hear *This Is Jazz*, the Rudi Blesh show, but I did get to hear Eddie Condon's *Jam Session* Saturday afternoon show for a while before they took it off the air locally. There was an old wind-up phonograph—this is one of those wind-up phonograph stories—but right after the war Dad got a Philco, one of these terrible Philco radio/phono combos where you open a door and *slide the record in,* so that it gets scratched up. I think Philco had decided to go into the record business around that time. [*laughs*]. It never happened.

Bob Koester on the floor of the Jazz Record Mart. Courtesy Bob Koester.

Having learned to like jazz, I started going around jukebox operators. And we had a wonderful store there, the Record Shop, owned by a guy named Irving Albert.

And he'd bought a jukebox operator's stack—somewhere in Kansas—and swapped a lot of the blues records with Rols [record store] here in Chicago, where Rose and, later, Tower was on Wabash. In his store there was this one area with all these fascinating names: Big Bill Broonzy, Tampa Red, Memphis Minnie—I remember she had a stack. I was getting into jazz and I discovered you couldn't get anything much from the 1920s and 1930s. And I liked the early stuff; I hadn't yet gotten my head into bebop. To me it was all the same thing, whether it was Sister Rosetta Tharpe, or Big Bill, or Louis Armstrong. To me it was all part of the same music. I still firmly believe that, and I wonder about people whose focus is a little narrower than that.

I met a couple of black jukebox operators and bought stuff from them and got my first Robert [Johnson]—six dollars for a hundred. I believe the Robert had been under water. But that really expanded me into blues. That's while I was still in Wichita, still in high school. I soon discovered a little racket. Glenn Miller's wife, Mrs. Miller, was not, I think, beloved of RCA. I think they had twenty sides out of the hundreds he made. And there were a lot of people who wanted Miller records, yet they were common in the secondhand stores or jukebox operators if you knew where to get them. So I did my first commercial thing; that was in my last year of high school. I ran an ad in a magazine called *Record Exchange* up in Canada, which specialized in Glenn Miller. I sold six of them, but that was enough—the ad was cheap!

So when I went to college I continued increasing my collection. I had, by that time, about three thousand records, and I'd say slightly under a thousand of them were blues records, because no one wanted blues records. You could pick them up. They were left behind by the collectors in secondhand stores. I remember going to one. It was a funny little store, a secondhand store a guy had, but he had apparently bought a jukebox stock, I think he said, from Oklahoma. And he was selling those records. He said, "Oh, you don't want to hear those. Those are nigger records!" And I saw the sign "Race Records," and I said, "Well, let me take a look at them anyway." And that was mostly what I bought. He had Peetie Wheatstraws and Big Bills [*laughs*] and all the good stuff. I've always been very fond of the late 1930s, early 1940s period in blues. I think it's vastly underappreciated and under-reissued!

Which of the names struck you? I'm trying to recapture the romance of that earlier period.

Well, you and I have always had a difference of opinion about Tampa Red, but I'm beginning to come around. The guy I liked was Big Bill, and I didn't know for years that was Broonzy. But I also was very fond of Blind Boy Fuller. I just picked up anything I didn't have, and if I had it I'd pick it up for trade. My early sales list when I started the Blue Note Record Shop in St. Louis, you'd see me selling E-plus Peeties for fifty cents, because some of those were things I'd bought in Wichita. Others I got in St. Louis.

It seems to me that Big Bill is mainstream, the median line compared to many others that were out there.

Bill picked up ideas from everybody. Yeah, that was pretty much him. To me, when I realized he was writing these songs, and then was writing Jazz Gillum's songs and Washboard Sam's songs—I've got a lot of respect for him as a writer. I divide blues artists into players and writers—singers, players, and writers. Some guys are good at all three. Most of them don't write that much. Sykes, Peetie, Walter Davis, Leroy Carr were very prolific. If we get an artist at Delmark and he's short on repertoire, that's where we start—Leroy Carr, Broonzy, Sykes, or Walter Davis.

Did you go to school with your record collection?

That was a problem. When I got out of high school, I had every design to be a cinematographer. But having been a little bit entrepreneurial, I thought I might end up a producer or director. I'd had the Kool-Aid stand, I'd almost had a paper route and sold greeting cards door-to-door and all that stuff, which is what got me into the film thing. I got an Excel toy projector and that bit me. I really wanted to be a filmmaker. But I decided I should get some business school first.

Wait, where did the film thing come in as opposed to the music?

Well, the film thing goes back, way back. I was always fascinated with film—the Saturday morning show and all that. I don't know when I started picking up at the local camera shop *American Cinematographer,* which is put out by the American Society of Cinematographers, and getting into it. I got a movie camera when I was in high school. That was really my first love; that's what I wanted to do. I had an old Victor movie camera, a sixteen millimeter. The only gig I got, my father was involved with the Kansas Geological Society, and I would go on field trips and take pictures of outcroppings and guys tromping around in their boots and stuff. I just really had the bug. So I was going to go to business school first. My parents insisted I go to a Jesuit college; we were an ardent Catholic family. I figured, "Well, if I go to Loyola in New Orleans or Loyola in Chicago, I'm going to get seduced by the music." And the only other Jezzie school was St. Louis University, where the first band I recorded, the Windy City Six, played a block north, where Tab Smith played a half-block east. And two more blocks is Charlie Thompson, the last ragtime guy, a 1916 contest winner from the Booker Washington Theatre. And a few steps from there, the Peacock. It was a black jazz club where people like Bird and Billie and Johnny Hodges would play. So I got seduced by the music when I was in St. Louis.

Add to that the fact that at that time St. Louis was a blues town on a level almost to rival Chicago . . .

I barely knew that. I was pretty sure Peetie was from there. I don't think I was aware of [the area in St. Louis called] Deep Morgan, which became Delmar, but I knew that some of those Paramount artists were from St. Louis. I may have known about Walter Davis; I don't think so, though . . . I don't think he mentioned St. Louis town in any of the records I had. But I learned that pretty quickly. Walter cut his last records for Victor within my first year or two there. I went there in the fall of 1951, and I left in the fall of 1958. I went to a meeting of the St. Louis Jazz Club, which decided not to try to cover both modern and trad because of the arguments people would have. Bebop wars were on in those days.

Bob Koester and George Spinks with dates. Courtesy Bob Koester.

And I met several people who influenced my life greatly: Vivian Oswald, who was the secretary, and her husband, Bob Oswald, and we have a Barrelhouse Buck McFarland record that he recorded in his home studio in his basement. We used his studio for quite a few of our sessions when I later started the label. I met Charlie O'Brien, who discovered all the blues guys. I met George Hocutt, who later was a distributor of Delmark Records. George and his friends used to smuggle me in to the clubs when I was underage. They used to surround me and we'd all go in. [*laughs*] They wouldn't even ask my age, because I wasn't good at all at faking it. I didn't even like to drink. I'd buy one beer and make it last three or four sets. It was pretty inexpensive that way, particularly since most clubs didn't even have a door charge. I once went to see Miles Davis and saw two sets for one fifty-cent beer. [*laughs*]

The blues people that you were listening to—and who came out of St. Louis—at this point did you realize that they came from St. Louis?

References in the songs was all I had. Of course I thought St. Louis Jimmy might have been from there. [*laughs*] I figured that out!

Well, that seems like a much later development as researchers went around and established all the blues strongholds. Your generation was listening and knew what they liked, but at this point did they necessarily associate styles with particular schools of blues?

I sort of figured out that Eddie Miller was from the St. Louis school, because I had an Eddie Miller record and he sounded like the St. Louis guys. That whole Jimmy Yancey thing did come from Doug Suggs, who apparently was from St. Louis, so if they had that Yancey thing, I figured they might be from St. Louis. But I never suspected . . . I had "Down on the Levee" by Speckled Red, but I didn't know about "Boots' Place" being in St. Louis. I had "Third Street Going Down" by Peetie, and I figured that was by the levee—you know, black bars on the levee. I first began to learn more and more about the St. Louis blues scene when Charlie O'Brien, who'd been a uniformed cop—incidentally he'd been on the beat at the Pin-Up Lounge, where the Windy City Six played. That was the first trad band I recorded. He later made lieutenant, plainclothes. Charlie's parents were both killed in holdups—two separate holdups—and he was raised in an orphan's home. And he had this veneration for older people, which worked very well for him when he was working his job in the ghetto and he wanted to look up old jazz musicians who'd played around St. Louis.

St. Louis detective and blues researcher Charlie O'Brien. Courtesy Mike Rowe.

Well, the jazz club had done a pretty good job of locating most of those guys. The jazz guys would be in the musicians union, and the vice president of the union was on our board, Elijah Shaw—a drummer but a great musician. So I suggested that he look for blues artists. We knew that Edith Johnson owned a restaurant somewhere. We heard that Virginia Liston lived there. We never turned up anything about her. So I gave Charlie a list of artists that I thought were from there: Ike and Henry Brown, and Edith and Mary Johnson, and Alice Moore. And the ones that were still alive he found, and he found others. And Mary Johnson happened to mention, "Oh, you're looking for old blues artists. I saw Speckled Red the other day." And that's how Red turned up. Charlie brought Speckled Red up to my little old second-floor store, Blue Note Record Shop, at Delmar and DeBaliviere, and we went down to a nearby tavern where he played some piano, and I thought, "God, I didn't think I'd ever hear this kind of piano live!" Raggedy, pre-Sykesian piano.

To me Sykes is the guy who codified blues piano [*laughs*] forever after. Through him to Otis Spann and then to countless white and European guys, I guess. [*laughs*] Red just fascinated me, and I had to record him! And of course several of his sides were still in print. Well, actually they'd just been deleted on the Brunswick label when the ten-inch LPs went out in 1955. But it seems to me when I saw him they were still in print. I don't know when Charlie brought him out—1955 or '56 was the deletion time for ten-inch LPs.

Wasn't there a situation with Brunswick where in order to renew the copyright they had to press them again? And so they went with vinyl and pressed twenty or twenty-five records?

No, that's the Champion story. They pressed 175 or 200 of the Freddie Shayne Champion record and shipped that out to their branches. Doug Jugstra—Doug Lee, he calls himself sometimes—worked for Decca in Kansas City, and he saw them in a warehouse. So he contacted all the branches and said, "Hey, send me all these records!" They never made any attempt to merchandize them; that was to maintain the Champion trademark. And these were flex records. They were not easy to break. Paul Garon wound up with them when he bought Doug's collection.

I wanted to ask you about Speckled Red. Was he from St. Louis or Atlanta?

He grew up outside of Atlanta, and as I recall, there was a lynching and a burning of the body in whatever the small town was—it may be in a liner note somewhere—and so the family moved to Atlanta. And then he went on the road playing piano. We know he recorded in Chicago and Memphis and apparently wound up in St. Louis in the very early 1930s, possibly immediately after Memphis. Red actually used to talk about working in sporting houses: "I was just in the whorehouse to make a little noise for the people, make them know there's a party going on!" He knew musicians that had never recorded—James Hemmingway is one that comes to mind. When I played him a Charlie Spand record, he said, "Well, that sounds like . . ." And he gave some nickname; he'd never learned the guy's name. And of course his eyesight was very bad, so showing him pictures didn't help. He had these nicknames, and it doesn't much matter, because none of them had ever appeared on record. But he had one guy—"Dad"? I think it was Dad—Dad was the first guy he learned from. Red had a tune called "Dad's Piece." I think it came out on the *Primitive Piano* record reissued on the Sirens label and recorded at the same session as the Delmark Speckled Red.

Red was a fascinating guy, and the thing I really regret about all the Speckled Red sessions was some idiot would bring a bottle of booze. Once it was the guy who went down to get him and gave him a bottle, and by the time he got to the session, he was—because Red could not play well when he was boozed up—and, I think, could not handle very much booze. He was an albino, and I think there was something about his system, perhaps diabetes or something, but it didn't take him long to get there. He was very economical. He'd say, "They'll buy you drinks all night, but nobody will buy you a sandwich." [*laughs*]

Tell me about Edith Johnson.

Edith was the first—and easiest—person to discover. Edith and Jesse, her late husband, had operated the Deluxe Record Shop, and if you bought a race record that had been purchased in St. Louis, it darn near always has a Deluxe Record Shop sticker on it. Charlie put two and two together—or heard somewhere—that the Deluxe Restaurant and the Deluxe Taxi Cab Company were both owned by Edith Johnson. So he walks in, and up over the bar is this picture of Jesse Johnson, and that's how he met Edith. And Edith told him about Mary and mentioned Walter Davis—and who else?

Jesse had died during the Depression. Jesse once promoted a concert of Duke Ellington, McKinney's Cotton Pickers, and Fletcher Henderson at the Booker Washington Theatre, which he promoted by dropping leaflets from an airplane around the corner of Market and Sixteenth Street—and had lost quite a bit of money during the Depression. The closing of his record shop and the Depression seemed to have worked on his mind, and I've had several people tell me stories of Jesse standing at the corner of Sixteenth and Market Street, handing out dollar bills to people, liquidating all his assets, but somehow he held on to the cab company and the restaurant and Edith was still operating it. You'd walk in and she'd be back there slinging hash—and the thing was, she had a gig at city hall! It was a secretarial job of some sort, but she would go to the restaurant on her lunch hour and be a restaurateur—and actually waitress/manager—and then she'd go back to her job. And then in the evening she'd be there in time for dinner.

That was quite a block, because just off of Market and Jefferson—if you walked out of her restaurant and turned left, you'd go into Market Street, and catty-cornered from there was the Booker Washington Theatre, or the vacant lot where it had been. If you went up to the corner on the right, her brother-in-law, Stump Johnson, had a shoeshine parlor. Then across the street from that was the Grand Central Hotel, and the desk clerk on at least one shift was Henry Townsend. I had his Columbia record! I never could find any of the other ones. I ran into Henry when Roosevelt Sykes came into town. I was told by a jazz researcher in New Orleans that Roosevelt Sykes had just played New Orleans and was coming to Chicago. So I picked up the *St. Louis Argus,* the black newspaper, and there's that classic photo of Roosevelt Sykes adjusting his tie. That's a great shot. I don't think that's ever been used on [a] record cover! So I went down to see Roosevelt, and his guitar player was Henry Townsend.

Another experience was finally deciding—the Calumet Hotel, where Walter Davis worked, was only two blocks from one of the record wholesalers. So I decided that before I go to the wholesaler, I'll go see Walter Davis. I walked up to the counter, and I said, "Pardon me, sir. Are you Walter Davis?" And he said, "No, I'm not Walter Davis. That's Walter there by the door." So I walk to the door—"Walter Davis?" He turned and said, "Yeah?" I said, "You don't know me. I'm Bob Koester and I love your records. I just wanted to meet you." And he said, "Oh, here—meet Robert Nighthawk!" I had the Nighthawk States record ["The Moon Is Rising"], but I hadn't listened to it yet. It was one of them *new* records—I didn't think I'd like it.

I had Robert Lee McCoy on Bluebird, and I knew that Robert Lee McCoy was a guitarist on Speckled Red Bluebirds. I had Peetie's Buddy or something like that on Decca, with Robert L. McCoy. And I had Ann Sortier, but I didn't know that was Robert Nighthawk. And I wasn't all that crazy about Robert McCoy's playing on some of those records. I thought it was a little too jazz-oriented, sort of like George Barnes on those Broonzy records—great stuff, but it didn't always fit in.

Another thing that happened—and this happened several years earlier—when my first shop was on Laclede, just a door east of Grand; that would have been mid-1953. A kid walks by, playing harp. I think that was the first blues harp I'd ever heard. I said, "Hey! What's your name?" "Malcolm Simmons." "Do you play at a club anywhere?" And he said, "Yeah, I play at the Polka Dot Inn in East St. Louis." Well, I didn't have a car, and I'm not going to go to East St. Louis anywhere except Collinsville Avenue, where the mob had a couple of clubs. [*laughs*] I'm not going to East St. Louis without a car, so I never went. But he was working with Robert Nighthawk at the Polka Dot Inn. That was the first I heard about any live blues bands.

The first band was not in St. Louis but in East St. Louis. We're on our way—the Dixie Stompers—on our way to an afterhours jam in East St. Louis. St. Louis closed down on Saturday night at midnight. There's two Catholic ideas about the Sabbath. French Jansenists would say, "Keep holy the Sabbath; close the bars at midnight." In Chicago it's the much more enlightened view [*in an Irish brogue*]: "Aww, sure, it's Saturday night. Let the lads stay open an extra hour!" [*laughs*] But it was good business for East St. Louis that they did that, because the clubs could open in East St. Louis and pick up some slack.

So we were on our way to a jam and I had to stop for directions. I stopped at a place that looked like it had been a gas station with a house. So I walk in and there's an old bar, with a crap game going beyond the bar. I ask directions but I hear music coming from upstairs. It's "One-Arm" John Wrencher as a sideman with James DuShay's String Wizards. That was the first blues band I heard—it was pretty good! I remember they had a little kid—he looked like he was twelve years old—playing this piano. In between sets I checked it out, and half the keys did not work; a third of them weren't even there. And this kid was able to make music on this. And the drummer—well, it took me a long time to like drummers, and amplified guitars. I wanted to hear the down-home stuff. But that was the first blues I heard. I followed those guys around to places on Biddle Street and different places.

What about the business end of your music endeavors?

Such as they were! I first had the Blue Note Record Shop. I opened at Laclede and Grand. Maybe it was an omen or something, but it had been the Pig Pen Inn barbecue stand. When we moved in, the line of demarcation between the ghetto and the white area moved—unfortunately, it regressed a little bit—about twenty feet and the place was tiny. It was three hundred square feet at the most. I had done business out of my dormitory as K and F Sales. I met this guy Ron Fiester. Ron collected music from the late 1930s, and we'd argue about who got to keep the Billie and Duke 78s. Anything else would be, "Aw, let him have it if he wants it." He wanted to turn it into a commercial record shop. I then learned for sure that Walter Davis was still alive. Ron worked at the Victor distributor there—Interstate Appliance Supply. He was pretty active in the record department there, and Walter Davis came in to buy his new record. He made those last four sides for Victor. I think that was the first time I learned that Walter Davis was a St. Louis guy. It took me a long time to go and see him, because word was that he was with the church now and wasn't much interested in doing blues. Of course there was no white audience for blues.

We moved after the first year at Laclede to Delmar and DeBaliviere, and I stayed there—at two different locations—until I left St. Louis. Eventually we moved into an artist's studio, and we found a piano for the hauling. This was walk-up retail; we were on the second floor. I only sold traditional jazz and big band, because my friends Harry Morrison and Ken Schitzmeyer had a shop called Modern Music in St. Louis, and they had the money for the inventory. I didn't have the bread. Dad—in the early days, until my younger brother, Ed, went to school a year later—gave me an allowance of a hundred dollars every month. Dad had paid the dorm rent and the tuition and the books. So I had a hundred dollars a month to live on.

I later worked as a busboy in Garavelli's Restaurant, which is, sadly, gone. [*laughs*] It was around the corner from the campus. I would get two twenty-five-cent tips for a two-

and-a-half-hour gig—and two meals. So I didn't need the hundred dollars. I would buy records with the hundred dollars, and then on the second Monday of the month I would go to the St. Louis Jazz Club meeting, and I was selling records you couldn't get anywhere else in St. Louis because they weren't distributed locally. I would sell records there and keep a few bucks. That's how I built up the thing. If you find a Glenn Miller in a salvage store for ten cents and sell it for $1.25, that's a pretty good margin.

Were your clientele black or white?

Mostly white, because blacks could not get into most of the Dixieland clubs. I've been asked on several occasions, "How come black people don't like Dixieland?" "Because you wouldn't let them in!" [*laughs*] "You kept them out of the clubs!" We'd occasionally get black customers, but not often. I remember one lady came in and she wanted to use the bathroom.

Right across from the Laclede store was a great big rolling lot, and every year the Royal American Shows traveling carnival would occupy it for several weeks—always around exam time. I guess it was around the early spring. I remember once hearing a really good trumpet, but I had to get my term paper done, so I didn't go see him. And the next day they were gone. It turns out that was Punch Miller; since he's on Broonzy records it's okay to mention him here. So this black lady came in from the Royal American, and she's like, "Wow, a white man is letting me use his john!"

And was I rewarded for my bravery in allowing this mixture of the races in my store. [*laughs*], because she said, "I see you like those old records. I've got a lot of those. Would you like them?" She wanted to give them to me, and she was thrilled when I gave her pretty good money for them: King Olivers, some Jelly Roll Mortons, and a bunch of Ma Rainey Paramounts—four of them! You remember a strike like that! So I said, "If any of your friends . . ." And she later had a friend call me up, and that was nice. Charlie O'Brien, once in a while, would find records. When he was in a black home, if he was there on friendly duty he would bring up the subject: "Got any old records?" I don't think, to his credit, he said, "You better sell 'em to me, because I'm a cop!" We didn't have the kind of corruption in St. Louis we have here.

Did you manage to graduate?

No, I was asked not to return for a fourth year.

So you missed Punch Miller and still didn't get a degree?

Yeah. [*laughs*] Well, my accounting grade tells the whole story: A, B, B, C, D, F! And they just said, "We don't think you're very serious." My next worry was the draft; Korea was still on—the draft was on anyway. I remember standing in this enormous gym [*laughs*] with three thousand naked guys jumping up and down. The most ridiculous thing I've ever seen. I'd had rheumatic fever in high school, and the doctor said, "Any history of rheumatic fever?" "Yes." He gave me the benefit of the doubt. He wasn't sure he heard anything. With all the noise I don't know how he heard anything.

By that time I had recorded four or five LPs—maybe six? So I decided I'd try and make this serious. I'd been publishing a thing called *Jazz Report* since about 1953. I got help from the St. Louis Jazz Club, because we'd incorporate their monthly meeting notice and they would pay for the mailing, because it cost them to mail it anyway. Eventually I started listing records in it—78s. We ran articles and stuff like that. Of course we had ads for Delmar Records; we named it after Delmar Boulevard. I always thought if we had a budget label we could name it Morgan. [*laughs*]

Our store did seven or eight or nine hundred dollars' mail order each month and one, two, or three hundred dollars' local business. It was a tiny, tiny business, a very limited area. Although I did always carry three modern jazz records that you could not get anywhere else in St. Louis, because they were distributed out of Chicago, not St. Louis. One was *Jazz at Massey Hall*—essential Bird and Diz with Bud Powell, Mingus, and Max Roach. It was always there. Another that was always there—mainly because I couldn't sell it—was "Sun Song" by Sun Ra. I stocked it on the Transition label but later bought the master for Delmark. That might have been one of the reasons I went to Chicago. I said, "Anything this strange, I want to be around it!" I never heard Sun Ra in the flesh until after he left Chicago.

Anyway, it was a pretty rough existence. I would go home in the summer, it would be so hot and sweaty in St. Louis that you couldn't sell records. Air conditioners for homes and small business places were just coming in; in fact, the record distributors would sell them during those lean summer months. I would go back to Wichita and work. I remember one summer I worked in a typewriter shop; I'm pretty good at taking apart an old Underwood. Another year I worked at McCormack Reaper as an inventory clerk. Then I decided to stay in St. Louis; so I was a parking lot attendant—until the boss went on vacation and his son fired me so he could hire one of his buddies. I wasn't a very good parking attendant. [*laughs*] I didn't know how to handle a car that didn't have a gearshift! [*laughs*] I guess it's good I got out of there before I wrecked somebody's transmission!

I was later a waiter. The Dixie Stompers got a gig at a bar in the South St. Louis area called Jackovack's, right next to the Scullin Steel mill. This wasn't a nightclub area at all, but this Nick Jackovack was a brach, tambour, and bass player in a tamburitza band. He had this bar and had a little banquet room in the back. We would take over the room and collect a dollar at the door, and I and my friend John Wilhoft would wait tables. We got a split of the door money with the band, and we made more money than the band did, because we got tips too. But I got busted there one night when John couldn't make it [*laughs*] and I was trying to handle all these tables, and three kids showed us phony IDs. And then when the cops came, they showed them their real IDs and I got busted. I spent the night in jail—a $250 fine and a criminal record! I hope it's been expunged—I don't know! [*laughs*]

When did your recording activity start?

I knew very well the history of jazz record businesses starting with labels like Session and Dial and Commodore and Keynote—even Prestige—coming out of record stores—and Riverside coming out of the mail-order business. So it just seemed as though, "If I'm gonna stay in this, this would be a good place to go." And I think subconsciously I must have known. I started the store per se in 1952 and did the first record date in 1953, and that was the band at the Pin-Up Room over on Olive just off of Grand Avenue. By the time I got to doing it, the band had moved to the Windemere Club at Delmar and DeBaliviere and was being fronted by the clarinet player who had been working there—by the way, with a mixed band. It had been an all-black band, except for him.

The pianist had been Chester Lane, who left town to go with Louis Jordan. That was Joe Smith's band, a black Dixieland band. Originally a clarinet player named Norman Mason, who's on the Fate Marable record and the Jelly Roll Morton Gennett session (and one of our Dixie Stompers albums), but Sammy was brought in to front the thing when Norman decided he didn't want to work six nights a week. So it wasn't quite the band I wanted to record, but it was still good enough to record, and the band wanted to have records to sell. So we recorded them in Bob Oswald's basement, which, unfortunately, had kind of a dead sound; he didn't believe in reverberation. [*laughs*] I put the record out—and did a very amateurish job. I printed the covers on glued paper and ruined a lot of jackets, because they'd wrinkle up. The paper really wasn't thick enough. We pressed about 487 of those.

What format did you record in back in those days?

It was a Concert-tone tape recorder at 15 i.p.s. [inches per second]. In mono, one mic—one *good* mic. And we arranged the guys according to sound levels; that's how you balance the band. It was on two reels. We lost that master. These were ten-inch LPs—red vinyl—pressed by Research Craft in Los Angeles. I was just like a little kid waiting for Christmas. [*laughs*] And then we recorded Sid Dawson; that would be in 1954. Sid Dawson's Riverboat Ramblers. Sid was a trombonist. He had played the Barrel [in St. Louis] with Dewey Jackson and Don Ewell, who are also on Delmark now. He was very active during the trad revival in St. Louis of the 1940s and early 1950s. He moved to Chicago, found a backer, and put a band together. Unfortunately, I didn't catch his first band, because he had this wonderful clarinetist, this great trad clarinetist—sort of like Edmund Hall. Bob Schraeder. I wish I knew where he was now. [*laughs*] I'd make him learn to play again and record him!

With the second band he couldn't afford that many sidemen. He was backed by Ish Kabibble [a comedy singer and musician with Kay Kyser's Orchestra]. We did that one, and then I met a guy named John Chapman at a George Lewis concert in 1953. He wanted to put a band together to play that kind of music. We sort of helped form the band called the Dixie Stompers. That's the closest I ever came to any kind of talent management or anything serious like that. We ultimately did two ten-inches and then a twelve-inch LP, and in recent years we've done two CDs with a reunion of the group. I was going to put out—it seems to me we listed a ten-inch LP by Speckled Red and another by Big Joe Williams, *Piney Woods Blues* and *Dirty Dozens*. But I just wasn't able to get it done by 1955 or '56, whenever it was—what I call the "ten-inch crash."

I was not in touch with industry trends; I always felt that there was no point in reading *Billboard*, because it was irrelevant. Had I watched *Billboard* I would have realized that companies were going to—virtually over a weekend—get out of the ten-inch LP business.

I remember I went down to the Columbia distributors and paid a $1.90 for some Columbia ten-inch LPs—they sold for about $3.00 then. The next night I bought the Sunday papers, and there's this double-truck ad: "Entire catalog of Columbia Records ten-inch LPs at $1.49!" [*laughs*] I stormed into Columbia on Monday, and they said, "Oh, you can buy anything you want for a dollar." But almost all the inventory was over at Sticks, Baer, and Fuller, a St. Louis department store. [*laughs*]

At that point I had had covers printed for an album by Walt Gifford. We had issued one George Lewis record. I bought the George Lewis masters. We had covers printed for the second George Lewis record, the Walt Gifford, and an album called *Motor City Reveille* by Frank Gillis's Dixie Five from Detroit, which we had on lease at the time. And I'd love to say I did the Speckled Red and Big Joe, but I felt those were doomed projects, that trad jazz may not sell very well, but I had investments in these other masters. The only good thing about the blues records was that it didn't cost nearly as much to pay one guy to play—or maybe two, with J. D. Short—but I should get the trad records out and keep my label going. So the Red and the Big Joe were expanded to twelve-inch LPs, and I didn't get those issued until after I moved to Chicago.

Who recorded those? How did they get done—and where?

The Big Joe Williams[es] were recorded in my office, partly—and in John Chapman's living room—and in the living room of either John Harford or his friend Paul Breidenbach, who were bluegrass musicians. Harford later became known as John Hartford and wrote "Gentle on My Mind." You can hear him talking, and he's asking, "Did you know Jimmie Rodgers?" That's John Hartford [*laughs*]—the inside scoop here! The Speckled Red was recorded in the home of a wonderful old guy named John Phillips, who , now that he's gone, I can say is said to have spiked his Manhattans. He made wonderful Manhattans. He got me into Manhattans; he would spike them with absinthe. John had a real appreciation for blues piano. He had all the Andy Boy records. He just thought it was great and he was having the time of his life. He had his piano tuned for us and wouldn't let us pay him anything.

It was my feeling that blues records [were] going to sell so poorly. Bob Oswalt wanted fifteen bucks an hour for his studio. We had several different sessions. We had one at General Insurers, and that's the one where somebody got Red drunk. We did a session at the Dixie Stompers pianist/leader John Chapman's house, but Chapman's piano, you didn't have to hold the sustain pedal down—it sustained anyway. We have issued Speckled Reds made by other guys—at that house, and I would guess someday we'll probably issue the other Reds we have. The thing I regret about Red is that we never recorded his pop song performances. I thought, "That's too commercial." And he did tunes nobody's done for years—"If I Had a Million Dollars, *I know just what I'd do,*" and "Georgia on My Mind"—but also some really obscure stuff! I'm just ashamed of myself that I didn't see that this was something to record. He wasn't just a bluesman; what he played was blues, but he could extend it those extra four bars and learn these other chords. One session was held when Erwin Helfer stopped in St. Louis on his way back from New

Orleans. He had a good mic and a Concertone recorder, and three tracks appeared on his *Primitive Piano* album.

Was it difficult to get him to do the unexpurgated version of "Dirty Dozens"?

It's my recollection that it was at John Phillips's. I'd heard him do that a couple of times. There was a beauty parlor almost across the street from the building Red lived in at Sixteenth and Franklin. One night he was in there—he'd always look around—"There ain't no women around. Okay, I'm gonna play the *real* 'Dirty Dozens'!" So this happened at John Phillips's house. Happily, it was captured on a good piano with a good engineer, with Red in great shape. [*laughs*] It took time to learn how to deal with Red and make sure he stayed dry for a while. Of course when the CD came along, censorship had gone its way to its deserved place, and we were able to issue those two takes and another one—"I Feel So Good," which we thought was just a little too raw for LPs. [*laughs*]

How about the Big Joe Williamses? How did those happen?

Somebody once said I discovered Joe Williams. Well, Joe Williams never really disappeared. At the time I met him, he was making the Vee-Jay records. Joe Williams heard at Joe's Music, the leading shop in the black neighborhood, that there was this crazy guy out at Delmar Boulevard who liked old blues. There was a Joe's in East St. Louis and one in St. Louis. I don't know how the proprietor knew me. He might have met me at a wholesaler's warehouse; in those days you used to go to wholesalers to pick up your records. But he told Joe about me, and Joe showed up one day with an old Columbia brochure with his picture in it to prove that he was *the* real Joe Williams. I wasn't there, but they told him I'd gone to pick up records and that I would be there the next day. So he came in. And there was some more music I never thought I'd hear outside of records! Joe always needed a few bucks and Red always needed a few bucks, and so I kept a little book—ten bucks here or twenty—and that was hard-bought money for me.

How did you decide to record Joe?

Oh, I had to! I made sure he wasn't under contract. Actually he had just done his Vee-Jay session, and we had to wait a while for that option to drop. And that's why we had to wait—I think it was 1957 or '58—until we got into the sessions. When I first met Joe, he invited me to come down and hear him in this real shanty. They were in the older Biddle Street section of the ghetto, along Franklin and Delmar. There were houses that had outhouses behind them, even though they were in the city, and this was one of them. And there was this funny—it looked like it had been a backyard—and somebody had boarded it over. I went down there and Joe had put a band together. A guy named Little Hat on harmonica, Joe's cousin J. D. Short, and Joe on guitar. J. D. also doubled on clarinet—not very well—it was an old E-flat clarinet. And Little Hat just didn't fit in. I always thought it was a shame we didn't just do some solo stuff with him blowing and singing, but he was definitely tetched.

Was Joe playing a nine-string guitar at that point?

Yeah, yeah. It's probably the one that's in the front showcase at Jazz Record Mart.

Any idea when he added those strings?

Well, he added those strings so other people couldn't play the instrument. And he didn't quite understand how it was tuned. You'd ask him, and he just tuned them like he thought they should be tuned. [*laughs*] I don't know enough about the instrument to say anything more, but he didn't want anybody playing his instrument, and that was his way—it made him unique. And sometimes he had ten strings. I think he mentioned that he had ten on the Trumpet label. Maybe he was bragging, but I think one of the records says, "Big Joe Williams and his ten-string guitar." But he was amazed that I had all five of the Columbias, I had three or four Bluebirds, I had the Trumpets.

He claimed he was the Joe Williams on the 1929 Vocalion until I got hip, and then he admitted that was "Jackson Joe" Williams—he was from Jackson. And he claimed he was King Solomon Hill. And because he made these claims—which we didn't believe when he made such idiotic statements such as, "Sleepy John Estes is alive and living in Brownsville, Tennessee"—we didn't believe him. [*laughs*] We found out that damn near everything else he told me was actual fact—total truth! But he lied about those two record sessions, the only times he ever lied to me. He claimed to be Big Joe and His Rhythm on Bluebird. Most of those were Joe McCoy, but there were a couple of sessions where it was someone else. He claimed it was him, but he didn't need to. It was so silly.

When I first met you, you were totally fascinated with him. Did you feel like that when you first met him?

It was a love affair, man—the man was marvelous! When we recorded the Dixie Stompers at Westminster College, it was to my undying regret that I didn't record the intermission music. The first intermission was by Speckled Red; the second intermission was by Big Joe Williams and J. D. Short. With J. D. you had to pay him in front. You could give him some money, and give him some money, and when you finally gave him enough so that he was paid in full, then you could record. With Joe you give him some money, give him some money, do some recording. Then you owe him money. He understands that. [*laughs*] He'll come around and get twenty bucks a week until it's paid for. That's pretty much how it happened.

There were other people I would like to have recorded. Mary Johnson we did in fact record. We issued it on a budget CD of female blues vocalists. We did a session for the Dixie Stompers' second album. It was recorded in a marvelous nightclub. It was called the Yacht Club, and it was a barge anchored in the Mississippi River on the waterfront, and we had Mary come in and do a couple of gospel tunes. This is "Signifyin' Mary," but she had become a gospel singer. But a couple of the guys in the band took the attitude that she should accompany the band [*laughs*] rather than the band should accompany her. So over the years, we did issue the instrumental stuff and one Dixieland vocal. I don't like Dixieland vocals, but you've got to give in once in a while. Mary had recorded for Atlantic, and people said, "That ain't the same lady." But I'm here to tell you it definitely was, because she had acetates of those same four titles. Now, I haven't heard the Atlantic records, but I guarantee that's got to be her. She lived with her mother—she had been Lonnie Johnson's common-law wife—and her mother would never let her forget that she had lived in sin.

Not long before that recording session, I was on the board of the St. Louis Jazz Club and I would get the talent. I'd suggest ideas and they'd okay it; it was just like a rubber stamp. They didn't want to go out and look for stuff; they were too busy listening to records. Some of them lived way out in the country. I lived half a block from the clubs, right on a block with five clubs actually! That's why I was at DeBaliviere and Delmar; I could save bus fare. So we did Speckled Red at the meeting and he got paid. It's not like some of these bars—"Oh, come on down and play for us—we'll buy you a drink. Maybe a sandwich even." Red played one, I think; Joe and J. D. did one. Usually it was a band—they wanted a trad band. Every once in a while you could get away with something else.

I remember once we did four pianos: Charlie Thompson, the ragtime guy; we did Speckled Red; we did George Reynolds, who I never heard at any other point—he was from the ragtime era; and Gus Perryman—no relation to Speckled Red. He was Singleton Palmer's pianist in his Dixieland Six. And there was one other guy—Lawrence Henry. He worked in a funeral home, so he could never work gigs, but he could come out on Monday nights. We've got some tapes on him. He tried to sound like James P. Johnson, only not as good. [*laughs*] So the Dixie Stompers did an St. Louis Jazz Club session with Mary Johnson, and right in the middle of [*sings*] *"Move on up a little higher,"* she goes, *"My man left me!"* [*laughs*] She came down afterward and she was blushing. She said, "Bob Koester, you made me sing the blues! Don't tell my mother!" [*laughs*] I sort of hoped that would happen at the record date, but it didn't. She did a couple of her gospel songs.

How long were you actually in St. Louis? And how/why did you leave?

From 1951 to 1958. I used to make trips to Chicago and visit Bill Russell and John Steiner at Paramount Records on North Ashland. In fact, the first records I ever bought to sell at the St. Louis Jazz Club I bought from Bill and John on Paramount and American Music. I would go up there and he was helping people dispose of record collections, so I would get collectors' items that I could sell for a lot more than what they were dumping them for. I got a letter from John once, saying, "I'm thinking about retirement and will want to dispose of my Paramount properties. I'll help you with financing, but get going, young fellow." I put that letter upside the wall and that was my motto, because I decided if I'm going to run the kind of store I'm going to have, I better be in a bigger market for it.

And the clincher was when the local furniture store started discounting records. None of the stores would discount; there was discounting in Chicago and New York and L.A., but not in the smaller cities. So someone cracked that, and I thought, "If I have to be in a discount market, first I better get on the ground floor, and I'd better be someplace where I can sell some modern jazz." I don't know where in the heck I thought I was going to get the capital, but I actually made quite a bit of money selling those cutout ten-inch LP's. I got back all the cost from all the paper I threw away when the ten-inch LP died, buying up all the inventories of Paramount, American Music, Riverside, Blue Note, Prestige, et

Bob Koester at Seymour's Record Shop, forerunner of his Jazz Record Mart. Courtesy Bob Koester.

cetera, ten-inch LPs for distressed prices and selling them at the regular price. People still wanted them, and they didn't come out overnight on twelve-inch LP, so I made a pretty good buck on that stuff. I remember we got Riverside ten-inchers for fifty cents apiece and sold them for three-eighty-five.

I have always dealt with the "obsolescent" formats, which means I'm doing pretty good with LPs these days. [*laughs*] First it was 78s, then ten-inch LPs, then mono LPs—now just any old LP. That paid my bills and gave me some money. I bought a car. My parents were moving to Turkey, and I had to get the collection out of their house. So I had to make two moves; I had to move my collection up to Chicago, which I had been doing. I went home on the train, bought a 1950 Buick, and came back with the 78s and got it moved. I remember when the ten-inch X Vault label originals came out and Riverside was doing their ten-inch originals, I decided it was folly to have these valuable 78s, so I was selling those off to capitalize myself.

Anyway, I decided to move to Chicago. So John loaned me the money to buy Seymour's Record Mart. I moved in August, and in March I bought Seymour's Record Mart for—I don't think I'd better say, but it wasn't very much. Seymour wanted to promote his records [Seymour and His Heartbeat Trumpet] and get out of the retail business. Most of his inventory was on consignment from a one-stop, so I didn't have to pay for that. I just brought his own stuff. John did that loan and was very patient in waiting; it took me years and years to repay him. What I did was not nice. I was still paying off a partner I had on the label for the first LP, John Gailbraith. So it took me forever to pay the two guys back, bless their hearts. But guys like that really gave me a leg up in the thing. So I moved to Chicago and bought Seymour's.

Where was Seymour's located?

That was at 439 South Wabash—the Auditorium Building—at that time it was just the Roosevelt University Building. I had to move out of there when they refurbished the auditorium. They moved the bookstore over to the Wabash side, so I had to move out. That's when we moved to Seven West Grand. I think I only issued one record while on Wabash; that was the Walt Gifford traditional jazz record. The business at Seymour's was really good for the first six or eight months, and then it slacked off quite a bit. I went on a binge and recorded seven albums—two each with Albert Nicholas and Ira Sullivan. Jimmy Forrest with Grant Green, and one with John Young.

And when we moved over to Grand and State I really had a tough first year. I remember we bought thirteen thousand Prestige 78s for two cents apiece. It was Prestige, United, and States—fifteen thousand with the two added labels. Two cents apiece! That was nice. There were some I just threw away. I got five hundred copies of a Billy Taylor on Prestige. They didn't sell very well. At first I would just throw them in the trash whenever I needed a paper sleeve. [*laughs*] The sleeves might cost more than the pressing. Prior to that, when I was still at Seymour's, I'd bought United Records Distributors' inventory. He just waved his hand at about four or five thousand records and said, "Wanna give me sixty bucks for all that crap?" Trumpets—not very many Sonny Boys—Blue Lakes, Parrots; they were all labels that had gone out of business. But the Prestige and the OKehs and Uniteds were still stuff you had to reckon with the label owners. Prestige, this was the early 1960, the United—they hadn't been pressing anything, but they were getting rid of stock through United Distributors.

Those kinds of things helped out a great deal, but I remember Joe Segal worked for me at Seymour's, and I had to let him go when we moved to State and Grand. Oh, we were moved by some interesting people! Paul Garon had worked in the store, but he had to go back to Louisville for some reason or another. And he had a bad back, so he couldn't help move. But some visitors came looking for blues artists in 1962 when we moved from Wabash to Grand and State. It was Joe Boyd, with Warwick, his brother. Joe later had the Marshmellow label. He set up Elektra Records in England and Riverboat Enterprises, which was a wholesale house in Boston that sold a hell of a lot of Delmarks; they outsold our New York distributor. I never had a distributor in Boston before that. [*laughs*] Also, Geoff Muldaur, who later married Maria. I guess she's still well known for "Midnight at the Oasis." She's an awfully good singer.

I don't think people realize the logistics involved in handling a collection of 78s. If they think of records, they think of LPs. I don't think they have any notion of owning three thousand 78s.

At the Jazz Record Mart we feel we should stay in 78s because I need the exercise. Steiner and I came very close to cutting the Paramount deal. In 1965 we actually designed an album cover called *Louis Armstrong and the Blues*. We were going to feature Ma Rainey and Trixie Smith and Coot Grant and so forth. We delayed printing Junior Wells's *Hoodoo Man* so we could print a two-up [two different covers printed simultaneously] on a big sheet of paper, and then we save money by chopping it up for each album. And I figure we lost some sales on that, but Steiner and I were finally not able to come to grips with it.

The reason we didn't get Paramount was that his license to Riverside Records from the very early 1950s did not have a term, so that license is still in effect. And the Riverside assets

Bob Koester at Jazz Record Mart counter. Courtesy Bob Koester.

were sold eventually to the Fantasy label, and they have the rights to those too—whatever Riverside kept in print. And John made another deal with Arnold Kaplan; he sold him the Paramount Eagle. He sold the Paramount trademark to ABC. He was suing ABC, and the deal was they would buy the Paramount logo from him for a certain amount of money—and it was a pretty good amount of money—and to settle the lawsuit, Steiner was pissed off because ABC wouldn't send the mail sent for him. And something fairly important never reached him in time. So he went to Ashcraft's law firm and started legal action.

First came Estes. Dave Blumenthal was making a documentary in Brownsville, *Citizen South, Citizen North*. He came in the store to talk to Joe Segal because he wanted to film one of Joe's Monday night jam sessions, which he did do. And he had this excellent Danish photographer doing the camera. Unfortunately, the Danish photographer didn't know how to operate an Oricon movie camera, which is a totally professional sixteen-millimeter camera. Dave went down to Seymour's to talk to Joe Segal, and he happened to mention that he had filmed Sleepy John Estes down in Brownsville. Joe Williams wasn't lying, was he? I should have listened to the old guy. [*laughs*] So that's how we found Sleepy John. Sadly, the film was no good—none of the footage he shot—so he had to scrap the whole darn documentary.

We had known a guy named Sam Estes, who had worked at Davis Congress Shop, a marvelous clothing store next door. Ramsey Lewis used to go there and get his clothes, and then he'd come in the store and buy a record. I remember Sam was really getting along in years and he was slowing down a little bit, but I guess he really knew his trade, the tailoring trade. And I remember once going in there and thinking, "I'll call him Sleepy Sam." But then I changed my mind; I thought that was rather unkind. But if I'd done it, we might have found John a year earlier. He was John Estes's brother! John and I got off the train after a rather circuitous route to Chicago to do a couple of college concerts on the way. I said, "Well, John, where do you want to go?" He said, "I'd like to go to 437 South Wabash." I said, "Don't you mean 439?" He said, "No, it's a place called the Davis Congress Shop. [*laughs*] My brother works there." He had never noticed the similarity between the two addresses, not being able to read. He could read; he just couldn't see.

How did you actually make the contact with him?

Well, I wrote to him. I didn't get an answer, so I wrote him again, and I didn't get an answer. We set up a concert, one at Westminster College; John Randolph, another saint, set that one up for us. Then Archie Green at the University of Illinois, and he set up a third one at Purdue. There were three concerts on the way from Brownsville. So I decided I'd go down there. So I went down there and I took John to the store. He needed groceries and he wouldn't even let me go in this place he lived. It was a hovel, a terrible place. Anyway, I overspent and didn't have enough for the bus ticket. I called the store Jazz Record Mart, and Joe Segal says, "Man, we're having a terrible time."

And this is weird—Joe went next door and borrowed money from Maury Davis at Davis Congress Shop so I could bring John to Chicago. I had to go to Jackson to get the postal money order. I had to go to Jackson because the bus stop in Brownsville is a flower shop that closes at five thirty. I had enough money to get to Jackson, but some of John's people came in so late we nearly missed the bus. They had a breakdown. They had a really old car. I remember John in this old car. Eventually we got on the bus, we did the concerts, and we came to Chicago. We got acquainted, and later, of course, we brought in Yank Rachell from Indianapolis and did the *Mandolin Blues* record; a little later we did *Broke and Hungry*, and then we went to Europe. And I was Sleepy John Estes's lead boy. I'm proud of that.

In the Delmark catalog *Hoodoo Man* [Junior Wells] was 612; *West Side Soul* [Magic Sam] was 615. What were 613 and 614?

613 is *Brownsville Blues*, with Sleepy John. And we had done 608 with John. We'd done a whole lot of sessions. The first time we recorded Sleepy John Estes we recorded fifty-four titles, just him with guitar. The second time and the third session were done the same day—the first session with "Knocky" Parker added to John and Hammie Nixon and Ed Wilkinson, the bass player.

There's a cute story. I needed a way to get to Milwaukee; I didn't own a car. Ed had a Volkswagen. I said, "Ed, look, if we go to Chicago it's forty-one and a quarter for a record date. If not, I'll give you twenty-five bucks and buy you dinner." So we got there, and he was a good bass player. He'd been the tuba player in the Dixie Stompers and had moved to Chicago. I remember he asked me if I wanted a bass or tuba. I'd never heard him play string bass. So he strapped the bass to the top of the car and we got there. E. D. Nunn of Audiophile Records had been recording another one of Knocky Parker's ragtime albums. Knocky was a professor at Kentucky Wesleyan, I believe, who had played with the Light Crust Dough Boys and Bill Boyd's Cowboy Ramblers. He had recorded extensively with them in the 1930s. He was an ardent blues fan. He once came to St. Louis just so he could play four-hand piano with Speckled Red. I can't imagine anybody else capable of doing it—or wanting to—but he did!

Anyway, he was finishing up his album. We had to wait a little while until he finished up this last tune. And he asked if he could sit in. He loved Sleepy John, and he really loved blues! God bless him! He became known as a ragtime guy, and he really wasn't that particular about ragtime, but he loved blues—Jess Stacey, Jelly Roll Morton, et cetera. So we did a session and then he had to catch his plane. So we broke for lunch and then came back with just guitar, the harp, and the bass. We did a lot of stuff—we were always recording John. He always needed money, and either he owed me money or I owed him money, but it was a constant stream of recording activity. The forty-one and a quarter would go through the union. We wasted a lot of the artists' money insisting that they go through the union because we were a union label. It was a horrible waste of money. The union never got any of the bluesmen any gigs.

Earlier, on one of my trips to John Steiner and Bill Russell's place, on my way to see Lee Collins at the Beehive in Hyde Park, Bill Russell took us to the Zanzibar, because he said, "You've got to hear Muddy Waters." And by now I'm so hip I know that Little Walter is going to be the harmonica player—only he wasn't. That was the first night I heard Junior Wells in person. I asked for "Key to the Highway." Muddy said, "Well, I do it, but this boy does it better." And Junior sung it—Junior does a great "Key to the Highway." So that was my first Chicago blues, but I had gone to hear several bands in St. Louis. Usually they'd give you phony names, because they thought you were a cop. [*laughs*] I think I saw Little Milton there once, and another time I think I saw Albert King. Of course, I knew Little Mack, who years later made records.

When I first got here I went to see Muddy at Smitty's Corner, at Thirty-fifth and State. There were two waiters there who'd made blues records. One was—"Red Nelson." Muddy called one of the waiters up on stage and he did "Dirty Mother Fuyer." It was a long time ago. I asked Muddy, "Where else can I hear blues?" Muddy asked me, "How are you traveling?" I said, "On the subway." He said, "Well, you can always get to the Green Door on Sixty-third Street and see a couple of young guys—Mighty Joe Young and Billy Boy Arnold." That was the second experience. I pretty quickly heard about Sylvio's, and Sylvio's had an El stop in front of the place, so I could go there. In those days it was no worry to go to Thirty-fifth and Indiana. It was a two-block walk. There've been times since then I wouldn't want to do that walk.

I later learned that one of the things we had going for us was that in those days cops would be much harder on anyone black committing a crime against a white person. I'm not too proud to say we took full advantage of that; we didn't even realize that was the case. So we'd walk to Pepper's and to the other places, and we tried to organize rides. I would go around and hear a lot of trad—Franz Jackson at the Red Arrow out on Harlem and

Thirty-ninth; Art Hodes at half a dozen different places. George Brunis was always at the 1111 on Bryn Mawr. Up and down North Broadway there were gigs. In fact, for a long time, I, Don Kent, and Paul Garon, and Leon Kellert would waste our Friday nights listening to records [*laughs*] until one in the morning, two in the morning. We could have been out hearing live music! But Saturday was generally the night to go listening to live music. I was generally out in the clubs on Saturday nights. And then when I found out about Theresa's, I was there Saturday *and* Monday.

Let's talk about how you made the connection with Junior Wells.

That was at Theresa's. I think that was when George Mitchell worked for me; he was running around all over the South Side. I would ask him to be careful not to get in trouble. Finally he said, "Tonight 'Sunnyland Slim' [Luandrew] is playing at Theresa's." And we went in there and he had his electric piano and he was playing. I loved the club. Anybody ever walked into Theresa's felt like they just walked into their own living room. It was just so "at home"—not down home, "at home." I went back the next week and it was Junior Wells. I had some Junior Wells records—a couple of Chiefs [record label], and a Profile [another label] or two, and all the Uniteds, those that had been issued. He was on USA by that time. I wanted to record him, and the first thing I said was, "Are you under contract?" He said, "I have a contract with Paul Glass at USA, but I don't think it will be a problem." So I went to see Paul—I was one of his customers—and he said, "As long as you don't put out a 45 [rpm] I don't have a problem with that." I said, "I might do even better than that and you can issue a 45 from the session on USA."

Junior said that there was a session—it might have been a rehearsal, because the tapes have never turned up—that Junior started singing, "*Oo-ah, ee-ehh*" [*sings with syncopation*], and Paul Glass thought that was a little too raw, a little too bawdy, and he didn't want to issue the thing. And he'd had a little falling out with Paul about that. I don't think he ever did anymore recording for Paul. Mainly it was the guy who had Chief, Mel London, that was Junior's main man for singles. Mel first had Chief, and then Profile was in partnership with Glass, and then he went to work for Glass as a producer. Then he went to work for Barney and did the overdub of the old Chief thing—"Cha Cha Cha in Blues" became "Cut My Toenail" or some such thing.

When you cleared the way around the contract what was the next step?

Well, first we cut the deal, and then he wanted to use Buddy. So I called up Leonard Chess and said, "I want to use Buddy Guy on a record." He said [*imitating Chess's gruff voice*], "Yeah, go ahead and record the son-of-a-bitch, but you can't use his name, *and* he doesn't sing!" Come to find out, this was just Buddy's way of letting Leonard know that there was a demand for his services. He was not under contract to Chess. Nobody was under contract to Chess. Muddy Waters was not under contract to Chess. But it was the best game in town, and I don't blame people for staying with Chess.

At that time Peter Balfour Brown was working for me—one of a string of Englishmen; we had one every year. It was some sort of program where they could come over and make money and not have to pay income tax, which was nice because it saved me some money too. So I said, "Pete, I need a pseudonym for Buddy Guy for this record." He said, "A buddy is a friend and a guy is a chap." So we called him "Friendly Chap." *Veddy* British! And I have to say I really thought, "I'm taking a chance here, man." I had one sideman on Big Joe's record; I had two sidemen, then three sidemen on parts of the Estes record. And here I am, I'm going to have a full band on the whole record. And this was not the stuff that the "folkies" were going to dig. But it was too dammed good. His singles were really getting over—the kind of stuff that I loved at Theresa's on Friday and Saturday nights.

So we rented the studio. And in the middle of the session Buddy's amp went *kerplunk*. So Stu Black brought the amp into the studio. Stu plugged Buddy's amp into the Leslie, the amplifier for the B-3 organ, and we kept the session cooking. And I was amazed because years went by before anybody noticed that Buddy Guy seemed to be playing organ on a few tracks. There was one tune with two takes: one take him on the guitar, and the second take him on the Leslie. Stu fixed the guitar amp and Buddy finished the date on his guitar amp.

How did you decide what the band would be? Did you leave that in Junior's hands?

I left it to Junior, and I've done so since and I think everybody should. This was the band at Theresa's—four pieces. It was the Buddy Guy Trio basically, and Junior fronted it, as did B. B. Junior and Detroit Junior sometimes. At Theresa's they used to say, "Theresa could hire and Junior could fire."

What about repertoire?

I let him pick that too. He had this tune, "Snatch It Back and Hold It," he wanted to record. That may have been the tune he had the argument with Paul Glass about. I thought it was a little too far out, a little too R & B-ish. But then I said, "This is the great stuff I hear every night." I remember Junior showed up fifteen minutes late for the first session, and I said, "You know, this is business," and he was early the next time. [*laughs*] I didn't sign him to an exclusive contract; he didn't want to be under contract, and because of that he was able to do the Vanguard anthology. And they slipped a little clause in there saying he had to do an album a year for three years. So he was with Vanguard, but he was actually under contract to the Four Brothers label, and the contract was sold to Mercury. So he was simultaneously on Vanguard and Mercury.

One of my favorite stories—when that contract ran out about a year into his Mercury deal, he was having some success with "Up in Heah," and he said, "Let's cut a deal for the next record." I said, "Junior, you're under contract. I can't touch you." He said, "No, let's cut a deal, and when the contract runs out, let's record before I get the next contract." And we agreed on a price. I remember it was in a limo. He had four gigs that night. He had done a sock hop or two in the afternoon. He was exhausted. So we went from Theresa's to the Checkerboard, and from the Checkerboard to a club on Thirty-ninth near Lake Shore Drive. Somewhere along the line we cut the deal, and then we went back to Theresa's for the evening. And I went home and I thought, "He's never going to remember the details." Two and a half years later he calls me up: "Well, I'm finished with Mercury. You better come down to the club and we'll talk about the new record." I went down to the club, and I said, "The first thing we better talk about is the price." "No, man, we settled that two or three years ago!" And he did the record for that money. This time around we could use Buddy's name. And he forgot to mention that Otis Spann was on the session, and Otis was the first guy to show up.

How many tracks were you looking for on the session?

The *Hoodoo Man* sessions? We had more than enough material for an LP, but, unfortunately, not enough for a second LP. There was fifteen minutes of additional material and some alternate tracks that we've issued since then. The fifteen minutes included a Buddy Guy vocal, a Buddy Junior duet, and another Junior. I could look up the titles, but I don't have the tape. That got lost before *Hoodoo Man* came out.

How did the connection with Magic Sam happen?

I was on the West Side a lot. By that time I had a car, and I was out on the West Side and I ran across Sam. I have to say I was still trying to get Otis Rush, so we put off recording Sam because we thought we could get Otis Rush. Bill Lindeman was constantly kicking my rear about "You've got to record Magic Sam!" Eventually I did, and that's about all there is to the story.

Where would you see Sam?

I think at the Alex—I've forgotten which came first, the L & N or the Alex. It seems to me I had seen him somewhere else many years prior to that—by now we're up to 1967. I'd heard his records; the first one I'd heard was one of those Chief things. Did he do "Round Square Dance" for Chief? It was something like that. It's like the guy whose first Otis Rush experience is "Violent Love" on Cobra. [*laughs*] It should be barred from the Cobra discography. And that happened to me years before with Muddy, back in Wichita. My very first Muddy—or maybe Wolf—had a sax on it. It was terrible! That was long before he did the things with J. T. Brown. I kind of liked J. T., but some blues sax players do drive you up the wall if you're a jazz fan.

Anyway, at the time, Sam was sort of partnering with "Shakey" Jake. The one thing that he and I agreed on was that the two of them were playing different music—that Sam's music needed a harmonica like a hole in the head. That might have turned me off of Sam for a while. Bill Lindeman may have mentioned this to Sam, though I don't remember ever mentioning this to Bill. But Sam came to me and said, "Let's do a couple of tracks with Jake; he's helped me out a lot. But I don't want him on the record." So we did those tracks, which we later issued on a Magic Sam memorial or something. We took the "outs" [outtakes] from his first two albums and did a third one, which enabled us to lay some more bread on the musicians and Sam's estate.

I remember a noted blues and jazz writer who loved blues but hated Junior Wells and Magic Sam once told me that Magic Sam steals tubes from his sidemen's amps. [*laughs*] I will not mention the guy's name, because he's a beautiful guy—he's done wonderful things. He was wonderful to me, but he's no longer alive or I wouldn't be talking about him. But he just couldn't abide Junior Wells or Magic Sam. And we got terrible ratings from this guy in

Down Beat. We got two stars on each record. By the time the Sam album came out, I told the editor, "Look, could you at least send the record to someone else?" And they printed a second review, a good review. Paul Butterfield once told me, "Aw, that Magic Sam—he's just doing that James Brown shit." I didn't mind that. To me James Brown is a blues singer. You may not want to put him on your show, but he's a blues singer. It's like gospel—blues but with four more bars.

I always thought *West Side Soul* was one of the most metallic sounding sessions I've ever heard, and that's a positive thing. How much of a hands-on producer are you?

Obviously I'm in no position to tell Magic Sam how to play his guitar. My recollection is that he came into the studio, and we did it. Now, there seems to be an impression that Shakey Jake had a lot to do with the session, and he may have. I didn't notice. And there is a difference between *West Side Soul* and *Black Magic*, the next record. I think *Black Magic* is a little looser and, quite honestly, more the kind of record I like. So Jake may have done some rehearsing and shaping up of things that I never would have done.

Is he anywhere on *West Side Soul*?

He was at both sessions that went into making *West Side Soul*, and he did the tracks I mentioned earlier that appeared on a later album, but he wasn't heard on *West Side Soul*. Sam didn't want him on it. It's understandable. It's like Buddy and Junior, basically they're playing different music—the stinging guitar and the relaxed harmonica. But Sam said specifically he didn't want Jake on the record.

And repertoire? Were you out at the clubs making notes about which tunes you'd like to include?

No, I'd have let him record. Oh, we *did* let him record "Sweet Home Chicago"! [*laughs*] By the way, we were going to call the album *Sweet Home Chicago* and call the later anthology *West Side Soul*, and I don't know why, but we switched the titles. By the time we were getting ready to release *West Side Soul* we had purchased Shakey Jakes's tapes of Magic Sam, Luther Allison, et cetera, and were going to issue that as a follow-up. I don't remember why we switched the titles, but I have no regrets that we did. *West Side Soul* was the best-selling Delmark release up to that point. We'd sold seventeen hundred *Hoodoo Man* the first year, and I think Sam's sold twenty-seven or twenty-eight hundred.

It's ironic that the whole "Sweet Home Chicago" stigma didn't exist at that time. That might have been the fifth recorded version of the tune. Now it's number five of fifteen thousand different versions. I've always regarded Sam's version as the definitive recording of the tune.

Yeah, I like to think so. That or the Robert Johnson.

So again, you're a rather benign presence at your sessions, aren't you?

I don't try to inflict my ignorance on the artist. I might have one or two ideas per album; that's about par. The one other thing about our version of "Sweet Home Chicago" was Stockholm Slim, the piano player Per Notini. I don't think Notini was on the payroll at Jazz Record Mart, but he was hanging around. I think Otis Spann was going to be on that and couldn't make it at the last minute. But who do you use to replace Otis Spann if Sykes is out of town? [*laughs*] So Per came to the studio and sat in, and it worked out very well.

With a piano in a mix you want to try and bring it down. It's one of the few times I do exert my personal taste. I can't tell someone how to play it, but I know how I want to hear it. And I have arguments with other label owners about how loud the guitar should be. Some guys like the guitar to be louder than the voice. To me, blues is a verbal/vocal music, and if you can't hear the vocals, can't hear the poetry, it's like a person who goes to the opera to listen to the orchestra. I think a lot of us white people are like that. That's one of the differences between a Delmark mix and some of the other blues labels. To me the emphasis on the instruments is a little bit weird—me, who used to buy Bessie Smith records to hear Joe Smith and Louis Armstrong. [*laughs*] I eventually learned to listen to Bessie.

My involvement damned near ends before I walk into the studio. My main job is to keep the engineer out of the way of the musicians. Of course I've never said that to the engineers, because they are important. We had Stu Black, and occasionally Malcolm Chisholm, and these guys knew how to record blues. They'd done it before and they had a lot of good ideas. They didn't want to wire the guitars directly into the console. They knew to put a mic in front of the speakers and get some of that ratty sound. And that's important. I'm told when Mike Bloomfield and Paul Butterfield and their band went to New York the first two times, they wired everything direct and didn't get any of that good sound. That's why it took them a third trip—they finally talked them into mic-ing the speakers. [*laughs*]

With Otis Rush, the first time I went to see him, I walked into the Copacabana and the first thing I hear is a trumpet—so maybe I'm in the wrong club—but it sounds okay. I walked back—trumpet, alto, tenor, baritone, Little Brother Montgomery, Otis Rush, Ernest Gatewood, and I forget who else on drums. It was a damned orchestra. It was great! And I generally didn't like blues bands with a lot of horns. Well, you know the guy on the Cobras went from Otis Rush to Duke Ellington and stayed with Duke until Duke's death—Harold Ashby. It's very weird. Friday night I heard Little Brother Montgomery with Franz Jackson's All-Stars at the Red Arrow—trad. Saturday afternoon he played solo at the Hollywood Show Lounge on Randolph Street, about where city hall is, close to Clark Street. Cocktail piano, boogie-woogie—if you want, he'll play that. And Saturday night I heard him with Otis Rush—Little Brother Montgomery. People have asked, "What is Delmark number 610?" It was going to be Little Brother. I wanted to do a session with Otis. I wanted to issue the Lee Collins sides and then the four sides that turned up later on *Blues Piano Orgy*. We held that open, but I never got a chance to record Otis with Little Brother.

How did you start seeing J. B. Hutto?

Somebody—I'm not sure who, it might have been Charlie Musselwhite—told me about J. B. playing at Turner's. I had some of the Chance label records, so it was obvious we were going to record him if we possibly could. I went out to Turner's and I talked to him.

The most interesting thing about Turner's was its location—Thirty-ninth Street and the El. You didn't have to be afraid to go there. It was right across the street from the station;

it was literally under the tracks. It was a shallow building, a one-story building; I suspect it's still there. Turner's was two storefronts; most blues bars were once storefronts. In most situations one's a storefront, and it was always a bar. And the other one was once a store. And this second storefront is usually where the band was, Pepper's was. Quite a number of joints were like that. Turner's was two storefronts with the bar located in the middle. It was a horseshoe-shaped bar with the bandstand at the end of the bar, and behind the bandstand were the washrooms. And if you went around to the other side of the bar there was another room, which was usually pretty much empty. I never sat there; you couldn't see the band from there. There had been a beer garden—you could see that it had been a beer garden, but it had been shut down before I ever went there. Turner said the neighbors complained.

When I first went in there they had a little sandwich thing—I think maybe they made ribs there—but that disappeared real quick. One weird thing was Turner's had a neon sign. I don't think it worked, but there were neon tubes there. I don't think it said "Turner's Blue Flame Lounge"; I think it just said "Turner's." It was a dollar at the door and you got a beer. That was the way of keeping the riffraff out—like a one-drink minimum and a twenty-five-cent entry fee. Turner had one waitress, who during the day served as the barmaid when Turner had business away from the place. It was a small operation. When we first went in there, the band got five bucks a man per night—and free drinks. J. B. Hutto would come all the way from Harvey on public transit to get to the gig and to go home. If he had a gig somewhere else, he'd load up his amp and carry it on the bus. I don't know how you'd do that—the CTA [Chicago Transit Authority commuter train] to Randolph Street to the South Shore and then probably a bus at the other end. He did that two nights a week.

Oh, and the story Chuck Nessa tells about me—have you heard this one? We were just sitting there watching the band. I was there with Nessa and my wife. Turner is wrestling with a guy on the floor, and all I remember was Turner reaching in his back pocket, where he kept his little short pistol. And Nessa claims I jumped in and began pulling the guy off of him. And J. B. Hutto says, "I ain't gonna record for this motherfucker. He's crazy!" And somebody besides Chuck Nessa was there and said, "Yeah, it really happened." I guess I saw red. We booked J. B. Hutto at a place in California—the Ash Grove, I think it was. And he came back—came back to Turner's. I came in and Turner said, "You cost me money. Now I got to pay them eight dollars a man!" [*laughs*] That was 1967 or 1968. I later saw what the people at Theresa's got, and I was surprised—it was pretty good bread. It was a good gig. I could see why everybody in town would come around and sit in. [*laughs*]

The shooting at Turner's was more recent. After J. B. Hutto left town, Buster Benton was playing there. One of these real jerks that show up drunk and maybe high. The first time I noticed him, he's getting pushed out of the women's room. And the second time, he's being expelled from the men's bathroom. I don't know what that was about! After he get's expelled from the men's room, he's hitting on a couple of people, and they're just saying, "Get away from here." Then he walks up—there were a couple of people in there that night—an unusual couple—I'd never even seen their prototype before there. One guy looked like he might be a famous basketball player. He was so tall and erect—with a suit yet! He was with an absolutely gorgeous girl. She looked like she was the queen of the ball—really beautiful! And this idiot comes up behind her and pushed the guy so he falls into her. There was an "I" beam in the middle of the floor. He pushed her to the floor. She comes up and she'd bit her tongue, bit her lip, and she's bleeding. And they left.

So then this idiot starts heading for our table. Then the tall guy walks back in and shoots him—two shots, right across our table. They say pistols don't sound like you think they're going to sound, and that's true. "Snap—snap!" Snap a pistol in your face. He goes down and we split. I went across the street and there were two cops—two guys—and they were parked under the El. And I say, "Hey, there's been a shooting at Turner's." They looked kind of perplexed, nonplussed, guilty—and quickly split. They never did show up. We got in our car and went home. And there was a guy with us—someone you know, I don't want to mention his name; it would embarrass him. He was so screwed up, because he was right near the guy with the pistol, with his back to him. But he had this terrible guilt attack that maybe he could have prevented the shooting. We thought maybe the guy had died. It turned out he did live. This was the only shooting I ever witnessed in all the years in blues bars. My rule always was if they got a chain up at the door, you're going to be safe, because they're going to keep the idiots out. And Turner was pretty strict; he kept a neat house.

Then we recorded Arthur Crudup, and I used the classic system. It was the way Bunk Johnson was discovered: "Arthur Crudup, Blues Guitarist, General Delivery." We sent it to Clarksdale, Mississippi, and he was in Virginia. He wrote back and we recorded him. That was a lot of fun. And we did three albums with Arthur, the last of which—I think he was only under contract for the first one. He recorded for World Pacific, and then we did non-contractual things after that. His last session, which we have not issued, is the most different Arthur Crudup. He was in a highly emotional state. If you think Arthur Crudup has a high voice—he went up about two more octaves. I was embarrassed, but he loved it and wanted to hear it. We paid for an extra hour of studio time just so he could listen to the session.

What did you find him to be like personally?

. . . . I always have to explain my use of the word "simple," meaning uncomplicated. He was a straightforward man who loved his wife very much, who didn't have an ounce of feeling of being in show business. He had, to my knowledge, never played in clubs. We went out to the Key Largo once, where whoever it was that was appearing asked him to sit in later in the show and didn't put him up until the club was almost empty.

He would say that his lyrics came out of the sky, which was like the Bukka White recordings—*Sky Songs:* "They just fell out of the sky." And a lot of them were floating couplets, but really great stuff, you know. He once told me he was glad we'd found him, because he was thinking so much; he'd just lost his wife at the time we discovered him. And he said he had contemplated suicide. He said, "I'd be walking alongside the road and those trucks would come along, and I just felt like throwing myself out there." Of course he didn't—he didn't believe he should—so he didn't. He was a very ethical guy, who was not well treated by the trade. Shortly before he died, he was being handled by Dick Waterman, and Waterman had arranged for a $75,000 settlement on some of his copyrights. I believe what happened was some publishing company bought Lester Melrose's interest in a couple of his songs that Elvis had recorded. They got to the office, and the guy wrote a check for $38,000. They said, "Take it or leave it." Waterman said, "We'll leave it." A month later Arthur died, but eventually they paid double what the original settlement was! Yeah, a very nice taste! I was told it was $150,000 or $250,000. It was a great ending! It's too bad he didn't live to see that.

Wasn't Crudup the guy I once heard you talk about living in a cardboard box under the El?

That was when he was in Chicago. Melrose found him on the street. It was Melrose—it wasn't Broonzy or Tampa or any of those guys—living in a cardboard box under the El across the street from where Turner's later was, literally trying to get his train fare home. A lot of his blues are very, very personal. A lot of his verses may be floating couplets, but they're personal to him at the time, totally out of his own thing. We could never get him to do "Dust My Broom," though we did locate a tape of him doing it and we'll find a way to issue that someday. These artists were my favorite charity. People come around and want money for the policemen or the firemen. Screw that—I'm giving to the bluesmen!

I had toured Europe in 1964 with Sleepy John Estes, American Blues Festival—Horst Lippmann and Fritz Rau—who really did pioneer touring blues artists in Europe. There had been tours in England in the 1940s even, with Lonnie Johnson, Big Bill—and Memphis Slim was already living in Paris along about the time they started. I think this tour was their third one; they had done two before that. Anyway, this show was Howling Wolf, Sonny Boy Williamson II, Sugar Pie DeSanto, Willie Dixon, John Henry Barbee, Sunnyland Slim, and Clifton James on drums. Oh, Lightning Hopkins was on that tour too, and Chris Strachwitz was on the tour with Lightning. Well, anyway, you could see what a star-studded tour that was.

Because Sleepy John was blind, Lippmann and Rau offered to help me come with him. They didn't buy me a ticket, but they did give me the benefit of their group rate and the free transportation on the band bus—from the airport to the hotel and to the concerts and sometimes to adjacent small cities like Oberhof and Strasbourg, where we went on a bus. Most of the other cities we went by plane. I was Sleepy John Estes's lead boy. It was great. I'd never been to Europe before and have only been back twice—the next time was my honeymoon. Anyway, I would spend most of my time with John. I got so I could lead him up escalators. I tell that to blind people, and they say, "You must have been good." The first time it was traumatic for John—"Okay now, John, take a step. It's going to be moving." [*laughs*] I helped him figure out the currency. And Hammie was along too. It was great! I'm on buses every day with Sonny Boy Williamson, and they were usually tour buses with a mic up front that the driver used to make announcements. Sonny Boy would sing and play on that mic—constantly—to the point that one of the guys got a little upset. The tour was great exposure for John—and great for his psyche too! He was no longer this guy living in an unheated sharecropper's shack; he was a star. People asked for his autograph. He'd write, "Sleepy J E." One guy in England asked, "Would you mind finishing it out?" [*laughs*]

First we land and it's miles and acres and kilometers from the Frankfort airport to Baden-Baden, and they kept a secret from all the artists that there was a gambling casino there. [laughs] I knew it was a spa, but I didn't really feel the need to take the waters. But it was a charming little town, and it's the locale of Sudwestrundfunk—Southwest German radio and television studio. And this was a studio bigger than some of the sound stages I've been on in Los Angeles. It was just an enormous studio where they spend three days shooting this TV show, and then they do a concert—in the concert hall. We stayed in a hotel away from the downtown area. It was right by the railroad track, which isn't as dowdy as it sounds. In Europe you can have a railroad track and it's still a very nice neighborhood. Across the railroad tracks was a Yugoslavian restaurant, and we ate there most of the nights. I certainly did—I love Yugoslavian food. I remember the last night, after the concert, as we walked into the restaurant, everybody in the restaurant—and this is two hundred, two hundred and fifty people—stood and applauded. They'd heard about the concert. Before that they were just a bunch of Americans. [laughs]

Then there was a trip in a plane from Strasbourg to Copenhagen. I did a little business with Storyville [record label]; then Sweden—Guttenberg, Stockholm—the Sports Palace in Berlin, where Hitler made his famous speeches; the hall, the Koncerthus in Stockholm, which is where they hand out the Nobel Peace Prize; and then back to England. Well, by England I had gotten sick and tired of one-nighters, and they had a week of one-nighters in England, and John was getting around better, so I opted off the tour for that week and hung around London with Bob Dixon. We stayed at Bob Dixon's house, the guy who did the discography. And that was charming. They had a charming little place with a fire in each room that you turned on. They had these heaters and a charming garden. Then the London subway system. There is no other, a great subway system—it was fun!

Oh, John Henry Barbee, he was on that tour and very, very sick, very ill. In fact, he died shortly after we got home, but he was happy to be there. Here's a man who made one Vocalion record. I would play it for people and they would think it was Leadbelly. I'd say, "Did you know that Leadbelly recorded for Vocalion in 1938?" And I'd put in on—"My God, that is Leadbelly." But he was so good, and thank God he did that record for Storyville, because I think that's the only record he ever did besides the single. The story of his discovery was kind of interesting. He was known in Chicago as "John Henry"—and not highly respected, apparently, because he didn't work in clubs and didn't have a band. But Willie Dixon knew about him. I believe that Lippmann and Rau had the 78, because they were at Dixon's house and John Henry came in. They start talking and they realized that this is John Henry Barbee. He had changed his name because he had a ruckus in Mississippi and had to get out of Mississippi. So it wasn't until they were in England, and he's being interviewed by Fred Joslyn of *Jazz Journal*, a real sweet guy, nice man. And Fred says, "So John Henry was a name you used, but John Henry Barbee is your real name?" "No, no, no. I had another problem in another part of Mississippi." And Barbee was not his real name! [*laughs*] Barbee was a pseudonym down in Mississippi—before he came to Chicago! [*laughs*]

Jim O'Neal of *Living Blues* magazine and Bruce Iglauer of Alligator Records, both give you credit for lighting the fire under them to initiate their projects.

Well, Bruce Iglauer used to come to the store on breaks from college in Appleton, Wisconsin. He had a radio show there and we used to send him samples. He came in once and said, "I'm going to graduate soon, and I want to come and work for you. I want you to show me how to start a label, and I want to start a blues magazine." I said, "Great!" Though Jim and Amy put the magazine together, Iglauer is the guy who made it happen.

By that I mean he took the magazines around to all the stores and mailed out the subscriptions and all that. Our contribution was pretty minimal. Of course we sold them in the store. When I bought the Lincoln Avenue place, we had some space in the basement where Jim and Amy set up their Varityper to do the typesetting. And Diane Allman, who was a member of the committee and a pretty good photographer—she now runs a postcard-collecting business—Diane and her brother constructed a photo lab in our basement, a darkroom. It was a part of the basement where there was a sink, so they had a pretty good start on it. That was about our contribution. I believe we let them have our sample mailing list with deejays and people they should send at least one freebie sample to. Iglauer worked for me for a while. We had a system. When we did sessions, he would sit in the studio and he could catch vibes that I might not catch sitting in the booth. And he'd come back—he was my snitch! [*laughs*]

He doesn't know this, I think, to this day, but I was going to let him produce Luther Allison's second record. I was going to mix it, but I was going to let him produce it. Because when we did Luther's first record, we did a lot of tunes we didn't put on the record, because they had, even at that point, been over-recorded. So I needed somebody to find some song material, and we talked about it. But Bruce went to a hotel where Luther was staying; he was staying somewhere up in Wisconsin by this time. He said Luther was nude the entire time—I don't know what that was about. But Luther said, "I ain't gonna record for Bob." We had picked up his option and given him a small advance on the second record, which simply got written against the first record—and pretty quickly too. He felt he should be on a larger label, so he just sat out the two years. It's kind of sad. Around that time he had the first of several managers who were very uncommunicative to us. We thought it was the first record that, even though it was a quickie, at least got his foot in the door. And going another two years without another record was not a good idea. But he did wind up on Motown. I suppose he got pretty good money, but I'm not

Bob and Sue Koester, 2013. Photo Steve Cushing.

crazy about the records. I believe those records got remixed for the Japanese market, and I hope the CD reissue came from the Japanese remix, because with the first ones, you could tell it was a [Barry] Gordy product. Instead of just letting him do his thing, he [Gordy] tried to push him into the Motown mold.

I remember those things used to sit in the bins for years at a quarter a piece.

They were out of print real quick. One track on that, by the way, is in the film *Cooley High*.

What about the beginnings of the Alligator label?

Bruce wanted me to record "Hound Dog" Taylor. Two things—first, I had never heard Hound Dog Taylor doing a set in a club. Somehow if I got there, he didn't. I don't know why. Most of the Hound Dog I had heard, he used to come into Turner's and sit in after hours or in between sets with J. B. It was interesting because they would fret each other's guitars. It was like two piano players interlocking their hands. It was good and I thought that would be a good idea, but generally when I heard Hound Dog he was four and a half sheets to the wind. And he was always doing the same one or two tunes, and he would never finish them. Right in the middle of the tune those long fingers would go up in front of his head and he would stop playing. There were other reasons we didn't want to do Hound Dog. We didn't have any money. We'd just bought the building on Lincoln and we were having some trouble making the payments. We had young Bob and wanted to have another child, and I thought that was a little more important than expanding the Delmark catalog at that point.

In fact, all of a sudden in 1967 we got real active with the Jimmy Dawkins, the Luther Allison, the second Crudup, and the second Magic Sam. And *bam*! Those six or seven records came out in a period of six months, if not a year, and it got pretty slow after that, and that's because of the family and buying the building. So Bruce asked if I would mind if he went ahead and did it. And I said, "Sure! I know you're going to start a label sooner or later, and if you believe in this artist, then you should be the guy to record him." So he did it. And he stayed at Delmark and he was pretty good about not doing Alligator business on Delmark time. If he had to make a phone call he'd make it during his lunch hour. Once in a while he'd ask if he could leave early if he got his work done, to go to Ohio with Hound Dog, but he was very conscientious about it. Of course with two strong personalities we'd have arguments and he quit a few times, but I'd say, "No, no, stick around." Then one time he quit and I said, "Okay." [*laughs*] But we never had a hassle about him doing Alligator business on Delmark time. I have to give him credit for that. And he's been very nice over the years in mentioning Delmark in interviews, which you wouldn't really have to do. He and I do not discuss mixes. I don't think I discuss mixes with any other record producers. He produced more records that were rock fans' first blues records than we did—maybe even more than Chess did—and that's saying something!

JOHN BROVEN INTERVIEW

Presentation of Louisiana Music Commission plaque by famed record producer J. D. Miller to John Broven, Bayou Bar, Lafayette, Louisiana, April 1982. Photo Paul Harris.

I was born in Maidstone, Kent, England, in 1942—that's in the southeast of England—and was raised in what was then a little village called Polegate, outside of Eastbourne in Sussex, on the south coast.

What did your parents do?

My father was an electrician who did a variety of jobs, including farm manager, before finishing up with the local electrical utility company called Seeboard. He was in charge of transformer substations throughout East Sussex and part of Kent. My mother was a post office worker. She had a little bit of a sabbatical when she was raising my sister and myself, but she started in the post office in the 1930s, which at the time was quite unusual for a woman, and then she started her career again at Polegate.

Was your father in the service during the war years?

He was in what was called the Home Guard. Because of his specialty as an electrician he was not called into service overseas. But he was in the Home Guard, which was ready in case of invasion, which luckily never happened.

Where did you go to school?

I went to school in my junior years at Polegate. Then I went to Bexhill Grammar School. I started there in 1953. That was the equivalent of high school and college over here these days. Really that was where my interest in music started. It was the rock 'n' roll era, and we were smack-bang in the middle of it. My first awareness of rock 'n' roll was when my cousin Judy visited me. She said, "Have you heard of Elvis Presley?" And of course I hadn't.

Then I looked in the *Sunday People* paper that day and saw a record chart, and there was "Heartbreak Hotel" by Elvis Presley. That was 1956. That sparked my interest—what was all this about? Then my father purchased a radiogram which included a record player. The first records he brought home—I can remember—were "Blueberry Hill" by Fats Domino, "Only You" by the Hilltoppers, and "Rock Around the Clock" by Bill Haley. Those were the old 78s. And we were off and running.

It was a confluence of events. I guess all these things are. At grammar school there were a few keen rock 'n' roll fans, but one of them was Mike Leadbitter, who became the cofounder of *Blues Unlimited* magazine. So we were there as teenagers. Mike had already assumed a fascination for American music, particularly with rock 'n' roll, and then taken it into rhythm and blues. We had the big pop hit artists like Elvis Presley and Guy Mitchell, then the Everly Brothers. Mike was already starting to dig beneath the surface with his intrigue and natural instinct for searching out. And I just liked the feel of the rock 'n' roll and rhythm and blues records that were coming out at the time.

How and where did you guys listen?

Mike actually lived in Bexhill and I lived in Polegate, which was about a twenty-mile train journey every day to grammar school and back home again. But Mike lived in Bexhill and was part of the gang that used to meet at a coffee bar at Bexhill seafront on Sundays—wet and windy and blowy Sundays. But they got friendly with this café owner, and they encouraged him to put records on the jukebox that weren't necessarily in the mainstream.

Just to explain, there was a label called London, London-American. It was licensing from a lot of the American indie companies. Obviously they were looking for the American hits to release in England, but they also, by doing deals with labels—for example, labels like Atlantic, Chess, Sun, you name them—they had literally almost every notable independent company. For example, London was releasing songs by Chuck Willis which were hits over here in the States—"C. C. Rider," which did nothing in England. But Mike and then his friend Simon Napier would encourage the café owner to put "C. C. Rider" on the jukebox. It was very much an underground thing, very much a cult thing, which started from very small beginnings but then started to grow.

When you guys finished what would be high school here in the States, what did you do at that point?

There are two sets of exams in England. One was O [Ordinary] level, which was at the end of the fifth year in grammar school. Then you went on to the next stage, which was the A [Advanced] levels. Mike got totally distracted, and though a very bright individual, he came out with just one O level, which meant that he wasn't invited back to take the A levels. He was totally distracted by the music and was digging into not only mainstream people like Chuck Berry and Fats Domino. I remember one record was the Jiv-A-Tones' "Flirty Gertie." It was totally underground. It wasn't even rhythm and blues, just good rock 'n' roll. So he was starting to dig into the lower levels of catalogs. So he wasn't invited back to grammar school. Music was taking a bigger hold on him. So he started to work as a clerk in a company called the British South Africa Company. It was a mining company in South Africa which had an office set up, for some reason, in Bexhill-on-Sea. His friend Simon was about two years older than us, and his parents were in the antique furniture business. When Simon left school, he automatically went into the family business.

I was in the same class with Mike. We were together in the fourth form and the fifth form—1957/1958—which of course were the great rock 'n' roll years. Then Mike flunked his O level exams. I carried on to the A level course, and because we didn't live in the same town we did drift apart for a year or so. Then we met up again briefly when he decided to sell his record collection. Mike was never very good with money, and I learned that he was selling off his rock 'n' roll singles. I met him one evening, and for very little money I can remember buying from him "The Fool" by Sanford Clark and "Blue Suede Shoes" by Carl Perkins. Everybody knows the record now, but then it hardly sold a bean in England, because it was the Elvis Presley version which took the limelight. That was a pretty rare record, which I bought for two and sixpence—literally a few cents. Another one was a really prized item, which is a very rare London EP [extended play] by Bo Diddley. Not only was I buying rare items, but then it was great music, particularly the Bo Diddley EP. I can still remember the tracks: it was "Bo Diddley," "I'm a Man," "Bring It to Jerome," and "Pretty Thing." You put it on the record player, and it was just something you never heard before in your life. Those records just had tremendous echo and tremendous rhythm, and Billy Boy Arnold's harmonica, also Lester Davenport's, had a most unreal sound. In fact, it took a little while until I realized it *was* a harmonica. It was out of this world—totally mesmerizing.

I had lost contact with Mike. Then in 1960 he wrote to me and said, "I'm starting to compile label discographies, particularly the independent labels, and of some of the individual artists," which at that time nobody had done. You had the jazz discographers, but nobody had started to look at blues and rhythm and blues. And then coincidently I came across *Cash Box* magazine, through patronizing a local record shop in Eastbourne, called Davis's. We used to go there every Saturday morning, like most of us record fans in England. The guys who all met in later years, you realized, were all doing the same thing, but we all thought that we were all doing it on a solo basis. Every little town had a record shop, and there always seemed to be this coterie of teenagers who used to descend upon it on a Saturday morning, and these record shops used to have all the latest releases. The London label, which I mentioned, they always had four or five weekly releases. Around 1959 or 1960 you had "What'd I Say" by Ray Charles, "Ooh Poo Pah Doo" by Jessie Hill, and so on and so on. But this record shop, Davis's, for some reason subscribed to *Cash Box* magazine, and the guy kept them all in this nice pile in the corner of his office.

I said to him one Saturday morning, "What are those?" He said, "They're *Cash Box* magazine—would you like them?" It was about fifteen months' worth of magazines; it was a weekly magazine, as you know. I got home and started looking at them, and it just gave a totally new view on the American record scene. Not only were the new records being reviewed, but you had the news stories and the charts, of course—rhythm and blues charts,

Top 100—and also the advertisements and information about disc jockeys, distributors, one-stops, and jukebox operators. So that was opening our eyes even further. So when Mike wrote to me and said, "Can you help with the discography?" I said, "I just got hold of these *Cash Box* magazines," and that was it! He had to see them, and we arranged to meet. Then we started to have weekly record sessions. We're talking about 1961 now; that was when we were together—that's Mike and Simon—and the record sessions were held at the family shop on London Road. So I guess we sparked each other.

Just out of curiosity, what kind of career were you headed for?

These days everybody goes to university, but in 1960, certainly in England, university was only for the very elite, the blue-blooded part of the population. You had to be exceptional even to be accepted into the second-tier universities—let alone Oxford and Cambridge, which were out of reach for all except for the born geniuses. So if you accepted that it was only the exceptional people who went to university and you had a decent education, you looked around for jobs. There were banking and insurance and teaching. Salesman's jobs were quite popular at the time, I seem to remember. I always had it in the back of mind that I'd like to try banking, so when I finished the A levels I applied for jobs in the big banks, and it was Midland Bank that made the offer. I didn't regret it. It was a terrific career which lasted, in my case, about thirty years. I became a branch bank manager, then I became a corporate manager with an East Kent area of responsibility. It was a job where you had a definite career pattern, you made that gradual progression. As long as you recognized that and took your time, it was a great time, where you really learned the craft. You went through every segment of the banking office, so when you became a branch manager you understood how everything operated.

[*laughs*] That runs so counter to everybody else involved in this music—a responsible profession!

Well, there you go! Music was always a serious hobby with me. I was content to develop the music in tandem with the banking career. Certainly in the early days there was no question where the sustenance was coming from—from your regular monthly salary from the bank, not from indulging yourself in the music. There we were in Bexhill. Mike was writing to journals like *Jazz Journal* and any other people or collectors interested in rhythm and blues and blues music. He got a few replies from interested collectors, and that led Mike and Simon to form what was called the Blues Appreciation Society. That was in 1962. It was simply a forum of people interested in

Blues Unlimited magazine.

blues and rhythm and blues music. I think the intention was to send out a regular newsletter. And of course the natural next step was to turn the newsletter into a magazine, and that's how *Blues Unlimited* came about.

Can you describe the original newsletter?

It was duplicated, not printed, and it was just a single page. I've got one somewhere. It was a duplicated letter made on what we call a stencil machine. You typed out this letter in stencil form and then put it onto a roller. Then just turn the roller, which was inked, and out came the letter. It was a very simple and cheap form of printing. That was how the newsletter was produced.

How many issues of the newsletter were produced before it was turned into the magazine?

I would say no more than three. It was a very quick process. I believe Simon contacted a magazine—it was in Holland—which invented the name of *Blues Unlimited*. They decided that they had come to the end of their run. In effect, Simon took over the name of *Blues Unlimited,* which was a brilliant piece of forethought on his part. It was just a fabulous name, which conveyed the coming blues boom which was happening, but it also meant that it would encompass rhythm and blues music so that the two went hand in hand. So having made the decision to start the magazine—I wasn't part of it—the co-founders and co-editors were Simon Napier and Mike Leadbitter.

I was a friend of them both, and when they made a decision to start the magazine, they said to me, "Would you like to write for the magazine?" Well, I never had any ambition to be a writer. I hadn't even thought of it! I was just an interested record collector and a friend of theirs. They said "Yes, you must write for us!" So with the very first magazine—I've got a copy of it here—it was headed *Blues Unlimited,* subtitled *A Journal of the Blues Appreciation Society*. In fact, it was edited by Simon Napier. Mike wasn't even a co-editor then. The price was one and six pence. Let me try and convert the pound, shilling, and pence into dollars terms for you—that represents something like ten cents. [*laughs*]

Issue number one was April 1963. Perhaps I can read aloud the first paragraph:

> This is the first of what we hope will be many issues of our magazine. When, last May, we founded the "Blues Appreciation Society" our ultimate aim was to publish just such a magazine, as one seemed badly needed in this increasingly popular field. It will be published at about 5 weekly intervals, and future contributors include John Godrich, Dr. H. R. Rootmaaker, Derek Coller, Henry Vestine, as well as the writers in this issue.
>
> Our "B.A.S." activities will carry on as before, in conjunction with this magazine. (Well, it didn't really—the magazine took over. [*laughs*]) Ideas for improving our service are still very welcome and will receive our closest attention. We hope to salvage many of the fine ideas laid down by Max Vreede's original society, and further details will be published here.

It was Max Vreede—he was from Holland—who invented the name *Blues Unlimited*. And so for the first issue I was invited to write on whatever topic I wanted. [*laughs*] And at the time, I was very interested in Excello Records, the great Southern blues label in Nashville. I'd been in correspondence with Excello and had letters from the boss, Ernie Young. And he put me in touch with Jay Miller, who recorded some of the great blues artists like Lightning Slim, Lonesome Sundown, and Lazy Lester and Slim Harpo. So I wrote an article on Jay Miller based on those letters, but also based on the records that I'd been buying. It was done, if you like, from a record collector's viewpoint. So I didn't actually do any interviews. Remember this is 1963. America was three thousand miles away on another continent, but it was very much from a fan's viewpoint.

Mike Leadbitter and Simon Napier. Courtesy Mike Rowe.

Just to take the thread through, my interest in writing these articles and doing a few record reviews manifested itself in a trip to New Orleans in 1970, when I started research for my book, *Walking to New Orleans* [published by *Blues Unlimited* Books, 1974]. It's now published in the States as *Rhythm & Blues in New Orleans* [by Pelican Publishing Company]. That was really the first book on New Orleans rhythm and blues music. Then the US publishers asked me to do a follow-up, and I wrote *South to Louisiana: The Music of the Cajun Bayou*. That came out in 1983. So from small acorns the first article was on Jay D. Miller, from Crowley, Louisiana, and Excello Records, and in 1983 I finished up writing a full-scale book on south Louisiana music.

The magazine was printed on the same duplicating machine that the Blues Appreciation Society newsletters were printed [on]. I can still remember, Simon's parents had moved the antique shop to 38A Sackville Road in Bexhill, which is quite near the seafront. They gave him the attic room to play around with the magazine. So there he was sitting in the attic room with his typewriter doing the stencils for *Blues Unlimited* number one; just flicking through it I can see there were sixteen pages. I seem to recall that for the first issue there were two hundred copies. So there were two hundred magazines, sixteen pages each, so you can just imagine there were, what, sixteen hundred double-sided pages with Mike, Simon, and I running up in a line catching the pages off the duplicating machine and then stapling them together. It was very much [like] Henry Ford's conveyor belt system, and it was a very simple one at that. Mike and I gathered the pages together and Simon had the stapler, and that was *Blues Unlimited* number one.

It was a perfect time to start a blues magazine, because the rock 'n' roll era had really ended around 1959 or 1960, but there were all these collectors who had started buying these records, particularly on the London-American label, who just wanted to find out more about the roots of rock 'n' roll. *Blues Unlimited* really brought together a whole generation of enthusiastic collectors who just wanted to know more about the roots of the music.

How long did you actually stay with the magazine?

I continued right through until the late 1970s. My banking career was taking root, and there was a period when I was transferred by the bank up to Weybridge in Surrey, away from the home. I lost a little bit of touch with Mike and Simon, and for a year or two I did hardly anything research-wise while finishing bank exams, but I always saw writing for *Blues Unlimited* as a very interesting and fascinating *hobby*. I was always there, but more heavily involved sometimes than at others. In the meantime they were starting to go great guns. The long and short of it was that Mike took over editorship after issue number one hundred in 1972. Simon had really done what he wanted to do, but he had a tiger by the tail. He'd finish one magazine and he had to start another. He was working until one and two o'clock in the morning just turning the magazine out. But they were very lucky, because there was this groundswell of enthusiasm. They were attracting some of the best writers. We were all young, and people like Mike Rowe were suddenly appearing on the scene. I can remember Neil Paterson. And then you had the great Paul Oliver, who wrote an occasional article. The magazine in a sense reflected the British R & B boom of the mid-1960s.

With the sponsors that appeared in *BU*, did you solicit sponsors, or did they come to you?

It was really through record company advertising. The initial issues were supported entirely by subscription; it was all done by mail order. But Simon's parents were in the antique business, and Simon had a natural instinct, a real mind for small business. He knew what a profit was, what gross takings were, what expenditure was. Mike just had no idea. [*laughs*] He was, if you'd like, the visionary. Mike was busy doing research and encouraging collectors. Not that Simon wasn't, or that Simon wasn't interested in the music. By the way, this was another interesting contrast: Simon's interest was in prewar blues, touching on gospel and hillbilly, whereas Mike was more into down-home blues and rhythm and blues. But between them they covered the whole spectrum of black music as we know it now. It was a very happy confluence that they had these different fields of expertise, which included business and research of the music.

Can you talk about Mike's legacy?

What happened with Mike . . . I have to say as time goes on, I'm just more and more aware of his genius—to think that he invented blues discography and launched this magazine. Classical and jazz were the elitist musics. Rock 'n' roll and rhythm and blues were totally ignored by the academic institutions as inferior. And it seemed as though rock 'n' roll was destined to die out as had been predicted; they said it wouldn't last. But rock 'n' roll is here to stay. Mike really was responsible for sparking the interest in blues in England—in Europe—and contributed in sparking the interest in the States as well. His work is seen in *Blues Unlimited*, but it's also seen in his blues records discography [*Blues Records, 1943–1970*], which is the bible of blues discography. The first one [*Blues Records, 1943–1966*] was published in 1968 by Hanover Books, and it still stands up forty years later. He really

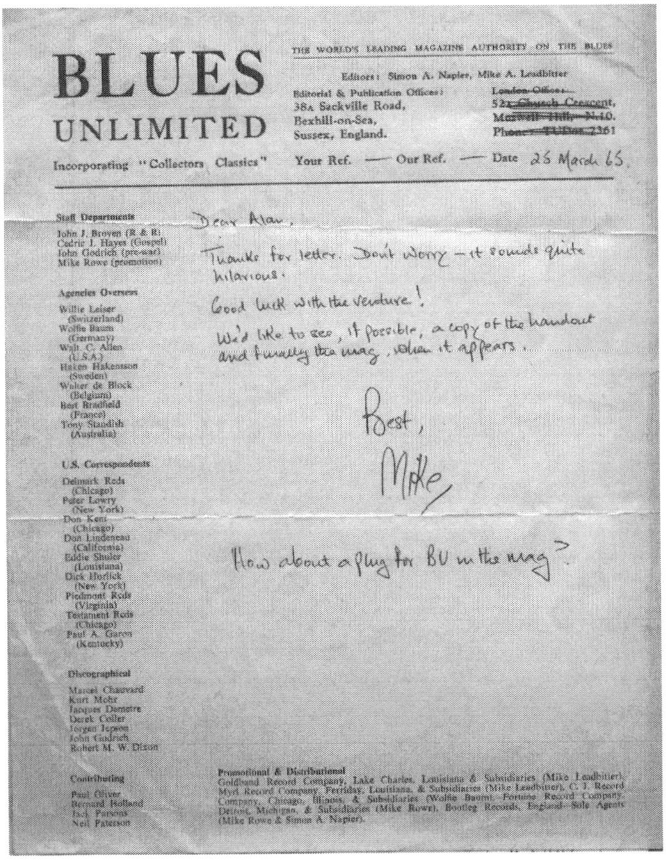

THE WORLD'S LEADING MAGAZINE AUTHORITY ON THE BLUES

BLUES UNLIMITED

Incorporating "Collectors Classics"

Editors: Simon A. Napier, Mike A. Leadbitter

Editorial & Publication Offices:
38A Sackville Road,
Bexhill-on-Sea,
Sussex, England.

~~London Office:~~
52 ~~Church Crescent,~~
~~Muswell Hill, N.10.~~
~~Phone: TUDor~~ 2361

Your Ref. — Our Ref. — Date 25 March 65.

Staff Departments
John J. Broven (R & B)
Cedric J. Hayes (Gospel)
John Godrich (pre-war)
Mike Rowe (promotion)

Agencies Overseas
Willie Leiser (Switzerland)
Wolfie Baum (Germany)
Walt. C. Allen (U.S.A.)
Hakan Hakensson (Sweden)
Walter de Block (Belgium)
Bert Bradfield (France)
Tony Standish (Australia)

U.S. Correspondents
Delmark Rcds (Chicago)
Peter Lowry (New York)
Don Kent (Chicago)
Don Lindeneau (California)
Eddie Shuler (Louisiana)
Dick Horlick (New York)
Piedmont Rcds (Virginia)
Testament Rcds (Chicago)
Paul A. Garon (Kentucky)

Discographical
Marcel Chauvard
Kurt Mohr
Jacques Demetre
Derek Coller
Jorgen Jepson
John Godrich
Robert M. W. Dixon

Contributing
Paul Oliver
Bernard Holland
Jack Parsons
Neil Paterson

Dear Alan,

Thanks for letter. Don't worry – it sounds quite hilarious.

Good luck with the venture!

We'd like to see, if possible, a copy of the handout and naturally the mag, when it appears.

Best,

Mike

How about a plug for BU in the mag?

Promotional & Distributional
Goldband Record Company, Lake Charles, Louisiana & Subsidiaries (Mike Leadbitter), Myrl Record Company, Ferriday, Louisiana, & Subsidiaries (Mike Leadbitter), C. J. Record Company, Chicago, Illinois, & Subsidiaries (Wolfie Baum), Fortune Record Company, Detroit, Michigan, & Subsidiaries (Mike Rowe), Bootleg Records, England—Sole Agents (Mike Rowe & Simon A. Napier).

Mike Leadbitter letter. Courtesy Alan Balfour.

had to work at it. He didn't do it alone; he had a network. But he was the coordinator, the conductor of the orchestra. He made a very interesting field trip to Texas and Louisiana in 1967. He covered many artists down there that are no longer with us. If he hadn't done that work, the research field would have been that much poorer.

I'd just like to go on record in saying how much I respected the work done on the postwar discography—and what a monumental task the postwar volume would have been in comparison to the prewar discography, with all the independent labels to track down.

Well, that's right! It was literally done from a blank slate and filled in from a variety of sources—the *Cash Box* and *Billboard* magazines were a terrific research resource—and the records we were buying. You had record auctions and you'd see a Cobra label recording listed that wasn't included in your latest discographical listing. Bit by bit you piece things together. It was literally a gradual gathering of information. Mike's book was a result of his personal intensity. He just had this natural instinct to explore and research. And this was in the days before computers! It was all hand-written, and then it had to be typed out. It was a tremendous piece of work and a lot of hard work as well.

The original book was authored by Leadbitter and Slaven, referring to Neil Slaven. Can you talk about the role that Neil played in the research for the book?

The research work was Mike's, and Neil came into it when the first *Blues Records* was published. He offered to act as secretary. Now, who knows if the book would ever have been published without his work in the role of secretary? Mike handed in the info sheets, and Neil dutifully spent hours and hours typing it out, setting it out ready for the publishers, who would then have to re-input it to produce the book. Neil was associated with Mike Vernon's *R & B Monthly*. Mike Vernon, of course, is known as the founder of Blues Horizon Records, which was one of the important British blues and R & B labels of the 1960s. So Neil came up through *R & B Monthly*. He started producing blues records for Decca. It was at that stage that he became friendly with Mike Leadbitter and acted as secretary for that first edition of the postwar *Blues Records* discography. Then after Mike died, Neil took over production of the expanded version for the issues that came out under the Paul Pelletier banner in the 1980s. Again, those expanded versions couldn't have been done without the original work, which over time has proven to be so reliable. Mike achieved a lot, but to think that he died in 1974 at the age of thirty-two. You think, "How much more would he have achieved?" His legacy is with us, and it doesn't do any harm to remind people just what a genius he was and how much he had achieved.

Simon was more low-key. He was content to keep the wheels of the magazine rolling without seeking any personal publicity. After *Blues Unlimited* number one hundred—that was 1972—he really felt that he'd had enough and handed the reins over to Mike, who became sole editor. So Mike was editor from 1972 to 1974, which was when he unfortunately died of meningitis. He'd suffered from tuberculosis—and unfortunately didn't follow through with the treatment that was required. Then the tuberculosis manifested as meningitis and he died very suddenly in October 1974. So then the question was "What to do?" and a committee of five of us got together and decided to carry on the magazine. That was Mike Rowe, who people may know as the author of *Chicago Breakdown*; Bez Turner, who was the secretary; Bill Greensmith, the photographer and [who] has written a book with Henry Townsend—he now lives in St. Louis; Neil Slaven, who's now associated with *Blues & Rhythm* magazine and does a lot of liner notes on blues releases; and myself.

So that committee carried the magazine through. I left about 1978. It was purely on the basis that my bank career was advancing to such an extent that there was danger of conflict of interest. The magazine was carried on into the 1980s by Mike Rowe and Bill Greensmith, until Mike eventually ran out of steam. It finished [with] issue number 149, which was in 1987. But in the meantime, I suppose it was in my blood and we saw that issues of *Blues Unlimited* were becoming less and less frequent. So with Bez Turner, who had been with *Blues Unlimited*, and Cilla Huggins, who did all the production work for all the later stages of *Blues Unlimited*—we got together in 1985 and started *Juke Blues* magazine. That magazine continues to this day under Cilla's editorship—and [she] does a very good job, a very professional magazine. And it's not an easy climate in which to produce a blues magazine. You might say that *Juke Blues* was in a sense the offspring of *Blues Unlimited*, and *Juke Blues* retains all the values that *Blues Unlimited* gave us.

What happened to Simon?

After leaving *Blues Unlimited*, Simon then became a director with Flyright Records. Flyright was a roots label. I had a hand in the start of that with Robin Gosden in the 1960s. But then it became a much more professional outfit in the 1970s. Simon ran it in conjunction with Robin and Bruce Bastin, another writer for *Blues Unlimited*, who has done some notable work on East Coast blues, culminating in his book *Red River Blues*. Flyright was very much involved in blues, rhythm and blues—roots music generally. Flyright was a combination of a record label and a distribution company. Bruce was the head of the record label; Simon was the businessman who really held the company together. Robin Gosden came in to head distribution, and the three of them made a great success of the business. Flyright was in a sense an offshoot of *Blues Unlimited*, and it shows just how influential the magazine was. Then Simon had a heart attack and died in 1990. He was fifty-one years old. His legacy was very much *Blues Unlimited*. If it hadn't been for him and his business sense, combined with his love of the music, I doubt that *Blues Unlimited* would ever have become the institution that it became. It nurtured young writers and researchers who then took it a step further.

Did *Blues Unlimited* have correspondents in the States?

Yes, we did. Again, Mike became very interested in the history of the Delta and the Delta blues. I guess today everyone knows about Robert Johnson and Robert "Junior" Lockwood and Sonny Boy Williamson II and Elmore James. But in the early 1960s the research books were not there, and so you had to do the research for yourself, and *Blues Unlimited* became a central forum for interested parties. Subscribers came not just from England but from the rest of the world, including the United States. Once you had an American write in—say, for example, Jim O'Neal was an early subscriber—you'd write to Jim and find out that his interest was in Delta blues. So Mike struck up a relationship and would say to Jim, "Perhaps you ought to interview Lillian McMurry of Trumpet Records." Or Johnny Vincent of Ace Records, or whoever. And David Evans wrote in—names that are now very familiar. Pete Lowry was another one. He had a great interest in blues from the East Coast, and so he struck up a relationship with Bruce Bastin. So, yes, it was very much a two-way thing. Sadly, Mike's Delta blues manuscript, which he was working on at his death, remains unpublished to this day.

How did you happen to focus and write about New Orleans?

Again, I have to put it down to the influence of Mike Leadbitter. The very first trip that I made to the United States was in 1970. And again, it was a collaboration with American subscribers to *Blues Unlimited*. I went with Mike and Robin Gosden. Mike, Robert, and I flew out from London in 1970. Our first port of call was New Orleans. We stayed at the house of one of the *Blues Unlimited* subscribers, the mother of James LaRocca. James was a subscriber, and it was pure circumstance that his mother, Connie, ran a record label in New Orleans in the early 1960s. We had no idea that his mother had a record label—Frisco. So that was a good start. On that first trip, during the first three or four days the first person we met was Professor Longhair, who had just been rediscovered. He'd been totally forgotten in the latter stages of the 1960s. We met Archibald, the great blues and boogie pianist; we met Huey "Piano" Smith and the bluesman "Boogie" Bill Webb. It suddenly hit me—"Here you are in New Orleans," so many great artists from the 1950s were still around, and yet there'd been no attempt to document their careers. So that was the spark for *Walking to New Orleans*.

When we got back we wrote a series of articles for *Blues Unlimited* on the trip called "Behind the Sun," which included our trips not only to New Orleans but through south Louisiana, through Cajun country, up to Shreveport, up to Memphis, then Chicago. Blues at that time, commercially, was a dead music. It really was dead over here in the US. Yet all those great artists from the 1950s were still around. When we got back, Mike said, "Well, what are you gonna do?" I said, "What do you mean?" He said, "It's about time you wrote a book." [*laughs*] I was more or less pushed into it. "What's the subject going to be?" "Well, I think New Orleans is a terrific subject which needs to be done." And that really was the start of the research. The book came out in 1974. But in 1973, having written a first draft, I knew where both the strong points and the weak points were when I visited New Orleans again. At that time, the people just didn't move from the city, so ninety percent of the original participants were still alive—and still there. It was terrific for me. James LaRocca drove me around, and I had the tape recorder. The artists; the record men; Cosimo Matassa, the studio man—everybody was so willing to talk about the past. Hey, presto! There was *Walking to New Orleans*!

Were Paul Gayten and Dave Bartholomew still in the city?

Dave Bartholomew was; Paul Gayten was out in Los Angeles. So actually I didn't interview Paul Gayten for the book. Dave Bartholomew I did interview for the book. I remember Fats Domino gave me the runaround. [*laughs*] But apart from him, people like Allen Toussaint, Earl King, Clarence "Frogman" Henry—everybody on the scene was just so willing. And then you had studio men like Cosimo Matassa and Marshall Sehorn. What was good about them was that they provided a different point of view from the artists. I felt I was able to give a pretty comprehensive story of how the New Orleans R & B scene operated in the 1940s, '50s, and into the early 1960s.

Has anybody ever interviewed Annie Laurie?

No. A friend of mine, Opal Nations, was trying to contact her a few years ago, but not to my knowledge. Paul Gayten gave me her phone number a number of years ago. I called her in Atlanta. She denied being Annie Laurie, but she had such a distinctive voice that I'm positive it was her. I remember she said, "Annie Laurie? Who ever heard of Annie Laurie?" She was laughing, and what could I do except take no for an answer?

Johnnie Allen, Charlie Gillett, Bill Millar, Ray Topping, and John Broven, Marylebone, London, 1981. Photo Paul Harris.

Were there any predecessors to *Blues Unlimited* that you are aware of?

Yes. There was a magazine in Belgium called *R & B Panorama* edited by Serge Tonneau. Another influencing factor on *Blues Unlimited* and Mike Leadbitter was *Record Research,* which was Anthony Rotante, Len Kunstadt, and Paul Sheatsley. They operated out of Brooklyn, New York. They were publishing label lists of the independent labels. I remember they did Chess/Checker; they did Modern. Those publications were very important in the compiling of the postwar blues records discography. And *Living Blues*—that was the early 1970s—that was a natural extension. *Blues Unlimited* couldn't do it all. So Jim O'Neal and Amy and Bruce Iglauer all came in. They did a tremendous job of sharing the load of blues research. They were very much part of it. I suppose you can say that blues research was inspired by the jazz discographers, going right back to Brian Rust and Hugues Panassié in the 1930s and 1940s. Kurt Mohr, who just died in 2007, was another European who did some great discographical work. The framework was there and Mike just took it one step further.

We were very lucky in England in the 1960s because of the groundswell of interest in blues and rhythm and blues. We started to see some of the great American blues artists come overseas. To a man, to a woman, they were all astounded at the reception they received. They were treated like heroes. Here in the States there was nowhere near the adulation. They got a great reception and people were genuinely interested in their music. So it wasn't just the latest hit record or latest LP which was important; it was their entire catalog. We began to see—well, you name them—Muddy Waters, Jimmy Rogers, Jimmy Reed, Little Walter, Sonny Boy Williamson, Lightning Hopkins—the list goes on and on. That helped to cement the interest being generated by *Blues Unlimited*, *R & B Monthly,* and other magazines

Over here in Chicago the guy who's been the main motivator on the blues scene over the years is Bob Koester. It seems that Paul Oliver was the similar guiding force in the UK.

Paul was an inspiration to us all. He was a generation ahead of us—a little bit older—but Paul was always supportive and encouraging. I think sometimes we were coming at it from the rock 'n' roll end, which was a little bit foreign to him. He came from the trad jazz era of the 1940s and 1950s—a lot of jazz in his background—and the prewar blues, of course. But he accepted us and saw that we were adding to the existing canon. Again, totally supportive and encouraging, even if our music was sometimes a little foreign to him. Bob Koester of Delmark Records was terrific as well. I know that Bob set up regular correspondence with Simon; they were in contact all the time. I had a similar correspondence with Don Kent, again from Chicago. Don would give me the lowdown on who was appearing on the West Side and on the South Side—Muddy's latest record [*laughs*], "Little Brown Bird," with an organ. How could this be? Nobody was trying to outdo each other. They say during the 1960s you had causes. I think that blues and rhythm and blues was our cause. It was backed up, of course, by the civil rights struggle; we felt that we were doing a good thing. One thing I must say about Bob, he always used to finish up his letters with a terrific analysis and assessment of what was going on in Chicago. And then invariably his letters would end with a little phrase—"Not for Publication." [*laughs*] If Bob wrote that once, he wrote that literally a hundred times! I met him in 2006 in New Orleans, and he's still as enthusiastic for the music as he ever was.

Note: From 1991 to 2006 John Broven was a consultant for Ace Records of London, producing over 250 CD reissues. In 2009 he had another book published, *Record Makers and Breakers: Voices of the Independent Rock 'n' Roll Pioneers* (University of Illinois Press).

MIKE ROWE INTERVIEW

I was born in Plymouth, Devon, in 1938. My father was a bus conductor, and later he worked in the dockyard, just a typical working-class family. I went to school in Plymouth.

Wasn't Plymouth one of the cities that took quite a bit of punishment during the war?

The city was a naval center with the dockyards. The whole city's center was destroyed. Yes, Plymouth had several nights of absolutely concentrated bombing of civilian residential areas. There were a lot of casualties in Plymouth; I don't know how many. My father was in the RAF [Royal Air Force] and stationed in Scotland, but my mother had a nervous breakdown and so my father was transferred locally. Then my mother, my brother, and I moved to Cornwall, in the country, where we had relatives. And after that there was no more bombing of Plymouth. [*laughs*]

Mike Rowe, Chicago, 2006. Photo Robert Barclay.

People talk about your earliest memories, and they say the earliest kids can remember is four or five years old. Well, in my case it was age two and a bit, because you look out the door and you see the house across the street going up in flames—it was such a vivid image—and it stays with you. I remember my brother and I—I'd have to have been two and a half or three. We'd go down through the bombed houses collecting shrapnel, bits of metal from the bombs, which was still warm. There's a nice family story which you might be amused by. We lived in the ground-floor flat. Upstairs there were two old spinster ladies. During the bombing an incendiary bomb came crashing through and luckily landed in the garden. The two old ladies, who obviously were very worried and upset, called to my father. And to calm them down he said, "Don't worry—it's one of ours!" [*laughs*]

Mike Rowe with Moody Jones and family, 1974. Photo Jim O'Neal.

There were two entries to blues: you either came through jazz, or you came through rock 'n' roll. And if you came through rock 'n' roll, you came much later. As a kid in school I had no interest in pop music—or any music at all. One day on the radio I heard a Humphrey Littleton jazz record, and I thought, "That's the music for me!" So I started as a jazz enthusiast. I then read up absolutely everything I could find on jazz, and a lot of articles involved blues. There was one musical paper called the *Melody Maker*, and there would be one page on jazz reviews. Max Jones, a famous English critic, used to write the page, and some weeks he would have a page on blues records. And that's what got me interested in blues. I thought, "What's blues? What is this? I must investigate."

In those days, if you wanted to hear a blues record you had to buy it first. So I ordered a Leadbelly record—"Good Morning Blues," Leadbelly and Sonny Terry. And from the very first bar, I was hooked, and that was that. I think this might have been about 1951. I was still in school, but whenever I could afford it I bought records; half were jazz and half blues. There were a few blues records that had been issued in Britain at the time, like Sleepy John Estes or "Crippled" Clarence Lofton. And eventually when they started a Vocalion subsidiary there was wonderful stuff like Montana Taylor.

Who was doing the reissuing in the UK?

The Gramophone company, which comprised HMV, and Parlophone. Parlophone had reissued OKeh, and HMV had the tie-up with RCA Victor. And then later London had a tie-up with the independents like Chess and Sun. These were all 78s. The first microgroove recordings—ten-inch LPs—hit the UK a little later than the States, around 1954. There was a "T-Bone" Walker ten-inch LP on Capitol and a Leadbelly ten-inch on Capitol. I was lucky. There was a major jazz collector who lived in Plymouth, John Langmead. He was a Bessie Smith enthusiast, and he started the Plymouth Jazz Club with a couple of other friends. I got to know him, and he invited me around to record sessions at his house and introduced me to records like Tommy McClennen and Tampa Red—"Big Maceo" especially.

I was lucky; not many kids had the chance to hear this kind of music. Even luckier, one of the jazz record specialists, Peter Russell, opened up a record shop in Plymouth. Peter was a friend, and he knew I wanted to listen to the music. I used to spend all my free time down there listening to the records, and eventually, when I could afford it, I'd buy a record or two. I spent every available penny buying records. Then I went to college in London and the collecting dropped off for a few years, and it didn't really pick up again until I started work. It actually got very serious when I started buying records from the States rather than records that were issued here or imported by the jazz record shops. This was the early 1960s.

The main sources were Randy's in Gallatin, Tennessee, and Ernie's in Nashville—and Jack's Record Cellar in San Francisco. We used to get lists and catalogs from the States. By this time there was a growing crowd of blues fans. We used to swap information. When a lot of us started buying 78s, we were just buying blind—with the postwar records anyway. So we were all discovering new artists. We would gather at somebody's house and we'd each bring a few records, and the one that sticks in my mind—my friend Dave said, "I just got this new Jimmy Rogers record." And I thought, "Jimmie Rodgers—he's a white country singer. What's all this about?" [*laughs*] So he put on a Chess label *Jimmy Rogers* record and blew us all away!

I was equal parts prewar *and* postwar blues fan, but I had a special interest in Chicago and postwar down-home artists, but I suppose if I were more interested, it's because the records were more available. I could actually buy a Muddy Waters Chess 78, but it would have been a struggle to buy a Robert Johnson 78. My other interest was blues piano and boogie-woogie, which is a big, big interest—Crippled Clarence, Montana Taylor, Pinetop Smith, Albert Ammons—a whole host of them, and a lot of very obscure ones as well. What I was experiencing was probably happening all over the country, as it turns out.

Eventually Mike Leadbitter and Simon Napier in Bexhill put an advert in *Jazz Journal*, which was a magazine we bought each month because there was usually a page of blues reviews. They put in a small ad saying they were forming what they called the "Blues Appreciation Society." So I wrote to them, and there was such a response that they decided it wasn't really going to be a society—they were going to put out a magazine. From the beginning I was a subscriber—and learning. We were all learning, but there were others who were far ahead of us. I was living in London and they wanted a kind of "London address" for the magazine. I was kind of co-opted. [*laughs*] We were then moving into the American Folk Blues Festivals, and we were getting [around] visiting American bluesmen and women over here, and so generally we all met up at the concerts before—if we could—and interview the artists and publish the results. It was a fanzine, you know?

I've always been fascinated that not only were we learning about the blues singers, but that they were learning to talk to us. How did that work for you, and who did you talk to?

We talked to all the artists that came over, who were generally amazed that anybody had even heard of them, let alone their records, or that people wanted to talk to them. I think we engendered a tremendous amount of goodwill among the artists, which was really nice. And some were amazing,

Mike Rowe with Grace Brim, 1974. Photo Jim O'Neal.

like Little Brother Montgomery, who had the most amazing memory. Big Joe Williams, despite the incredible life he'd led, was another mine of information. Well, all right, some of it may have been a bit exaggerated, but a lot of it was on the money. Others weren't very good at talking and weren't used to being interviewed; other people just talked, and they were a joy to talk to.

Let's talk about your involvement with *Blues Unlimited* magazine.

I was there at the beginning, but I was a very minor player because I just didn't know as much as Simon Napier and Mike Leadbitter and John Broven. And so I would contribute reviews from the beginning, and then we eventually got into interviewing, visiting American blues artists, of which there was a kind of trickle. And it just developed from there. Eventually I was doing more interviews, more reviews. And then in '66, I made my first trip to America and wrote a series of small articles on the trip, really. My summer holidays, you know. What I did on my summer holidays. Well, I walked down Woodlawn, and I interviewed Johnny Shines, who was sitting on his doorstep with a battered guitar, et cetera. It was quite like that.

Can you talk about your years at *Blues Unlimited* after Mike Leadbitter died?

When Mike died, Simon Napier wanted to finish the magazine, but we wanted to continue it. There was John Broven, Bill Greensmith, Bez Turner, Neil Slaven, and myself—five of us to carry on the magazine. We took over and carried on. Then gradually Neil dropped out because he got a job as a roadie—I think with Deep Purple. Broven dropped out because he got a job as a bank manager, and he thought the bank would look rather askance in his interest in running a blues magazine. So it was down to three of us, and that continued for a period. Then Bill moved to St. Louis and married this beautiful black lady. Bez wanted to leave and start another blues magazine, *Juke Blues*. *BU* lived on despite the fact that Bill lived in the States and I was running it on my own with help from Tony Russell. The final problem was a financial crisis when we didn't get paid by a distributor, and then it just collapsed. We carried on quite a while—from issue number 116, when Mike died, and we finished around number 150 or something like that. The one thing I'd like to mention is how indebted I am—and we all were—to people like Chris Barber and Paul Oliver, and in the States to Chris Strachwitz and Mack McCormick and Don Kent.

Tell me the story of doing *Chicago Breakdown*.

There was a publisher called Studio Vista and they were doing a series of blues paperbacks. You may have seen some of the series: *Memphis Blues and Jug Bands*; *Blacks, Whites, and Blues*. There was a super one recalling the blues. There was the Derrick Stewart Baxter book, *Ma Rainey and the Classic Blues Singers,* and absolutely great recalling the blues. Yeah, so, the Chicago volume was supposed to be part of this set. But as I started to write it—and you ask where the information came from and what happened—it just became more and more. And by the time I was like halfway through it, Studio Vista had gone out of business. And so a friend of mine whose father had a publishing house and was also a blues fan and actually had a British blues band— Stewart K. had bankrolled the band Dr.

K's Boogie Disease, and he said, "I will publish it." And eventually that's how it appeared under the Edison Books imprint.

We have a picture of what the book entails, what purpose it really serves. When did it occur to you that that would be the purpose, the mission of that book?

I think all I planned to do was really lay down a first rough draft of the history of postwar Chicago blues. And I expected there would be further volumes that would certainly supersede it. There weren't. I can't even believe that there's been nothing written since '73, yeah.

Do you see any shortcomings in the book?

Oh, God, yes. [*chuckles*]

Let's talk about them. There's so much good material in there. What was not on the mark?

There was some information that was wrong, okay? Now, it may not bother a lot of people or be recognized by other people, but to me it hurts that I totally misidentified some sidemen on recordings. But the only other thing was that a couple of other important singers were rediscovered after I'd published, and those I would love to have been in the book. Little Hudson, who I did interview and did discover, and Blue Smitty, who I didn't and would loved to have included his story, because I remember a wonderful *Living Blues* article on him.

I think the thing that strikes me is that it took two guys from England to put everything in perspective. How did you manage, being in England, to put an American music in perspective so accurately? And if you have any theories, why didn't it happen here?

First of all, I had made several trips to Chicago and I had met the artists and I'd interviewed them, and so I had an idea, a seed, as it was. Why didn't it happen here? I could give you an analogy on this. There was a book on Sussex folk songs, or was it Sussick folk songs? But anyway, it was on a county of Southern England, and it was done by an American. So this is the other side of the question. It may be that there's a romance of faraway places. It may just be accidental. But it's not uncommon to find that books on specialist topics are often written by people who may reside thousands of miles away.

Mike Rowe with Jim O'Neal 1974. Photo Amy van Singel.

So you wouldn't say that segregation and race relations in this country would handcuff any American author in their appreciation of this music?

I wouldn't have thought so, actually. You know, it never bothered Jim O'Neal or any of the *Living Blues* writers, for instance. I think it may have just been in the right place, right time, wrong place, wrong time.

What were some of the major hurdles in doing the research and in assembling it in a cohesive manner that began to draw a picture?

It's the timelines, I guess. At any given time, take a snapshot of Chicago, all the bands playing in clubs and that, and you might be able to identify personnel et cetera for a large proportion of them. But a week later it all would change. And so in some ways it's like a map of the stars where you're looking at stars that have died millions of years ago but their image is still out there. You know, that's the analogy I would draw. That was a difficulty, but it was not, not enormous, I think. It was just nice to be able to find any kind of documentary evidence of where the clubs were and who played in them in any way.

What were your resources for the actual history of the city?

There's a great book called *Black Metropolis* by St. Clair Drake. There were three: there's *Black Metropolis*, which I think is volumes one and two—two volumes of that—and *Black Chicago* by Allan H. Spear. And these were wonderful, wonderful sources for the history of the development of all the black areas.

Was there anybody that you used as a sounding board as you assembled all this material?

Actually, no. Maybe I should have had somebody like that, but there wasn't anybody. There wasn't anybody to read it. In fact, my editor, Tony Russell, was a carryover from the Studio Vista days. He edited that series of monographs. And Rick Kay employed him to edit *Chicago Breakdown*.

I'd like to say that you did a magnificent job and it stands the test of time. I wonder if you would have any interest in a follow-up about the decline of this whole movement. Wouldn't it be a sad volume to write?

It would be. I don't think I'd have the heart for that. But certainly I wouldn't mind updating it as it is, being able to add Little Hudson and Blue Smitty and all the other stuff that has emerged. Today I had the enormous pleasure of talking to the Reverend Uncle Johnny Williams this afternoon. He came up with at least three or four guitar players I'd never heard of in my life. I think one was Bob and Andy, two guitarists on Maxwell Street. And then there's—I can't recall the other name, but somebody that he'd played with a lot with on Maxwell Street. But these are not names that exist in any kind of blues pantheon.

Who did you have it in mind that you really wanted to meet?

I wanted to meet everybody. But I wanted to meet Eddie Taylor. I wanted to meet Floyd Jones.

Good taste.

[*chuckles*] And this was effected by Walter Horton, who had come over the previous year. That was about the '65 American Folk Blues Festival. And we'd got to know him. He was friendly and he offered to show us around. So when we got to Chicago we phoned him up. And he took us down to Turner's that night; we saw J. B. Hutto. The next day, he took us to see Floyd on his job. And in the afternoon, over to see Eddie Taylor, who was playing that night at the Black and White Lounge on Ogden Avenue. And it just snowballed, really. And it was just through kindness of people I met that we were able to do this.

What were your impressions? You'd listened to the records. What was your impression in actually being in the clubs here?

It was that "Okay, there's a difference," but some things were so much the same. At the Black and White Lounge, Eddie Taylor's immediate opening to "Backdoor Friend"—I mean, the sound was absolutely wonderful, sort of great, bell-like tones off his Gibson. And it was just like the blues on record, you know, that I'd been listening to.

Who else did you have it in mind to see? And did the reality of meeting them, hearing them live up to expectations?

Johnny Shines was a great, great moment when I phoned him up. He said come on down in South Woodlawn. And we get there and he hasn't got a guitar. So we go down the road to a music store, and we hire a guitar for the afternoon for him to play. These were just wonderful little moments that you treasure.

Were there any major disappointments in personalities or performances in people that you'd heard in the glory years of the fifties, the late forties? Anybody that you'd run across that was a disappointment?

No, I think not then. Okay, I don't want this to sound like some simpering kind of end of view, "Everything's all wonderful and everybody's all sort of lovely." But at that time, no. Later on, certainly yes. And I was very disappointed in people who were my heroes.

Who in particular?

Jimmy Rogers, who by the time he was touring—we never heard him live in Chicago. He wasn't playing. He had sort of semi-retired then. And the only time we heard him live was when he started his career up again. And there were a couple of awful gigs at the Hundred Club on Oxford Street, where the place was packed with people who treasured his early Chess records. And he was drinking heavily and the show was just totally [a] disaster. And I thought, "This is so sad. This is somebody who really would have had the audience at his feet. And it's degenerated into nothingness now."

Talking of drummers, somebody I absolutely always adored playing drums, apart from Willie Nix, was Johnnie Mae Dunson. And I went to see her and there was a set of drums. Her niece was playing about on the drums, fancied herself as a drummer. And there was the most desultory kind of attack on the drums you could imagine. And I think Johnnie Mae could stand it no longer, and she elbowed her out of the way, picked up the drumsticks, and went *bang!* into it. It was wonderful! Absolutely! I hope to see her tomorrow.

You haven't seen her this trip yet?

No, I haven't. I was very worried about her, because I heard she wasn't well and I was concerned. But I was so pleased to see that she's on the bill.

How about some adventures that you've had with musicians out there when you were here? You told me about seeing Floyd and Johnny Shines. Who were the other musicians you saw?

What do you want? The stories of madness?

Absolutely!

This is the other thing, you see, we didn't really touch on today that we were interested in. We were serious about research and that. But we liked to have fun as well. And there were moments . . . There were just things that happened that really sort of tickled us, and we've enjoyed ever since. I mean, perhaps it's a case of you had to be there, but I'll try. There was a great moment with Sunnyland Slim at Jimmy Walker's house, and Sunnyland came in. Sunnyland had some of the JOB [record company] tapes. Jewel [record company] bought most of them, but Michael, Joe Brown's son, had been sort of just hunting the odd tape here and there. And Sunnyland had one of the JOB master tapes. And he bought this from Michael, and I think there was probably about a quarter of it not used. And he and Jimmy had this long discussion about what he was going to do with it. And it went on and on. You know, more and more bizarre. And then finally Jimmy—Jimmy hit on it, and he said, "Sunny, I'll tell you what you do." He said, "Yeah, what's that?" Jimmy said, "Put something on it." [*laughs*] Sunny looked at him and he scratched the knot on his head, and he said, "Yeah, I believe I'll do that."

The other one was we were going to an Eddie Taylor gig. We'd spent the day with Eddie. And we were going to the White Rose in Phoenix, which, as you know, is way down south.

Panel discussion at Chicago Blues Festival, 2005. *L to R*: Neil Slaven, Mike Rowe, moderator Jim O'Neal, Bill Greensmith, and Bob Hall. Photo Robert Barclay.

Playboy Venson was going to be his drummer. So the gig was, I think, starting about ten thirty. So eleven o'clock, we're outside Playboy's apartment and throwing stones up at the window and so on. Something like a pirate adventure or something. [*chuckles*] And Playboy, who was in bed, appeared with his cap and an eight-inch cigar in his mouth, looking out the window. And they were discussing this gig that, you know, had started half an hour earlier and it would take another hour and a half to get to it. Not surprisingly, we never went, which is really disappointing, because I was looking forward to that.

That's two, you know, little vignettes. There are others, but many are not repeatable. But I've got one last one about England, okay? You better not broadcast this anywhere. [*chuckles*] In the American Folk Blues Festival tour, John Wrencher was over with Homesick James. And whenever we went to a gig or whatever, there was one famous London groupie who was hideously ugly and just generally grotesque. And she was always hanging around John Wrencher. And she was there every night, absolutely with John. And then the last night, she was with Homesick. And we said to John, "John, what happened? Wasn't that your girl?" He said, "Yeah, but I sold her to Homesick." There's one I'm saving for the book, because it's one that Floyd told me. Every time I went to see Floyd, he would tell me a bit more of this story and said, "Mike, don't you write that up!" But now is the time.

Thank you very much for taking the time out to do this.

My pleasure. You know, it's just been so nice. I'm very touched that people actually want to talk to me about a book I wrote thirty years ago.

RAY FLERLAGE INTERVIEW

First of all, Ray, how do I correctly pronounce your last name?

Well, it's up for grabs in our family. But we say Fler-laydge. We used to say Fler-ledge, and then every time I was on radio for about fifteen years, every announcer would say Fler-laydge. And my present wife liked Fler-laydge better than Fler-ledge, so we compromised and now it's Fler-laydge. [*chuckles*]

With me is Ray Flerlage, and Ray has a brand-new book. It's mostly photographs, but there's also some light text. It's called *Chicago Blues as Seen from the Inside*. Ray, if people dig into this and read just the first opening pages, the thing that I recall was that you were going to do this many years ago. When were you going to do this originally?

Originally we were talking about this in 1965. It was a very specific project to do a book on Chicago blues. The people involved in it were people you would have heard of: Mike Bloomfield, Pete Welding, and a guy named Willie Hopkins, who was the editor then, the art editor, of *Chicago Scene* magazine, one of my best outlets for photographs until it folded. Everything that I was selling to folded, you know, during that period. But in any event, we won some prizes from—I forget—one of the local printers. And design prizes for a cover in which some of my minimalist-type shots of Pete Seeger were featured. And so Willie and Mike and Pete Welding and I would huddle together and had very definite plans about a book on Chicago blues, and we all had the wherewithal to do it. They finally decided to leave Mike Bloomfield out of it, because he was so enthusiastic that his enthusiasm would bubble over and lead us away from reality. So as it turned out, Pete Welding had a chance to go to the coast and work on his doctorate in folk music. He left Chicago. Mike Bloomfield had a chance to work

Ray Flerlage. Photo James Fraher.

with Bob Dylan and later with Paul Butterfield and all these people where he won his great fame and fortune and killed himself with dope. And Willie Hopkins had a chance to become art editor of *Look* magazine.

So they all skipped Chicago, and I was sitting here with plans for a book and nobody to plan it with. So I didn't really do anything about it except dream for a great many years. And then I started to get calls from various people. And a man named Charles K. Cowdery called me and said he'd seen some of my stuff when he was working with one of the companies that used my things in advertising. And he liked them and was thinking of doing a book himself, and he'd like for me to work with him. Well, you know, I'm a little tired, you know, not too ambitious at this point. And I wouldn't want to get involved in a lot of stuff for no rewards. So we talked and talked and talked. And finally he gets a publisher who would come up with printing costs and he leaned on me real hard—and Charles is pretty good at leaning on people hard. And we ended up doing a book called *Blues Legends*. And so people started to see some of the things, and I started to get more calls and more interest in my work.

And then in 1995 a film editor saw some of my stuff when she was working on *Eric Clapton: Nothing but the Blues* with Martin Scorsese. She saw some of the things that I'd done at the Trianon Ballroom with Bobby Bland and with Jackie Wilson. And the Trianon Ballroom was a fascinating vast expanse, and the thing that caught her attention was the . . . were the scenes with heavy smoke and the spotlights cutting through the smoke. A very dramatic effect. She said, "I've never seen anything like it before." And she said, "It opened a whole new world to me." And I thought it was the usual flattery of people, you know, like to make you feel good. But she kept calling. And over the next five years she kept calling. And she finally came to Chicago with half a ton of gear that she carried in herself, recording gear and video gear. And she taped, videotaped twelve hours of interviews with me and she did all the work. She did the lights and sound and everything. Then she told me that she was going to use this as the text for the book that we were going to do. So we started talking about a book.

And then Jack David of ECW Press of Toronto stopped in to see me. He wanted to do a book on Chicago blues. And, fortunately, Lisa was in town—Lisa Day. And so we all sat down—Jack David, Lisa Day, my wife, and myself—and hit on a plan to do a book. And Jack David asked Lisa if she would take over the editorship of the job. So the fact that she was the editor made the book into a different type of thing than I had expected to do, because when I talked with Jack David, I told him—as I've told everybody else—you know, "I just am tired! I just really don't want to go . . . do a whole lot of work." He said, "It will just be a photo book. You've got the prints already. It will be a simple thing. You can come up with some song lyrics and just captions." So I said, "Cool. It doesn't sound like a big job."

But Lisa's idea was that she had to get my voice. She said, "I want your voice!" So she kept saying, "Will you do an introduction to this section? Will you do a commentary on this section? Will you explain this?" And before you knew it, I'd written half a million words or less. [*chuckles*] And I finally ran out of steam, you know. And she kept heaping so much stuff on me that I finally said, "Well, you know, I'm getting confused, and I just don't know how to keep up with it." So Charles Cowdery—my old friend from *Blues Legends*—said, "I'll help you." He said, "I'm a professional writer. That's my business. I'll be glad to help you." So I said, "Okay." I talked with him and gave him a bunch of my loose notes and gave him some phone interviews and stuff like that. And he came with a whole lot of text, and then we reduced it and redid it. And took out some of my polysyllabic attempts at style and made it into readable text. So then I wrote some more and wrote some more and wrote some more and we ended up with a book!

And essentially—I don't know if I've gotten this correctly—it's basically a picture book and it's sort of like Ray Flerlage grabs you by the hand and runs you by all the prints and says, "This is sort of this session. This was what was going on at this time." It basically sheds a lot of light on the work that's there. All the pictures.

Yeah, that's correct. It's basically a book only of photographs, but this other stuff gets inserted to describe the pictures. And then there's a section at the end in which individual pictures are explained and identified for personnel and date and all that kind of stuff. But what Lisa and also Chuck were interested in doing were getting my own reactions to what was happening and to the meeting with these wonderful people. And my life experience, you know, which became very different from normal life experiences, you know. And the "why," you know—they want to know why. And all the people that I've talked with in interviews and stuff like that are interested in "why would you want to live like that?" And I want to live like that because it's good stuff, you know.

Is it accurate to say that essentially you're a white American who went to live in the black community?

That's correct.

Starting when?

Well, actually, it's very specific. During World War Two I was working at a radio chain, Crosley Radio in Cincinnati, and I was doing publicity work. I was writing publicity for the various artists who appeared there for newspapers. I then had an offer from *Cincinnati Post,* and I moved to the *Cincinnati Post* because it was more specifically the kind of writing job I'd always looked for. They had me interview classical musicians. I'd gotten very interested in classics and pretty knowledgeable. And my first interviewee was Marian Anderson, whom I had admired tremendously since hearing her Schubert records—"Ave Maria" and other things. To me, a demigod. And she was such a wonderful woman. Such a wonderful person to talk with. She talked to me—I think I took too much of her time, actually, when I thought of it later—but she chatted with me all of a Sunday afternoon. And one of the things I noticed was that instead of talking about herself, she was talking about the Finnish experiences of her accompanist—Kosti Vehanen, I believe his name was. She was telling me stories that he had told her rather than talking all about herself. And she talked to me like I was an equivalent of herself, you know. As important as she was. I mean, it was a wonderful experience! Warm experience.

Then I was muscled by the draft board to get a wartime job, that the *Cincinnati Post* would not keep me out of the draft. I was married and had children. So I had the opportunity to go to the Wright Aeronautical Corporation, right outside Cincinnati, where they were making aircraft engines. I went up there and started to tell them all the practical information, all the practical knowledge. I had all my practical capabilities. And the guy said to me, "Look, the reason we're interviewing you is because we understand you have a musical background." [*chuckles*] I said, "Well, what does music have to do with aircraft engines?" He said, "We want somebody to handle the employee recreation program, and we're thinking about an industrial music program. And we thought that you might be the person to do it." So I said, "Yeah." I then told them all the stuff that I had done musically. So I was hired and I became the director of industrial music. People laugh at that because the job was to play records on the public address system. And also to organize and rehearse employee groups of musicians.

But before long I ran into problems with discrimination. This is the first time that I had the opportunity to meet a lot of black executives. They had a number of very outstanding men, and they treated them with great dignity when everybody was together. But when the black executives were not there, they would talk about them like sub-citizens, to say the least—demeaning references to these outstanding guys. I couldn't see it. I couldn't see how could you look at this man and not see a serious, important human person equivalent to yourself? They could not see it. And I *could* see it. And then they started giving me trouble about the employee recreation rehearsals. The best groups I had were the black groups. Some of them were on radio. Some of the white groups were not even good amateurs; they didn't even know how to play their instruments. They were trying to learn and trying to learn to form groups, and yet they wanted me to give the white employees preference in the rehearsal times and make the black guys come in when they were not about to work, or when they were not just leaving their shifts—which would have meant disbanding the groups. They would not come out . . . you know, make special trips out to the plant just to rehearse. And I said, "No, these groups are the best groups I have, and they've got to have the preferential slots."

So we didn't get along too well. But from that time I just had formed friendships there. I formed friendships with the black executives. I started to form friendships with the workers in the plant, the plant foremen, who were not executives but minor operators. And I must confess, I was sent to a lot of the employee recreation affairs as the semiofficial plant representative to the interracial groups. And there were a lot of very pleasant, friendly people, including some very friendly, lovely girls [*laughs*], and I must confess that that had a lot to do with my conversion into a white-black man. [*laughs*] But in any event, I formed a very close alliance, a very deep feeling for the people I associated with, the black people I associated with, and a great resentment of the discrimination against them. And as I knew people as individuals and saw what they had to go through, I identified with—if you can put it—the suffering, you know, and more with the sufferers than the one inflicting the pain. I would rather do it, really. And then I had a second marriage. My first marriage disintegrated with the move from Cincinnati. I moved to Chicago.

Just out of curiosity, with the experience you were going through and your identification with black Americans, did that strain your marriage? Did being a black-white American not go over big at home?

Now is the time for obfuscation. I would like to say that I was faultless here, but I was not faultless. My marriage had been a little weak, and with my interest in the black community it became weaker. But I would not say that it was the racial strain or the racial difference that caused the split. We were splitting anyway. We were having some insurmountable difficulties. And we remained friends the rest of our lives. We have always remained friends. And yet we could not make it anymore. And I had to move back to Chicago. The war came to an end and I didn't have anything going down there. And I had some opportunities up here. My father was the general auditor of the Pullman Company, and I had a chance to get some employment up here. However, it was not satisfactory. And I would look for other outlets. And I started giving talks on folk music and blues and stuff like that. And that led to a job with *People's Songs* and directly into pretty much permanent identification with blues. And, of course, more logically, then identification with the black community. And actually a lot of writing for black publications. And then I had an opportunity to work with *Ebony* magazine, rather an odd connection.

While I was with *People's Songs*, some of the people who had attended my lectures decided that I would be a fit subject for a dramatization they were doing on *Ebony* magazine. Sinclair Lewis had a novel called *Kingsblood Royal*. And it had to do with a white man, like myself; rather than becoming identified with the black community, he found that he had a smidgeon of black blood in his family. He was looking to see whether Kingsblood . . . the name Kingsblood meant that he was descended from royalty, but he found that instead he was descended from blacks. And this terrible shock disintegrated his marriage too. And I was asked to play the role of Kingsblood. And when it appeared in *Ebony* magazine, and *Life* reprinted it and *Time* had reprinted it, and that ruined my job at the Pullman Company, because the people in the office saw Flerlage as Kingsblood, the black man, the white black man. And they said to my father, "Isn't that your son?" And he comes to me and he says, "What's this?" I said, "Well, this is the best job I've had to date!" And, oh, he was unhappy. As a matter of fact, it led to one-sided fisticuffs. And so I then concentrated still more on other jobs.

My goodness, we're talking about light-years ago, aren't we? It would be not so much of a leap today, since culture seems to have moved closer and closer, or white culture seems to be black culture by and large—at least entertainment-wise.

Yes. Right. Every encounter I had tended to cement my conviction. I had a chance to interview Paul Robeson, and I have never, never run into a human being with as powerful an aura, if you want to call it an aura. He just vibrated not only power, but you could say humanity. Like Marian Anderson, you had the feeling when you talked to Paul Robeson that he was looking at you as his equivalent, white or black. You had the feeling that humanity sort of—yours and his meshed, and you could see it working the same with women as with men. I mean, my God! You'd see him waiting to go to the airport and there would be crowds of people around him, and perhaps more white women than anybody else. [*chuckles*] Just gazing at the man. But with me, he talked in a very relaxed, friendly, unpretentious way.

But the thing I noticed about Robeson was that . . . I tried to make conversation. I would talk about this, I realized instantly that he knew more about it than I did. I'd switch to another subject; he knew more about it than I did. Switch to a third subject; he knew more about it than I did. I never hit a subject that Robeson didn't know a damn sight more than I did and could articulate it better. He was a powerful person. I would imagine if he were alive today, I'd have a terrible problem deciding who was the greatest man alive today—Robeson or Nelson Mandela. I mean, tremendous personality. Of course, I never met Mandela, but from everything I hear about him, or from the people who met him, he has the same kind of thing, except he has this magnificent humanity that encompasses the ability to forgive incredible injustice. Robeson, of course, they beat him down. He was . . . The conspiracy against Paul Robeson was one of the great tragedies of our time, I think. I saw a show in which Harry Belafonte said very much the same thing, you know. And he said the people that destroyed Paul Robeson are still out there. And I presume so.

When you talk to these people, did they have any clue as to who you were and the path you were on? Do you think they had any notion of that?

[*laughs*] I don't know how they did; *I* didn't! If they knew the path I was on, I didn't know the path I was on. You just play it by ear. But I've always felt, you know, a lot of times people say . . . in effect, they're asking, "How do you have the moxie to walk into all these places as though you belong there?" And especially when you are with . . . In my case, when I was with a black woman, they would often feel tentative. And I'd say, "Damn!" You know, you just go there like that's where you should be! You know, you look at somebody. They're not going to challenge you if they know you know that you . . . you're where you ought to be. You belong there just as much as they do. Why challenge you? No point!

I was just thinking, it's many years later, but I know when I got out of high school I went to the South Side, and I was the only white face for miles. Of course, this was, again, three or four decades from the time you were doing it. And I don't think it was quite so uncommon at that point. But even that, at that point, to me it was like a different world!

Well, it was. It was a very difficult thing at first. I remember when I first went to Chicago and went on the South Side and went to visit this beautiful lady. And I was up there to visit this beautiful lady at that time. And I was going to visit her no matter what. But I got off the El, and the only compromise that I made was that I put on a big wide-brimmed hat. [*laughs*] I don't know how that would help me with my light skin and blue eyes, but I put on a big wide-brimmed hat. And I started to go toward the stairs going down, and the ticket taker called to me and said, "You'd better not go down there." And I just still went toward the door, and one of the security people said, "You know, you don't want to go down there."

Are these black folks admonishing you at this point? Or white?

White—white people advising me not to go down. And you know, it made me think. But I couldn't think . . . I wasn't going down, because that's why I was here. You know, I was going to go down, but it was . . . it was a thing to do. You know, it was something that you were aware that you were doing, something that required decision. But I went down, and although I've had some difficulties with some people, every time I've had difficulties with a black man I would have had the same difficulty with a white man in the same circumstances. In other words, I never was accosted or attacked or anything of the sort without a fairly good reason, you know—like fooling with his woman or something like that. And the same thing would happen if I fooled with a white guy's woman. You find people are estranged pairs; they're sometimes very watchful, each of the other's activities. But I, for the most part, was amazingly welcome almost wherever I went. I've had the welcome mat, and even better than the welcome mat, nothing at all. You know, just, you come in and you're just there. You're just one of the people there. And again, I've told Chuck a couple of times, it's hard to believe in some cases.

A couple of times I had to pass, reverse passing, to get an apartment. And people, I suppose, decided to believe me when I passed as black. I didn't look it, but I had to get an apartment. And I was taken for black when I worked at the Studebaker plant, because I always traveled in black cars with black friends. And people came to me and said, "The word is going around that you're black!" I said, "Well, you know, so what? It happens that I'm not, but that doesn't hurt me to have that reputation. My friends are black. I ride with black people. I live with black people. Sure. Cool. Everything is fine."

But I've had . . . One of the funniest stories, one of the strangest stories I have. There was a very black guy, one of a group of friends that I had friendly associations with. My wife at the time, a black woman, took me to all these affairs. And this guy was known as a preacher. I'm not sure exactly what his occupation was, but he was known as a preacher. And he was telling some stories, some of the "in" jokes in which they use the N-word and all this kind of stuff, black among black. And he was using all the words, and somebody walked over to him and whispered in his ear [*chuckles*] and he turned and he looked at me. His eyes just popped! He had thought that because of my association and because of my ease in that . . . in spite of my whiteness, I was black. And he was telling these stories. He could not believe he'd been telling these stories with a white guy sitting there. But we got over the problem very quick, you know.

Of course, nowadays there are a lot of television programs in which you see people, if possible, whiter than myself with lighter eyes than myself, which you look at now and they say they're black. And you still find it very difficult to believe. But with all the intermixture in our society, there're many more black people that you see walking on the street than you realize. You know, white black people. And I happen to be a white white person, but I think I could pass very easily, you know . . . I remember a guy named Jazz Gillum. Ever hear of Jazz Gillum?

You betcha.

Okay. Folkways was doing a Jazz Gillum album—that is, it was a shared album. It was with a couple of other guys.

Was it Stidham?

Arbee Stidham and James Brewer? Was it James Brewer?

It was Big Bill Broonzy.

Well, in any event, I knew Broonzy, but I never photographed Broonzy. I knew him when I was at *People's Songs*. But at any rate, Gillum was not performing anywhere. And I was used to photographing people performing. But in this particular case he was not performing, so I asked him to come over to the place we were living—Lake Meadows. So Broonzy came over and he had this very formal type hat on, and he looked like a guy who was very self-conscious sartorially. But Gillum was pretty dirty and, well, I hate to go into all of it. But he looked like he might be living on the street when he left us. And he liked the change from his regular living quarters so much that he stayed there about nine hours. It got to be a problem, but the interesting thing about Gillum was that although he made a poor impression physically, as we talked to him I was astonished by the poetry of his language—it's very interesting.

He was telling me, for example, about living in the South and about coming north. He played the mouth harp, played the harp. I think he played other instruments, but he used to play on the street corners for pennies and whatever, used a tin cup. But some of the white clowns would come and ask him to perform for them specifically. And he would for a while, and then they would get him to go out with them. They would take him out on some country road or something like that for a group and get him to perform and to dance. And if he stopped dancing energetically enough, they would start shooting at his feet! So he told me, you know, "When you leave the South, you better leave running, because walking is way too slow." And I said, "Huh?" He said, "That's how this 'Key to the Highway' came about." He said, "Lester Melrose asked me to do a song about a highway." There was a song out then, very popular. I don't remember what it was. I don't remember whether he told me specifically. But there was a highway song out there. So Lester Melrose asked Gillum to do a song about a highway. So he said, "I was thinking about 'Key to the Highway.' I was thinking about *'better leave running, because walking is way too slow.'*" And so he ends up with this song. And he said, "They end up giving it to Broonzy." He said, "But it's my song." He said, "Melrose gave it to Broonzy for his own benefit."

In your opinion, in speaking to Jazz, do you think that he was mentally stable? Was he in his right mind, in your opinion?

When he talked with me, yes. Yes. I think he was . . . I think he was at a low ebb. I think he was at a low ebb. As I say, it looked like he might be living anywhere he could, as his clothes looked very disordered and they were dirty and crummy. But he still wore the hat and he still . . . He looked like a guy who was accustomed to being sharp. I think the pictures in the book will show that here's a guy that was accustomed to looking sharp, you know. When I took pictures of him, he had the old horn—you know, the old acoustic horns and all that kind of stuff to add color to the photos. And so at any rate, I found him an interesting guy. He was the guest who came to dinner and stayed a little too long. [*chuckles*]

Well, I think the reason I ask that is because I believe that he was regarded as mentally unstable by the time of his death. Was it about 1966, I think?

M-hm [yes].

That somehow basically just doing irrational things led to his death.

Oh, I see.

And I just wondered . . . When was it that you actually . . .

About three years earlier. At the time I talked with him, I did not have that impression. Neither did my wife. You know, we just figured he stuck around a little too long for our other social arrangements. We had other stuff that was going to go on, but Jazz liked it there and . . . The only thing I could say about irrationality is that I did have an appointment with him to come back and he didn't show. And some weeks or months later I got a postcard indicating that he had tried to come visit us and we weren't there. But he did not come when he was expected. And you know, he didn't leave a card at the time. I got this card indicating that he had come. So that was irrational but not totally nutty, you know.

Well, a lot of times in the black community, when you head for irrationality, it's in no uncertain terms. It's not a subtle thing. I guess Billy Boy Arnold was the fellow who is saying that he saw Jazz in a tarpaper shack and it was 100 out and 110 in the shack, and he was stoking a fire.

Oh, God! That's too bad. Sorry to hear that.

Can I ask you some impressions of some other people that you have photographs here?

Sure.

It seems to me that in the history of blues—particularly of the first white guys getting involved—that Mike Bloomfield was a key figure. It seems to me that he doesn't retain much of a reputation at this point, other than being there first. I think people tend to dismiss his abilities as a player. I just wondered if you think that's an accurate perception or if you have a different perception of him.

No, I certainly have a different perception. I think he was regarded as a major talent, I mean, a superb guitarist. You know, I don't necessarily follow his musical trends, the stuff he was doing. You know, I'm not all that much on Jimi Hendrix and stuff like that. But Mike could play a tremendous guitar. But also, I feel, a miraculous talent in that in between takes of the Sleepy John Estes session, he would go to a piano and play very impressive barrelhouse piano—Big Maceo–type stuff, you know. And as a matter of fact, one time I had him on one of the radio shows and he played himself out of the studio. He played for so long and so loud, the station manager asked him to cease and desist! [*chuckles*] But he played a helluva lot of piano. Also, you'll see him in here [Ray's book]. Big Joe Williams would get him up on stage playing string bass, acoustic bass behind him. I think Mike could probably have played anything he tried to play. He just had this immense musical talent.

So you think he was a talent, not just a novelty?

Oh, no. No, I think he was an astonishing musician! I think he was a genius—not using it loosely, but a person so gifted in so many areas I would tend to think of having a kind of genius. And I think he had it. A nutty guy but very, very nice, friendly, easy . . . but you know, if you saw him with Wolf or Muddy or John Lee Hooker, he was irresistible in his admiration for them. He would talk to them, and the adoration in his eye just broke down any of their resistance. He looked at them, you know, like he was looking at a minor god, and they would give him anything he wanted. Tell him all the things that were going to help him take their business away, in a sense, make more money than they made.

But people like Muddy were very philosophical about that. He was aware that some guys like Mike would make more money than he was making, probably. But he said, "Still it helps expand the market for our work." But, no, any of these guys would be glad to help Mike Bloomfield, because he so obviously was very sincere, and also they knew that what they were telling him, he was intelligent enough and perceptive enough and musically acute enough to use. And he used it! I mean, they could tell me stuff all year long. I wouldn't even know what they said, you know. But he knew.

Were you around for his decline?

No. No, we ran together quite a little bit. I used to . . .

Was he a student when you knew him? Was he *ever* a student?

If he was, I didn't know that aspect of his life. I think it was Pete Welding who introduced me to Mike. And my association with Mike was primarily going to these various interviews and stuff like that. And I was the only one driving a car, so I was their wheels. I was Pete's and Mike's wheels. Although a lot of times I'd run into Mike other places, and other guys had cars, I presume. Butterfield and Charlie Musselwhite. Charlie was a sweet character, and I guess still is. I haven't seen him for a long time. But when he talked with these guys, it was very, very impressive.

I wanted to ask you about Muddy. When we were talking earlier, and I said I was totally prepared to dislike Memphis Slim because I thought he'd be a little artificial, a little too polished, and it disappeared the moment I met him. What was your impression of Muddy?

Well, I got to know Muddy, I guess, kind of slowly. I remember when I shot some stuff in Pepper's in 1961. I didn't carry away any feeling that I knew Muddy. He was aware of my camera. I don't think I was there by invitation. I think I just went there for *Rhythm and Blues* magazine. I did a cover or something for them. Or maybe *Chicago Scene*. I was doing a lot of stuff for *Chicago Scene* then. But Muddy was aware I was there, and he—in some of the photos he looked at me. But for the most part, as always, I tried to get stuff while they were performing. And I walked away from that session without any feeling that I knew Muddy or had any association or anything like that with Muddy or anybody in the band at all. Because at that time I didn't think of anybody in any band except the leader. You know, if I went to photograph Muddy Waters, Muddy Waters was the only one that I was more or less aware of. I wasn't even aware then of Spann or any of these other people—I was not. Later I found out that the sidemen that I photographed were kind of interesting too. You know, they were part of the band.

But it was not, I think, until I went to interview Muddy at his home that I started to get to know him. Although, having been at Pepper's in '61, I shot him again at the Chicago Opera House during a jazz concert at the Opera House in 1963, and cameras were not allowed. I fortunately had some Leicas that were quite quiet, and I just shoot from one seat, you know—not move around at all—with a quiet Leica. And I got a lot of good stuff. And I had the feeling some of the shots looked like Muddy's looking right at me—you know, eyes right on the camera. Now, a photographer can make himself feel that people are looking at him, and they forget that when a musician sees a camera lens he's not looking at the photographer; he's looking at the camera lens probably. You like to think that . . . "Oh, he recognized me! Oh, Muddy recognized me." [*chuckles*] Clear across the opera house! But he saw a camera lens. But he's looking right, right at me. So again, I don't know whether he recognized a familiar face or not.

I guess my question here is did you find him sincere and admirable? Because I know that when he first came to town, there were established musicians—Big Bill and others—who took him under wing and helped him and pointed him in the right direction. It seemed like that was sort of a tradition among the musicians. I know he helped a lot of the young white guys. He also helped a lot of the black musicians who came to town. If you got to know him, did you find that element about him?

Yeah, yeah. That's one of the phrases that always stuck with me. As a matter of fact, I always wanted to write an article about it, or have a chapter in the book on it, but it didn't work out—"Camaraderie of the Blues." They didn't have an apprentice system, but they didn't need an apprentice system, because they helped each other just automatically without going through apprenticeship. But Muddy had the reputation among other musicians and among everybody who knew him, if somebody like Buddy Guy or somebody like that comes to town, and he hears that he doesn't have a job and maybe doesn't have a place to stay or doesn't have a square meal, they said, if Muddy wouldn't send anybody across town, he'd make a pack of sandwiches and he'd carry them over there himself! And a few bucks.

Muddy to me, I mean, I just say I love Muddy. I mean, I can't look . . . I look at a picture of Marc PoKempner's book, *Down at Theresa's*. He's got a picture of Muddy about ten years after the last shot I took of Muddy. And I just look at that picture and I just love it, because he was just such a sweet guy. I just love Muddy! He was so utterly natural. Just like, again, like Marian Anderson, like Paul Robeson. He talks to you like you and he are just equivalent. Okay. He's world famous. He's the greatest bluesman in Chicago—maybe—and you're just some little old stumbling photographer. But you would that think you were a king like he was. I call him up to photograph Otis Spann for Prestige Records, and Spann would be rehearsing in his basement. It turns out that he's rehearsing with James Cotton. And it's just as easy as if you talked to an old friend. You call Muddy and he answers the phone, "Yeah, come on over" and such and such.

I remember when I was photographing Spann—just a little insignificant thing. But I walk up the hall and Muddy's sitting there in the kitchen with part of his family. And he's all stripped—he's wide open here. And I look at the son-of-a-bitch. He looks like a prize-fighter! I said, "God damn! He's the same age that I am, born in 1915, and he looks like he could take on Joe Louis or Mohammed Ali and here I am all, you know, going to pot." And it don't seem right. He's up all night, you know, with booze and the gals and yet he looks one hundred percent. No, but you'd sit down and you'd interview him and you could talk about anything. You could talk about Old Fitzgerald; you could talk about anything. And he'd just chat with you like an old-time friend, you know. No, he was great. And I would say so was Memphis Slim [John Chatman]. But Muddy was less sophisticated and, in a sense, maybe sweeter. I don't know.

Maybe not as calculated.

I don't feel . . .

Is that an insulting term to use, you think, for Slim?

Yes, yes. I think . . . I think rather than "calculated" I would say "sophisticated," "urbane." He's very experienced in the ways of the world, you know. Not down-home anymore, like Muddy still was kind of down-home in some ways. I liked both of the guys very much. But I feel more . . . it's hard to say. I like them both very much. Maybe I feel a little more warmth for Muddy, but I certainly like Slim as much as anybody I've met. Sunnyland Slim is another great guy—one of these guys who would always help somebody else. Always help the other guy. Always extol the virtues, even of his rivals—another sweet guy.

I know that our generation of white guys, Sunnyland was the guy who took us all under wing and helped us out. Lord knows what he thought of our playing! He just said, "Well, maybe they're trying." [*laughs*]

Oh, he's a nice guy. I remember Sunnyland said to me one time—you know, I just said I liked Memphis Slim very much. And I'd mentioned to him something, that I'd photographed Memphis Slim. And I was doing an article about Little Brother Montgomery for an album that Folkways was putting out. I was doing the liner notes. I asked him about his opinion of Little Brother and he said, "You know, Memphis Slim . . . Memphis Slim would get up off of his piano stool for *me*, and Little Brother can play rings around me!" Now, that's a sweet thing.

The esteem that he had for Little Brother was amazing.

Yeah. Now, Little Brother I knew perhaps better than anybody else. He gave a party for us. Some of the pictures are in there—the party Little Brother gave for us. And he had a guy from Germany here—Karl Gert zur Heide. He wrote a book about him. And Oliver Alcorn and a whole lot of people, a very nice thing. And Sunnyland was there and Big Walter Horton and Little Brother. And I knew Brother and his wife, and he had us over there several times. And I saw him on a regular basis. I knew him very well. And yet to me it's astonishing that when I go back to the oldest records that Little Brother made and then listen to those we did for Folkways, he did not change. And that's a plus. But also, it's all sounds so—I don't know the word . . . "disingenuous." He always sounded so utterly unsophisticated—so *utterly* unsophisticated in his singing. The way he sang sort of—just out. You know, just untempered in any way—very interesting. A little like some of the oriental people who sing just wide open, just wide open with no tempering of the voice, but very interesting. And his piano style—I've never quite fathomed what it is about his piano style that makes so many musicians say, "He's one of the *greatest* of them!" I can hear greatness in Otis Spann. And I could hear greatness in Jimmy Yancey. And Art Hodes—I love Art Hodes's playing. Brother, with the best will in the world, and I have a deep feeling for Bro, but—his wife called him L. B., by the way—but his . . . I've never quite understood the power of his music.

In other words, you've had to take the words of the people whose music you *do* respect—Sunnyland and Spann, who I'm sure all pointed to him and said, "He's light-years ahead of us."

Yes, yes. But to me it's incomprehensible. [*laughs*] You know, the power of his . . . I can hear everything he's doing, but I can't understand the great power of it versus that of Spann. Spann just goes right to my gut. You know, if I see a record with a nine-minute blues by Otis Spann, boy! Everything else's got to wait, because if he has a chance to stretch out, and *nobody* can play the blues like Otis Spann! And there's another sweet character—my God! Talk about an unsophisticated guy! But natural guy.

Those of us who have been collecting records a long time have grown up with your photographs, and we're familiar with some of the classics that can be found in the book. Are there any photography sessions that didn't make it? Are there sessions that were just a total loss?

Yes, there's one that I think was the worst of them all. There are a couple of examples in the book in which I acknowledge that it's a goofed-up session. I'm not exactly sure why it was goofed up. But I did a session for *Rhythm and Blues* magazine just before they folded. I did a successful session with John Lee Hooker, with Pete Welding and Mike Bloomfield interviewing Hooker at his hotel. He was staying at the Sutherland Hotel. He was not *performing* in Chicago, so I didn't have a chance to get him in performance. But I photographed him during the interviews, and I got some really good stuff of him, very natural, very extensive stuff. And then I was using sun guns. I don't remember all the particulars about sun guns, but it was a semiprofessional type floodlight that I used for fill-in and backlight. And most of my stuff I did with available light, you know, without extra light. But in some things I needed some light to lift up the light in the room.

This would be like a little handheld kind of thing?

No, I use it on tripods. But the problem with the sun gun, as I remember it—and it took me a long time to remember what went wrong with this session—but sun guns, once you turn them off, you can't turn them on again until they get cold. I'm not sure exactly why. But I had turned the sun guns off, and they were my only fill light. And Hooker all of a sudden said, "You know, I'm going to call Muddy and see if he'll drop over." Well, you know, it just sounded like talk for a minute. I didn't think you could just pick up the phone and ask Muddy Waters to come over! But—and I didn't know they were old friends—but

Welding and Mike and I said, "Well, it's worth sticking around." So we stuck around, and Muddy did show. But I didn't have any fill light. And I did not make the correct adjustment. Maybe I couldn't.

But *Rhythm and Blues* magazine went out of business then. And I had sent them the only proof sheets. And I have a vague memory that did I at one time—or did I dream that someone had shot Muddy Waters and John Lee Hooker together? I was very busy at the time. I was doing a lot of stuff: I was traveling; I was doing radio shows; I was going to Roosevelt College; all sorts of stuff. I was working a day job, all this stuff. And I totally forgot, since I didn't have the proof sheet. And then, about three years ago I guess it was, I ran across some of my correspondence with *Rhythm and Blues* magazine, just at the time they went under. And there's an indication that, no, that's not a dream. I *did* do a series. So I went through all, all my negatives of that period, and I finally came up with John Lee Hooker and Muddy Waters. Oh, Christ! Here is a great treasure. And I took them to the processor, and what did I get back? Near junk. I mean, I don't know what went wrong, but they were all underexposed and under-lighted, and oh, a terrible feeling. Here's this great moment with these guys, you know, goofing off together and all this kind of stuff. And that's when Muddy was talking about Old Fitzgerald with me and all this kind of stuff. And totally ruined.

So I talked with Jim Frayer. Do you know Jim? Jim and I are kind of tight. And I asked him, "What can I do about this film?" And he came over and looked at it and said, "Well, maybe you can have it intensified. Maybe you can get something out of it." So we took it in and had it intensified, and it got worse! So I finally decided, "Well, damn it. I'm going to have some stuff printed anyway." So that was a ruined session. There's some very junky stuff. Several people have printed it, and they will continue to print it just because of what's in it. But it was a ruined session in that sense.

And then there was another one, one of my most famous pictures—and this is irrational, really irrational. Another thing for *Rhythm and Blues* magazine. I had a B. B. King thing and I had a tight deadline. And so I just had this one session at the Trianon. And one of my good friends, who is now deceased, one of the nicest guys in the city, one of the two black photographers who when I started took me by the hand, gave me their contacts, sometimes developed my film for me—free of charge, introduced me to their girlfriends . . . shit! [*chuckles*] I mean, incredible guys! Anyhow, Jim took these things home. I was in a big rush. I had to get the stuff. But Jim was very gregarious and he was subject to be developing film, and maybe somebody'd come in and maybe turn the light on or something like that. At any rate, this B. B. King stuff was light-struck! And I had to have it. It was a big job, you know, and I had a deadline, and so, as happened very many times, I just spent the night going through these proof sheets, going through the proof sheets. And I find all this light-struck film, and finally—I kept zeroing in on one little patch—and here's a little patch with B. B. King almost looking like a human being. And I decided to print it. And that is one of the most popular things I've ever had. It just happened to catch him. And it looked like it was intelligently planned. [*laughs*] So some of my best stuff, it looks like it was intelligently planned—it was goofed up!

And other stuff of that same session with B. B. King, also light-struck from different angles and also in the book. And one of them, I still am not sure had any justification for being printed. But Lisa Day, who has this fantastic eye—she's the film editor who pushed me into this book—she wanted the thing printed full negative instead of cropped tight. I'm trying to get a section out of the negative that looks like a successful exposure. But she said she'd like to see the thing full neg. So we've got it in there in which the right-hand side is nothing but blur. Weird, just blur. And I call it the "Jean Cocteau shot," as it reminds me of *Beauty and the Beast*—you know, the Jean Cocteau? These wonderful fairy-like things. And if you look at that thing over on the right-hand side and several people looked at it and said, "If you look real carefully at this blur, you'll see a couple of faces poking out of the background." [*chuckles*] So it's one of those failures that is working.

Do you think that the future of photography in the world of computers, that there's going to be a time when people are going to look at this stuff and find a process and restore it to what it might have been originally? Or do you think once it's cast, it's cast?

I've got to confess I have nothing but admiration for the photographers nowadays who understand the current processes. Guys like Marc PoKempner and I'm sure Jim Frayer, they know what's happening. I don't know what's happening. But I cannot believe that you can take ruined film and make it into a successful image. Because if it's not captured, there's nothing to restore. If it's not in the emulsion, I don't think there's anything you can do with it. You can do . . . I mentioned intensification, but about all it does is increase the contrasts, and sometimes it loses some of the, I guess you can say, nuances. I don't believe that, like you say, when the die is cast, I think it's cast.

Well, I know they're going to restore all the sound. So we'll see. [*laughs*] Hey, I also wanted to get your impressions, just off the top, of the Little Walter session, because I think, at least in my mind, that's one of your most famous sessions. In fact, I think it's probably—if there were of the whole gallery of photographs of Little Walter, those are probably the flagship.

Yeah, I certainly feel that that's one of the most thorough, complete shots of anybody I ever did. My relationship . . . A lot of people ask me, you know, Little Walter had a very ferocious reputation. You know, he was a . . . face all scarred up with knife wounds. And I guess he inflicted a lot of knife wounds, and I think he got killed with getting kicked in the head in a fight. So he did not have a pretty reputation. But, again, it's not necessarily the winning personality of the photographer that makes a guy smile. When he sees the photographer, he sees a camera lens. And while he might smile for a camera lens, he might want to kick you in the gut. But Little Walter and I never had anything but pleasant relationships. He walked up to me on Maxwell Street, and I guess if he introduced himself, I didn't get it, because I didn't know who he was. He asked me to take his picture, and I did take his picture and sent it to *Rhythm and Blues,* and they ran it as an "unidentified Maxwell Street musician." And I later found out it was Little Walter playing a guitar instead of his mouth harp. And I showed it to Bob Koester and other great authorities on the blues, and they said, "That can't be Little Walter, because he plays the mouth harp." But he had already made recordings as a guitarist.

But, you see, even great authorities sometimes have like my Melrose lack of information. I'm not saying I'm one of the great authorities, but I'm saying *some* of the great authorities don't know everything that's happening. At any rate, he didn't take the trouble—There's a lot of people who come up and say, "Take my picture," they don't think they won't *see* the picture unless they give you their name and address, which he did not do. So I didn't send him the picture. I don't know whether he ever saw it. Next time I saw him it was in Theresa's, and whether he recognized me or not, I don't know. He smiled to me, but maybe he smiled because I had a camera. So every time I saw him, he smiled. And he also smiled at this Mandel Hall session at the University of Chicago. But, again, I'd like to think that he recognized me and smiled at me, but maybe he saw a glistening camera lens and smiled at it.

But he was so turned on that night. I've never seen a musician, any musician anywhere, as turned on as Walter was that night. And I don't know what it was, but he was utterly ecstatic. He was just in seventh heaven, smiling and grinning, and making obscene gestures, and strutting and fooling around with the guitarist, and just totally dominating the stage. While he was up there, I don't think anybody could see anybody else. Fred Below was up there behind him, and Below was one of the great blues and jazz musicians. Below was up there behind him, but Walter had that stage. I don't think anybody that night performed like Walter. And just shot after shot, each frame—I did not have to select frames. When I later looked at the stuff, frame after frame after frame after frame—each frame was part of a sequence in which he was just raising hell up there! He was all bent over, all bent back, hollering, yelling, gesturing, playing the harp, singing, everything—just going utterly crazy up there. And I think it probably is the greatest single session that I've ever had, in spite of some of the great Muddy sessions. But Walter—it was an amazing performance! So, yeah, I think it was possibly the tops.

Would you talk a little bit about this Wolf session at Silvio's? How did this come about?

Yeah, that was interesting too. That's one of the interesting stories actually. Again, I think it was *Rhythm and Blues*; it might have been *Chicago Scene*, but I think it was *Rhythm and Blues* that wanted me to get a shot of Howling Wolf in 1961. More likely it was *Chicago Scene*, because I think *Rhythm and Blues* started a little later. But either they knew or I found out he was at a place, a little dump called Mr. Lee's Lounge. I forget now where it was. I think it was on Vincennes around Seventy-ninth or something like that, I believe. I've got it in my notes. But for a long time I could not figure out where that was, and I ran into some obscure notes in my piled up—you should see my piled up junk. They were making jokes about that yesterday when I shot a session. [*laughs*] One of the guys said, "How did you ever find any of these prints?" He said, "I saw your place once and I wondered how you ever found anything to make a book!"

So in any event . . . at any rate, at Mr. Lee's Lounge, I went in there, and it was great for available light. Like I said, I started out wanting to do everything with available light. No fill-in light, you know, just 100 percent reality. So I went there without any fill-in light and it was a dark place. It was a dark dive, and there were no accommodations for photographers. I don't remember whether I'd made arrangements out front, whether they knew I was coming, but I had . . . I guess I just had my two Leicas there. I didn't have any of the lenses that . . . super-sensitive lenses that I later got. But I realized that I couldn't take anything with normal exposures, because there just was not enough light. And they didn't have any table for me, a place to set up a tripod or to use my elbows or the back of a chair for a tripod. So I just had to do what I could do, and I shot, as I recall it, over the bar at Wolf. And it seems that he was performing alone, which is rather odd for Wolf, but I don't have any indication that there was another musician. And so all the shots were just of Wolf himself. And the only thing I could do was take shots with . . . it wasn't a slow shutter, but in terms of the light, it was a slow shutter. And every time Wolf's head moved or he went through his usual gyrations, what happened on the film was there was a streak across the film. And a lot of time when his mouth was open, it looked like the teeth made a tooth mark across the film. So, goofing around with it, I saw some of this looked really animalistic, very wolfish, you know.

And so I printed some of these blurry things and they were very crazy, and somebody printed them. And Phil Chess, when he was offered the things, he said . . . he used some of his language that I don't think we can put on here . . . but he said, "Fuck—fuck all that stuff." He said, "It looked like an x-ray!" He said, "I don't want to print anything that looks like a god-damned x-ray!" So he turned it down and printed some of the less interesting stuff. But somebody—I guess it was *Sing Out* magazine, I believe—printed some of the blurry stuff. And Wolf had apparently seen it. I don't think I showed it to him. But at any rate, he hated it! And when I went to interview him with Welding, with Mike for *Rhythm and Blues* magazine, Welding wasn't there. First thing he said was, "I'm no animal! I'm a man!" I said, "Well, you know, you use the name Howling Wolf, and some of your performance would make you think . . ." He said, "Look, if you had wanted to see what Wolf was really like, you'd have come to Silvio's." I said, "Well, okay. How about I come to Silvio's? When should I come?" He said, "Come next Sunday." So, in other words, I have an invitation by Wolf to go to his lair. [*chuckles*]

It was so funny—I was so shook up by the opportunity, I went over there. This time Bloomfield wasn't with me. And I wanted to carry a bunch of stuff. I had a whole bunch of . . . and I was in so interested in doing this session. I got over there and unpacked all my stuff, and I'd forgotten to bring any film! [*laughs*] So I got him to agree that I would come back the next week. So after going there without any film, I went the next time. And he was very nice about it. And I walked in Silvio's and sat down, and Hubert Sumlin comes over to me with his nice big smile and puts a sixteen-ounce tumbler and fills it with hundred-proof bourbon. I had made some comment about liking bourbon and they took me seriously. [*chuckles*] So I started this session with sixteen ounces of bourbon, and I was trying to be very clever about it, just a little at a time, a little at a time. Then when Wolf came in, he set me up with another one. So both of them were sort of watching me out of the corner of their eyes to see what was going to happen. But it was a marvelous session. Wolf was very "on." He had invited me. He wanted the camera there. He was not going to resent the camera this time. And he did a lot of his antics, but also there was a lot of camaraderie that a lot of people didn't realize happened with Wolf and his crowd too. A lot of friendliness between the guys. And you see some of the breaks, you know, and Wolf acting very gregarious and friendly. And actually very friendly and pleasant to me. And it was a very nice session.

One mystery that I've never solved: I have a picture of Wolf going over to a table and in a very charming way—smoke over the table, nice picture—shaking hands with a guy who looks to me like Sleepy John Estes. And I showed that to Koester, and I asked him, "Is that Sleepy John Estes?" And he refused to give an opinion. I said, "It looks like Sleepy John to me." And he said, "Well, I don't know." I said, "Well, was he in town at that time?" "Well, I think probably he was in town at that time." So that may be Sleepy John Estes. I think we should run a contest. I have that picture—"Is this Sleepy John Estes?" And then I have another picture of Pat Hare; I think it's Pat Hare. He's the guy who wrote that song "I'm Going to Murder My Baby" and then he went out and did it! [*laughs*] And I've got this picture of—I think it's Pat Hare, 1961. It's his lead guitarist, and he has quite a sinister look on his face and he's all blurry. Now I'd like to run a contest—"Is this Sleepy John Estes? And is this Pat Hare?"

Part of the text that you write in the book was your reaction to seeing Son House, and I have to tell you that I shared that 100 percent. I'd seen Wolf and seen Muddy and not as many as you saw, you know, being here so early. But I considered seeing Son House like a religious experience, even though it was a film clip. I thought, "My God! I've never . . . I've seen Wolf. I've seen Muddy. I've never seen blues this intense!" And it just struck me that you talked about how it affected you. And I just wondered if you'd give voice to that here.

Yes. I really wish somebody would do a series based on the sequence that I have of . . . I had a chance to meet Son House at Pete Welding's house. Pete and I were pretty tight. And before his concert, I had a chance to meet Son House. And he was this Southern gentleman type, beatific, all smiles, all . . . all subservient-type smiling. And I didn't have too much idea of what he was going to be like. I think I might have heard some records. But I always liked the idea of one . . . one artist, one instrument. You know? That's the pure blues. There's one guy doing all his own accompaniment. So Son House gets up there on the Mandel Hall stage. And he sits down on a plain chair, one man, one instrument. And he looks around with this sort of subservient smile, and all of a sudden he starts to think. And his face—I've always thought of it as a metamorphosis—his face starts to change and you see trouble coming over his face, and then trouble turns to sorrow and you can think, "He's thinking about 'what they done to me,'" like the down South experiences of Jazz Gillum. Horrible stuff. And then it becomes more and more insufferable-type pain. Then he actually starts to sing.

And it's just like cries of pain almost. And yet he has this very dramatic, percussive, classical term—ostinato. He has an ostinato bass. It's a continuous, repetitious, just simple, repetitious what in the piano would be the left-hand accompaniment. And just keeps repeating itself while he's churning out this tragic story as, for example, "Death Letter Blues."

"I found my baby laying on the cooling board, and I say to my baby, 'Baby, I love you more than I love myself.'" And it just brings tears to your eyes, because it's just like he's reliving it. It's not a performance; it's like a man reliving an unforgettably painful experience. And it's something that I've never forgotten.

And I find other people writing liner notes get that same feeling having watched Son House. And I had the most, the biggest resentment I think I've ever felt about a recording session when I heard one of the Son House recordings when the producer wanted a particular song and Son misheard him and started a different song. And he had barely started the second song when the guy interrupts him and said, "No! I wanted you to do such and such!" But good God! I mean, he had another great creative experience starting to go on tape, and he cut him off so that *his* sequence could be imposed on him. But just like with Robert Johnson, I feel you're hearing an act of creation. Not so much as with Johnson, the change of the words, but a different take on the projection.

Do you think . . . since we weren't there, that we would have had the same experience that we both profess with Son House if we'd seen Robert Johnson or if we'd seen Charlie Patton in person? The intensity is like a bolt from the blue.

I don't know. I don't get the impression from Robert Johnson that I would get that same kind of . . . There's a different kind of intensity. I think he's . . . I get more of a—for better or for worse—poetic inspiration from Johnson. Charley Patton, I wouldn't be surprised if he come across a little like Son House. One of the performers showed how he performed. He'd sort of get down on one . . . way bent over on one knee, and I get the impression that he was *very* intense. So I kind of imagine that he might be a little like Son House.

And perhaps Willie Brown. Because I get the feeling that maybe there's that same kind of intensity at work there too.

I don't recall having heard Willie Brown. I'm sorry. I must have missed him.

I think he started out as a traveling companion of Patton and then later drifted over to House. But only two sides.

I must have missed those!

But Son House—what fervor!

Oh, yes. And you know, I've been told . . . They'd say, "Okay, you heard Son House when he was over the hill, when he was past his prime." I say, "Oh, God! If he was past his prime, for Christ's sake, I don't think I could have stood it when he was in his prime!" Because it would just be like molten steel.

JIM O'NEAL INTERVIEW

I was born November 25th, 1948, in Fort Wayne, Indiana. Both of my parents were from Mississippi and they returned to Mississippi after six weeks, so I never knew Indiana. My father was a minister at the time, but he became a doctor later, and my mother was a teacher.

What part of Mississippi were you from?

The Gulf Coast, really—around Biloxi, Gulfport. And I still have a lot of family down in Hattiesburg. Later in life I moved to the Delta, but I didn't know anything about the Delta when I was growing up.

Can you explain how you got interested in blues? Did you listen to rock 'n' roll like most blues fans?

Jim O'Neal with James Cotton, 2012. Photo by Claire Pittman and courtesy of Webster Franklin.

Yeah, I listened to rock 'n' roll and I started collecting records when I was in third grade. The first records I bought were Fats Domino and Elvis Presley. I would just listen to the Top 40 radio, and eventually when the Rolling Stones and the British groups came along, I started buying LPs and reading the liner notes about who wrote the songs and tried to trace them back. That's when I realized that most of the rock 'n' roll music that I liked was blues-based—people like Muddy Waters, Jimmy Reed, and Howling Wolf. By that time I was in Chicago in college.

Was there any one particular tune or artist that was a breakthrough for you into the blues?

No. I can actually remember hearing blues on the radio down in Mobile, but I didn't recognize it as blues. I don't think any particular rock 'n' roll record got me interested in blues per se. It was only after I listened to some blues that I realized that that's where it came from, that it really hit me. And the first blues album that I bought was at a Kmart in Mobile, which is where I went to school—from the third grade to high school—in Mobile, Alabama. It was

Jim O'Neal vintage photo. Courtesy Jim O'Neal.

an Albert King record and I spent forty-seven cents on it. But I'd heard that he played at the Fillmore and so I thought he was somebody I should check out. And then I listened to it and I said, "Wait a minute—I've heard all this stuff before." And I was hearing licks from Eric Clapton and Electric Flag and all kinds of other groups, and that really turned my head around. Then I started buying B. B. King and Muddy Waters, and pretty soon I realized where it all had come from.

Was this before you came to Chicago?

Actually this was while I was home from college one summer. That was in the middle of my college career. I went to Northwestern in Chicago. My parents had gone there, and in fact that's where they'd met. Like I said, they were both from Mississippi, and so I was trying to follow family tradition. At that point I wanted to get away from the South. It was during the civil rights era. I just didn't like a lot of the Southern attitude towards things and I thought I wanted to be somewhere else, and Chicago seemed like a fun place to be. I didn't know anything about the blues or where it would lead me, but I'm glad it did. I went to Northwestern and I ended up in journalism.

Did you see live music while you were here as a student?

In 1969 I started going around. I met Amy van Singel, who was a student at Northwestern. She was much more advanced in the blues than I was. I would ask her, "Do you know about Mike Bloomfield?" And she would say, "Do you know about Big Joe Williams?" It turned out she had worked for Bob Koester at Jazz Record Mart and Delmark Records in Chicago. With her I went to Jazz Record Mart and saw a whole store full of blues albums. That opened my mind to the fact that there was this whole other world out there—a blues world. And of course Bob Koester was always a great blues contact for people who wanted to find out what was going on in Chicago, where to go to hear music in the clubs. From Bob we got a club list and started going primarily to Theresa's—also to Pepper's Lounge and a few places on the West Side. It was basically wherever we could go and they wouldn't check our IDs at the door, because we weren't twenty-one yet. Pepper's and Theresa's were the big experience, and going to

Jim O'Neal and Amy van Singel, vintage. Courtesy Jim O'Neal.

see Otis Rush at Pepper's was the big changing point in my life. That was more powerful and intense than anything I'd ever seen—of any kind of music.

Who did Otis have in his band at that point? And who else appeared at Pepper's?

I think Bobby Davis was on drums. A lot of people regarded him as a show drummer, but he could really play—Otis liked him a lot. Ernest Gatewood was on bass. Jesse Green was around too.

And Otis was in good shape back then?

Otis was magnificent! I still think there was nobody better than Otis at his peak. Even on an average night he was better than 90 percent of the rest on their best nights. As for other artists at Pepper's, I remember Earl Hooker came in one night. I didn't get to see much of him. He died in 1970. Junior Wells was there a lot—also Fenton Robinson and Lefty Dizz, Little Mack—Hound Dog Taylor once in a while. There was just an endless parade of them.

Where was the original location for Pepper's?

That was at Forty-seventh and Vincennes. Then a couple of years later Pepper's moved to Thirteenth and Michigan—blues in the Loop. It wasn't really in the Loop; it was south of downtown. There were a lot of mirrors there. I remember seeing Howling Wolf there once, and he got so disgusted with the band that he told them all to get off the bandstand and he was going to play guitar himself. I remember he sat there for half an hour tuning his guitar and nothing much ever happened. Mighty Joe Young—he was there a lot too.

Wasn't the original location really hot gang turf?

Yeah, that was probably the most dangerous place we could have gone, and that was the place we went the most often—that and Theresa's. There were some near incidents at Pepper's, but it didn't generally involve people coming to hear the blues, because it was gang territory, and if you wore the wrong color hat you could be in trouble if it was red or black. Black was the color of the Blackstone Rangers. Once in a while there were some minor hassles on the street—some of the gang members would start talking or something—but nothing ever actually happened. One time I was in there . . . One of the first times I went in there, I went with some friends from college, and I was naive about the whole experience. Anyway, it was like being in a whole different world. This young guy came in and sat down at the table with us and began beating out a rhythm on the table with his hands and spelling "Beware" like we were going to get killed. [*laughs*] But we made it out alive.

Jim O'Neal and Amy van Singel, 2012. Courtesy Jim O'Neal.

Who was at Theresa's when you were going there?

Theresa's featured Buddy Guy and Junior Wells together a lot—and separately too. That's when Phil Guy had first come to town, so sometimes it was Phil Guy. Sammy Lawhorn was there. He wasn't with Muddy Waters anymore at that point, but he was around. Byther Smith sometimes. They had these great jam sessions on "Blue Mondays," and sometimes James Cotton would come by. Sometimes the obscure artists were there too. I remember one night Charles Clark was there—the guy who recorded "Row Your Boat" for Artistic/Cobra back in the 1950s—he came by one night. But it was Junior Wells more than anybody else. I think I saw Junior more than I saw anybody else during the time I lived in Chicago. They had a guy Sleepy, the bartender/the doorman/the assistant; he was always helping out. Theresa was there, and Carl Jones, the guy who owned C. J. Records, was behind the bar sometimes, or Junior was behind the bar sometimes. He was also kind of the security guard. He made sure nothing would ever happen at Theresa's. Everybody was always telling me, "You're going to get killed going down there"—not specifically Theresa's, but to the South Side or West Side in general. But people like Junior Wells had a real protective attitude toward visitors who came to see them. They wanted to make sure that nothing happened. So sometimes they would walk you out to the car or just make sure that nobody was hassling you.

I heard that Carl Jones actually lived in an apartment above Theresa's. I'd also heard that Junior Wells's mother lived above the bar.

I believe Carl did live above the bar. I don't know when Junior's mother stayed there, if she did. I know later they lived further south on the South Side.

Did you manage to finish school?

Yeah, I got a degree in journalism in 1970. Amy graduated with a degree in English and went back to get a master's, but it got interrupted. We got married during that time, and then the draft came along and I was doing alternative service at a mental hospital in Chicago for two years. Then I did go back and get a master's degree. But I didn't really use it very much, because I was already publishing the magazine—not that that was the great goal of most of the journalism students at Northwestern.

Amy van Singel, Beth and Paul Garon. Courtesy Jim O'Neal.

You were seeing live blues in Chicago. Did you have much interest or exposure to prewar blues?

I was interested in it. I thought the mission we had set out to do was to document that the blues was a living tradition, so the magazine was always more oriented toward who was still active, who was still playing. I always did have an interest in prewar blues, and Paul Garon, who was one of the founders of *Living Blues,* was our prewar expert. He had a great collection of 78s, and he had known Big Joe Williams and a lot of those people too. But he was a source of information and inspiration. I was interested in Tampa Red and the people who weren't around anymore. He was still alive, and I did manage to track him down and interview—well, I spent time with him—I didn't do much actual interviewing. I think you spent some time with him too.

Where was Tampa when you caught up with him?

Tampa was living in an apartment on Fifty-fourth Street. I think I'd gotten his address from Blind John Davis, who gave it to Bob Koester. Willie Dixon and others warned me that Tampa had "flipped his wig," as Willie Dixon put it. I wasn't even sure it was safe to go there, but he wasn't dangerous—he'd just gotten kind of senile. He'd had a couple of breakdowns earlier after his wife died. But he was a nice, gentle man, I thought.

That was my impression as well. I'd heard that he was a pyromaniac. After meeting him I thought, "This is the gentlest man in the world."

There were stories that he was hard to get along with, or had an attitude. But we don't know what he was like earlier in life. I'm certainly glad we got to meet him.

The fact that Wolf looked up to him, that said volumes to me.

Yeah. Everybody spoke well of him as far as being an influence. Even Muddy and Junior Wells, they all looked up to him.

Let's talk about how *Living Blues* began.

I think *Living Blues* began as another offshoot of the crowd that was hanging around Bob Koester. I remember in 1969 there had been a sign-up sheet at Bob Koester's store for anyone who wanted to contribute some stories to a blues magazine, to send them in. I think Dick Shurman was going to be the one who put the magazine together at that time. Of course it wasn't *Living Blues*; it was just an idea for a magazine. I think I wrote up a concert I'd just been to, which was my first blues concert, at the Kinetic Playground, which was B. B. King, Albert King, and Paul Butterfield. Not long after that, I saw a Howling Wolf concert with Paul Butterfield at Northwestern.

In any case, Dick Shurman left town and that magazine never got started. In the meantime Bruce Iglauer came to town and went to work for Bob Koester as a shipping clerk. Bruce and Amy and I had gotten together to go hear music, and we started talking about having a magazine—"Why isn't there a magazine here?"—since I was in journalism and we were all interested in it. And it just sort of grew from there, because we were all anxious to get all the information we could about blues. And it was kind of weird because the best source of information at that point was a magazine from England, *Blues Unlimited,* which some of us had contributed to at times. It seemed weird to subscribe to a magazine from England to find out what was going on on the other side of Chicago. So that was how it all got started.

Living Blues magazine. Courtesy *Living Blues* magazine.

Did you use *Blues Unlimited* as a template? And if so, were there things you felt you needed to do different, or thought, "We can improve on that"?

Just by the fact that they were in England, thousands of miles away from the actual artists, except when they were on tour or visiting over there, it gave them a whole different perspective. The articles were like "We're on a blues safari and here's our stop in dangerous Neverland." And *Blues Unlimited* was more orientated on records and discography, which I was always interested in too. We always thought that the advantage *Living Blues* would have was that we were right there where the blues artists lived. We could talk to them; we could do interviews and get their take on what the blues were about and get more personal stories that way. So I think that was the difference. But we always felt we were comrades with *Blues Unlimited* as well as competitors.

Were there ever any alternate titles considered for the magazine beside *Living Blues*?

I can't remember if we had any other titles. Bruce Iglauer actually came up with the title *Living Blues.*

What was Bruce's background? I know he was working as a shipping clerk. Did he have a degree, and if so, what was it in?

Bruce had come from Lawrence University in Appleton, Wisconsin. I don't remember what his degree was in, but he had graduated. He had promoted a few blues shows while he was there and had been into folk music before that. He had a little experience when he showed up in Chicago. He got a lot of balls rolling when he got to Chicago with *Living Blues* and Alligator Records.

Bruce Iglauer in Alligator Records office. Courtesy Bruce Iglauer and Alligator Records.

So Bob Koester was not the one who initiated the idea of *Living Blues* magazine?

Well, Bob was always very supportive. He didn't recruit us, so to speak, but he was one of our central gurus, I suppose you could say. And he did loan us the money to get the first issue out and let us use the Jazz Record Mart if we needed a place to interview someone, which we did a few times. He was always there with information, and he gave me my first paying writing gig—writing liner notes for a Magic Sam album. He was crucial to the genesis of *Living Blues,* but he wasn't the creative force behind it.

What was involved in getting an issue of the magazine published? And how long did it take?

Well, I'm not sure any of us had any practical experience. I had done some work on high school and college newspapers, but it wasn't the same as laying out, designing, and publishing your own magazine. Bruce and Diane Allman, another of the co-founders, did a lot of that work in the beginning. But basically this is before the age of computers and word processing, so on the first issue the actual text for the magazine was typed on an IBM typewriter that we borrowed from the *Chicago Seed,* which was an underground newspaper. So if you look at that first issue the text is all typewriting. You would type out the text and then wax it down to a page, and the printer would shoot negatives from that page and then print it.

We found a printer in Chicago who had done a lot of the underground press work. He printed some of the first issues. Then we went to Port Washington, Wisconsin, where later issues were printed. The printer would collate all the pages and staple them together, and then bundle the individual copies in bundles of fifty or one hundred. We'd have to drive up to Port Washington in our station wagon and get the magazines and bring them back down and bundle them up. Bruce would get them out to distributors. Amy and I would address them all to the individual subscribers. So we did the whole thing.

There must have been something about going to Port Washington, given its blues tradition.

Yeah, Port Washington is where Paramount Records began, but there didn't seem to be much evidence of it when we were there. Certainly there's been more that's turned up in recent years. People have offered a lot of money to find any relics of the Paramount label. We would stop at junk stores there, and I was hoping I'd find a Charley Patton 78, but nothing much ever happened. The printer up there was also the publisher of the local paper, and we talked to him about the Paramount label, but I don't think he was very aware of it. He thought that was very strange, that Paramount would have an office in Port Washington, which was, as he called it, "a lily-white town." It was one of those towns where if you were black, you weren't supposed to be there after sundown. Of course there's a lot of towns like that in the Midwest. But that was just an odd place for a great segment of recorded African American history to have happened.

I guess you didn't look on top of all the sheds and work barns?

I had heard that some of the old metal plates from the Paramount masters were being used as the roofs for chicken shacks and chicken coops and barns. [*laughs*]

Back to the magazine—was the layout you used to shoot the negative real size?

Yes, it was 100 percent; it wasn't on a computer screen. Everything was done with paper or typewriter, and later, when we got a typesetter, we still had to type the text onto paper, which was printed by a photo process, and then paste or glue that onto the layout paper.

Then you would leave space and cut out a black square wherever the photos would go—black cardboard or construction paper. Then you would give the photos to the printer and indicate which photo went into which space. Every once in a while those would get mixed up and you'd have the wrong photo with the wrong caption. It was a completely different way to do it.

One time we were advancing beyond the typewriter stage, and we'd gotten this thing called a Varityper. It was like a typewriter, but you could select different fonts on it. It was huge and made a huge thud whenever you struck a key—and we were living on the third-floor apartment at that point. The neighbors downstairs called the police and said we were playing drums upstairs! [*laughs*]

Who else were contributors to the magazine in the early days?

We had a couple of other Chicago people who were on board for a while—Tim Zorn and Andre Souffront; it's been years since I've heard from either one of them. But once the magazine got around, we started getting people who did news and reviews. We couldn't pay anybody, so it was just fans who cared about the music and sent things in. We eventually got a list, a staff of what we called contributing editors—like Tom Mazzolini from San Francisco, who started the San Francisco Blues Festival, and Pete Welding from Los Angeles, who contributed to the early issues. We got a little bit from Paul Oliver, who was the leading blues expert in England. He didn't do much magazine writing at that point, but he was always in touch with us. It was just whoever was a hard-core blues fan who cared enough to write about it in the news end in the early days. Sometimes it was white blues musicians who knew what was happening in the black community; they would send material in. I remember Anson Funderburg would send things in, and every once in a while we'd get a letter from Charlie Musselwhite. It was just a network of fans. It wasn't ever much of a big business—or any business at all, actually.

How did you know when an issue of the magazine was ready to go to press?

I think we usually knew when a magazine was finished: it was when the pages we had allotted for it were filled up. [*laughs*] Sometimes the things we were waiting for didn't come in. A lot of times that was my stuff more than anybody else's. [*laughs*] And sometimes we'd get something finished—I remember with the Thomas Dorsey interview or the Houston Stackhouse interviews, one of those long ones—and it was much longer than we realized, longer than we had allotted in the magazine. What a normal editor would do is just cut some of the text. You wouldn't have it all, but you'd get the essence of it. But what I preferred to do was shrink the text, so instead of it being in twelve-point type you'd shrink it down eight- or nine-point type, which you could barely read, but it would all be there.

I guess one of my real surprises came in making my first record. You were expected to pay up front for use of the recording studio and pressing plant, yet record distributors wouldn't pay you until much later in the process—if at all. How did it work in publishing a magazine?

We were obligated to pay for the magazine when it was printed, although we did get extended some credit as time went on. The more credit we were extended, the more different ways we had to come up with to make money—eventually that's where the *Living Blues* Cookout came from. That was an event that we had every year at the club B.L.U.E.S. on Halsted Street. It actually started at Elsewhere on Clark Street. But that was a fundraiser where we would invite musicians to come and play and have a picnic or cookout or fish fry, and we'd sell records to try and make money to pay the printer. That became one of the sources of income once a year for a while. But as you say, it kind of caught you in between: you're obligated to pay for the product a long time before you actually collect any money from it from distributors, because the distribution system is set up where they pay you. Well, it used to be that they would pay you in 30 or 60 days. Now I'm in the record business again and it's 150 days. [*laughs*]

And everything we made from an issue of the magazine went back into it to get the next issue out. We started making some money to support our activities and pay our rent by selling records. At the same time we'd be going around to clubs on the South Side or visiting musicians and interviewing them. There were still stores where you could get a J. B. Lenoir record for a dime or a quarter, and I could sell them overseas for two dollars. I could advertise them and sell them to someone in England. That was big money then. I wish I had some of those records now.

I remember you got me started on the Reverend J. M. Gates. Long before Johnny Parth made everything available, you had a stack of eight or ten Gates 78s, totally beat up. I was just fascinated—I bought them all. I don't think I even had a 78 stylus at that point, but I was off and running.

There was a guy who used to work at Bob Koester's; his name was Bob Baron. He was a student at the University of Chicago. I remember he was the guy who clued me in that you could go to the South Side and find these records. That became a regular thing wherever I went. If I went down South to Memphis or Mobile, I would find the black record stores that had been around a long time to see if they still had anything left. A lot of times the older material wasn't regarded as anything valuable, so that would be on a table or in the attic or in the basement—for a quarter.

It all comes back to me now. Your basement used to be a regular stop on my record-buying Fridays—Jazz Record Mart, Sounds Good, Jim and Amy's—and then Wax Trax on Lincoln Avenue.

Another way that the record business worked was that we would get advertisements from these small record companies. And even though an ad in *Living Blues* didn't cost much for an independent record label, that was a lot of cash to pay out. So often what we would do is trade them a box of records for an ad—they'd take out an ad and we'd get twenty-five records or whatever it was. And we'd sell the records through our mail-order catalog and get the money back that way.

Let's talk about the features in the magazine.

I guess the *Living Blues* interview became the centerpiece of each issue, which would be an in-depth interview with a blues artist. That hadn't been done much, not that kind of in-depth interview. There had been features on particular artists, but they were usually shorter and they were in the writer's words, often not even quoting the musicians. There were many narrative articles, but even there we would try to get the writers to quote the musicians. You get more of a sense of their personality; it wouldn't be a simple objective listing of facts. So the interviews and those kind of articles were the main focus.

We felt an obligation to cover the popular artists of the time but also to dig into the woodwork and find the guys who were playing the juke joints or ghetto blues bars. Or maybe people who weren't playing at all but that you'd heard about—guys who were just sitting at home but would play if someone would book them. That became a big thing too. Once we'd interview someone, we'd always get offers—from a booking agent, or a manager, or a record producer. I managed to stay out of that for a long time, but I did eventually get involved in it. [*laughs*] A lot of the time we—or *Blues Unlimited* or the Swedish blues magazine—would be the only one to interview some of these artists, so we were their only connection to the outside world. If there were gigs coming in Europe or after a while, the festival phenomena started. We ended up being the middlemen for a lot of things, and we were booking agents when we had to.

I remember that issue number one presented an interview with Howling Wolf. Who did the interview? And what was Wolf like to talk with?

That interview was done by three of us—Amy, myself, and a student from Northwestern named Jim Lovel. It was done originally for Amy's radio program at WNUR, the college radio station at Northwestern. Amy wasn't "Atomic Mama" at that point—she hadn't gotten radioactive yet. I think at that point she was "Big Mama." It was *Big Mama's Blues Show* at WNUR, and then it became *Atomic Mama's Wang Dang Doodle Blues Show* on a couple of FM stations—WXFM and then WNIB. As for Wolf, he was very patient in answering our questions. I wish that I'd known more what questions to ask.

In terms of the interviews, how much of a sense of desperation did you have trying to interview the aged, trying to catch up with them before they're gone?

When we started the magazine it was called *Living Blues,* but one of the first things we found was that every issue we had to report some more deaths. I became a prolific obituary writer. At first we didn't realize how important it was to get to some of these people, but it became an important issue. In general, blues is very well documented—perhaps over-documented—at least in comparison to other kinds of music.

Who got away that you wish you could have caught up with?

Well, you talk about prewar artists—one of the reasons I didn't go to see Memphis Minnie or Gus Cannon was because I thought that had already been done, and if I was going to talk with older musicians I should find somebody who hadn't been done, like Tampa Red. And I felt I should concentrate on the contemporary scene, artists who were out there playing. I figured those were the people who really needed our support, people who were trying to make a living from it. They may never make a living from it, but at least trying to have some sort of career. Slim Harpo died just before he was scheduled to play at the

Ann Arbor Blues Festival. He was always one of my favorites, and I regret not being able to see or talk to him. Lonnie Johnson was another one from that period.

Didn't he die in 1970? Spann and Hooker too?

Lonnie died in 1970, Spann and Hooker too—and Slim Harpo died just before that. And J. T. Brown died just around that period. That was a batch of the early obituaries. Brownie McGhee wrote a remembrance of Lonnie Johnson for us in *Living Blues*. Once in a while we would get artists to write. That was a good thing.

Over the years that you were with the magazine, which were the favorite interviews that you did?

I was always real close to Houston Stackhouse. He felt kind of like a grandfather to me, but it was easy to just sit around the house and talk to him, because he would come to Chicago to play and I'd offer him a place to stay because he didn't want to pay the twelve dollars for the hotel room [*laughs*] that the Quiet Knight nightclub would provide for him. That made it easy to just to sit and talk with him. He was a wonderful source of history and had a great way of telling stories. I always had a fondness for him. I was always glad that I finally got to interview Junior Wells. He was probably the blues artist I saw in Chicago more than anyone else, although it could be the greatest show or something you'd like to forget, depending on what his mood was at the time. I thought that he represented something that was real important in that street sense of Chicago blues. So I was happy to finally get an extensive interview with him. I had actually wanted to do one earlier, but he'd always wanted to be paid. Somehow we worked it out where he didn't have to be; perhaps it was through an agent or something.

Any surprises in Junior's answers?

There were some questions that arose about some of the recordings that I wasn't sure about—and I'm still not sure about. When you try to sort out discography in an interview, details are always kind of fuzzy. Just some of the stories, the way he came up with Muddy. It may have printed different ways here and there. I thought he did a good job of telling it.

What was his mood like when you talked to him?

On one interview we sat in a van outside the Checkerboard Lounge for about an hour or two. He was perfectly willing to talk—anything I asked he was off and running. I think the other interview was outside Buddy Guy's Legends nightclub. I think he was just trying to be earnest, not jive or boastful about stuff.

How deeply immersed was Junior in the artists that came before him?

He had an appreciation for artists like Tampa Red and Forrest City Joe. And he was childhood friends with Junior Parker—that wasn't before him—they were contemporaries. Those are two artists I don't think people would usually connect, but they were actually boyhood friends in West Memphis. And of course the first Sonny Boy, he was greatly influenced by him. He did have an appreciation for what came before. And he was one of the artists who helped keep it contemporary as the years went by. So he had a good sense of the past and the future.

I always find that delightful—guys that I think are good artists and also have a sense of the history. I've always felt that about Billy Boy Arnold.

I agree. Billy Boy has an amazing sense and a perspective on the whole history too. He can tell you what happened when, and how that influenced who, and what that means now! [*laughs*]

I think the last time I talked with him he told me a story about a recording session with Blind John Davis and Big Joe Williams, and how Big Joe was being particularly belligerent until Blind John stood up and slapped him and got Big Joe back in line. And Big Joe was regarded as a rough character in his own right, and here a blind man slaps him down. We forget, I think, that Blind John was actually a pretty big man. We always saw him seated at the piano, but when he stood up he was fairly tall.

I spent a lot of time with Blind John Davis. It came about through my interest in Tampa Red, but I wound up spending more time with Blind John, I'd take him to gigs. They'd call him "Big Johnny" sometimes too.

Any other favorites among your interviews?

Thomas Dorsey, I'm always glad that we'd interviewed him. "Georgia Tom." He became known as the Father of Gospel Music as Thomas A. Dorsey. He'd done some of the most risqué blues when he was a bluesman, and then he became this revered gospel figure. It was great talking to him, because he didn't put the blues down in any way. He always regarded the blues as valid a way of expressing the human condition as gospel was.

How did that interview take place, Jim?

We just called him on the phone and asked if we could come over to his house, and we went over a couple of times and interviewed him. Amy had a radio show at different times during that period, and some of those interviews we would record for the radio. So Amy would open with some of the more general and biographical questions for the radio audience, and then we'd follow up with the more specific questions like "Do you remember Stovepipe Johnson?" and stuff like that.

At this point you both felt you were knowledgeable enough to ask intelligent questions?

We read what we could on him. I suppose there were always more questions we could have asked. That was one of my big regrets with Howling Wolf—at that point we really didn't know enough to ask him any really good questions. As time went on . . . The more research we do, that helps in the interview too—when you can dredge up some kind of obscure detail from the artist's past or some record they made that they might not have thought about in years to get things going a little better. At that point we had it a little easier than folks do now, because most of these artists hadn't been interviewed a lot. And now, with so many blues magazines and newsletters and radio shows, some of the interviews become stock questions and answers. It gets fairly boring or even irritating to the artists.

And you say that some of these interviews were done with broadcast sound quality?

There were a few. We had a reel-to-reel tape recorder and sometimes we would record things at the radio station. A few of them survived on reel-to-reel, but mostly we were recording on a cheap cassette recorder with the cheapest cassettes we could find. It took me a little while to realize I shouldn't be taping over the interviews. [*laughs*] I did lose a few of the very early ones that way. But we were a print medium and our primary purpose was to get the words in print, so we weren't quite as concerned about audio quality. I could have spent the money on a better quality system, but I never did. Instead I spent the money on records. [*laughs*]

Many years ago you gave me copies of extended interviews with Jimmy Reed and Eddie Boyd for use on my program, which drove home the point about print media and disregard for sound quality. It was the first time I realized the difference between print and broadcast sound quality. Those were both wonderful interviews, by the way.

The Jimmy Reed interview was another interview I'm certainly glad we did, because at that point in his career he was fairly difficult to get to. Not because he was difficult, but just because circumstances of his life made it hard to pin him down. And Eddie Boyd just had so much to say. Some of the bluesmen were such great storytellers and had so much to say. They were great historians themselves that you could just let the tape roll and you'd get something great. Jimmy Reed took a lot of work, because I had to spend a lot of time trying to track him down. I stood outside in the snow for two hours one time listening to him play upstairs. No one would answer the door! [*laughs*] Jimmy wasn't with his family, with Mama Reed, at that point. He was with Johnnie Mae Dunson for a while, and then he lived with his cousin Levi Reed for a while after that.

Didn't some of the family act as insulating agents trying to keep him out of the reach of the rest of the world?

Johnnie Mae was very protective of him. He had epileptic seizures and had a well-known alcohol problem in earlier years; although he had stopped drinking at the time that I met him, and there was great effort made so that he wouldn't be tempted again. A lot of that was just keeping him away from everybody.

Were there any real disappointments among the interviews? Any disasters on the launch pad?

There were some interviews that other people did—that I thought were really good—that never got printed. There was a Clifton Chenier interview that Hammond Scott had done. And another one with "Gatemouth" Brown that was real interesting and extensive—they both got erased. [*laughs*] But as far as people that I tried to interview, some people just are not very talkative. Otis Rush isn't. So to do an interview with him we had to interview him more than once, and we interspersed the interview with quotes from other musicians to fill it out. The ones who have the most to say musically aren't always the ones who have the most to say in interviews.

I was always fascinated with your involvement with Cadillac Baby.

What happened was in my record collecting and interviewing I'd met Cadillac Baby, who had a record label called Bea & Baby back in the 1950s and 1960s. He had a little candy store where he had records for sale at Forty-fourth and State. He still had a stock of records on his label and he wanted to sell them. We told him he should advertise them in our magazine, so he started advertising them and people would write in. He found out there was some interest. So he decided he would do an album, and he announced in one of his ads in *Living Blues* that you could order this album from Cadillac Baby—except that the album didn't exist. And people started writing in, so he decided he would go into the studio and do something.

So he got Sunnyland Slim and "Winehead" Willie Williams and Homesick James and some others together and went into the studio. And he wanted to make it seem that it was recorded live in his club. This was the club he'd had many years earlier and was no longer in business. So he announced, "This is Cadillac Baby, live from the show club in 1958!" And the few of us that were in the studio would applaud, so we were the live audience. So he put that album out. It came out pretty good, but it wasn't a live album. Some of these were his old Bea & Baby recordings, but some were new. The label from England, Red Lightning, licensed a lot of his older material too and put a series of albums out.

Eventually you handed off stewardship of *Living Blues* magazine. How did that happen?

Amy and I had been publishing *Living Blues* out of our house in Chicago and also trying to run the record label Rooster Blues. It was a lot of work, and it got to be more than we could handle, really, trying to keep the magazine going, because Amy couldn't work on it full-time, and in order to make enough money on it and do all that, we'd have to bring in another income, which would be me trying to do a mail-order business or work freelance jobs, or Amy getting a job as a typesetter or working for a magazine or something. So she learned a trade from what she learned doing *Living Blues*. She got to be a professional typesetter from what she learned working on the magazine. It was overwhelming, plus I was still spending money collecting records. I had this huge record collection with lots of unfiled material—photos and clippings and all sort of memorabilia about the blues.

We'd gotten in touch with Bill Ferris at the University of Mississippi and through some conversations with him found out that the Center for the Study of Southern Culture at Ole Miss was doing some publishing and other documentary projects, including educational projects about the blues. They were actually interested in publishing the magazine, and we felt that would be great because we could still edit it. They could have all the headache of publishing the magazine, and we could get some money from it. But the deal was we would get fifty percent of the profits. [*laughs*] Yeah, there was the key. As the years went by there were no profits. But they kept the magazine going, and eventually they made an agreement to pay us a little bit once in a while to make up for the lack of profit.

And Amy and I got a divorce at the same time. She and I stayed together the whole time we had something to do with *Living Blues*—it kind of all fell apart at the same time. I continued to edit the magazine while living in Oxford, and then I resigned as editor in 1987. Oxford's a nice college town in Mississippi, but the pull of the Delta was too strong on me. I didn't like not being in the Delta, where all the blues artists were. Every weekend I was leaving Oxford and going to Clarksdale or Greenville or Indianola, so I figured I might as well be over there and really be into it. I had a little money from selling the house in Chicago to invest in something in the Delta. But the university has been publishing the magazine for twenty-three years now—they've certainly shown a commitment to it and I still work with the magazine. They send me articles and I proofread them for accuracy. Also I still do some writing for the magazine.

How did Rooster Records get started?

I had managed to stay out of the record business for a while, but in retrospect I wish I'd gotten into it earlier. But I'd been helping out on occasion. Once in a while I would go to a Delmark session. Those are the first recording sessions I ever went to—Luther Allison and Junior Wells—some of those early Delmark sessions. Sometimes companies would come to town. There was a record company called MCM that came to town from France in the mid-1970s and wanted to record a whole series of albums. They wanted to set up and record in the blues clubs, so I helped them do that; I helped to make arrangements and took pictures for them. Also, Ralph Bass was a noted record producer who recorded a series of blues albums in 1977. He had been very active with the Chess label and other labels earlier in his career. He was sort of out of touch with the scene at that point, so he called *Living Blues* to advise him on who to record.

I was able to get Jimmy Johnson and Magic Slim and Eddie Clearwater and Carey Bell and many other people recorded then. But I hadn't really done anything on my own. The more I saw how some of these other sessions were being done—give the artist two hours in the studio and tell him to record some blues, or two hours on the bandstand while you ran tape on them. And I thought there were a lot of blues artists around town who hadn't had a good representation of their work recorded or hadn't been recorded at all. So it actually came about with friends of ours from England, Mick and Cilla Huggins. They came over and decided they'd like to get involved in a record label. They actually had one thousand dollars! It's just like we started *Living Blues* with three hundred dollars; now we started Rooster Blues with a thousand dollars. [*laughs*] The artist I picked to do our first recording was Eddie Clearwater. I hadn't seen him a lot but I always liked him, and I thought he hadn't come near recording what he could. So we recorded *The Chief* album then and followed that with Larry Davis, and then Magic Slim, also Carey and Lurrie Bell.

You were also busy keeping the 45 alive.

Yeah, I always liked 45s. I still do. I wish they still made them. [*laughs*] We did 45s sometimes as collector items. We did a red vinyl Hound Dog Taylor 45 which came from an old session he'd done for Cadillac Baby. And we did a blue vinyl Little Johnny Jones 45 which was an unissued acetate I'd gotten from Johnny's wife, Letha. And we also put out some 45s, and the idea was to get them put on the jukebox or played on the radio—on a more commercial level in the black community than in the white collector's community. Once in a while we had a little success, like with Larry Davis. And when I moved to Mississippi I did a 45 on "Booba" Barnes. I always felt proud of that—that I recorded a 45 that you could hear on a jukebox on Nelson Street in Greenville, Mississippi.

Where did the Billy "The Kid" Emerson 45 come from?

Billy the Kid was one of those artists that was kind of off the scene when we got into it, and I was somehow introduced to him. He was one of those artists that had a lot to say, a great recording history, and so we did a *Living Blues* interview with him. He had some tapes he wanted to do something with. Mostly they were tapes of himself, but he had some sides with Matt Murphy and with Lacey Gibson on guitar. We never did get around to doing a whole album on him, because after the 45 came out he got back into the church, became a preacher, and said that the bishops told him he shouldn't be messing with the blues anymore. I believe he's back in Florida now.

The first Rooster Blues sessions were in 1979; the first records came out in 1980. Originally it was a partnership between Amy and me and Mick and Cilla Huggins in England. After two or three years Mick and Cilla decided they'd had enough of it. They could see where the record business was going. [*laughs*] But I thought we'd gotten off to a good start with it, compared to the way things developed later. After I moved to Mississippi I focused more on recording contemporary Mississippi blues like Booba Barnes and "Super Chikan," Willie Cobbs, who was in Arkansas. I left Mississippi in 1998 after I'd gotten married and had a couple of kids and moved to Kansas City, where my wife was from. I couldn't keep the label going the way things were.

In the past the blues artists were part of the family; if they needed money I would loan them money or a place to stay. But once I actually had a family with kids to support, it got harder to keep the blues end of it going, at least on a business level, so we ended up selling the record label to a blues fan and businessman, Robert Johnson, from Connecticut. It looked like it was going to be a great future; here was someone with money who loved the blues—and who was willing to pay me to produce records—I actually got paid to produce the records. But that only lasted a year or two until he saw the way blues record sales were going. The label's been pretty much inactive for the last four years. He's agreed to license some of the material back to me so I can put it out on a new label called Stackhouse, which was the name of a record store I had and the name of one of my favorite blues artists, Houston Stackhouse.

Let's talk about that. How did Stackhouse, the store, come about?

I moved to Mississippi in 1986 after *Living Blues* was transferred to the University of Mississippi. That happened in 1983. The university started publishing the magazine, although I was still the editor. I was still living in Chicago, and there were problems trying to coordinate the material and the content of the different issues of the magazine.

I was in Chicago and the layout staff was in Mississippi. I guess it's done more often now with computers and the Internet, but at that time it wasn't. So I ended up moving to Mississippi to edit the magazine from there for a while. That was in Oxford, Mississippi. But after a year of that I decided I'd done what I could with the magazine, and I went to the Delta—to Marigold and then to Clarksdale—to start a store and a recording studio, a store called Stackhouse. Patti Johnson was my partner at that point, and we were looking around the Delta for a place to have a business. We ended up in Clarksdale because that's where it seemed people were more interested in trying to develop something. There was an old store there that had been called the Creamboat. It was shaped like a steamboat with a couple of fake smokestacks on top of it. We were trying to think of a name for the business—something like "Smokestack"—and "Stackhouse" came out of that due to the fact that I'd been close to Houston Stackhouse and I knew his son, Houston Stackhouse Jr., in Helena, Arkansas, who was with the Blues Foundation in Memphis. When we opened the store, the Stackhouse family came over for the grand opening. We opened it on Muddy Waters's birthday in 1988. I think "T-Model" Ford played at the opening. So I stayed in Clarksdale until I moved to Kansas City, operating the store, and we put a recording studio in back of the store—and the record label.

Who did you record at Stackhouse?

Willie Cobbs, Lonnie Pitchford, Lonnie Shields, Super Chikan, Big Jack Johnson, Monroe Jones, Robert "Bilbo" Walker, also Jerry Ricks. On occasion we would rent out the studio. Jimbo Mathus recorded there. We had a temporary studio across the street, and Eddie Shaw recorded over there. Whenever there was enough money to pay musicians—and pay a recording engineer for a couple of hours—we tried to do something. So it was kind of a sporadic operation. When a bunch of money came in from something, we would spend it right away recording. I used to spend it on records; then I spent it on sessions instead.

Let's talk about some of the blues people that you've met over the years. Did you have a favorite above and beyond all others?

Joe Willie Wilkins, I think, as a blues spirit and musician is someone I think of a lot. He's the first person I would have recorded for Rooster Blues if he hadn't died that year. He was the guitar player in Memphis who played with Sonny Boy Williamson II in the earlier years. And Houston Stackhouse used to live at his house in Memphis, so I would go visit them. At that point in my career they were the elder figures in my life that I looked up to. He was just wonderful to be around and did a lot more with his music than anybody ever heard—just not on record. B. B. King is someone who's inspirational to me today. I get a similar feeling from him today.

Will you talk about Willie Nix?

Willie Nix was one of those legendary figures who recorded back in the 1950s for Sun and Chess and RPM, also Chance and Sabre. He had disappeared from the scene. He'd been in prison or gotten into something else and had resurfaced during the early years of *Living Blues*. Steve LaVere found him in Memphis. Steve LaVere used to be a regular contributor to *Living Blues* too. He did an article on Willie Nix. Then Willie dropped out of sight again. It was through Joe Willie Wilkins, several years later, that I found out that Willie Nix was still around. He had a piece of paper that Willie Nix had written his name on, and the name of the town he wrote on the paper was Leater, Mississippi, which actually was Leland, Mississippi. So I went down to Leland. I was living in Chicago, but I made these regular trips down to Memphis and Mississippi just to interview people and report on what was going on.

Willie Nix was what Lee Jackson, a Chicago player, always described as "a little aviatic," which meant that he was a little "flighty" or in a different world—or had a different mindset than the average person. [*laughs*] He was quite a character. He would recite jive poetry: "long and lean—ain't never had enough—and all that stuff." I drove around Leland with him just out in the countryside; he wanted to show me some stuff. We'd stop and visit some people. Most of the people around Leland just knew him as a wino. They didn't think anything about him being a musician or that he'd ever been famous. He *had* been famous; Robert Junior Lockwood played in his band. Willie was a pretty big name around 1950 or '51 down there. But nobody believed it in later days. So we'd stop and there'd be a bunch of guys hanging out somewhere, and Willie would get out of the car and say, "Look—look! He [meaning O'Neal] came all the way to see me! Look at his car—you can tell he ain't from around here! I'm tellin' you, I made records!" And I'd say, "Yeah, he did." And I'd try to verify that all the people on the scene knew who he was.

But he never had much of a career in the later years at all. He'd learned guitar from Joe Willie Wilkins, and I heard him play a little guitar at his house and he sounded just like him. He was better known as a drummer. That's what he did on his records. He sang and played drums with people like Walter Horton and Willie Johnson—a lot of great Memphis and Chicago musicians. He actually moved to Clarksdale after having lived in Leland all those years. It was in the 1970s when I went to see him the first time. After I moved to Clarksdale he decided he would move there and he wanted to make a record. He wrote some new songs—"Look Out All You Young Hookers—Nix Is in Town." [*laughs*] He made friends with another friend of mine, a deejay named Andy McWilliams. They would go around places together, and Willie Nix would tell him he wanted to set up in front of the Chinese grocery store and play, because that's the way they used to do it. That's the way they used to get crowds. This is back forty or fifty years ago. In Willie Nix's mind it was still like that. In the end it was kind of sad nobody knew much about him. When he died, we just heard that he died—in 1991, I think.

Weren't you also a fan of Ike Turner?

I always had an admiration for Ike Turner's music, regardless of what happened in his personal life. He was a pretty notorious character, but I always thought his contributions to music—to blues, to rhythm and blues, and rock ' n' roll—have not always been acknowledged, certainly not as much as they should have been. So I went to Los Angeles. I knew he was living out there. I made a trip out there to an address I had for Bolic Sound Studios, but it had burned down. The building was still there, there were master tapes in there, but it was all charred and burned. I couldn't find him that trip.

A couple of years later I heard he moved to East St. Louis briefly to make a comeback there. This was after he and Tina had split up. I did end up spending a few days with him at the house he had there in East St. Louis. There were musicians coming in and out. I would try to talk to him—to try and interview him. He would sit still a little while, but he was always going a mile a minute. He'd be going somewhere and trying to do something, and he couldn't understand why anybody would want to know about all that old stuff, because he was always trying to find something new that was going to be a hit. I kept in touch with him over the years. He moved back to L.A. right to that area.

Finally when I made the deal with Bob Johnson for Rooster Blues, I introduced Bob to Ike Turner to try to get Ike to do a blues album. Ike had pretty much done it on his own. I didn't really have anything to do with it except making that connection so he could get the album out. It did put him on a blues path, and I just got a new CD from him the other day. It's another all-blues album, called *Riding with the Blues*. I think a lot of people regarded Ike as dangerous. But the thing I learned about Ike, despite the violent image and the criminal associations, or abuse associations, was that he was actually a shy person underneath and can be very funny and entertaining to be around. A lot of people have a great fondness for him, and other people wouldn't trust him at all, so . . .

Tell me about the Mississippi Blues Trail project.

Doing the research and writing for the Mississippi Blues Trail historical markers with Scott Barretta, who is another former editor of *Living Blues*, has been reinvigorating. When we started the work in 2006, a lot of people probably assumed all the research on Mississippi blues had already been done, but we've found lots of new information on the famous artists and learned about many bluesmen we didn't know about. Tracing the history of blues in areas outside the Delta, like Natchez, Columbus, Hattiesburg, and the Mississippi Gulf Coast, has been especially interesting, and very little of that history can be found in books and magazines. We're planning on at least one book based on all this research. There is so much more genealogical information available now than there once was—in the census reports, military records, city directories, and other online sources—and we've spent a lot of time doing interviews and searching through material at different libraries and courthouses. The fact that the blues trail is officially connected with the state of Mississippi has made it much easier to get local people and organizations interested in contributing information, too.

I've been fascinated by some of the local stories about blues artists who grew up in Mississippi but moved to Chicago at an early age, because those Mississippi years have often been dismissed with a couple of sentences in the old biographies we've read, some of which I wrote! For instance, Magic Sam came up under an old black fiddler in a community around Grenada, where the popular black music was breakdowns, and you can hear that in some of the music he recorded later. And Otis Rush was married and working his own farm in his mid-teens in Mississippi. Plus it turns out that the birthplaces, dates, and names of the artists aren't what we've thought them to be in a lot of cases. I'm glad I've had the chance to help peel away some more layers of blues history, and I'm glad the state of Mississippi realized that its blues history was worth documenting and promoting. Considering the past racial history there, it's pretty amazing. When the Otis Rush marker was unveiled in Philadelphia, where the civil rights workers were murdered in 1964, the white mayor talked about it as part of a healing process for the community.

I've always regarded the work in documenting and promoting the blues as a benign second front to the civil rights movement, a unique opportunity to associate, and hopefully to communicate, an alternative to the confrontation of the 1960s. Does this work generate a similar sense for you?

Yes, for me it does, especially since I grew up in Alabama when all of that civil rights activity was going on. It seemed kind of far removed to me at the time, since Mobile was fairly calm compared to what we were seeing on the news from Selma and Birmingham. So when I got into the blues a few years later and saw what a struggle the black musicians were still facing, becoming an advocate for the blues gave me—and all of us at *Living Blues*—an opportunity to do our part to support a form of civil rights and artistic rights in our own small way. I also realized that the white attraction to black music was, or could be, a factor in improving race relations, although there were some negative feelings too over the fact that white bands often made a lot more money than the black blues artists whose songs they were singing. That was one of the reasons we tried to focus *Living Blues* on the African American tradition.

Later when I was living in Clarksdale, when Patti Johnson and I were concentrating on recording and promoting Delta blues, we were making some kind of statement on behalf of African American artists. I remember that when we met a black chiropractor from another town, Batesville, who heard what we were doing, he said, "What, you mean they haven't burned crosses on your lawn?" Thankfully, Clarksdale was past that then. People generally just left us alone to do what we were doing, and there were a few who were genuinely supportive. I guess the strongest civil rights statement I helped disseminate was the message of Willie King, who had a lot of songs that came out of the struggle in Alabama. I recorded him for Rooster Blues after I had sold the label but I was still producing. He was pretty critical of local politics and race relations in his songs, and I was actually afraid there might be reprisals against him. But he was never worried. He did a lot of great work for his community, and in the end he became a folk hero.

RICHARD K. SPOTTSWOOD INTERVIEW

Dick Spottswood. Courtesy Dick Spottswood.

I'm better known as Dick. I was born in Washington, D.C., in 1937. My mother stayed at home, and my father was a mid-level executive at the telephone company. I've always enjoyed music. People used to dump old recordings on me when I was a child. I enjoyed the sound on them more than I did the late-era swing music and the pop crooners that were commonplace in the 1940s. I thought some of those older dance bands on acoustic records were kinda cute—maybe a little cooler too, although the concept of "cool" hadn't evolved yet. But I was a little kid—I wasn't listening to anything systematically. I heard some early jazz—I guess Bix Beiderbecke and Louis Armstrong, Jelly Roll Morton, and King Oliver. That was really the first thing that reached up and grabbed me. I heard something in that blues-influenced music that I hadn't heard in popular music before. I didn't know that at the time; it was just an element that instinctively appealed to me.

I always had a collector mentality and accumulated a fairly broad-based collection, because I liked early country, I liked blues, I liked gospel music, I loved early jazz. And years later I came to discover there were wonderful riches to be found in old foreign-language music catalogs. I was ten when I first heard Oliver, Morton, Beiderbecke, and those people—the early jazz I really fastened on to. There was a big legend on the old Columbia 78 rpm disc album by Bix Beiderbecke. A banner on the cover said, "Jazz as it should be played." Previous to that I thought of myself as really not liking jazz much, but I sure liked Bix's music, so it told me to keep listening for more so-called hot jazz from the 1920s. That was very much to my taste and temperament—and still is today.

There are so many different directions that your career has gone. Where shall we start? With the folk boom era?

Well, I was never very fond of what was called—what is still called folk music. I don't like the music of urban folksingers. I don't dislike it either, but people assume I'm involved with that, and I'm not. I've always had problems with the other way the term "folk music" is used, in a pseudo-anthropological way that we apply to people whom we consider exotic, quaint, inferior, or simply "other." Calling their artistry "folk music" seems condescending, so it's a word I avoid.

So you probably wouldn't be the ideal guy to lay out what the folk boom era was then?

Well, the folk boom or folk revival never had much to do with serious folk music, did it? Peter, Paul, and Mary; Joan Baez; Tom Paxton; or Tom Rush all specialized in composed popular songs. What does that have to do with what we normally think of as folk music, or at least what we used to think of as folk music? Like I said, it's a term I avoid, because I can't use it without having to define it and underscoring what it is and what it isn't. When I edited that collection in the seventies called *Folk Music in America* for the Library of Congress, I hadn't thought that one through yet.

I'm just trying to make the connection with the reemergence or rediscovery of a number of prewar bluesmen.

Well, I would maintain that that had as much to do with rock 'n' roll as with the folk revival. All of a sudden when Robert Johnson and Charley Patton and those old people became chic, the guitar had become rock's emblematic instrument. It had more to do with old voice-and-guitar guys than it did with the people I had previously thought as more important—especially the women—Ma Rainey, Bessie Smith, and Ida Cox, blues matriarchs in the pre-rock era. Somehow or other Charley Patton and those people were conceived of as being of a different order. People who liked Charley Patton usually did not like Bessie Smith. I always found that incomprehensible until I figured out that young blues fans were people looking for prototypes to validate their rock sensibilities. However, the people who were elevating the Charley Patton et al. included significant New York collectors like Pete Whelan, Bernie Klatzko, and Jim McKune who liked that music in addition to Ma Rainey and "King" Oliver and the early jazz people. Pete Whelan is writing a novel based loosely on the early life of the New Orleans cornetist Freddy Keppard. He's never lost that enthusiasm and neither have I. We like Charlie Patton and we like Son House—we just don't think the sun rises and sets on them. There are record collectors who prefer old guitar blues to everything else. They tend to make record collecting seem kind of exotic and the people who indulge in it weird misfits. Prominent collectors like Joe Bussard and R. Crumb enjoy being part of the humorous stereotype, and of course the popular press eats it up. [*laughs*] The problem, of course, is that sometimes that's true. I don't see that book collectors and art collectors are subject to the same degree of ridicule. Maybe we collectors had it coming—I don't know. I don't like it very much [*laughs*], but I guess it's ok.

How did the Mississippi John Hurt era come about?

I was just out of school and working in the undergraduate library at American University in Washington, D.C. John Edwards, an Australian record collector who died in 1960, had made a tape of some scarce 78 rpm discs for Pete Kuykendall. Edwards owned a scarce copy of John Hurt's "Avalon Blues." I'd never heard it before, and as soon as Pete played me the tape I immediately picked up on the line *"Avalon's my hometown—it's always on my mind."* Well, it seemed like a no-brainer to go get a map, or an atlas—whatever was at hand—I think I went to the library and found Avalon, Mississippi.

This was 1963 and this ne'er-do-well friend of mine, Tom Hoskins, was going down to New Orleans for the Mardi Gras. I suggested he stop by there if he could. Avalon was an "if-you-blink-you-miss-it" kind of little town, and the first person he asked directed him to Hurt's doorstep. Tom determined that he was musically still viable, and we arranged to bring him to Washington to record some songs and appear briefly at some folk and coffeehouses. There was a place called the Brickskeller in northwest Washington, across from Rock Creek Park—I forget what street it was on—and a little coffeehouse on Ontario Place, where Hurt became something of an artist in residence.

That fall his family moved to D.C., where he frequently appeared if he didn't have other commitments. He was invited to the Newport Folk Festival in 1963, where he was a very surprising success, due in no small part to a comfortably modest demeanor that projected extremely well, even from a large stage. Although he wasn't performing in the usual, theatrical sense of the word, he was a brilliant and engaging performer nonetheless, with a quiet magnetism that appealed to people. Skip James and Robert Wilkins were at Newport with him in 1964, but, great as they were, they seemed withdrawn and taciturn by comparison, so they never hit it off with the public like Hurt did. Ironically, Wilkins and James were able to copyright eventual hit songs, and Hurt never really did.

Dick Spottswood with Mississippi John Hurt. Courtesy Dick Spottswood.

Tom Hoskins; my wife, Louisa; and I were partners in a corporation we formed when John Hurt's reputation grew and it looked like there might be money involved. But we learned that it was possible to be famous without getting rich, which is what happened. Louisa and I were not businesspeople. We failed to do what we should have in order to protect our interests and wound up leaving the corporation.

So Dick Waterman was never a part of the situation while you were there?

No.

When you made the recordings with John Hurt, was this the beginning of the Piedmont label?

Yes, basically we created a record label in order to present John Hurt. That was ill-advised. None of us were prepared for the record biz. We should have made arrangements with the Vanguard label or somebody like that who was equipped to do business on a larger scale. But when Piedmont started, it wasn't clear that Hurt was going to be the runaway successful performer that he was. It took about seven or eight months to realize he was pretty good and reasonably profitable. He never made a bunch of money, but I think if he had lived a little longer and collaborated with somebody more skilled at business than we were, everyone—especially the Hurts—would have been better off.

Prior to Piedmont, did you have any experience in recording anybody?

I had actually made some pretty good on-site recordings of Fred McDowell, the previous spring [1962] while I was still in school. Louisa and I recorded him in Como, Mississippi, in his home and surrounded by family and neighbors. The recordings came out extremely well, and they're still available on the Rounder label. I recommend them if you haven't heard them.

Can you run down your involvement of the era when all the prewar bluesmen were being rediscovered?

The folk boom era, or folk revival, which is what we call it in retrospect—of course, we rarely define an era until it's over—what those years made possible was the research and the legwork that was necessary to engage older performers who could still be found and who still had some good music left in them. I recorded and was involved, in one way or another, with John Hurt, Frank Hovington, the Reverend Robert Wilkins, and Skip James. Beyond blues, I remember Dennis McGee, the great Cajun musician of the 1920s, who still sang and played brilliant fiddle half a century later.

"Jabbo" Smith was a pioneer trumpeter, singer, and songwriter, and Louis Armstrong's only serious competitor in the 1920s. Lorraine Gordon, Manhattan's jazz rainmaker, once married to Max Gordon of the Village Vanguard, was Jabbo's manager when he decided to perform again after 1970. Lucky for him, too! Lorraine was very professional, very organized, very aggressive. [*laughs*] In 1964 I located him in Milwaukee and brought him to Washington to supervise the reissue of his first records. He wasn't playing at the time, because his teeth were in bad shape. A dentist/jazz fan, Al Vollmer, fixed him up so he could play trombone, whose embouchure was larger and more comfortable. Jabbo hadn't played music for years, but his artistry was still impressive. He was also a very good composer, and he wrote several new songs for a musical called *One Mo' Time* that also featured him in the pit band. The tunes sounded like ones you heard all your life, but they were all originals. He performed with the show from its 1978 debut until 1982.

So the reemergence was a happy experience for him?

Oh, yes, yes, yes! He was earning only a modest living as a driver for a car rental company. He'd take a rental car from one place to another as needed, and I think he was living on food stamps. It was not a good situation, and he was very happy that people remembered who he was. He went to live in New York, where the musical was based. But before that we assembled and reissued his early records, at least the ones under his own name, and put them on two Melodeon long-play records.

Tell me how you discovered Robert Wilkins.

That was a little comedy of errors. Bill Givens, who at the time was Pete Whelan's partner—a real character too—in the Origin Jazz Library label, they put out those first Charley Patton reissues and the guitar-heavy country blues collections of the early 1960s. Bill insisted that he located Robert Wilkins in Memphis, which made sense because that's where he made the records, but he didn't have the address. I went to the telephone company in downtown D.C. and found addresses for two people named Robert Wilkins in the Memphis phone book. I put two pieces of paper and a sheet of carbon paper in the typewriter, typed two different addresses at the heading, and wrote to both, "If you are the Robert Wilkins who made records et cetera, et cetera." And I got an answer from one of them. [*laughs*] It was that easy. By then he was the Reverend Robert T. Wilkins, of the Church of God in Christ, and a professional herbalist as well. He came up to Washington to record, and he went to the Newport Folk Festival in 1964.

I have to say, of all of the early heroes I was fortunate enough to record again, Reverend Wilkins wasn't just as good as he had been on early records—he was a damn sight better! His strongest recordings, I say with all modesty, are the ones I made of him in 1964, including the long, immortal performance of "The Prodigal Son." In retrospect you could really see how it captured the Rolling Stones' imagination. It was a powerful performance. He still loved the blues and liked to listen to old records of people he once knew. He would have played the blues in an instant. But his faith and his livelihood depended on his congregation and his church, and he was not going to do anything to offend his people. I didn't blame him. It wasn't my place to intrude into that world and say, "Well, you should really perform blues again, because all of us white folks don't want to hear you play gospel." That record sold very poorly. Great as it was, it generated little interest beyond Mick Jagger, who covered "The Prodigal Son" on a best-selling Rolling Stones set. Wilkins was recorded later on in uncongenial settings with a loud electric guitar—it was maybe eight or ten years later—and nobody seemed interested in him after that. So we were lucky to have those calmly made, controlled, deliberative studio recordings of his from 1964. I think those were maybe the best live recordings I was ever involved with. Our relationship never really ended, but he returned to Memphis and took up his pastoring duties full-time.

Dick Spottswood. Courtesy Dick Spottswood.

Wilkins assigned publishing rights for his songs to Wynwood Music, as had John Hurt, Dorsey Dixon, Skip James, Bukka White, and several people who were writing original bluegrass and country songs in the D.C. area. Pete Kuykendall started Wynwood around 1962. He was a talented, resourceful guy who had a strong influence on D.C. bluegrass after 1957. Among other things, he played Flatt and Scruggs's "Foggy Mountain Breakdown" for the future actor/director Warren Beatty when both attended Arlington [Virginia] High, long before it became the celebrated leitmotif for [the 1967 film] *Bonnie and Clyde.*

Pete agreed to publish the songs, none of which we thought had any commercial potential, to copyright and protect them. In exchange, he agreed to do all the recording, production, editing, and everything. In other words, he presented us with final masters of Hurt, James, Wilkins, et cetera prepared for release. So Wynwood was in place with "The Prodigal Son." The Rolling Stones came out with that record *Beggars Banquet,* whose original cover is now quite collectible. It showed the Rolling Stones standing at urinals in a public men's room, and on the wall in place of the graffiti are the title and composer credits for each song, including one that says "The Prodigal Son" by Reverend Robert Wilkins. Well, that cover, because it involved watching the Rolling Stones pee into ceramic pots, was withdrawn, another image replaced it, and at the same time Mick Jagger's name was substituted for Wilkins as composer of that song. So Pete was able to write a letter to whoever was representing the Stones' publishing—"Dear Sir or Madam, We have a copyright number 'so and so,' but the song was published by Wynwood Music." That was all that was needed. Wilkins continued to collect money on that for the rest of his life. And it was there for Skip James—twice! He was still alive when Eric Clapton's band called Cream recorded "I'm So Glad" in the studio in '68 and then did a live version in 1969. Both were very well-selling records and basically paid Skip's medical bills before and after his death in October 1969.

Those songs turned out to be extremely important for those people. When "Hard Time Killing Floor Blues" was selected for the 2000 film *O Brother Where Art Thou,* and the soundtrack from that movie sold a gazillion copies, the song earned impressive royalties. Only recently have legitimate heirs of Skip James been located. There's been money waiting in escrow for them all these years, including the *O Brother* royalties. You can imagine [*laughs*] some poor individual down there in Mississippi or Texas getting a six-figure check from somebody they never knew. [*laughs*] I'm detailing the story to show that music publishing isn't all about stealing.

Did Piedmont do a Skip James record?

No, by the time Skip James was in place I'd started a new label named Melodeon that prominently featured Skip James. Pete Kuykendall and I recorded him in December of '64. Earlier that year Skip had come up to Washington for surgery on what would turn out to be terminal cancer. While he was in the hospital he wrote "Washington D.C. Hospital Center Blues." The cancer wasn't really caught, and that's what killed him five years later. But he had a few good years in between that surgery and what finally took him out.

Wasn't there some involved litigation concerning the John Hurt estate?

What happened was that John Hurt seems to have remarried—or at least had a common-law relationship with the woman who was always presented as his wife, a very smart and lovely lady named Jessie Cole, who claimed to be a distant relation of Nat Cole. But it turns out he had married a lady named Gertrude around 1917. She lived well past the century mark and claimed in a lawsuit that they were never divorced. She claimed to have papers, including a marriage certificate that would prove it. So on that basis they tried to get all of the proceeds that at that time were going to John and Jessie Hurt's son, John Junior—they called him "Man" Hurt. But John Senior had a couple of children with Gertrude, and inevitably there were conflicting claims.

The only place to go to for money was Wynwood. Unlike Reverend Wilkins and Skip James, Hurt didn't have any hit songs. There were small and steady accumulations of royalties, but they had all gone to John Junior. And then for a while they were held in escrow while which branch of the family got what was sorted out. Ultimately they were able to settle amicably, because neither side had any basis for depriving the other of a share of the royalties.

What else was on Piedmont besides John Hurt and Robert Wilkins?

We did a couple of little anthologies which were fun to toss off—they kept the presses busy along with our main orders. We did a collection of twelve-string-guitar players, including George Carter—the first and last time anybody ever heard of George Carter—and Seth Richard, another obscurity. It was a good collection. There was an LP of semi-pornographic things: Bo Carter, Frankie "Half-Pint" Jaxon, things like that. Oh, there was an anthology of early ragtime—you know, ragtime from early source recordings, early ragtime songs, military bands and banjo solos, and a wonderful recording of a Scott Joplin rag from Memphis in 1928. Though it was labeled "Easy Winner" [another Joplin title], it turned out to be "The Entertainer."

Well, they say that man proposes and God disposes. On the twenty-eighth of August 1963, not long after visiting Newport with John Hurt, Louisa and I were marching on Constitution Avenue. That was the date of the March on Washington and the Martin Luther King "I Have a Dream" speech. We would have been near the steps of the Lincoln Monument listening to that speech, except that I got a severe stomach cramp. I went home and it soon developed into a debilitating variety of ulcerative colitis that later was named Crohn's disease. It almost killed me. I was in and out of the hospital and active or inactive, depending on my condition at any given moment, for a period of five years, from 1963 through 1968. During this time there wasn't much besides the Crohn's. It was all I could do to tend to what work I could manage and keep my head above water. There were times when I could function and times when I couldn't. And it was one more reason I wish I had avoided the record business. My wife, Louisa, and I—it really took over our lives. It was ultimately very corrosive, and I've stayed the hell away from it ever since, except to make records for other people.

Most of the collectors that I've talked with over the years have told tales of managing their collections: stories of the logistics of owning and moving so many records, stories of divorce and having to sell their collections. Have you ever had similar experiences?

I sure have. I wasn't somebody who had a whole lot of resources I could use to collect records. I couldn't compete with the guys like Pete Whelan and Nick Perls, who had money to go after good records on the collector market. When I was young I just got what I could. I'd buy records from the Salvation Army or go out and knock on doors and ask people if they had old records. I'd give them nickels and dimes [*laughs*], whatever I could afford. I didn't have any money. Still, I built up a pretty good collection over the years. Finally it occurred to me to reconsider collecting when I saw four-figure sums—this was in the late seventies and early eighties—attached to an awful lot of the records I had by that time. I didn't have much in the bank, and I didn't know what the rest of my life was going to be like. I didn't like having something that big, bulky, heavy, and fragile, and I didn't like the idea of having to guard them against flood, fire, and other possible calamities.

It was a valuable collection by then, and I didn't feel like being the custodian. So in 1982 I offered a number of attractive individual discs in a mail auction. A dealer from New York named Bob Altshuler offered an attractive price for my early jazz, blues, and gospel 78s. It was a pretty generous deal, and taking him up on it was the smartest thing I ever did. I put the money in mutual funds when the Dow Jones Average was still below eight hundred. The income freed me to write, produce records, and do freelance work, whatever I wanted to. So God bless that record collection. I was sad to see it go, but on the other hand, I never looked back. And I haven't stopped collecting either!

Did having the collector mentality influence or guide you in terms of your schooling and trying to acquire a degree?

Well, I graduated from the University of Maryland in 1960 with a philosophy degree and a minor in languages. In my senior year I fell in love with a lovely lady, Louisa Hill, whom I met in a music class. We married at the year's end, and I served active duty with the Army Reserve before enrolling in the library school at Catholic University. At the time, librarians were in very short supply and they were looking for males in what was then a female-dominated profession. Males tended to get better-paying administrative jobs—I doubt if that kind of sexism is still as pervasive. I liked books, learning, and libraries, and the degree seemed like a good idea, if only because I couldn't think of anything else I particularly wanted to do.

I came out of Catholic University with a degree a year later and did library chores at American University for a while. It got tedious to me, and by the time John Hurt emerged from the Mississippi countryside in March 1963, I was ready to move on. I didn't have a business temperament, but, despite reservations, I started a record label because of John Hurt. I discovered that everything I suspected about my business abilities, or lack of them, was true.

But you asked about record collecting. Being guilty of that myself, I've observed collectors like Joe Bussard and others being characterized as quaint and obsessed in the popular press. You can collect at extreme levels. A guy on the West Coast has publicized his standing offer of twenty-five thousand dollars for a 1930 record by the Delta bluesman Willie Brown that collectors haven't found so far. It sounds like a load of money, but this collector has paid hefty prices for premium discs for years. If he's inflated the market across the board for blues records, he's also increased the value of the rare ones he already owns. [*laughs*] My collecting activities dropped off after Bob Altshuler bought my collection in 1982, but I like to find a nice 78 myself once in a while, and I enjoy keeping up with fellow addicts.

When did your work for the Library of Congress take place? And how did that happen?

I'd known about the Library of Congress and I'd known curators Rae Korson, Bob Carneal, and Joe Hickerson since I was in my teens and twenties. When someone of consequence like John Hurt or Robert Wilkins or Dorsey Dixon or "Chief" Ellis was available, I would ask them if they wanted to record for the Archive of American Folk Song—to contribute to that great collection and to be there for posterity. In '74 they hired me to do a fifteen-disc annotated anthology called *Folk Music in America*. I was on that job for three years. My resources included commercial documents, Library of Congress recordings, and new recordings made on location. After the project was complete, I went back briefly to the public library world and then got a large grant, a series of grants actually, to prepare a discography called *Ethnic Music on Records* that was published by the University of Illinois in 1990.

The library's Archive of American Folk Song began in 1928 with Robert Gordon, who was sort of an on-and-off employee then. Some of his earliest recordings were on a home disc recorder, a very primitive apparatus that was available at the time. Later John and Alan Lomax traveled the South collecting music on improved recording machines: the music Americans played, listened to, and enjoyed on a sort of pre-commercial level in those days. There were lots of fiddlers, banjo pickers, convicts, and blues singers in reformatories and penitentiaries, that kind of thing. Americans making music in their hometown, home life situations.

What format are the field recordings? And how are they stored?

Wax cylinder recorders were used as early as 1890 to record Native American songs at the Smithsonian's Bureau of American Ethnology. The Library of Congress has cylinders made by John Lomax as late as 1932. Better-sounding uncoated aluminum discs replaced them in the spring of 1933 when the Library of Congress acquired a Presto Model Y portable disc cutter. There are some experimental discs made by John Lomax at a black church in Alexandria, Virginia, when he was trying to learn how to work the damned thing. Then in 1937 they began using acetate-coated aluminum blanks. They were less hissy, but they haven't aged as well as the earlier uncoated aluminum discs, because the acetate coating has tended to separate from the aluminum base, making the discs unplayable. By comparison, the library's pre-'37 uncoated aluminums play back with some hiss, but they continue to hold up well.

And just out of curiosity, are these recordings actually stored on shelves?

Oh, yeah, I handled and listened to any number of them there. [*laughs*] I couldn't believe people were paying me to have so much fun. I encountered so much great music that had never been heard since the time it was recorded. What a wonderful job!

Do they receive and archive commercial recordings as well?

The Archive of American Folk Song has been rebranded as the Archive of Folk Culture. It's not in charge of published products, which go to the Motion Picture, Broadcasting, and Recorded Sound Division.

The other night I had a record that you and Bruce Bastin did with Frank Hovington.

Oh, I'd forgotten about Frank! That's a record I'm really proud of. That record almost didn't get made, because Frank was avoiding us [*laughs*], but we just outfoxed him. That was more Bruce Bastin's idea than mine. He was visiting from England and staying with me over the July 4th holiday in 1975. I had a Nagra recorder on loan from the Library of Congress, a small reel-to-reel recorder that could make studio-quality recordings on location. Frank lived out in the country near Frederica, Delaware, had no phone, and previous attempts to record him had been unsuccessful. Bruce proposed that we ride over from D.C. to see if Frank was at home.

We threw the recorder in the backseat of my 1972 Volkswagen and took off the morning of July 5th, with no expectation that our trip would be successful. But when we arrived Frank was there with his wife, Winnie, and their family—friendly, cheerful, and welcoming to their unexpected guests. With no preparation or reservations, Frank just sat down and tossed off one great performance after another. Jesus, he was good! [*laughs*] It was an event that ranks right up there with recording Robert Wilkins, John Hurt, and Fred McDowell in my memory, and they were among the best performances I ever had the privilege to record. Thank you for reminding me.

And you've reminded me of McDowell. Would you tell that story?

I'd heard Fred McDowell on that 1959 Atlantic record set that Alan Lomax did, *Sounds of the South*, and I'm thinking, "Wow! It would be nice to get some more music like that." I was still in school in 1962 when my wife, Louisa, and I set out over Easter break and drove down to Mississippi to see if we could find Fred McDowell. We were lucky, and Fred and Annie were as welcoming and hospitable as the Hovingtons. However, they had a dog that was less receptive and went for me when I left the house to get something from the car. When I was a kid I used to be a newspaper carrier, so I knew how to deal with dogs. This one was especially mean. He came after me with his teeth bared. We were inside a fence, and there was no way I was going to get through the gate in time, so I just turned around and ran after the dog. [*laughs*] I screamed at him and scared the shit out of him [*laughs*], but I also lost my voice for a week.

Fred was apologetic, of course, but he was also vastly amused. It broke the ice, made us friends, and I'm sure it made the records better. It also helped that family, friends, little kids, grandparents, and neighbors hung out with us and kept things informal. I didn't try to shush people. Most were impressed with the recording apparatus, and they had a sense that it was an important event. They were fun to be around, and if people were talking or clattering dishes, we just moved the mic a little closer. Being in his own living room with family and neighbors, Fred wasn't uptight with the intrusion of us white folks—and you've heard the results! Bruce edited a Flyright LP in England, and Rounder issued it stateside.

What did you record on?

I think it was a monaural full-track Ampex that Pete Kuykendall loaned, along with a mixer and a couple of microphones. I was able to put one mic near Fred's voice and another on his guitar. I had headphones on and was sitting right next to him, but because there was extra room noise from our audience I couldn't hear a damned thing through those headphones, which were only good for playback. But somehow the tapes got made and they were wonderful.

Louisa and I went to visit Memphis Minnie shortly after making those records. She was entirely paralyzed on her left side, living with her sister in Walls, Mississippi—a couple miles south of the Tennessee line near Memphis. Minnie wanted to hear some of what I'd recorded. [*laughs*] I brought the tape recorder in from the car and let her hear some of Fred's music through the headphones. She made this terrible face [*laughs*]. and she said. "That's how I played when I was just learning." [*laughs*] And I could see where she was coming from. Fred's music sounded superb to me, but I was of a different race and different time with different sensibilities. In her prime Minnie had been a superb guitarist, and I could see where she'd be dismissive of a country guy who, to her, couldn't do a damned thing but run a steel bar up and down the strings.

Let's talk about your series of discographies.

Ethnic Music on Records was an outgrowth of my Library of Congress time, and the discovery that foreign-language music on early records could be pretty exciting. I included examples wherever they fit into the *Folk Music in America* collection, and what I heard made me want to hear more and learn about the vast catalogs of foreign-language records made by immigrants to America, along with Native Americans, Hispanic Americans, Americans from Central and South America—everything that was germane in North and South America.

The only English-language components were Irish and West Indian, but those were treated for marketing purposes like other foreign-language series. They were assigned separate number series in the catalogs and directed specifically at the appropriate minorities. A lot of black music and white country music was marketed on a broad non-regional basis, but target audiences for Albanian records and the Trinidad calypsos, for example, were specific, because much of the music in those days had limited crossover appeal. I didn't include Hawaiian music, because I saw it as American pop music with a regional flavor, and the crossover component was so pronounced that there was no way to tell where real Hawaiian stuff left off and where Bing Crosby took over.

In order to meet the criteria a recording had to have been made before 1942 in the United States or its possessions. I scoured the record company archives—Edison in New Jersey; Columbia and Victor in New York; and Decca, Brunswick, and Vocalion—all those labels out in California. Not all of them had a complete surviving set of written records, but I took what I could and learned what I could. And I discovered that there was enough material, preserved material, to put together something approaching a complete discography of the foreign-language material in the United States, including cylinders made at the World's Fair in Chicago in 1893 and later field recordings. The cutoff was July 31, 1942. After that the nature of record production changed very greatly. So it turned out that, with multiple indexes, there was enough material for seven volumes.

What years were you actually working on this series of discographies?

I worked full-time on them for five years—from 1978 to 1983—and then on an as-needed basis until the book was published in 1990. I've been logging new information ever since, and an updated online edition now looks possible.

Was this completed volume by volume or as a complete series?

In those days we didn't have the computer tools that we have today. When I began the project in 1978, I organized everything on five-by-eight cards and kept them in shoe boxes—and traveled around the country with them. The cards were arranged by nationality and then by performer. So after bringing all that material back home in half a dozen boxes, I got several word processors and hired a bunch of literate kids to input my handwritten information. In a couple of cases these word processors, which were all leased, went to live with these people, who were paid by the hour with funds from the grant. The Library of Congress Automation Office took word processor files and made one gigantic program to print the discography. Because we had to enter accents, special non-English-language characters, and other things by using a lot of elaborate punctuation marks and certain numbers in coded sequences, it was pretty tedious. But once that was done, you pushed a button and a big printer next to the mainframe computer in the basement of the Library of Congress would print out a complete four-thousand-page discography. The first time it came out of that printer, it was exciting indeed, having evolved in the space of five years from file cards in shoe boxes to something you could publish as a book.

You've also had a great deal of involvement in bluegrass. How and when did that happen?

Growing up in the D.C. suburbs, it wasn't music I'd been routinely exposed to. I remember being at a high school party around 1953, and there was a bunch of 78 rpm records stacked on a record changer. The music was normal pop music for the time—Patti Page, Frankie Laine, music of that ilk. Somehow or other a copy of "Foggy Bottom Breakdown" got into the stack, and when I heard it I stopped whatever I was doing and went over and stuck my ear up next to the record player and savored every little drop of that one. I didn't even know it was a banjo. I'd never heard a banjo sound like that.

By 1953 I think the 1949 original had gone out of print. I couldn't find the record for a while, but I knew I wanted to hear more music like that. I came to know Mike Seeger at that point. Mike had already learned about that music (it wasn't called bluegrass yet), and he said, "You should listen to Bill Monroe. You should listen to Jim and Jesse. You should listen to Charlie Monroe and Mac Wiseman." So I started listening to WGAY, WARL, and other local country stations and discovered that I liked the instrumental sound of that music, especially the hot Earl Scruggs and Bill Monroe breakdowns. It took me a year or two to appreciate that Lester Flatt was just as great as Earl Scruggs and that there was more to the music than just high-speed virtuosity. By 1955 I was listening to more retro-style country music. The best part is that was popular music from my own generation being made then and there in my own time. I could hear it live, on radio, and on new records, and it was great stuff I could relate to. So I liked that and I also liked avant garde classical music—the fifties were a very good time for that music too.

Except for records, I didn't get to hear the classical music as much, but in 1954, I guess, Buzz Busby had a band with Scott Stoneman's fiddling and Don Stover playing banjo. They played at a cheesy little bar at Massachusetts Avenue and Sixth Street Northwest. During the school year I could ride a bus downtown Friday nights and hear subsidized concerts by the Budapest String Quartet for a quarter at the Library of Congress. When they were over I'd walk six blocks down Massachusetts Avenue to the Pine Tavern and Buzz Busby's Bayou Boys, the other string quartet. [*laughs*] It occurred to me that I probably couldn't do that at any place outside of Washington, D.C. I was a kid, I didn't have any money, but I could get all that great entertainment for next to nothing, which is what I had at the time. I loved bluegrass—still do.

How about the magazine *Bluegrass Unlimited*?

In the spring of 1966 the Stanley Brothers made an appearance in the D.C. area that went virtually unnoticed until after it happened. Pete Kuykendall, Gary Henderson, Dianne Sims, George McCeney, Dick Freeland, and a few others—we thought there needed to be some sort of systematic effort to promote personal appearances. So that's how *Bluegrass Unlimited* was born. I was the unpaid editor for four years. Dianne was nominally the secretary; she had done secretarial things before, so we bought a mimeograph machine at a government auction. She taught herself how to type stencils, and we'd run the magazine off on the mimeograph machine every month. We'd put big piles of paper on her dining room table, and the local pickers would come over and collate the magazine pages, staple them, put them in envelopes, and attach address labels.

Basically we got the magazine out like that entirely with volunteer labor until 1970, when Pete Kuykendall took it over. Pete has a gift for organizing and administration, and he turned *Bluegrass Unlimited* into a more than viable organization. There are a lot of full-time employees down there right now, and that's with the depression and the Internet cutting into magazine sales. I don't think they've had to fire anyone—yet. I keep my fingers crossed.

And let's talk about your radio show.

That was an outgrowth of *Bluegrass Unlimited* when we decided there should be a radio component. Public radio in Washington was still in diapers at that point. It was still called National Educational Radio in 1967 when I signed up to do a series of half-hour broadcasts at WAMU on the American University campus in northwest D.C. They amounted to little lectures designed to meet the educational model, liberally sprinkled with musical examples—every program a rhetorical theme or topical point. We weren't paid, and I quit after five years when I got tired of doing them. And so Gary Henderson, a veteran country music programmer and a much better radio host than I am, took the program over and the station really grew it. It was WAMU's primary income source until *Morning Edition* took hold in the 1980s, and news, public affairs, and lightweight weekend entertainment came to dominate NPR. Today WAMU supports a Bluegrass Country channel twenty-four/seven on the Internet, an HD channel in Washington, and on a low-powered FM transmitter in Reston, Virginia. Bluegrass helped pay the bills at WAMU-FM for a long, long time, and we're lucky it till has a place there.

My Bluegrass Country identity these days is the *Dick Spottswood Show*, more informally known as the "Obsolete Music Hour." It's got a foundation of bluegrass, but as you might gather, it also covers other styles I like. The aim is to expose bluegrass people to the roots of their music along with some other, less market-driven styles called folk music, but there's some primitive stuff. Last night I featured a little suite of French-language things, early recordings—Cajun from New Orleans, patois Kalinda from Trinidad, Martinican émigrés who settled in Paris in the late 1920s, and a Canadian lady singing Nashville country style, complete with fiddle and steel guitar and sung entirely in French. [*laughs*] I love that kind of thing. I love the music that's unexpected—unexpected connections between Bob Wills and the blues, between King Oliver and Wade Mainer, Duke Ellington in a washboard band, and other surprises. Johnnie and Jack and "Fats" Waller each recorded a mid-thirties pop song, giving it a different spin. I like to play their versions side by side, because I enjoy the contrast. It's the story of how diverse music has become in America—and not just as a result of the "new age-y" self-conscious experimentation. A lot of it has just evolved that way.

Let's talk about the ARSC. What is it and how did it start?

Well, ARSC, the Association for Recorded Sound Collections, was born in a meeting that formed an alliance between institutions—specifically institutional sound recording collections and their curators—and private collectors. It seemed to be a viable reason to keep and maintain an organization, because the institutions had the resources to send their people to those conferences at no cost to the individuals themselves. Hobbyists and private collectors like me have to go on our own hook, pay for our hotel rooms and meals and all that. The private collectors tend to hang out with each other or where their subject specialties are discussed. Classical music people were off in one corner, jazz people in another one, and techno-geeks always have lots of toys and protocols to talk about. Collectively everyone's interested in the preservation of historic sound across the board, and these days ARSC is focused on arbitrary and capricious copyright extensions that have attached to sound recordings, primarily because there's no federal law governing ones made before 1972, and conflicting state laws—especially in New York and California, where entertainment industry interests prevail—tend to confer eternal ownership of recorded music content to rights holders. ARSC has combined forces with libraries and other organizations seeking reasonable solutions.

Do you think that extending copyright protection is a bad thing?

Absolutely! With copyrights the old model was twenty-eight years. I'm talking about print. Sheet music, anything in print, was copyrighted for twenty-eight years and you could renew [for] another twenty-eight years. That provided protection for over half a century. Why does recorded music need to be protected any longer than that? The people who want access include historians, institutions, people who want to hear and study older music. Under existing laws institutional collections are theoretically liable for making preservation copies of deteriorating recordings, commercial and noncommercial recordings.

Once upon a time, if you wanted to copy a recording for your own use—your own study—and you were making a single copy, this did not constitute publication; it constituted fair use. That's no longer the case. Rights holders are theoretically able to litigate and say you don't have the right to copy something because its contents don't belong to you. Rights holders who profit by skewed legislation include record companies, publishing companies, and businesspeople who successfully lobby in the name of artists, composers, and other content creators [and] are the ones who profit by draconian laws aiming to protect recordings into perpetuity. When Sonny Bono died in a 1998 skiing accident, Congress extended copyright protection of intellectual property across the board for another twenty years in tribute to him. It wasn't enough that he made all those bad records; his legacy prevents us from hearing the good ones. Thank you, Sonny!

JACQUES DEMÊTRE INTERVIEW

I was born in 1924 in Paris. Jacques Demêtre is a pen name I've used over the years for all my written work. My parents came from Russia, émigrés after the Revolution in 1917, who came to Paris. My father was a classical composer in the style of Alexander Scriabin, a Russian composer. My mother was a painter, the daughter of a well-known painter in Russia. My parents met and married in Paris. Until the war I lived in a Russian atmosphere, always speaking Russian at home. I went to school and learned to speak French, which I spoke outside my home—with my friends at school, on the streets, and in the shops—but as soon as I got home we spoke Russian. Also, before the war I wasn't interested much in music. I wasn't interested in the music of my father; it was too complicated for me. I was more interested in the songs of Charles Trenet, a French singer. So there was little to indicate at this point that I would become interested in blues.

L to R: Willie "Big-Eyes" Smith, Otis Spann, Jacques Demêtre, and Muddy Waters, Chicago, 1959. Photo Jacques Demêtre/Soul Bag Archive.

I was too young to serve in the military when the war began and too old when the war finished. [*laughs*] So I didn't serve in the military, but during the Occupation people born just a few years earlier—in 1921 or 1922 or '23—were sent to Germany to work in the factories. It was called the *Service du travail obligatoire,* or STO—the Obligatory Work Service. I was too young for that as well. I was in the streets when the army of LeClerc liberated Paris. But I wasn't killed [*laughs*] or wounded or anything—I was lucky.

When the Germans came to France in June 1940, they occupied the northern half of the country. The Nazis regarded jazz as low music, music of an inferior people. We thought that they would forbid this music altogether, but it was a paradoxical thing. Only American jazz was forbidden, both by black and white musicians. Also American jazz tunes were forbidden, so many of the American jazz standards were issued in France with alternate titles during this time. For instance, the tune "Some of These Days" was issued as "Baby of Love"; or "St. Louis Blues," which was issued as "The Sadness of St. Louis"—you know, Louis the French king, St. Louis [*laughs*].

At the start of the war I was living in the south of France, where things were more relaxed, there was a less restrictive regime. Hugues Panassié, a well-known jazz critic, had a weekly radio program and played records by both black and white American jazz artists. In 1942 I moved to Paris and was living with my father. At that time there were very good French musicians, who had played with black jazzmen before the war. Some were very good and made records. For instance, Django Reinhardt—even though he was a gypsy, a people whom the Germans viewed as inferior—made very good records during this time. So I started to buy jazz records, especially the records by Django Reinhardt. And this was how I became interested in jazz and swing—music with improvisation.

There was a label called Swing, which was started before the war by Charles Delaunay and Hugues Panassié. I tried to find these records, but it was rather difficult because they were rare. I had to go to the flea markets in the north of Paris. There I could find records by Django Reinhardt and Alix Combelle with Le Jazz de Paris, who played in the style of Count Basie. Also there were two or three Negro musicians who were living in Paris. Harry Cooper was an American Negro who became a French national, and because of that he was allowed to record and made very good records for the Swing label. He was playing in a café called Le Cigale. And near Cigale was a movie theater for German soldiers. And as the crowds from the theater let out, the German soldiers would pass by the club and they'd say, *"Jazz ist gut! Der jazz ist gut! Sie sind gut!"* [*laughs*] And there was a very good piano player, Leo Chauliac, who played in the styles of Count Basie and Fats Waller. He gave a concert in 1943 at the Salle Gaveau. He was performing with another organ player, Michel Ramos. I attended, and half the audience were German officers—and they applauded right along with the rest of us! Incredible!

After the liberation at the end of the war, the major record companies started to issue records by American musicians. At that time I had a good collection of jazz records. I was buying records by Louis Armstrong, Duke Ellington, Count Basie, Lionel Hampton, and Benny Goodman—swing and the big bands. But after the war, the music changed and bebop was invented, with Charlie Parker, Dizzy Gillespie, and Kenny Clark. I was very disappointed—it wasn't a music that I liked. I didn't have any of the bop records, and I wouldn't listen to it on the radio. For me, it got worse and worse. So I divorced bebop. [*laughs*] But I was already listening to blues even before bebop became popular. So even if jazz hadn't changed, I had already discovered the blues. Even before I discovered the blues singers, I was always interested in the blues that were played by the well-known jazz musicians.

I understood that the blues were something different, something deeper than the standards, or George Gershwin, or Cole Porter, or Irving Berlin. That was all good music, but much lighter in a sense than the blues. The major labels also issued records by blues artists like Bessie Smith, Leroy Carr, Lonnie Johnson, and vintage records by Big Bill Broonzy. These were on Columbia and Victor. And then there were illegal labels as well, Jazz Society and Jazz Document, which reissued the old-timers—sides by Blind Lemon Jefferson and Crippled Clarence Lofton. These were all on 78s. So I became more and more interested in blues. I was also reading *Jazz Hot* magazine with articles by Panassié and Delaunay. The prevailing opinion at this point was that with the death of Bessie Smith shortly before the war, blues had died. There were no more blues singers, no more blues—only jazz. But then around 1949 or 1950 a label called Vogue began to issue records, and that was a revelation—modern blues records by Muddy Waters, John Lee Hooker, blues shouters like Wynonie Harris and Eddie Vinson, also gospel sides by Spirits of Memphis and Mahalia Jackson. I began to understand that the blues wasn't dead—it was still alive!

There was a man François Postis, who owned a record shop in the middle of Paris, and he sold all the new blues records. I came by frequently and we became good friends. He told us, "See—the blues aren't dead! Listen to these records by Muddy Waters, by John Lee Hooker and 'Champion' Jack Dupree." We were listening to "Honey Bee," "Rolling Stone"—the classic recordings Muddy did for Chess. And then in 1951 Big Bill Broonzy toured Europe and came to Paris. This was organized by Postis. Big Bill performed in Paris accompanied by Blind John Davis. Postis also organized a solo performance by Blind John Davis in a small club near the record shop. I had the opportunity to sit very close to Blind John and watch the way he played. I was fascinated and became even more of a blues enthusiast.

The records were 78s up until 1954. Then came microgroove records—first ten-inch LPs and then the twelve-inch LPs. My first impulse was to tell everybody, all the jazz fans, that the blues wasn't dead. But it also occurred to me that while it was good to hear modern blues, the fact that so many black people were still listening to blues meant that their situation in life hadn't much improved. It's ironic—we're happy to hear the music, and blacks might have been happy to play it, but I understood that the blues was born from the racial situation of the blacks.

Originally, in the years before the war, Hugues Panassié and Charles Delaunay were close friends, almost the same person—like Laurel and Hardy! [*laughs*] They founded the magazine *Jazz Hot* in 1935 and started the jazz record label Swing in 1937. They organized concerts with Coleman Hawkins, Django Reinhardt, Eddie South, and many others. They were close friends for many years. It surprised many of us when a rift came between them, and how vehement the rift was. That was about 1958 or '59. Charles Delaunay wanted to promote bebop musicians and Panassié was against that. Even though my tastes didn't favor bebop, I was on the side of Delaunay, because Panassié was too insulting. You may not agree with someone, but it's unnecessary to belittle them. There was a jazz critic, André Hodeir, and Panassié denounced him by calling him *Mauvaise Odeur*, which means "bad smell." [*laughs*] I agreed with Panassié's opinion of bebop, but not his style in denouncing it. Panassié seemed to be a very angry man—it was just his nature—while Delaunay never really responded to the attacks.

After the split each of them had their own music magazine: *Jazz Hot* continued to be run by Charles Delaunay, and Panassié had the *Bulletin of the Hot Club of France*. I disliked Panassié so much that I decided to write for *Jazz Hot*—plus I thought I could make a case for the blues with their readers. Readers of the *Hot Club of France* already were familiar with the blues. *Jazz Hot* carried on until just a few years ago, while the Swing label was taken over in the years after the war by a man named Kabakian—"Mr. Kaba," as he was known. This is the same man who owned the Vogue label. So the Swing label and its affiliate label Jazz Selection were taken over by the Vogue label. Delaunay also went to work for the Vogue label. Kaba died many years ago and none of the labels exist anymore.

In 1953 I went to London and met a man called Bert Bradfield. He owned a record shop, and when I went there it was like paradise. He had stacks of records by the RCA/Bluebird artists—Tampa Red, Big Maceo, Tommy McClennen, Big Boy Crudup, and Big Bill. I bought what I could afford and brought them back with me to Paris, and I made arrangements to buy records from him by mail. He sent me sides from the Bluebird catalog and Decca as well. The one that I never could find was Kokomo Arnold—it was very rare. So I collected a cross-section of blues artists and styles. I began to recognize the different styles from Mississippi up to Chicago—also from the Eastern seaboard up to New York. Panassié wrote and recommended various blues artists in his articles, but he never talked about their styles or their influences. Charley Patton to Robert Johnson to Muddy Waters—or Blind Boy Fuller to Brownie McGhee. Panassié never wrote about this aspect of the blues, but the network of styles and influences was becoming more and more clear to me.

In 1954 I met a man Gerard Conte, who was a lover of New Orleans jazz. Conte was writing for *Jazz Hot* because Delaunay realized he had to present more than just bebop and he made space for traditional jazz. Gerard Conte started to write articles on New Orleans jazz. Then Gerard Conte introduced me to Charles Delaunay, and Delaunay was very nice to me because he was half Russian too; we had that in common. And he told me, "You write what you want, and I'll never change one word of what you write." So I wrote articles starting in 1954. I wrote about Muddy Waters and John Lee Hooker, Sonny Terry—all the people that I knew.

After I started to write this series of articles, I met Paul Oliver. Paul, who was in England, wrote me a letter. He told me, "I've been reading your articles and they're very interesting—as much as I can understand in French. I want to meet with you and have a discussion on the blues. I'm coming to Paris. Can I meet you?" So we met and he told me a very interesting thing: "You have to listen very carefully to the lyrics, because blues is not just music for entertainment. There is meaning, a story in the lyrics. These are stories about being in prison, about unemployment, and about living and traveling as a hobo." And he wrote a wonderful book, *Blues Fell This Morning*. Paul Oliver was a big influence on me. This was another step in my coming to a deeper understanding of the blues.

You've told me that you spoke French and Russian, but in order to comprehend the lyrics of blues tunes you'd have to understand English. Did you speak and/or read English?

Yes, I studied English in school for six or seven years. At that time I spoke much better English than I do now. So, yes, I understood most of the lyrics. In recent years I've had little opportunity to speak English and have forgotten much of what I knew.

Did you understand that often the lyrics referred to real events and real places?

Through the blues you can hear the history of American Negro society during the twentieth century. Some of the records sing about authentic events—the Natchez fire [of 1940] or the 1927 flood in Mississippi and other catastrophes.

Before you started writing your articles were there other people writing about blues?

Panassié was writing about blues—also a writer from Belgium, Serge Tonneau. He had a blues magazine—*Rhythm and Blues Panorama*. I wrote some articles for him. Also François Postis wrote for *Jazz Hot*. Another writer who was very important to me was Kurt Mohr. He was a discographer who introduced me to the practice of discography; if you write an article about an artist, you should include a discography of their records. And he told me, "It's not enough to simply listen to the records. You must meet the artists whenever you can." When Sammy Price toured France in 1956 or '57, Kurt told me, "You must go to meet him at the station, stay with him as much as you can, and ask him questions about how he lives." So that's what I did. Every time a singer came to Paris I met them.

After Sammy Price I met Brother John Sellers; then Sister Rosetta Tharpe came to Paris in '58. I became her chauffeur and drove her from the hotel to the theater. And every time I met these artists, I asked them about their careers and their lives in the United States, about the lives of black people in America. I wasn't just interested in the music, but in the racial-political climate as well. Eventually we decided that it wasn't enough to listen to the records, nor to meet with the visiting artists. We decided that we had to go to America. So in 1959 a friend, Marcel Chauvard, and I decided we had to go there and see how these people lived.

Marcel was a friend and a blues fan, who also wrote articles on the blues. It was strange—Marcel's father was a butcher and Marcel worked with his father in their butcher shop. Kurt Mohr's father worked for SDN [Société des Nations], the international society in Geneva. And my father was Russian. We were such different people, but we all came together as close friends because of the music. Marcel and I made the trip to America together in 1959, and I remember Marcel died in 1968. It was a sad and curious story. We made our landmark trip together to the US in 1959. The next year Marcel returned to America without me. And on this trip he fell in love with a Negro woman named Lillian. He came back to

France and was very unhappy. He told me, "I think I am really in love with her and want to get married." So he wrote and asked her to come to Paris and they would get married. But at the same time, he was afraid to tell his father and his family that he was married to a black woman. He thought his parents were racists and would be against the marriage. So he and Lillian were married, but he never told his family that they were married. He would visit his family each week—but alone; he never took his wife. Each week they would ask him, "What's new?" And he would say, "Oh, nothing."

Finally Marcel and Lillian decided they would move back to Chicago, but it wasn't so simple, because he was still working for his father. By this time he was running a photography shop, still working for his father. So they set the date to come back to Chicago and he came by to see me. I asked him what he was going to do about the shop; he couldn't just abandon the shop without explaining to his family. So my wife offered to talk to his parents and explain the situation. He got angry and told her never to do that. A few days later Lillian phoned me and said she had tried to call Marcel at the shop and no one answered. She was worried that something might be wrong. She went to the shop and it was closed. Marcel had disappeared. So she opened the shop and they found Marcel dead of a heart attack. He died from the stress of his situation. He couldn't leave without having to explain that he was married to a black woman. We met his parents at the funeral, and they said, "What a fool our son was. We already knew. We found out through his sister that he was married—we knew. We were just waiting for him to tell us. We were more than ready to accept her." And Lillian went to see them, and they said, "You're like our daughter. Why didn't you come to see us?" But it was too late. She went back to Chicago and I lost contact with her. She was a little older than Marcel, so I think she may be dead. Quite a sad story—like a blues story!

Champion Jack Dupree and son with Marcel Chauvard, New York City, 1959. Photo Jacques Demêtre/Soul Bag Archive.

On our trip to the US, which took place in 1959, we had no financing. We paid out of our own pockets—like a vacation. First we went to New York City, because I had contact with Champion Jack Dupree. I wrote an article about him. This was before I met him. Somebody gave me his address and I sent the article to him. He wrote back

Jazz Hot magazine cover. John Lee Hooker outside Joe Von Battle's shop, Detroit, 1959. Photo Jacques Demêtre/ Soul Bag Archive.

to me and told me that he was glad to read the article and invited us, if we ever came to New York, to stay at his home. So Marcel and I stayed with Jack Dupree for almost a week. He took us to clubs and introduced us to many blues musicians. We saw Sammy Price and Lafayette Thomas, who at the time was playing guitar with Sammy—also Larry Dale and Jimmy Spruill. We saw Danny "Run Joe" Taylor—also Henry Glover. We met Bobby Robinson, who had the Fire/Fury/Meteor labels. We went to the office of his record company, where we were introduced to Allen Bunn—"Tarheel Slim"—and his wife, Little Ann. We also saw gospel artists. We went to churches, and the Apollo Theater held a special gospel night with Alex Bradford, Clara Ward, and the Spirits of Memphis. For us it was an unforgettable experience.

Then we took the Greyhound to Detroit. We had the address of Joe Von Battle's record shop on Hasting Street. We told him we wanted to meet some blues singers, and the first thing he did was to call John Lee Hooker. Hooker showed up and I took a picture of him out on the street. He was surprised to meet blues fans from France, but he'd already recorded for a label for white listeners. I remember he told us, "They want me to be the new Leadbelly." They wanted him to play acoustic guitar, but he told us that electric guitar was his thing, not acoustic. I think he was a little insulted. He stuttered when he spoke but not when he sang. I had already heard about that from a friend who met Hooker earlier. And we went out to the clubs in Detroit to see live blues. We saw Little Sonny Willis on harmonica and Eddie Burns, who played with Little Sonny at the Club Carib. They also had a piano player, Prince Albert. We met Floyd Taylor and Emmitt Slay. Also K. G. Fuller, who played piano at a white club. And we saw Little Eddie Kirkland at a black club, but back then he wasn't wearing a turban. [*laughs*] Joe Von Battle gave us many records on his own label, JVB, including a record by One-String Sam. The man played a guitar with only one string—"I Need a Hundred Dollars." [*laughs*] We only spent two days in Detroit.

Then we went to Chicago. Our main reason to visit to the United States was to come to Chicago, and our first stop was the Vee-Jay record company. Our friend Kurt Mohr worked for the Odeon record label, which reissued Vee-Jay records in Europe. He met Vivian Carter and Jimmy Bracken [the Vee-Jay founders] in London. And when they heard about our trip to America, they told Kurt to make sure we came to visit at Vee-Jay. Vivian and Jimmy were there, but not Abner—and he was the real chief. We waited for him, but finally we had to leave. We were going to catch a taxi, but Jimmy insisted that his friend would take us to a good blues club, and his friend took us to see Buddy Guy. There was another club nearby where we met Sunnyland Slim, Dirty Red Nelson, Tiny Topsy, and Matt Murphy. We met Muddy Waters and his band at Smitty's Corner. Pat Hare, James Cotton, and Otis Spann were in his band at the time, and Memphis Slim was performing at the club with Muddy as a special guest. Little Walter also performed as a special guest with Muddy at Smitty's Corner. I got an interview with Little Walter. People later told me that he was often angry, but he wasn't with me. He was a very kind man. Sonny Thompson was at Smitty's as a special guest as well. We also met B. B. King, who was staying at a hotel near ours. We saw him perform at a theater. Other bluesmen we met were J. B. Lenoir and Eddie Boyd along with Elmore James and Homesick James, and we saw Eddie Taylor.

We took photos of everybody we saw, and they're all included in my book. Day after day we were out at the clubs meeting musicians. Sometimes we would visit them at their homes. We saw Howling Wolf at his home. We went to the home of J. Mayo Williams, the impresario who worked for Decca before the war. We wanted to meet the old-timers, and he gave us addresses for Kokomo Arnold and Tampa Red. We went to see Tampa. At that time he was renting a room, but the landlord didn't have any idea who he was; he had written "Hudson Whittaker" on a label on the door. I took some shots of Tampa holding his guitar, but he didn't want to play. Also he wouldn't tell me very much about his life or career; he said he was writing a book and it would all be in his book. He was a quiet man, not very tall. But for me it was a very emotional moment to meet such a great artist. I think his records with Big Maceo are among the best blues ever on record.

We met St. Louis Jimmy, a very clever man. We corresponded afterwards, and his letters were well written. He was a good writer, an educated man. We got to meet Little Brother Montgomery. Surprisingly, Little Brother was working regularly with Otis Rush! I saw Brother perform with the band, and then I met him again at the office of Mayo Williams—it was Mayo Williams, St. Louis Jimmy, and Little Brother. Brother played piano and St. Louis Jimmy sang "Going Down Slow." We were used to hearing them on record, and so it was exciting to see them perform in person.

Jacques Demêtre with Kokomo Arnold at Kokomo's Room, Chicago, 1959. Photo Jacques Demêtre/ Soul Bag Archive.

Mayo Williams gave us an address for Kokomo Arnold. The first time we went to his home but he wasn't there. The landlady told us to come back the next day and we finally caught up with him. At first he really didn't want to speak about his career as a musician. He told us he had nothing to do with music anymore—he'd forgotten all about it and didn't want to speak about it. But Marcel and I showed him the articles we had done in *Jazz Hot* magazine—we carried a supply of *Jazz Hot* to show the various musicians we met. In *Jazz Hot* over ninety percent of the musicians featured were black. Kokomo was impressed and agreed to tell us his story—when and where he was born, how he started to play bottleneck guitar, how he was working in a steel mill in Chicago. He'd made a record. Mayo Williams heard it and wanted him to record for Decca. Kokomo wasn't interested and refused on several occasions; he was a bootlegger and preferred his liquor business to a career as a musician. Every time somebody came to convince him to make records, he would hide out in the backyard with the moonshine. [*laughs*] But Kansas Joe McCoy took him to the studio with his guitar and urged him to play. He finally agreed but was reluctant to be involved with other musicians. He complained about going to New York to record; the city was too noisy and always smelled like fish, he had to ride elevators in the skyscrapers where the studios were located, which gave him a headache. "It smelled bad, smelled bad." There are a couple of pictures of him in our book. The first was the picture we took when we visited him in 1959, and the other was a vintage photo he gave us, which has become quite famous. It showed Kokomo, many years earlier, drinking a bottle of whiskey.

Kokomo Arnold at home, Chicago, 1959. Photo Jacques Demêtre/Soul Bag Archive.

He also explained the origin of his name, Kokomo. There was a mystery surrounding his name. Some thought it was an African name; others thought he was named after a city or town where he lived. But he explained that he was simply named after cocoa—a chocolate-flavored powder—it was a drink mix. He showed us his recording contract. He saved it because he wanted to prove that he was the real Kokomo Arnold and not an imposter. He was working in a factory. He said all his fellow factory workers were very jealous that he would make more money for one three-minute record than they would make in a month. [*laughs*] We asked him if he'd like to be recognized again, to be famous, and he told us, "Why? I have a good life. I work in a factory, go fishing on Sundays. What more do I need?" At the end of the interview a bunch of children from the neighborhood came to see Kokomo and wanted him to play. So he told us the interview was over, that he had to go play with the kids. He was a picturesque man. [*laughs*]

Curtis Jones was another old-timer. We met him in a hotel where he was staying, but it didn't have any customers. He lived in a single room at the end of this long hall, but nobody else seemed to stay there. He told us he wanted to play again and be recognized by the public. We wrote about him in the series of articles we did for *Jazz Hot*, and he wrote to me after our visit. He wasn't very literate; his letters looked like they were written by a child. He wanted to come to Paris and play in the Blind Pig, a club in Paris. He said that the articles in *Jazz Hot* helped him and so he was able to come to Paris to perform. But he wasn't successful; he was very shy, and when he played he wouldn't look at the people. He played wonderful music, but he just looked down at the piano and didn't connect with the audience. Eventually he went to Germany, where he died in poverty. On the other hand, both Memphis Slim and Champion Jack Dupree came to Europe and were very successful. They were good performers, and between each tune they'd tell stories to make the people laugh. They'd tell anecdotes that entertained the audience, which Curtis Jones was unable to do. He made great records but wasn't a good performer.

I saw Memphis Slim several times, and he was very successful. He made many records—in fact, he made too many records. [*laughs*] Big Bill too—too many records. And Brownie McGhee and Sonny Terry—a flood of records. [*laughs*] I understand, you make a record, you make money. But it's not always good for your reputation.

We were in Chicago for two weeks, but we still weren't able to see it all. We had to go back to Paris. When we got back from our trip we wrote about our adventures in the US, which were in a series of articles in five consecutive issues of *Jazz Hot* magazine. Then a year later another magazine, *Jazz Journal*, reissued the articles translated into English. Finally, many years later, I was working for *Soul Bag* magazine, writing stories and record reviews. I was friends with the owner, Jacques Perin, and we saw each other all the time. He told me he thought the articles of our trip would make a good book, and that's how the book was published. They decided to reissue the stories with the English translation included, one page in French and then that same page in English. There was a preface written by a friend of mine which was in French only; otherwise everything was published in both French and English.

I see from your book that you have all sorts of photos. Did you bring back any audio recordings from your trip?

No. No. We had no tapes, no recorder. And actually it was one of the reasons we had such good relations with the musicians. Since we had no recording equipment, the musicians had no reason to be suspicious that we would record them and issue records without paying them. We didn't bring a recorder. At that time recorders were big and heavy, very awkward to handle. Also I'm not very technically minded. I wouldn't have known how to operate a recorder. So it made us more trustworthy in the eyes of the musicians. We weren't able to record our interviews, but I kept a notebook to write down what the musicians told me.

Did you have anything to do with the Chronological Classics series?

Yes. The man who produced this series, Gilles Pétard, was a friend of mine. He asked me to produce three different CD sets: *The Story of the Blues*, with two CDs, for which I donated records from my collection and wrote the liner notes; another was *The Anthology of the Blues*, also with two CDs; and another was *Just the Blues*, with three CDs. Altogether I produced three packages devoted to blues, and two discs devoted to gospel, plus another disc for the Golden Gate Quartet, and another for Mahalia Jackson. But Gilles Pétard was having financial problems, and the series has since ended.

PHIL SPIRO INTERVIEW

I was born in New York City in 1940. My mother, a housewife, was also born in New York, although her parents came from Russia. My father was born in Mława, Russian Poland (yes, there is a stroke through the letter *L*; it's pronounced like a *W* in English), where the family name was written as "Szpiro." The judge who naturalized my father's brother as a US citizen advised that nobody would ever pronounce it right or spell it right, the *Z* got dropped, and it became "Spiro" for those who ended up in the US. All but one of the family who stayed in Poland died in the Holocaust. In Poland my father had been apprenticed as a watchmaker to an older brother who had made the town clock, an important undertaking at that time and place. His parents sent my father to the US to avoid his being conscripted into the tsar's army.

When he landed in New York City in 1911 at age sixteen, he was already a skilled watchmaker and jeweler, and he spoke Polish, German, and Yiddish, but no English. By the time I knew him, he claimed to have forgotten his Polish and German, and he spoke English with no discernible accent. During the 1920s he started a successful clock-importing company and made many trips to Europe, but was wiped out by the Depression, and went back to retail watch repair, engraving, and jewelry; along the way he picked up optometry. By the time I was old enough to be aware of such things, he had an office in Manhattan, three stories up looking out over Lower Broadway—a great place for a kid to view the many parades after the end of the war. When I was ten my father had a heart attack, and we followed the conventional wisdom of the time and moved to a warmer climate—in our case, Miami.

Phil Spiro at the Waldorf Cafeteria, Cambridge, Massachusetts, winter 1963–64. Photo Dick Waterman.

Miami was a shock. It took us a long time to get used to the overt signs of segregation—"White" and "Colored" drinking fountains, restrooms, waiting rooms, schools, bus seating, et cetera. It would be years before the Cuban revolution made Miami into a Latin American city, and while I lived there it was a Southern city that also had a lot of people who came from the North. I'd gone to unsegregated public schools in New York, and I went to segregated public schools in Miami. At school most of the kids were native Floridians with Southern accents and attitudes, or immigrants from the North like me, with just a very few who had Hispanic surnames, from Venezuela or Cuba. Many kids hunted snakes in the Everglades, or hopped up cars that sometimes sported Confederate flags, and in that regard Miami and its people were little different from other Southern cities—Robert E. Lee's birthday was a school holiday.

I spent weekends and vacations at my father's store, running errands for him, going to wholesale parts suppliers for watch parts—"material," in the trade—or to plating companies and engravers for specialty work. He was a master watchmaker, but my father was not particularly dexterous, and it would sometimes take him three or four tries to get a part seated properly. And it is exactly the same for me when I build a computer. I learned patience from my father.

I was admitted to MIT in 1957, but I could not afford to go, so I spent my freshman year at the University of Miami. The next year I got a loan and transferred to MIT as a sophomore in aeronautical engineering. I took a co-op plan that had five months of work in the real world, which I spent at North American Aviation in L.A. I did trivial data analysis and graphing, including some small work on the X-15, now in the Smithsonian, and fifty-odd years later, still the fastest airplane ever piloted by a man, 6.7 times the speed of sound.

Because I was on a co-op plan, I had to take courses every summer thereafter. If I had been taking a regular course schedule with the usual vacations, I would not have developed an interest in music or a later, oddly connected interest in computers. Had music not been the bright, shiny distraction that it became for me, I'd have stayed in school, and I would not have become a computer programmer. And because I met my wife, Elaine Chow, at a symposium for computer professionals, there is much more than just work and music involved here. It's every aspect of my life that's worth talking about.

During the summer of 1960 I ended up in a new dorm. A guy a few doors down from me had a banjo. He played what I learned were Carter Family and Woody Guthrie songs. His name was Emerson Griswold, and he was a year behind me, studying mechanical engineering. Understandably, he preferred being called "Griz," and it suited him. He had previously played trumpet and cornet, but had lost his lip and had taken up the banjo.

I had heard all the pop music of the day on the radio, and some classical as well, but I had never developed an interest in music. If you asked me what kind of music I liked, it would have been like asking me what kind of sewing stitch I preferred. But I was captivated by what Griz was playing. I'd never heard anything like it before. This stuff was somehow different, and had substance to it, something I had not run into before—or at least not noticed before.

I asked Griz where I could hear more of this kind of music, and he recommended the MIT music library. They had everything! They had the anthology. They had Charters's *The Country*

Blues book and LP, and his Blind Willie Johnson LP, which made a profound impression on me. They had rooms where you could play records. They had Library of Congress LPs. They had Ewan MacColl and A. L. Lloyd's incredible set of unaccompanied Child ballads on Riverside. They had lots of Folkways LPs, including Pete Seeger, Woody Guthrie, and Leadbelly. They had almost all the English-language traditional music that could be had on LP at that time. The MIT music library did just about everything but stick a guitar in my hand.

I absorbed all of this like a sponge, indiscriminately at first, but eventually establishing preferences. If some people came to traditional music through the back door of the Kingston Trio, or through the front door of growing up with it in their home, I was the guy climbing in the side window, listening almost exclusively to traditional music of many kinds without any of it having been a part of my life previously, but shaping my musical values as though I had grown up with it. I was okay with formal schooling methods, but learning this way—diving into interesting material—was much more fun. So I read and listened and read some more. I learned about the folk music coffeehouses around Boston and frequented them as often as I could afford. At the Turk's Head in Boston I met Geoff Muldaur, who had a tape of Blind Willie Johnson 78s that had not been on the Charters LP, which cranked up my interest in blues and underlined how little had been reissued on LP. I met a fellow who had a folk music show on the campus radio station, began sitting in on his shows, and took over as announcer when he left school.

I hung out a lot at the Club 47 in Cambridge, where I heard performers in many different styles. The most influential for me were Rolf Cahn and Eric von Schmidt, who separately and together played a wide variety of styles, with an emphasis on blues. Eric did wonderful things, reworking material from Furry Lewis and some of the Library of Congress field recordings by Smith Casey and "Sin-Killer" Griffin, and Eric's music increased my interest in country blues as such. Rolf was an entirely different story. He was a very serious flamenco guitarist as well as a good blues guitarist, although not in the country blues tradition. His approach to blues was through jazz and intricate guitar work, but hanging out with him was not so much about blues as it was about music in general. Rolf once remarked of a flamenco singer whom he admired—I think it was "El Pili," a guy who practiced his singing with his head in an empty refrigerator, the better to hear what he sounded like—that "he's so good that even his mistakes are interesting."

By my senior year I had spent so much time on music that my grades had become terrible, and I dropped out before I flunked out. I eventually went back and finished with a degree in aero, but that would be years later. In 1961 I was just another MIT dropout in a city full of MIT, Harvard, and Boston University dropouts, and other than music, I was adrift.

For a few months I lived on a cot in a friend's dorm room. I found a job punching a desk calculator at a rarefied research facility in the extreme boondocks and got a cheap room near Harvard. I saw Griz only occasionally; he had started working part time for Keenan and Keyes, redoing their famous—to engineers—steam tables, which, for the steam engine nut he was, was like a monk being asked by the pope to help rewrite the Mass. For the job, he had to learn how to program a computer, unusual in those days, and he liked it a lot.

I had no knowledge of computers, but I figured that if he liked working with computers, I might like it too.

I got a job at the MIT instrumentation laboratory as a computer operator in the group that had just started designing the guidance computer for the Apollo lunar mission. I punched cards, changed tapes, rewired plug boards, and I even did a little programming. I barely knew what I was doing, but I was learning about computers, and I liked it as much as Griz had. He graduated in 1962, and we then shared an apartment in Boston on the cheap side of Beacon Hill, a few doors down from where the Boston Strangler had struck the month before we moved in. I found a job as a computer operator and junior programmer with Itek, a company that developed the first satellite cameras. Griz was doing high-powered work at MITRE and he could soon afford a place by himself. I couldn't, so I needed a new roommate.

Al Wilson was a friend I had met at Club 47 through Laurie Forti, and I had spent time with Al at his parents' house, where he lived, listening to Muddy Waters, Howling Wolf, Bo Diddley, John Lee Hooker, and George Lewis records. We both had a developing interest in country blues, and in September of 1963 we moved into a rat-trap apartment in Cambridge. I owned a few records, but no record player. Al had even less money than I did, but he had a record player, some good records, and a cheap Stella guitar, which he played pretty well. Somewhere along the way I bought a 1930s National steel-body guitar that a friend had got from his grandmother's attic but had found that it was not very good for the kind of music he played. I thought that it might be good for blues.

Al was mostly unemployed except for a few harmonica gigs and brief work as a bricklayer for his father, who was in construction. We didn't have a telephone, and when we needed to make a call, we walked a block and a half to the Laundromat's pay phone. Anyone who wanted to talk to us had to come in person or send a telegram. We had little money, less heat, one fork, and no plates. We both ate out, but occasionally I would roast a hot dog on the stove using the fork. Al's room was in front; mine was in back behind the kitchen. In the year that we shared that apartment, Al shoveled out his room exactly twice—once for Booker and once for Son. He took in a garbage can and literally shoveled. When I got back home after finding Son, I found that Al had converted my room into a kind of planetarium, with paper maps of various sky segments pasted over the window and the door, with holes punched for major stars. He must have spent days making those maps, copied by hand and eye from an astronomy book, using pencil and paper. Al was around twenty-one, and I was twenty-four, so none of this seemed particularly odd to me.

From September 1963, when we moved in, till April 1964, we both played a lot of guitar, read extensively, and listened to a lot of records. Al introduced me to the superb OJL series of country blues reissue LPs. Between us we already had both RBFs and soon bought all the OJLs. The RBFs were a really good survey of the field, but the OJLs were something else—the quality and quantity of the music on them was nothing short of inspirational. Charters's work, the Robert Johnson album on Columbia, and Lomax's field recordings on Atlantic had got me seriously interested in country blues, but it was the OJLs that totally hooked me, and Al as well.

This brings up a point about the blues revival that has not had the attention that it deserves: that the record collectors made it all possible. Without them, almost all the great old guys would have disappeared into the dust of history, simply forgotten. Without the record collectors and their research and reissues of the early sixties, like the OJLs, there would not have been much of a blues revival. An enormous debt is owed to Sam Charters and Harry Smith and Moe Asch in this regard, but it was the OJL reissues that energized wider interest in the music among neophytes like me. Also, they enhanced the popularity of the music after the spate of rediscoveries and stimulated the major record companies to open their vaults to a degree. The OJLs, particularly the incredible *Really! The Country Blues*, changed everything. Bringing giants like Charley Patton, Tommy Johnson, and Son House into the game added a new dimension.

With the history of country blues opening up with each reissue LP, our horizons widened and our tastes became more individual and well-defined. Al and I both appreciated the jug bands, the guys of the Georgia twelve-string school, like Barbecue Bob and Blind Willie McTell, and the ragtime guys, like Blind Blake and especially William Moore ("too sad for the public" was our catch phrase), but our main focus was the old Delta blues greats: Patton, House, Robert Johnson, Willie Brown, Tommy Johnson. We weren't sure where Skip James fitted in, but we knew he was great. Not all of our musical heroes were on 78. There was Howling Wolf, Big Joe Williams, and John Lee Hooker, all still making records. And Lomax's field recordings on Atlantic and later Prestige had great music that was only about ten years old, and some of it was the equal of what we heard on OJL, particularly Fred McDowell's work.

McDowell was the complete musical package, very original yet very traditional, great voice, and guitar that was both economical and explosive. He could make you dance around the room when he did driving material, but he was as deep as Robert Pete Williams. A very important bluesman, and as I later learned, a charming, funny, very cool guy. Al thought so much of Fred as an exemplar of what blues should be that when he noticed a seriously un-blues-like and very un-McDowell-like note in one of Fred's cuts—it was perhaps a second or a sixth, I've forgotten which—he could not believe his ears and went into a funk for hours, wide-eyed and muttering to himself in disbelief that Fred could actually have done something like that. That was as close to a dogmatic approach to music that I ever heard from Al, who was always open to new music and new ideas, and I

Phil Spiro and Al Wilson at the Loft coffeehouse, Boston, Massachusetts, winter 1963–64. Photo Dick Waterman.

suppose in this case he was having trouble recalibrating one of his assumptions. Since those early days, I've often seen Al referred to in print as "Alan," which of course was his given name. But the only people I ever heard who actually called him Alan were his parents, and [as] far as I recall, he always introduced himself as "Al."

The two of us played together in public just once, at Jim Pope's coffeehouse, the Loft, but I was never in Al's league as a musician. Within a few months Al had become a remarkably good bluesman, while most of my effort went into record reviews for *Broadside* of Boston, my radio show at the MIT station, and my job at Itek, where I was now doing fairly serious system programming for the lens design work. That all changed in April, at least for a while.

Booker White, a country blues great of the 1930s, had been found the previous year by John Fahey and ED Denson, and was doing a gig in Boston. Thanks to a phonetic spelling by a clerk at a record company in the thirties, his public name had become "Bukka," but the letters we exchanged later were signed "Booker," and his full name was Booker T. Washington White. He needed a place to stay—a common problem for folk-circuit performers of the period. Al and I immediately volunteered.

During Booker's stay with us, Al and David Evans, then an undergrad at Harvard, spent time with Booker in what might be called an informal interview. Both David and Al were versed in what little was known about the mysterious names on the country blues reissue LPs, and they hoped that Booker could add to that meager store of knowledge. Booker had been one of those mysteries until the previous year, and as a musician of the same time and place as the other Delta and Memphis greats, he might well know something about those other musicians.

I was at work while Al and David had their session with Booker. When I got home Al was bubbling over with excitement about Booker's information, which was that Son House had been seen in Memphis a year ago! House was known for a very few electrifying cuts from 1930 on Paramount, two of which had been reissued on OJL, and for a larger, less intense set of cuts recorded in Mississippi for the Library of Congress in the early 1940s by Alan Lomax. No one had heard of House since then. His few recordings spoke for themselves, and he was an important figure in country blues in spite of his obscurity. He was up there with the best of Delta blues, one of the greats. The only information about House was minimal: his first name was Eugene; he had lived in Robinsonville, Mississippi; had been a part-time preacher; and sometimes wore a cowboy hat. It was said he was short and fat.

Booker had told David and Al that a friend of his in Memphis, a woman named Lillian Glover—generally called "Ma Rainey" for her vocal abilities—had mentioned in passing that she had seen Son House in Memphis the previous year. Once I heard of this, I went to the Laundromat pay phone and called Lillian Glover to verify what Booker had said. Booker had got it right. Ma Rainey confirmed exactly what Booker had said, that she had seen Son House in Memphis the previous year and had spoken with him. She hadn't found out where he was living, but she said she would be glad to help look for him. Thus when last seen by someone who knew him by sight, Son House was in Memphis—a reasonable place for an old Delta bluesman to have been seen.

After getting that unambiguous confirmation, my decision to look for Son House in Memphis took about a microsecond. It was too good to pass up, but I didn't know what to do about it.

I had some vacation time coming and I had a great boss at Itek, Ed Radkowski, who would probably let me take the time off when I wanted to. Ed had already taken a chance on me and had given me my first real programming job.

There were just a few difficulties to overcome.

Any such trip should include Al and David. But Al had a gig to play at the Club 47, and David still had classes at Harvard, so I had to find other people who might be as crazy as I was about this almost unknown musician.

Flying to Memphis cost more than I could afford. It was too much to expect that House lived in Memphis proper or even near Memphis, so a car was a necessity. I didn't drive and I still don't. I grew up in New York City and environs, my parents never had a car, and I've got pretty poor vision. To look for Son, at least one person with a car was necessary. And we'd need a tape recorder on principle—you don't go looking for an old bluesman without a tape recorder. If this was to happen within some approximation of my limited vacation time, we'd need a second driver if one could be found.

The obvious person to try was Tom Hoskins, who had famously found John Hurt in Avalon, Mississippi, while driving from D.C. to New Orleans, thanks to John's 1920s recording that went *"Avalon's my home town, Always on my mind."* I had briefly met Hoskins at the 1963 Newport Festival. Sometime between the '63 Newport and the spring of 1964, Hoskins was in Boston for John Hurt's gig at Cafe Yana. Al and I were flattered when Hoskins wanted to tape our music, and he taped a few other Boston area people as well. Nothing came of the tape, of course.

When the time came to plan the trip, Hoskins was the logical choice—he'd been there, done that, had a car, and probably a tape recorder. Off to the Laundromat pay phone again. Hoskins wasn't interested. I don't recall why he wasn't interested—could have been he quite reasonably didn't trust the tip, or was busy, or just didn't care to do the trip. He recommended Nick Perls in NYC as someone who might be interested. I had never heard of Perls, but Hoskins assured me that he had a car and a tape recorder, and knew about blues, being something of a record collector.

I don't clearly recall which came first—calling Perls or talking with Dick Waterman. I'll assume that my vague recollection is correct and that I spoke with Perls first.

Nick lived with his parents, who owned a leading art gallery in New York City. Nick had a VW Bug, a competent tape recorder, was indeed a record collector, and had a recommendation from Hoskins. Perls's participation would make everything possible, and I wasn't inclined to look beyond that—I was twenty-four, after all. Nick was very interested, and thus the trip was a go.

At the time, Cambridge had *three* all-night cafeterias in tiny Harvard Square—Albiani's, Hayes Bickford, and the Waldorf—all gone long ago, victims of changing times. Albiani's was large but was not a welcoming place, and Hayes Bickford was okay but small, so most of the folk scene hangers-on like me ended up at the Waldorf when the coffeehouses closed. It was large and comfortable. You met people there without trying to; there was always someone you knew, usually sitting with someone you didn't know, but introductions were natural. Thus I would run into people I knew well and people I knew "from around" at the Waldorf or the coffeehouses.

I think I had Dick Waterman in mind at the time. I knew him somewhat better than just "from around," and he was generally known to have been a journalist and photographer, and he had written for *Broadside*. Even though he had been involved in a number of bookings, including Booker White and John Hurt, for some reason I thought of him then as a photographer first and foremost. I don't recall any details, but I did run into him at the Waldorf, we got to talking, and I mentioned that I had a hot tip on finding Son House. To which Dick replied, "Son *who*?"

I hadn't heard of House myself till the previous year, so I was not much taken aback by Dick's response. However great I thought Son House was, I hadn't forgotten how unknown his name was to most of the world. The conversation eventually came around to doing the trip, and, if my chronology is right, I asked Dick if he was interested in being the second driver on the trip. As a photographer and professional journalist, he would be a great asset, and clearly he had a high level of interest in the music, even if he hadn't heard of House. I might have asked Dick before I spoke to Nick, but I think I'd got Perls on board before I ran into Dick at the Waldorf. Whatever the sequence of events actually was, Dick signed on.

Asking Dick was the best possible thing that I could have done at the time, but like so much in life, it was dumb luck on my part that I ended up with a guy who would do more for the old music and the old musicians than anyone had a right to expect. I can't praise Dick's contributions to the music enough, but that was yet to come, and we were both just speculating that this harebrained trip was worth the time and effort.

Somehow (I can't recall any detail) Dick and I ended up at the Perls residence in New York City. We stayed there overnight. There was an original Modigliani on the wall of the guest room; I believe it is now in the Metropolitan Museum of Art.

I'm dependent upon the article I wrote in July 1964 for *Broadside* of Boston for the details of our trip to find Son House. They were as accurate as I could make it while it was all still reasonably fresh in my mind, and I can't do better than that today, nearly fifty years later.

We crammed suitcases, tape recorders, a camera bag, sleeping bags, mic stands and booms, maps, books, and other trivia into and on top of one very small, very red Volkswagen Bug. We drove straight through to Memphis.

In Memphis we found that Ma Rainey was not in, so we went with Booker to visit friends of his and we did some taping. It was two or three days before we found Ma Rainey at home. She said that she had found out that Son had been in Memphis to visit relatives whose names she had not learned, and that he had left town for parts unknown. Our hot lead—the only reason for the trip—was a dead end.

We were discouraged, but since we were there we decided to check a slim older lead. Gayle Dean Wardlow and Bernard Klatzko, while searching for information about Charley

Patton, had learned that House had lived in Lake Cormorant, Mississippi, or so it said in an OJL reissue LP. We enlisted the aid of Reverend Robert Wilkins, another recently rediscovered bluesman who lived in Memphis, and had been found by Dick and Louisa Spottswood. He proved to be an old friend of Son's and agreed to help us. With him, we went to check out Lake Cormorant.

Lake Cormorant was a virtually nonexistent town about twenty miles south of Memphis, off highway 61. We pulled off 61 and spoke with a group of women who were chopping cotton. Reverend Wilkins was from that area, and he quickly found out that House had relatives in Lake Cormorant. Another woman told us that Son's brother-in-law or cousin or some sort of relative lived a few miles away, on a nearby plantation. The people we spoke with there had heard of Son House but did not know of any relatives of his. Someone said that Son had gone to New York years ago but had been back a few times to visit. They suggested that we see Fiddling Joe Martin, who lived near Clak's [*sic*] store. Martin, they said, used to play with Son.

Martin's place was easy to find, but Fiddling Joe had gone fishing. He had been picked up by someone using Woodrow Adams's car. Although Woodrow was off working, he would know who was using his car, and perhaps where Joe was.

Adams worked as a tractor driver on a large plantation. For three hours the four of us in a heavily loaded Beetle ground and bumped our way through the maze of fields. Woodrow's wife turned up, Woodrow's car turned up, but no Fiddling Joe, and finally Woodrow himself turned up, driving a tractor. He didn't know where Joe was, and Joe had not been using his car.

Rev. Robert Wilkins and Phil Spiro get a lead to Son House in a cotton field, Lake Cormorant, Mississippi, June 1964. Photo Dick Waterman.

Woodrow agreed to find Joe and to set up a recording session in Memphis the following evening. Woodrow and Joe played guitar and drums in a three piece group with John "Piano Red" Williams, who lived in Memphis and, of course, played piano.

We felt that we might be getting somewhere. Because of Reverend Wilkins, doors that had been closed were opened to us, or, more accurately, were opened to Reverend Wilkins. Without him I have no doubt that we would have hit a dead end as well.

We met Joe the next night at Piano Red's place. Joe proved to be a thin, energetic man of about fifty; he had burned his hand sometime in the past and had taken up drums because, he said, he now felt uncomfortable when playing guitar. We asked if he knew Son. Hell, yes, he knew Son! Son had lived in New York for years, but Joe didn't know Son's address. He knew that Son's stepdaughter had been married to Benny Brown Junior and that Benny Brown Senior, then in the Memphis VA Hospital, should have Son's address.

We said we would visit Brown Senior in the hospital, and Joe agreed to try Brown Junior, who lived nearby in Robinsonville.

Brown Senior was in the hospital for what was said to be a minor ailment, and we were allowed to visit him. Reverend Wilkins again went with us and made things happen. Brown Senior didn't have Son's address, but he was sure that Son lived in Rochester, New York.

We still needed an address, and it was back to Mississippi to see what Joe might have found out. Joe took us to meet Benny Brown Junior, who had been out when Joe tried to reach him earlier, but Brown said that he had not heard from his ex-wife in years—she remarried and was living somewhere in Detroit. She married Grace Strong's son, so the Strongs should know something . . .

Mrs. Strong said that her boy was indeed married to Son's stepdaughter. We could probably reach him by phone, when he finishes work.

We called Mrs. Strong's son, J. W. Smith, in Detroit—"Just a minute. I have the address here somewhere . . . Saw him last year . . . Oh, yes, he still plays the old music . . . Here's the address."

Hardly believing our luck, we went back to Memphis and sent this telegram: "If you are the Son House who recorded for Paramount in the thirties and the Library of Congress in the forties, please call person-to-person collect in Memphis."

But Smith had made a mistake in the address, and the telegram could not be delivered. For two frustrating days, we called Rochester and Detroit before we finally reached Son on the phone on Father's Day.

Son was puzzled as to why we had been looking for him and how we knew of his music. No one had showed any interest in his music in over twenty years. He said he could still play, but hadn't played much for about four years. We told him we would see him in Rochester in a few days.

I hung up and turned to Dick, who was grinning from ear to ear. Whatever it was that I had started to say ended up as "*We did it!*" Well, we hadn't quite done it yet, and Reverend Wilkins had made it possible, but at that moment it certainly felt like we had done it.

Nick was in our room, taping Solomon Henderson, one of the many fine blues men and women we taped during the trip. After much mutual congratulation, Nick finished taping Henderson, and we started planning for our unanticipated trip to Rochester.

We also had a ghost of a lead to Skip James from one of Piano Red's neighbors. Seven years earlier James was supposed to have gone to Poplar Bluff, Missouri, from Kansas City. We drove straight to Poplar Bluff from Memphis, about 150 miles, but we found not a trace of James. We left for Rochester after a single day in Poplar Bluff. We later learned that Skip had been found in Tunica, Mississippi, about 10 miles from where we had been in Robinsonville, by John Fahey, Henry Vestine, and Bill Barth while we were looking for him in Poplar Bluff.

When we hit Rochester we filled up with gas and asked the station attendant where we could find a cheap motel. He rolled his cigar around his mouth and said in a strong Bronx accent, "You go to a cheap motel, you get your head bashed in." Strange that I've remem-

Classic Son House Discovery photo, taken in front of 61 Grieg Street, Rochester, New York, June 1964. *L to R*: Nick Perls, Dick Waterman, Son House, Phil Spiro. Courtesy Dick Waterman.

bered those exact words, but other than the cigar, he looked and sounded remarkably like my uncle Jack. The oddest thing about this was that in my job at Itek, a photo-optical company, nearly every senior person I worked with had once worked in Rochester or at least had gone to university in Rochester—Kodak, Xerox, Wollensak, Bausch and Lomb, University of Rochester—the city was the optics capital of the US. Nobody at work had mentioned getting their head bashed in. We didn't expect Rochester to be that kind of place, but I recall that we took the gas station guy at his word and went to a decent motel.

We had sent Son a telegram, telling him when we hoped to arrive, and he was expecting us. Son was supposed to be a short, fat man, according to various sources, and there was no one of that description in view. There was a thin man of average height sitting on the apartment house stoop. I asked him if he knew which apartment Son House lived in.

"This is him," said Son House.

He wasn't short, he wasn't fat; his first name was Eddie, not Eugene; and when we eventually asked, it turned out that he hadn't been in Memphis in fifteen years. The hot lead that had sent us off to look for him, the *only* reason we went, was rubbish in the first place.

But we had found Son House.

We stayed in Rochester about three days. We all asked questions of Son, but not that many at that time. We relaxed the intense focus on digging up the facts and details about his life that we had needed in order to find him. We knew all the obvious questions, of course, and we asked some of them, but because he said that he was seriously interested in performing, we faced a time constraint—the upcoming Newport Folk Festival.

When I put the trip together I didn't have anything in mind beyond finding Son, with no thought given to what might follow. It was only after Son said that he could still play that the notion of him having a shot at a career entered my skull, and I doubt it was much different for the others. But until we saw Son in Rochester and heard him play, we had no idea what might be possible.

The idea of Newport surfaced once we had some reasonable cuts on tape. I'll bet it was first voiced by Dick. Both Dick and I had some knowledge of the people and the workings of the folk music scene, and we felt that with a decent tape we could probably get Son on the bill at Newport, even though it was just a month away, and that would make a tremendous difference in establishing a career for Son, just as it had for John Hurt the previous year. As Dick and I both knew people who were directly involved with Newport, this was not just wishful thinking. So we concentrated on taping during our short stay in Rochester and left most of the rest for later. We had so many questions, but most would have to wait.

Unlike Reverend Wilkins, Son didn't seem reluctant to play blues, not that I could tell. The reluctance that I recall was about not having played in so long a time. What that means for *any* guitar player is pretty nasty stuff—poorly remembered fingerings, tunings, melodies, and words; no calluses on the fingers, making fretting difficult and making extended playing painful; et cetera—a musician's nightmare. People who don't play an instrument usually don't realize how much neuromuscular learning and muscular development go into playing an instrument and how quickly much of it can leak away with disuse. If you play continuously from your teens to your seventies, you retain almost everything, even compensating for age to some degree, but a multi-year absence from practice means you are almost starting all over from scratch. The mind may remember, but the muscles don't, and they have to be almost completely retrained to some approximation of their old level of strength and coordination, and that takes months for most people. That you used to be able to do these things makes retraining that much more difficult, because you feel that you *ought* to be able to do these things easily, but you can't. Not that Son complained—he was interested in performing, he was motivated, and he did his best.

Waterman and I tried to buy a suitable guitar for Son, but the best that our joint budget could do just didn't match my steel-body National for impact. So even though Son had never played a National in the old days, he used mine until it was stolen at a gig in New York City.

Dick and I both knew people on the Newport board, but it was Dick who almost immediately got Son a Newport appearance, based on the tape made in Rochester. At that time Son was still an unknown name to most of the people who were likely to attend Newport, but the *Newsweek* article about the near-simultaneous rediscovery of Son and Skip, and the fact that Newport had chosen to book many other important country blues performers that year—both helped things along. Dick wrote an article for the *National Observer*, and I had one published in *Broadside*, but the short *Newsweek* article on Son and Skip undoubtedly reached the most people. It was Dick's quick action with *Newsweek* and Newport that got the ball rolling.

My *Broadside* article incorrectly attributed Booker's information to Al's questioning. It was actually David Evans who had asked the important questions about Son, not Al. I never thought to ask either David or Al about this at the time, simply assuming it was Al. Forty-odd years later, David mentioned in passing that he had been the one who had asked Booker about Son. I was dumbfounded and embarrassed about my error. I've taken every opportunity since then to rectify that error. Why didn't Al say anything? Maybe it was because he didn't think such credits were important, or perhaps he never read my article, or perhaps because we were both caught up with getting Son ready for Newport, but I simply don't know.

Al was there for most of Son's early gigs, including ones outside the Boston area, and I have no doubt that Son's process of recollection and reflection about his music went on during that period, as long as he and Al were together. Son had not played in years and remembered only a small number of songs. Al reminded Son of the old songs that Son could no longer recall, using both guitar and records. He didn't *teach* Son how to play them; he *reminded* Son what and how he had played in the past. I was there and saw much of it as it progressed. Al became something like what Willie Brown had been for Son in the old days—a friend, a like-minded and respected musician, someone to share musical ideas with, a second voice in the music when appropriate. Al could certainly reproduce Brown's guitar work as well as Son's, but that wasn't the point at all. The mere presence of such a person was beneficial for Son on a psychological level as well as a musical level. Son simply enjoyed playing with others who understood his music, and Al filled that bill to a T. Al helped him remember and relearn, but Al was also there as a friend and supporter who understood and shared his music, and I think that role was more important to Son than being reminded of what had gone on before. Al was unstinting in his support, and over time, that made a tremendous difference.

Dick's father was a doctor, and he had Son see a neurologist at Massachusetts General Hospital in Boston, one of the world's great hospitals. The neurologist said that for anyone else of Son's age his tremor was a minor issue and was just something one had to live with, but because of Son's occupation it couldn't be ignored, and he gave Son a prescription for a medication that should help—and did. With the medication, whatever it was, Son could play reasonably well when reasonably sober, and he had no problem with the medication. Dick took on the responsibility of balancing alcohol and medication.

All these years later, recounting what happened with Son sounds like a badly plotted movie that no one would believe, because coincidences don't happen in that quantity in real life. We go to Memphis on a tip that was totally wrong, and we end up finding Son anyway—in a Northern city which we've never been to before, one to which I'm connected by my work in computers. Son wants to perform and have a career, but his skills are very rusty and need practice. I know someone who is eager to and able to help Son regain his old form, probably the best person in the world for the job, who, by the way, happens to be my roommate. Son needs publicity to get his career started, and it happens that Waterman has a *Newsweek* music critic for a brother-in-law. We get Son a practice gig and discover he's an alcoholic with a tremor and needs medical assistance if he is to have a career, and, fortunately, we have a doctor at our disposal who instantly directs us to a top neurologist who saves the day. We have no money to buy Son a decent guitar of his own, but I happen to have one available for free that enhances his onstage image and becomes identified with him. What an implausible story! But the medication helped with the tremor to the point where Son felt ready for Newport, and we did too, if more than a little uncertain of the outcome.

Newport Folk Festival 1968, with Taj Mahal and Phil Spiro. Photo Dick Waterman.

It took years of hard work by many people long before 1964 to discover the remnants of country blues, but if you look for a starting point for what has been called the "blues revival," the 1964 Newport is a great candidate. An unprecedented number of first-rank country blues musicians were assembled under one roof to appear before the largest audience ever to hear such music—literally "under one roof," as most of them were staying at one of the huge old Newport houses that the festival used to accommodate performers. I recall seeing Fred McDowell, Skip James, Robert Pete Williams, John Hurt, Sleepy John Estes, and Hammie Nixon at the "blues house." There were other great traditional performers at Newport that year, like Robert Wilkins, Doc Reese, and Elizabeth Cotton, but I didn't see them at the Miantinomi Avenue house. On one of the nights before the start of the festival, the house turned into an all-night party of most of the finest country bluesmen alive in 1964. I remember watching Robert Pete Williams, who was sitting on the edge of an old claw-foot bathtub, playing guitar while beating a different time with each foot. Al was playing harmonica and, amazingly, managed to add something. The 1964 Newport had a wealth of traditional music of all kinds, but I missed most of it.

Soon after our arrival at Newport, Son was taken to the hospital with bad abdominal pains that as far as I know were never fully diagnosed. He did not play at Newport in 1964. But by that point his career as a "rediscovered bluesman" was well launched. Not incidentally, and somewhat accidentally, Dick's career as booking agent, manager, and all-round protector of the old guys was also launched—not that any of us imagined such a job at the time.

Again, I've got blanks in my memory. I had to check with Dick to see if he recalled any details of Son's hospital stay, as I cannot. In an email, he said: "Not only did you take Son to the hospital and visit him there, I know that you took the bus from Boston down to

Newport *after* the festival to visit him. You also took care of the details of him being released from the hospital and put on a bus back to Rochester." I was glad to hear that, even if it didn't jog my memory. After Newport, Son had other gigs, of course, many of them, and I became less and less involved.

By September 1964 I was doing well enough at work to be able to afford a place by myself, and I moved to an apartment near Harvard Square, while Al moved to Somerville with Bob Wilfong, who can be seen and heard today as "Fongster100" on YouTube.

I had room in my new place to put up Son during gigs, and of course Al visited. But by this point I had realized that I did not have what it took to play a part in Son's career, even though I felt responsible. While I had a role in negotiating the recording contract with Columbia, Dick was doing the heavy lifting. He coped with the various crises in a way that kept Son on track, balancing medication and alcohol, finding gigs and making sure that contracts and gigs were as they should be, and that Son got paid his royalties and for his performances. I could not, and I left it all to Dick, and that proved to be the right thing to do.

I had almost no contact with Nick Perls after the trip. Some years later he sent me a letter complaining about my slowness in reviewing his records for *Broadside*, but that was it. During the trip we were three guys who at best were together only through common purpose and at worst were very different people who knew each other not at all. By some miracle we all got along okay during the trip, doing what was necessary, but I never felt much affinity for Nick, who was privately dismissive of the people who were kind enough to share their music with us, just as Dick describes in his book. I would not be surprised to learn that Nick would have been happier if we had turned up a Son House 78 instead of the man himself. He never said anything at all like that—it's just how his attitude struck me at the time. As far as I know, he went on with his life after the trip and was a founder of Yazoo Records, which in turn did excellent reissue LPs.

By 1965 Son's career was progressing well, with a Columbia LP and many gigs. I was still doing what I had done before, as was Al, but that changed when John Fahey came to town to play at Dave Wilson's Odyssey Coffeehouse in Boston. Naturally Al and I showed up at Fahey's gig—both of us had all his records, but we had never met him and knew nothing about him other than that he had found both Skip and Booker.

Fahey had forgotten more about blues by 1965 than I ever learned and is a major figure in the blues revival, in spite of being one of the most impossible people I've ever met, doing his best to drive away wives, friends, and audiences—yet everyone, myself included, cut him more slack than he deserved. He had access to Joe Bussard's collection—one of the best collections of 78s in the world—and had an encyclopedic knowledge of blues, which he chose to publicly scorn. "Enigmatic" does not begin to describe him, and anyone who ever knew him will have many bizarre stories to tell. But without John, Skip James would not have been found. Without John, Booker would not have been found, and thus Son House would not have been found. I respected John's musical abilities and his accomplishments, but that's all anyone could respect about the man.

Fahey and I made the same mistake about guitars. We both owned steel-body guitars, because we had independently concluded that they ought to sound good for blues, so when we found Booker and Son, we each put our Nationals in the hands of our rediscoveries. In Son's case it was because we couldn't afford to buy him a good wooden guitar, and that may also have been true in Booker's case. Both Booker and Son were happy to have a steel-body to play, but what that accomplished was making two already sloppy guitar players sound a bit sloppier, and somehow started a widespread belief that National steel-bodies were the guitar of choice in the thirties, which was not remotely the case. No itinerant guitar player in the Delta of the 1930s could afford an expensive steel-body, and only a very few people recorded with them in the thirties. At least it didn't seriously affect Son's or Booker's music, which of course had been created on cheap wooden guitars with high action, but the Nationals made them both sound muddier than necessary.

I admired Fahey's music, and at his request I set up recording time for him at the MIT radio station, and of course Al came too. Fahey had got hold of a vina and was not having all that much success with the complex Indian instrument. Al picked it up and took to it as though he had played one for years, but he'd never even seen one before. John was both pissed and impressed. Beyond Al being in the studio with John during the recording session and participating in some of the cuts, I don't know what transpired between them, so I don't know how or why Al decided to go to L.A. with Fahey, but that's what happened, and that led to the formation of Canned Heat. I saw both Al and John many times afterwards during gigs, John on his own, and Al with Canned Heat.

Over the following years I had progressively more intense jobs and less time for music. I gradually dropped writing and eventually radio shows as well. But I had one last musical interaction with Al Wilson in 1969 or 1970.

I was working in Boston for a company that was applying artificial intelligence methods to optical character recognition. On board was Stu Nelson, who also had a small grant from Stanford University to investigate aspects of using a low-cost ($8,000) minicomputer as the basis for a musical instrument. Up to that point electronic music had all been produced by analog equipment, as in the *Switched-on Bach* record. Stu's notion, which we all shared, was that you can't make interesting music with a device that takes minutes to set up a single note. The concept Stu was working on is familiar to everyone today as a digital synthesizer. He hoped to be able to bring the cost down to eventually around the $25,000 mark, low enough that major groups like the Beatles could afford to own one and play around with it without specialists needing to be in attendance on the machine. The further hope was that such a group could become familiar enough with the device to develop decent music of some sort on it, as we all thought that what passed for electronic music at the time was far from musical, and that the problem was the human interface—or lack thereof. We had an electric organ keyboard to start with, but everyone felt that if at all possible, this "music machine," as we called it, should be able to cater to musicians other than piano players. I signed on to help locate experimental musicians to give us advice about how they as experienced experimenters in music would like to use an instrument that could make any sound they wanted, in real time. What would the ideal interface look like for them other than a conventional keyboard?

By coincidence, Al was in town for an extended period, and he was very interested in the project. He attended the project meeting and later came up with a list of thoughtful ideas that could be useful for players of stringed instruments. On the other hand, the experimental musicians, like the guy I located who played bottleneck piano—he reached into the piano and fretted the strings with a bottle—were so used to fighting the limitations of their instruments that they had no useful thoughts about an instrument that could be anything they wanted.

Phil Spiro with wife Elaine Chow, late 2000s. Photo Michael Erhlich.

The company relocated to Los Angeles, I stayed in Boston, and I lost track of the project. Of the four or five musicians we spoke with, only Al had useful ideas. That project meeting was likely the last time I saw Al. I think his death was an accident, but opinions don't matter much about that sort of thing. I was lucky to have been a friend of his, however short the time. He was a brilliant musician and, at heart, a scholar.

I haven't seen Dick in about thirty years, but we have the phone and email. I'm delighted at how things turned out for Dick, and for Son, and for the many other old guys Dick watched over. They had a day in the sun, made some money, and finally had well-deserved recognition.

Sam Charters's books and records, particularly the Blind Willie Johnson record and liner notes, played a major part in getting me interested in country blues. I applaud Charters for sending so many of us off on our various musical quests, and I thank him for inadvertently changing my life. The unselfishly shared research of Gayle Dean Wardlow and Bernard Klatzko enabled Son House to be found. The great OJL reissues of Pete Whelan and Bill Givens made the old guys live again, and I can't possibly thank them enough for that.

I've not touched a guitar in perhaps twenty years, and I now know how Son must have felt when we blew in from outer space and asked him to play for the tape in Rochester. It was a hell of a thing he did in his old age, picking up the guitar again after so many years and playing for large, strange audiences of admiring young white college kids, competing with his younger self on the old, reissued records. That took guts.

CHRIS BARBER INTERVIEW

I was born on the seventeenth of April 1930 in Welwyn, a small town thirty miles north of London. My mother was a teacher and my father was an economist statistician.

You would have been a schoolboy during World War II. Can you talk about your memories during this period.

Sure, I remember it quite well. I didn't see any fighting [*laughs*]—luckily, I was too young. The war was about to begin, and we knew it was about to begin. I was from a political family. My parents were political people, they were left-wing. In the US "left wing" meant you were communist, but in the UK in the 1930s this meant you were the only people in the country who realized what was wrong with the Nazis. We could see war was coming. We just didn't know how soon our government would wake up, see we had to get in there and stop Hitler. What we did was find a cottage in the country where my mother, younger sister, and I would live while my father, who worked for the government, would stay in an apartment in London. He wasn't going to be called into the army, because he was needed for government work.

Chris Barber and Ottilie Patterson. Courtesy Chris Barber.

So from 1941 to 1945 I went to school in a place called Royston. Royston was four miles from a village called Bassingbourn, which had a large airfield outside it, and that airfield was the headquarters of the Eighth Air Force. So we had all the B-17s—all the Flying Fortresses—stationed four miles away from us. My friends and I used to get up before breakfast and cycle up to that airfield and lie where the main runway crossed the road. They had wire netting about two meters high, and we'd lie in the ditch outside the road as the B-17s came back from their raids. As they came in you could see most of them had dead front-gunners. It was a very dangerous position to be in, in the nose of a B-17; they mostly got killed. That's the airfield where Glenn Miller gave his last show and the next day flew out to Paris and didn't make it. Once, from the hill where the farm was, I wandered across the plain and below me and still flying was a German V-1. That was a rocket-powered drone—kind of a little airplane with a pulse-jet [engine]. It went *boom-boom-boom-boom-boom*. What happened was they just put enough fuel in it to reach where they wanted, then it would crash and explode. You would hear it stop, and when you heard it stop you took cover. It would come straight down and explode. So that's the nearest I got to it.

At the beginning of the war I had a little radio set. Kids didn't have personal radio sets in 1939 and 1940; they were quite expensive. But I had a little Bakelite radio, and we used to listen to the radio all the time, because our troops were overseas and fought in France and then came back and fought back against the Germans, and of course we used to listen all the time. I used to listen to the AFN—American Forces Network—Willis Conover, for example, who I met later. I heard things on there that were kind of jazz. And the BBC, which was always an old-fashioned kind of radio station . . . The rumor—and I believe it's true—was that the disc jockeys doing record programs on the BBC had to sit wearing dinner jackets at the microphone in the studio. [*laughs*] Very smart; it was an important job, you see.

The BBC—one of the channels they broadcast—they made it a kind of war work helper. What they did was put on programs called *Music While You Work*, which were relayed to all the factories building airplanes and that stuff—so you heard music all day. The problem was they had no jazz programs at all—the BBC didn't play jazz records. Jazz records were released in Britain before World War II, blues records too. But they weren't the sort of thing the BBC would play. However, if you play music on records sixteen hours a day, chances are at some point or other you're going to make a mistake and put on one you didn't mean to. And at the end of the record the disc jockey, or what they call a presenter in Britain, said, "That was so and so and so and so—I think that was jazz." And I thought, "I like that!' So then I began reading up. I had books and so I could look up who that was, and I began to get the whole idea, and the story began to sound interesting. So I began listening to jazz. I would listen to AFN and they would have the March of Dimes campaign, and I would send in a request for what jazz there was on V-Disc.

America had already acquired the consumer madness society forty years before we did in Britain—buying loads of things which you're never going to use; don't even try to use them, just sell them or throw them away. My friends and I used to cycle up to the Eighth Air Force base. And at this base was a dump where all this stuff was being thrown away never used, or used once and thrown away. So on that dump was a pile of pocket books, what we call Penguins in England. In this pile of pocket books was a book called *Really the Blues*. *Really the Blues* was a book written by a musician called "Mezz" Mezzrow, with Bernard Wolfe. He was quite a stalwart on the Chicago jazz scene of the 1920s. The book tells it like it is, exactly. Where the music came from, what it was, that black music is the real thing, and why white people managed it pretty well—not always, but then again, not all blacks managed it perfectly either. But the whole story was there. I read that book, and I read it and read it again. And if you read that book, you didn't need to read anything else. I was the original "jazz kid." I was thirteen! Then I wanted to hear some records of this music.

Before World War II in Britain jazz records did not sell—not much—nor blues records either. By the end of the 1920s all the blues records were on what they called the "race list," and many of the great jazz records were in the race series too. Of course, in England that didn't make any difference. The British division of RCA Victor, HMV—His Master's Voice—issued records now and again, like Jelly Roll Morton, which in America had appeared in the race series and would only be found in stock in a store in a black area. In Britain they were in stock here and there, but not much. The people who bought them then in Britain would almost certainly have been students, medical students; they like more extreme things and they have inquiring minds.

It so happened that Royston, where my school was, was only fourteen miles from Cambridge, one of our great universities. The point is that one of the few places in Britain where a record store would have jazz records in stock was in Cambridge, and there was I—in Cambridge. I was learning the violin by this time. My father had played the violin when he was in school, and he bought me a violin when I was at the school in Royston. There was nothing to do around there at all, so perhaps I might try practicing the violin. I used to have to go for a violin lesson every week, and the violin teacher in the area was an old French guy who lived in Cambridge. So every week I had enough money for a bus ticket to Cambridge and back.

Now, it so happened that the price of a bus ticket was roughly the equivalent of one dollar. And at that time, just like in America, the price of a 78 rpm was one dollar and five cents. I had enough money for a 78 rpm record each week, which was rare; kids didn't buy records in those days, or have record players. Well, I had a bicycle and I thought, "I'm going to Cambridge for a violin lesson, and I want to buy a record, and what I've got here is a dollar for a bus ticket. Why don't I take my bicycle—I can hold the violin in my left hand and also the handlebar—and with my right hand grab the back end of a delivery truck and get pulled along free to Cambridge?" Which I did—every week.

So that meant every week I was in Cambridge, and after my violin lesson I had some free time before I would find a truck to pull me back, and I had enough money to buy a 78 rpm record. So I bought one every week. I went into the record store, and I said, "Do you have any jazz records?" He said, "Yes, we have some. I don't know where they are, but they're here somewhere." So I began poking around, and he said, "Come around the counter. There's some catalogs there. See what you can find." So I looked in the catalog and I found them. I found where they were, and I began pulling them off the shelf to see what they were. Of course, a record store that kept jazz records in stock, there was a good chance that students were going to buy them when it suited them. But the store hadn't reckoned that the war had started and all the older students were called up right away into the army. The students were gone, and all the records were still there. So the shop was pleased to have someone buy them, even at one a week. So I bought them.

How many of these records were by British bands, and how many by American bands?

None. I didn't buy British bands. I knew about jazz. I bought real ones! [*laughs*] The British companies—Parlophone, which basically speaking was the equivalent of OKeh and Columbia labels in America—and HMV, which was RCA Victor. On the Parlophone label there were Bessie Smith records and Louis Armstrong's Hot Seven [his early band]. HMV had Jelly Roll Morton and Duke Ellington—I bought those. I didn't even want Glenn Miller [*laughs*]—that wasn't jazz! I was very strict. So that's what I was buying, and some of them I have the copies still! I think I did get one actual copy.

There had been an organization in the late thirties called the British Hot Blues Society, or something like that, and they persuaded the English label Decca to release a couple of blues records. They released a Sleepy John Estes and then a Cow Cow Davenport record. I got those from the store in Cambridge—and the Bessie Smith records. About 1939 and 1940 American Columbia began putting out albums with half a dozen 78s inside them by various artists. They had a Louis Armstrong Hot Five album and a Bessie Smith album, and those albums were automatically available to the British arm of the company if they wanted to issue them. They had the masters to press them, so they did. Parlophone put them out, and on the Bessie Smith, which Columbia had issued in America, Parlophone not only put out the album but found they had some masters that had come over to them in the 1920s which were never issued at the time, so they put them out as well, which was very nice.

So by the time the war finished and I went back to London, I had sixty or seventy jazz and blues 78s. And for a kid of fifteen, it didn't happen very often, even with regular records. The pop culture hadn't come in yet, where we were all buying sounds all the time. Once I got back to London, I thought, "Well, there must be some jazz around here somewhere." I somehow found out about a couple of stores in London—small record shops, which did, in fact, specialize in jazz. So I went to see them and began talking to them. When discography was more or less invented, I had a copy; I got this music and I bought it. [*laughs*]

I knew there were several amateur jazz bands playing traditional jazz, and they even sang the blues a bit, but they weren't seriously trying to play the music properly; they were just trying to enjoy themselves the best they could. The dictionary definition of an amateur jazz musician is—a jazz fan who has access to a musical instrument. [*laughs*] I went to see a band—I saw an advertisement for a band that played in some club in South London. This is about twenty-five miles from where I lived. I managed to get there to hear them play, and they were trying to play like a band would play in the twenties, but the only similarity was that they had the same lineup of instruments. They played the same tunes, but they didn't have the feel, shall we say.

They were led by a pianist named George Webb, who died last week at the age of ninety-two. He had one decent player who sounded like he could really play, but even then you realized he was an amateur—like a tennis player before he went on the circuit. Then a trumpet player joined that band. His name was Humphrey Lyttelton. Humphrey was from an aristocratic family, and it's said that as an officer in the army he landed on the beach at Anzio carrying his trumpet. [*laughs*] It's like [Bix] Beiderbecke—always a bit mythical.

And when I heard him play, I thought, "My God, it *can* be done!" I never thought it was even worth trying, because the original players were all so amazing—and so extraordinarily skillful, with all those wonderful ideas. And I always thought, "You can't do that if you didn't start out there." But Humphrey's playing said, "I'm going to get this stuff right—and do it," which he did.

So I used to go and see this band with George Webb—the first band I saw. The trumpeter, Lyttelton, joined them and took the band over. I used to go and see them every week in the club where they played. I wanted to be a trumpeter. I watched the trumpeter, because as far as I was concerned the image of a traditional jazz player was the picture of Louis Armstrong, and he's tooting his coronet up in the air, with his eyes looking up above him. So I went to watch the trumpet player, actually the cornet player was who he was.

Now, I was the keen guy—I always sat on the front of the stage. The others would sit in the back of the hall on chairs, but I always sat on the stage. But if you want to watch the trumpeter you can't sit in front of him, because you couldn't see him, so I sat to one side, in front of the trombone player. One day the trombone player tapped me on the shoulder and said, "Chris, you want to buy a trombone?" And I couldn't think of what to say. I said, "How much is it?" He said, "Six pounds," which at the time was about twenty-five dollars. I couldn't think of anything but the fact that I had six pounds in my pocket—so I bought it! [*laughs*] I couldn't think of anything else to do! So I bought the trombone. It was terrible, it wasn't worth it, but still I bought the trombone.

Then, naturally enough, when I got it home I put the records on, on the wind-up gramophone—or the electric radiogram, as they called them—and played the trombone along with it. Having played the violin, not very seriously, about three years learning it, I was aware of scales and the things you do to practice music, you know? And of course the trombone and the violin are similar in one respect: the notes are not found for you; you have to create the positions for yourself. On the violin there are no frets or anything; trombone, same thing. So that helped. I was used to being able to create notes by putting my fingers a quarter of an inch up, creating the next semitone. So I just began practicing with the records. My mother didn't like it too much. My mother appreciated music, but she was a simple Yorkshire, all prim and proper. And I was an amateur playing noisy jazz. She didn't like the sound of it too much, really.

I imagine that it would be brutal listening to a novice violin player.

Well, the violin is quieter. The trombone is really loud. [*laughs*] I don't think my mother liked to hear me on the violin either, to be honest. But I played my records quite loud, and I played along with the records. Anyhow, that was the beginning of it.

So I was one of those guys that had access to a musical instrument. I found some friends with the same ideas as I did, and we started a band. We used to practice, and it wasn't very good. Some got along fairly well, and some just gave up when they found they couldn't play properly. At least they had the decency to give up when they couldn't play right. [*laughs*] And eventually the amateur band we had played some gigs, and then we did a broadcast on the BBC, which by that time had a *Jazz Club* [program] once a week at six thirty on Saturday evenings, for an hour. We played on that a couple of times. At that time we were comparable to an American band like Lu Watters. I didn't like that band too much; the blues part was missing. So then I had this amateur band going. We started up in '49, when I was nineteen. By the way, in my first amateur band was Alex Korner, who had been a schoolmate of mine much earlier.

By the time I was twenty-two I was really pissed off, because we were never getting any better. In an amateur band what happens? You've got a group of friends, and you're not from the same family, so you've all got different time off, you know, different evenings when you're available. Some can't make it at all. So you've seldom got the full band there most times. If you're lucky, you play once a week. And once a week is not enough to teach yourself an instrument and the music at the same time—you're just not going to make it. There was quite a bit of jazz going on at that time, a reasonable amount, a bit of jazz and a bit of blues.

In 1951 we had this thing called Festival of Britain; it was like a World's Fair thing. They had a concert at the Royal Festival Hall in London, and there was a thing called the National Federation of Jazz Organizations, which was bumbling old idiot people, unfortunately. It was a good idea. They said, "We've got to get some Americans to play," so they had Ralph Sutton on piano and Lonnie Johnson on guitar. They got them to play on their own and to play with bands that would fit. You could hear the real thing now and then, and you had the records. Once you got to hear the real thing live, when you heard Lonnie Johnson live and then you heard the record, you tried to adjust the tone and volume on the record to get the sound you heard when he was live. So you learned, which was good. Eventually around 1952 three guys, who each had an amateur jazz band, playing once a week, they were never going to get any better. I mean when you play once a week, you get through and you've made the same mistakes that you made last week, and you aren't going to get any better, because you just don't play enough. So the three of us met up, and it so happened we each led our own amateur band and we each had plenty of free time.

By this time I was going to become a mathematician like my father, but I failed some exams, so that didn't work. So he said, "What about music school?" I said, "I've got a band already." He said, "No, I mean take it seriously." I said, "Fine." So I got into music school, which meant I wasn't doing anything all day. [*laughs*] I had plenty of free time, and another friend of mine played the clarinet. He had a band and the same idea, and he was studying art, so he had nothing to do all day. And the other guy played the guitar and banjo. He was doing his military service, and, luckily, he was actually stationed in London, so he could get away in the afternoon quite easily. So we sat there drinking tea and coffee in the afternoon in a restaurant where musicians hang out. And we were trying to work out how the hell we were going to play this music properly, because we weren't getting enough playing. You had to play every day to get the hang of it. So we said, "Let's form a band that plays full-time and does nothing else." One of them said, "How are we going to get enough money to live on?" Well, we were all living at home anyhow—we could keep doing that. So we formed a small band.

Chris Barber and band on tour with Sonny Terry and Brownie McGhee. Courtesy Chris Barber.

The clarinet player was Monty Sunshine, who joined up with me, and he was the player who played on my only hit record, a tune originally done by Sidney Bechet called "Petite Fleur," recorded back in 1959. And the other guy, who played banjo and guitar, was Anthony Donegan—known as "Lonnie" because he'd been on the concert when Lonnie Johnson was in town, and the announcer for the concert got confused and announced my friend as "Lonnie" Donegan. [*laughs*] He recorded "Rock Island Line," and that was a worldwide hit in 1954. So we formed this special band, and after all these years that band has changed only gradually and I'm still leading it now. It's been fifty-five years, quite a long time.

When we got this first professional band together, we had planned to have the trumpeter who had played with me in 1954, Pat Halcox, and then we had drummer Ron Bowden and Jim Bray on bass. We were going to turn professional in March of 1953, and if we could get ourselves over to Denmark we could play in some jazz clubs every night—and get ourselves together in the provinces before hitting the big time, you know? That was the idea. It was all set and we were going to do that. We were going to stay in the houses of various fans over there, and that would be nice. At the end of '52 we played a couple of live sessions in London, and some guys heard the band and thought we were really great. But then Pat Halcox, the trumpeter, came to me and said, "I'm terribly sorry. My parents are holding me to a promise I made that I would do my studies. They've kept me since I left school and have been doing further studies and working as an apprentice. I promised them I would follow through until I had a qualification of some kind that I could make a living with—rather than taking a dangerous step and becoming a musician. [*laughs*] So I can't turn professional with you."

But within a week we heard the great Ken Colyer, who'd been in New Orleans. Ken had joined up as a merchant seaman on a shipping line that traveled between London and Mobile, Alabama. Of course, merchant seamen never did have passports; they had an identity card. So he simply jumped ship in Mobile and went to New Orleans. He had a trumpet and he went around sitting in. This was around 1952 and '53. He eventually was noticed. [*laughs*] He couldn't have been too hard to notice, mainly because he was the only white guy in most of the places. [*laughs*] With Louisiana state law at the time, it was illegal for black and white to be onstage together. What happened was they picked him up on Christmas of 1952—and he didn't even have a passport, much less a visa—so they threw him in the parish prison. Well, he was a genuine guy; he just liked the music and he was well-behaved. So they said, "We're going to send you home." And they sent him home, which was great, because if you get deported from anyplace they send you home first-class. [*laughs*]

So he had this great journey on the bottom of a big liner. And he wrote his song "Going Home" then, because as far as he was concerned, his home was in New Orleans. He felt more at home in New Orleans than he did in England. The music he loved was there—everything he wanted to do was there—but the Americans were sending him home. So he wrote the song. He said, "If home is where the heart is, my home's in New Orleans." I did say to him afterwards, "Ken, I know you got away and went home to England, but did you think that when you went the police might not be so friendly to your black friends with whom you sat in at the clubs?" He hadn't thought of that.

Anyway, he was coming back to England. We heard he'd been deported and I sent him a letter quickly before he could leave saying, "Listen, we've got this band. It's really good and we're going to have a professional band playing all the time. We like all the same things you do. What about joining us?" He said yes, and he came back and joined us. So we played with Ken, and we felt that since Ken had been in New Orleans, and no other of the serious jazz and blues musicians in Britain had even seen New Orleans, much less been there, we said, "We better call it your band." So we called it the Ken Colyer Jazz Band. And that was fine.

Unfortunately, he had a brother who was a real pain. He was a control freak, you know. He didn't play an instrument—he didn't do anything worth having—but he wanted to prove he'd done it. So after about a year—in front of Ken, who was a very quiet man, didn't have much to say—but he told the clarinet player and myself that Ken was "really fed up with the rhythm guys. He's going to throw out the guitar player/banjo player and the bass player and the drummer. You and Monty are catching on fairly well—you can stay." And I thought, "Well, half the tunes he can play on his trumpet I taught him, because he couldn't work them out by himself. Thank you very much!" [*laughs*] But we said, "No, the rhythm section is great." The recordings of that band you could hear it—it was a very good rhythm section. And we said, "We'll never find another one as good as that." It was a co-operative band. It was a co-op band to begin with and we'd invited Ken to join it. And we said, "There are six of us—we're five—you're one, and you're out!" [*laughs*] So the boys said, "Chris, you better be the leader. You seem to have some understanding of what you've got to do." So I led the band and that was it.

Ken Colyer was a genuine musician. He loved the blues; he loved jazz. He really understood the feeling of the music very, very well, but he was the most inarticulate man, very hard to deal with. To say he didn't have the gift of the gab is understating it. You could feel that he was embarrassed because he couldn't express himself. Instead he'd just get angry and shout at you. Which is a shame, because he had great instinct—great instinct. Anyway, that's what happened.

So after a year I became the leader of the band and it carried on from there. And by that time Pat Halcox—the guy who couldn't join up with us in the first place—had convinced his parents that he would do all right and make a decent living, because we already were. So all of a sudden, within a year, the music that we played—which the English media, who had a genius for stupid nicknames—had named what we call traditional jazz "trad." And within a year we were the biggest live attraction in show business in Britain. The first two years that we did it, none of the other players in popular music even noticed what was going on. You'd think that they would try and copy our band, but, no, it took them two years to do it. So we had it by ourselves for two years.

Part of the success was because jazz could spread through all the clubs that were called jazz clubs, or blues clubs, or beat clubs—like the Cavern in Liverpool. Most of my jazz friends played in the Cavern, and the Beatles were one of the local amateur bands that played during intermission. The reason that it could take off—unlike America, where in a place that sold alcohol you had to prove your age with an ID card—in Britain, although you couldn't sell a drink to people under eighteen, people over sixteen were allowed to be there, like with a family, as long as you didn't sell a drink to them. So if people decided to have a jazz club night in these little dance hall pubs, kids over sixteen could be there. In America kids over sixteen had nowhere to go. And the traditional jazz thing just struck a chord with the British public.

In 1954—when we just got started, really—was the first time we did shows with Big Bill Broonzy. I must tell you that the skiffle group with Lonnie Donegan and Dickie Bishop—myself on bass and Ron on drums and Big Bill—was an absolutely wonderful sound. I couldn't persuade our recording manager to record it. He insisted on recording Big Bill with musicians who couldn't play that type of music at all. He did the same thing with Sonny Terry and Brownie McGhee later. Because I had records with Sleepy John Estes, Lonnie Johnson, Brownie McGhee, and Big Bill, to me that was a part of the music, and I wanted a band that could cultivate that as well.

My first amateur band was based on the King Oliver Creole Jazz Band in the repertoire and lineup on those marvelous 1923 records of King Oliver. Oliver's band had two trumpets, a clarinet and trombone, a banjo and bass, piano and drums. We had all that plus a guitar as well. The guitar player was Alexis Korner, who I went to school with, or as I like to say, who went to school with me. My piano player in that band—who played a kind of ragtimey style like Lil Hardin Armstrong played in King Oliver's band—also played Maceo Merriweather piano solos. We were doing that in 1949 and '50. So we had a blues session in the band.

There were two aspects to it. There's the kind of blues like 1920s blues, where women sang vaudeville songs; I mean, some sang vaudeville songs and some sang real blues songs. So while Bessie Smith sang "Kitchen Man" and stupid things like that, she also sang wonderful blues like "Work House." So that was the thing. So we wanted to do that and we also wanted to do urban/country blues, like Muddy Waters on the South Side. It wasn't saxophone music; it was kind of country blues played with more urban intensity. I just felt I wanted to able to do that too. It was part of what you had to do. If you couldn't understand that, you couldn't possibly understand New Orleans jazz. It's all part of it; they go hand in hand. The only real difference between blues—as it's called by a lot of fans—and New Orleans jazz is the instruments it's played on. It's the same music, but it's mostly played on guitars and not trombones.

Would you describe the skiffle segment of your program?

Lonnie Donegan loved singing. We had Leadbelly records; I had 931 on Perfect—he sang that very well. I played the bass and he played the guitar, and he sang that very well. I played that when Sonny Terry and Brownie McGhee came to Britain. They toured with my band in '58 and we had a party at my house, and I put that record on and I said to Sonny, "Who's that?" He said, "That's Blind Lemon Jefferson." Now, if *he* wouldn't know who that was, who would? I thought, "Well, then, we're doing something right." It's like the real thing should be, so that's what we tried to do. We had "Rock Island Line," and Lonnie sang a lot of things he later turned into hit records.

I had a 78 rpm record, a Paramount record called "Hometown Skiffle," a 1929 sampler record. What they did was dub—rather badly—their new releases. They played Blind Blake or whoever it was, and halfway through they had a guy talking and clinking glasses as though it was a party, and then they dubbed in a half of another record—all part of the next month's new releases. Anyway, they called it "Hometown Skiffle"—you'll find it listed in the discography. So I had that record, and by this time I had acquired from a friend of mine in England the magazine *Jazz Information*. There we read about Dan Burley, who was playing skiffle, what he called skiffle music. We thought that was a good name; it means rent party, hometown bluesy blues, so we called it skiffle. So what we did—it wasn't during the intermission; it was just a part of the show—after we did a few rip-roaring fast New Orleans numbers, then it was time for some blues, so we did some skiffle. And it got so popular that we would end the first half of the concert with about five skiffle numbers. We'd say, "Shall we do the skiffle now?" [*laughs*]

And would the rest of the band breakdown or just sort of sit out during those numbers?

Yes, sure. They didn't play on those, just like I didn't play on "Petite Fleur," the clarinet solo. It was just Lonnie, with our drummer and myself on the bass. I had learned the bass at music school. I liked that music, while our regular bass player was hardly a great blues enthusiast; he was more of an old-time jazz enthusiast. So that was the lineup, and it was just Lonnie carrying the guitar. And what happened was he had a friend called Dickie Bishop, and we had some very nice records of light skiffle, I would call it, which were on Folkways—stuff with Woody Guthrie and other guys joining in. So we had Dickie Bishop and other guys joining in. So that was the skiffle bit. If you make a record, an album—at that time we didn't know if we were popular, or would be—they tried to make the cast of the recording more interesting by saying, "There's not only jazz, but a skiffle group too!" It was just us trying to play country blues.

I've read that your band became the most popular and successful in the UK during this period. Perhaps you can talk about the band's popularity.

Actually it wasn't just in the UK, but in all of Europe. Well, after World War II Britain was still rationing food and clothes and things until 1952, which was quite a long time to go without luxuries. And popular music was still firmly based in 1930s dance music. Our sort of music, once it began to get good, broke the whole country open. When we were invited to go around the country and play, we found ourselves in some ballroom where there was a kind of a dance band playing, and the proprietor of the ballroom expected us to play quicksteps and foxtrots and waltzes, which we weren't much good at. With quicksteps and foxtrots you just play jazz and call it a quickstep or foxtrot. But the difficulty was with waltzes; we weren't much good.

At that time we were twenty or twenty-two years old, and the kids who liked what we played were seventeen or eighteen. We had an audience that was probably five years younger than ourselves. They obviously wanted something more lively, and they'd seen some movies with jitterbugging in them and they tried doing that—"jiving," they call it in Britain; then later they called it rock 'n' roll dancing. That's what they did—or tried to do. The problem is if you go to a big dance hall and you've got a thousand people dancing, when they did the quicksteps and foxtrots, they circulated around the floor—even when they're all together, they circulate en masse. But when you were jitterbugging you stayed in one place and took up six times as much space as the other couples did. [*laughs*] So the ballroom owners said, "Don't play any of that rock 'n' roll." What they meant was don't play anything you could rock 'n' roll dance to, because all the people doing the foxtrot and quickstep got kicked. [*laughs*]

So then the fans began asking us, "Would you play a cha-cha-cha?" We don't play a cha-cha-cha. Well, it worked out that the ballroom proprietors didn't know what a cha-cha-cha was. All they knew was you didn't dance together and circulate around the floor; you just stood in one spot, and the couples didn't stand together either. So the kids worked it out. They could jitterbug dance and get away with it in the ballroom, because I would announce, "Muskrat Ramble Cha-cha-cha." [*laughs*] Of course the management of the ballrooms proved themselves to be as stupid as I thought they were, because they didn't know the difference! In fact, I remember one time we were playing in some local town hall in a provincial town somewhere. It was a dance on a Saturday night. We were the name band and there was a local band on the stage, and we were going to play the second and fourth sets. The manager came to me in the dressing rooms and said, "You must be very careful. You mustn't play any of that rock 'n' roll here." At that particular point I could hear his local band playing "Rock Around the Clock." [*laughs*] So I said yes and ignored him. The audience wanted to see us, they came to see us, they paid money for tickets to see us—not the local dance band—and they wanted what we did, so we did it.

The whole of Europe took up the music that we played. I guess "traditional jazz" is one way of putting it, and "New Orleans" in a way, or "Dixieland" in America, like you'd hear from Eddie Condon in New York. But it was quite a bit different—a bit more skillful, to be honest, and less funky feeling. It swept the whole of Europe, quite extraordinary at the time. I think from 1954, when the band really took off, to something like 1959, we saw very few venues without a sign out front saying "Sold Out." From the time I took the band over in 1954, we had six resident weekly jazz club nights in London—that is to say, six jobs a week! And we played 52 weeks a year. We did 312 gigs that year in those clubs, plus sometimes the other night, which wasn't in use. People would ask us to play somewhere else, so we'd play there too. We probably did 330 or 340 gigs that year.

You must realize that in 1954 in Britain nobody owned a car! No new cars were on sale in Britain, and there were no new cars until 1957 or 1956. The war effort during World War II had really drained the country tremendously. So we hadn't really learned to drive a car—we hadn't even *tried* to drive a car yet—until we were twenty-four, because there wasn't really a chance. So for all the gigs in London we would go to them by underground train, the subway system. The London subway system is very effective. It even goes out into the country about fifteen miles on each side. So we were doing that all the time and trying to catch the last train at night, the last train leaving about midnight. We used to make it home most times. [*laughs*]

Within about a year of that we began to be asked to do other things as well, which meant taking a night off from our regular clubs and playing a concert somewhere. In England there's a society called the Lord's Day Observance Society. They were formed by religious people years and years before that to prevent the country from becoming a den of iniquity of having people out dancing on Sundays. There was a law passed in the seventeenth century which is called the Lord's Day Observance Act, which says that you are not allowed to be onstage in costume on Sunday playing to people. So you couldn't put a play on—I guess you *could* put a play on if you didn't wear costumes. [*laughs*]

What happened was this: In Britain at that time people didn't go on holiday, they didn't go abroad, they went somewhere else in Britain. All the places they went to on the coast had theaters which had a summer show, a summer stock theater—sort of a vaudeville show, a couple of comedians and a singer or two, even jugglers. But on Sundays they couldn't do that. None of that was possible on Sunday, because it was against the law. And then someone had the bright idea that they could put a concert on. A concert? Well, you would have thought a concert at that time was going to be guys in dress suits. Then there were bands that became quite popular. They were show bands, and they were all wearing costumes—like one of them wore these wild tartan dinner jackets. They couldn't go onstage like that; it was against the law. But in the end a jazz band playing in ordinary clothes, they couldn't argue about. So we got asked to go and do concerts in theaters.

Now, playing in clubs as we were first—in America you think of a jazz club with a legal capacity determined by the fire department, held about sixty people. Most of ours held three or four hundred. Of course they didn't pay any money; the money you paid to get in was very small, but, nevertheless, those were big places. Playing those was very hot. We didn't have any air conditioning in Britain at all at that time. It was really hot, full of people. But when we found ourselves in a concert hall or theater, on the stage where there was space,

Chris Barber and band with Howling Wolf and Hubert Sumlin. © Sylvia Pitcher, London.

most of the jazz bands used to huddle in one corner, because they felt awkward being spread out on the stage. But my band instinctively filled the stage up by spreading out and felt comfortable doing that. So that made us look extremely good on stage compared to the other bands. So that was a part of it, but only a part. It really was just the right moment.

I started leading the band in May of 1954. The first thing we did was record an album for Decca. We'd made an album for Decca with Ken Colyer playing a year earlier, which was quite special. Then we bust[ed] up, and as we were busting up, Ken Colyer's brother was talking to a man from Decca about doing a second record, but he didn't mention that all the band was leaving. [*laughs*] The man then came and chased me. "We signed Ken up. What about you?" "We'll do one—we'll do a record. Love to!" So we did an album, and the album contained Lonnie Donegan, the banjo player, playing guitar and singing "Rock Island Line," which I played the bass on and which became a large hit record. That was on our first album. The fans liked the jazz we played—and the skiffle group, as we called it—and that caught on somewhat. We had quite a monopoly in the business, really.

In the time span we were talking about, 1954 to 1959, how many records did your band manage to make?

We made quite a few. We were involved with different companies—about twenty albums, I would think. Let's see—seven ten-inch LPs and about ten or twelve twelve-inch LPs. The first records we did were for Decca; that was the record with "Rock Island Line" on it. The record with "Rock Island Line" came out in 1954 and was selling like hell. I knew a guy who worked at Decca, and he said, "You should put out a single of 'Rock Island Line.'" It was so far away from anything that they understood as popular music that they just couldn't believe it, so it took them a year to put out a single of "Rock Island Line." We sold a whole lot of LPs, and we should have just stuck with those, because if you bought the LP you got "Rock Island Line," two tracks of the skiffle/blues stuff, and six tracks of the band. And if you heard the band you might come and see it later. It was better from our point of view, because it sold the whole package. We then did two more records for Decca, which were concerts at the Royal Festival Hall in London, which was a new concert hall built in 1951. We were the headliner band—this was in October 1954 and January of 1955. Those were both on twelve-inch LPs. That was Decca.

Then a fellow who was a friend of mine—he's long dead now, Dennis Preston—we talked to a guy who was the first in Europe to do a lease-tape deal with record companies, where he'd prepare the tape completely, got it all ready, organize the band, and then sold the whole thing for a royalty. In Europe nobody had done that up until then. In America people like Norman Granz had been doing it for a long time, but in England it was a new thing. So he said, "Come on, we've got a good deal with a record label. We'll get something going and it will go very well," because Decca was not disposed to be interested in what we were doing at all. The head of the company was totally disinterested. In fact, my friend, who actually worked there, went to see the boss: "Their 'Rock Island Line' is a hit. This Chris Barber Band's really good! I think they might go sign with somebody else if we don't interest them in staying." The boss said to him, "Oh, give the boy a radiogram." That was an old-fashioned piece of furniture with a radio built in and a record player on top. So my friend said, "I believe he has one, sir," and walked out. [*laughs*]

So we signed with this person with the lease-tape idea. First there was this company called B-Side Up—a British company that sold radios and early TVs—and they thought that was a record label. So we had a contract with the producer fellow, and he had a contract with the record company that paid him a royalty and he gave some of that to us—not much, but some. They were called Pye. After being with them for three years he changed and went with EMI instead, on our behalf. So we were with EMI for three years, from 1958 until 1961, and after 1961 we left, mainly because he wasn't interested in our music, really. He loved the music, the same as I do, but he was certainly disinterested in any condition whether we played it or not. At a session I would say, "I want to play that back. We need to do that again and get that right." He said to me, "Chris, don't take it so seriously. Let's face it—in ten years time we'll both be sitting back in an armchair, with a nice dot of brandy, playing Duke Ellington records." "Well, I want my records to come out properly." He never saw the point of us doing it; he thought it had all been done already. But at the end of that time we didn't sign with him again. We got different deals at different times—so onward!

Let's talk about Ottilie Patterson. Please tell me about her.

Ottilie was—and is—somewhat unusual in a sense, because she's half Latvian and half Irish. [*laughs*] She loved the blues. We played it, and she sang it—it was fantastic! She played the piano and she loved boogie-woogie, and she had some blues records. She met a guy in Belfast who was a great, serious jazz enthusiast who used to, when there were any youngsters around, play them all these red-hot jazz and blues records and make them play properly and think seriously about them. Then she heard a record of the Ken Colyer Band—the first and only album we did with Ken Colyer. She said, "That sounds good. I must go to London and find them!" So she came over.

She was teaching art for a living at that time, and she came to London to try and find us. She found us and came up and sang with the band—and it was very good. We offered her a chance to sing with us. At that time she had to go back to teaching, because to get a government grant to study art, you had to promise that when you were qualified you would teach for a couple of years so they wouldn't waste the money they had invested in you. She said she had to go back. But when she got back they couldn't offer her a full-time job at all—and she just quit. So six months later she came back and joined us and sang with us from that point on. Ottilie joined the band in January of 1955, because the first thing she did with us was sing at the Royal Festival Hall.

At what point did Lonnie leave the band?

While we had a contract with this manager for Pye Records—we had "Rock Island Line" out on Decca the year before, which was a tremendous success and had everybody playing skiffle music. So part of the deal we did with this guy Preston, the manager, was to record Lonnie's skiffle group, which included myself on bass; Lonnie on guitar; another guitarist, a friend of ours named Dickie Bishop; and the drummer, Ron Bowden.

It was almost like a country group, really. Like in America Woody Guthrie would sing with Sonny Terry and Brownie McGhee—like that, more or less. In 1955 we had two EPs [extended play records]—it looked like a 45 but had four tunes—of Lonnie and the skiffle group in the top ten at the same time. That's how popular Lonnie was. That was pretty extraordinary. And the influence of that was fantastic. It was a co-operative band, and Lonnie was our partner and he began to get offers to go and do solo stuff with a lot of money for himself. And he said, "Listen, fellows. I've got to go. There's a lot of money there." I said, "Well, you'll make a lot of money in the band too." He said, "No, I'm just getting paid like everybody else." I said, "Right now we're benefiting from your record. In five years time it might be the clarinet solo making the money." He said, "Na-a-a-h-h." The funny thing is five years later we had a hit with "Petite Fleur," and the clarinet supported us all! But Lonnie went on to become a vaudeville star. It was March of 1956 he left. His career was very successful. He had a lot of hit records—that's how you measure success in the business. He was really big-time. He did very well indeed. He died only a few years back now, but he was very successful.

Did you and the band ever appear in any "Hollywood-type" movies?

We took part in one very serious movie, which is called *Look Back in Anger,* with Richard Burton and other great actors in it, 1960 or 1961. It's a play by John Osburn. There was a thing at the time that the country, England, was going nowhere—nothing was happening in the country. And the younger men were all angry because nothing was happening, and they called them "angry young men." And the playwright John Osburn wrote this play about an angry young man, which Richard Burton played. It was set in what appeared to be the Marquee Club. It was the newest thing I've ever seen in Hollywood. They made a set to look like a jazz club in Britain, and it actually looked like it! [*laughs*] My band played in the club.

In the movie Richard Burton played the angry young man—a bit of a lout, and he plays trumpet. He carries the trumpet with him and plays blues phrases all the time, which my trumpeter did for him. He did a wonderful job of miming to the music, so that when you see him on the screen he looks like he's playing music. He couldn't play at all, but he knew how to pretend, where we in the band were all hopeless at pretending. [*laughs*] We actually play music but looked like we didn't know what we were doing! [*laughs*] The music in the movie is nice, and it's exactly how we sounded at the time.

We were different from the other traditional jazz bands because we started to play the blues, which is a vocal music and we had somebody to sing it, so we learned how to play it. Accompanying a singer is something that all too many jazz musicians are terrible at. Most of them don't think it's too important and don't listen to them much. That was great help to us. Having worked with Big Bill already in 1954 and again in '56, we were on tour with him and Brother John Sellers and we wanted a chance to work with real people. These people teach you without really trying to, because they play things right—the way it's supposed to be done. If you play things the wrong way, you stick out like a sore thumb—you feel it, you know? That's how you learn it.

The musicians union in Britain, having had a row with the American Federation of Musicians in America in 1938, wouldn't allow American musicians to play in Britain. We would like to have had real jazz musicians to come over and play with us, but they weren't allowed to. And the musicians union in Britain was communist, which didn't help at all. I remember going to the general secretary of the union, who was about as important as the teamsters in America, without the mafia. And I said, "Listen, we thought Louis Armstrong was giving up, but he's playing now, touring around the world, but he can't play in Britain. If we can get him to come and play solo with a British band, that would be fantastic! We'll all learn so much more about the music, and the public likes it so much now. That will be even better! We'll get so much work from it and it'll be good for all of us." And he said to me, I kid you not, "Why do you always want an American trumpeter? Why don't you get a Russian trumpeter?" [*laughs*]

So we discovered, quite by chance, that singers in America—folk singers and such—couldn't join the AF of M, because they weren't musicians. They joined the American Guild of Variety Artists, if they had a union at all. And in England it was the same thing. Neither of those federations cared a damn about work permits or Americans coming over. All they wanted was 2 percent union dues. So that was it. Okay, if we can do that, who are we going to get? Well, we thought, the first thing is, many of the great blues artists that are still playing and recording would not be accustomed to playing in front of white audiences, and this might put them off.

It could be difficult for them. We didn't want to embarrass them and have them not know what to do, even if I knew that all they needed to do was what they did perfectly and what we wanted to hear. Well, we knew that Rosetta Tharpe had been playing in clubs with "Lucky" Millinder's band, and in front of mostly white audiences. Clearly she wasn't worried about that. And the same thing with Sonny Terry and Brownie McGhee, because they did the music for *Cat on a Hot Tin Roof,* the play on Broadway. They worked with folk audiences in America who were mostly white—in fact, Woody Guthrie and his following. So we got Rosetta Tharpe to come over first, and that was absolutely, mind-bogglingly wonderful—the best, immediate unexpected experience ever! She acted as if she'd found a band like she'd never heard before—and needed to have all her life. That was flattering, and she wasn't given to flattering people. We had the most marvelous tour with Sister. She and Ottilie got along well together; she had that with Marie Knight for years. Some people said, "You've already got a singer. She and Ottilie will be at each other's throats—rivals!" That was stupid, ridiculous! It wasn't so at all, of course.

The most important thing, we found, we asked some critics who came to see our concert and they all said, "How dare you get up and play with Rosetta Tharpe? How dare you? You're ruining their music with your crappy English music?" And I said, "A, if we hadn't got the money and brought them over here, you wouldn't have heard them at all! And secondly, they like it." And we actually tried hard to persuade Rosetta Tharpe to sing a song or two by herself. It was hell-going difficulty to get her to do that. She wanted the band there all the time, because she loved the music. It moved her. The same thing with Sonny Terry and Brownie McGhee. Luckily, they were used to playing by themselves, playing in a folk environment where people would get up and do songs just like they were. It was the most marvelous experience the first time we brought them over.

And then just after Rosetta Tharpe had toured with us in 1957, I was a part of an organization called the National Jazz Federation in Britain. The musicians union had finally agreed to allow Americans to work in Britain as long as there was an identical exchange going to America, which was difficult because there was no demand for English bands in America at all. So the people just used fake contracts, and the union accepted it because they were stupid. So small America modern bands were coming over—the Modern Jazz Quartet and Gerry Mulligan—and the Modern Jazz Quartet became lifelong friends of mine. John Lewis said to me, "Who have you brought over here?" and I said, "Rosetta Tharpe, Sonny and Brownie." And he said, "Why don't you get Muddy Waters?" I said, "I don't know how to reach him. Do you send him a postcard to the first cotton bush on the left at Stovall's Plantation or something?" [*laughs*] John says, "No, he's got a Cadillac and an agent!" [*laughs*] I found out later that Chess bought him a Cadillac and he didn't like it—he never used it!

So we arranged for our agent here to book Muddy to come over in October of 1958. And again, that was wonderful, a fantastic experience! By that time we weren't nervous about playing with these people, but then on Muddy's records we noticed they had just a bass and drums in general. They had horns on a record or two, mostly just clarinet or sax. And most bands wouldn't have known what to do with Muddy's numbers, but we did. I know when he did the first concert with us we hadn't had time to rehearse with him in Newcastle, North England. He turned up there and we told him what we were doing. He heard us playing the first half of the concert playing jazz from New Orleans, that kind of stuff. He didn't say anything much about it. He didn't say, "What's that shit?" or "Can I get some of that!" I said to him, "We're going to start off with 'Hoochie Coochie Man.'" He said, "Yeah, yeah, yeah." [*Chris starts to sing the opening riffs.*]. "Yeah, yeah." I said, "What key?" "A." "Okay."

Ottilie Patterson and Muddy Waters. Photo Terry Cryer. Courtesy Chris Barber.

So the second part of the show we just did three songs and then called on our guests. It happened that particular theater, when you came on the stage, there were windows in the door, so you could see what was going on. And of course we could see them. There were Muddy and Otis Spann peering through these two windows and listening to the Dixieland we were playing. So I announced them and we played the opening riff. [*Chris sings the ominous opening riff.*] And their two faces lit up like watermelon eaters! They knew we were on their wavelength. So we kept playing and they came out. We dropped [the] volume down. It was the most impressive, exciting feeling. They didn't expect us to know or care about their music. We had a great time with them.

How big was the theater?

It seated three thousand; it was a concert hall. It was actually the city hall of Newcastle-upon-Tyne—in the North of England. It was a venue for concerts, and we'd been there more than anybody else, actually, because we were so popular. I remember when we first got going in 1956, and we played that concert hall in Newcastle five times in one year. It was full every time. In recent years I've been over there playing as an extra musician in Van Morrison's band. Van Morrison has, for years, been the biggest attraction—an established artist, drawing people to his concerts all the time. He played Newcastle twice in one year and that was it. We didn't realize how popular we were. We could have been more forceful in our demands on some promoters, couldn't we? [*laughs*]

How did you make contact with Big Bill Broonzy?

Well, Big Bill had been brought to Europe. I believe the first time he'd been brought to Europe by the Belgian guys—Yannick Bruynoghe. They had contacted him in America. They found him and brought him over to Europe. The first time I saw him he did a concert in London, in a big concert hall. The concert was Mahalia Jackson with Mildred Falls, Big Bill, and an English jazz band opening the show. I went to that concert, and it was funny because Big Bill was really upset. He thought it was quite naughty to put him on a concert with the wonderful, sanctified Mahalia Jackson. He thought it was insulting. He thought he shouldn't be on with her. But she didn't worry about Big Bill being there at all! [*laughs*] He was really worried: "I hadn't better say anything too risqué with Mahalia on the concert." The unusual thing was that Bill sang spirituals normally when performing, quite a lot. Traditionally speaking, in America—historically speaking—the blues places were not places to sing spirituals; likewise, blues were not allowed in church. It was profane music. To me—blues or spirituals—you can't say one's more important than the other. There are different techniques in the singing style, more so in recent years than in the 1920s.

During the time that Bill was there with you, did he work with the band or play solo?

Well, he may have done one or two songs by himself, but in general the whole point was that we wanted to play with him. In New Orleans kids one and two years old were exposed to gospel music in the church, by being there and a part of it. We took that mind to play that music when we were in our twenties. Then we had to try to acquire that background, the understanding of it, that they had acquired from birth because it was all around them. In England it wasn't all around you at all! We wanted to get ourselves in it as far as possible, because we wanted to be able to play that music, or at least not embarrass or annoy the real people whose music it was. Anyway, we were very keen to get a hold of that and play with all the right people if we could. We didn't have as much chance to play as we would like to have had. And in trad jazz in England it became a thing to sing like Al Jolson. But we said, "No, that's the way you sing if you can't manage the black style properly!" [*laughs*]

Big Bill loved playing with the band. My memory of Bill was he would stand with the guitar and was just singing and playing to enjoy himself. And what he would play and sing would be "I'm Looking Over a Four-Leaf Clover" or "Won't You Come Home, Bill Bailey?" songs—not blues. He loved singing "When Did You Leave Heaven?" and other ballads; he loved those. We asked him, "What do you want to do?" And he wanted to do those, and we did them with him. He was in the spotlight for forty minutes, and during the course of that time he would sing a blues or two, but he would also sing the pop tunes as well. The records that he made during the 1940s for Columbia, he had horns—saxes and things. He was used to having instrumentalists around. He obviously liked it. He was happiest when there was a band playing with him.

What was the itinerary like on his tours with you?

In those days we played practically every day—somewhere. Sometimes concert halls, other times jazz clubs. You had jazz clubs in Chicago or Bourbon Street in New Orleans.

In England a jazz club might hold three or four hundred people. But we played somewhere almost every day.

How long were your tours with Bill?

When he came in 1954, he been brought over by the guys in Belgium. Jumping Jazz in London said [they could] get him some work in Britain. So they found him a room where he could stay, and they arranged for him to come and play in different jazz clubs with different bands—or on his own, whichever people wanted to do. I think he was there for about two or three weeks. When we toured with him in 1956, we brought Brother John Sellers on the bill as well. We did about twenty concerts in three weeks. We traveled around a lot; we got in various cars and traveled around and took him with us. Same thing with Rosetta Tharpe; we had about four weeks, playing every day virtually with Sister in 1957.

Sonny and Brownie were here longer than that. We did a concert tour kind of thing, about twenty gigs. And then we did some clubs and other things. They stayed about six weeks, and then they stayed on in Europe after that anyhow. Our tours were in April and May in 1958, and they stayed after that. It was the first time they'd been out of America at all. Sonny and Brownie were a funny couple, because Sonny was blind—or almost blind—and Brownie, having had polio, didn't walk too well. Brownie would lead Sonny around, because he could see, and the quote from the Bible is "the halt leading the blind." [*laughs*] Brownie would say, "C'mon, Sonny. Sonny, let's do this—let's do that." And Sonny would say, "You're just jealous. I'm a better blues singer than you are!" [*laughs*] They had no problems—nobody gave them any trouble.

One time we had Big Bill Broonzy with us in a town called Nottingham, a nice gig in a jazz club. It was like a big dance hall that held a thousand people. It was run on Thursdays by the jazz club. We played there, and after the job we had Big Bill and we went to the hotel afterwards. It was the night porter—not the manager—and he said, "We don't have black people here." So we just turned around and walked out, all of us. We went and found another place and ask[ed] the clerk, "Do you rent rooms to colored people?" He said, "We rent rooms to people with money. Do you have money?" I said yes. "Then you can have rooms." [*laughs*] Bill, he was a lovely guy. He just did what he did; there was no doubt about it.

You know, in England, because of the colonies, we've always had lots of black people in Britain—not huge numbers, but a lot. And most of the black people there had money because they were government people. This goes back to 1937, to a Jamaican guy called Larry Constantine. He was a preacher, but he worked for the government and he went to a restaurant in 1937. He made a reservation, and when he got in there they wouldn't serve him. He took them to court and won the case. The restaurant was fined. So there has been a basis for many years against racial discrimination.

Did you make records with them while they were there?

Many. We have three CDs out called *Lost & Found*. Those were the recordings of our concerts with Rosetta Tharpe, Sonny and Brownie, Muddy Waters—with Howling Wolf, with Sonny Boy Williamson II. They're all valuable. You can even see bits of them on YouTube. They came out two years ago, totally unexpected to me. Blues magazines tend to know what the real thing is, and you didn't expect them to be terribly welcoming to British people, who have a reputation for being stiff-upper-lip types. Every blues magazine in America gave us five stars for that record. In fact, one said, "I'd like to give you ten stars, but I'm only allowed to give you five—so I give you five!" The best review we had came from a guy who played guitar in Muddy's band, Bob Margolin. He reviewed records for *Blues Revue* [*Quarterly*] in America. He gave us a brilliant review. It seems to me he understood where we were at; he saw the point of why we did what we did.

The first time we were in Chicago, we went to America with the band in February 1959. It was set up as an exchange deal under the musicians union arrangement with Woody Herman; he wanted Woody Herman to work in Britain. We didn't play Chicago; we passed through, having played somewhere else. When we got to Chicago, the American manager took us down to see the Prudential Building and some of the buildings in the Loop area. When we toured with him in October of 1958, Muddy had told us to come and see him, and this was only a few months later. So we got taxis to go down and visit at Smitty's Corner at Thirty-fifth and Indiana. We came in and Muddy was immediately very welcoming. He announced us as his friends from the state of England [*laughs*]—and of course he wanted us to get up and play.

As it happened, we had a trailer with all of our equipment that we pulled behind our station wagon, but we hadn't brought it with [us]. So Muddy announced us as singers, without hardly asking, really, because he knew Ottilie sang the blues. And as Ottilie said, "Singers—you can't say you left *that* behind; it's your throat." It was amazing because, in my opinion, the best band Muddy ever had was when he had Francis Clay and Jimmy Cotton with Spann and Pat Hare on guitar—that was a beautiful band. So Ottilie sang Big Bill's tune "Southbound Train." She sang that with Big Bill himself only a few months earlier. So she sang [*Chris sings*], *"I wonder why that southbound train,"* and the entire audience raised their right hands and said, "Yeah!" That was . . . [*tearing up, voice breaking*] quite warming! It meant that she had conveyed not just what the words were, but what it meant: you don't want to go down there, but you somehow would like to do it. Do you see what I mean? Southbound. His audience wasn't joking; it's just what they did. They would have done that if Muddy had sung that. Eventually we did play there with the band. The next time we were over, he brought us in and we played our normal stuff there, and they loved it. We got standing ovations! And that was from Muddy's crowd—nobody else's. Nobody knew we were coming. Muddy's crowd was older, first-generation immigrants from the South. The place only held about sixty people, and as Muddy said, "My crowd drinks whiskey!" [*laughs*]

About 1961 or '62 we were in the States, and Ottilie and I were staying in Muddy Waters's house on Lake Park. And Muddy had a gig in Gary, Indiana. So I went along as a member of the band. We went along in the Chevy station wagon with Killer, his bodyguard—who really wasn't a bodyguard at all—and Jimmy, who was his mascot—Jimmy Oden, St. Louis Jimmy. We got to this club, which was a smart kind of place, and I played the first set with Muddy's band. Muddy didn't sing until the last number, as usual. This was a very cultured club. The people were dressed beautifully. That was the time when black people in America had the style. Anyway, at the end of the first set, as I came down from the stage, I had been playing and I wanted to get to the john. I went past a group of about eight people, very smartly attired. As I went past, this girl leaned back and said, "Say, are you Chris Barber?" I said, "Yes, I am." She said, "Is that your record, that 'Petite Fleur'?" I said, "Yes, it is." She said, "I don't like it!" [*laughs*] It was coming from an era of music that even her parents couldn't remember, so why would she like it? But it was put very frankly—so nice!

How did the recordings with Louis Jordan take place?

We were touring America and we were in New York City at the time. We looked at the marquee billing at the Apollo, and the Apollo had Louis Jordan for the week. I didn't know he was still working, but there he was, you see? So Ottilie and I went to see him. The billing was Louis Jordan and His Tympany Five, with guest star "Handsome" Sonny Stitt. And the great thing was at the end of the show Louis and his baritone player were jumping up in the air and doing the splits, and Sonny Stitt was beaming all over his face. He loved it! That shows that they didn't just love this over-intense modern jazz; they loved having a good time too. But also I was amazed to find that Louis had Teddy Bunn on guitar. I didn't know Teddy Bunn was alive still. And he was still playing without a pick. It was exciting to run into him. I had all his records; Louis Jordan's too.

So I said to Louis, "Would you like to come to England sometime?" He said, "Of course!" So we got back and I fixed it up to do a ten-day tour of England, which was utterly fantastic. I was thirty-two years old, and I had a band that was no slouch; Louis Jordan was then fifty-seven years old, and playing with him was like being dragged along by a wild horse. The thing was he didn't reckon on singing blues, and if he sang anything serious, he would put humorous interjections into it. He said, "You must not bring your audience down." [*laughs*] He was marvelous. He could have sung blues all night and no one would have minded. We made an album with him—it's out as well. There's one track on the *Lost & Found* set where he and Ottilie sing a duet of "T'ain't Nobody's Business" which is beautiful—absolutely terrific.

There were folks who have since become big names—Eric Clapton, Peter Green—who used to see your band during the skiffle phase. Can you talk about that?

They didn't come during the skiffle thing. That was too early for them. They came during the blues thing. Alex Korner joined my band playing guitar in 1960 or '61. They came to us to see Muddy Waters. For example, Eric Clapton and Jimmy Page came to hear Sonny and Brownie with us. That's how they came to steal one of their songs, their very first hits. That's when they came to see Muddy Waters, Rosetta Tharpe, and Sonny and Brownie. By that time they were into black music, blues, and we were the only ones that brought over the real thing. And Eric has been a great friend of mine ever since. I'm preparing a couple of albums for my eightieth birthday, which is next month—a kind of "Chris Barber and Friends" thing, and he volunteered to do it for me for nothing, to play for free. That was very nice.

DAVID EVANS INTERVIEW

David Evans, Malibu, California, July 1966. Photo Marina Bokelman.

I was born in Boston, January 22nd, 1944. I grew up in a solidly middle-class family mostly in Massachusetts. I spent a good part of my early years, up until fourth grade, in Lexington. Then my father, who worked for Prudential Insurance, was transferred to Dallas, Texas, and we lived there for four years—1954 to 1958. I was young, between ten and fourteen, but it gave me a little bit of exposure to the South—and even to blues, though I wasn't aware of it by that name, through the radio. These were the years that rock 'n' roll was coming on the scene, and R & B. You had radio stations with white deejays of the Dewey Phillips sort playing black music. I listened to it as I entered adolescence, so I guess you could say I had a "Southern Exposure." [*laughs*] It wasn't enough to get me hooked on blues. I never saw any of it live, but in some subtle way it gave me an orientation through the radio—and an opportunity to discover a bit of Southern black culture and life. We were classic New England liberals, not flaming liberals [*laughs*], but for the South my parents' views would have been considered pretty radical. Of course this was the era with the Supreme Court decision when integration was a possibility. The schools remained all white, but there was an awareness that things were likely to change. It was an interesting experience for me.

But then we came back north again to Massachusetts and lived in North Andover, and I got into a prep school as a day student at Phillips Academy. I was totally out of music at that time. In Texas I had taken up trumpet and then played baritone horn briefly in the school band, classical stuff and marches. But then in prep school I was just too busy studying to be involved in music. I listened to radio and rock 'n' roll of the late 1950s and very early 1960s, but I was studying Greek and Latin and got into Harvard, starting there in 1961. I graduated in 1965 as a classics major. Harvard from 1961 to 1965 was one of the hotbeds of the folk revival and the blues revival. I'd go around the coffeehouses just exploring all these new cultural opportunities, like any college freshman. I got exposed to folk music—first the Kingston Trio variety and then quickly on to Pete Seeger.

I had a scholarship at Harvard, and one of my duties—we had to do a little work there—was scraping uneaten food off the plates in the freshman dining hall. And the guy next to me, also working with me, was a day student at Harvard. I was living in a dorm then. He was into folk music already, and he started singing these songs while we scraped garbage off the plates—like work songs. [*laughs*] I liked the songs and we talked about them. He oriented me, mostly to the Weavers, and that was okay. I liked them better than the Kingston Trio. They seemed a bit more authentic in some way. Then in reading liner notes there'd be mention of Leadbelly and Woody Guthrie; that's how I started exploring. Then there was a very good record store in Harvard Square. I'd go over there and buy the occasional album. Then I went to coffeehouses. We went to Club 47, where they had people like Jim Kweskin's Jug Band, also Tom Rush and Jackie Washington. I got to see the Fugs [*laughs*], the Holy Modal Rounders; others I've forgotten—Dave Van Ronk, Eric von Schmidt—the whole list of people who were active in the Boston–New York–Cambridge axis of folk music. I liked it all and I gradually gravitated more toward the real thing; Leadbelly was a favorite at the time.

Then in 1962, in my sophomore year, there was a concert by a guy named Sleepy John Estes, who had just been rediscovered. I think I was familiar with one song of his through Sam Charters's book *The Country Blues* and the Folkways RBF album that went with it. I got ahold of that book, and of course I had the Robert Johnson album and a few other things. I was branching out. There were probably about twenty blues LPs altogether, and I probably had half of them. So I went and saw Sleepy John with Hammie Nixon. I could hardly understand a word he was singing, but it sounded so neat. I went out and bought the first Delmark album—"Delmar" at that time—by Sleepy John.

Sometime around that concert, possibly even before, in the record store at Harvard Square I ran into Alan Wilson, who lived in the area. He had just dropped out of Boston University in his freshman year and was trying to make a living playing music, giving guitar lessons, and working for his father as a bricklayer. We would run into each other in the record store, and then he'd come to my dorm and we'd listen to blues records together. We'd discuss the music—our favorites, what was good, what wasn't good. Through all of this I got deeper and deeper into country blues. Meanwhile more people were being rediscovered—Big Joe Williams

Al Wilson, Malibu, California, July 1966. Photo Marina Bokelman.

had been around on the scene, Jesse Fuller, Brownie and Sonny. Then John Hurt popped up in 1962, '63, and I got to meet him and hear him. I would be there every night. Back then the blues artists generally would have kind of a residency at a coffeehouse for a week or three or four days. So I got to meet John Hurt.

Also by this time I wanted to play the music too. I wanted to learn everything about it. I wanted to hear all of it, and I wanted to play it as well. Actually I'd first gotten a banjo during the folk music phase. I still have it, but I've hardly ever played it. The strings on it now are about forty or fifty years old. [*laughs*] Then I got a guitar and tried to learn everything on the Sleepy John Estes album, everything by Leadbelly. I got the Pete Seeger instruction books and records on how to play the twelve-string guitar like Leadbelly. And just like everybody else who was trying to play blues, we learned about half the songs on the Sam Charters's *The Country Blues* album.

Then the Origin Jazz Library records started coming out—Charley Patton. And you could hear Son House and Skip James, and that brought it to another level along with the Robert Johnson LP. And Leadbelly kind of faded into the background of my interest, although today I realize how great an artist he was. I was drawn to the Mississippi and Deep South sounds, the esoteric sounds, the music that Origin Jazz Library was issuing—that was my standard of excellence. Then those people started to be rediscovered, Son House and Bukka White. Bukka was rediscovered, and he came to Cambridge and stayed with Al Wilson.

Al was rooming with Phil Spiro, a friend of his who had a folk music radio show. Somehow—I guess through Phil's radio connection and friendship with the owners of the coffeehouse where Bukka was playing—it was arranged to have Bukka stay with them. That was the typical thing in those days, a cost-saving means: folk artists from the South would come to Boston, and the owner of the coffeehouse would find some die-hard fan who had a guest room and would put the artist up. It saved room and food costs, and that person would deliver the artist to the gig. It also gave them the opportunity to hobnob with a legendary blues singer. This was fantastic for Alan, and I was a friend, so I got to spend a lot of time with Bukka. This was in 1964, a year after his rediscovery. We talked with him and interviewed him. Bruce Jackson was also at Harvard. He was on some post-graduate fellowship as a folklorist there. He was a little older than Alan and me. So we kind of brought him in on it and we all interviewed Bukka together. I think Al and I asked as many questions of Bukka as Bruce did. In fact, we knew more about blues than Bruce did; he was more into the prison songs. Bruce had already done some fieldwork in Texas prisons and Indiana prisons, and some of that has come out on records.

One time when Al and I were talking with Bukka, typically you run a list of names of other blues singers by him—"Did you know so-and-so?"—hoping that they did and that they might have a lead to someone who would be the next rediscovery. Son House was one of those people. The name rang a bell with Bukka, and he said, "Yeah." And another blues singer he knew, Lillian Glover, "Memphis Ma" Rainey, told him that she had seen Son House recently, coming out of a movie theater in Memphis. So this seemed like a tremendous lead. "My God! Son House is still alive in Memphis!" [*laughs*] So we told Phil Spiro, who told his friend Dick Waterman. They cooked up an expedition and got Nick Perls. I think Nick was kind of the money man for the project. Waterman had the car, and they went off in the summer of '64.

They drove to Memphis to meet up with Bukka and Lillian Glover, who told them she had no idea what they were talking about! [*laughs*] Meanwhile the Reverend Robert Wilkins had been rediscovered—he knew Son House too—so they went to him. They also knew that Son had some connection with Robinsonville, having done a Library of Congress session there. So they went to Robinsonville with Robert Wilkins, asking around, and they got a lead. I believe it was a relative of Son's wife. The rest is a well-known story: Son was living up north in Rochester, New York, so they headed back and connected with him. And by November of 1964 Son was in Cambridge staying with Phil Spiro at his place. Alan and I interviewed Son extensively. It must have been one of the first lengthy interviews Son did. The results of that became a series of articles that Al wrote up in *Broadside of Boston* that later was published by *Blues Unlimited* as a booklet. You could meet these rediscoveries, sit right up close to them, watch them play, and ask them questions.

Son was a bit rusty and Alan helped him get his music back. Al had learned things off the records and would demonstrate it back to Son and refresh his memory about repertoire. It's sometimes been described as "teaching" Son House. I wouldn't call it that. It was more a case of refreshing Son's memory and both encouraging and stimulating him. Son had some severe problems with alcohol and some ambivalence about resuming a blues career. I think he was in a more religious phase of life at the time of his rediscovery. Playing the blues again was probably as much as anything an opportunity to increase his income to buy more alcohol. [*laughs*] He didn't go into it wholeheartedly. At the time of rediscovery he was a bluesman who had fallen on hard times and lost his popularity. He had given it up. He always had a religious impulse that was as strong as his blues impulse, and as he got older the religious impulse became dominant. He had a more or less settled, steady existence—and probably a manageable alcohol problem at the time of rediscovery. This threw a big new factor into his life. I think Dick Waterman, who managed his career, handled it pretty well. In any case, it was great getting to meet Son House.

I didn't really meet Sleepy John and Hammie; I just went to the concert. But I did get to meet and spend a lot of time with John Hurt, Bukka White, Son House, and then Skip James. He was rediscovered and I got to meet him and see him many times and talk with him. I did get to see Sleepy John more as he got back to Boston. Those were the main ones I would see. Fred McDowell came through once and I got to see him.

Out of curiosity, had the Son House Library of Congress sessions been made available on microgroove at that point?

Some had. I believe three or four tracks on a Library of Congress album came out in the early sixties, maybe around '61 or '62. I think Marshall Stearns put it together. The recording information said Robinsonville, Mississippi. That was a huge clue right there.

We also knew from discographies that he had recorded a piece called "Clarksdale Moan," another big clue. So we were certain he was from somewhere in the Delta. There was a whole album of Son's Library of Congress material, but I don't think that had been issued at the time of his rediscovery.

Also, in regard to your conversations with the various rediscoveries, I'm sure you gathered biographical information, and you've said that you would try to generate leads to other bluesmen or women who might still be alive. How much of your conversation centered on tunings?

Sure, we saw what tunings they used, what keys they played in. Of course Alan and I tried to learn the portion of that material that appealed to us the most. It was great. You could get right up close and personal with the artists; you could sit three feet in front of them. Some of them drew a better crowd. Mississippi John Hurt always drew a big crowd, but if you got there at the right time you could draw a front-row seat. I saw Skip James any number of nights. There'd be twenty-five or thirty people there. Skip James didn't seem to generate any crowd at all due to his aloof personality.

Alan was more active interacting in a musical sense. Alan would often play along with these artists. He worked most closely with Son House and recorded some with Son. He was also playing some harp and even a little guitar with Mississippi John Hurt at Café Yana in Boston. Al was very good and almost always played appropriate music. He was kind of in a class by himself. We were both able to pick things up by listening to the records. We both had good ears, especially Al. I was a full-time student, studying Greek and Latin—I had homework—but Al was just out there hoping to be a musician and make money. He really wasn't making much of anything, and his personality—he was kind of a nerd—a very nice guy and a dear friend, but he was struggling socially. But it meant that he had a lot of time on his hands and could put more time into being a musician than I could.

Another musician we got to know was "Babe" Stovall, a much lesser known artist—not a rediscovery, but a good Mississippi blues and folk musician. A young guy named Marc Ryan, who had dropped out of Brown University and moved to New Orleans, met Babe there, in New Orleans, and decided he would use his contacts in the New York–New England folk scene to try to get a tour for Babe. Marc played guitar and would play along with Babe and act as a roadie. He was Babe's "white boy." [*laughs*] So Marc called me up—I was on the folk scene, and he thought I could help get a gig—and they wound up, Marc and Babe, crashing in my dorm room, which was against the rules. I interviewed Babe and learned a lot musically. I can still

Al Wilson with Robert Pete Williams, Malibu, California, July 1966. Photo Marina Bokelman.

do a lot of Babe's stuff; several of his pieces are staples in my repertoire. But he was another guy I interviewed.

Al Wilson with Fred McDowell, Malibu, California, November 1966. Photo Marina Bokelman.

All those interviews bore fruit in publications: Son House through Al Wilson's articles and booklet, Bukka White through a chapter I later co-authored as part of a book on three Tennessee folk singers—I did it with Jack Hurley, a colleague of mine here at the University of Memphis—and Babe Stovall in an article I did for *Blues Unlimited*. So that gave me some writing experience.

I graduated in 1965, and what do you do with a classics degree? Well, you go on to grad school. [*laughs*] But I was so hooked on blues and related folk music—as a musician, a record collector, and a researcher—that that was what I wanted to pursue academically. I guess it's fortunate that Bruce Jackson was at Harvard. I discussed my future plans with him. He had a residency in the same dorm that I was in, so he was very accessible. He told me about the academic field of folklore. At the time there were just three graduate programs in folklore—Pennsylvania and Indiana Universities and UCLA. He'd been to Indiana, and he went through the pros and cons of the three programs in regard to music for me—and suggested UCLA. That seemed attractive, because California seemed attractive anyway to a lot of people; this was 1965, "California Dreaming." It was the "Promised Land," as Chuck Berry put it.

Al was planning a move out there. We didn't move out there together, but we moved there about the same time—in late summer, early fall. I would get started in the fall semester in 1965. I actually still continued a little bit of classics, even taught a first-year Latin course. I got an assistantship in classics the first year and got one in the folklore program after that. So Al went out there trying to be a musician. We even roomed together for several months. He was always broke and couldn't contribute too much to the rent, but he was a friend and we had many discussions and listening sessions about blues—and continued seeing all the same people when they'd make their West Coast swings: Son House, Bukka White, Fred McDowell, Robert Pete Williams.

Skip James stayed with me and Al in the spring of '66. I had a duplex in Venice, California, near Santa Monica. Skip stayed with us for several days. We interviewed him and recorded some pieces, but we never used that material, because other interviews came out. Al was a huge fan of Skip's. Skip was God for Al. Then later, near the end of spring, I moved in with my girlfriend at the time, Marina Bokelman, and Al got some place in

Santa Monica; this is 1966. Then first Fred McDowell and then later Robert Pete Williams stayed with Marina and me, and Al would come over and we had sessions. So we got to see and meet and interact with the cream of the blues revival.

Were the rediscovered bluesmen you met and talked with surprised that white guys were taking an interest in their music?

Yeah, generally they were. They were pleased, of course. They were retired—and on the downside of whatever careers they had. Very few had ever been full-time musicians; perhaps Bukka was for a few years. I don't know if Son was ever a full-time musician. They had been recording artists, and some had played for Southern white audiences, but the Northern white audiences were a different thing. They were seriously interested in their music and wanted to learn it; they didn't just want to be entertained by the local black musician, with all the social implications of that relationship. The young whites were liberal, mostly, and certainly had a different social attitude that the musicians could eat at the same table and sleep at their houses and be treated like royalty. This was a pretty new experience, a bit strange. But they mostly took to it, and it must have changed their attitudes and their outlooks on life and the opportunities that they hadn't anticipated. These were people in their fifties, sixties, if not their seventies, and we were all in our twenties, most of us. I think they all handled that pretty well.

Son House lived in the North quite a while and slipped into that role rather easily. The others all lived in the South, and like Fred McDowell, in the rural South, or like John Hurt, small-town Mississippi. And some probably had not had much contact with whites other than work situations. John Hurt lived in the same town all his life and had friendships in his community and got along well with the white folks, but it was under the regime of Jim Crow. Most probably had only superficial contact with white folks, and then to have people who took them seriously as artists and wanted to know about their lives and their way of life, obviously you respected them greatly. This must have been an extraordinary experience for them as much as for people like myself and Alan. Any number of the blues singers have autobiographies based on interviews, and each seems to include a chapter on their relationship with the newfound white audience. I think in most cases it was almost all positive from a social point of view. I don't think there were too many rip-offs or exploitations business-wise. I believe John Hurt was badly used by Tom Hoskins, although he did live better than he had before his rediscovery. And some of their financial expectations were never realized. I don't think Skip James got as much out of it as he thought he deserved for his artistry. [*laughs*] Although I don't think he was ripped off in any way.

Was Al having any kind of substance abuse problems during this time?

I don't know that it was ever a problem. Of course there are allegations and maybe some evidence that he died of an overdose—possibly accidental, possibly deliberate. Also he'd had a pretty bad car accident shortly before that, and it may have been a brain aneurysm. He used drugs, but mostly he drank a lot of beer. He liked to get high, but that was the thing in the sixties. I'm pretty sure he didn't do hard stuff—heroin—as far as I know. He'd been around and living with some junkies in Cambridge and was disgusted with them. They were stealing from him and things like that. I think he steered clear of that stuff, and cocaine hadn't come in yet, so he didn't have any exposure to that. It was mostly beer, marijuana, and LSD. He wanted to experience highs and psychedelic trips. When it came to marijuana, he had already gotten a hold of some and had some experience with it in Cambridge. I wasn't interested in it and didn't drink too much then. I was a student—I graduated and went onto grad school—and continued to be a student. And then I got a job. I've only had two jobs. [*laughs*] I've been employed all my life. Al lived a much more hand-to-mouth existence. This was California, and marijuana was coming up from Mexico and was readily available. Then LSD was around and Al tripped on that.

At some point—I think it was the fall of 1966—Canned Heat started. We met Bob Hite—you meet people with similar interests; he loved the same kind of music. So Al and Bob and Henry Vestine were forming Canned Heat. Marina and I would go over to Bob's place. She actually made a documentary film as a student project—she was a grad student at UCLA also—on Canned Heat as they were forming in the early days, before they got famous. Bob Hite was always having record-listening parties. He and Henry Vestine were big, big collectors. With the success of Canned Heat, that meant more money—and more rare records in their collections. [*laughs*] Suddenly they became *major* collectors. They were the rivals of Nick Perls and Bernie Klatzko and all these legendary East Coast collectors. You had to have money, even then, to buy the rarities, though the prices would seem ridiculously low by today's standards.

You've talked about your interest—and Al's interest—in prewar blues. Did anybody acknowledge or have an interest in postwar blues?

We were starting to get interested in it—the Chicago sound and postwar country blues. John Lee Hooker, Lightning Hopkins were the main kind of postwar things we were interested in. Now, Bob Hite liked the shouters—guys with jump bands—because he grew up in California, and they have that stuff in L.A. But Al and I were much more country blues. Al liked electric guitars. Way back in the Cambridge days he was into John Lee Hooker electric stuff and Muddy Waters and Howling Wolf, more so than I was at first. I kind of got dragged into the Chicago sound by Al, but it was an acquired taste for me. I was very much a country blues purist. Al was a little more experimental; he was into jazz—I wasn't. He was into Indian music. He was a bit ahead of me in his tastes and his exploration. I was exposed and learned a lot through my friendship with him.

When I was in Cambridge I was learning to play guitar. I didn't have a lot of time, but I got pretty competent, at least looking at who else was playing on the coffeehouse scene. I learned pretty quickly, and Al was a quick learner too. I think we were pretty good. On my last CD I put a couple of pieces with me and Al on there. I think they were pretty damned good considering what the competition was—young white blues players of the sixties. We were trying to sound like Son House, Bukka White, Skip James, and other people like that. This was on the coffeehouse scene. There were very few festivals; you had to be a star to get on the festivals. Coffeehouses were the place to start. You might say the slots were pretty well taken, between the rediscoveries and the discoveries, the authentic older folk artists and your Jim Kweskins and Tom Rush. It was hard to break into that scene, and when you were trying to sound like Sleepy John and others it was even harder. The audiences generally wanted something a bit lighter; maybe if I were doing the John Hurt repertoire or Leadbelly, or had formed a jug band, we might have made it. But when you're playing slide guitar and moaning and groaning like Son House. [*laughs*] And, then again, Son was around and on the circuit and people could see him.

We would play at hootenannies; there were a lot of those. Jim Kweskin ran a hootenanny at Café Yana in Boston, near Fenway Park. Al and I would go there almost every Sunday, and Jim liked our sound and sometimes he would play along with us. So we got some exposure there. We got a few coffeehouse gigs together in places around the Boston area. Transportation was a bit of a problem, getting to these places, because I didn't have a car then and Al didn't drive. Maybe he did later in his life—and had that wreck. His eyesight wasn't very good; he wore thick glasses. He wasn't blind. That was just a blues nickname—the "Blind Owl." [*laughs*] Al got a few gigs shortly before moving to California, in the summer of '65. He got some gigs on his own at a coffeehouse in Cambridge, but the whole student body wasn't there, so there was nobody to see him. He was the opening act for folk acts.

When I got to California we played and I kept my skills up as a musician, but I didn't have that much ambition to have a musical career. By grad school I wanted to get an advanced degree and become a professor and study the music. I had started doing fieldwork. I wanted to write about it. I wanted to research it and play music on the side, both as a way of understanding the music and for the enjoyment. Al, on the other hand, needed to make a living and wanted to be a musician, saw himself primarily as a musician who also knew a lot about the music and who could be a student of it. So he and Bob Hite and the others formed Canned Heat. Their story is well known. By the time Canned Heat got big and was on the road, I didn't see that much of Al. I saw less and less of him, very little in 1968 and 1969. He died in 1970. Al was on the road with Canned Heat, and I hardly saw him at all during the last year of his life. Even before that I saw very little of him, because Canned Heat was on the road so much.

David Evans with Robert Pete Williams, Malibu, California, July 1966. Photo Marina Bokelman.

I was a grad student by this time. I'd gone to UCLA in the fall of 1965, and I was working on a thesis. It had occurred to me while listening to country blues that it was, to a great extent, a type of folk music—there was a tradition. I could hear lyrical, musical similarities in the blues of various artists—especially the Mississippi artists—that seemed to suggest connections, either direct influence from one another or a type of collective participation in some folk tradition. And becoming a student of folklore in the folklore and mythology program at UCLA was an opportunity to investigate this.

Tommy Johnson especially seemed very central to the concept of a blues tradition. His blues in particular seemed very connected; they had lots of similarities to blues of other Mississippi artists, including, of course, Charley Patton and Willie Brown. Meeting Babe Stovall in '64—Babe had known Tommy Johnson briefly and spoke about Roosevelt Holts, who he said had known Tommy better and played more of Tommy's music. So I thought here was a possibility to get an understanding of Tommy Johnson and find further musicians who had known him, learned from him, or interacted with him.

I knew that Tommy was deceased by that time; that seemed to be generally acknowledged by everyone. But he died not too long before, in 1956. So it seemed like there should still be people around who knew him and played like him or learned from him. This was one of my main motivations to look into traditions and connections between blues musicians in an academic sense—and to find, encounter, and document good music. [*laughs*] Not only the tradition of Tommy Johnson, but I heard other traditional elements in music by people like Skip James and Fred McDowell. So it seemed to me perhaps local traditions needed to be investigated, or different blues communities. Skip told me of other musicians in his community in Bentonia. And Fred McDowell told me about other people around Como, Mississippi. So that was my goal: to investigate as many of those traditions as possible. To branch out from a known quantity such as Skip or Fred McDowell or Tommy Johnson and his circle and find more people, more connections.

And this theory is what you refer to as the "Drew school of blues"?

In my book *Big Road Blues*, and to some extent in my book *Tommy Johnson*, it was a book about local styles. There's nothing complex about it. Drew was just the name of a town I fastened on; it could be Dockery's or Cleveland or any nearby town. But the idea was that in the small towns and the rural South, musicians were somewhat localized, performing in a community. They would learn from and interact with one another—they were connected. Of course, one had to take in the factor of phonograph records and their influence in bringing in new styles and repertoires. And some of the musicians were more itinerant than others. Charley Patton made occasional trips to Chicago and Gary and down around New Orleans. Tommy Johnson moved between Crystal Springs and Jackson and then would go to the Delta in the fall. He seems to have learned much of his basic style in the Delta from people like Willie Brown and Charley Patton; there are such strong similarities in style and repertoire. So basically it was the idea of a local style.

I saw another distinctive tradition around Bentonia with Skip James, Jack Owens, and Cornelius Bright—also, most likely, Henry Stuckey. Skip James learned from Stuckey, although Stuckey never recorded. [Gayle Dean] Wardlow did interview him, and he and I went there again in '66, but Henry had just died. Then there were others who performed an occasional song or two, perhaps represented by Jimmy Holmes, who is active now. In fact, I made the first recordings of Jimmy in 1989, I believe. Como and Senatobia seemed to be yet another local style, a local sound. In fact, Como and Senatobia seemed to be an entire folk music scene, and blues is a part of it. One could draw connections between Fred McDowell and Ranie Burnette. But Fred moved into that area; he hadn't been living there all that long. He grew up in West Tennessee and lived around Holly Springs for a number of years, somewhat far from Como and Senatobia. And the styles are quite distinct from one another. The Bentonia sound is quite different from that of Tommy Johnson.

I also had an interest in urban scenes, Jackson in particular. I haven't fully developed it, but I did contribute to the understanding of music in Jackson. Then another scene was in Tylertown, Mississippi, with Babe Stovall and Roosevelt Holts. There you had influences coming in from Tommy Johnson, with Roosevelt Holts especially. Roosevelt had lived up in Jackson for a time and kind of followed Tommy up there.

I think that in my book I exaggerated the isolation or amount of localism of the styles. As I've thought about it more over the years, I now feel that a lot of these artists were more itinerant and more influenced by outside sources—especially records—than I might have estimated at the time. Now, there were some, like Jack Owens, who *were* very local and didn't go out at all. A trip into town was a big trip for Jack. [*laughs*] But others did get around. Even if the idea of a local style is a little bit shaky, I think I did uncover a lot about the process of tradition at the local level. I did establish a folk quality, a traditional side of blues, that it did participate in an oral tradition as well as a popular music of the mass media. I could do something like that for Bentonia, show the connections between Skip James and Jack Owens and others. The sixties and seventies were about the last possible time one could've done that. If only I could have been there in the 1920s and the 1930s. It was a fairly short-lived development in folk song—the blues as folk music in the first half of the twentieth century—and by the sixties and seventies it was becoming vestigial.

I'd gotten my master's degree in '67 and wanted to go for a doctorate. Unfortunately, UCLA didn't have a doctoral program in folklore at the time. It was a kind of interdisciplinary program in any case, but they were planning to establish one. So I continued to take courses with the expectation that they would have the program established, but by the end of the spring quarter in 1969, I had taken all the class work I could at UCLA and I wanted to work and get a job there. Frankly, I was concerned about the draft and the Vietnam War. If you stayed, either as a grad student or working in education, you were draft-deferred. I did take a physical and then they introduced the lottery system. I remember I had a very high number—well up in the two hundreds—which meant I was unlikely to get drafted.

So I got my first real job. It was a teaching job at California State University in Fullerton, out in Orange County about fifty miles southeast from Los Angeles, in the anthropology department as a folklorist, a music specialist—ethnomusicology. I hadn't really been trained in ethnomusicology, though I sort of eased into it [*laughs*] through the study of folk music. The anthropology department was a very free-thinking department. They had a jazz musician on the faculty, Fred Katz, who played jazz cello. [*laughs*] He was sort of a free spirit, and there were several other free spirits in the department. So I guess with my unorthodox background I fit in as well as anybody. We also had quite a crew at UCLA. My professor was D. K. Wilgus, the ballad scholar of an older generation, who was mostly interested in Anglo-American music but included country and western music—and folk music on commercial records—the relationship of folk and popular music. That was a fairly radical interest within folk music. D. K. himself was sort of an ex-radical back in the thirties and a campus leftist at Ohio State. He had made a pilgrimage to Mexico City to visit Leon Trotsky—something that is not well known, but he was rather proud of that. [*laughs*] D. K. encouraged a lot of us folkies.

Generally the folklore academic programs were not encouraging. There were only three of them: Pennsylvania, Indiana, and UCLA. Pennsylvania had Ken Goldstein, who had done a lot of fine work, including blues recording for the Prestige Bluesville label, although he was a ballad scholar also. He was pretty encouraging. Bill Ferris went to Penn for his doctoral work, but Indiana had Richard Dorson, a very eminent folklorist, one who hated folk music and almost forced every folkie in Indiana to study and do a dissertation on something else, like superstitions or folktales. Dorson was something else, a great scholar, but discouraging of folk music. He just didn't like young people with beards and guitars or long hair. [*laughs*] D. K. was my professor. Archie Green was there at the time, a great scholar of labor songs who later published his book *Only a Miner*. He was there in some kind of adjunct capacity.

The John Edwards Memorial Foundation was there, this great record collection that John Edwards, an Australian collector of hillbilly music, had donated. The foundation had also acquired a great blues 78 stash from Peter Tamony. He was an amateur scholar of language who bought up all these old Columbia and OKeh store stocks of blues records in order to study the dialect usage. He transcribed the lyrics and then had no use for the records anymore [*laughs*] and gave them to UCLA. There was this treasure trove of old 78s there. The students included myself, Marina Bokelman, and John Fahey, who got the first MA degree in folklore from the program a little bit before I did. I think I got the second.

Since you invoke his name, was Fahey any influence in your interest in Patton?

Not really. That probably came through Alan Wilson. As I said, Al tended to be a little bit ahead of me in discovering things and would often lead me to things. Al knew John better. John was coming to the Boston-Cambridge area, and I think I may have met him there once or twice before coming to California, but Fahey was more or less settled in the L.A. area, a grad student at UCLA also. Al helped him a lot in transcribing his music. Al had good ears and a very good understanding of rhythm, pitch, and so on. I learned a lot about transcribing and analyzing music from Al. Fahey was also there pursuing his performing career—and recording. I didn't know Fahey all that well; he was a pretty strange guy. We had common interests in the music, but his personality was certainly different than mine. Another person there was Barry Hansen, who later became Dr. Demento. He's still around in the L.A. area.

John and Barry and Al and I went out to John's girlfriend's birthday party in San Bernardino, at which John got drunk and proceeded to beat her up. We had to drive John home and he was puking out the window. I was the only one who could drive. Barry had a motor scooter, Al couldn't drive [*laughs*], so I was the designated driver for the "Great San Bernardino Birthday Party," which became the title for one of John's better-known pieces. That's the story behind the "Great San Bernardino Birthday Party."

John came along when we found Rubin Lacey—John, Al, and me—maybe Barry too—we were all kind of associates. But I didn't stay around John much and didn't follow his performing career. If we saw anybody it would be Skip James or Big Joe Williams at the Ash Grove. Al was not a student, but he was around a lot. Barry Hansen, Al, John—and Pete Welding came and entered the program. He never did get his degree; he decided that academia was not for him. He liked a more freewheeling writing style. He was a good researcher, and he brought Testament Records with him. I helped him with some recording sessions, a little bit with Johnny Shines and more so with Fred McDowell—an album of Fred's on Milestone. Fred came out there around '68. I explored Fred's older repertoire, the stuff he had learned in his earliest years, when he was living in Tennessee—in Rossville—a lot of it without bottleneck. I got him to resuscitate a lot of that music. So the Milestone album of Fred's is somewhat different in sound and orientation than the usual Fred McDowell record, another dimension of Fred. You'll see my name somewhere in the credits, and I was the guy who stimulated Fred to pull a lot of that material out of his memory.

Another study I did was in formulaic lyrics. This was something that I recognized very early in my listening to blues. When I was at Harvard—you know, I told you I was a classics major in Latin and Greek—one of my professors was Albert Lord, who had done fieldwork in epic singers in Yugoslavia back in the 1930s. He had just published his book *A Singer of Tales,* in which he explicated the so-called oral formulaic theory. He and his mentor Milman Parry had developed this theory of how epic songs were composed. I took a couple of courses from Albert Lord and got to understand that theory, which also applied to ancient Greek epics—to Homer, the *Iliad,* and the *Odyssey*—which I had studied. I heard something similar in blues, just through the recordings. So that was one of the ideas I applied to the study of blues in my fieldwork: applying Lord's methodology, rerecording people on different occasions, singers who knew one another, learned from one another. That was a great inspiration to me. I tried not to apply that theory too literally, because blues is very different from oral epics. And of course the culture is very different as well. And, in fact, when *Big Road Blues* was published, Lord was a reader and wrote a very nice blurb on the dust jacket. I was proud of that—he was a very, very eminent scholar.

As I mentioned earlier, UCLA didn't have a doctoral program. I took enough coursework for a doctorate, but there were no more courses for me to take, so I had to get a job at Cal State Fullerton, expecting that UCLA would establish its PhD program and I could apply all my units to that and write my dissertation. Well, things dragged on and on and on, and the PhD never got set up. But fortunately UCLA did set up an individual studies program, basically a design-your-own-PhD interdisciplinary program. I did that with the help of my professors, and I wrote a dissertation in 1975 and got the degree in early 1976. The dissertation was called "Tradition and Creativity in the Folk Blues," and in a slightly condensed version this became my book *Big Road Blues*. The title of my dissertation became the subtitle of the book *Big Road Blues*. The book wasn't published until 1982; there were some delays at the University of California Press—I don't remember quite why. Then about a year after I got my interdisciplinary degree, UCLA did actually establish a folklore PhD.

Big Road Blues drew upon the Tommy Johnson research but didn't focus on biography so much. I had gathered more biographical information on Tommy Johnson in the years since the *Tommy Johnson* book came out in '71. I continued to go back and interview Mott Willis and Mager Johnson and others, but in *Big Road Blues* I concentrated more on the songs and tradition—basically how the tradition worked, how people used traditional elements, what some called formulas of musical elements and lyrical elements to put those songs together. I took a look at the repertoires of Mager Johnson and Mott Willis, based on my fieldwork, and compared their work to Tommy Johnson and Charley Patton, Willie Brown, and others—and developed that theory of the "Drew tradition." Since that time I've become interested in the individual personalities—some of the great musicians—as I was with Tommy Johnson. I've published some on Charley Patton. I've done some work on Blind Lemon Jefferson. My interests gravitate between the individual and the tradition.

And how did that earlier book, *Tommy Johnson*, happen?

During the 1960s I had been writing articles for *Blues Unlimited* and *Blues World* from my fieldwork and had two albums come out in '68: *Goin' Up the Country* and the Roosevelt Holts album [*Presenting the Country Blues*]. Paul [Oliver] knew of my research on Tommy Johnson. I had corresponded with Paul, and I met him in '68 when Marina and I went to Europe for a blues convention that Simon Napier and Mike Leadbitter [editors of *Blues Unlimited*] organized. Canned Heat happened to be there on tour, so they attended. It was quite a gathering of English and American blues enthusiasts. Nick Perls came over. Bob Groom came down from Cheshire. I'd made connections with a lot of people in Great Britain, and Paul invited me to contribute a book on Tommy Johnson to this series, and we included a record to go with it on the Matchbox/Saydisc label, *The Legacy of Tommy Johnson*. Basically I wrote it up as a reconstructed biography on the life of Tommy Johnson and the musical scene as well as his songs and their influence.

I was teaching at Cal State Fullerton from 1969 until 1978 when I came here to Memphis. In 1978 I was still teaching at Cal State Fullerton. I was in my ninth year then. Out of the blue I got a call from the University of Memphis. They were establishing a PhD program in ethnomusicology—this was in the music department—with a specialization in Southern regional music. We had a musicologist here, Efrim Fruchtman, who played viola da gamba and studied baroque music as a musicologist. His wife was also a musicologist and on the faculty. He wanted a PhD program badly but couldn't get one approved; you have to get approval all the way up to the Tennessee legislature. He figured out a way to get one established by this regional emphasis. Elvis Presley had just died, Stax and Hi record labels had just gone down; and the Memphis scene seemed like it had collapsed, but it generated a lot of attention doing so. There seemed to be this sense that we need to make a preservation effort before all this disappears. So he basically made a proposal for a PhD program, outlined what it would be, and gave it this regional emphasis—the only way he thought he could get it pushed through all the levels of approval. It did, and they needed somebody to run it, to teach the courses, and nobody in that music department had any competency in that area.

I think Efrim was hoping to expand it into his area of musicology once it got established, which in fact we've done, although he's retired and passed away a few months ago. They were thrashing around, trying to recruit somebody to head the program. Robert Palmer, the journalist and blues-rock researcher, had done some guest teaching there, and I had been in correspondence with Palmer. He had broad interests—fife-and-drum music and all kinds of things. He mentioned me as somebody who might be good for this, and they called me and asked me to apply for the position. I did and they interviewed me and one other guy, and I got the job. It seemed like a great move to make. I could build a doctoral program right in the area of this music that I was interested in, an hour from Como and Senatobia. So we moved. By that time I had a wife and two daughters, and we came here in 1978.

Let's talk about your various field trips. To start perhaps we can simply list the year, the locations, and briefly list some of the people.

The major portion of my research for both my thesis and my dissertation was compiled during a series of field trips in the years 1966, '67, '69, '70, '71, '73, '76, '77, and 1978. Remember that before I ever went into the field, I'd gained experience doing interviews with the various prewar bluesmen appearing in the coffeehouse circuit during my undergrad years. Actually, when I think back about it, I'd had an earlier trip—my first trip into the field. This was late summer of '65. I graduated in '65, late spring, early summer, and by the end of summer or early fall I drove across the country—by that time I had a Volkswagen [*laughs*]—to UCLA. I drove by way of New Orleans, and I met Babe Stovall and Marc Ryan. I stayed with Marc for a while and we made a trip with Babe up to Franklinton, Louisiana, where he had spent some time. He was originally from Tylertown, Mississippi, which is in the southern part of Mississippi. Franklinton was just across the state line, in Louisiana, and for some reason many people from Tylertown had moved to Louisiana. Babe's friend Roosevelt Holts lived in Franklinton. He was originally from Tylertown as well.

We recorded a session of Roosevelt; Babe played on a few. There were some other people that came by. It turned out that Roosevelt was the local bootlegger. Franklinton was a dry town. He would drive over to Bogalusa and stock up on alcohol and bring it back to Franklinton. Everyone knew when he was making his runs—at least all the drinkers did. He had just gotten back with a shipment, and all the winos and regular customers converged on his place, and there I was with my little red Volkswagen with Massachusetts plates trying to record him. It turned out to be a big party—a drinking blues party—and some of the customers were musicians too. One of them, L. V. Conerly, was playing; Roosevelt was playing; and his brother, who was kind of a drunk but played good harp, was over there. Roosevelt was a teetotaler. He used to be a big drinker, but he gave it up for medical reasons. He was a hustler, always had been. He was a very good singer and guitarist in a Tommy Johnson/Jackson, Mississippi/Charlie McCoy/Johnny Temple kind of style.

The cops suspected him of bootlegging too, and the local policeman was walking his beat outside Roosevelt's house. I have no idea why he didn't come to the house to investigate, because there was this strange Volkswagen car from Massachusetts there. This was 1965 and Franklinton was a real Southern town [*laughs*]; everyone drove a pickup with a shotgun on a rack in the rear window. The cop was out there and Roosevelt saw him out the window, grabbed his shotgun, and pointed it at the cop. He kept him in the sights of his gun while the cop walked his beat. For some reason he didn't come to the house. It was sort of scary. It might have been the beginning and the end of my fieldwork career. [*laughs*] That was the first session.

Later that same trip Marc and I drove up to Crystal Springs, Mississippi. Roosevelt suspected that Tommy Johnson's brother Mager was still living up there, and he was, sure enough. So we met him and talked with him. We also met Ishman Bracey in Jackson. We had learned through reports by Gayle Wardlow in *Blues Unlimited* that he still was living there. So I think we just found him in the phone book and went to talk to him. We didn't record or interview either of them. The only recording I did was the Roosevelt Holts session, and that was all music, hardly any interview, because it was so chaotic, though we got good recordings there. Some of them have been issued.

What kind of equipment were you using to record?

Back then I had a Realistic reel-to-reel model from Radio Shack. Radio Shack was something new at the time, and Realistic was their store brand. But I had a good mic, an Electrovoice. I still have the microphone. I used it to record myself with Alan Wilson. I found a couple of tracks from 1964. It was a pretty good mic for back then, and I got decent recordings of Roosevelt. Mono, of course—stereo was unheard of then, although Alan Lomax had recorded in stereo as early as 1959, but I think that was a machine he got from Atlantic Records.

Anyway, I went on to UCLA, and Al and I in the spring of 1966 interviewed Skip James and recorded him out there. We did just a little bit of Fred McDowell when he stayed with me and Marina, not much. We did a lot with Robert Pete Williams in '66—that was great stuff. Al participated in those interviews and wrote a series of articles about Robert Pete in *Little Sandy Review*. Harry Oster's Robert Pete recordings had been issued, and we knew about his work. And Alan had some contact with Harry; Al transcribed some music for him. He could read music and had a very good ear, and Harry paid him to transcribe some stuff. It was good income for Al, though I don't know why Harry wanted obscure material like Emmanuel Dunn transcribed. But we knew of Robert Pete and were huge admirers of his, especially Al, who thought Robert Pete was right up there with Skip in seventh heaven. [*laughs*]

Marina Bokelman, Malibu, California, July 1966. Photo David Evans.

Robert was paroled in '65 or '66 for some brief appearances, and then he had to come back. He was actually paroled to a farmer or a plantation owner—he worked for a white farmer—but his ability to go out of state to perform was limited. It was kind of a halfway house system. It was convict labor, a vestige of the Jim Crow system, but it gave him some limited freedom. I think he got his full freedom in 1965 or 1966, and it could be that his tour to California was his first real extended time out of Louisiana. He was amazed at the mountains. He rode the bus out there; he'd never seen the ocean. He was probably the most isolated artist to come on the scene, in terms of experience in the world and white people. I think most of his interactions with white people had been pretty negative, or superficial at best, up until then. He was illiterate. He came a mighty long way. I thought a lot of Robert Pete. He served a sentence for murder. Whether it was self-defense or not I can't say, but he was really an example of the possibilities of rehabilitation. He really made something out of his life. As a musician he was a true original; plus he started up a salvage business with his children—iron and metal—and managed to have a productive life and left a great legacy.

Going back to the South, that started in the late summer of '66. I did a field trip with Marina Bokelman. We just self-financed. There were no grants; we didn't know what a grant was. [*laughs*] I'd had an assistantship there and I saved a little money. We drove in the Volkswagen back across the desert on Route 66, back to Louisiana first. We stayed with Robert Pete and his family. That was pretty amazing; they made us welcome at their house. He was living in Baton Rouge, kind of on the outskirts but still an urban setting. He had about seven or eight kids—a lot of children—and they lived very close to the bone. We recorded him and he took us around to people that he knew: Isaiah Chatman; he was a friend and neighbor of Pete's who was more modern. He played with, I believe it was Lonesome Sundown, in that Excello style. Also Sally Dotson; she'd been a former girlfriend of Robert Pete's—and Robert Pete's sister; she played a little piano. Also Robert Jenkins. Some of these were people that Harry Oster recorded. Pete took us around and we were in his world. There were no white folks around, and I'm sure they wouldn't have approved of it.

Then we went on to New Orleans. Babe Stovall from Tylertown took us around to some of his friends who had also moved to New Orleans: O. D. Jones and Dink Brister. I recorded them as kind of a string band. Then we saw Roosevelt Holts again; we saw Babe's older brother, Myrt Holmes, and recorded Roosevelt. Then we went up to Jackson, Mississippi, and then to Mager Johnson, Tommy Johnson's brother, to record and interview him. We interviewed Ishman Bracey. We couldn't record him; he wanted fifty dollars a song—the same thing he'd gotten in 1928 from Victor Records. That was way out of our league financially [*laughs*], but he was willing to be interviewed for a much smaller compensation. We interviewed H. C. Spier with Gayle Wardlow. Spier lived in Pearl City, just across the river from Jackson. I found Johnny Temple and interviewed him. I didn't do much recording in Jackson except for Ishman Bracey. And then we found Tommy Johnson's other brother, LeDell Johnson, and recorded an interview with him and a few songs, mostly sanctified tunes. He was a preacher by that time.

Then we went on to Bentonia. When Skip James stayed with Al and me earlier in '66, in the spring, he told us about Cornelius Bright, who lived right there in town. We found him just asking around and recorded him. And Cornelius told us about Jack Owens, this older guy that lived out in the country. So the next night Cornelius took us out there to Jack's and we recorded him. That was a major discovery of mine. I revisited Jack many times up until his death in the mid-nineties. I had almost a thirty-year relationship with Jack, and with Bud Spires, who played harmonica with Jack. Bud was the son of bluesman "Big Boy" Spires, who had abandoned Bud and his mother and went on to Chicago many years earlier. Bud was going blind, sort of an industrial accident. He'd been hauling farm chemicals which got into his eyes, and he was starting to go blind, so he took up the harp to play with Jack. He always liked Jack's music and hung around with him. Jack encouraged him and wanted to help him out in his condition and bought him harps. And Bud just developed a sound compatible with Jack's playing; that was pretty much the extent of Bud's playing.

From there we went back to Tylertown and found Herb Quinn, a great old string band musician, and Isaac Youngblood, and then back to New Orleans, where we recorded Arzo Youngblood. These are relatives of Tommy Johnson; they played in that style. "Boogie Bill" Webb lived next door to Arzo and he heard music and came over, so I guess you could say I rediscovered Boogie Bill Webb. [*laughs*] Those were the highlights of our trip in 1966. I don't believe I've left anyone out.

In 1967 I planned another trip. I learned in 1966 from LeDell Johnson that Tommy had interacted with Charley Patton and Willie Brown and had been up in the Delta around Drew and Dockery's. I wanted to go up in the Delta. I hadn't really spent any time in the Delta in 1966; I just didn't have the time. I had a few leads, a few names, and Marina and I went first to Cleveland, Mississippi. I have to say that the Delta work was not as productive; the '67 trip was not nearly as productive as the '66 trip. Basically I couldn't really find anybody around Drew and Cleveland who was still playing music. I did talk to one guy in Cleveland that was highly recommended—I've forgotten his name. He was very reluctant to play. He said he was rusty and had all kinds of excuses, even though everybody said he was great. I think he was just suspicious.

This was still the 1960s, and even though the Civil Rights and Voting Rights Acts had been passed, there was still a lot of fear and suspicion, especially among the older generation. Usually we were able to overcome it, but not always. People were just hard to find in the Delta. Everybody had moved around. Sharecropping had pretty much come to an end, and all the old people had been thrown off the plantations because their labor just wasn't needed anymore. They moved and nobody had telephones. It was just very hard to find people in the Delta.

We came back to Crystal Springs, and I did find Mott Willis, a second cousin of Tommy Johnson's. He was a little bit older than Tommy and a wonderful musician, who also gave a lot of information as well as recorded music. I would say he was the best discovery of 1967, and I revisited him a number of times in subsequent years. Also in Crystal Springs we found Houston Stackhouse. George Mitchell had recorded Stackhouse just a few days earlier. I forgot to mention that I had gotten to know George Mitchell in between the field trips in 1966 and 1967. I had a lot of leads that I thought of exploring in '67, but I knew my time was somewhat limited. So George and his wife, Kathy, were planning a trip to Mississippi, basically to find blues singers and record them. I don't think it had any particular focus beyond that, just to find good music. He was planning the book which became *Blow My Blues Away,* a series of interviews. George asked me for leads and I gave him a number of names, especially from Fred McDowell. I didn't think I was going to have time in '67 to go to Como. Fred had told me about Othar Turner and others, and I told George, and I also told him about Houston Stackhouse, who many people had told me about and who I had intended to find. George followed up on several of those leads, and he was the first to record Othar Turner and through Othar found R. L. Burnside and any number of great people. George had a very productive field trip in 1967.

Houston Stackhouse was in Crystal Springs. I went back there to visit Mager Johnson and he told me Stackhouse was there. As it turned out, George had recorded Stack in Helena with Robert Nighthawk, just a few days before. I then recorded Stackhouse with Ditty Mason, who was a local musician there in Crystal Springs, and a local bass player, Willis Kinebrew, and some with Mager; they were at Mager's house. That was a nice session, and Stackhouse told me about various musicians he'd been associated with—Tommy Johnson and Robert Johnson. I really didn't get to do much of an interview with him, but fortunately others, like Jim O'Neal, later interviewed Stackhouse extensively. The session I recorded was a bit tense in the sense that somebody in the neighborhood that they all knew had died recently and the funeral was that day. They were a little reluctant to play blues on the day of his funeral. So it was sort of a low-key session.

I'm proud to have been one of the first to record Stackhouse. Parts of that session were issued on the Wolf label. Besides Mott Willis and Stackhouse, the best man I did record was a gospel artist up in the Delta, a man named Robert Johnson. He was a former bluesman who had been known as Robert Nighthawk. He was neither *the* Robert Johnson nor *the* Robert Nighthawk, but he was a very good singer and musician in his own right. I recorded him in Skeene, Mississippi. He was still sharecropping and had a large family. He had formerly been a blues singer, had known Charley Patton; he was one of Charley's young acolytes. I told George Mitchell about him, and George later recorded Robert Johnson. I believe it may have been later that same year.

I wanted to mention that we went up around Robinsonville. I wanted to see Fiddling Joe Martin. I had interviewed Jake Martin, the musician of Charley Patton's generation.

He was living in Mound Bayou, and he told me he was kin to Fiddling Joe Martin, a name that I knew from the Son House Library of Congress recordings. I believe Dick Waterman, Phil Spiro, and Nick Perls had interviewed Fiddling Joe when they were looking for Son House. I thought Fiddling Joe was somebody I should interview, and he was living up in Robinsonville. We went up there and he was playing with Woodrow Adams at the time.

I did a nice session with Woodrow Adams, my first experience with electric blues and recording a band. I had a mono Nagra tape recorder that I had borrowed from UCLA. So I tried to record a whole band with one microphone. [*laughs*] Well, it was only a three-piece band: Fiddling Joe on drums, Woodrow on either harmonica or electric guitar and vocals, and a younger nephew of Woodrow's playing bass lines on a guitar. It was very primitive electric Delta blues music. This was at Woodrow's house, and his wife was pregnant and about a day from giving birth, and she was groaning in the next room while we were playing blues. There were liberal quantities of moonshine there. Fiddling Joe got roaring drunk and fell over into the drum set. [*laughs*] It was quite a session. We made some good recordings there. We also interviewed Fiddling Joe and Woodrow as well. I was able to write little profiles of them in *Blues World*—or *Blues Unlimited.*

After that I believe we went back down through Tylertown. I was revisiting people. That was one of my purposes: to record people on different occasions. I was studying the traditions, how blues were learned and created in a traditional environment. I wanted to study variation—not only find musicians that had learned from one another and interacted with one another to compare their versions of songs but also the same performer on different occasions to see if he would vary songs.

After you had recorded these guys, were they interested in hearing themselves?

Oh, yeah, and I always had headphones and did a lot of playback. Most of the machines at that time had built-in speakers, and everybody would crowd around—relatives and friends. In 1965 I had the Realistic recorder from Radio Shack. Then in 1966 I used a Wollensak. It was built like a tank [*laughs*], solid and rugged. But I used good microphones, and then in '67 I graduated to a Nagra. These were things I borrowed from the UCLA folklore program in '66 and '67. Then I was writing my master's thesis in '67 and got my master's degree. It was called "The Blues of Tommy Johnson: A Study of a Tradition." There I laid out what biographical information I had accumulated on Tommy by that time and my ideas about how the blues tradition worked, a kind of tradition in which he was the central figure and how his work related to the work of all these people, including his brother, Mager.

In 1968 I didn't make a field trip. Marina and I went to Europe, just as tourists, to drive around Europe and Morocco in a Volkswagen. Then in March of '69 I made a short trip to the South from California by myself. I had acquired my own recording machine, an Ampex. It looked like a suitcase [*laughs*]—and a single microphone for it. I had some problems with it; it had a slightly wobbly, echoic sound to it. The recordings were quite listenable and usable; some of these have been released, but I wasn't entirely happy with them. It was a fairly short trip. I think the first place I started out was Helena. I interviewed Peck Curtis there; I think Stackhouse had given me his address. I got a long interview from him. It didn't have much to do with Tommy Johnson, but he knew a lot of blues artists and I ran a lot of names by him. I got a lot of interesting information from somebody who knew Stackhouse and Sonny Boy II. It was more modern blues than I was usually interested in, but I'm glad I did the interview.

Then I went on to Memphis and stayed with Furry Lewis for two or three nights in his apartment on Fourth and Beale. That was an experience too. He recorded and we got a very nice session and interviewed him. That interview I transcribed. Meanwhile I came into communication with Bengt Olsson. I don't remember how I met him. He was in and out of Memphis. Perhaps we met through correspondence. He had been doing research in Memphis and by 1970 was writing this book for Paul Oliver and Tony Russell's series of blues paperbacks, which included my own *Tommy Johnson*. Bengt, for some reason, had not interviewed Furry Lewis and asked if I had. As I said, I had interviewed Furry, and Bengt asked if he could use it. I gave him permission and sent him the transcription. He just published it as his Furry Lewis chapter without any acknowledgment. [*laughs*] So that whole chapter in his book is my work. I stayed with Furry right there on Beale Street.

Beale Street was at the end of its tenure as a major musical and cultural center of black Memphis; in fact, much of it was torn down shortly after 1969. But you could still get a sense of what it had been. I guess I didn't know it at the time, but every other fan and researcher in the country—and the world—[*laughs*] had also visited Furry Lewis or was visiting about that time, staying with him a night or two and recording a session. Many sessions from around 1968 or '69 seem to have been issued. My material hadn't been issued except for one gospel track, but I've got some very nice recordings of Furry. He was in good form back then. All of his other buddies—Will Shade and all—had just died, so Furry was the only one left. I believe I had inquired about Gus Cannon but never could run him down. I really regret that, because Gus never was adequately interviewed, in my opinion.

Although I live here now, I never did spend much time in Memphis in my early fieldwork. I did go to Memphis briefly in '67 to find and interview Dink Bankston, another musician in the Charley Patton/Tommy Johnson circle. Gayle Wardlow had also interviewed Bankston. It was LeDell Johnson who told me about him, and Gayle followed up with LeDell and also got the name of Dink Bankston. I believe that Gayle got to Bankston first. There were no recordings of Bankston, to the best of my knowledge. He was through with playing and not in particularly good health. I think we both interviewed him in '67, and I believe he didn't last too much longer. Both interviews were rather cursory but still valuable. He was born near Crystal Springs but moved to the Delta and finally to Memphis.

It was hard to find people in that tradition. There were real problems in the Delta with people moving around and nobody having addresses and not yet being able to afford telephones—you couldn't find anybody. The old system had fallen apart, and a new social network hadn't emerged yet. Add the residue of fear and suspicion from the old days, and that made it very frustrating to do fieldwork in the Delta in the 1960s. The Delta had always been an area in flux; people had always moved around a lot. People came in there to work and moved on. It was all exaggerated around 1967, '68, '69.

Anyway, I finally got to Fred McDowell in 1969. I went to Como. I'd heard George Mitchell's recordings from that area in '67; the fife-and-drum tradition was still thriving. As far as traditional music went, that was the mother lode. I think Alan Lomax had recognized that already on his '59 trip, following up on the earlier recordings of Sid Hemphill he had done in '42. Then Alan traced Sid again in '59 and through him found Fred McDowell, the Pratchers, the Young brothers, and so on. We knew through Fred McDowell that a lot of that was still around. George happened into it in '67 and found R. L. Burnside. But George didn't seem to be doing anything further with it. In 1969 I had hoped to record Joe Callicott. I had heard through the grapevine—again through Gayle Wardlow's research—that Joe was around Nesbit. Unfortunately, Joe had died a little bit earlier. So I went to Como and visited Fred, who was gracious as always.

Fred had stayed with Marina and me back in 1966, and I had seen him on tour a few times since then, so we had stayed in touch. Fred took me out to Othar Turner's. We met Napoleon Strickland. George had recorded Napoleon playing fife; I don't know if he recorded anything more of Napoleon. It turned out Napoleon played very good harmonica plus pretty good guitar. He was sort of a Fred McDowell disciple. He wasn't as good as Fred, but still he was good. And he played this one-string instrument that I had heard about from those recordings of Eddie "One-String" Jones. So I recorded him on that. We built one on the wall of Othar Turner's house. It was March of 1969 and there were no picnics, but I recorded a bit of fife-and-drum music indoors at Othar's house—Napoleon playing fife and Othar playing snare drum; I forgot who played bass drum—and I interviewed them.

Then they told me about Ranie Burnette, a guitar player/singer who lived in Senatobia and who had long played in the area. I visited him; he lived in town. I did a long recording session with him and recorded him in subsequent years as well. He was very good in something of a Fred McDowell style, simpler, in what's often called "hill country." I have a lot of recordings of Ranie. Only a few of them have been issued; in fact, I recorded him for the High Water label when I came to the University of Memphis. We did two tracks on High Water—"Hungry Spell" and "Coal Black Mattie"—and then I put "Shake 'Em on Down" on an album for the Library of Congress that I did and Rounder later reissued as a

Napoleon Strickland, R. L. Burnside, Abe Young, David Evans. Senatobia, Mississippi. c.1980. Photo Cheryl Thurber.

CD: *Afro-American Folk Music from Tate and Panola Counties, Mississippi*—world's longest album title! [*laughs*]

Ranie was really good. I later tried to promote him on the circuit, but he was already, even at that time, easing into retirement from music, or at least out of blues. He was a church guy and he joined the Masons—in an effort to be a more upstanding individual, as opposed to a blues guy. [*laughs*] He was married and had a nice house in the Senatobia area. I did get him a few gigs, including an overseas tour in 1980, also a tour of Minnesota and North Dakota. Arne Brogger, who used to work with Steve LaVere promoting the Memphis Blues Caravan, got Ranie up there. But Ranie wasn't comfortable in that setting with those kinds of audiences. I think he was used to being background music in a rowdy juke setting, where people just wanted a beat. He wasn't used to a concert setting with people listening silently to him. And then he didn't want to play blues on Sunday either.

Also in 1969 I went to Bogalusa and saw Roosevelt Holts and stayed with him for a few nights—the second convicted murderer that I stayed with. [*laughs*] Roosevelt had settled in Bogalusa; he had a sister who lived there. I recorded him and he took me around to some of his friends: "Blind Pete" Burrell, a gospel singer and guitarist, who's still living, I believe! Blind Pete was very, very good. I issued several tracks of his. I also saw Esau Weary, about the only pianist I ever recorded. I just didn't run into many. In the rural South there just weren't many homes with pianos. Esau was in that old-time sawmill, lumber camp tradition of Louisiana. Bogalusa was a big sawmill town. Esau lived a little bit out from there in a place called Angie. We had a hard time finding a piano. Some lady that Roosevelt knew—a middle-class, proper lady, a schoolteacher—had a piano there. Roosevelt was a bit of a rough character, but somehow he convinced her to let us use her piano to record with. We only did four pieces, including one with guitar. He played guitar as well. I don't think there was anything more in '69. It was a fairly short trip.

Then in 1970 I took another field trip on my own. By that time my department at Cal State Fullerton, where I had started teaching, had acquired a Sony 770—a stereo tape recorder—and I borrowed a couple of good microphones from Pete Welding. This was my first experience in stereo . . .

Nothing like the sound of a single guitar player in stereo!

Well, one mic on the guitar, another on the voice. We were coming up in the world. I pretty much covered old haunts. I wanted to explore more in the Como/Senatobia area. I was quite excited by what I found there in '69 and what George Mitchell and others had found. So I went back, and I don't know that I found anyone new that year in that area, but I did record some of the same people: Ranie Barnette, Othar Turner, and Napoleon Strickland.

I also went out in '71, '73, '76. Those were the main trips. I saw Jack Owens again. I had seen him in '69 and then again in '70. Also Mager Johnson and Mott Willis again; I believe it was '71 I saw Mott Willis. I saw Roosevelt Holts again in '70. I recorded his neighbor, Eli Owens. He had sort of a folk style, very gentle finger-picking and singing, with a very large repertoire. I wish I had worked more with Eli. I visited and recorded him on three different trips. He was an artist with good potential and in fact did make many recordings, of which only a handful have been issued. I don't believe anyone else ever recorded Eli. He played the guitar and a bit of harmonica—and a mouth bow, which may have been the first recordings of an African American mouth bow in the United States. He also could play pan pipes; they actually were a set of tuned whistles. He didn't have a set of pipes, and he tried to make a set just to show me what they looked like, but the cane was green. I did get a mouth bow from him. His hands were occasionally a bit arthritic; it sometimes affected his guitar playing. He used to rub them with alcohol a lot just to be able to play guitar.

In '71 I got married and went with my wife, Cheryl—she's now Cheryl Thurber, which was her maiden name—on trips in 1971 and 1973 and later. I did a lot of work around Como and Senatobia. We stayed with Othar Turner and his family. I did a lot of recording of fife-and-drum music. I made some recordings of Jessie Mae Hemphill in '73, but her guitar and amp had problems, and her repertoire was undeveloped at that time. I met Jessie through George Mitchell. He recommended her; he had interviewed her. He thought she had a lot of potential. He had heard fragments of her playing on guitar but never recorded her. There's a chapter on her in his book. There also was Compton Jones, who played a one-string instrument and would beat on a washtub and whistle, sort of simulating a fife-and-drum band. Much of his music stayed on a level similar to children's music, but he had carried it into adulthood and was teaching his music to his children and other neighborhood children. He was an interesting person to record. I would revisit Ranie Burnette and record fife-and-drum music at picnics there in the summertime.

I started recording gospel music and preachers. I had developed the idea to record folk music in a black community in the area around Como and Senatobia just to survey the entire range of music—the blues, fife-and-drum music, church songs, gospel quartets, and so on. So I began recording sermons, congregations, choirs, and gospel quartets as well, there in the area. I didn't find anymore good blues singers. I did do a brief session with R. L. Burnside in 1973. He was playing at Othar Turner's picnic. It was mostly instrumentals. He was there in the afternoon and there weren't many people around, because it was so hot. He and a drummer were playing. It wasn't a stellar R. L. session by any means, but I met him, and later, after I moved here to Memphis, I would see a lot of him and record him. He'd recorded for George Mitchell and the Adelphi label and was getting around on the scene. I didn't find any other major blues artists around there. I recorded Ranie Burnette, Napoleon Strickland, extensively. Fred McDowell was already well recorded, and then he passed away in '71. So I concentrated on the folk music in that community, but I haven't really done a lot with that material. Seventy-three was pretty much revisiting people, including Jack Owens, Roosevelt Holts; I believe Herb Quinn was still living. I also revisited Mager Johnson and definitely saw Mott Willis.

In 1973 my father retired from working for the Prudential Insurance Company after many years. My parents lived in the Boston area and wanted to get away from the snow. They thought about retiring to Portugal, but that didn't work out well, and so they retired to Savannah, Georgia, because it was like Boston—an old colonial city. [*laughs*] They had time on their hands and asked me if there was anything they could do to help my research. I knew Blind Willie McTell had some connection to Statesboro, Georgia, which is not far from Savannah. So I suggested they start asking around about Blind Willie McTell and see what they could find. I had been able to reconstruct something of Tommy Johnson's life and thought maybe something similar could be done for McTell. Very little was known about him. So they did, and amazingly—this was around 1975—they took it seriously, particularly my mother, who's still living. They found any number of people who knew McTell, some around Savannah and Statesboro, and they found old friends of his and eventually found his half-brother, Robert Owens. They also found some cousins of his up around Thomson, Georgia, and eventually Kate McTell, his former wife, living in Wrens, Georgia. They interviewed all of them and got a treasure trove of information about McTell. Cheryl and I would visit those people from time to time, driving all the way from California in '76.

I did follow-up interviews with many of the people my parents had found. My mother recorded all these interviews on a little cassette recorder, and she knew next to nothing about blues, but she had very good instincts and knew which questions to ask. I had briefed her about McTell and sent her cassettes of his music. So she had some background, but it was mostly dogged persistence in following up leads. I never could find any musician that played like McTell. In fact, I don't think there really were any. Nobody sounded quite like him. There is nobody else.

Buddy Moss was around in Atlanta but wasn't too welcoming. He'd been in prison in the 1930s, and it killed his career. He was very suspicious, rather embittered. I did meet him but never did an interview with Buddy Moss. We did all this follow-up interviewing about Blind Willie McTell, which eventually became extensive booklet notes for the John Edwards Memorial Foundation album that received a Grammy nomination. Bruce Bastin and I put that together—Bruce doing Buddy Moss, and Curley Weaver and I did the McTell portion.

Unfortunately, my father passed away later in 1976, so I flew to Savannah at the time. I received a lead—from Pete Lowry, I believe—for "Blind Log," an associate of McTell's. Unfortunately, Log had suffered a stroke and could no longer play guitar, but he was in otherwise good shape. While I was there I interviewed Blind Log and got a lot more information about McTell. These were trying circumstances for me, since my father had just passed away unexpectedly of a massive heart attack.

Then the following year George Mitchell, who lived in Atlanta, had been putting on a festival in Georgia, a folk festival. He'd gotten a grant to do research to find folk artists in Georgia—or to hire somebody to do it. So George hired me, which was great [*laughs*], because it became an opportunity to visit my mother and get a little income from it. We tried to do some recording in Savannah. My mother had found a few musicians in Savannah. She did other things besides McTell; she did other folklore—traditions and folktales and so on—mostly just as a hobby, something to do but which might help me as well. She had developed a few leads, but we never did find any artist that was outstanding. One, Embry Raines appeared at the festival. We found a white guy there that played a tenor banjo, Buck Lanier. And we found a guy in Porthole, Georgia—it's a little town near Statesboro—Ira Coney, "Tiny" Coney they called him. He was a younger blues singer/guitarist; by that I mean in his forties. He had known McTell slightly. McTell was more of his father's generation, who had been a musician as well. Tiny played gospel on Sundays and blues during the week, in a somewhat more modern style, though he had some solo material; he even had some Bahamian music. He worked on the docks in Savannah with some guys from the Bahamas. He had an interesting repertoire that he didn't do much anymore, but he could still recall it. Those were people we found, and I reinterviewed Kate McTell in Thomson but again couldn't find any musicians that amounted to anything around there. So for the investment of the grant money in terms of finding musicians, I wasn't entirely satisfied.

Of the various artists and sessions you recorded during your fieldwork, what has been issued on record or CD?

I've had several albums of my field recordings issued. The first one was on British Decca, later on Rounder, called *Goin' Up the Country*. That was in 1968. And then later that same year I had one by Roosevelt Holts on Blue Horizon, Mike Vernon's label in Great Britain. And then through knowing Pete Welding I did some on the Testament label—a fife-and-drum album, a Jack Owens album in 1970 or '71. I did one for Chris Strachwitz on Arhoolie—*Roosevelt Holts and Friends*—one of his lesser-known albums but very nice. I'd gotten to know Frank Scott and did an album for his Advent label, a gospel album called *Sorrow Come Pass Me Around*. I was supposed to have a record to go with my book *Big Road Blues*, but Frank closed the label down before that could come out. I did two other records for British companies—one called *The Legacy of Tommy Johnson* that accompanied my book *Tommy Johnson*. It was on the Matchbox label, a very rare album now. I did one called *High Water Blues* for Bruce Bastin's label Flyright. I also did a Houston Stackhouse record on Roots—that was later in the seventies—and one for the Library of Congress, but that was somewhat later too. It came out around the time I moved to Memphis in the late seventies and then later was reissued on the Rounder label on CD.

So I had done a number of albums of field recordings and had the idea to set up a label through my university. I never wanted to run a record label myself. I had one very bad experience. In 1969 Roosevelt Holts kept bugging me to put out a 45 by him. He wanted something on the jukebox; he thought he was going to be a star again. And he was really good. He had started playing electric by that time; he had a solid-body guitar and a little amp. He knew Boogie Bill Webb from years before, and I had rediscovered Boogie Bill in '66 when Bill wandered into his next-door neighbor Arzo Youngblood's recording session. So I reunited them; they hadn't seen each other since the 1940s. This was in New Orleans, and there was this teenage drummer that Bill knew. He was about fifteen years old, so we got him and we recorded them together—a whole band, two electric guitars and drums. And we got some nice stuff, a version of *Big Road Blues* and a slide guitar piece by Roosevelt in an early Muddy Waters style. So I took these two tracks from the session and got a 45 pressed on the Blues Man label—Blues Man number 100. I thought this thing could make some money and satisfy Roosevelt; he might have some kind of career.

So I sent a couple of boxes to Roosevelt. He was living in Bogalusa, and he took it up around Tylertown, where he had a lot of friends. Well, he had spent some time in Parchman in the 1930s for murder, and so as far as the Mississippi authorities were concerned, he was an ex-con. So he was selling his record to his friends. And Roosevelt had kind of a big mouth—he used to brag a lot about himself—and the cops got word that he was around selling records, and they arrested him for selling without a retail license, some BS charge. And they put him in some horrible jail out from Tylertown. It was like some medieval cell or something, a tiny little room with bars on it. They confiscated his car and fined him five hundred dollars to get out and get his car back. I got a phone call from his sister in Bogalusa: "Roosevelt's in jail. What can you do to help him?" I was still a student at that time and didn't have a decent salary; putting out the record had been a labor of love. I thought maybe it would make some money. So I sent some money, then tried to raise some money and did a petition, and his family got some money together. Somehow he got out, but that was a disaster and scared me away from ever wanting to own a record company.

Of course, I saw all the financial problems Pete Welding had; Testament was a labor of love as well. Now, I'm in Memphis in '78, and I thought if the university could set up a record company, well, that would be fine [*laughs*]—put out records with other people's money. [*laughs*] My dean was very sympathetic to that idea; he wanted to see this degree program take off. So we got High Water Records set up as a division of the university, which of course is the state of Tennessee, and two affiliated publishing companies: Music River Publishing Company with BMI and Mississippi River Music Publishing Company with ASCAP. We called the label High Water, calling up the Patton connection; also connecting to the Mississippi River and at the same time invoking the term for the mark of excellence.

Then I got a grant from the National Endowment for the Arts. It was almost money dumped in my hands, so to speak. The university got the grant, of course. Bess Hawes, Alan Lomax's sister, had a position with the National Endowment for the Arts in the folklore area and was in charge of various grant programs, and she almost suggested to me to do a program to document contemporary folk blues in the area and put out 45s. The idea was to stimulate this music, to get it on the scene in terms of commercial music—a 45 that could go on jukeboxes and get radio airplay and help local artists in their careers. That was probably a naïve idea, if you think about what popular black music sounded like in 1978, '79; disco was supreme at the time. [*laughs*] We did get enough of a grant to record four artists.

Bess must have thought we were going to record people like Jack Owens. Her brother Alan had come to Mississippi in '78 on this video documenting project. It's a funny thing; we drove to Memphis from California with a big moving truck, a rental truck. I drove it myself with a big record collection. We arrived there in '78 on the first anniversary of Elvis's death. There were all these people here; it was very hard to get a motel room. We bought a house. My wife had done that in advance, so we eventually moved in there, but one of the first things we did was to go to Othar Turner's picnic. He always had his picnic the last weekend in August. So we went there, and who should be there but Alan Lomax with his crew—a sound truck and video crew. [*laughs*] What I thought was going to be another great picnic and we'd be the only outsiders, and there was Alan Lomax. He had recorded Jack Owens and several other people on that trip. And I think that Bess expected that I would put people like Jack Owens on these 45s.

My own thought was to find people a little bit younger who might still have some commercial viability and could actually get some airplay. So I selected Jessie Mae Hemphill, who had started developing her sound at that time; Ranie Burnette, who might have some residual appeal—he did play electric guitar. I really thought, "This is going to have to be electric guitar if these records are going to get anywhere." Both Jessie and Ranie played country blues but on electric guitar. Then I picked R. L. Burnside, who had started up a family band, the Sound Machine, with his two sons and son-in-law. I thought that was an interesting sound; it was country blues but with elements of R & B. And then I selected Raymond Hill as sort of a link to the past; Raymond was in Clarksdale and had played saxophone on "Rocket 88." I went to Clarksdale because I heard Raymond was there; for that matter, Jackie Brenston was still there, though he no longer was involved in music. I thought about reconstructing the Kings of Rhythm; of course, Ike Turner was long gone from there, but there were still some people around. Raymond Hill had his own ideas and basically wanted to put together a group around himself, including some younger musicians he was working with. I was never entirely satisfied with the results of that, but we got two interesting songs, one by him and another by his wife.

We put out these four 45s thanks to that grant. We recorded them at this studio that we rented in Memphis. Then we had to try and market these records. The radio stations were not as interested in that music as I thought they would be, and it was hard to get them on jukeboxes. I ran into the realities of the commercial music scene, including payola and everything else. I thought everyone would be glad to play and promote these records. I was very naïve. [*laughs*] Contracts, mechanical royalties—I knew nothing about these things as a folklorist; none of us did. But I learned a lot about the music business, and we did get a little bit of radio airplay. Rufus Thomas—God bless him—would play a record by a local artist. He played Jessie Mae, and Ranie Burnette even got a little airplay. We also got them on a few jukeboxes. The project was not a total failure, and the records came out and the artists were documented—some for the first time. And we got additional material, enough for whole albums by Jessie Mae and R .L. Burnside. Altogether High Water had nineteen 45s and thirteen LPs, mostly blues and gospel.

The last major production was around 1990. We did a licensing agreement with Hightone Records out in California; I'd known Bruce Bromberg from my days in California, and he was one of the two partners in Hightone. They wanted to license twenty CDs, an amazing deal. They were particularly interested in Junior Kimbrough and R. L. Burnside and Jessie Mae. I'd made a prospectus of what we had; it was a twenty-CD prospectus and they went for it. They put all of our blues and gospel vinyl back out with previously unissued stuff. Kip Lornell, our first PhD graduate—of course, he'd already done work on his own in the seventies—he recorded gospel quartets in Memphis, a cappella groups, and we put some of that material out. In the eighties I had recorded Hezekiah and the House Rockers in Natchez—another interesting group, a unique group with a trombone and three generations of musicians.

Around that time people started coming to Memphis. There was an awareness that there was still a blues scene in the area. Gérard Herzhaft, the French scholar, got in touch with me and came to Memphis. I took him around to see people. He had connections in France with Vogue Records. He was very impressed with Burnside and the Sound Machine, and with Jessie Mae in particular. He persuaded Vogue Records to start up a series of albums, contemporary traditional blues. The first two—the only two, in fact [*laughs*]—were Burnside and the Sound Machine and Jessie Mae. Unfortunately for me and blues in general, Vogue decided to lease the entire Chess label catalog, and they put all their efforts into that.

Then I discovered an urban blues scene in Memphis. I'd never done much with urban blues. I found this scene quite by accident. It was an underground scene, and I was driving around McLemore Avenue deep in the ghetto of South Memphis and saw a sign on the door of a club, a place called Willie's Lounge: "Live Blues Saturday Night." So I went there Saturday night and walked in the door, and—wow!—blues coming off of the bandstand and about 200 people seated at tables. It was the Fieldstones, a great blues band. And they were more modern than what my tastes had been up to that time. I could recognize the quality of the music—and the scene itself. I never had really been in urban blues clubs. So I followed the Fieldstones almost every Saturday night. They'd be there and then they moved to another place—the J & J Lounge, on Mississippi Boulevard, and finally to Green's Lounge. And other musicians would sit in with them. I got to know all the members of the group and members of other bands—the Hollywood All-Stars, and eventually a group of musicians broke away from the Hollywood All-Stars to form the Blues Busters. There weren't a lot of bands in Memphis, but there was an urban blues scene at these lounges. Usually each band would play a night each week, sometimes two nights on the weekends. And the same 100 or 150 people would come out and follow them every weekend.

In addition to your fieldwork, the books, and your adventures in the record business, I know you have worked consistently through the years as a singer/guitarist focusing on traditional blues. Can you talk a bit about your playing?

As a grad student I played very few public gigs. They had a little festival at Cal State Fullerton. I remember playing there. But I mostly just played with friends. It was not until I came to Memphis that I started playing more in public, accompanying older musicians at first, sometimes touring with them, playing festivals and concerts. We formed a jug band here in Memphis with Hammie Nixon and Van Hunt. She [Van] had sung one side of one record in 1930 with the Noah Lewis Jug Band, and she was still active as a singer. She was on the side "Selling the Jelly"; it was on one of those Origin Jazz Library jug band albums. She was living right near Beale Street and was quite a singer. She had an extraordinary repertoire but was quite a difficult personality. She was kind of a prima donna, hard to work with. Hammie Nixon, on the other hand, was a wonderful person—just this jolly old guy. I learned a lot about entertainment from Hammie, and I loved playing with him. We had this jug band, the Beale Street Jug Band. There were five of us and we played a number of concerts and festivals—three young white guys and two older black musicians. We played the World's Fair in Knoxville, Tennessee, in 1982.

Then I played second guitar with Jessie Mae Hemphill; I did that for about ten years starting in 1979 to the late 1980s. We had a tour of Europe—Germany, Holland, and Sweden—in 1980. It was three weeks with Jessie Mae and the fife-and-drum band; that was my first European tour. Then I did one in France with Hammie and R. L. Burnside. I would play guitar with Hammie—Sleepy John was deceased by that time—and act as road manager too; that was 1983. Hammie died the following year. In 1986 I had two tours with Jessie Mae and Hezekiah and the House Rockers. On one tour we had Son Thomas; it was sort of a traveling blues festival, a Mississippi blues festival. On the other one we had Boyd Rivers, a gospel guitarist from Mississippi. Then I did another tour with Jessie Mae in France in 1987.

On all those tours I would do a few solo pieces; it gave me a little experience facing an audience. But then in 1988 I did a little "State Department tour," playing and lecturing in Colombia. Then in '89 I did a tour with Johnny Shines acting as road manager and as his left hand. He'd had a stroke. He could still sing and had a good right hand, but his left hand was pretty much paralyzed, so I would try to play appropriate things to give the guitar some sound, and he would chord. Between the two of us we managed to be the Johnny Shines of old. [*laughs*] We did sixteen concerts in France and Italy. In '89 I took the Hollywood All-Stars, another Memphis blues band, on a tour of Peru and Ecuador and Venezuela, and I would do a few songs of my own as an opening for them. I had the Fieldstones in Venezuela in 1990, and again I would do a few pieces of my own. It wasn't until 1991 that I had a tour of my own. That was in Great Britain. I got a gig through a British friend who hooked me up with a guitar festival near Liverpool. I did that and my friend got a string of gigs in Great Britain stretching from the Liverpool area down to London. My wife, Marice, went with me; we'd just gotten married in 1990. That was a nice tour and gave me confidence.

David Evans's one-room country shack, August 1966. Photo Marina Bokelman.

Then in 1993 I started touring steadily; by that I mean one to three times a year in Europe. I also got another tour in Venezuela in 1996. I haven't been back to South American since then. I met an agent in Germany, Volker Albold. He was in the former East Germany, and he wrote a book in the last days of the German Democratic Republic, a book on blues—one of the very few from behind the Iron Curtain. After the Wall came down he came to visit us in 1993. I played a few pieces, and he was looking for talent to book. I hooked him up with Robert Belfour, who I'd gotten to know and had encouraged. In fact, I recorded an album for Volker. He had a label called Hot Fox Records. I had a couple of tracks of myself on that; those are my first issued recordings under my own name. That came out in 1994. So I've been going to Europe every year since 1993. Last year I had two tours, the year before I had three, and three the year before that. I played in about fifteen countries. Not too many people get to Latvia, Slovenia, Czech Republic, Slovakia. [*laughs*]

I've got another tour set up for this year in Germany, Austria, France—and maybe Italy. And I'm working on two more maybe later in the summer, generally in the summer or on my spring break. Last year I had a tour on my spring break in the Czech Republic, Austria, and Poland. So I've gotten to Eastern Europe quite a bit, which has been interesting. Some of it not long after the changeover, particularly East Germany, which in 1993 was pretty rundown.

CHRIS STRACHWITZ INTERVIEW

I was born in a little village in Lower Silesia [southwestern Poland] in 1931. During the war we lived on a big farm, and I was lucky to get out of where we lived before they grabbed us. You see, we left before the Russians came in—that was in February of 1945—because we were considered capitalists and would not have survived. We eventually took a train to a friend of the family; she actually was a nanny when we were little. She was in Sondershausen in Thuringia [in east-central Germany], and that's where we met the American forces coming in, thank God. Then we heard "This area's going to go under the East Bloc." An uncle from Braunschweig came and got us, and we lived near Braunschweig for two years. Two of our great aunts managed to get us out of Germany via Sweden. My mother's mother was an American. She died very young, and her two sisters were very keen about my mother and her survival.

Chris Strachwitz in the Arhoolie Record vault. Photo Philip Gould. Courtesy Arhoolie Records.

I came to the US in 1947. In Germany we didn't really have much schooling, except a private tutor came from time to time, so when I came here—I was sixteen—they put me in ninth grade. As soon as I got here I was sent to school in Southern California, and I heard all this amazing stuff on the radio, hillbilly music over XERB broadcasting from Rosarito Beach, Baja California. I heard Mexican music in the afternoons over a station in Santa Paula. And after I graduated and went to Pomona College, I heard gospel music Sunday nights over KFVD from the St. Paul Baptist Church and rhythm and blues from Hunter Hancock, who had a program—also over KFVD—called *Harlem Matinee*. It was just the beginnings of black programming on radio stations; it really started about that

Chris Strachwitz. Courtesy Arhoolie Records.

time in 1949, '50, right in there. And there were an amazing amount of live broadcasts in those days. I remember a live blues broadcast from some auditorium in L.A. It was conducted by Gene Norman. Some of that was actually issued on Modern label 78s, like "I'm Gonna Let Him Ride" by Helen Humes—I remember that. Those were taken from his live radio broadcasts. It was just wild. I heard a real amazing hillbilly string band over a radio station in San Bernardino on Saturday mornings. It was just a barrelhouse and ragtime hillbilly band. Back in 1947 over XERB, every morning they would broadcast these fifteen-minute programs devoted to the Armstrong Twins, Floyd and Lloyd! They had a song called "Three Miles South of Cash in Arkansas"—God, that stuff was so good! And "T-Texas Tyler," and the Maddox Brothers and Rose! Later I found out that Four Star Records would buy blocks of programming on that station, and it blasted all over the West Coast. During the daytime it covered the whole of Southern California. It just opened my ears to all of this music.

I saw a movie called *New Orleans*—this was also in 1947—and it just blew me away. This was my first meeting with New Orleans jazz. The film includes Louis Armstrong, but playing with the Kid Ory Band—"Kid" Ory on trombone, Barney Bigard on clarinet, "Zutty" Singleton on drums, that real New Orleans–type jazz band. It was just a fantastic rhythm band, and the music was so well recorded in that movie. Billie Holiday and Meade Lux Lewis are also in it. I remember asking my friend, walking back afterwards, "What do you call that music we just heard?" "Oh, man, that's New Orleans jazz." And so I looked for everything that was available or becoming available at that time, like the Victor album of 78s by Bunk Johnson. I literally wore those records out and made [them] turn gray. [*laughs*] This was right after the war, and Victor had a very thin layer of shellac. As soon as you wore that down, you got into that gray crap, that filler in the middle. That also happened with some Modern records, the early ones. [*laughs*] Oh, boy! Those were the days!

So I liked New Orleans jazz and the hillbilly music and gospel music; this was in the early 1950s. Once I got to the L.A. area I also heard various ethnic groups. They would have programs on Saturday morning. There was the polka hour, there was the Yiddish hour, and Ukrainian hour. It was just this amazing array of vernacular music that blew me away!

But traditional jazz was what you were buying?

Yeah, that was my first love, but I could hardly afford to buy much of anything. But I did buy traditional jazz, and also some hillbilly records like "Remember Me" by T-Texas Tyler, and "Oklahoma Hills"—that was my first encounter with hillbilly music and New Orleans jazz. I was in high school at this time and graduated in 1952, and then I went to Pomona, down in Southern California. That's where I really got into the rhythm and blues and the New Orleans jazz more, because a friend of mine, Frank Demond, who still plays from time to time with the Preservation Hall Jazz Band, we would go to the Beverley Cavern. We were there every night and I just about flunked out. He was too smart—he didn't flunk—but just to hear the George Lewis Band every night! And they didn't have freeways back then; it took us hours and hours just to get to L.A. I also would go to L.A. on my own, because I couldn't get anyone to go with me, to some of those blues concerts that Hunter Hancock would put on at the Olympic Auditorium. There I heard a blues singer named Smiling Smokey Lynn. He had the longest god-damned guitar cord—that was before Chuck Berry—and he hopped all over the stage like a praying mantis. And they had vocal groups. Man, it was some experience! And the audience was mostly what we called pachucos—you know, Mexican American kids. A lot of blacks too—hardly any gringos—but there were some. The radio was so democratic; it would go to anybody who could tune it in. That had never happened before. Before that this minority music was only heard over the jukeboxes in the ghettos. But all of a sudden in the early 1950s all of this stuff became available over various little radio stations.

So I fell in love with this American music, and I was so enthusiastic about the George Lewis Band. I think it was before I went into the army. I was going to Berkeley. I had transferred because I just about flunked out of Pomona, so I transferred to U. C. Berkeley. In those days it was easy to get in to. I heard that if you joined the Big Game Committee—you see, I didn't give a shit about football, but I heard about this Big Game Committee that dealt with the game between Cal and Stanford—that if you joined that committee, you could determine what band was going to play a big concert on the campus. So I did that, and I told all the kids on the committee, "Listen, the best god-dammed music you'll ever hear—let's go over to the Club Hangover in San Francisco!"—where the George Lewis Band was playing an extended engagement. So we went over there and it just blew their minds! They never heard a rhythmic powerhouse black ensemble New Orleans jazz band. There was no rock 'n' roll yet. There was R & B, but most white kids didn't listen to that. But here was this traditional band that just played rhythm, just this powerhouse machine. It was almost like a small Count Basie Band with so much feeling; George Lewis was so unique. And they said, "Yeah! Let's do that!" So we brought him to Wheeler Auditorium. The late Phil Elwood emceed, and the place was packed.

George Lewis and all those kind of bands were popular back in those days. It was before rock 'n' roll, and any halfway hip people would go to dance to jazz bands—traditional jazz bands, not the beboppers, you couldn't dance to them, but the traditional jazz bands. Here it was Bob Scobey, Turk Murphy, Bob Mielke, but the George Lewis Band was just so much more powerful than anything they'd ever heard. And then I also went to R & B shows emceed by Jumpin' George Oxford over KWBR in Oakland. He would have a program every afternoon doing pretty much the same thing Hunter Hancock did in L.A.: playing all these blues and jump bands and all the vocal groups—all the R & B stuff—Lightning Hopkins, the Clovers, the Dominos, Muddy Waters, Howling Wolf, Big Jay McNeely, Joe Houston—all mixed up! [*laughs*] It was fantastic—the early years of all that music, and I was just lucky to grow up during that time. It was the first time the white-Anglo world was exposed to all this powerful music if they dared to dial into these radio stations.

So how did you get involved in the record label business?

I was totally fascinated by the little tape machines that started popping up, although mostly cheap and really bad ones. I remember when I was still at Pomona, Frank Demond and his friends had a Dixieland band. I remember the Storyville Stompers, and we organized some dances there at Pomona at Stoddard's Canyon with his band. We also broadcast over the local college station and just had a good time with it. So I started making little recordings on a really horrible primitive recorder, sometimes off the air. As time went by and I came up here to Berkeley about 1953, I started recording people like Jesse Fuller, who was all over the place here, and K. C. Douglas. And I would record traditional bands like the Bob Mielke Band, who played over at a place in San Francisco. I just loved the idea of taping stuff.

And already in high school I had ordered a disc cutter from a catalog, a real primitive disc-cutting machine. These were acetate-covered aluminum discs you had to buy; they were twenty-five cents, something like that. It was really a basic cutter, but it worked. There was a lathe, a cutting head. You put that on the disc and it would cut just like a professional one. But you had to blow away the cuttings; it didn't have a suck-up device. You spoke into a microphone and it had a little amplifier. And I would record stuff, weird stuff like people talking. I'll never forget when our Latin teacher came in the room and I asked him if he had any comments. And he said, "Yes. The rich get richer and the poor have children." [*laughs*] I never forgot that true saying. And I also ordered a little oscillator. In those days you could have a little broadcast station that would have 1.5 watts. This was a small school on top of a hill, and the other kids sometimes bitched about Strachwitz blocking out their favorite radio stations that were broadcasting syrupy shit like Doris Day and Frank Sinatra. Here was Strachwitz playing this hillbilly music! [*laughs*]

What was the name of the cheap tape deck you had?

I can't recall the first one, but once I came to Berkeley, I think I got a Wollensak. I'd met people like Bob Geddins, who was making blues records here in Oakland. I'd gone all over the place and met a lot of these people. I was looking for 78s, and that's how I made my first money. I'd buy them cheap at old stores and from jukebox operators and then auction them off. In Europe they were paying me a dollar or two dollars and fifty cents for records I picked up for ten cents or a quarter. I picked up anything that said "blues singer with guitar" on it. [*laughs*] Nobody knew much about this stuff. I knew some of the names—Lightning Hopkins, Howling Wolf. But the early stuff was hard to find, like Washboard Sam and Jazz Gillum. But Jazz Gillum had a big hit even in the 1940s with "Key to the Highway." I remember that being played by Jumpin' George.

I remember I decided to really make a go of it after hearing Lightning Hopkins in Houston in 1959, and I bought a Roberts recorder—a Japanese copy of an Ampex recorder, but they left out all the important parts. [*laughs*] I thought this was a better recorder. I should have kept the old Wollensak; it was probably more reliable. The first year it worked, when

I went to Texas in '60. A year later it gave out. It would over-modulate everything, and I couldn't figure out what the hell I was doing. Apparently some circuitry in it went out of control. It ruined a couple of sessions.

There was a bunch of piano players we recorded in Houston—Buster Pickens was one of them—and also one session with Lightning, but it was so chaotic anyway. You see, I had met Sam Charters here in Berkeley, who was playing in a Dixieland band. He was already working on his blues book, *The Country Blues*, and he became intrigued by my Lightning Hopkins records. At first he didn't particularly care for him; he was into that old music, like Blind Lemon Jefferson. I thought those were awfully tinny and crappy sounding. [*laughs*] They didn't have the beat I liked—and the ferociousness that the postwar blues had. But then Sam suddenly sent me a postcard from Houston saying, "I found Lightning Hopkins. He lives here in Houston. This fellow Mack McCormick is trying to be his agent." So I took a pilgrimage to Houston. My sister needed her car driven back to Albuquerque, and I figured, "Heck, that must be most of the way to Texas." [*laughs*] Well, it wasn't quite, so I took a bus the rest of the way to Texas in 1959 and met Mack McCormick there—and saw Lightning Hopkins at his place.

I think I was probably the first fan he'd ever encountered. The other white people he'd encountered were either folk scholars or record people who just wanted songs out of him. But I just adored his music; he was one of my very favorite singers. [*sings*] *"Hello, Central, give me two-o-nine. I wanna talk to my baby, she's way on down the line. Buses don't stop running—trains don't allow me to ride no more."* Just that lonesome voice with his ferocious guitar. Lightning invited us to come out to this juke place where he played that night. It was just a tiny little beer joint with maybe half a dozen people in it. He was blasting away with his electric guitar, a drummer behind him, singing about all this shit that was happening to him—how his arthritis was acting up and how the chuckholes were covered with water and he could hardly get to the job that night. He just rhymed it all up and made it into songs. He pointed at me and said, "Whoa, this man come all the way from California to hear poor Lightning sing." I had never heard anything like that. Most of the blues I'd heard was pretty much patterned stuff; they knew their songs and they did them. But he was like an African griot—you know, just make up stuff. Later I found out he had a bag full of lyrics—from his previous songs, or "Texas" Alexander, or whoever he learned from—that he would toss in there.

So did you make a record with Lightning on this trip?

No, the first year I didn't make a record with him. I was a schoolteacher then, making seven thousand dollars a year. I didn't have a pot to piss in. But he was already hip to all this stuff by the time I got to him. If I had gotten to him some years before and got his confidence, he probably would have let me record him in the beer joint, but by this time he was strictly on his trip of getting one hundred dollars per song that he was used to, to put on tape. He and Mack almost had a fight outside the god-dammed beer joint where we were trying to make a recording. He had also become somewhat self-conscious about what he would want to put on a record. And I had technical problems trying to record his sound with one mic.

Front to Back: Mack McCormick, Lightning Hopkins, Luke "Long Gone" Miles, and unknown. Courtesy Arhoolie Records.

Can you tell me about Mack McCormick?

He was an extraordinarily well informed person who knew the world of Texas better than anyone you could imagine. He knew that the "big wheel" politically wasn't the governor; it was the Texas railroad commissioner who ran the state. He knew where all these weird little underground ethnic groups were. He knew where these Creoles were living, and he had already heard something about zydeco. He was an amazing guy. He's still alive, but he is hard to get to talk to. He was an extraordinarily well informed person. And he knew more about the old blues than I did. I was just a fan of rhythm and blues. He said, "Chris, Lightning's stuff isn't all that original. He always puts in lines that he learned from Texas Alexander." I'd never heard of the guy. Mack once told me, "Listen to this lyric about *'If you see a mule run away with the world, let him go ahead.'* Isn't that an amazing poetic statement?" And the more I think about it, it sure as hell is. Lowell Fulson also used that verse on a record.

How did you make connections with Mack McCormick?

That was through Sam Charters, when he sent me that postcard saying, "I've found Lightning Hopkins." He gave me Mack's address. He said, "This fellow Mack McCormick is trying to be his agent." That's how I got in touch with him. So when I made connections with Mack again in 1960, we went out to Navasota, because Lightning had just left for California. He was scheduled to play the Berkeley Folk Festival [*laughs*], and he'd just left with John Lomax Jr. Mack didn't have a car, and I had a little old beat-up car, so Mack said, "Let's drive out in the country. I'm sure we can find blues singers that are just as good as Lightning." Of course I was suspicious, but it was an amazing adventure for me. I'd never encountered anyplace like Texas. I think there's just no other place in the world like that! With all these plantations, with these ethnic groups mingling, with these Creoles and the blacks and the Mexicans and the Bohemians—it was just a new world to me.

So we drove out towards Navasota. We happened to be going toward Navasota, and I saw people chopping cotton on the road. I had already learned to be something of a detective with my friend Ken Mills and then Bob Pinson, a collector here in California who eventually sold his records to the Country Music Hall of Fame, which started that collection of which he was hired to be curator. We had driven together toward Dallas, where Bob left me; he had relatives there. In Dallas and Fort Worth we started doing some detective work looking for "Lil Son" Jackson. He wasn't in the phone book, but his first name is Melvin, because I saw that on the records as composer credit. So Bob suggested we go to the library and look at old phone books.

There he was listed in the early 1950s and we phoned that number—and there he was! Another time I stopped on the corner where some black guys were playing cards or dominoes. This was in Fort Worth too. I asked them, "Any of you ever heard a guy called 'Little Brother'?" I heard him on a 78 on the Talent label; the Talent label was based in that area. And one of them said, "What you want with him?" They all thought we were bill collectors, or sheriffs, or some such thing. I said, "Well, I like this record I have by him." And so one of them came up to me and said, "He used to hang around with Black Ace." Now, "Black Ace" was a name Paul Oliver had sent me. Prior to our trip in 1960, Paul sent me this long list of people who made records back in the 1920s and 1930s in Fort Worth or Dallas. And I remembered Black Ace. Such a name you couldn't forget! So I said, "Where can I find Black Ace?" [*laughs*] He says, "He comes to this tavern right around the corner every evening about five o'clock, and you can't miss him, because he's got 'Ace' written on his white shirt." It was pretty close to five, so I went to the beer joint, and sure enough this guy walks in with "Ace" written on his white shirt. I said, "Are you Black Ace?" He says, "Yes, sir." That's how we met Black Ace.

So I had done some detective work before, even in California with a guy named Ken Mills. We would go snooping around in Los Angeles, and we found John Hogg, who was a cousin to Smokey Hogg. We just became detectives—I probably should have opened a detective agency. So on the road to Navasota these people came to the fence and said, "What are y'all looking for?" I said, "Are there any good guitar pickers in these parts?" And they said, "You have to go to Navasota for that." Now, Mack had the idea that . . . "Tim Moore" ["Tom Moore's Farm," sometimes known as "Tim Moore's Farm or "Tom Moore's Blues"] that Lightning had made a 78 about on the Gold Star label. It's a powerful song if you've ever heard the record: "*Ain't but the one thing that this black man done wrong—moved his wife and family on Tom Moore's farm. If you ask Mr. Moore for five dollars, he'll haul off and give you ten*"—just to keep you deeper in debt. Or if your woman runs off and leaves, you ask Mr. Moore to have her brought right back. Mack had an idea that there was such a person, and he said, "Look, Chris, let's just ask at a feed store. If anybody knows anybody in the town, it's at a feed store." [*laughs*] So we walked into the first feed store we saw in Navasota.

Now, Mack didn't act like a fan; he had a gruff way, like a policeman. "Does Tim Moore live in this town?" "Yes, *Mr.* Moore certainly does live in this town." "Well, how can we get ahold of him?" "There's a telephone right there. He's got an office over the bank building. You can probably call him." That's what we did. And Mack—as cocky as he is—asked him all sorts of questions. I thought Tim Moore was pretty nice to us. And Mack said, "Can we visit your plantation?" "Well, you'd have to make an appointment. I don't really have time right now." Finally Mack asked him, "Is there anybody who plays for your hired hands on weekends or suppers?" I remember Tim Moore saying, "Yeah, there's a fellow people seem to like around here." "Do you know his name?" "No, but you can go ask Pegleg at the railroad station. He probably knows his name." We had no trouble finding Pegleg, and he's the one who gave us Mance Lipscomb's name. And that's how we recorded that first record that same evening, in Mance's little shack. That became my first record. I had recorded other stuff before. I had recorded Lil Son Jackson on my way down but didn't finish the thing. I met Black Ace, but he didn't have any guitar strings. So I told him, "Go get some strings, and when I come back with Paul Oliver we'll make some recordings."

The Mance Lipscomb was the first, because Mack said, "Chris, this is the most amazing discovery since Leadbelly. This man is a songster." He was a pre-blues artist. At first I thought he was an awfully sweet guy, but I didn't consider him a rough blues singer like Lightning. [*laughs*] But that became my first record. I had seen Mack the previous year when I first met Lightning Hopkins. But the previous year I took a bus from Albuquerque. In 1960 I had driven down to Houston, and then I finally drove through Louisiana and up through Mississippi and then met up with Paul Oliver and his wife, Valerie, in Memphis. That's where we made an appointment to get together. And then we drove back down through Mississippi, and Louisiana, and Houston, then Navasota and Dallas, and finally back to California—the three of us with a trailer full of 78s.

Did you do any recording as you passed through all these states?

I'd written to Harry Oster in Baton Rouge, because I knew he had his Folk-Lyric label with all that Cajun music and also the blues singers, those Angola things. I believe I stopped at his place, either going to New Orleans or on the way back, or both! I recorded Butch Cage and Willie Thomas there. New Orleans was my favorite stomping grounds, because there was so much addictive music there. In 1960 there was still some pretty good stuff around—Billie and Deedee Pierce, the Kid Thomas Band, even George Lewis was still playing. And the whole Preservation Hall scene was starting up. I knew Ken Mills, who actually started it, who was the first one, but he was no businessman, so then the Jaffees took it over and it made it a real deal.

From there I drove through Bogue Chitto, Mississippi. I had contacted the lady who put out Trumpet records. I was totally enamored by a record on her label by the Hodges Brothers, a hillbilly duo who had "The Leaves Is Falling on the Ground." I wrote to her and she told me that they lived in Bogue Chitto, Mississippi. So I stopped there, and they lived in literally a one-room country shack with their mother. It was unbelievable. I'd never encountered this primitive aspect of America.

I drove through Mississippi and made the stop in Clarksdale and met Wade Walton, the barber. He was a wonderful host. That's where the police stopped me. Wade was in my car, and I had California license plates. The light had just turned yellow, and I thought instead of coming to a screeching halt, I'd just go through it. Yeeoowww! Here comes the siren. "All right, what you doin'? Let me see your driver's license. What kind of business are you in?" I started thinking real fast: "I'm in the record business." I'd heard that if you got stopped by the police, especially with a black person in the car, you'd better be on business. That was the only legitimate way you can be with someone of color. "Yeah, I'm in the record business." "Do you have any proof of that?" I had a stash of 78s in boxes on my backseat that I'd just gotten from some jukebox operator, and I pointed to them. "I got all those records in the back." And he shined his light in there. "All right, but we don't drive with them niggers here. You better take him back where you found him." And he let us go, but that was a shocker.

Then in Memphis at the Peabody Hotel, Paul and Valerie were there. He recorded a whole bunch of people there in Memphis, including Charlie Burse and Gus Cannon—and Bo Carter. They were all on their last go-round. I recorded Sam Chatmon in Hollandale, Mississippi. I believe he may have been on the list Paul gave me. It wasn't easy to find people, but I was really impressed with Paul. I thought he was sent by the BBC, because he had a small tape recorder; it was just a jewel. It was very small and it had a fantastic microphone. He was really interested in the stories and the history of all these people. I mean I was basically just a fan, you know? I think meeting Paul and Mack helped me a lot in trying to document this music. I became fascinated by the oral history of all these people.

When you and Paul got together and recorded all these people, how did you decide who was going to retain the rights to which recordings?

That was pretty easy. Paul wasn't interested in doing much taping to be issued as records. He was doing his documentary, which was primarily talking with them, and getting their stories and a sampling of their music. He did that pretty much all over the place. It was one reason why he would tape and document, say, a Gus Cannon. Because I didn't think they could play much anymore. But Paul was fascinated with their history and all they could tell—it was amazing! To me, I was much more interested in a guy named R. C. Smith, who just walked into the barbershop in Clarksdale because he'd heard there were some guys making records there. Of course we were not the first to do that. The Bihari brothers of Modern Records did that extensively. When they drove around down there they had Ike Turner with them, who was a piano player and who was arranging all those down-home sessions that they did for Modern Records. If the word got out in those days, people who wanted to make records would come out of the woodwork!

Were the two of you prepared to pay everybody who showed up to record?

I think Paul did pay everybody a small token. I only paid them if I felt I got a record out of it. Money was so relative. To the guys who'd made commercial records, like Lightning or Lil Son Jackson, they had a precedent; it was a hundred dollars a tune. To most of them it was just fun doing it. I gave Mance Lipscomb, I think it was thirty-five dollars after the first session. It was all I had with me at the time. The next time we came through, he told us, "My wife, when she saw what I had in my hand, she said, 'Mance, that's the most money you ever made playing for the white folks.'"

Who else would you have seen on that trip?

We also met Alex Moore. That was bizarre! Paul and I went back to visit Black Ace again, and we happened to be near some little bar and took little notice of a fellow sitting on the porch. Then we walked in and Paul asked if anybody had heard of this fellow Alex Moore. And they said, "Yeah, he's sitting out on the front porch." [*laughs*] A totally bizarre incident—there he was! But then we had a hard time finding a piano. Alex Moore knew a piano teacher and she let us use her piano in her living room.

Can you go into more detail regarding the Lil Son Jackson session?

We found his phone number in the library, in a phone book from 1952. We called him up, and he said, "Yeah, that's me. We can meet tomorrow at the parts store where I work." And that's where Paul Oliver took that cover picture of Son standing with all those old hubcaps and stuff. That's where we met him, and he told us that he'd quit the music business—he was actually working in a used auto parts store. He didn't really want to fool with the music business anymore. He said he got into a bad accident in fifty-something-or-other and he quit making records. He said, "I didn't want to fool with that stuff." I said, "I'd really love to put down some of your old things." He finally agreed, but he wanted a certain amount of money—I've forgotten how much it was—but I didn't have quite that much with me. My whole budget was something like eight hundred dollars. So I said, "If you record some numbers, I'll come back and pay you the rest of the money."

After he got home that day, he made at least a part of that record in his living room. It was awfully hot; he didn't have air conditioning. Also, he had just eaten something and I thought he sounded lazy. I'll never forget the time that Bob Geddins once told me, "Chris, if you ever make a recording, don't feed your musicians before you done cut the record." [*laughs*] That was well said. They get lazy if they eat a bunch of fat; they just get bogged down. But they shouldn't be starving either—you can't work. Little Son Jackson wasn't a very exciting guy. He just had his unique sound and style.

Bob Geddins. Photo Pat Monaco. Courtesy Dan Kochakian.

And did you ever get Black Ace to get his instrument together?

I've forgotten whether I bought him the strings or how it happened, but when I came back with Paul he had gotten it together, and that's when we recorded him there.

The two of you did Buster Pickens as well. How did that happen?

Well, Mack found him in Houston. There were a bunch of other piano players, and the next year I recorded them all. And that's when that damned recorder gave out. I remember we did a whole bunch of piano sessions and they were all over-modulated. It was a real pisser.

Didn't Paul come away with an LP by Buster Pickens on Flyright?

Oh, that's right. I did record that in 1960. I didn't think it was all that great. Yeah, sometimes he wanted me to record certain artists that I didn't think were all that interesting, and I think Buster was a case in point. And there was another one—Joel Hopkins, I think. There was a weird label in England that put out ninety-nine copies of each item. But I don't recall who recorded those.

So where did your adventures with Paul and Valerie ultimately lead you?

We went all the way back through Mississippi and southern Mississippi to New Orleans and then back to Baton Rouge with Harry Oster—then back to Houston, back up through Navasota, and to Fort Worth and Dallas for Alex Moore and Black Ace. And then we drove west. By that time I had a god-damned trailer full of 78s [*laughs*], and my car couldn't make it up the grade when we came to the California border—that's a big steep grade. I remember we had to go back down the hill, and I had to hire a truck to pull me over the mountain. [*laughs*] We finally wound up in Reno, Nevada, where my family was living. I think that Paul and Valerie flew back from there. But I've seen him many times since then.

How and when did your record company start?

The Arhoolie thing happened as we were driving back from recording Mance Lipscomb. That was really the first amazing recording I did. I had recorded Son Jackson earlier, but I didn't think the Son Jackson was all that great. I was thinking of names like "Delta" or "Southern" or "Gulf," and Mack suddenly said, "How about Arhoolie?" And I said, "Arwhat?" [*laughs*] And then he explained to me where that appeared—on that Library of Congress record Negro Work Songs & Calls. And I said, "Well, maybe that's not a bad idea." I cut out the *W* in there, and then my friend Wayne Pope designed that little guitar insignia, and that's how Arhoolie was born. The first recordings were done in 1960, and the first records were issued in the fall of 1960, in September or October.

What would an initial run be on an Arhoolie record?

I think I pressed 250 and we had them pressed at Record Research Craft down in Los Angeles. I ordered solid black jackets from Modern Albums, because I liked the way Folkway albums looked. My friend Wayne Pope, who designed the logo, was working at a printing company, and he said, "Chris, if you want to do like Folkways does—slicks glued to the album jacket with a flap wrapped over the spine—I can do that on gummed label stock." That's what we did. We did 250 sheets on gummed label stock. We sat there in his kitchen with sponges and wetted down these slicks and glued on one after the other. It took us a long god-damned time! [*laughs*] So that first run of albums was homemade. And he printed that booklet that Mack McCormick wrote on Mance Lipscomb; that was also modeled on Folkways.

Chris Strachwitz with Mance Lipscomb. Courtesy Arhoolie Records.

What was the reaction to the Mance Lipscomb record?

There was quite a bit of reaction. In 1961 I got a phone call from a lady working for the brand-new Reprise label. She said, "This is Frank Sinatra's label and we're doing some interesting things. We want to do some real folk music, and we're going to issue some of Big Bill Broonzy's things. Can we license your Mance Lipscomb record?" I said, "No, I kind of like the record, but you can go record him yourself; he's got a lot more songs." So she contacted Mack McCormick, and I think they made their records in Houston. And when both of those records hit the market—"hit the market" is a misnomer; we snuck ours out—all of a sudden the *Saturday Review of Literature*, Pete Welding, reviewed both of those records and it caused a sensation. We heard from distributors and people all over the place. This was really it, as if we had discovered this amazing songster who knew all this repertoire from black rural Texas—everything from blues to Spirituals, reels to ballads, children's songs, and on and on. That caused a big stir. The *Saturday Review* was an important magazine at that time.

Chris Strachwitz with Big Joe Williams. Courtesy Arhoolie Records.

Let's talk about Arhoolie 1002, your next record. Who was the artist, and how did it happen?

That was the most amazing! That was Big Joe Williams. It was the fall of 1960, and I was still working on the Mance Lipscomb record. I was living and teaching school in Los Gatos, which is south of here, near San Jose. And I was constantly going to visit Bob Geddins; on the weekends I'd come up to Berkeley and visit Bob Geddins. I liked the guy and I was constantly searching for records he put out. To me he was the guru who taught me more about recording than anyone else. On one particular visit he said, "Chris, let me play you a tape here—see if you like it." He pulled out this tape, and the first note I heard, I thought, "My God, this is Big Joe Williams." I said, "Where did you record him? Did you go to Chicago?" Bob Koester had just put out a Big Joe Williams LP. He said, "No, man—he's right here. I just bailed him out of jail. He pulled a knife on some old lady that was messing with him. I paid his bail. You can find him. He's staying at this funky-ass hotel on San Pablo Avenue—him and his wife and his little boy." So I visited him and I said, "I've got to go back to teaching on Monday." This was a Saturday. He had some friend from Texas, who a few days later drove Joe down to Los Gatos, where I was living in this little shack near Holy City.

Anyway, this guy and another fellow brought Big Joe down and his wife, and his boy. I had a friend of mine who had a slightly better microphone than I had. I had an Electrovoice 664 that I used for that whole trip in 1960, but I knew that the Electrovoice 666 was the better mic. And this fellow I met in San Francisco said he would come down and let me use his 666. I hung it up from the ceiling in front of Big Joe's singing and his amp. He was so torn up that night because of the whole thing about being arrested and having somebody go [post] his bail—he was on parole. He was totally spooked out and under such emotional stress. I don't think he's ever made a more powerful record than that one. I even had his wife sing a couple of spirituals. I'm putting out another record by her about the Oakland blues. That was unbelievable. And the guy that brought him, he came from Texas, and I asked him if he knew "Tom Moore." He said, "Oh, yeah." And he knew the best version of "Tom Moore." I taped it, but I made the fatal mistake of sending that original tape to Mack McCormick; I knew he was collecting all these versions of "Tom Moore." He never sent it back to me! [*laughs*] That still pisses me off to this day.

You had records by guys in the Bay Area. How did those happen? How about Mercy Dee Walton?

Somebody told me there was this piano player in or near Watsonville, which is south of Santa Cruz. Anyway, I went down there and there was this guy with a big turban on his head [*laughs*], playing in a cocktail lounge for a bunch of gringos. There weren't any black folks there. Of course, by the first note, I knew who it was. He couldn't change his style to play like Nat Cole—no way! [*laughs*] I said, "You must be Mercy Dee." He said, "Yes, sir." "I've got to record you." I kept in touch with him, and he moved to Stockton.

There was this guy, Ken Goldstein, he put out records for Prestige. He told me he wanted a full LP of Mercy Dee. I can't recall if I had recorded Mercy Dee first—I think so. Anyway, that's how I first met Mercy Dee and began recording him. By the time he was back in Stockton, he was trying to play for the black field hands that were still out there in some numbers. This was during a time when most field workers were black. There weren't that many Mexicans yet, and the Okies had sort of disappeared, so there were still a lot of black field workers at that time, particularly from Texas, who came to work here in the Central Valley. I remember West Fresno—I went to West Fresno with Ken Mills—there was a real blues scene working there, because there were a lot of black field hands in those fields. They had this little section in West Fresno—they call it Jericho, I think—where all the winos would hang out and where all the honkytonks were. It was a tough world.

And didn't you do K. C. Douglas?

Yes, he was actually working for the city of Berkeley all this time. He was like Jesse Fuller, almost—people knew him. This guy Sam Eskin had made an LP of him on the Cook label, mostly playing Tommy Johnson songs that K. C. had learned. But K. C. wanted to do new songs. He wanted to have commercial records out. So we tried a 45 on "You Know You Didn't Want Me." I tried to do music for the black music market—you know, 45s. That was one of them. I believe the first one I put out was "Lady Luck" by Mercy Dee. A guy named "Rockin' Lucky" on the old KSAN—the old AM station in San Francisco—and he would play the stuff. He had a record shop in East Oakland. If you gave him one hundred 45s, he'd play the hell out of your record. He'd have this great spiel on the air in the evening: "Hey, baby—Okay, I'm gonna play this record. Call up and tell me should I 'shake it or break it?' Should I shake or break this record? You want me to shake it? Okay, I'll keep playing this record. You want me to break it? Okay, I'll get rid of it!" [*laughs*] He was a character; he was from Orange, Texas. Man, he just played the blues. He played that "Mr. Charley" that Lightning had out on the Candid label, over and over! Man, that was the first time I ever heard a story-song like that on the radio.

So you didn't lose your shirt pressing 45s?

Oh, yeah! [*laughs*] Well, we didn't press that many. I mostly pressed them locally. Bob Geddins had this funky little record-pressing plant out in East Oakland, so we didn't have to press too many—I think five hundred. And you had to give Rockin' Lucky a hundred anyway, and then I had this black guy who was distributing some of them to jukeboxes. Olin Harrison was his name. He also carried some weird folk label [*laughs*]—and Mexican records. I remember he had the Cima label, which intrigued me. I heard some really good conjuntos on Cima, out of San Jose. Anyway, it's an amazing world out there, and records were a happening thing in those days. Everybody tried their luck. Today, unfortunately, it's the end of the line.

How about Clifton Chenier?

Clifton Chenier was the greatest. I met him by hanging out with Lightning Hopkins. Horst Lippmann from Germany, who was doing the American Folk Blues Festivals with his partner, Fritz Rau, contacted me and said, "I hear you can get along with Lightning Hopkins real good. My French promoter says I can't put on your shows unless you bring Lightning Hopkins." I said, "All right, Horst, we'll meet in Houston and see if I can talk Lightning into it." He knew that Lightning was very reluctant to fly anywhere. So we met in Houston, and before Lippmann arrived I hung around with Lightning. One night Lightning says, "Hey, Chris, do you want to go hear my cuz?" I said, "Who's your cuz?" He says, "Cliff." "Cliff who?" "Cliff Chenier." I had in my head the sound of "Boppin' the Rock" or "Ay-Tete-Fee"—more R & B. I wanted real low-down blues, but I thought anyplace that Lightning would go, yeah—let's go.

So he took me to this teeny little beer joint in Frenchtown that was kind of on the southeast side of Houston that was in the ship channel area. I'll never forget driving toward this joint. The rats crossing the road were just *huge*—I'd never seen such big rats! I've seen big roaches in Houston, maybe four inches long, but these rats were at least a foot long! [*laughs*] When we got there, here was this lanky black man with a huge accordion on his chest—and just a drummer behind him—singing the most low-down blues I've ever heard, in this weird patois. I don't speak any French; I didn't even know what it was at first. I knew from meeting some of these Creole guys, that's what it was—a Louisiana French-style language. Since Cliff knew Lightning well, he came over to the table after he played a couple of songs, and Lightning introduced me and said, "Here's Chris from California. He's a record man." "Oh-oh! You're a record man? Let's cut a record!" [*laughs*] I haven't got a pot to piss in, and he's saying, "C'mon, man, we got to make a record!" I was intrigued—I loved the sound he had. So I called up Bill Quinn and asked him if he had his studio available the next day, and he said, "Yeah." I told Cliff, "Bring yourself and that drummer. That sounds fantastic." He said, "All right, I'll be there!"

The next day I'm at Bill Quinn's studio, and here comes Clifton Chenier with not just a drummer—who was real good—but with a whole god-damned band! A guitar player, a piano player, and an electric bass player. The electric bass player plugs in his piece-of-shit amp, and it goes, "Putt-putt-putt." The god-damned cone had separated from the paper! So the amplifier was totally useless, and you can't get anything out of an electric bass unless you have an amplifier and a speaker. So we ain't got no bass—good! [*laughs*] All right, that's taken care of. And the guitar player had an old army surplus amp. He plugged it in and literally the god-damned thing started smoking. I said, "Shit! Put that fire out! And get rid of that guitar!" Again, he had an electric guitar—he couldn't do shit without an amplifier. So we were down to piano, drums, and accordion! And Cliff says, "Yeah, man, I got to have a piano—that makes it sound better." So we recorded "Ay Ai Ai," *"underneath the evergreen"*—and I forget what the flip side was—but it was all in English, and a nice blues. They only did three or four numbers. We put that out.

I was lucky to get "Pappy" Dailey to distribute my stuff. Dailey was a big distributor, and Clifton had a sufficient name in that area. I remember visiting Dailey, because I was always interested in how these guys operated. I remember he said, "I can take some of that stuff. I can sell that down here." We did sell a few—not that much. Anyway, I made a little money out of it.

The next year I told Clifton, "Listen, I want to make an album." He wasn't too big on that. He said, "I just need those jukebox records." I said, "Look, you made the jukebox record; now I want an album. But I want some of that French stuff; I don't want the English." [*laughs*] "Oh, Chris, that ain't hittin' on nothin'. I wanna make rock 'n' roll records." He finally said, "Okay, if you wanna make an album, I'll make half of it rock 'n' roll and half of it French." I said, "Okay, let's do that." I forget which half we did first, but that next year—1964, I believe it was—we were in the Gold Star studio. He started recording and he made this thing, a low-down blues in French, and that's just what I wanted! I remember Bill Quinn standing behind me, and he said, "Chris, that will sell down here! It's got that sound." Just a drummer and his brother played a rubboard. And sure enough, Clifton comes running out of the control booth and says, "I gotta call my old lady. She's gotta hear this one!" Just one take—that's all he ever did—and he poured everything he had into it. And the engineer was real good; he got a real bottom out of that bass drum.

I asked Clifton, "What are you going to call that song? What did you sing?" And he rattled off this French. I didn't understand a word of it. I said, "How do I spell that?" He said, "Spell it any way you want to." "Can't you help me?" [*laughs*] It was probably a good thing we didn't spell it any way I wanted. "Cliff, can I call it 'Louisiana Blues'?" He thought half a minute and said, "Go ahead, call it 'Louisiana Blues.' That's a good idea." So we called it "Louisiana Blues," and I think that was the smartest move we ever made, because if we'd have put that weird French as the title, nobody would ever have played it. So the disc jockeys played it on the Houston station and over in Louisiana. That sucker got on all the jukeboxes. The flipside was "Zydeco Sont Pas Sale." That record was really the one that made him the king of zydeco. It was an old song that they all knew. But it was so tough—just him, the drummer, and the rubboard. He made that accordion talk.

He did a couple more, including the "French Waltz." One side of the LP was the wonderful French stuff, and the other side was what he called rock 'n' roll, like "Keep on Scratching" or some silly thing. That first album did nicely, especially the singles, "Louisiana Blues" and "Zydeco Sont Pas Sale." And I think he finally became proud of being the king of this Creole music—and the king of zydeco. When I first met him I asked him, "What do you call this music?" He said, "We call it 'push and pull' or just 'French,' we call it 'La-la' music, we call it you name it. Some people call it zydeco." He just rattled off a whole bunch of phrases that they associated more with the dancing—when you go to a dance and they play this "push and pull" music.

How did you acquire the material from the Gold Star label?

I met Bill Quinn, the owner of the Gold Star label, on one of my first trips. That's where I did the first Clifton session. He was an older man. He'd recorded some of the earlier Lightning records, plus a bunch of other Texas blues—some Little Son Jackson, "Thunder" Smith, and L. C. Williams. He had the studio, but he no longer had any interest in being in the record business. During one of my trips I asked if it would be possible to license any of his material. He said, "Sure." There were two volumes of Gold Star Lightning Hopkins and then a Texas anthology.

How did the "Juke Boy" Bonner happen?

Well, with that one I got in touch with Mike Leadbitter. He was really keen about him and he turned me on to him; that's how that happened. I thought Juke Boy was a really interesting poet. He couldn't get his thing together on the guitar. He didn't have a style like Lightning. He was a great poet and was a much more aware songwriter, but his records never sold. It was terribly sad to see him live this horrible existence that he had to live. He worked in these little beer joints and wrote a column in this local black paper. I tried my best. The one with the drummer was a pretty good session, and I think a couple of the singles did get played on the local R & B station in Houston, but it just never really clicked.

How did you manage to tap in, finally, to Chicago blues artists?

That was Pete Welding. He lived in Chicago and he was working for *Down Beat*. He was my first big contact. Of course there was Bob Koester, but I knew he was already recording stuff, so there was a little bit of competition. Pete was really keen about Johnny Young, so he did all of that. The way the Earl Hooker and Johnny Littlejohn happened, Buddy Guy was out here in Berkeley playing in a little joint. He was a really sweet guy. I remember talking to him. I told him, "I want to go to Chicago. Do you know any guys you feel are underserved on record, that are really good artists but have hardly made records?" He said, "Yeah, Earl Hooker and John Littlejohn." So those records were really from Buddy Guy telling me about them.

I went to Chicago, and Willie Dixon was really helpful with the Littlejohn record. I'd met Willie in Europe on the folk blues festival. The Earl Hooker sessions I did myself, but I probably should have used Willie Dixon. [*laughs*] I did the best I could. Earl was such a diverse artist; it was just amazing. But he didn't want to play blues all the time. Like in that overseas film, that footage that's available from those blues festivals in England. They caught him backstage and instead of a blues song, he sang "Walking the Floor Over You," the big country hit for Ernest Tubb. He was really pissed at the blues freaks who only wanted blues; he wanted to play everything. Elijah Wald, in his book about Robert Johnson, points out that many artists, including Lonnie Johnson, didn't particularly want to be blues singers, but that was the category they got stuck into. They said, "Hey, why can't I sing like Bing Crosby?" Earl came out here to do the second record and started recording for other labels out here, with mostly white bands. I got to know him pretty good on the trip to Europe in 1969, and he was pretty sick by then. I liked the guy very much. It was just sad.

I see another name that most people won't recognize—Johnny Lewis, the slide guitar player. How did that happen?

I believe this was John Steiner; I know I went to Steiner to record him. I don't remember. Perhaps Charlie Musselwhite told me about him. You'd have to reread the liner notes. [*laughs*]

Can you tell me about the Blues Classics series?

I think Origin Jazz Library started putting out old blues, and Folkways had done it all along. Meeting Bob Pinson and his hillbilly record collection helped me put out our Old Timey LPs, great old early country classics. I felt the same about blues. Only a few were trying to reissue old blues records, so I thought, "Someone should do this and pay the artists if they are still around." And I met Memphis Minnie in Memphis before she died. It was an English girl, Joe Ann Kelley, who sings and plays like her, who told us where Minnie was. And I thought, "There ought to be a way to make some money for these poor people."

That was my reason for putting out the first Memphis Minnie. I sent her a bunch of royalties, and I still have some of those letters she tried to write thanking me; she was already partially paralyzed. And I got the sweetest letter from Blind Boy Fuller's widow: "Dear Mr. Christ [*sic*], I sure appreciate you sending that check of yours . . ." And I just loved to do it, and if I could find the people still around I would pay them something for it. There was all this great music that wasn't out there, and I thought, "Somebody ought to pump it out there." So that's what happened. Now it's a flood, an inundation—they've reissued every record by every artist, but back then it wasn't so saturated and we called it "liberating the people's music"!

Let's talk about the trips you took to Europe with the blues guys.

The first one was with Lightning Hopkins. Horst desperately wanted him, and Lightning finally said, "If you go with me, Chris, I'll go." We had met up in Houston. We took a plane to New Jersey or New York. That was fairly uneventful; it was an American plane. Then we transferred to an Air India plane in New York to take us to Frankfort. I remember very vividly, it was one of those back-loading planes. We were already sitting in our seats, and from the rear came in the pilot and co-pilot and the personnel. And Lightning suddenly turns to me and says, "Chris, are these people going to fly this airplane?" And I said, "Yeah, I think they're probably perfectly trained for this." Later on, when we landed in Frankfort, poor Lightning was totally incapable of playing. When we got to our hotel, he tried playing—and couldn't. We called a doctor—and he couldn't find anything wrong with him—because we thought maybe he'd had a stroke or something.

I think he was just absolutely scared to death because the only familiarity he had with East Indians was the hoodoo people in Louisiana. And guys like Lightning—and I've met a lot of other people down there—they take that so seriously. If you put a hex on somebody, if you get a "mojo hand"—Lightning sings that song *"Going to Louisiana, get me a mojo hand. I'm gonna fix my woman so she can't have no other man"*—to him that was super-serious stuff, and I think he was deathly afraid that these East Indians were going to crash us.

Thank God we had a whole week in Baden-Baden, and he recovered enough at the end of it to be able to do that TV show. They saved his part for the last day. But that was scary. Otherwise we had a good time, except that he could never get the right food. But he liked that lager beer that comes in those German bottles with a porcelain cap and you could click it shut. Even on our farm, that was the most common way. People would drink soft drinks out of bottles like that; you could always stop them up again real easy. Anyway, Lightning said, "That's the best beer!" They tried to give him all these pilsner beers; he didn't like that shit at all. [*laughs*] Horst got along with me, in part, because I was German and, secondly, I knew Lightning.

So the next year I came back—this time it was with Fred McDowell and "Big Mama" Thornton. Jim Moore, her manager, insisted on going too. Oh, boy! I did make that nice record with Fred McDowell and Big Mama together over in Europe. I wish we had done that on the stage. They would jam together on the bus or in the hotel. It was just some wonderful times! I remember "Doctor" Ross, the harmonica boss. [*laughs*] We used to call him the "Flying Eagle." He used to stand in the middle of the aisle of the bus and spread his wings out: "I'm the Flying Eagle!" [*laughs*] Oh, man, we had some amazing times.

And Sonny Boy Williamson [II] was this amazing character! I remember one time at a hotel in Sweden I knocked on his door. I thought maybe they'd want to go down and get something to eat. He and Sunnyland Slim would always room together. Sonny Boy opened the door and said [*Chris's gruff-voice Sonny Boy imitation*], "How you doin', Chris?" And the whole room was steamed up—totally steamed up! I said, "What are you guys doing?" "Oh, man, we're just cooking a chicken in the coffee pot here." They had stuffed a fucking chicken in the coffee pot—and were steaming it! [*laughs*]

Sometimes on the buses they wouldn't stop often, and these guys would always be drinking whiskey, especially Sonny Boy. So in Berlin they gave him the hugest bottle of whiskey I've ever seen; it was about two feet tall. I don't know where the hell they got it, but they were always drinking. And since the buses wouldn't stop, he would piss in an empty bottle. And Sunnyland was pouring it out the window—I was sitting right behind them—and I got this shower coming back at me. [*laughs*] "Wait until we stop to pour it out!" Priceless adventures!

In Stockholm during the daytime we were all sitting around doing nothing. Sonny Boy came down, and we all ask him, "Where are you going?' [*Chris's Sonny Boy imitation*]: "Oh, the newspaper wants to talk to me about some shit, you know." So he went on his way. And when he came back I asked him, "Hey, man, what did you tell them?" "Oh, they just want to know how long my dick is—and that kind of shit!" [*laughs*] I don't think he ever told a true story in his life!

I think Sonny Boy was almost as tall as I am. I'm about six foot four, so he was a pretty big guy, but he was sort of stooped over already, so he looked like this kind of hulk—with a bowler hat on. And he had these suits made in England, with one color on one pant leg and a different color on the other leg, and then with the opposite colors on the jacket—unique-looking clothing. [*laughs*] There were some really bizarre stories.

Sometimes I used to sit next to Howling Wolf. He seemed like a really insecure guy in a way. He knew that weird voice he had is what put him over, but he couldn't play guitar worth a shit and he couldn't play much harmonica, but he knew people were scared of his physical size. One time he came out on the stage in overalls and had a broom [*laughs*], singing "Dust My Broom." It has nothing to do with a broom! In fact, I think that's how I finally found out what "dust my broom" meant. I asked him, "What does 'dust my broom' mean anyhow?" "Oh, man, that means you're gonna cut out on your old lady. You're gonna leave her—you're gonna split."

He scared the shit out of most people. He looked like a huge man out of the Congo or something, but he was really sweet, just talking to him—he would tell me all kinds of shit. Just a sweet guy, but I hear he was pretty nasty to Hubert Sumlin a lot of the time. He was a rough guy, I guess, but most people have a rough side and sweet side. They were rough guys who lived in a tough world. They had to survive, but they were great human beings. Big Mama Thornton was the same way. She lived in this unbelievably rough environment. But they all had hearts like gold.

Chris Strachwitz. Photo Alain McLaughlin.

Did you see a lot of Big Mama out in the Bay Area?

Oh, yeah, sure. That was another really sad thing. She got gigs very infrequently, so she couldn't really afford to keep a steady band. "Bee" Houston was the best guitar who could play behind her. But her manager, Jim Moore, every time she got a halfway decent job, like at the Fillmore, he would hire these god-damned black lounge musicians. He called them jazz musicians or whatever. To me, they had no clue what blues was all about; they were mediocre at best. I'm issuing a book with four CDs, *Hear Me Howling*, including all kinds of music I recorded here in the Bay Area during the 1960s, including a concert by Big Mama here on the University of California campus with this incompetent band. And in the middle of one song, she literally starts yelling at the saxophone player, "Hey, you! Mr. Nothin'—can't you do nothin'? You're just nothin'!" [*laughs*] And you will hear that the frigging band *couldn't* do nothin'. [*laughs*] And she was singing her ass off. The sad part was, she was always saddled with these "do-nothing" musicians. She could sing her heart and soul out, but it wouldn't do her any good. The people always wanted to hear "Ball and Chain," because Janis Joplin made a huge hit out of it. I felt so sorry for Big Mama. I think the best record we ever did with her was with the Muddy Waters band.

How did it happen that the recordings which originally appeared on Downbeat and Swingtime labels were added to your catalog?

That was in 1961 when I came back and found out that most of the recordings I made were over-modulated on that god-damned Roberts recorder. That's what it was. It was a cheap Japanese imitation of an Ampex recorder. I heard that Jack Lauderdale, who at that time, 1961, operated a bunch of motels, used to own those labels. I tracked him down, stopped in and visited him. I said, "Would you be willing to sell some of those recordings?" I was particularly interested in the Big Joe Turner and early Lowell Fulson sides. And he said, "Sure." I think I bought all the sides by Joe Turner and early Lowell Fulson sides. He wanted two hundred each for each artist. The Big Joe Turner sides were actually on tape, but they were recorded on an early German tape machine, and the speed was not exactly fifteen inches per second but a variation on that speed. I went to Sierra Sound here in Berkeley, and Bob DeSusa had a rheostat he used to find the proper playback speed. All the Lowell Fulsons were on acetate. I was totally in love with the real early ones where he just played guitar and sang with his brother Martin accompanying. Those were tough records, like "River Blues Parts 1 and 2": *"If you ever been on the river in 1910, where Bud Russell drove the women like he did the ugly men."* Pure Texas country blues!

And that's how I bought those, and I at least had something to release on Arhoolie! And he gave me a whole bunch of 78s—stacks of them! [*laughs*] Boxes full I hauled out of there. Then I gave his name to a British fellow. That was my mistake, I shouldn't have done that. He had the Black Lion label, and he bought all the rest of it. He was supposed to let me have some of it in return, but he never did, the bastard. There were the later Fulsons and Jimmy Witherspoon, and I really wanted the Smokey Hoggs on Excelsior. I think he owns a bunch of that early stuff.

How did you happen to add the Sonny Boy Trumpet label recordings to the Arhoolie catalog?

Since I met Sonny Boy on our trip to Europe, I then visited him in Helena, Arkansas, and I got his signature on a contract that he was selling me the Trumpet label sides. I neglected to do a live recording with him, which is what I should have done. Those Trumpet label recordings got me in trouble. I was sued by Lillian McMurry; it was the only time I was ever sued. We finally settled out of court. I paid her, and I'm now the owner of the Trumpet label recordings that I put out. I was only interested in those items that I had issued on my Blues Classics label; I didn't like the later sides with all the saxophone. Also I did the recording of Sonny Boy as he did the King Biscuit broadcast.

I issued it first as an EP and then included those recordings on the CD of Trumpet sides. I hung a very cheap microphone in the studio on my Uher tape recorder. I hung it from the studio microphone. They were just using one mic for the little band; I just hung mine next to it. Houston Stackhouse and Peck Curtis were the band that day. It was the last time I saw Sonny Boy, and it was when I took all those pictures of him. I believe that was about a month before he died. The stupid thing I did that day, when I was searching Helena for Sonny Boy that day, I saw a guy walk out of the joint with a guitar in one hand and an amp in the other. I asked him, "Where can I find Sonny Boy?" He told me where I could find him. Instead of asking him who he was, which I later surmised—it was . . . Little Boy Blues [Robert Nighthawk?]—you know, he made records for the United label," a wonderful slide guitar player. It would have been a wonderful session, a totally missed opportunity. Yes, indeed.

How did you get access to the Harry Oster recordings?

Oh, God, I always admired those recordings. I think he wrote to me, "Chris, I really don't want to be in this record business anymore." He was up in Iowa by that time, teaching up there. I remember he also sent a note to George Buck in New Orleans, who still resents the fact that I got the recordings, and not him. I'm sure glad I did. [*laughs*] So I drove up and visited him one year and signed the agreement. I bought the whole catalog from him: all the Angola recordings; all this great Cajun stuff he did, including a lot of unissued ballads from other Cajuns he recorded; of course, "Snooks" Eaglin and the Reverend Pearly Brown—this bluegrass band—"Snuffy" Jenkins and then this bluegrass band from Louisiana, the Louisiana Honeydrippers. He also had all kinds of other stuff—Peggy Seeger.

Oh, also he had a Jesse Fuller! I combined his Jesse Fuller with the one I had from Cavalier Records in San Francisco to make a CD. I should have just left LPs alone in those days. I made a mistake trying to make CDs longer; people didn't really appreciate it. I want to put out a package, "The Best of Harry Oster," with probably four CDs and a book. But I am not sure we can afford to do it. I still don't know what to do with the Harry Oster package. Unless you do something spectacular, nothing sells anymore.

Didn't Harry do the Robert Pete Williams?

Yeah, that's how I got in touch with Robert Pete when he got out. I'm sure that was through Harry. I recorded him some myself, but the classic material was the stuff Harry Oster recorded. Harry did "Angola Prisoner Blues," which included Robert Pete Williams, and then I did two Robert Pete CDs. But I think some of those were from Harry Oster tapes, but I'd have to go back and look that up.

What are you doing these days? Don't you have some involvement in recording Mexican folk music?

This is a whole separate chapter but very dear to me. As I told you earlier, as a young student I heard Mexican music on the radio, way back in the early 1950s. And I always liked it. And when I came up here, I would go to a little restaurant in the Broadway district in San

Francisco. They had a little mariachi with just one trumpet; those were so nice and funky. And every time I drove to Texas I heard this stuff on the radio, and in San Antonio you were just inundated with it. I just became totally enamored with it. It just fits that area somehow. And I just loved American polka music—and the Czech/Bohemian music that's down there in Central Texas. And here's this Mexican polka music that has this totally different sound to it. It's distinctly unique. And the duet singing is just like great hillbilly music, especially the real norteños from Mexico. With the Tejano musicians, I've always had trouble because of their duet singing not being as strong as the guys from Mexico. For example, I recorded Flaco Jimenez. He had one really great guy that sings good with him, Fred Ojeda, but most of the guys he sings with don't sound as Mexican as they ought to, because they're Tejanos. [*laughs*]

So I got totally into this, and I got into the recording of it by meeting this young fellow who was a law student out of Austin, Texas; he was actually out of Boston, Jerry Abrams. He put me in touch with Rumel Fuentes, who lived in Eagle Pass. They all knew this little conjunto over the river in Piedras Negras—Los Pinguinos del Norte, the Penguins of the North. I was totally enamored with them when I heard them. The accordionist was such a sweet guy, and they had this down-home style and they played in all these cantinas down there. By that time I had a Magnecord tape deck, in the early 1970s, and it was always in my trunk on my trips to Texas. I literally took my tape deck across the river. I tried recording them in the cantina where they were working, but the owner said, "No, man, you're disturbing our customers." So we went to a bar next door. There was hardly anybody in it, but Rumel and a few friends did the hollering and the *gritos* [cries]. We did this live recording in a cantina, which nobody had ever done before. I didn't know how it would sell, but it did stir up some interest.

From that point on it just became one of my manias. I reissued a lot of old Mexican border music records. You see, as I traveled around looking for talent, going through Alabama or Georgia or Mississippi or Louisiana, if I didn't find musicians, I would always look for old records. Same thing in Texas—I would hunt records constantly. And this Mexican music was unbelievably well documented on hundreds of little labels. [*laughs*] And that just became a mania for me.

Historically it's more interesting text-wise than any American music I know of. Blues has some interesting ballads, like "Tom Moore," and hillbilly music has some interesting ballads that deal with contemporary events, but the Mexican stuff is really potent. It deals with this conflict between Mexicans and gringos. It just haunts me. Some of the live recordings are on Arhoolie, but I started putting out many of the reissued sides on the Folklyric label. I originally got the Folklyric label from Harry Oster but used it to reissue all sorts of ethnic music that I really like and feel should be documented. We've done Puerto Rican music; we've done Cuban *sones*, Texas Bohemian/Czech music, early *tamburitzen*—you name it. [*laughs*]

PAUL GARON INTERVIEW

I was born in 1942 in Louisville, Kentucky, and lived in the same house until I was twenty-one. My father was a doctor. I continued to live in Louisville for another ten years until I moved to Chicago. It was blues that brought me to Chicago. Around 1959 I walked into a record shop in Louisville and heard somebody playing a record that was fantastic. I'd never heard that kind of music—I thought it was great. It turned out to be the first Sonny Terry and Brownie McGhee on Bluesville. I bought that record and a Jimmy Reed record as well, and then I started going around buying Sonny and Brownie LPs and had no idea that there was more to the music than that. I thought, "Hey—I've discovered a great folk form!" But little by little I started discovering how much more was out there. I worked in a record store, and I started to ask customers if they had any old records. The store was in an African American neighborhood, so I ran into a lot of people who had 78s, and every once in a while I'd actually buy some—and that introduced me to many, many more names. I remember buying the book *Country Blues* by Sam Charters and being impressed by everybody in there—and not particularly Robert Johnson. I don't remember how I heard about it but I drove to Chicago because they had a great big record store called Rose's. I was looking for an LP by Big Joe Williams on the Delmark label. It never occurred to me to go to Delmark—I just wanted to go to a big store and buy the album—and I did. I bought the record and came back home and never heard of Jazz Record Mart.

Paul Garon. Photo Steve Cushing.

But Chris Strachwitz stopped at our house for a chat. I'm sure he told me things as well, but I just can't remember what got me into the wider world—beyond Sonny and Brownie. When I came to Chicago, I was staying at the YMCA at 800 South Wabash. I came to hear live blues at the Blind Pig or the Fickle

Pickle, music that Bob Koester was organizing—but without knowing anything about Koester. I came because Big Joe was there. I don't recall how in particular I heard about Big Joe. After I got the Brownie and Sonny bug I was buying a lot of LPs by mail—there was Folkway and Savoy and all these different labels, and they would send promos. One of the first LPs I got was an Arhoolie sampler. It had Big Joe and Lil Son Jackson and Black Ace, and each artist had one cut—and somehow in all this I heard about Big Joe Williams. So I came to Chicago: I got to see Big Joe and I got to watch his fingers, and somehow I got the nerve to talk to him afterward. He pointed to Bob and said, "If you like those old records, that's the guy you ought to see." So that was the big tip-off. This was all between 1959 and 1961. I visited Chicago maybe five or six times. In 1961 or 1962 I came up to Chicago to work for the summer, and I worked for Bob Koester at his Jazz Record Mart, then located at 439 South Wabash. That was very formative [*laughs*]—I don't remember if I was still at the YMCA. I remember that Koester had this bed/cot thing that you could sleep on—but just barely. It was in the attic of the store, which was where his collection was—and it was so hot up there. I can remember that if I laid perfectly still, I was okay; but if I rolled over, sweat just poured off me [*laughs*]. I also discovered Maxwell Street because the bed was missing a caster and Koester said, "You know, if you go down to Maxwell Street, you'll not only hear a lot of great blues, but you can buy casters." I said, "Is there a caster store down there?" "No-no, go down there. You'll see. You'll find a thousand casters!" So I went down early like he told me, five o'clock—and it was amazing. And my mind expanded once again! [*laughs*] People playing on the street—and your choice of casters!

Koester was my main mentor in those days. My blues education those first five years was strictly from Bob. It was a pretty good place to start, plus I got paid for working in the shop. And when he sold his 78s, I got matching privileges, so if I was willing to match somebody else's highest bid, I'd get the record—and boy did I! I couldn't afford the two or three rarest things but I got many, many great records from Bob. He had decided to sell his own personal 78 collection to finance more years for Delmark—this was his longstanding collection that he had been working on for years. This must have been around 1966 because shortly after, 1967, I served as the best man at his wedding, and I finally moved to Chicago because Bob wanted me to run the shop for a month while he was on his honeymoon. After that I drifted away, and that was probably the end of Bob's influence on my blues preferences.

Most of the Jazz Record Mart/Delmark employees had the privilege of meeting and associating with the artists on the label when they dropped by. Did you meet any of the Delmark artists?

Sleepy John Estes's first session for Delmark was held at Audiophone studios in Wisconsin—E. D. Nunn had this Audiophile label, and his was the studio for the first Sleepy John sessions. So I drove together with Bob and Sleepy John. That was huge excitement, and I had my steel-body National. Even though I was clumsy and useless, I was able to play along on two songs, but I wasn't good enough [*laughs*]. Koester let me play, but I was fucked—I didn't know what I was doing—you know, strum-strum, and I don't think I was even in tune. So after a couple of tunes I dropped out. But I got to watch the whole session, and that was pretty exciting. And of course, with Big Joe Williams you couldn't avoid meeting Joe, and I was very fond of him. In fact, I played behind Big Joe for a couple of years after I first moved here. It was very irregular—I mean, I wasn't his partner or anything. If he had a North Side gig that happened to coincide with my being at the shop, then I played behind him. I had the same arrangement with Johnny Shines a couple of years later. But the people coming through Koester's were just amazing—you could meet anybody! I met Yank Rachell in Louisville because we had managed to get him a gig at a coffeehouse, and then one day I was sitting in the JRM talking to somebody and Yank came walking in. They may have been gathering together to attend one of the American Folk Blues Fests. There were so many names in the back of my head and people I wanted to see. Elmore James was one of those people. Well, he never did walk in, but one day in the early 1960s somebody posted a three-by-five card on the cash register announcing his death. I never talked to Tommy McClennan, but Koester said, "He's in so and so hospital if you want to go see him." I'd heard his record and thought he was tremendous, but I was scared to go to a hospital and see him. I didn't know what to say to somebody I'd never seen. So I didn't go. I remember reading in Honeyboy's biography, just recently, that he had picked Tommy up from the gutter and got him back in shape and was going to play again. But it just didn't work, and he was drinking more and more and more. He was staying with Honeyboy, and Tommy said to him, "Just take me back to the jungle. That's where I want to be. I don't want to be messing around with you and trying to stay in your house—I just want to drink wine." So they took him back, and then he was in the hospital and he died. It would seem as though he lived as late as 1962 or 1963, but I do remember Koester offering me a chance at a visit.

Was Jazz Record Mart located on South Wabash during you entire tenure with Bob?

No, they moved. But fortunately my knee gave out about a month before they moved the store. I've had trouble with this knee—in fact, both knees—forever. They kept me out of the army and other things, but in this particular instance they kept me out of helping to move the store—and I was glad to be out. I had surgery on the knee and went back home for the summer in 1962, just before Koester decided to move the store to 7 West Grand.

I would see blues singers regularly at the Blind Pig and the Fickle Pickle—I don't remember which came first. Then I met Don Kent—he was my first blues buddy. He told about places like Big John's where I could see Muddy, and then Koester told me about places on the South Side. He started taking me to places like the Checkerboard and Theresa's—mostly the South Side.

Charlie Musselwhite has mentioned Big John's. Where were these places located?

Well, I really didn't know Chicago then, and so they were just streets. I think one of them was on North Avenue in the Old Town area, near where the cinema is located—just west of Wells Street. When I moved here, there was something of a blues scene there—Mother Blues was on 1305 North Wells down by Schiller. I went there a lot to see Howling

Wolf and Otis Rush—and Buddy Guy. Curtis Jones was at the Blind Pig one night. Curtis, unfortunately, had a dismal end. He was an expatriate, but unlike other blues expatriates his years of poverty and nonsuccess continued. Having seen him at the Blind Pig, I could see what happened. He was the most nondynamic, unassuming person. You don't expect blues performers to be like that—you expect them to be "out there" for you—and he just wasn't. He made dozens and dozens of records, but in person he just had no élan. He had a tough life. He was one of the first bluesmen I read about who spent time in the mid- to upper plains—he talked about going through Nebraska and working there for a couple of years. I don't think of blues singers in Nebraska. It's possible he was just beaten down by the years. The folk boom was going on, and all these blues singers were soaring—and he just didn't make it. He died in Germany and was buried in a pauper's grave. Six years later they sold the grave space because no one was keeping it up, and buried someone on top of him. Just terrible things—what a story! But I think those were the main people I saw when I was still visiting Chicago because I didn't move here until 1967 or 1968. During that time Chris Strachwitz and Bob Koester were still my main source of blues information. At that time I became rabid about looking for 78s in Louisville. I bid in many auctions—mostly prewar. I actually did "door-knocking" in Louisville with only mediocre success—most of what I found there was postwar. I bought that, but to me the prewar was the great stuff, that's what I was really looking for.

It seems as though there was no great following for postwar at that time . . .

That's the way it seems to me—but again, I was pulled toward that world. When I met Don Kent he was 98 percent postwar. He'd take me to see Muddy Waters because to him, that's what the blues were. He's changed since. Also Jim O'Neal and Amy [van Singel] were big postwar fans. Like so many others, they came in through rock 'n' roll, and they were used to the electric guitar licks you'd hear in electric postwar blues. They didn't really discover prewar blues until I got a hold of them [*laughs*]. I discovered while still in Louisville that if they came from the folk world, they would like my stuff, but if they came from rock music, they'd prefer postwar blues, so I would play them some of that. I was a proselytizer. I went overseas in 1965, before I lived in Chicago full time. Blues Unlimited had started in 1965, and I wanted to meet Simon Napier of Blues Unlimited—I already knew Mike Leadbitter from his visits here; I met him once. And I wanted to meet Paul Oliver—that was my big goal. I remember writing to John Godrich, clumsily trying to find out what the drug laws were in England [*laughs*]; I planned my visit for the summer of 1965—and I'm fairly sure that BU was up and running by that time. There were thousands of people—you've got reviews and discographies and all sorts of names. Francis [Wilford] Smith—that was another name I heard about. And I was able to meet all these people. They all hosted me in their houses—they were wonderful. Francis was wonderful—he had a great collection, but I was never invited to browse it—he would play anything. That's kind of what you do when you go to someone's house and they play things for you. He had these two little girls, and they were just so disciplined that my heart went out to them. They were invited down to say hello, and they came down to the living room in their night dresses and both said "Hello, I'm glad to meet you. Good night now." No running through the house or making noise—uh-uh—a very well-run house. He was cartooning at that time for *Playboy* and a number of other well-known magazines—that was his living. His cartoon name was Smilby.

I eventually met John Godrich. I met all these people at other people's houses—I don't remember where, but John was from Wales and must have come into London. Robert M. W. Dixon, his partner, was there. And Pete Whelan of *78 Quarterly* came in with a little 78 case—a case that might hold twenty-five or one hundred records. He had sold his whole collection but he was keeping what he had in the case. I didn't really know who all the big names were at that point, but I knew about Pete because his OJL label had started issuing records in 1963. His case was filled with Electrobeam Gennetts and records that you never, ever see. I've been collecting now for forty years, and I've only got two or three Gennetts—and that was his specialty.

Were you able to meet Derrick Stewart-Baxter?

He wrote the book on Ma Rainey, but no. I liked the book, but I didn't meet the jazz people. I did meet Paul and Valerie Oliver, and they were very warmly encouraging. Paul has been encouraging to me for decades—suggesting that I write for the Blues Series and getting me to write for the *Blackwell Guide*. He was the impetus for that. He was a mentor—indirectly. We never indulged in theoretical discussions, but his writing was very influential on my writing. I've always thought of him in that context. One thing I always liked about Bob Koester was if somebody came into the shop asking for a Paul Butterfield LP, Bob would say, "You know, you can hear the same music by the guy who wrote it over here on this record."

I've heard that at one point in your life you had a problem with drugs.

That was why, in part, I went to England. It was legal over there. You get signed up with an MD and you can take care of things without any problem. I was very open about it while I was there. I know a lot of stories circulated about that [*laughs*]. That was a big problem for me during the 1960s and on and off since then, but the 1960s was when it was bad. I had many painful joint problems—my knee, my back. Because of the joint pain my father, who was a physician, gave me very powerful painkillers all through my teens. And that's how I got my start. I moved out of the house when I was twenty-one—that would've been late 1963 or early 1964—and all of my drug problems were pretty well established by that time. I wasn't being treated in the sense that I was bedbound and getting treatment. I had a father who was a doctor and a medicine cabinet full of everything. None of it was off limits—and that did the trick. It was mostly high-powered pills, and I had them with me at all times. I either got them from home or had a prescription my father would write for me. The druggist was a good friend. Louisville was not a big place and my father had a large medical practice—and at the time these drugs were not considered that dangerous. Every time they came up with a new narcotic, it was supposed to be a great cure that wouldn't addict anybody, and the next thing you know it was worse than the last one [*laughs*]. In that sense I was lucky. I was a medical addict—but not a street addict, so I didn't have to score when I went places. That was a big difference. When you get to England, you find that everybody's like that—that's their arrangement. Again, that's why I went to England—not only could I get everything I needed, I could also get treatment and get off it in a hospital. Over there you're not a criminal. What I had to do was find one of the four doctors in London who bothered with addicts and go to her and simply have her say, "Okay, I'll treat you." She probably sent my name and address into the home office and thus I became registered. This was 1964 and 1965—I was there in '65. They counted their addicts as 560. There were 560 addicts, that's all. It wasn't a big problem yet. So in that sense I *was* registered, and I was registered with Lady Frankau, who was the most famous in giving heroin to everybody, though she was stingy with me. The first time I met her—I was on this side of the desk and she was the other side, and there was this guy sitting over there, and it turned out he was from the home office. I had no idea he was anybody or what they were talking about, but I told them what I was doing, that I was an addict and I needed something legal. And he asked, "How did you hear about Lady Frankau?" And she interrupted, saying, "Oh don't ask him that question! Let me work with this man!"

Did she provide you with prescriptions or drugs?

Prescriptions to get drugs. And you took the prescriptions to Boots, which was the biggest pharmacy chain. They had two all-night drugstores, which meant if you had a prescription for August 2nd, you could go there at midnight. And there were always people hanging around at midnight hoping they could bum something off one of the people who were getting a refill. This situation lasted only about three or four months. I went over in the summer and came back about December.

While I was in England arranging to go into this hospital, my father was talking to the [US] Treasury people over here—in those days they were the drug agents. They wanted me to go to Lexington, which was a half-hospital–half-prison for addicts. That's when my father decided if I really got off drugs over there like I said I was going to, he would put me in a place over here, but it wouldn't be Lexington. He guaranteed the Treasury guy that he would put me in a place—otherwise they were going to say, "We want him." He made that deal. I wound up coming home from England, home for a few days. I thought I would go into drug rehab the very day I got back, but it took a week for someone to be released and make another bed available, so I was home for a week before I went in. I wasn't in particularly good shape physically at that time, and I thought maybe it would be peace and quiet for a while, but I didn't realize how long it would be—eight months—but I finally got off everything on my own.

The person I got to know best during my time in England was a fellow named Charles Radcliff, and he had written the first attacks on white blues for a magazine called *Anarchy* in 1965. I got to England in 1965 in time to see one of the American Folk Blues tours, but he told me about an earlier tour that had Lightning [Hopkins] and Sonny Boy II on the same bill. Charles had gotten himself in with the "in crowd," and when Charles came in the room Sonny Boy was just leaving. So Charles talked to Lightning a little bit and Sonny Boy came back and put a bottle of whiskey on the table, dropped some money on the table, and said to Lightning, "Here's your change." Lightning grabbed Charles and said, "He got this for me (referring to the bottle) and this is my change—Is that right?" And Charles said, "That's not even close to right." And right away Sonny Boy started squawking, "Why you white son of a bitch, you better not say nothin' about what I do here!" And then Lightning would talk to Charles and say, "Don't you worry son. Don't you worry about him at all." Charles said, "Well, I think there should be a little bit more money." And then Sonny Boy would throw down another pound note—instead of the five or ten pounds he was supposed to. Sonny Boy was saying "I'll kill you!" and Lightning saying "I'll protect you!" Charles said he was amazed he got out with his life! [*laughs*]

It seems as though Sam Charters's overall body of work has in recent years taken it on the nose with so much criticism, yet everybody I interviewed for this book talks about what an influence his work was. Are you among those influenced by Charters?

It's true, but I felt he treated a couple of people in that book badly just making presumptions—like Kokomo Arnold was dropped by Decca because he was too boring, or Bo Carter was dropped by Bluebird because all he could do was double-entendre crap. He was obviously making it up since they were not people he interviewed personally. I was sort of rude and quite hostile when I did reviews of him in my *Blues and The Poetic Spirit*, when I did my special chapter of denunciations of people—that was the first edition; they took it out later. Then I met him later and he asked me to do an appraisal of his and his wife's archive of material, which they were giving to the University of Connecticut—which was his wife's school. He said, "I know you're not fond of my writing. I just wanted to make sure you could do this job for us or would that color your decisions?" "That was forty years ago and I really don't have anything against you," I told him.

So all was forgiven—until . . . The Living Blues symposiums were at Oxford, Mississippi. I was in charge of a Robert Johnson panel. Charters was the guest of honor and was going to give the keynote address. As it happened, four of us were in the Memphis airport when the bus came to take us to Ole Miss. It was Charters, Elijah Wald, Steve Hoffman, and myself. All of us are on the bus and none of us had ever met. I'm putting this panel together and I'm trying to get everybody involved to tell me what they intend to talk about. I wanted to use this information in my general introductions for everyone and Sam wouldn't answer. He started saying, "What's all this Robert Johnson crap? When I go to a record store I don't look for Robert Johnson—I'm trying to find the latest hip-hop hits." And I was thinking "Oh, Christ . . ." [*laughs*]. The Robert Johnson panel had Elijah Wald, Patty Schroeder, myself, and somebody else. And right in the middle of the panel presentation, Patty was speaking and Charters pipes up from the back of the hall: "I'm listening to this panel on the Blues and I don't see a black person up there." And so I'm thinking this is why everybody calls him an asshole—because he is one! Elijah stands up and says, "If there's any African American in the room who wants to speak, they can have my seat, certainly." Luckily, there was an African American, one of the Sacred Steel group, who stood up and talked about the great contribution that the white Living Blues people happen to make and he wanted to continue to hear them, and that got things back on track. So then when the panel that Charters is going to be on comes up, I'm still trying to get him to tell me what he's going to say. He says, "Well, I think what I would like to talk about is how a white critic like me can't even get his next book published." At that point I lost my temper and really cursed him out. "I've spent days trying to get you to tell me what you wanted to talk about. We could have discussed how to work that particular subject in your conversation, but on its own that's got nothing to do with shit!" It did not go well. The evening's entertainment was out in some rural location—I didn't go.

The next morning the conference was over and we were all leaving, and Jim O'Neal told me that Charters was looking around frantically trying to find me to apologize. "So try to find him," he said, "I think he's leaving in a couple of minutes." And I did find him and he was totally abject and said, "I know I shouldn't come to these things because I'm always such an arrogant son-of-a-bitch." And I said, "Don't worry about it Sam—it's really nothing, nothing, nothing." And I'm thinking, "Yeah you are—Yes you are!" [*laughs*] So I started off being greatly influenced by Charters, then not liking him, liking him again and helping to appraise their collection—and then not liking him again [*laughs*]. That was my Charters adventure—he was a complex person. His book was the introduction to the blues for hundreds if not thousands of people, but I think his reputation deservedly belongs with his field recordings—that was his main contribution, finding Lightning Hopkins and producing *Chicago/The Blues/Today!* I still think that's one of the best anthologies to come out of Chicago. Sam just did thousands of things like that. His book *Country Blues* was a pioneering effort, but his recordings will be the things that last.

When I first moved here, I met a couple of people who were students at Grinnell. I'd gone to Grinnell for one semester—didn't like it and switched to the University at Louisville. I hadn't met any of these people. They'd started a year later, but they were correspondents at the Jazz Record Mart when I was there working for Koester—so I had their names and they moved here. They lived below The Midway in Hyde Park—something like 6200 South Kenwood. They told me about the annual University of Chicago folk festivals. So I started going to those. It was at one of my early U of C folk fests that either Jim or Bruce tapped me on the shoulder, introduced himself, and said, "We're starting a Blues magazine, and Bob Koester suggested that you'd be a good person to have with us because of your knowledge of prewar blues." The magazine was at that point mostly the efforts of Jim and Amy O'Neal and Bruce Iglauer. They had talked to Diana Allman, Tim Zorn, and Andre Souffront, but Jim, Amy, and Bruce were the core group. So that's how I met them—I didn't know any of them prior to that. Bruce hadn't started Alligator Records yet. I think after our first meeting I was telling my folks about it, and I told them the names of everybody and my father said, "What was Bruce's name?" "Iglauer." "Is he from Cincinnati?" "Yes—I think he is." And dad said, "That boy's your cousin." And it's true—we really are cousins—once or twice removed. He'd gone to school in Appleton, Wisconsin, but he came from Cincinnati. At the time, I was so deeply into frogs and Beasley and the logo that Bruce asked if it would be trespassing if he named his new record label Bullfrog. I said yes—and that's why we have Alligator today [*laughs*]. Right away I felt the real lines of labor were being drawn, and Jim, Amy, and Bruce were going to do all the work—which was true. They were really the nuts and bolts of the organization. I went to all the meetings—and I knew more than any of them, certainly from a historical perspective—but Bruce singlehandedly did distribution, which was a huge pain in the butt. Jim and Amy did everything else. I lazed around and tried to write things, frequently—but I wasn't the dynamos they were. We became good friends with Jim and Amy and around 1978; we lived above them, and we met many blues people downstairs.

I find it ironic that anybody, under any circumstances, would refer to Jim O'Neal as a dynamo. And who did you see at the University of Chicago folk festivals?

I saw the most dynamic act I'd ever seen, which was Ed and Lonnie Young with their cane fife band. That was so impressive! It really floored me. I'd just gotten the LPs—the Lomax sessions on the Atlantic label—exactly! I still play that stuff all the time. What I enjoyed at those festivals was the blues and the bluegrass stuff. And they always had a highlight act like Bill Monroe or Don Reno, but they always had great headlining acts. I think I saw Lightning Slim, shortly after he was rediscovered. It was just a thrill that the guy was still around. This was the late 1960s—shortly after I moved here.

How did you get into the book business?

My uncle had a big bookstore in Louisville. I worked there off and on for a long time, and he constantly fed me books. Birthdays it would be a book, Christmases it would be a book—just on general principles it would be a book. And that worked out because I was bookish. If I hadn't been, nothing would have come of that. My uncle was kind of the culture wing of the family and the one I took to, so I grew up with that. And my mother was very literate—constantly reading a book because she got them from her brother, my uncle—the same person. When I graduated from Louisville with a BS in sociology, I decided to pursue a career and apply for state jobs in Chicago—for social work, any kind of social thing—so I came to Chicago long before I discovered the blues. But when I came here I discovered Barbara's Bookstore. It was such a fun place and she was looking for someone early on, but I found out what the salary was and said, "I couldn't possibly live on that." So I recommended that she hire Franklin Rosemont. Barbara knew me as a customer, so Franklin got the job. After a year working for the state—it was a cool job working as a test administrator—I got promoted to counselor, but it was far away and I didn't want the commotion. I told my boss I'd prefer to skip the promotion and stay on as the test administrator. So that was cool, but then three weeks later she said she'd like me to work in reception for a while, so I decided to check out the job at Barbara's Bookstore. I went to Barbara's, and by then Franklin was working there and spoke up on my behalf and convinced her to hire me. I wanted a full-time job, and so I became a night manager. That's how I got into books, at Barbara's.

I was at Barbara's from 1968 until 1973. Then I worked for Logan Bros. for a year. They were a medical book jobber. Then I moved to Avon Paperbacks as a rep. I was with them from 1975 to 1980. Then I spent two years at Playboy Paperbacks, and they went under. Before that, Beth and I had the idea of becoming book dealers ourselves—rare books. So while I was working for these companies I would try to get all my calls done instantly and go to the used bookstores and look around. That's how we built up our first stock. When Playboy crashed in the early 1980s, we did our first catalog—1981, I believe. And we've been doing it ever since. We were mostly mail order, and the store didn't come into being until 1998. We were downtown near the Newberry Library at that time. In 2004 we moved up to Evanston.

When did you and Beth meet?

We met here in Chicago. During the time I worked at Barbara's Bookstore—around 1972 or 1973—we had a rep who would stop in from Avon Books, and he hired one of my workmates. This guy he hired went on to become a sales manager at Avon Books, and he hired me to take his place. And when I became a regional manager, I hired Beth, who worked at Barbara's Bookstore to take my place. We met at a party sometime in the mid-1970s but didn't particularly see each other. At the place I lived before Wrightwood, Beth lived next door in the back—so we kind of knew each other. And then when the job opened up, I thought she'd be a good person to ask. I had no personal interest. She was out west with a boyfriend she was ready to dump. That was 1977, and Barbara's Bookstore was sort of the nucleus.

As the resident prewar expert at *Living Blues*, how were the topics chosen for the articles you wrote?

I usually picked things. I remember Jim asked me to write an obituary for Lonnie Johnson. I wrote the obit—and Brownie McGhee wrote one AND Steve LaVere wrote an obit for Memphis Minnie. Both his Minnie obit and my Lonnie obit appeared on the same page. But usually I just had an idea for an article. *Living Blues* did a Robert Johnson issue, and I wrote an article about why he wasn't so great and who his forerunners were—that kind of stuff. But I think my leadership role, if you can call it that, came to the fore when Erwin Helfer had gotten pissed about our anti-white attitude, which was stoked mostly by me. Jim, Amy, and Bruce had no disagreement with that attitude. But Harriet Choice, the jazz columnist, called us into her office for a conference and lectured us on how our views were so narrow and then wrote an entire column about why we were wrong. So we did an editorial about why we were right. I wrote that editorial and so became the official articulator of the position whenever it came up. That subject came up about once a decade. Then in the 1980s and 1990s I wasn't with the magazine much. The subject of white blues came up again, and Larry Hoffman, who started with *Guitar Player* magazine, took the heat that time around. So *Living Blues* asked me to write an article about it again, but by this time I believe Jim and Amy were no longer with the magazine. That particular issue served to renew my link with the magazine.

Were you the guy who had a problem with Nick Perls?

No—Nick humorously said that Peetie Wheatstraw was the guy who ruined the blues. Well, that's a good statement, and obviously what he was getting at was that anybody who's a fan of Charley Patton, Skip James, and Son House and found themselves having to listen to 161 sides by Peetie Wheatstraw is going to get bored pretty quickly [*laughs*]. But I thought he misplaced the blame by saying it about Peetie when it was actually Leroy Carr who led the way with same-y sounding piano/guitar duets. Peetie was only following in his footsteps. No, Nick and I were always on friendly terms. Don Kent told me that Nick admired me because I played guitar—which I don't really understand—but my 78 recordings were among the sides he borrowed for his reissues. So we stayed friends down through the years. At one point he was going around with a record player and recorder going through various collectors' collections, searching for records for his reissues, so we all knew him. He'd tell Don Kent, "I hope when Paul comes over, the subject of his book doesn't come up—because I didn't like it very much." But then when we got together he'd say how much he liked my book [*laughs*]. Nick was the first person I knew personally who died of AIDS. He was in seclusion for several years at the end, and we all wondered what was going on—and then we heard of his passing.

When did you do the Peetie Wheatstraw book, and how did it come about?

I met Paul Oliver when I was in England in 1965. He was a very congenial host. The next year I started sending little pieces in to *Blues Unlimited* to Simon Napier. By that time I was already a Peetie Wheatstraw nut and had most of his records. Simon's introduction to the article said something to the effect that I was a Peetie nut. The article was about how I had met some characters, long after Peetie was dead. When I was first working a record shop in Louisville, a short black man with a hat came in. He was about fifty and very jivey and jerky. He jumped around a lot and snapped his fingers, and without any introduction at all he started saying "I'm Peetie Wheatstraw, the devil's son-in-law." That was all he said. I could never get him to tell me what that meant. And he was behaving bizarrely in the store. At that time I was also walking through black neighborhoods knocking on doors, asking to buy records from people. While one woman was selling me records, I came across a Peetie Wheatstraw record. I said, "Oh, Peetie Wheatstraw—I'll have to buy this." And she said, "Yeah, he's one of my favorites too. In fact, we just saw him last month in Arkansas." My thought was Peetie's been dead for thirty years [*laughs*], but there was another example of someone mentioning Peetie. Then I got a note from Paul Oliver suggesting I write a book on Peetie. He said, "Why don't you do a Peetie Wheatstraw book for this new series I'm starting? Stein & Day is going to publish them in the US and Studio Vista's going to publish them in England." But I didn't give it much thought. I didn't know what to do. I'd never written a book before. Then at the Ann Arbor Blues Fest Paul Oliver was the emcee, and when I went to see him he had a copy of his book, *Savannah Syncopators*, from the series. He gave me a copy, and I said, "If I did a Peetie Wheatstraw book, would it look like this?" "Exactly—they all look like that—many photos and text all the way through."

So then I decided I wanted to do it—and I went home and did it. It took about a year, I guess. But that's how it got started.

A friend of mine, Diane Allman, who was a photographer for *Living Blues* magazine and one of its founders, went with me down to St. Louis and East St. Louis. We interviewed anybody we could find who knew Peetie—which at that point was principally Henry Townsend and Teddy Darby. She took pictures and I did the interviewing. Both Henry and Teddy were great informants. They knew Peetie well. Darby could well have been in the fatal car wreck [that killed Peetie]. Darby said the owner of the car had gotten it just recently and it was a Buick. Peetie came over and said, "C'mon man. We're gonna blow this Buick out." But luckily Darby's wife wouldn't let him go. Peetie was riding in the back seat when the car ran into a standing freight train. They hit it hard enough to actually move the freight cars a bit. Peetie died a few hours later. His wife actually heard the crash down the block but had no idea Peetie was in it. Darby told me that after Peetie's death he didn't really have the heart to play anymore. Playing with Peetie and the guys was so much of what he did that it just didn't seem like fun after the crash.

Later, I talked with Peetie's brother, who I met in Cotton Plant, Arkansas. Studio Vista had sent me a copy of the dust jacket for the Peetie book while the book was at press. The proof arrived the day I was leaving on this trip, so I just put it in my breast pocket and took it with me. I went into Cotton Plant knowing that Peetie was buried there. I stopped at a funeral home, which turned out to be a white funeral home. They let me know they wouldn't know where a negro was buried and told me to go ask at a garage—really. So we went over to this garage where there were a couple of black guys hanging out. I told them who we were and that we were trying to find Peetie Wheatstraw's grave. The guys went into the garage and didn't came out again. So we went in to see what was going on and there were six or seven guys there and they were all talking about Peetie. They were saying, "Peetie Wheatstraw, the Devil's Son-in-Law, the High Sherriff of Hell!" and they were laughing. For them it was a great memory. These guys were all in their forties, so it was clear they didn't know Peetie. One of them said, "You know, you could talk to his brother—he lives right over there," and he pointed through a vacant lot to a house on the next block. "Yeah—Sam's over there." So we went to Sam's house. There was a little fence and a gate with a woman sitting on the front porch. I stopped at the gate and said, "Hello—we're looking anybody who can tell us anything about William Bunch." The woman totally ignored me. I said the same thing again and she didn't even look up. I was baffled—no response at all. I said, "We're writing a book on Peetie Wheatstraw." And she jumped up and said, "Peetie Wheatstraw!" And then she ran to the door and said, "Sam, Sam—somebody here wants to talk about Peetie Wheatstraw!" Sam came out—and he didn't look very friendly. He was old and frail, and he came out to the gate to invite me in. I showed him the proof dust jacket from the book and he really didn't like that. I hadn't seen that kind of negative reaction to it before, but he clarified it for me. He said, "I told him many a time to stop, to just put all that junk down but he never listened to me." He wanted nothing to do with the book. And he didn't want to talk about Peetie. I heard much later, like in the past five years, that there were some people in the South doing some Peetie Wheatstraw research. There was this minister—and I believe he was a relative—and he wouldn't let Peetie be buried in the good part of the cemetery. Peetie was buried closer to the road, out of the cemetery proper without a marker. That was shocking.

Did you talk to Charlie O'Brien?

No. I don't know what the deal was there. I know Koester mentioned him to me. I may have just been reluctant to speak with an authoritative stranger. Not for any real reason—just my own neurotic bullshit [*laughs*]. But no, I didn't speak with him. I had this feeling that I knew who I was looking for down there. One of the people, I believe it was Mary Johnson, lived in a Cabrini Green–type highrise. I just said, "We're not going in there. That's an interview we're not going to do."

Did anybody here in Chicago have connections to Peetie?

Big Joe Williams. Big Joe knew a lot, but the problem was always how did you strain the truth out of all that he said. According to him, he was in the car that night but they got into an argument and he got pissed and they had to let him out of the car [*laughs*]. I may have included that in the book but with no guarantee of credence. I don't remember where I got this, but apparently they had a rehearsal hall in St. Louis that served the same purpose as Tampa Red's house in Chicago. That was the meeting place. You had Peetie and Henry Townsend and Darby, who were all on the Decca Label. I've forgotten who mentioned this, but it was someone who had a great deal of affection for the hall—they knew the address, and Big Joe said you wouldn't visit St. Louis without stopping by this rehearsal hall. He said sometimes you might be looking for a playing job, but mostly it was just social. Charlie Jordan was always there. We didn't know that Charlie was crippled, but he was shot in the legs or the back and walked with crutches. No one seemed to know the story exactly, and the more people you asked about it, the more limbs were disabled. They got him in the head and the foot and the right arm! [laughs]

At that time of our discussion here today, you've recently reissued your book on Peetie Wheatstraw, *The Devil's Son-in-Law*, which was originally published in 1971. How did that come about?

I think that, simply by terms of the standard contract, the publishing rights to the Peetie book reverted to me when the original publisher, Studio Vista, let them lapse. I remember Studio Vista had apparently cleared out their warehouse because I was able to get twenty copies of the book in paperback from Red Lick Records. This was about ten years after the original publishing date. So the book was officially out of print. I had been friends for years, since 1968 or 1969, with Franklin and Penny Rosemont, who were part of the surrealist movement that I'm part of. They are the people who have steered the Charles H. Kerr Company, an old radical Chicago publisher that's been around since the 1870s. They always liked Peetie. They had heard all sorts of great things about Peetie from everybody who was interested in blues, but they hadn't really heard his records. So when they started listening, they liked Peetie, and I think they saw a biography of Peetie in the

Charles H. Kerr list as being a good example for the Proletariat Lives series. They do a lot of biographies—if you're a dockworker and an anarchist agitator—that's the kind of books they've always done. True—it wasn't written as a radical book, but there were always little touches of that perspective. It was essentially a straightforward biography from the lyrics, supported by testimony of three or four people. So they wanted to publish it again. I said, "Great—I still have the pictures. Everything's ready." They were used to doing things like that. *The Invisible Man* was a famous race-study black novel from 1952. I know I edited a number of pages on Ralph Ellison in my Peetie book because in *The Invisible Man* Ellison brings into the story a character who's pushing a cart full of old blueprints, and the man introduces himself as Peetie Wheatstraw. As it turned out, Ellison actually knew Peetie and had actually played trumpet with him once or twice in St. Louis. So I went into more detail on that than I had in the original book. And the reissue gave me the opportunity to include anecdotes that came in after the original book went to press. I added to the appendix and to the discography. I featured microgroove reissues of Peetie's and their original 78 release numbers, which I was very proud of. For both the Peetie reissue and the Memphis Minnie book I tried to offer composer credits. On the Peetie discography I was able to do that because I had almost every record. It was easy to note who had composer's credit, and that's not a standard feature in most discographies. And because there was a lot of confusion in those names, it was a lot of fun to play around with. There were a lot of credits to Hairston—and nobody's ever connected anybody named Hairston to Peetie. Was that somebody who organized the sessions?—I don't know. Bunch [William Bunch was Peetie Wheatstraw's real name] was one of the main composers—that and [Charlie] Jordan, because Jordan was on so many of Peetie's record. So it was often Jordan and Bunch.

Oftentimes wouldn't they assign composer's credit to anyone who wanted to pocket a few extra shillings?

That was my feeling, and I mentioned it in the book. While you can clearly see whose name is there, you can't tell who really wrote something. Very late in his recording career some of Peetie's lyrics got very poetic, in a romantic sense—things I would call stilted. And yet one of the most outstanding in its sense of "badness" had a Bunch credit on it. It sounds like something somebody got out of a pop song somewhere. It was so atypical of Peetie's usual lyrics, and you'd like to think that any tune with his credit listed was written by Peetie. While Peetie recorded for Vocalion, most of his work was for the Decca label, which meant it was not in the Lester Melrose review. Melrose's name wound up as composer on many of the recordings for which he was A&R man. Jack Kapp was at Decca, yet his name never shows on any of Peetie's record, nor does "Ink" J. Mayo Williams's name ever turn up.

Let's talk about your book, *Blues and the Poetic Spirit* . . .

At the time of the Peetie book, I was getting radicalized. It was very fresh for me to think of blues with a radical perspective. Those were the kind of questions I started asking myself and trying to think of the blues with new perspectives. I was talking to a friend who's a major in philosophy at Northwestern University. I was telling him about my ideas and about my search for new ways to look at blues. I mentioned blues tunes as protest songs—even though blues songs were not protest songs in the sense of union songs, I felt that they were somehow. He said, "Well, you could try to investigate end-view negation." Think about blues—if they didn't change anything, maybe they still preserved the function of negation. Here we're defining negation as to negative-ize something; to be against it; to see the negative view of something; blues was an attempt to negate the oppressive aspect of white society. Obviously, blues wasn't a change-bringing music that brought people into the streets and led to strikes, but blues and the types of things it sang about were spoken from a position of oppression. Even if it didn't make any difference whether somebody was having a great time or a poor time, the music was expressive of any of these emotional states. But I was trying to say that it seemed to me that, at least for the people, it was effective as a measure against oppression even if it wasn't a change in the social structure. So you can say, at least philosophically, that blues negated at least some of the effects of the oppression. I thought the clever part was him saying that you could say that blues preserved this function of negation for black people throughout its decades. So that spark of light against oppression would remain within the people; even if the strike wasn't called and people weren't led into the streets, by preserving the spark you're preserving the function of negation. Preserving a concept owned by a people that they would be able to use at some point. And you could say that blues led to soul and the civil rights movement, at which point it went beyond where I was going anyway—it wasn't really going to the civil rights movement. I think that notion set me to writing, and that's where *Blues and the Poetic Spirit* came from.

I worked on that for three or four years. I was still working in a bookstore and was working as a publisher's rep and starting to travel—but I was still working on *Blues and the Poetic Spirit*. The odd thing about that not everybody knows—I finished the book and it was very short, and I sent it to William Morrow, who had published a lot of black music books. They published Leroi Jones. They were obviously interested in the subject. I got a letter back that said, "We didn't even look at this. We won't look at anything less than 75,000 words." My recollection is that I had about half of that. So I started adding bits and pieces here and there. Right about this time I had my first serious depression—and this was a bad one. I couldn't do anything. I couldn't work on the book.

But I took it to one of our surrealists' meetings, and I said, "Here's the manuscript—get to work. If anybody has anything to say, put it in there. And maybe someday I'll be able to look at it and decide if I want to use it or not." Only one person took me up on it, and it was Franklin Rosemont. He was my mentor as a radical. He added quite a bit to the book and made the book a bit stronger. While Franklin was looking at it, Tony Russell comes to town and he stayed with me. I showed him the manuscript that Morrow had rejected. He said, "God, I think this is great the way it is—we'll do that!" It turned out he was starting a new series, which were the Edison Blues books—including Mike Rowe's *Chicago Breakdown*, there was another on R&B I've forgotten the title—and then my book was the third in the series. And then once again the series went out of business [*laughs*]. So I was in a quandary: Tony liked the book the way it was and Franklin was adding all these things to it. It was about a year later and I'm starting to come out from under this depression, and I started to look at it and I actually liked some of Franklin's stuff. I said, "Let's compromise and send the new, different manuscript back to Tony and see if he likes that as much as the one he originally liked." And he did. So that's how that one came about.

Much of this book involves examination of lyrics. Did you decide beforehand that certain blues genre covered activities in everyday life and concentrate on those? Or did you concentrate on particular artists? I would assume, in those early years, that even the most diligent collectors probably had limited access to the overall range of artists. Did you assume that you were familiar with a wide-enough array of artists that you could represent them accurately?

I think I had a pretty wide exposure. This was the early 1970s, and the first exposure that anybody outside of the New York Blues Mafia had was Sam Charters's book *Country Blues* and Paul Oliver's *Blues Fell This Morning*. Each book was accompanied by an issued LP. You had to buy the record separately, but each book had a companion LP. Also, the Prestige Bluesville series had just begun. The first blues record I ever heard was the Prestige Bluesville *Sonny Terry and Brownie McGhee*. They did about seventy records in that series, and Folkways did Memphis Slim and Big Bill Broonzy. OJL [Origin of Jazz Library] label started about two years later. With that I thought I'd really arrived, though I have to admit that I listened to the Charley Patton LP and thought, "Oh—well maybe I'll try him again some other time." I put that away.

Not long after that OJL issued *Really the Country Blues*, which was their response to Charters's *Country Blues* LP. That LP had many tunes and artists that really hooked me. I think that within a five- or six-month period, I began to really like the Patton LP. I also grew to appreciate the Folkways Lightning Hopkins LP that I didn't like originally. I really grew into some of these things, and after fifteen years of collecting and listening there was quite a bit out there. But—this is kind of the thing you hinted about [earlier regarding] biography versus lyrics and how one thinks about this. I was inevitably more influenced by *Blues Fell This Morning* than I was by *The Country Blues* by Charters. *Blues Fell This Morning* was similar to what I was doing. Oliver's book is arranged sociologically by topic—gambling blues, et cetera. And *Screening the Blues* was published with a specialized focus on that same idea. I really followed the Oliver pattern even though I thought it was [obvious] to independent thinkers. I liked lyrics so much, as did Don Kent, who was a very early listening buddy. It was clear to me a lot of people would listen to blues and not pay much attention to the lyrics. If blues were your main dancing party music, you weren't required to listen to the lyrics. I think I saw a surrealist aspect to those lyric categories.

So I tried to talk about introductory material, a scathing chapter about blues books I didn't like. I talked about the psychology of the enjoyment because I thought we should confront the question, "Is blues a happy music—is blues a sad music? Is it a sad music made by happy people, or vice versa?" There's room for everything there. I tried to give anecdotes about how negative things in art can make you feel good. And if it were connected to an anecdote, I tried to give credit to its source. And that was a guy who wrote an analytic book on art. He said that he was a platoon leader in World War II. They were dug in and expecting the Japanese to attack—what a mood you'd be in a situation like that [*laughs*]. And he heard some mumbling going around in the foxhole, which he thought was a little nuts. So he wandered over to that area and there were two guys in a foxhole listening to a radio drama about soldiers dug in waiting for an attack. He thought, "Isn't that amusing?"—the art of the drama is more appealing than the reality. These guys would rather hear a radio play about an attack even when facing the real-life event. This was very eye-opening for me because it showed that none of this is simple. You can't say blues is a goodtime music—or blues is a sad music—there's just too many directions.

Then I had a great chapter on the white poet. I guess we'd done our *Living Blues* statement already, but that was my own volatile chapter, and I got a chance to really let go. I discussed white blues at some length—why I thought they were inferior products. I also tried to discuss other effects of race relations and surrealism because I was a psychoanalytically oriented guy. I tried to do some writing on how black people functioned in the dreams of white people. There were two or three articles, and each of the articles was more than one page—although not many pages. Again and again, black people showed up as father-type images. Sometimes they appeared as invading brother and sister images. I didn't try to psychoanalyze white listeners or say who they were, I was just trying to point to the fact that there were more things. But the real thrust of the white blues chapter was me trying to say how crappy white blues players were. That was the main goal [*laughs*].

This would be around 1975. Who were the white blues players at that point?

Butterfield, Bloomfield—Barbara Dane, Jo Ann Kelly, all were in play. It was mostly local blues bands—Charlie Musselwhite, who had been a good friend. We messed around at Koester's together. I still have contact with him.

Do you think Charlie offered his music to be taken seriously by the traditional blues audience?

I think he would like that. I believe any white blues player would be honored if their music was sought out and enjoyed by black listeners—but obviously that's not what keeps them going. To me, the original identification patterns are not there anymore. It used to be black music for black people in black culture. Once it's gone from there, even though it may be acoustic and similar, I just don't have any interest in it. The real source of my problem with white blues is that when I see a white person take the stage and perform, I think they're totally full of shit. Nothing could be less appealing, regardless of what it sounds like. It's just a very human reaction, and I've tried to do a very human thing and rationalize it, analyze it, justify it—all these things—but I just have this primitive reaction that this is wrong. I think the reason white blues is popular is because there are so many white people with the primitive notion that "Oooh this is really wicked!" And they like that. They like it much better than hearing a black person. So in that sense white blues is bound to be successful because so many white people would prefer to hear black music played by white people. We may not know them, but they're out there. And they keep saying, "We're keeping the blues alive." Maybe—but there's no way for people like me to enjoy it.

I never knew that Da Capo was going to do an edition of *Blues and the Poetic Spirit*. Da Capo had a series of reissues they did in red cloth with no jackets. These were slated to go straight to libraries and places like that. They were going to do *Blues and the Poetic Spirit* in the series. I never would have heard about it except that they called me to see if I still had the original photos. In the original issue of the book the photos were way too dark. Some were actually ruined because they were too dark. That was the first I heard someone wanted to reissue the book in this country. So I gathered the photos and sent them to Da Capo and I asked them about a paperback edition, and they more or less said "Fuck off!" [*laughs*]. Then I think there must have been some personnel changes at Da Capo because the guy who had been personally insulting about a paperback edition was gone, and the next person I talked to actually wanted to do a paperback. That was the first I heard of that—and they did a paperback. And that was the first time many people in this country had seen it. It took two or three years. Now hardcore blues fans keep track of blues books on either side of the pond.

Do you know Ray Templeton? His name shows up quite a bit on the Real Blues Forum on Facebook. He posted a statement on the forum, not to me personally, that he always thought it was interesting that there was a bookshop where he would order the new books when they came out—this was in England—and when he heard that *Blues and the Poetic Spirit* came out he gathered his money together to go over to the shop and buy it. When he got there and gave the guy his money, the guy said, "This is so you" [laughs]. I never responded because I didn't know Ray. So then it was out in both countries. Reviews were very mixed. A lot of people didn't like what they regarded as hostility to white people. For some reason Stanley Dance took a grave dislike to me in regard to that book and followed me around for a while doing the same thing with the Memphis Minnie book—very condescending and nasty. In a way I think *Blues and the Poetic Spirit* has become my most important book. A lot of people liked it because it echoed their feeling about white blues even if they didn't realize they felt that way. I believe a lot of black people liked it because it made something positive out of black experience—particularly the blues experience, which had always been portrayed in a negative way. It did become a favorite for a while.

City Lights is a publishing house located on the West Coast; Lawrence Ferlinghetti owns [it]. That's where a lot of the beatnik things entered. City Lights was the main publisher of the "Beats"—Allen Ginsburg, Jack Kerouac, and Lawrence Ferlinghetti, who was one of the poets himself. He's still writing and running the show in his nineties. His righthand person was Nancy Peters, who was part of our surrealist thing. That was my "in" at City Lights. I knew them in passing—not well, but I knew them. There was a guy working in the basement with the bookshop (but not with the publisher) called Paul Yamasaki. I was at a book convention and a friend said, "I was talking to Paul Yamasaki the other day and he said they were talking about reprinting *Blues and the Poetic Spirit*." I hadn't heard about it, but when I got back, I wrote to Nancy and told her I had heard that they were thinking of reissuing *Blues and the Poetic Spirit*. I got a call a couple of days later, saying, "No—but that's not a bad idea. Let's talk about it." The book originally was published in 1975, and the City Lights edition came out in 1996, twenty years later. So that's how that came about.

It would seem to me that lyric analysis was one of the few things that early researchers could do. You weren't required to go into the field, locate and interview the artist or his family or acquaintances. It was you and the record—armchair research. You couldn't really know anything other than what the artist told you in his recording.

I wasn't there for the beginning of 78 collecting, but I think it probably required the inspiration generated by an artist's imagination as expressed in the lyrics of their songs to motivate collector/enthusiasts to do the hard biographic research. Again, I tend to follow Paul Oliver, the main disciple of lyric analysis on the subject. If you took all the lyrics out of the body of the work of each *Blues and the Poetic Spirit* and *The Blues Fell This Morning*, there wouldn't be many blues singers names in there at all. Most of them appear as footnotes to the lyrics at the end of the chapters. You don't have many people by name or biographies in those two books. Paul's book *The Story of the Blues* made up for that ten years later. It's full of biographies. *The Story of the Blues*, was a book of biographies, the history without any lyric analysis—it was St. Louis, it was New York, it was Mississippi. It was a comprehensive blues history leaving aside the subject of the song content. It was a listing of style or genre, genre location, and timeline. And by this time I think Charters had done his *The Bluesmen*, which was more biographies. So I think most blues fans would agree with you. So many blues fans are interested in finding out more about the musicians and their lives. I would never make it as a biographer. I think it's a quirk in me, but emotionally I don't seek people out. I'm not usually comfortable meeting new people. I try to avoid it. In the case of the Peetie book, I believe I was more social at the time, but even back then there were only so many people you could talk to, and talking to Koester probably told me more than I ever knew before, simply because he was from St. Louis and he knew all these names. To write a real biography and to have to interview fifty or sixty people—to me that would be horrifying [laughs]. Part of the problem for me is I realize I'm allergic to people—and even I'm turned off by that. I think that's one of the things that led to not a falling out but a cold shoulder with Chris Strachwitz and me. I wrote to him. I asked him something about Memphis Minnie. I had a lot of ideas about Minnie and lyric analysis. I knew he'd been in touch with Minnie and her sister Daisy. I approached him with these ideas. In return he wrote a rather harsh letter, saying, "Minnie's sister's still alive in Memphis. If you don't go down and talk to her and everybody else down there, you shouldn't do the book." But that was when I first realized that somewhere between the Peetie book in 1970 and working on the Minnie book in the late 1980s, I had a problem with other people. It's an interesting question. I thought a lot about it since you contacted me.

I foresee an end to biographical research. There just won't be any sources out there. After you've combed the archives, talked to acquaintances and family, at some point the sources dry up. Perhaps the body of lyric analysis will be wrung dry as well. Do you see this as a dead end?

No. What will evolve is society, and new ways of thinking about things will come around. Perhaps they won't even look at blues any more. But let me give an example of new ways. Twenty-five or thirty years ago, people didn't really have an idea of what kind of archives were out there to comb through. You can go to county seats all over Mississippi and take down these seats' ledgers with marriages and death certificates. I'm sure Gayle Dean Wardlow and Jim O'Neal did years' worth of this. But at that time the notion that the 1890s census could be found online was inconceivable. The website Ancestry.com is where the ardent statistics people hang out. Every week it seems they find a new residency for people they never knew even lived there. In that sense, I believe the research will continue. Another thing is that there seems to be a new blues scholarship with Elijah Wald and several other people—Marybeth Hamilton. To me the only interesting thing about Marybeth's book was the chapter on Whelan, Klatzko, and McKune at the end. All of the earlier stuff about Howard Odum, Guy B. Johnson, and Dorothy Scarborough I've known for years and was touched on by Oliver and other people. The thesis of the book was *how* do we determine that the Delta blues was the deepest, darkest, most moving music. How was it decided? Why that region, that style? And who were those guys to decide that issue? I don't think any of those guys did that until we got up to Whelan, Klatzko, and McKune. Odum and Johnson might have been some of the earliest people to discuss blues and do lyrical analysis, as was Dorothy Scarborough, but none of them criticized Delta blues—they didn't do that. But the collectors of the late 1940s—they're the guys. Those are the guys who created Paramount-mania, who created Patton-ism. That's where all the collector values got their names. It might have been a less interesting book without the other material, but the Delta fetish is a fairly modern invention—perhaps going back to the 1950s but not the 1920s. Her book was largely about blues critics. It was one of the first books to look at "us" as if we were worth looking at. Many people have done this. The German Neala Schleuning has a section on the surrealist theories of Paul Garon [laughs]. Again, these are new perspectives, new ways to look at blues.

In 1976 a surrealist group here did an international surrealist exhibition. We had people from sixty countries plus three hundred items and many artists. We called it "Marvelous Freedom Vigilance of Desire Reunited." It was a huge exhibition, and it was very successful. We had this space on the corner of LaSalle and Grand. You walk up this concrete ramp and you're in this huge spacious hall. We were able to set up a relationship with the guy who lived there. That was our exhibition space for several months. Then parts of it traveled to Wisconsin, and a couple of places downstate, and Gary, Indiana. Recently we noticed a group of black artists at Columbia College were having an art exhibition, and they were calling it "Marvelous Freedom Vigilance of Desire Reunited." So we got in touch with these black students and they were thrilled. They couldn't believe their inspirers were alive, that we gave them recognition and wanted to see them! We went to the opening, and it was a wonderful time. They bought all of our books, most on surrealism, some on blues. After a while at the opening I began to get fatigued and said to Beth, "Let's go sit over there where all those tables are." There was this older black guy there, so we sat down and began to talk with him. Beth asked who he was. His name was Stan West, and he taught a class at Columbia College on blues as literature. I was impressed and introduced myself. He said, "Oh my God—I teach your book! This year we're having a section on white blues—would you like to come and talk to the class?" [laughs] I never would have thought that 2013–14 would be significant blues-wise for me, but it's all sort of happening now: There's this great exhibition. I'm going to talk to the class. City Lights is going to do a new edition of Memphis Minnie. Angela Davis has a book on blues. There are two novels that are supposed to be blues novels, and a handful of articles—one of which is mine. A year ago I would never have predicted any of those things going on. To me it's just amazing, but I'd rather see that going on among black people than to hear about a new white blues band that's performing.

Let's talk about the Memphis Minnie book. How did that get started?

It was the mid- to late 1980s and I was reading a lot of literary theory and feminist criticism, and I felt like there was a way to look at women's blues that neither I nor anyone else had tried before. I thought it might be worthwhile. So Beth and I both started buckling down and reading and listening, listening, listening, and transcribing lyrics. Minnie had always been a great favorite, so nobody had any hesitancy about making her the subject of a biography. I later found out, from a technical aspect, that there were many problems. I've heard this several times, and I don't know if it's true—the Angela Davis book on blues women had three focal points—and that Minnie was the fourth one but she backed off of Minnie because there wasn't enough biographical data. She was doing biographies. She did Ma Rainey and Bessie Smith. I heard of another woman who was working in the field of radical history, and she was going to do a history of Mary Marcy, who was a very early manager at the Charles H. Kerr Company in Chicago. She changed her mind about the project, once again finding out that there just wasn't enough data out there to make it a project. We didn't think that was a problem with Minnie. I'm glad it was an independent project; if I had been submitting the Minnie project as a thesis, they probably would've told me no.

The way the book is set up, the first eighty or ninety pages are a straight biography—that probably could have made a second entire book the size of the Peetie Wheatstraw book, but the next two-thirds of the book were filled with lyric transcriptions and analysis of many of her songs. It was the analysis of those songs that saw many blues fans back away. Many readers didn't like the analysis. I've run into this hostility before, and it more commonly originates from England than anywhere else—I have no theories on why that is. But we were having a good time compiling. It became a Da Capo original. Da Capo has done a huge number of blues books. They were very fond of books on blues and jazz. I sent the book around, and I thought with two previous books under my belt and great subject matter for my project, I'd have had no trouble getting a publisher. I was wrong [laughs]. Many publishers just said no. I sent them chapter samples and outlines. It was all sort of fragmentary, and I was trying to get a feeling if they even wanted to see more. It just wasn't working well—all I got were refusals. A couple of academic presses sent the material out to readers; I got a couple of snotty refusals but also a couple expressing encouragement. But around the time the book got to Da Capo, a friend in Louisville said, "My grandmother left a trust that's supposed to further the cause of women in the arts in Kentucky. I'm sure we can finagle something. I'll bet we can get a couple thousand dollars." The trust was called the PACE Trust. Two years earlier they put five thousand dollars into a Greil Marcus book that Harvard published. PACE came through with a grant that made a great difference with my book. I got three or four thousand dollars. It was enough to offer Da Capo a thousand of it—and I got it back as an advance, so it hardly mattered. The main thing I wanted the money for was to run a Library of Congress search for the composers of every Memphis Minnie song—and we ran out of money before we got to Kansas Joe McCoy, but we did get every Minnie tune researched. In the discography it shows whether the Library of Congress had it at all, if they had it as nothing at all or if it was listed as by somebody. I'm very proud of that—that's something that doesn't usually show up in discographies. No one's ever mentioned that, but I thought that was cool.

Why did you offer Da Capo a thousand dollars?

They saw the book and said they really liked it, but it was well over three hundred pages. They wanted to take a bunch of chapters out. They weren't very happy. Then there was the University of Illinois Press—they wanted me to take a bunch of chapters out. They said, "You can always publish them as articles elsewhere." I didn't want to take any chapters out, and so it was on to Da Capo, who were more encouraging. It was at this time that I got the PACE Trust money. I called Da Capo and talked with a woman named Bea Freidlander. I said, "If you got a thousand dollars from the PACE Trust as a subvention for publishing this book, could you do it without taking any chapters out?" "A thousand dollars? Sure!" That really made economic sense as far as they were concerned. Since then they've done a number of Da Capo originals. The Skip James biography was one; Steve Calt wrote that. But at that time I don't believe they did many—or any—blues books. They were leery. They're essentially a reprint house. When you're a reprint house, you just take an old copy of a book and shoot it, make your plates, and print the book—whereas this was going to require typesetting and a handful of new expenses. That's what they were thinking about. But the book got a lot of attention. It did very well and went through three or four printings before it finally disappeared. We were both very happy with it.

Was this the first book you'd done while you and Beth were together?

Yes.

And what was Beth's role?

She wanted me to do all the writing instead of having two people taking turns writing chapters. We talked about what we wanted to say in various chapters and how we were going to handle it. Many of the newfangled ideas were mine, while she focused on the whole package—what ideas were we trying to present of a woman in blues. Beth played a critical role in all the interviews, especially when we were interviewing Minnie's sister and sister-in-law. She was able to get them to open up much more than I could. We had such a difficult time getting them. Daisy Douglas Johnson was Minnie's younger sister and the one who cared for Minnie the most after Minnie had her strokes. But there was also the sister-in-law, Ethel, who was older and knew Minnie earlier. Daisy wasn't born until

1915, and depending on which of Minnie's birth dates you regard as accurate, Minnie may have been as old as seventeen when Daisy was born. Daisy never liked the idea of talking about Minnie—at least not in modern times. Back in the 1960s Minnie was still alive, and Blues Unlimited was sending checks and Chris Strachwitz was sending checks: Daisy was an important spokesperson. Minnie had her first stroke in 1962, and her husband, Son Joe, had a stroke just before that and died shortly after the stroke, so the last decade of her life she was more and more incapacitated. She died in 1972. By the mid-1980s Daisy had left the whole blues thing behind. In later years Daisy hadn't wanted a gravestone or a ceremony or anything to do with it at all. Beth and I decided we were going to go down to Memphis anyway, to prowl through the library and prowl through the newspaper morgue and see what we could turn up. Somebody told us to go to the Mud Island Museum—that there was some Minnie sheet music there. We went to the museum on this little tramway across the trestle. We asked about the Minnie sheet music, and in fact it was a handwritten sheet of music. I don't know that Minnie ever had or even could write sheet music, but the museum who received it from Minnie's family presented it as Minnie's writing. I had doubts about its authenticity but wasn't going to argue with them about it. They said, "We got this from her niece—and she still works here right down the hall." So we went and talked with the niece. And we were telling her our troubles. She said, "Let me talk to Daisy and you call back tomorrow or the next day. Let me talk to her first." When we called back, they said she would talk to us, but she wanted a signed agreement and a cut of the proceedings. We were thrilled to do that. We went to a folklore center and borrowed a typewriter to type up an agreement in a motel in Memphis. We took it over to Daisy to sign it and had her son there as a witness; she wouldn't sign until it was notarized. So we got it notarized. She signed, and the agreement said she would get twenty percent of any proceedings, which was twenty percent of anything I would get.

Did she realize how slim those pickin's were likely to be?

I told her that in advance, but I don't think that she or any families involved ever realize how little profit this kind of book will bring. Why would we be doing this if there weren't all sorts of people out there ready to buy the book? I think what Daisy got was ultimately twenty percent of my advance because that was the only money I ever got. I think that the book earned back almost all the advance [laughs], but there wasn't a lot in it for Daisy. We became very close to Daisy, and she became very friendly and introduced us to Ethel. Ethel had even more memories. Ethel was one of Minnie's sisters-in-law. I don't know which brother she married, but Ethel's was where Minnie would stay whenever she came back to Memphis; be it an overnight or for six months, she stayed with Ethel. Minnie's husbands—first Kansas Joe and then later Son Joe—both stayed at Ethel's with Minnie. She stayed with Ethel up until the time she had her strokes and then she went to stay with Daisy. Beth got along superbly with both of them and was able to draw out memories from them. But Daisy reminded me of Peetie's brother, who's response was disbelief that anybody would rate this much attention for having lived a blues life. Daisy had a hard time accepting that, but her family prevailed, and many of them thought this was an exciting project—and she didn't. To her the project brought back memories of the years she had to clothe, wash, and feed Minnie every day, which was not necessarily a fond reminiscence. But she did get into the project, and with Ethel there the two of them would laugh about the things that Minnie did. That helped to encourage the flow of ideas. Ethel was the only one who knew Kansas Joe and remembered their tune *When the Levee Breaks*. People think of it as a Minnie song even though Kansas Joe did the vocals. Ethel was around for the 1927 flood. She remembered the song, and to her it was very realistic. She remembered the family having to move because of the flood. They all went back to their houses after the flood. It was obvious that Ethel was more comfortable with the blues life than Daisy was. Daisy had, in fact, in the 1940s gone to Chicago to find Minnie and had actually gone to a couple of club dates that Minnie played. Daisy said she liked them, and we have a photo of Daisy in Chicago looking very smart in the 1940s.

Who were your other sources of information?

Well, we had your interview with Brewer Phillips—and Jim O'Neal helped. Jim was able to transcribe many of the interviews he had conducted with various other blues people who made mention of Minnie and what they said about her. He would always ask people about Memphis Minnie. He had interviews with Memphis Slim, Homesick James, Jimmy Rogers—stacks of people all with recollections of Minnie. We were more interested in prewar informants, but there weren't many. When we first started planning our trip to Memphis, one of the people we were going to talk to was Rev. Robert Wilkins, but he died before we got there. There was another woman we wanted to talk to—her name was Hunt, something that started with a "V" Hunt. We talked to David Evans about how to get in touch with her, and he said, "Well, you know she charges a lot of money—and so does Bukka White"—and we had already spent our money on composers' credits [laughs], so that fell by the wayside. We were able to find various things in archives but, as Angela Davis said, "There just wasn't much." And now in recent years, because so much Census Bureau data is available online, and people like Bob Eagle spend ten hours a day perusing the data, they've discovered many things about Minnie that we didn't know. The information places her in a certain county when she was ten years old—and then ten years later places her in a different county—then ten years later she's no longer in the household. It gave us much more solid biographical information. These items and so much more were included in the revised edition of the Minnie book. We also found new photos that are included in the revised edition. Jim O'Neal found a postage-stamp-size photo that no one had ever seen. He also found some Minnie stories in the [*Chicago*] *Defender*—often making passing reference to Minnie. He found one reference of Minnie playing in Florida, and we never had any idea she was ever even there. Robert Pruter, during his research, took photostat shots of perhaps fifty Memphis Minnie ads in the *Defender*. We know that she played certain clubs on certain dates because we have ads for the gigs. Bob sent them to us because they weren't quite on target for the theme of his books. He actually sent these while the original version had gone to press—so we didn't get a chance to include them in the original. But they are in the revised edition.

Were there any outstanding Minnie anecdotes you've run across in your research?

Jimmy Rogers remembered that a group of people were sitting around a table. The group included Little Son Joe and some women. He said Minnie was jumping all around and she didn't like it. She either came up to the table or leaned across the table and threw a shot of whiskey in Son Joe's face. It burned his eyes and he had to be led out of there. I've heard that she could be rougher than that. Johnny Shines said that he heard that Minnie had cut off some guy's arm. "Cut it off or shot it off—that's what they told me!" She was such an odd duck being part of the all-male crowd—and she was a part of it, not an adjunct. I think everybody had their tales. Memphis Slim objected to some hypothesis that she played at such-and-such club because in his mind street players wouldn't have been able to work in that club. He could play there on piano, but they wouldn't have a street player with a guitar in there. And the Billy Boy Arnold story was wonderful [laughs]. If you want to talk to someone about the earlier generation of blues singers, Billy Boy is really at this point an elder. I'm seventy, and I think he has me by four or five years, but what was great was he was walking into a club with Big Bill and he couldn't get over it. He said, "There I was walking down the street with the great Big Bill." He was Billy Boy's idol. They're both blues guys but of different generations. Billy was really excited whenever Minnie or Big Bill would let him come up and play a tune. And now he's taken his place as one of the elders. But that's really one of the problems. For the people who were born in 1890 or the 1900s or 1910—there's nobody around today that knew them then. They didn't really know them as a child. Although there was a story—I believe it was Eddie Taylor who said that Memphis Minnie babysat for him when he was a baby. Memphis Minnie was friends with his mother and she would babysit sometimes when his mother went out. And then there were the stories from Brewer Phillips.

The thing I remember best is that Phillip always said that Minnie didn't like Big Bill and was very suspicious of any business dealings with him—that she didn't trust him. Did anybody else say that?

No. I thought that was real interesting. All I can think is that there must have been an incident that happened with money and Big Bill around that time that just changed her mind. I've never heard from anybody about an argument between Big Bill and Minnie. But then when you think about it, we don't have that many people who were there all the time. The people who were around were Tampa Red, Big Maceo, Washboard Sam—all the people in the Lester Melrose stable and all the sidemen in those sessions. Nobody's talked to any of them. Jim had a story. Memphis Minnie had a wig—and she had a puppy. She'd put the wig on the table and gone to bed. When she woke up in the morning, the puppy had destroyed the wig, ripped it to shreds. She hit the puppy and chased it with her guitar and the puppy ran out the door and never came back [laughs]. I guess the puppy knew that was no longer its home.

When the Minnie book came out, were there any great revelations in it?

While we don't have information on early Minnie, when it came to blues survival there were a lot of people on her case. Right away Georges Adins from Belgium did an interview with Minnie. That was in the late 1950s, early 1960s, and this may have been before her stroke. There's data in there that has led to ideas that may not be right—like whether Minnie ever did marry Casey Bill Weldon. According to our findings there's no reason to think so. We were able to get some of those things straightened out. Chris Strachwitz liked Minnie enough to reissue two LPs of her stuff and sent money to Daisy. There was always interest in Minnie, and people were always looking into her story, so the broad outlines were known—there were no real revelations.

Did you contact George and Ethel McCoy? Wasn't she supposed to be their aunt?

No. Bob Eagle posted on the internet lately, and he said, "I've been looking and I don't see anywhere that George and Ethel could be related to Minnie." For one thing, their name is McCoy and Minnie's name was Douglas. If the McCoys are related, it would have to be through Joe's family. I think I've read that they never knew Minnie well, but they played some of her songs. They weren't on our list to talk to.

Which brings us to the subject of blues and surrealism. What can you tell me about *Living Blues* #25, the issue that included the supplement on surrealism?

Odd as this may sound, I really had very little to do with the issue of *Living Blues* that featured the material on surrealism. No, really. Amy, who did all the typesetting for *Living Blues* was also doing a huge amount of typesetting for surrealists, like the magazine *Arsenal*. She got to read a lot of surrealist material because she was doing all the typesetting. And she would talk to Franklin and Penny Rosemont when they would come over to pick up typesetting. I suspect one of them suggested to Amy that maybe they could do a whole issue about surrealism and the blues. Obviously, I was going to be included in it, but it wasn't my doing. I was in on the writing, but I wasn't in on the fomentation.

Let's do it like this—tell me how blues and surrealism are related as you see it.

I was attempting to look at blues lyrics in a surrealist's way that involved what a surrealist conception of poetry was. I think I quoted Peter Guralnick somewhat negatively, and he's always thought I've hated him, which is not true at all. It was in *Feel Like Going Home* in the introduction where he said something like " . . . yes we thought blues was poetry but we can see that on the printed page it just doesn't stand out." I felt that's the wrong kind of poetry—looking for versification as a standard aspect of poetry while surrealism thinks that poetry is a much more powerful thing. It establishes principals of revolt, and it was revolt I see running all through the blues that I wanted to make more obvious. It was like a thin red line running through there, but most people don't see it. Every once in a while, a singer sings something that sounds like protest. People see that, but that's all they see. In *Blues and the Poetic Spirit* I was really trying to get people to see how it's a different kind of poetry there—that's what we're watching for. If you think of poetry as a principal of revolt, and I realize you can't just make up your mind to do that, but if you can make up your mind to do that or can follow me trying to do that, then I think you can see why I see more in the blues than a lot of other people do. All I was trying to do is let people see what I think. I grant you ahead of time that not many people are going to go there, but I just throw that out there and say, "There you go!" But I did the best I could, and I tried to re-elaborate the same thing in *Woman with Guitar*. The whole second half of the book *Woman with Guitar* re-elaborates these principles and has a chapter between the hard biography and the interpretive part that lays out all the principles we were trying to use—Why is analogy important? Can we use analogy? I quoted André Breton at length on the analogy question. For me, as I became more of a surrealist I started seeing blues in a different way. That was what was exciting about it. It's still an exciting concept for me, but unfortunately as I grow older I don't become more articulate.

I can see why you would pick the people who created blues as ripe for revolt. To me it's amazing that element isn't more overt. When you mention protest songs, it reminds me of Mack McCormick's notion that perhaps two out of ten thousand blues tunes were protest songs—a minuscule number—and probably delivered at the request of these researchers—but protest songs were what many white researchers might have expected from the folks who composed blues.

One thing that people don't realize when we're talking about poetry is if you say something clearly, like "I'm an animal," people know what you mean right away. But when a poet has that "I'm an animal" thought in his head, he expresses that notion in a much different way than simply making that statement. Writing poetry about being an animal is far different than simply stating "I'm an animal." Poetry's a different thing. Why do we like it? What does it do? And this all applies to blues lyrics. As poetry, it has to elaborate on the original simple statement or it's not worth writing. One of the reasons I see poetry as the revolt principle is that it's the opposite of protest songs. A protest song says straight up, "Boss, get off my back." It's not a metaphoric statement, it's not a poetic statement. It's a straight-ahead remark set to music. Willie King, who died approximately five years ago and recorded for the Rooster label, started getting into this type of outspoken protest song. As far as I was concerned, that wasn't the way to go. Black freedom isn't something that was going to come from playing blues records, I'm aware of that. Singing about "get the boss off my back" may get people charged up enough to do something. So it's two different things, but to me the blues becomes more interesting if you don't say it "Boss, get off my back" but if you elaborate it in some poetic way that adds something to it, makes you think about it differently, perhaps connect it with thousands of images—things poems can do. So now we're looking for the protest songs and the line of protest that runs through it. It's a subtle thing. These are the kind of things I've been thinking about since we talked—how to elaborate that.

In the late 1960s Franklin and Penelope Rosemont, my very close friends—Franklin is now dead—went to Paris to meet André Breton and all the other surrealists. They went around 1965. They did meet Breton and they did meet the group. They went to meetings at the café every day. And they came back here with the idea of starting their own group—which they did. Three or four years later that group found me—I had just moved here. I'll tell you a quick story here. It may seem labyrinthine, but it really isn't. When I went to England in 1965, I couldn't find a place to stay. But through the blues crew Mike Leadbitter and company, they dug up Charles Radcliff and Diana Shelly, who said I could come and live with them. I thought that was very cordial, as I was going to be there some months. I went over there the next day with my guitar in hand, walked into the room that was going to be mine, and there was some guy packing up his guitar to walk out. We introduced ourselves and he left. His name was Eric Clapton, and my name was Paul Garon—and you can see who became famous [laughs]. I had never heard his name—it meant absolutely nothing to me. I was there for three months. I was a junkie. I don't think Diana liked that part at all but she put up with me and they were huge blues fans. We stayed up all the time talking about blues. I had been in it much more deeply than they had at that time, and I was able to turn them on to a lot of stuff—especially Charles. He was the person who wrote the first anti-white blues article I'd ever seen. That was in the mid 1960s in a little magazine called *Anarchy* that came out of England.

By the time I went into the hospital to quit my drug addiction, I believe Charles and Diana had had it about up to here with guests. Some of my friends from the States had come over and just started flopping at Charles and Diana's house because I was there. They really didn't like that, and I really didn't like it either, but I couldn't get them to leave. It was a very bad scene. Meanwhile, Franklin and Penny are going to go to Paris to meet the surrealists. They're going to go to England first and stay with this wonderful couple they heard about—Charles and Diana [laughs]. They got over there and they're having trouble with immigration, who are demanding proof that they have a residence. They called Charles, and Charles said, "Oh no—ain't nobody coming here!" So Franklin and Penny went to France first. They met all the surrealists, and they had a great time. When that was over, they called Charles and Diana again. They had been guest-free for several months, so they welcomed the two. Franklin and Penny were all full of surrealism. Charles was interested in surrealism, but he wasn't a surrealist. They published a couple of issues of a magazine called *Heatwave*—nothing could be more obscure—and they published a piece of mine that I left behind.

Five years later I'm in Chicago. I'm walking down the street and I see this radical bookstore. I'm thinking, "I wonder if they would have a copy of *Heatwave*." So I go in and Franklin and Penny, who I haven't met yet, are there. I asked if they'd ever heard of *Heatwave*. They said, "Yes—why are you interested?" And I said, "I've got something in it." And they're thinking, "Who's this two-bit fraud who says he has something in our magazine? And we've never met the guy in our lives." But Penny, through some clever questioning, reminds him that they've published things that were already there—and, did I write something about addiction? "Yeah—that was me." "Are you the Peetie Wheatstraw person?" "Yes!" Then we became good friends. It has the charm of coincidence.

Surrealists have always been fond of those kind of happenings because they imply that so much more is going on than we know. As soon as I started hearing about surrealism, I got interested in it, especially the fact that there were black surrealists. I thought—and I think Franklin and Penny were already there—that the more radical aspects of the civil rights movement in America might be very open to a surrealist adventure. There was a mini-revolution waiting to happen with the Black Panther Party in Chicago handing out their papers. They brought their papers to Barbara's Bookstore, where we all worked. And I started thinking these are the same black people who produced blues. Somehow, I've got to show this is all of the piece—black resistance to white oppression—surrealism's goal that life is elsewhere. And the whole idea of liberation of the person. I think a lot of it comes—and this really goes into the white blues question—one of the things I think makes blues radical is who's doing it. The people who produced blues from the 1920s through to the 1960s have done it from a rather oppressed position. There has not been black liberation in a real sense for many of these people. They've been at the bottom of the pile. The pile is at the bottom to begin with—and they're at the bottom of that. That's kind of a ready-made revolutionary situation. To me, the very thrusting forward of their voice into white discourse is radical and of great interest to surrealists; they're speaking poetry from an oppressed position and not thinking that any of these people are elaborating revolutionary theory—I know they're not. They're producing poetry and song. It's inventive. It's often brilliant, and it's done in the midst of this oppression dynamic. To me, that proved two things: it meant the lyrics of the songs were real poetic statements of radical fervor, no matter what the words pronounced; and the reason it's so disappointing when you see a white person mount the stage with their guitar is all the positionality is gone. The very thing that made it so wonderful, such a statement isn't there anymore. Even if it was musical brilliance, its location and the structure, how it appears in society, has been completely undercut.

Were Franklin and Penny Rosemont white or black?

White. All of the surrealists in Chicago were white. When I met Franklin in 1967, he considered himself an anarchist. He was a partner in a conglomeration of about seven people around Solidarity Bookshop, which was on the 700 block of West Armitage on that school near Halsted. Several of the people there were black, but I think that crew fell apart about the time Franklin and Penny were getting interested in surrealism. I think there was a black woman who worked at the post office and another woman who didn't want to go in that direction, so they didn't become black surrealists. There were black people who were surrealists who we were in touch with all the time, but nobody in the group in Chicago. And nobody opposed us in the group back in the day—and I'm talking about Chicago. I think many people were surprised to find out I was white after I wrote *Blues and the Poetic Spirit*, particularly the "Whites versus Blacks" chapter. Years ago I read a book about pine-tree racism, and as I was reading it I thought, "These guys have to be black." Franklin and Penny had just been to France and met André Breton. They went to the meetings every day in Paris, and that pulled them out of the Solidarity group. Penny was in the print shop faction of SDS (Students for a Democratic Society), and I believe her faction got kicked out. They've always been radicals, and I believe they all met at Roosevelt University before my time. I met them at Solidarity, but within six months of my meeting them they were no longer a part of Solidarity.

MACK MCCORMICK INTERVIEW

Mack McCormick. Courtesy Mack McCormick Estate.

Both of my parents, Greg and Effie Mae McCormick, were X-ray technicians in the very early days of X-ray machines coming into hospitals and doctor's offices. They met at the X-ray school at C&O Hospital in Cincinnati. They split up soon after I was born. My father went back to Texas—he was a Texan, born in Waco—he lived in Dallas. My mother was an X-ray technician, but during the Depression the medical industry decided that men were the natural wage earners, and the limited number of jobs which existed were given to men—which meant that my mother, who had been professionally trained, had a license and a degree, couldn't get a job as an X-ray technician. So she worked at menial jobs moving from town to town—hoping that somewhere she could get back into the medical profession. I was with her through most of those travels, and it shaped my life. We moved first to Columbus and Cleveland, then a stint as medical aide on a Caribbean cruise ship.

A second marriage turned into the job of managing three boardinghouses in Houston, then about 1943 we went to a spot between Crichton and Prichard, Alabama, to run a chicken farm with seven thousand white leghorns, many with an eye disease. She toughed it out with good humor. Next in St. Louis we opened a nice lunchroom, the kind working people patronize, with a blue-plate special and an outdoor sign reading "Eat." The place was on busy Gravois Avenue, which is Route 66 through the city. We went to Denver at one point. She moved on to a wartime factory job as inspector of .50 caliber brass cartridges. For me, a large bump came when schools reserved available places for the children of the war workers pouring into cities. I had to skip a year in Mobile but kept abreast by reading, helped by a neighbor who explained knotty things but left me in a lurch when it came to algebra.

In St. Louis the only places open were in the technical school. I probably can still do spot welding or put a thread on steel bar stock using a turret lathe. In 1944 she finally found work with a doctor in Lakewood, Colorado, as combination receptionist, nurse, and X-ray and lab technician. At the same time, she became night manager of the Red Dot Motel on Colfax Avenue. I was appointed "Assistant Night Manager" responsible for discouraging midnight drunks wandering around the parking lot bellowing for Ida Belle. The Red Dot had previously been a hot bed palace. So about ten years later she finally succeeded getting back into the medical profession, but in the meanwhile we'd been in Columbus, Cincinnati, Huntington, West Virginia, Cleveland, Lakewood, and many other locations. During this time my mother would run into financial hard times and my father would offer to take me in—not to offer child support, just to take me in. He'd become a factory rep for DuPont x-ray film, traveling five states out of Dallas. So I kept coming back to Texas to live with him. I was very young, and my schooling got ridiculous. Texas schools were a year behind northern schools. If you went back and forth, you'd either be a year ahead—or a year behind. I came to Texas on three different occasions after being in the north somewhere. And each time I came to Texas and entered school they would insist that I take Texas history. So I took it the first time, and the second time I came back they would insist that I take the class again—out of the same book. And I would tell them, "I know about the Alamo—I can tell you the date of the Alamo; I know about Spindletop," which was the first oil discovery here, "I know about Howard Hughes"—and all the other things. And they would put me in a class for history with the same damned book. That made it pretty boring—just to sit there. Also, my father had the habit of shipping me off to private schools. In 1939 it was Morris School for Boys in the Ozark foothills near Searcy, Arkansas. I spent a year there going to Mass—but any time I got near the chapel, the priests would remind me that I could not take communion. They'd say, "Now Bob, you can't go to communion—you remember that. You just stay in your seat." I guess I heard that twice a day. They were worried about that—they said that to all the Protestant boys. The older students taught the younger ones gambling, elevated cursing, and stealing watermelons from a nearby farmer who came after us with a shot gun loaded with dried hard bacon rind. I ended up back with my dad in a downtown high school that had a pretty rough crowd. And, as often had happened coming in from another part of the country, the bully of the school would mess me around—I was a fairly skinny kid at the time. So I would end up telling the bully of the school answers to test questions so he could pass a course. High school was really sort of a black period for me.

I always found Texas a little strange, having grown up in northern cities. For example, I turned on the radio one time in midday and the Light Crust Dough Boys were there. Here I am, this smart-aleck Yankee kid, and I can't quite believe they'd put something like this on the radio. Later I got to like them, but at first there were a lot of things that seemed strange to me and I wasn't quick to enjoy them until some years later.

During the '40s when I was still traveling with my mother, I was spellbound by late-night radio remotes featuring the big bands. Les Brown from the Hollywood Palladium. Gene Krupa with Anita O'Day from the Steel Pier in Atlantic City. I even remember the address of one place. An excited voice came on saying, "We bring you the sound of Harry James and His Music Makers from Frank Dailey's Meadowbrook, on the Newark-Pompton Turnpike, Cedar Grove, New Jersey." Then, to my delight, we were living in Sandusky, Ohio, across the bay from the huge Cedar Point resort on Lake Erie. The Grand Ballroom booked twelve name bands, each for a week stand over the summer, with each band contracted for an NBC network broadcast twice a week. I bribed my way into a job. On opening night I found myself delivering mail to the Tony Pastor Orchestra and the two band singers, Betty and Rosemary Clooney. Two nights later an announcer and engineer arrived from WTAM in Cleveland to set up for the broadcast. Then I was moving radio equipment in place, moving microphones around during a sound check, and getting a phone for them to call the "long lines" department of the phone company to order a dedicated 600 ohm balanced line. Over that summer I was the official "go-for." I ran errands for the musicians. I did their shopping in town, but disappointed some by explaining Sandusky had yet to acquire a reefer dealer.

The world of popular music rolled by. Stan Kenton was making his first hit records. Woody Herman was unleashing an amazing sound. Bobby Sherwood experimenting with a piece titled "Bedlam" that appeared on record as "Sherwood's Forrest." Boyd Raeburn came with two remarkable singers, Ginnie Powell and David Allyn, and arrangers that delved deep into "progressive music" involving oboes, French horns, English horns. There were dull weeks, as when Eddy Howard sang "To Each His Own" three times a night. Buddy Rich's first big band appeared, with the leader in the habit of laying around—actually laying and napping—on the bandstand while the substitute drummer worked. Johnny Bothwell came with a band that some experts say never existed, though it can be heard on the album "Whatever Happened to Johnny Bothwell?" Jerry Wald was kind enough to teach me a few things on the clarinet. I loved the low notes of "September in the Rain," but it came with difficulty. No talent, no gift. Glen Gray had an astonishing cornet player. When I asked his name, he said, "I'm Bobby Hackett." Jazzmen of his caliber often had no regular work and would go on the road with one band or another until a jazz club called. Alvino Rey came with several electric guitars in a brightly decorated box at least ten feet wide, maybe eight feet high. One of his feature numbers was the "Mama Blues"—are you familiar with the tune? It was first recorded by a harmonica player from Dallas named Willie McCoy. The first edition of the "Blues and Gospel Records" discography by Robert Dixon and John Godrich arrived about 1964. It lists the first recording of "Mama Blues"—at least under that title—as by Willie McCoy. He made only six sides and then disappeared. In the 1950s, looking for musicians to record, people mentioned him, making me wonder if he had been one of the street musicians I'd heard. Then I found a snippet about him in an old Dallas newspaper. It said, in a comic tone, the police had hauled in a Willie McCoy to play the "Mama Blues" for them—a police pastime on slow nights. The police reporter left us that trace of him. He could have been there when I looked, but no one knew his full name. Other such items—perhaps the only information still possible to find—are waiting to be found in newspaper files or microfilm. Anyway, Alvino Rey played it on the steel guitar—an enormous steel guitar—it was a feature piece. I'd never heard it and was surprised to find out where it had come from. Rey had a conversation with the guitar. He asked, "Can you call your mama?" The guitar wails. He tells the guitar to call her, his steel bar whining along the strings. He comforts the guitar as it weeps—all this booming through enormous speakers. Thirty years later I recorded Billy Bizor's "Mama Blues." Music is a great ball that rolls in any direction.

Musicians who passed through the Cedar Point ballroom often suggested ways I could expand my horizons. The arrangers told me to listen to Delius and Ravel. They often worked at the piano near the dressing rooms while the band was on stage. Pete Rugolo and Ralph Burns were beginning to write arrangements—like "Bedlam" that would move the bands to a new life on the concert stage. A few of the musicians said great jazz wasn't much found among the swing bands. They said I should listen to records of small groups and gave me names of the most elegant, including Benny Goodman's quartet, Lester Young, and Rex Stewart. They told me to find a jam session, the kind where six or seven guys get together about two in the morning and close to dawn it peaks. When the Georgie Auld Band was playing Cedar Point, they were invited to Toledo for an after-hours jam with some of Count Basie's guys. It was one of the roughest places I've seen then or since. A chicken wire fence was stretched around a bandstand, which was at least seven feet above the dance floor. A sign said, "Do Not Throw Beer Bottles at the Band." At first the two groups of musicians, most of whom had never met, messed around talking about keys and the piece to begin with. They discussed "I Got Rhythm" and "Fine and Dandy." Then Count Basie settled the discussion, breaking in with the inevitable "Blues in C." My strongest memory is aggressive Georgie Auld going after Basie's tenor sax player, who must have been Buddy Tate. The others yielded to let those two swap sixteen bars back and forth. In jazz this kind of challenge isn't meant to decide the winner. They're looking for an exciting friend. After a time the two tenor saxes moved to a gentle mood, with the others joining in then. It was one of those momentous evenings that go unrecorded, and that was my introduction to jazz in its best tradition.

In the fall of 1946 I came down to Houston. Two weeks after I moved to Houston I followed Bobby Hackett's advice to listen to the musicians who stayed home in New Orleans with regular jobs in the tourist clubs. I hitchhiked over and learned something still not fully credited. From the late nineteenth century, perhaps earlier, four groups of musicians had shared much of the New Orleans repertoire. Small groups, hotel bands, brass parade bands, whatever—they flourished in competition. The four were: the downtown black working men, the formally trained uptown creoles, the various whites, and, feeling themselves a separate community, the Italians. Frank Frederico, Papa Celestin, Armand Hug, Jim Robinson, and a trombonist known as Walking John explained it.

In New Orleans, even at sixteen, I had no trouble getting served in barrooms. It was still a whorehouse town with open gambling across the river in Jefferson Parish. The

French Quarter was rich with music, tourists not yet so insistent on hearing the "Saints." The neighborhoods were full of music not meant for outsiders. New Orleans vigorously supports its live music. The jukebox is in second place. The HBO cable series "Treme" has moments of what I found in 1946. Walking about the city one day, on the upriver side of Canal, I came across a store at 439 Baronne Street with a sign reading "Records for Collectors." I went in there and I was absolutely fascinated. The store sold prized records, all 78s, primarily jazz and blues. I saw records—not the way they were in retail stores at the time—but in little vertical slots. They were in heavy shucks stacked on edge in vertical bins. There was a guy there who watched you as you went through the records because there's a trick you have to learn as you go through a stack of 78s—otherwise you'll put pressure on the rim and break it off. The clerk hurried over to ask if I knew how to flip through an armload of 78s. I demonstrated that peculiar skill junk-shopping collectors develop going through a stacks of 78s. A pile of twenty 78s weighs ten pounds. You hold them so the weight can't snap off an edge. I was just fascinated to see all these records. I began seeing Gennetts, Paramounts, a red disc with a Cameo label, Vocalions from the '20s, OKehs in the 8000 series, Columbia records with pictures on the label. On the wall a copy of Louis Armstrong's "West End Blues" was framed under glass. Then when I got to the swing section of the store, a fellow came out of the back of the store and came over and kind of watched me. We talked a little bit—he was the kind of guy who got to know all of his customers. He asked if I was finding what I wanted, then went over to the clerk. A moment later he returned saying the clerk told him I was from Texas, and when he found out I was from Texas he took a whole new attitude toward me. He asked a chain of questions. What kind of music did I like? Did I know Texas had many different kinds of music? And he told me a whole lot of things about the various records. Then he took me into the back and he showed me what he was working on. He had what was known as a veri-typewriter. It's a typewriter whose keys you could lift out and substitute a different font—there were four or five different fonts. He introduced himself as Orin Blackstone and told me he was working on a book, *Index to Jazz*. He was the first American to work on a jazz discography, and he has never gotten the credit or the honor he deserves. At that time the only discography of American jazz was by a Belgian named Hughes Panassie and Charles Delaunay, a Frenchman. The first discographies of American jazz came from a Belgian and a Frenchman. Orin was a breakthrough artist, and in that first set of four books he included an amazing amount of things, including the Light Crust Dough Boys, who had a repertoire that overlapped jazz. They would play things like "Clarinet Marmalade"—they would give the clarinet part to their fiddler. Orin was interested in a lot of Texas artists—Boots and His Buddies, Don Albert's Big Swing Band, pianists like Rob Cooper—and many other things. He took me to one particular slot of records, pulled out some and showed me the label. He said, "Do you see what it says there? It says DAL. That means this record was recorded in Dallas, Texas." Then he'd get out another record, and this one said SA, meaning the record was recorded in San Antonio. He had another with EP on it—that meant El Paso; it was a Mexican record.

He got out records with initials showing they came from Memphis and Hattiesburg and Hot Springs. He'd said he'd gone to all three towns and easily found the people involved. He went on, saying I could do a lot of good if I'd do the same. Get them to tell you who else was on a record. Something about their career—just information about their career and about the recording. Who influenced them. Find out what started western swing bands playing "Yancey Special," "Milk Cow Blues," and jazz standards like "Clarinet Marmalade." He showed me "masterpieces" by people I'd never heard of, then asked if I knew anything about KXYZ. Yes, it's the Houston station I listen to most often. The city's outstanding disc jockey, Bob Blase, has a jazz and swing band program. He showed me a Bluebird record by the "KXYZ Novelty Band," saying it would be easy to find out more about them. (It turned out not to be so easy. It called for a series of efforts, a hint of what was to come.) He wanted me to help understand the sources of music—the records that preserve it. As to Texas, he knew the Okeh company had come to Dallas in 1924. "Prairie Blues" and "Sentimental Blues" by Seger Ellis appeared on Victor about the same time. A while later I found Seger Ellis living only a few miles from my apartment. He'd been a famous singer and pianist, sometimes accompanied by Louis Armstrong on records. Yet he was forgotten only a few years after he'd given up his "Choir of Brass." The two piano blues were his first records, both influenced by pianists he'd heard along West Dallas Street. He'd recorded them when Victor set up at the Rice Hotel in 1925.

I knew a little about the record companies going around the cities. In the mid '40s Victor used the Dallas Athletic Club to record Bill Boyd and others. My father was a member of the club and arranged for me to watch a unit of engineers and producers moving around the country looking for new talent. Later, as old company files were gathered, we learned such units had stopped in seven Texas towns. Laredo, El Paso, and Brownsville for Mexican music. Many times in Dallas, San Antonio, and Fort Worth, only twice in Houston. They'd gone to most Southern towns, others like Minneapolis and Butte, Montana, and the Carter Family and Jimmie Rodgers had discovered themselves by showing up when Victor was in Bristol, Tennessee. The huge wartime hit "Pistol Packing Mama" was by Al Dexter, who made his first records in San Antonio. Orin named what seemed more than a hundred people he was interested in. I couldn't begin to remember the ones he brought out to show me. Over time I pursued many of them. Boots and His Buddies, Troy Floyd, Irene Taylor, Willie Reed, Joe Pullum, Rob Cooper, Bernice Edwards, Crystal Springs Ramblers, Gene Autry, Cotton Thompson, Andy Boy, Robert Johnson, Little Hat Jones, Dad Nelson, Chief Henry's Indian String Band, Bob Wills, Hermanas Barraza, Pedro Rocha, Milton Brown, Don Albert, Floyd Tillman, Texas Alexander, Eva Garza, The Hurricane of the Valley, a Mexican duo featuring *dialogos calle*—alley talk. Hattie Burleson, Mississippi Sheiks, Bo Carter, Coley Jones, M. S. Dillehay, Breaux Brothers, Cartwright Brothers, Bacova's Ceska Kapela, Jay McShann, Rambling Thomas, Simmons University Cowboy Band, Buddy Woods, Eddie and Sugar Lou's Hotel Tyler Orchestra.

I tried to locate the legendary Snoozer Quinn, who'd awed every jazz guitar player who heard him, but no one knew what happened to him. He'd made four recordings, none of them issued. I learned Prince Albert Hunt had been murdered outside a Dallas dance hall. I got to Blind Willie Johnson's house in Beaumont soon after he died. Five years earlier I could have put him back on records. Tried to locate Robert Johnson after hearing "32-20 Blues" recorded after the Chuck Wagon Gang finished for the day.

Index to Jazz was published in four paperback volumes beginning in 1945. They were tentative books meant to capture the attention of collectors. Readers were asked to add information from their own collection, to talk to musicians to find out who did a certain solo, to find out about others in the group. His plan was to put this added information in a revised second edition. I agreed to help, and before I left town Orin gave me the first two published volumes of *Index* and autographed one for me. That was on September 28, 1946. I still have them, torn and brown. And when I left New Orleans, hitchhiking back to Houston, I had been given the title—which I'm very proud of to this day—of Texas Editor of *Index to Jazz*. That's where my field research began—that day in 1946.

I never heard from him again. I'd sent him a lot of the information he wanted but never had the chance to use. That turned out to be my first experience with the sting of unpublished work. For some reason, in all the years since, I haven't really tried to find out what happened. When I looked, the internet only came up with an item about a New Orleans jazz club and magazine he started in the early '30s. Greenwood Press reprinted the original four volumes of *Index* in a single book in the '70s. On occasion Amazon's network of used-book dealers lists a copy for sale. In 1948 he published the first volume of the revised *Index to Jazz* in loose-leaf form. It covered A to E, from Copenhagen's Cecil Aagaard to Louisiana's Will Ezell. It's a rare book, though an occasional a copy turns up. Abe Books has offered it for twenty dollars. Information I sent for the new edition was included in the new A–E. Tiny bits are dug out now and then. Now every bio entry about Texas Alexander says his first name was Alger, something he'd told me while working his corner outside the Rice Hotel. The revised A–E at the time eluded a lot of people. Sam Charters, who'd lived in New Orleans and met Orin, told me he never knew it existed. There may be a hint of trouble on the title page. It has no publication date, and the address, 439 Baronne, is marked out, with "811 No. Rampart," in Orin's hand, written over it. Orin seemed overworked when I met him. Yet he took on more work. In addition to the monthly magazine, *Playback*, he brought out his first annual, *Jazzfinder '49*. Then trouble came along. Competition from England. Albert McCarthy and Dave Carey began publishing *Jazz Directory*. It had better looking typeface and was neater and widely advertised. It must have hurt Orin's sales badly.

Over the next few years I interviewed Joe Pullum, who told me about the differences between Fourth Ward and Fifth Ward piano players. Gene Autry laughed about his 1935 recordings in Dallas. Seger Ellis bragged about being one of the artists—along with Sophie Tucker, Paul Whiteman, and I think Ted Lewis—whose picture Columbia put on their record labels. Jack Sharpe, who claimed to be author of "St. James Infirmary," remembered the pianists he'd heard in Galveston and oil boomtowns. A neighbor described Blind Willie Johnson playing on a Beaumont street corner. Hanging around a Musicians' Union hall was a way to find what they called "legitimate" musicians. I liked the idea of gathering unique information, history likely to be lost if someone didn't make the effort.

How did you communicate with black people? Did that present any problem?

I'll tell you something astonishing. I have almost never had any kind of trouble that people seem to expect. I would often go into a town—this is over a thirty-four-year period now—I would see some people standing on a corner—usually men—I'd go over. I'd ask them some ordinary questions and gradually I'd work my way around to saying, "I understand you play a kind of forty-two"—that's a kind of domino game "—that they don't play anywhere else." And on one occasion with that question they'd invite me around the corner where people were playing dominoes—and they'd teach me the game and show me how the way they played the game differed from the people in the next county. And that, by the way, was the sort of thing that fascinated me—and still does—the regional variations and how close they could be. It happened in jazz and in all kind of folk arts—the way people build houses—in eastern Pennsylvania where the house-type changes every county or two.

Of course, I did meet people with whom I couldn't communicate very well. This is typical of what would happen. I was in a Mississippi town and I was asking questions. There was a group of eight or ten guys who were at college in Jackson—they came from this town—it was the weekend, I guess. And they started to get nasty with me—things like "What are you doing in our place? Why don't you stay in your place?"—that sort of thing. That happened many times in one form or another. And as soon as they started doing that, there was an old man who popped up on the front porch alongside where we were on the street. And he said, "You boys can't do that! This is a man—you can't do that to him! Get away!" So as long as there was somebody like that around—the few times I had problems there was always a fellow like that. Many people don't realize that there were a number of civil rights movements before the well-known one from the Kennedy era. I was a part of that era where people in the Carolinas were doing sit-ins. They'd go into a restaurant and sit at the lunch counter and demand to be served. Often the police would be called, but that succeeded fairly well with big corporations like Woolworths and Walgreens—places like that, who didn't want static from their southern stores. One of the things I liked to do, there's an intersection here—at Main and Elgin. It's a bus stop where the women who worked as domestics for the wealthy people in River Oaks would changes buses to go to the Third Ward—their home. Around four thirty or five o'clock you would find about thirty women out there, waiting for the bus to take them home. We got to going over there—these Texas Southern University guys and myself. I would go over to the Walgreens, which was right on that corner, and I would order four cheeseburgers and say "My friends will be coming," and when the cheeseburgers got set out there in front of four stools, these three university guys—all black—would come in and sit alongside of me. And if they could talk some of the women into it, they'd come too. The women didn't want to come in at first, but later on some of them came too. Almost every day they'd have to stand out there for around thirty minutes, waiting for the next bus. So they started coming in too—eventually.

What we were trying to do was to fill up all eighteen or twenty seats in the lunch area. So the store was in the position of having to kick us out—and we were the type of guys who weren't going to go quietly—they'd have to drag us away. Well, they called the police once but that didn't work very well. There were at least eight people there with the women, and the police didn't want to take that many people to jail because it would make the papers. So that was some of the early days of the civil rights movement—before the civil rights act was passed, which I think was 1964. The 1950s was the age of the sit-ins.

When it came to communication, there was one problem: as I got older, a lot of people assumed that I was the rent man—there to collect the rent. So I was quick to tell everybody I was not there to collect the rent. And musicians were sometimes quite suspicious—when I thought I was facing a musician, I always told them I was interested in music—because who knows what problems they had going on? Perhaps there was an arrest warrant out for them or they had drug problems—who knew what they were dealing with? So I was always quick to let them know I was interested in music.

Can you tell me the story of how you first met Lightning Hopkins—and what your involvement with him was?

I mentioned earlier that my mother was an X-ray technician. In 1947 she got a job in Houston as an X-ray technician/nurse/receptionist. She knew I was interested in records and musicians—one day she told me that one of the patients had come in and that he was recording and making records here in Houston. I didn't realize that records were being made here, so I decided to find out about him. A few days later, she said he was back in and "I asked him if you could come down and watch the recordings being made." So I did exactly that pretty fast. His name was Bill Quinn and his company was Gold Star Records, which is one of the very early, legendary companies.

There was a terrible monopoly in the record industry in the 1930s and 1940s—up to the end of World War II. Victor and Columbia, Decca and Brunswick prevented other people from starting record companies by trying to control the pressing machines themselves—and not pressing anybody's records. Then Capitol Records came along—founded by Johnny Mercer and several other music business people. They not only worked around the monopoly, they actually joined the monopoly. But the monopoly didn't last much longer because various individuals got hold of record-pressing machines—and Bill Quinn was one of them. The pressing machines, resembling huge waffle irons, were being acquired by outsiders. Bill Quinn, who started Gold Star records, liberated his machine from a Bridgeport junkyard. He got a pressing machine, which meant that he could make records—*if he could figure out what compound was used to make the records.* He experimented with all kinds of wacky compounds. If you could hear copies of his first fifty records, you can hear him experimenting with different compounds—some of which were terrible! They were awful sounding! The surface noise was as loud as or louder than the music. Then, over a period of time, you hear it getting better and better. From that point on—this is the mid-1940s, the years just after the war—anybody who wanted to start a record company could. And Bill Quinn was one of the pioneers. Then he got some hit records. "Jole Blon" became a national rage.

The day I went down there in about 1947, Lightning Hopkins was recording. He was pretty well known around town at the time. I heard the songs he recorded that day—some of which I heard again when they were issued on the Gold Star label. Then I saw him on the bus playing—several times. I knew that he rode a bus in the Third Ward—which is the guitar playing ward. You could often find him on this bus. He could ride free and he would play for the people on the bus and earn some change that way. In the 1950s there were several newspaper stories that were titled "Finding Lightning"—or "Searching For Lightning"—that kind of thing—which was idiotic because at that time I'd rarely run across a black person who *couldn't* tell you where to find him. [laughs] He lived in the Third Ward right alongside a railway siding—his house was readily pointed out. I think when I decided to talk to him about recording, I went over to Dowling Street, which is the main street in the Third Ward—and I asked somebody where he lived. They said, "Well, he's riding around right now—but he'll probably be back by in a minute." And there he was—driving down Dowling Street, sort of cruising—looking things over. So I hollered at him and waved him over. We started talking. People continued to come to town and continued to write articles about finding him. I guess the reason that entertained me so much was the fact that finding people like Mance Lipscomb or Barefoot Bill had involved a real effort! But finding Lightning was largely a matter of going down on Dowling Street and asking a few questions. If you didn't know to go to Dowling, then ask anybody anywhere and they'd probably send you to Third Ward. He was a very well-known figure among the black people—and a good many white folks knew about him too.

I'd had some contact in the commercial music world. I had recorded some things on assignment. The first records I made were of a swing band called the Buddy Ryland Band (1949)—an eighteen-piece band, in a progressive mode—like the Kenton band. Buddy was a trombone player. So I'm pleased to say that my recording work began in the 78 era. I also got some assignments to record some country artists who were here. One I remember: I recorded the Short Brothers—Jimmy and Leon Short—for the Coral label, which is a subsidiary of Decca. There were other sessions, which for some reason I'm unable to remember. I didn't pay for these sessions. I was contacted to take musicians or groups into the studio, and they sent me money to pay the musicians. I was actually in the commercial end of the music business, trying to make a living at that time. I would take them into the ACA Studios here in Houston. It's well known—a lot of the local labels in Houston used ACA—in fact, for a while I don't think there was another professional studio in Houston.

I first recorded Lightning sometime in the late 1950s. Lightning's first recordings for me were recorded in my apartment. They were very intimate recordings. When I recorded I used to do a certain thing. I would sit directly opposite him with a microphone between us—and I would get our knees touching. I'm looking directly at him and he's singing directly to me. Those recordings have an intimate feel because he's singing directly for me and I may reach over and squeeze his knee if I'm pleased with something he's done. I think it's very important to keep an artist aware of an audience—and if it's a recording that audience might only be one person. Frank Sinatra used to invite twenty or thirty people to his sessions—so my approach wasn't unique. I'd sit within a finger's width of these artists and got what I thought of as a very intimate feeling on his songs. With Lightning I was looking for his earliest songs—the ones he had learned along the line—the ones he had learned from Blind Blake's records, the ones he had learned while accompanying Texas Alexander. He'd also gone around the country a couple of times, and there was a song he learned while going to Friars Point, Mississippi.

There were problems with the recordings—the machine was bad. I tried on several occasions. Then I decided—and this is one of the landmark albums that I didn't quite finish—I decided I wanted to record his entire repertoire—not the songs he improvised on the spot, but the songs he had been singing much of his life. I recorded those—there were about one hundred of them. The first recordings I made with Lightning wound up on the Tradition label. Those were the first ones. Some of the discographies have got a list of all my recordings from that very first period. These were the ones done at my apartment. A number of them were issued in an album called *Country Blues* with an absolutely dreadful cover—and also *Autobiography in Blues*, which had a nice cover with a photograph of Lightning. These are microgroove recordings. That was the beginning. On those first two albums he was not amplified. I recorded several more albums by Lightning and then I got a contract to record him for the Prestige label. I did those—some with groups, some with Lightning amplified, and some acoustic. The thing I meant to do was to issue them all as a set. That didn't happen. A good portion of his repertoire was there, but it was scattered—and then there's material I have on master tapes that has never been issued.

I did a few things that horrified people later. Sam Hopkins had a tremendous inclination to repeat himself. And there were some songs he didn't want to do because they were too much trouble—or they involved re-tuning the guitar to an open tuning. So I would push him harder than most people did. Most people who recorded him just said, "Go ahead Lightning—do what you want to do." And they would get a lot of repetitious verses—verses you might hear on a lot of his other records. But I would say to him, "Give me the best verses you can." And if he got repetitious, I'd reach over and switch off the tape machine—and would say to him "This is not your best. So let's try again. Go off—have a drink and think about it and come back to me with a good version of it." I don't think that had ever happened to him before—where somebody just turned off the tape machine and said, "You can do better." But he very much needed that. If you listen to so many blues musicians—especially now that there are so many second takes and alternate versions available—it's easy to pick out those who, before they record, decide what a song is going to be. If you listen to Robert Johnson and listen to take number 1 of his song and then listen to take number 2 of it—there's very little difference between the versions. In fact, sometimes you could almost play them on top of one another. So here's Robert Johnson, who knew what he wanted to record—and there was Lightning Hopkins at the other extreme. He had no idea where he was going on in many cases. But he also had other kinds of songs—for example, his time at Rice Institute, Rice University now. It's right here in Houston, and there was a hurricane on the way. I had arranged for him to do a street dance, and they had built a big platform out there and they were literally going to dance on one of the streets. The crowd had just begun to assemble and Lightning was sitting on a folding chair up on top of that platform, which was maybe eight feet high. I'd set up his amplifier, and he was ready to get into it—and the wind started to blow pretty good. A gust of wind came that just blew him [laughs] about ten feet across the platform. So at that point we decided we weren't going to use the platform anymore [laughs]—he'd gotten to within a few feet of the edge of it—and we brought the equipment down to the street. He played a while and there was a little dancing, but after an hour it became impossible. The dancers went inside—and we went home. The very next day he came to me and *wanted* to record this new piece that he had written about the event from the night before. So I got out the tape machine and we recorded that. It showed that he was capable of doing that kind of thing. In another instance that's better known—we were recording an album for Prestige at ACA Studios on Fannin Street in downtown Houston. During a break in the session I went out to smoke on the corner—and there was a newspaper rack. There on the front page of the *Houston Chronicle* was a story: "John Glenn Circles the Earth Three Times." I bought the newspaper, took it inside, and I showed it to Sam—I always called him Sam. I said to him, "Here's what's happening at this moment. What about we make up a song about John Glenn going around the world?" Both of us sat down—I suggested ideas—he suggested things—and we worked them up into verses. Then we recorded a six-minute version of the tune "Happy Blues for John Glenn." That was issued on a 45 as a part-one–part-two thing by Prestige. And it turned into a small hit. I got a partial composer's credit—and I deserved it. The songwriter royalties have come back, and we each made a nice piece of money off that. And then when John Glenn went up in more recent years—what was that, maybe the thirtieth anniversary?—all of a sudden the royalties jumped up because a lot of disc jockeys remembered the record, got it out, and started playing it again.

One of the things I did during that period—Lightning wanted to make more money—so I wrote a lot of articles about him and publicized him. That's how he became internationally known—between the records and the articles and the interviews. I often tell people that for a number of years Howard Hughes was the most famous person from Houston. But then after Howard Hughes, Lightning became the most famous person from Houston. And that was under my management and due to my work on his behalf. People in Houston will say, "Now that can't possibly be true." But here's a fan letter that he got from Thailand, here's another letter from Germany—here's a club in Sweden sending him an award of some kind—plus all the records in the stores. Altogether I believe I spent five or six years working to promote and publicize Lightning Hopkins. After a while he became well known and no longer needed my services. But I'm kind of proud of having turned a local street singer into a well-known international singer.

In regard to discovering and recording Mance Lipscomb, I used to do grid searches. I'd search a county, road by road, back and forth. I might spend three or four days in that county and then go back to it again. I was working on my Texas book—and I had done a lot of the research before the Texas book got started. So I started with a group of counties that would measure, north and south, between five and ten counties. Then I came farther east and did the same thing with the adjacent counties. I kept going that way and I eventually wound up in Delaware—with a long, long strip of counties I'd been in. Now this wasn't limited strictly to music—it also included games, recipes, or crafts people—or whatever I could find that was distinctive of that area. So imagine a long strip that starts west of San Antonio and extends into Delaware. Now I did this over a number of years but I first heard of Mance Lipscomb in the earlier years. Back then some people told me he was a useless old man who couldn't really play. Then I met his nephew in Galveston—a fellow named T. Lipscomb. He was quite sick from diabetes. During the 1960s he had one leg cut off and then the other, and then died from diabetes. But he was the first one who told me that Mance was a good musician—well worth going to hear. Then I talked to Lightning Hopkins about it, and he more or less admitted the same thing—"He's an old man who plays old music"—but he didn't disparage him. Others had disparaged him as an old man who could no longer play. That's what lead me to Navasota on that particular occasion—I wanted to see Mance—and I wanted to interview Tom Moore.

Tom Moore was one of the white bosses in the area and was the subject of a much-played song generally called "Tom Moore's Farm" or "The Four Moore Brothers." The lyrics of the song describe him in some detail—two versions of that are on the Treasury of Field Recordings—one by Lightning Hopkins and one by an artist listed as "Anonymous." The reason for that is I talked to Tom Moore. He knew what a vicious reputation he had, and he was sensitive to the issue. He was proud of the property—he showed me all these photographs of the property—and he told me about the "good old days" when "black people didn't give you so much trouble." But when I asked him about the song, he got very uptight and defensive. He said to me, "You better not find anybody around here who's singing that song." Then, a few hours later, I was recording Mance, and I asked him about the song—and he was very reluctant to sing it. I talked him into singing it, and I asked him to tell me about Tom Moore. So on the Treasury of Field Recordings, Mance says something to the effect, "If Tom Moore knew I was singing this song on a record, he would come and burn me out"—and then he asked me *not* to put his name on it. That's why it appears as "Anonymous." When a full recording of Mance came out, those who heard both knew who it was, but it didn't get back to Tom Moore. And that was good because he was a very, very tough person who ran that area with an iron fist. In an era when you thought it was no longer possible, he was beating his workers as though they were still slaves. He had his people under his thumb—many who owed him money, and they were not able to leave or work on any other plantation; if they did, Tom Moore would go to that plantation owner and get his workers back. These are people in astonishing bondage as late as the 1920s and 1930s.

In the 1940s things began to loose up a bit, but Tom Moore's reputation persisted. The four Moore brothers owned huge tracks of Washington County and Grimes County, the county where Navasota is located. Those were originally slave farms, and they were built on river bottoms—very rich land. And even in the years before World War II, the landowners had such power that if one of the workers went into town and killed somebody and then went back to the plantation, when the sheriff heard about this he would call Tom Moore—or he would drive out to the gate where the farm began and send a note, by way of the gate tender, to Tom Moore and ask for permission to talk to him. He would wait until he got permission—then he would go in and talk to Tom Moore. And then Tom Moore would decide if this particular person—who had committed murder—should be arrested or not. If he decided he didn't want them arrested, he would say to the sheriff, "He's a valuable worker—I just can't let him go." Another time the sheriff might do the same thing—he'd come to Tom Moore, and Tom would say, "Yeah, you can take him—I don't need that guy." That's how that worked. "The four Moore Brothers bought Washington County—and now they're fencin' it in." It's one of the few, very rare songs of negro protest. Back in the early part of the 1930s in the early folk-song movement, there was a strong effort to find songs of negro protest. But I can tell you—there just aren't very many. If you listen to ten thousand race records and then ten thousand archival records, you will only occasionally come up with a real protest. And the reason is pretty obvious—blacks don't go around singing to each other about the conditions in which they live—they already know that. They want to hear something that's a wry comment on those conditions. But then when the Lomaxes got a hold of Leadbelly, they urged him to sing songs of protest. And if you listen to those early Lomax recordings of Leadbelly—he didn't really come up with what they wanted. They asked him about mean white people and he came up with Tom Hughes, who was the sheriff of Shreveport—who was kind of hard on black people—but he came up with Tom Hughes Town.

I used the same technique in recording Mance Lipscomb that I had used with Lightning—I would sit with our knees touching. There were some disadvantages in it though. I recorded Mance in his bedroom, sitting right alongside the bed. His grandkids lived in the house, and we could not keep them out of the bedroom. They were fascinated by the stranger and the recording machine. But I finally talked him into sitting down—if you walked across the floor it made a sound. So I was sitting opposite Mance, knee to knee, and the kids were just behind me. If they made any sound, I would motion to them to be quiet, and we finally succeeded. Later, Reprise Records wanted me to record Mance. That time we *did* go to ACA Studios and we did the same thing—sit knee to knee—and one of the moments of my life I never will forget is when he started singing "Motherless Children Have a Hard Time." My mother had just died, and I just sat there weeping—even now it's got me. As he sang that song he saw me weeping. We both were thinking of our mothers, which is one of the most emotional things anybody can do. Reprise recently reissued that original record along with some previously unissued sides from that same session. On the cover of the reissue it says: "With original liner notes by Mack McCormick." They not only include my original notes, they actually print those same notes twice! [laughs] I guess they had some space to fill.

The work that was done in discovering Mance was totally my work—nobody helped me with the real work. And that's true with most of the people you find—it takes a lot of work. You talk to a lot of people before they lead you to the person you're looking for. That's always bothered me—it's never been made clear just how much work was involved in finding Mance. Paul Oliver was not any part of finding Mance Lipscomb. Paul came along a few weeks after my original meeting with Mance, and he wanted to see Mance. So I went out there with him, and he recorded Mance for the book he was doing, *Conversation with the Blues.*

I was going to do an album with Alex Moore and Bobbie Cadillac together. He had known her since the time they first recorded. He was in Houston, and he talked to her in Dallas and asked her to come down so they could make this album together—I think it was for Prestige. I remember taking Alex down to the train station to meet her and how shaken and disappointed he was when she didn't step off the train. That's why Bobbie Cadillac didn't get recorded in the 1950s. She was a fascinating person—very nasty talking.

I found a second photograph of Blind Lemon Jefferson. I acquired this photograph from relatives of Lemon's that I located in 1963. His family lived in West Texas—half-brothers and sisters. I met them in Wortham. I had heard a lot of different descriptions of his health. Members of the family mentioned some things to me. In the photo he's standing upright. I looked at the photograph, and he was heavy—something just looked odd about it. I thought perhaps a doctor could suggest some things—I don't remember just what condition I had in mind. I loaned that photograph to Edmond Souchon, a New Orleans jazz musician who became a practicing physician. That made him the obvious person to ask about the condition of Blind Lemon Jefferson, which was apparent in that photograph. So I asked him what condition was suggested by that picture. He listed several afflictions which seemed likely. I also showed it to some doctors here who interpreted it for me—but this was fifty years ago, and I haven't seen the picture in years.

I've seen listed among your work research on the Thomas Family out of Houston—George, Hersal, Sippie (Wallace), and Hociel Thomas. Who or what were the sources for this particular research?

Well, it began with my knowledge that they had come from Houston. They were in Fifth Ward. I went out to Fifth Ward, which is the northeastern part of Houston. I asked around and somebody told me where to find the house—actually, two houses—that various members of the family had lived in. It was a very large family, and there were around fifteen people who played piano—either in the family, or close friends. They gathered at a place called Big Tree. It was an open area where people could dance on the dirt, and George and Hersal and all the rest played there. This was the early part of the century.

There was also another Thomas Family in central Texas—it was just enormous, and it went back a number of generations way back into the nineteenth century. They had string bands and tended to serenade houses. This may be the biggest musical family that I've ever heard of—just astonishing in size! Any town in that whole area, which might be a hundred miles across and a hundred miles, north to south, you'd hear of the Thomas Family and you might hear of the particular group hired by nearby people. The next generation of the family included Victoria Spivey and Sippie Wallace—both of whom I talked to, I would run into them at festivals. They confirmed a lot of things. Victoria was very interested in the fact that I lived in Houston, and she asked me a lot of things Houstonians would ask about.

Then I was a census taker for one year, 1960. I volunteered to do Fourth Ward—this is just west of downtown Houston, and I lived close by. So I did the census of this one particular area, which is about ten thousand houses. I went to every house writing down things the census asks, which included things like "What kind of toilet facilities do you have?" "Is the house disheveled?" and so on. But then after I asked the census bureau's questions, I asked my questions. And some people were willing to talk at length about them. And I've always regarded this understanding of the Fourth Ward pianists as one of the breakthroughs that I managed—just a staggering number of pianists that people had talked about who were there—or that had quit music. I met Edward Pickens, who was a piano player. He got interested in what I was trying to do—his interests paralleled mine. So Edward Pickens got very interested in this thing and he got into the habit of coming over to my house—we lived about a mile apart. He would come over—sometimes wake me up in the morning—and he said, "I found another one—you could record him!" He'd insist I go over, and he'd take me over to see this person. His information led me to Robert Shaw, who was then in Austin and who had been a member of this group—this very important group of pianists, which makes up an important example of how a cloister of musicians come together in a very limited spot. The pianists of the Fifth Ward had quite a different style than the Fourth Ward pianists. I could play a record for Alex Moore in Dallas—I would play a record for him and he would immediately know whether the pianist was the Fourth Ward or the Fifth Ward. People in Texas just knew these two distinctive styles. It might be somebody they'd never seen or heard, but they knew the particular style and the community it came from. I considered these very exciting experiences because they reveal how music works—not just blues, but every genre of music in the world.

I'm fascinated with Buster Pickens. I'm so glad the Buster Pickens LP was issued because I thought he was a wonderful artist.

What happened was that Paul Oliver came to town and I took him around to a number of musicians I'd located. He recorded a couple of them—Mance Lipscomb was one of them, Buster Pickens was another. That was the period when Buster Pickens was helping me. I did a radio program at that time at KHOU—that was a nonprofit station at the University of Houston—and I took Pickens up to the studio, and he was on my program on that occasion. After the program we recorded the stuff that was on his record. The engineer did the actual recording, and Paul asked him a lot of questions. Paul was gathering material for his book, *Conversation with the Blues*, and Pickens did that monologue about the Hobo, which is kind of unique—I've never heard anybody do anything quite like that. Pickens and I had grown quite close, but I remember I did one great disfavor to him. My interest in this music triggered his interest, once again, in making his living by playing piano. There was very little hope of that—and yet, by the questions I asked and the things he did to help, he got to the point where he thought piano players in bars was a thing that was going to come back. He was not making any money; his wife was working in a laundry and wanted him to go out and get a job. But because of what I'd done to stimulate his interest, he kept thinking that at any moment it was going to work out for him to play piano. And I had on some occasions gotten him hired at various places—and he *did* make some money—but it was not enough for him to continue. Pickens was in a bar on West Dallas Street—which is not in Dallas but is the main drag of the Fourth Ward in Houston. He was in a bar in Houston with his cousin and an argument developed, and his cousin shot him with a .22; Pickens died shortly thereafter. I was very shaken by his death and upset because we'd gotten very close. I enjoyed his company—he was a person from another world and he'd been so helpful to me, and we had a great time together. And I tried to help his wife with the funeral—it was just so sad. I dedicated my Robert Shaw record to Buster Pickens—in the booklet of liner notes there's a page describing what happened to Pickens.

I mentioned earlier my method of grid searching. I was doing a grid search across Texas. It was during this that I got to the Austin area and I heard the name Robert Shaw—not as a musician, but in a totally different context. He was famous in his town for his restaurant where so many people went for carryout barbeque. The restaurant was on Manor Road. I heard his name and thought that I should go there. He had moved to Austin and started a little, small store—an icehouse is what they're called here: it's kind of an open place where people go to get ice and groceries. And in this place back in the 1930s he played piano to attract people. Then he bought a bigger place sometime in the late '30s, and he stopped playing piano in public. Then when I saw him, which was 1964 I believe, I walked into his store—it was called Shaw's Store, on Manor Road. There was a customer there, and when he finished with the customer, I asked him if he was the Robert Shaw who had played piano in Houston and Austin. He didn't say anything, nothing at all. But he went over to a phone or some intercom gadget and called his wife to come over and take care of the store. His house was directly behind the store. So she came over quickly.

He still hadn't said a word to me but he simply stuck up his index finger and motioned for me to follow him. I followed him out the back door and to his house—and still not saying anything, he sat down at the piano and played the Ma Grinder. The Ma Grinder was the piece that everybody in the Fourth Ward had to play so people would understand that they were from the Fourth Ward. Though Shaw hadn't played in public for quite some time, he had continued to play all those years for his own pleasure. He knew the Fourth Ward repertoire, and he had never changed it or gone on to play other things. What he played for me—what I recorded—were pristine examples of the Fourth Ward, the best examples that exist. The Fourth Ward repertoire was not fully recorded in the 1930s. Pickens knew the repertoire, but he had gone on to other types of music—including popular music. But there was Shaw, with the repertoire just as though it had been preserved in ice. It wasn't long after that I started my own record company—Almanac.

I issued the LP as *Texas Barrelhouse Piano*. I should have called it *Fourth Ward Piano* because that's what it was. There was a session with Peppermint Harris for a label I've never heard of before or since. Next time I met Peppermint he was running a pressing machine at Houston Records, the plant I used when I started Almanac Records to issue Robert Shaw's *Texas Barrelhouse Piano*. Peppermint Harris pressed every copy of that album. That whole record pleases me—it hasn't had the attention I think it deserves. It may be my fault for not more thoroughly emphasizing how unique it was to find a community of ten thousand people who had produced 212 piano players—players who had, during at least a part of their lives, played piano professionally. That's why I consider this a landmark recording. My notes to this recording were probably not as extensive as they should have been in order to complete the story. It's the best picture of a single neighborhood's style that I know of—that's why it's so important.

After this album was issued on your Almanac label, wasn't it reissued on Arhoolie?

No comment. Well—I'll say this—it was bootlegged in two countries. One of the guys who bootlegged it told me, "There's nothing you can do about it because I live in another state than you do. To prevent it you'd have to sue people in every state in the union who did this." And since this business didn't bring in that much money, it wasn't feasible to bring such lawsuits unless you had a record company that was turning out a lot of product. And I've been told that even then, it's just not realistic to bring matters to a lawsuit unless there's a great deal of money involved. I remember contacting a law firm in one area where the record was being bootlegged. They sent back a letter telling me to send along a ten-thousand-dollar retainer and they would look into it. You run into a lot of problems with records. Nobody had told me about how the record business works. I put out the *Texas Barrelhouse Piano* LP and Nat Hentoff gave it "The Best of the Month Review" in *HiFi Stereo* magazine. It was a big, glossy magazine, and it brought me thousands of orders. A lot of small, independent record wholesalers ordered the record—sometimes in lots as small as five records. I sent the records out and then I sent out bills—but only a few of the bills were paid. So I started calling around asking people to pay the bill. Finally, I got a guy who told me the bottom line. He said, "Okay, this is a good record—you sold it. Now you put out another record that we need. If we need your next record, then we'll pay you for the first one. That's how the record business works. Didn't you know?" No—I didn't. I also found out that if you go into the record business, it immediately turns you into a shipping clerk. You've suddenly got boxes, packing material, trips to the post office—you're a shipping clerk.

Did you have any contact with Bernice Edwards?

Bernice Edwards was a major informer. She was another one I found through a series of steps. I was told she lived in Sunny Side, the suburb south of the Third Ward. She had been one of the extended members of the Thomas Family but later changed her loyalties and style to the Fourth Ward cluster. She was a major fountain of information, someone who explained lesser-known nooks and crannies of the black entertainment world. A lively woman in her mid-forties, she had owned a circus that traveled small towns in seven states in the US and northern Mexico. Texas, Oklahoma, New Mexico, Louisiana, Tamaulipas, Nuevo Leon, and Coahuila. The circus included clowns, trick riders, a lion tamer, plus a trapeze act. They were based in Freer, Texas, where I came upon a man who'd been a hot-dog vendor with the show. He told me the circus carried a special wagon with two or three prostitutes. He knew Bernice's married name, and with that it was only a matter of looking in the Houston phone book. She was quite open about having been a prostitute. She worked in some of the whorehouses along the Gulf Coast—and in the red wagon in her own circus. It's always fascinated me that so many of the female blues singers have backgrounds as prostitutes—and how often they were the stars of their houses. She named two other well-known singers who did the same. She made me promise not to blacken their names. But Bernice was not an ordinary working girl. She would show customers her records, telling them they'd be with a star. She'd then sing one of her songs for them and demand twice as much as the other girls. She made more money than the other girls because she could sit at the piano and play songs for her potential customers—which made her the place's outstanding woman.

Bernice Edwards had been a member of both the Fourth Ward pianists AND the Fifth Ward pianists. She had first been a close friend of one of the Spivey girls and for a while had lived in a house next door to the Thomas family. So she became a part of that group. Then she left town for a while, and then somehow—I don't know how—she merged into the Fourth Ward pianists. She was well known among those people, back in 1960 when I was meeting them. At first Bernice refused to see me. She said she was a devoted member of a church, was their pianist. She didn't want the members to know of her life as a blues singer. Yet she startled me, in a phone conversation with a stranger, saying she'd bought a circus with money from "whoring." On my next call she took the phone to the piano and played one of her songs. She wasn't out of practice. She admitted she'd often sing her "old songs" for herself at home. Bernice had religious convictions against what she was doing. Yet she tempted me by taking the phone to her piano and singing a blues about the Mexican border. My interest was stirring memories of good times. On the third or fourth phone call she agreed to see me. When I arrived, she repeated all her objections. After asking me a few questions and exchanging names of pianists we both knew, she began to open up. She answered freely, providing a good deal new to me. She sang more songs, some she'd recorded for Paramount in the late '20s, songs I first heard from her and only later from the original when they appeared on reissue albums.

Bernice had been recruited in Galveston at the age of fifteen by the Paramount scout Arthur Laibly. It seemed unusually young to me, but she said she was already being pimped out by a "gink" by then. Laibly talked her mother into letting her make the trip to Chicago. When he gave her the ticket, he asked her to watch out for and help another Paramount artist, a blind man who'd be boarding train in Dallas. On the way to Dallas, Bernice realized it might be Blind Lemon Jefferson. He had a reputation for grabbing women, lifting skirts so—his favorite joke—he could pretend to know the color of their panties. He'd name the color in a song, then challenge the woman to show her panties to prove him right or wrong. Occasionally one would take up the dare. Ray Charles did a milder version of it, singing, "See the girl with the red dress on?" Bernice admired Lemon's records and thought of him as a star. However, when he boarded the train, he demanded she help him to his seat and took advantage of that to grope her thoroughly. He was fat, smelly, and gruff. He insisted she guide him to the toilet, each time grabbing her in delicate places. Struggling with him went on most of the night. When she moved to another seat, he'd find her by scent or the sound of her breathing. When the conductor came through calling out that the next stop would be Peach Orchard, Arkansas, Bernice tried to distract [Lemon], saying he should make up a song about Peach Orchard. Next year his "Peach Orchard Mama" appeared. Lemon and Bessie Smith were the most popular blues artists at the time. I wondered if Bernice's story was concocted to put her in company with a celebrity. Now I have to apologize. When Max Vreede and other scholars gathered the Paramount master numbers, the sequence showed Bernice's first session had been interrupted for Lemon to record two songs—just as she'd said. She refused at first to record for me—then she agreed—then she changed her mind—back and forth because she was in the process of joining a church and abandoning the blues totally. Actually, she had abandoned the blues some years earlier, but when I visited her, it sparked her interest again, and she began rehearsing some of the songs she had recorded.

Bernice Edwards was part of the Fort Worth Catastrophe. You can look this up in *Blues and Gospel Records*. This session for Vocalion was held April 1935. Bernice was the one to describe the Great Fort Worth Disaster. It happened because they used an engineer other than one of the expert recording engineers who usually made records on the trips around the country. The one in Fort Worth typically recorded transcriptions of programs for distribution to radio stations. Apparently, he didn't understand how to cut 78s. The grooves on that particular session were too shallow. The needle would jump out and skid around. Their lab couldn't even copy them to make a new master. Only four by Bernice survived, none by Funny Paper Smith and none by Black Boy Shine except a messy duet with Bernice—"Ninth Street Stomp." Two that were lost were parts 5 and 6 meant to continue the four-part "Howling Wolf Blues" that he'd begun five years before. So we lost the last work of a giant, one of the most captivating song makers. That was the Great Fort Worth Catastrophe; it was one reason Bernice refused to record again. She had said no to Eli Oberstein, a Bluebird producer, who came around in the '30s. For several years she refused my invitation, then said yes. Those tapes are among the ones in hazard. The Fort Worth disaster did a lot of damage. Black Boy Shine was taunted in his hometown after he told neighbors his records would soon appear. The company never let him know they'd been ruined. Fortunately, Vocalion asked him to try again a year later. Funny Paper Smith refused to record again. When I first came across him in his rooming house, I had no idea and he didn't tell me who he was. He gave me an assumed name. He did say he'd made some records but wouldn't say any more about them. He said he had no interest in waiting for another record company to pay his money or what they'd said they'd do. Later, by a different route, I tried to run him down in Smithville—I mean, literally tried to run him down. When I came on the porch, he ran out the back door of his sister's shotgun house. I went after him, shouting the words "guitar" and "blues" until he got away in a clump of trees. There were other recording disasters.

Inexperience was frequently the problem. Breaking up, running too long, too shy. Then there can be engineering problems because the units so often came south in the worst of summer. That was the case in June 1937 during burning-hot days when Bob Wills and too many musicians crowded into a small studio on a warehouse floor in the time before air conditioning. After ruining takes for several days, the problem was solved by an army of fans blowing across tubs of fifty-pound cakes of ice. The engineer had a switch to cut off the fan noise during a take. It was nice and cool in the studio when Robert Johnson arrived two weeks later. Apparently, another disaster happened when Charlie Patton went to New York in 1934. I know nothing about it except the engineer was probably Ed Theroux. More than twenty sides were recorded and less than half issued. Was it Charlie falling apart or the engineer drinking? One of them, "The Delta Murder," particularly interests me. I heard stories of several Mississippi murders, usually the details of one mixed with another. But Charlie's record was made before some occurred, and he may have had an unmixed story. Also, there haven't been enough people interviewing the staff at record companies. Not even in New York, where so many collectors and writers lived. They should have talked to the people who called to confirm scheduled sessions. The people who filled out the artist address cards, kept track of titles, made out the contracts and paychecks. They can tell you a lot. An engineer like Vincent Liebler should have been the subject of a biography. He was the one Teddy Wilson and Billie Holiday preferred. He seldom ruined takes, and when he came on the talk-back, his voice was enthusiastic. No one likes a chilly engineer in the booth.

Vincent volunteered to go on the field trips. A man from Brooklyn, he liked to be astonished at the variety of music spread around the country. Another unexplored source were the territory salesmen and jukebox operators who took local talent to record. They thought of it as a feather in the cap. They could brag that records they brought about were on their own jukeboxes. The salesman who'd brought people into the studio would turn around and push sales in his territory, tell the retail people about finding the artist. All of them wheels that turn wheels.

My wife and I went to live in Mexico in early 1964. I was searching for an income. What I intended to do down there was go to a town called Paracho in the state of Michoacán. Paracho is the town that was established in the 1500s as the guitar-making center and the violin-making center of Mexico by Bishop Quiroga. He was an enthusiast of the book *Utopia*. He went up into the mountains of Mexico and decided that each village—as in the book *Utopia*—should have a specialty. One made copper pots, another did fishing, another made the musical instruments. And they all traded these things back and forth by the barter system. That was his idea—and the fascinating thing is those towns still do those same things. Paracho is the major guitar-, violin-, and bajo-sexto-making center in Mexico. My idea was to export those instruments to the United States because this was at the middle of the folk music craze. I put a lot of money into it, but I found I couldn't do it with all the licensing and paperwork to export guitars into the United States, added to all the paperwork required in Mexico; it just made it impossible. So I gave the idea up and came back here.

In 1965 the Newport Folk Festival invited me to bring up a prison worksong gang. This was Alan Lomax's suggestion because so much of their work had included prison songs.

Texas prisons were scattered over a large area—most of them were along the coastal land, south of Houston. They were old slavery farms. So Texas—and several other states—had reinvented the slave-farm system by busting a lot of guys, sending them to prison, and suddenly they're back under strict control—raising crops. In those days, Texas prisons returned a profit to the state, so of course there was a lot of emphasis on sending as many people as you could manage. Bust them, convict them, and send them on down here. That meant we could have more and more crops—cotton and cane and everything else. They don't do that anymore because it's been outlawed.

So Lomax suggested to the Newport people that they ask me to bring up a gang to demonstrate the songs. I had trouble finding people, but I finally found a halfway house that had a lot of ex-convicts. So I got together a large group of ex-convicts who knew the songs and had worked in the fields for years—but it didn't come together until a guy named R. G. Williams came up. He was one of the legendary song leaders in Texas prison-farm camps. I remember the day he came along. He got into the line. Everybody else was kind of working and singing a little bit. But he took that hoe—an I-hoe, which was not a garden hoe but a very special kind of hoe, a mean-looking hoe—he held that thing up and he started hollering and, by God, everybody started *working*. He set them to work like they had worked on the farms. Then he went along the line and picked out the people he wanted to keep. We did that for several days and finally we had a tight little group of five people—that's all Newport wanted to pay for, five—and one of those five people was Choppin' Charlie—the original guy that the song "Choppin' Charlie" was about. He was a legendary figure in the prisons. So I took this group up to Newport. I rented a car and drove them up there. I wanted to hear what they had to say, and it took us about five days to get up there.

During those five days you wouldn't believe some of the information that I heard—it was like a college reunion. One guy was on Ramsey, another had been on Darrington Farm, and they knew a lot of the same people—but often they wouldn't know what had happened to them. So they were exchanging all this information. I was simply letting them talk. I didn't ask them anything because they just began talking. Every time we stopped I would write down a whole lot of it. The one time they really startled me—somebody was asking, "Whatever happened to Old John?" And they said, "Oh—they cut him up." I asked, "Cut him up how?" "One night in the dormitory they cut him up and flushed him down the toilet. He wasn't there the next morning." They crushed his skull with hammers and flushed that down the toilet. So when the guards came around to do the count they came up one short. The guards knew that this happened from time to time. They understood what had occurred. That gives you an idea of life on a southern prison farm. Modern prisons have just a few people in a cell—sometimes only one. But most southern prisons—Parchman, Angola, et cetera—have dormitories with up to forty people in them. These dormitories would have a building tender—a convict who slept in a separate part of the dormitory that was fenced in so that the other convicts couldn't get to him at night. He would stay in the dormitory during the daytime to clean it up while the others were out in the field working. He had better food and better treatment, but the guards put him in a kind of intermediary situation. The guards wanted him to keep an eye on the convicts. He was the guy the guards would go to—and the convicts were afraid he was talking to the guards—so the average life expectancy of a building tender was about six months—maximum. He was the one who had all the tension. But this guy I mentioned earlier, R. G. Williams, he was a building tender for *ten years*. This amazed everybody—even people from other farms who had never met him knew he'd been a building tender for ten years—almost impossible.

So I drove this group up toward Newport. When we got to Central Park in New York, they were having a little Newport preview to attract people to the fest itself, and the prison group did their first performance before an audience there at the preview. It was hard to get them going because they literally had never been before an audience. In prison they were working and singing, but they didn't think of it as a performance—certainly not intended for an audience. So their first performance before an audience was in Central Park, and it made them a little nervous.

So then we drove on to Newport. There were perhaps two hundred performers over a five-day period. We checked in and they billeted many of the performers in the great mansions of Newport. Here were the ex-convicts and myself walking into this glorious mansion [laughs]—being assigned rooms. We started rehearsing. The Rhode Island state police escorted us out to a forest where we could start cutting down trees. We were directed to trees that were slated to be removed, and the guys started to work with a technique called double cutting. To understand the technique, think of yourself cutting a tree down. Now think of another person coming to help by standing on the other side of the tree. Each of you are using an axe and each of you are chopping a notch on opposite sides of the tree. Then two more guys come over to help—now you've got two notches and four axes with two guys work on each notch, standing to either side of the notch and taking turns chopping to the center. Timing is all important here. It's extremely important not to let your axes hit one another—otherwise, they'll glance off each other and take off a leg or a foot. So they practiced doubling cutting—trying to get back into the feeling for it. The Newport people had provided a long trough of dirt where the group could demonstrate hoeing. They also provided a large tree stump for the group to demonstrate double cutting. Keep in mind the group was not there to demonstrate the work but to perform the songs that accompanied the various work assignments. I was nervous. The group had only been before an audience that one time in Central Park, and that year's audience in Newport numbered around one hundred thousand—a huge sea of chairs, and behind those chairs thousands more just wandering around. This was the folk music center of the world during this era.

We were scheduled to do a sound check, but I hadn't gotten together with the people, and they agreed this would just be a rehearsal with a small audience, but the guys in the group would have a chance to get used to the stage and the microphone and get used to hearing themselves over the sound system—the notion of performing and hearing themselves at the same time—and get used to the stage lights in their eyes. They hadn't experienced any of this. So when we got to the stage where we were scheduled to rehearse, Bob Dylan and Mike Bloomfield were having a wonderful jam. They had done their sound check and now they were just jamming—it was Dylan, Bloomfield, and a couple of other guys. I waited for a while and then I went up to the stage, trying to get their attention—and I couldn't get their attention. In one of the Dylan books there's a photograph of me with Dylan and Bloomfield, facing each other. I'm in the middle, in the foreground of the photo, and it's clear that I have some business there. Just a moment or two after that photo was taken, I went over and unplugged all of them. I just pulled the master plug and said, "We need to rehearse—and we need it more than you do. You can jam anywhere but these guys need to get up here. I'm sorry I unplugged you—but we're next." By the way, that was the first time that Dylan performed using an electric guitar—that was a big moment in the Folk Music Scare. Bob Dylan was amplified and playing with The Band. A lot of people got pissed. Pete Seeger thought amplified music was a sin and an abomination, and he went wild backstage during their performance that night. Seeger couldn't stand it, and he wanted to unplug them during their performance. [laughs] He got an axe because he wanted to chop their electrical cables—and where do you suppose he got the axe from? He never did chop the cables—somebody restrained him. But that same night Alan Lomax and one of the managers got into a wrestling match. [laughs] It was an interesting time.

On the way up there, one of the convicts was a bookish kind of guy, so I gave him my credit card and asked him to keep track of the money spent. This was for the expense report I was going to turn into the Newport people. He was a meek, mild kind of guy, and one night, traveling through Tennessee, I was driving late into the night, and he was sitting in the front seat with me, started telling me why he was in prison. He had killed his wife. He told me all about it—the wrong that she had done and how he'd killed her. The next night he's riding up front with me once again—and once again he started telling me how he killed his wife, he described his wife and how he had killed her—only this time it's a totally different method of killing than he'd told me the previous night. I asked him, "How many women have you killed?" And he said, "Five." I said, "Did you go to prison for each murder?" He said, "No—only two." So he killed five women—not all in the same manner—but all in the same emotional state. Here I am—driving a serial murderer up to Newport. The others were murderers as well—but not in the same emotional sense. Now I'm driving this guy up there, and I've become very worried about him. I asked him more about what brought about these emotional states, because it was clear that his ordinary state was that of a meek, mild, bookish type of guy—but his potential was that of a homicidal maniac.

The next day as we were driving along I told everybody, "We need to reach an agreement on NO ALCOHOL—no alcohol whatsoever. Can you agree to that? If anybody starts drinking, I'll take you to the Boston airport and send you back—and you won't get paid." Everybody agreed. The second night we were there, there was a party for the entertainers. It was interesting at the party—here are these five guys who'd never heard of Peter, Paul, and Mary—or Pete Seeger, or any of the well-known performers. On the other hand, this prison group was the focus of attention. Everybody wondered, "These guys have been in

Texas prisons—what have their lives been like?" So a lot of people came up to talk. And I made a mistake—I said, "OK—why don't we all have just one drink?" So they brought drinks around, and then one of those things I'd heard about, but never seen, happened. As the waiter handed the drink to the fellow I've been talking about—Alfred Paul East was his name—as soon as he had the drink in his hand and the fumes reached his nose—he changed character. Just in that instant—he turned to me and said something antagonistic—something like "You think you're so smart. You always think you know what you're doing"—something of that nature. He remained that way—and he went on drinking. I tried to stop him but there was no way short of a rough-and-tumble fight. I ended up following him around because I couldn't tell what he might do—he was suddenly this other person. He was strange but took no threatening action until Pete Seeger's daughter, Mika, left the party and started walking down the street toward the house where she was staying. Alfred slipped out the door about a minute behind her. Earlier in the evening, when I first became concerned about Alfred's behavior, I sat with actor Theodore Bikel and told him the story of the five murdered wives. He became concerned and joined me to keep watch on Alfred. So the two of us headed out the door after Alfred Paul East, who was following Mika Seeger. Mika turned into one of the houses and Alfred eventually turned back to the party and shortly after went to bed. Bikel and I followed him to the place we were staying. We actually sat up all night and discussed taking him to Boston in the morning and to send him back. But in the morning I talked to Alfred and told him, "No more drinking or I'm going to call the police!" and he didn't.

I'm almost positive the group's performance at Newport was recorded—Vanguard recorded it, but it was never issued as far as I know. Parts of the performance went well—other parts didn't. The first song was a hoeing song, but the hoeing style was not what you might do in your garden—chopping up things. Prison hoeing was done mostly to clear land, and a lot of the work was done in ditches to remove big bushes and things like that. They would walk across an area in a line all working in unison. But when they used the hoe, which was called an I-hoe and had a heavy, long handle with a large piece of sharp metal, they would raise that up over their heads walking forward and bringing the metal hoe down with a very forceful chopping motion. That was the kind of work that was demonstrated on the first song they did. But as much as I had tried to acclimate them to the idea of working in front of an audience, when they raised those hoes up the group was just astonished at the size of the audience, at the number of people they saw—it was like an ocean of people out there. The hoes all came down at different times—instead of together—and the song went to hell. [laughs] The next song was better because R. G. Williams, whose nickname was "Forty"—he'd been sentenced to forty years and served twenty—he stepped forward and was obviously pissed. He wanted this thing to work, and he fussed at them so the next one went a little better. Then he decided they'd do the double-cutting on the tree. He later told me the reason he decided to do the double-cutting was because they didn't dare do anything wrong—if they did they'd kill one another. So he got himself and three others over there, and then it fell into place. The song and the work fell into sync together, and then maybe for the first time that audience heard and saw what a work song really was. The song made the work possible—made it possible to work over a ten or twelve-hour day.

When the performance was over, I had to stay—there were other things I had to do, but the members of the group went their various ways. The whole reason "Forty" participated was that he wanted to get to his brother's place in Flint, Michigan. His brother had promised to get him a good job. He was a tough guy after twenty years in prison, but he wanted to live the remainder of his life in a joyous way. And he did—I kept in touch with him for a while. A short time later he got married, and his brother got him a good job at the GM plant in Flint. Some in the group wanted to get away from Texas and make a fresh start—others went back to Texas. Choppin' Charlie went back to Texas. The reason there's a song about Choppin' Charlie—the song was recorded by the Lomaxes and several others—at first he was the strongest man around. He could do the most work. He was the toughest person around. But over the years he got to the point he couldn't keep up that kind of work. He got old and he got beaten down. That's really the point of the song—he starts out as a great hero, the great champion—but he doesn't stay that way. The latter part of his fame was that he would *pretend* to work. You would see him in a line of guys, and he would hold up that monster hoe—and he would kind of bring it down—or he wouldn't lift it at all—but he'd kind of move his shoulders as if he'd done it. He started as a great champion and been worn down to the point that he was creating an illusion of work. He was pretty old at that point. Well, he was old for a convict—he was in his sixties.

That particular Newport Fest put me in touch with a range of people who were giving folk festivals and putting up programs in World's Fairs, and it provided opportunities for me a few years later. I've done work for the Smithsonian, for World's Fairs and other festivals. I participated in World's Fairs starting with Hemisphere. Hemisphere was a half world's fair held in San Antonio. I did the concept for the Institute of Texas Culture, which is still there. It was built as a permanent part of Hemisphere. The program I did there, Texas Traditions, was one of the early days of the Smithsonian's American Folk Life. Before they had many resources, they asked us to just bring that same festival up to Washington—which we did. That was 1968—the same year as Hemisphere. Then I worked on Expo 71 in Montreal, and there were other World's Fairs I worked on—Expo 74 up in Spokane, which featured the Northwest Territory of the United States and the adjacent area of Canada—and even a little bit of Alaska. There was the Knoxville World's Fair, a Louisiana World's Fair in New Orleans. Again—all of this began in 1964 and 1965 when I brought the prison group up to Newport and met some of the people on the East Coast who wanted things from the South. I also worked for the National Park Service and for a couple of museums for which I created the concept for their "Living Museums"—one of which is a lumberman's museum on the northern tier of Pennsylvania. And the other is a museum which is now closed, unfortunately, in New Mexico. The Montreal Festival was the longest festival ever—to my knowledge.

The Smithsonian got an invitation from the Department of Commerce to take over and place a program in the US pavilion that had been built for the original World's Fair—Expo

’67, as it was called. This was 1968 or ’69, and the city of Montreal wanted to continue using that building and using that whole Expo grounds, trying to keep some of it going in the subsequent summers. So the Smithsonian asked me to a do a twelve-week-long festival of American folk life—sort of a satellite of the festival in Washington, D.C. They asked me to put that together—and I did. We had some well-established artists like Bill Monroe, Roy Acuff, and Ralph Stanley. We had Roosevelt Sykes, Teddy Wilson, practically everybody I admired—plus a lot of other people. It was both music and crafts people. If you were there the first night, you would have walked in and heard Ralph Stanley singing “A Man of Constant Sorrow.” Move past the main stage and you would have heard Jay McShann, who brought along Claude Williams—and together they were able to show us how Kansas City jazz was heard in its earliest stage, not with a tenor saxophone but with a violinist following the piano, going back to the late 1920s. It was a marvelous opportunity for the people in that area to hear American music. But it wasn’t restricted to music: it also included games, recipes and cooks, regional foods.

There were other things I was interested in. We kept a group of Navajo women who were on display making chief blankets—a special type of highly prized blankets from the late 1800s. As you passed this group of women, you could hear them talking in this sort of shuffling speech as they communicated in their Navajo language. And if you spoke to them, they would smile, but they didn’t speak enough English to tell you what they were doing. You might have seen George Lopez, from Cordova, New Mexico, who carved “santos”—saints from cottonwood. There’s a little part of Missouri that’s known as Little Dixie, which is very Southern. There was a guy there, a black man who had quite a reputation—I’d heard about him a number of times—he carved canes. He would carve two entwined snakes on the cane—beautiful work—and a little scary. It was the same as the caduceus, the medical symbol. Anyhow, he told me, as I bought one of his canes, that there’s nothing stronger in this world than two snakes wrapped together. I always kind of loved that phrase, but I had trouble getting him to allay his suspicions first—I don’t think a white person had ever come up to him, although I’d heard about his canes from white people.

That’s the type of thing the fest consisted of, but it changed people each week. It was a tremendous undertaking and was carried out by a small group of people. Those twelve weeks gave me an opportunity to interview people. To give you an example—you may or may not know that jazz musicians and blues musicians are a little suspicious of each other. There’s a small wall between them—one is highly trained musically and the other is self-taught, play by ear. They’ve never been immediately close. During that twelve weeks we had a week of piano there—Sunnyland Slim, Robert Shaw, Roosevelt Sykes—and we had Teddy Wilson. I introduced Sykes and Teddy Wilson when they first showed up, and they were friendly, but through the week I didn’t see them spend any time together. I went out there one day and I saw the two of them on opposite sides in the area in front of the main stage. So I kind of got them together and I said, “Both of you guys have been in entertainment for so long that you must have met up at some point—don’t you agree?” But neither of them could recall any meeting between them. Well, I kept after them about this and other things, and I saw them getting together and talking it over—which is part of what I was trying to do, to get the two to find out about each other, their music and their world. And then one day they both came running up to me together, and they said, "We figured it out—The Benny Goodman band was playing the Chicago Theatre." Teddy was featured in the quartet that performed from the Goodman band and Roosevelt, who'd had a popular hit around that time, was an extra added attraction at that show. And they each remembered standing in the wings, listening to each other, though they never met or got acquainted with each other. But that's the kind of information you can get if you have an artist around for an extended period.

Here are the recordings I produced that I consider landmark recordings: *A Treasury of Field Recordings*, volumes 1 and 2, *The Unexpurgated Folksongs of Men*, *Songs of Death and Tragedy*, *Mance Lipscomb*, *Ragtime Henry Thomas*, and *Texas Barrelhouse Piano*.

The *Mance Lipscomb* and *Texas Barrelhouse Piano* are recordings we've already discussed. *Songs of Death & Tragedy* and *Henry Thomas* are not my recordings but are albums that I compiled. These are from the 1950s and '60s. These are the records that I think of as "landmark recordings" because the music, together with my notes, were meant to reveal important parts of the music that was going on, more than just the recordings of an artist—not just what they were, but how they got where they were. I always felt that music belonged on records along with a comprehensive explanation of what the music was—and who played it. I was notorious for writing very long notes and some of the recordings have booklets with them—or did originally.

What label were the two volumes of *Treasury of Field Recordings* on?

They were first issued on the 77 label in England, and later Nat Hentoff recommended them to the Candid label, who issued them in this country. The connection with 77 came about from suggestions made in correspondence with English enthusiasts and scholars. I'd been in touch with Derek Coller since the late '40s, though it could have been Sinclair Trail or Brian Rust. Or maybe Doug Dobell contacted me. Doug had a much-admired retail record store at 77 Charing Cross Road, London, and was planning to start his own record label. He needed material. I provided his first three albums. The first album issued on 77 was *The Rooster Crowed in England* by Sam "Lightning" Hopkins. It sent greetings to England in "The Rooster Crowed in England" and "Blues for Queen Elizabeth." He improvised that one after a Houston visit by Elizabeth II. This was early in the blues revival, and those songs tickled interest over there. *A Rooster Crowed in England* was a limited edition—100 copies or less. I don't think anybody even knows of it today. The next releases on 77 were the two *A Treasury of Field Recordings* albums. These were an attempt to capture the spectrum of music thriving in a single city. Houston is musically diverse and rich. It was my hope the *Treasury* would inspire others to create a portrait of their town. New Orleans, Minneapolis, Miami would have been ideal. So far as I know, this it didn't happen. The *Treasury* may be alone in documenting one city's music.

The albums include a work gang from a prison just outside the city, a cowboy night-herding song, a local version of an old English ballad, "From a Foot Race to a Resting

Place" by Jealous James Stanchell, "Sand Mountain Blues" by Pete Rose, "Atomic Energy" by Jimmy Womack, a gospel quartet describing World War II. Plus the side-by-side versions of "Tom Moore's Farm" I mentioned. One volume of the *Treasury* has traditional music, the other regional music, some known mostly in the area. I planned a third album to include foreign-language music. More bilingual zydeco, Mexican rancheras and corridos, Czech dance music, polkas and mazukas, some from the Asians beginning to arrive. I ran out of money for fees, so only part was completed. More tapes in hazard.

When I first came to Texas, I wasn't all that happy with the state. I'd grown up in real cities—cities that had twenty-four-hour barbershops and huge newsstands. I was that kid who would stand outside of jazz clubs and listen. I was in Chicago, in Cleveland, in Denver, in Cincinnati—but here I am in Texas, and the sidewalks are not much used—except at midday downtown. Everybody drives pickups—everybody listens to country music. But after a while I said to myself, "Look—either leave town or get acquainted with town and get comfortable with it. It is not without its own culture. What you have to do is get involved with that culture and find things that you like." And a little bit later on I said to myself, "It doesn't matter what you like—if it is liked by the people who support it, that's all that's important." So the more I saw, the more I began to take an interest in the music of Texas—and then I went on to take an interest in the games—and particularly the cuisine, which is almost as rich as the music. So I came to like Texas because it offered so many riches to which I hadn't initially paid any attention.

With that in mind I went around recording all the various kinds of music that I could find in Houston. That was the concept on the two *Treasury* volumes—to do a panorama of music from a single city which was rich in music. The tracks were recorded, for the most part, from 1957 through 1959, and the albums were issued in 1960. The booklets that went with the records were about twenty-four pages each, with about ten photographs in each booklet. There were a couple of tracks that were not my recordings—a couple of prison recordings were done by Pete Seeger—but they were not good prison recordings. Most of the prison recordings from that period featured convicts that were herded into the dining hall and they sang work songs—but they did no work on them—which is an idiotic way to present work songs [laughs]. It wasn't until recording equipment became truly portable and had decent speed that you got good prison recordings. Nagras came along, and there was an EMI recorder that my brother-in-law bought for four hundred dollars that ran off batteries. I used it to record a selection on volume 2 of the *Treasury*.

There was a guy who played oil drums—not Bahamian oil drums—just oil drums that were filled with different levels of water and produced different tones. He worked on Galveston Beach and he did very long monologues—just the most eccentric thing. I recorded a long piece that was based on a standard religious song called "This Old World Is in a Terrible Condition." What he would do during this six- or seven-minute recording is comment on people in the crowd. He'd guess their occupations and try to relate his song "This Old World" to them and to their jobs. He had a washtub covered with chicken wire, and he expected people to throw money into it—the chicken wire was to keep people from stealing the money [laughs]. Sometimes the people would give more than coins—a dollar or five-dollar bill. On the recording when it came to that point, they'd hesitate to drop a bill in the water and you'd hear him say to them, "Don't hesitate—the water is fine!" The recording is very live sounding—you can hear the crowd, you can hear the waves once in a while, you can hear the cars with their horns. The artist's name was George Coleman—Bongo George. This is his initial recording.

Between the two volumes there's a whole range of Houston music. There's the first recording of zydeco—which is identified with the Fifth Ward, Frenchtown in Houston—referring to a French Cajun black music that came to Houston [with people looking] for war jobs during World War II—and then it encountered the blues. That original zydeco music was an amalgam of blues and what Louisianans would call la-la music. Zydeco is bilingual music—a combination of French and English. That was the earlier definition of it. That word was derived from the French word "les haricot," which was part of several songs. It graduated to become the word that referred to the music and the dance—and the occasion of a zydeco event or dance. Other black people, in addition to the French-speaking black people, started going out there and dancing. They enjoyed zydeco music, and they started hearing the word zydeco. They picked up on that word, and that's how zydeco really got its name—not from the French-speaking black people, though the word was in some of their songs—but from the other black people who came out there. They'd say, "Let's go to the zydeco, baby," or "I'll meet you at the zydeco." That's the way the word came into being, and finally it became known as zydeco music. A few people tried to spell it. I have some photographs of it being spelled z-o-r-d-i-c-o. There was a Lightning Hopkin's record that spelled it z-o-l-o-g-o. I have about fifteen different photographs of about fifteen different spellings, but then I decided how I wanted to spell it—which can be found in the booklet that accompanies the volumes of *Treasury of Field Recordings*. I am the person who established the spelling of it that you see today. The reason I did that is because I love the pattern of the "Z" and the "Y." The record was sent to Pete Welding, who was a record reviewer at the *Saturday Review*. A lot of his review had to do with the *Treasury* and specifically with the few outstanding things—like the zydeco music. It was a blues—"Baby Please Don't Go"—in both French and English. It wasn't the greatest recording, but it illustrated the music in Frenchtown. Anyway, Pete Welding talked about the music in several articles, and that made the music—and my spelling of the word—known to critics. Meanwhile, back in Houston there was a guy named Fred Marshall. He was a printer—the guy who made up all the posters that got nailed on telephone poles when an artist would come to town. At any given time you could find five or six posters on a given pole. The poster I'm looking at right now is for Clifton Chenier to appear at the I.L.A. Hall—International Longshoreman's Union—on October 7th. This is from back in the 1950s, and on it the word is spelled z-o-r-d-i-c-o. Well, I didn't like that spelling—and neither did Fred Marshall. So when I made my spelling available to him, he immediately adopted my spelling. So now it's happening on two levels: first, among the critics and the scholars, and at the same time it's happening on the posters because he switched over to that spelling.

And then the Frenchtown community itself used that spelling on their signs and on the slate boards in front of taverns. I'm very proud that both the critics and the local people accepted that spelling—and I'm credited, I'm proud to say, in the Oxford English Dictionary. I'm credited with the orthography—the spelling of the word, not the origin of it: the word was very nicely in place when I came along—but the accepted spelling, that's mine.

Then let's talk about another of the landmark LPs—the *Unexpurgated Folk Song of Men*.

I had several people I recorded independently, and then I gathered a number of people together at a session where we put cans of beer in a big tub filled with ice—and the people just sat around in a circle. The microphone was in the center, and when somebody had a song they wanted to sing, I'd move it closer to them. The singing of one person would inspire another person to remember a song. Both Lightning and Mance are heard here, but there are also a number of white participants; many of the songs and limericks are from England or Scotland. Some were quite charming. For instance, there's a Scots song called "The Ball of Kirriemuir." Other songs were extraordinarily ribald—and crude—often cruel to women. One of them was called "The Great Bloody Wheel." It was an English song. Most such songs are created in situations where there are no women—and in that situation men tend to think of women as acrobatic whores. I guess it's their loneliness, their unfulfilled desire that causes this bizarre reaction. The album was issued on the Raglan label—that was mine—just something I made up. It was my label, my production, my pressing. There were at least a thousand copies pressed—perhaps more.

This album, too, had a booklet—tracing as far as I was able each song to its origin and listing interrelated songs. This was a period when things were just beginning to change, but still material sent through the mail and deemed unsuitable would often be sent back to England or France. I was so concerned that the US postal department would regard this album as obscene and order us to cease and desist that on the back of the album I wrote something to the effect, "We claim the freedom granted psychiatric journals which print the monologues of deranged people, which are often highly obscene." In fact, I was prepared to go to Canada and mail it from there, or Mexico. But I never heard from the postal department. I sold many copies of this album for a long period of time. I believe it's regarded as a collector's item now. Somebody told me it was listed on eBay for three hundred dollars. Many of the lyrics to these songs were printed in books after they were cleaned up. I resisted that because a folklorist has no business fixing what is traditional in a community of people to suit himself. It's an outright lie—and I've written scathing reviews of people who do that.

Another of your listed "landmark albums" was *Songs of Death and Tragedy*.

That's part of Dick Spottswood's fifteen-volume set, *Folk Music in America*, which he did for the Library of Congress. I think he knew that I'd written a tragic play and was particularly interested in tragedy in dramatic form. He wanted me to do this specific album, and he sent me a tape of many things he thought might be appropriate. We picked out a handful of recordings, and then I suggested some others. Among the selected recordings was one I found—a "discovery." There was a musical group in San Antonio, Los Conquistadores with Jose Morante. He had written and produced a 45, "Homanaje a John F Kennedy," the story of John Kennedy coming to Texas and being assassinated. It's a typical *corrido*, a Mexican ballad. Morante had been at the airport to greet the president. Kennedy was scheduled to leave Dallas and go to either San Antonio or Austin. Morante had been brought into the ceremonies at the airport to honor the president. Jose Morante was waiting to see him get off the airplane. At first, everyone thought the entourage was just running behind schedule, but then he heard that the president had been shot—everybody was stunned by the news. He just stood there and waited. So that's why he wrote this corrido. I also wanted a version of America's greatest tragic story—"John Henry, the Steel Driving Man." Spottswood had recorded a version of that by a singer in Delaware, John Cephas—it was a good version. There's also an item by the Blue Sky Boys. This is another of my landmark albums—although it has the same disadvantage as other anthologies—people don't really want to listen to all of these different types of music. People invariably like one type of music over the others; so when you get to all the various types of music, you'll find in the Spottswood series it has a discouraging effect. But it's an enormously valuable reference work because he gathered all manner of American records in foreign languages—Czech, Hungarian, Chinese—and such things as street calls in Charleston, South Carolina. George Gershwin copied these calls in *Porgy and Bess*—like the strawberry street vendor. If you listen to all fifteen volumes in the series, you will increase your knowledge of American music tenfold. It's a marvelous set overall—I'm proud to have been a part of it.

How about the album with Henry "Ragtime Texas" Thomas? Which collection contains your liner notes—the OJL issue or the album on the Herwin label?

It was the Herwin album done by Bernie Klatzko. I consider this a landmark album because he brought together for the first time every record issued by Henry "Ragtime Texas" Thomas—that's twenty-three recordings. Then he asked me to write notes—which were very lengthy and were printed as a gatefold—not as a separate booklet but as pages inserted between the folding cover and incorporated as a part of the album. You open the gatefold and here are these extensive notes. I printed the first known information about Henry "Ragtime Texas" Thomas. I found where he was from and interviewed some people who remembered him. He was similar to Mance Lipscomb, in that Henry Thomas was a songster. His repertoire was enormous because he'd put two or three songs in medley form on a single recording. He sang parts of ballads, he sang reels, he sang material from the "coon song" period and ragtime songs—and he also sang some very, very early blues. He made a record that's just absolutely unique among all the records ever made—that's the one called "Railroadin' Some." That trip he describes—first coming through East Texas on the Texas Pacific line. He mentioned a couple of towns—I never did decide what it was—probably Turnertown—there's a Turnertown in East Texas close by to Louisiana. That was his area. Then to Shreveport, then swinging back to Dallas, and then all of a sudden he's off to Chicago, and he names all those towns—Sedalia, Joplin, and then he gets to Chicago and he blows that panpipe, which is the most joyous greeting at the point when they're going over Grand Crossing.

Chicago was always the biggest railroad center in the country, particularly for passengers. All the rail lines coming from the East had to cross over all the lines from the West. That place was known as Grand Crossing, and I believe it was located somewhere behind the stockyards—it's a place known by every hobo in America. Of course, his tune "Bull Doze" was covered by Canned Heat and given another title—"Going Up the Country." It's so obviously derived from the Ragtime Texas recording, but they gave it another name and took composer's credit. When it comes to blues covers, that one must have produced a great deal of money—just last year I saw it used on a car commercial. Every time it's played on network television, that brings in a lot of money both for the performers and anyone who claims composer credit. I also heard it in a movie just a few nights ago. Even though I didn't record Henry "Ragtime Texas" Thomas, I consider the album a companion piece to the two Mance Lipscomb records I made. Mance Lipscomb may have been the first person to call himself a songster. Mississippi John Hurt hadn't been discovered yet, and his records were hard to find, but when people finally became familiar with his repertoire, he was called a songster. So between Mance, John Hurt, and Henry Thomas, all of a sudden you had a new view—an earlier view of black music before the blues. They played blues, they sang blues, and Mississippi John Hurt was under pressure from the OKeh label to record blues—but later, when he was on the concert stage, you heard the rest of his repertoire. These were landmark records because they helped establish, so well, the concept of a songster. They help us understand that the blues go back well into the nineteenth century, but around 1910 we began seeing blues specialists—people who sang almost nothing but the blues. That first generation began around 1910. They did some recording, and then came the next generation, which would include Muddy Waters. These are the two great generations of the blues—which, by the way, is not unusual. Many great cultural events only last two generations and then suddenly they slip away. I don't want to disparage what came later. Perhaps there was a third generation with the electric guitar and early rhythm and blues—these are points I'd have to study before I offered an opinion. The blues specialists with their narrow focus stood apart very clearly from the songsters and their wide repertoires.

All together I issued about twenty albums and have another twenty albums' worth that have never been issued. I'm hoping I can find a company that will reissue the albums I put out and will issue the things that have never been issued. I had an album by James Tisdom that I was going to issue after the Robert Shaw LP. The title of his album was *South Texas Street Rambler*—that's what he called himself. He was marvelous singer who had a fantastic version of "Tom Moore's Farm," and he also added country music to his repertoire. There are four albums of prison songs, which include interviews and shouts and individual songs and gang recordings of several different kinds—hoeing songs, chopping songs, and several versions of a tune called "Chopping Charlie."

I have four books that are within inches of completion. On one manuscript, I collaborated with Paul Oliver on a book about Texas blues. Back then we had to depend on carbon copies and overseas mail, and that process worked so slowly that it stretched out over years—we started in 1959 and were still working on it in 1971. If we had email and photocopy machines—and the ability to talk back and forth all the time—that book might have succeeded. I contacted publishers here in the States and Paul talked to publishers in the UK, but by that time it had turned into a huge manuscript that would have been two volumes—and we could never find a publisher. I have another manuscript, an anthology of things I have written—ten or so liner notes and ten to fifteen magazine articles I've had published over the years—and again, I must say, those articles are unique research. The only thing left to do on that one is to type it into a computer. Still another, "Savage Joy," was read and pronounced ninety-five percent complete but it, too, needs to be typed into a computer for final editing. I had a book I called "Encounters." One of the chapters was called "When Bill Monroe Arrived Late and Roy Acuff Stayed Overtime." Roy Acuff was leaving and Bill Monroe didn't show up when he was supposed to—this was at the Montreal Festival. So Acuff covered, doing some of the sets Monroe was scheduled to play, and when Monroe's bus pulled in they had a conversation, which I taped. Actually, it was an extremely warm, friendly conversation. They had played together many times but had seldom in recent years had an opportunity to stop and talk with each other. That's why the conversation was interesting—they were catching up and Bill was apologizing to me about his bus breaking down. Other features of my "Encounters" book were interviews with working people—iron mongers, aircraft electricians, high steel workers, lumberjacks, et cetera. It also has interviews with celebrities, including Greta Garbo, who talked about her feelings about *Sunset Boulevard*, which was originally written for her. It has interviews with Frank Sinatra, who in 1951, when he was looking ahead and planning his concept albums, hadn't yet gone to Capitol Records, which is where he did those. It's got a freshman congressman's tales of the workings of Congress—and how he got boxed in from doing what he wanted to do. It had Dick Haymes commenting on the dearth of classical lyric songs—at the time I didn't appreciate how accurate he was, but in later years you can look back on it and see that the classical American song book began about 1920 and ended about 1945.

You might ask, "What happened to those books? Why weren't they ever published?" My answer is this: It's not a question of what happened to those books—it's a question of what happened to me. I did a lot of field work during the 1950s, '60s, and '70s. I also issued a number of albums and wrote a number of articles during this same period. Then in the mid-1970s—I was about forty-five—I began to experience mood swings, which got more and more serious. It got to the point where, in a manic phase—and these were unpredictable phases—I would spend excessive amounts of money and do dangerous things. For instance, I would frequently get myself into arguments with police officers who were taking a break at a nearby Dunkin' Donuts—and a lot of other excessive things. Other times during that period I would fall into a deep dark depression—not one of despondency, but one of an acute, severe lack of energy. Those cycles came about irregularly over the next twenty-five years. In manic-depressive illness there is a scale that goes from zero to ten—zero is dead and ten is when you are totally out of control. But there is a midpoint—five, you're in good shape, the illness doesn't have a hold of you—and when you get to six, slightly above midpoint, you're in what is termed "hypo-mania," the lower part of the manic phase. In that phase, as far as I was concerned I could control what I was doing—I could sit down and work on manuscripts, trying to get all the material I had gathered and prepare it to be published. But I didn't succeed to the extent I wanted to. That's what happened to the books—I was beset by a destructive illness. During the period of this illness I took twenty-one different antidepressant medications. None of them were distinctly helpful and some were nasty—like Butrans, which gave me two years of diarrhea as a side effect—and was very little help with my mood swings. What I was really doing during those years, when I was taking all those medications and trying to find help in various ways—and when I could, trying to write manuscripts—was waiting for the medical industry to come up with something that was useful, for me and for a lot of other people who were not helped by the antidepressants of the time. Then around the year 2000 they came up with something that operated on a totally different principal. In fact, these medications were used for people with epilepsy—but psychiatrists experimented using them on bipolar illness, and they were successful. So I'm still taking that medication, which has given me back a significant degree of control. However, in the meanwhile, I got much older and developed a number of other problems—including a type of blindness—a few years ago I was blind for three months. So all these problems kept me from finishing these books I was talking about. I think there are solutions to this situation. I would need to have a typist enter all this material into a computer and get all this information ready for publication. These are things I can't do because of limiting conditions—including my limited vision.

Did you meet Alan Lomax?

Alan Lomax had an older brother who lived here in Houston and whom I had known for some time. He was John Lomax Jr. Alan came to town to visit him, and John Jr. brought Alan over to see me. Alan was surprised that I had already done the *Treasury of Field Recordings*. After that, we had a cordial and mutually helpful relationship. In fact, at one time, we were working together on a project. He often was involved in the programs at the Smithsonian Festival of American Folk Life. By the way, those programs featured different states each year. The states were Pennsylvania, Texas, New York, Arkansas, Ohio, Kentucky, and Mississippi. Doing fieldwork on those programs was what gave me the opportunity to do field research. At one time Alan and I sat down with a map. He drew on the map the areas that he had covered, and I marked the areas that I covered, and he was amazed to find out I came out ahead of him. If you noticed my email address you'll notice it has the figure 888 in it, which is the number of counties in which I've done field research.

Our conversations certainly wouldn't be complete without discussing your research on Robert Johnson. What can you tell me about your research on Robert Johnson?

People who know my work would tell you that when it comes to Robert Johnson, I'm a major researcher. I've been after him since the 1940s. I don't know how far to get into this. It's information I used to believe was accurate—some of it's information that I originated—but I no longer trust or support a lot of that information. Robert Johnson recorded for the race record division of Vocalion in the 1930s. I'm sure you're familiar with a lot of the names on the race record labels—like Big Bill or the Yas Yas Girl—and many, many other people who appeared under what were obvious pseudonyms or nicknames. What I'm saying to you is—if you hold a 1930s race record, why would you trust the name on the label to be that artist's name? You've got so many examples where the listed name in not the artist's real name. Granted, you've got some like Tommy Johnson or Walter Davis which do list the artist's real name, but so many are simply not the artist's name. So now you're looking at a Robert Johnson record—why would you believe that name on the label was his real name? Everything written on Robert Johnson makes that assumption, and it's not an assumption that should be made by careful people—yet everything written on Robert Johnson assumes this. When I realized the assumption I had made, it threw a shadow over much of the work I had done. Much of the work I had done was simply chasing a person and that name. Part of the quandary of a name is that before somebody made a record, they were generally known in the various communities in the South by a nickname. If you heard about a person by a nickname, you'd also find out, in many cases, that in the next community down the line—because in almost every community the people in the community would give that person a nickname—so that the same person would be known in another community by another nickname. If you really think about that—how hard it is to really know anything about anybody because you've got all these communities, each assigning their own different nickname. Now it's true, after they make records, then it stabilizes things—now it's possible for them to get a better job and better pay by going around and telling people in bars and taverns that they are the person who made that record. That gives them a certain cachet and an ability to attract better crowds. I'm trying to make the point about how hard it is to know certain information for sure unless you can get the person themselves. If you can get a Son House or a Gatemouth Brown, then you can find out directly from that person—but short of that, it's so hard to develop reliable information.

There's also a second factor: besides the fact that many people are known by a variety of nicknames, then there's the fact that every time their records come out, there are lots of young people who imitate the songs and then go around and say, "I made this record." That was a problem with Peetie Wheatstraw, with Robert Johnson, with Funny Paper Smith, even with Blind Boy Fuller, which amazed me. There were three or four people I chased down in Alabama, each of whom was supposed to be Barefoot Bill. So these are the problems you encounter in fieldwork—and they just leave you uncertain about who's who. Robert Johnson is one of those very uncertain people. When I encountered some of these things, it just devastated my work because it meant that I had been operating on the basis of assumptions that could not be verified. I consider that shocking and am astonished that I would do that sort of thing because I knew that the names on race records labels could not be trusted—there were so many of them that obviously were nicknames, stage names, pseudonyms. I knew that—I don't know why I went along with the idea that the record label name was accurate. I never backed off and said, "Where is the evidence?" Realize that much of the information we have now regarding blues pseudonyms didn't exist when I was doing this work. It didn't become available until later editions of *Blues and Gospel Records*. Let's say it was illegal to make records in San Antonio in 1936 and in Dallas in 1937—so we have records that were made in those two cities. Now we are looking for the person we want to prosecute for making those records. In order to do that we have to get some evidence together that points unmistakably to that individual—you need evidence to make it a fair prosecution—and we don't have that.

So once I started applying these standards, a lot of my findings and information fell apart. I get dozens of letters about Robert Johnson—people wanting to help me with the research. For a long period of time I've offered those people a deal—I will give them, depending on where they are located geographically, leads out of my lead book—towns that need to be visited, people who need to be sought, and so on—if they, in turn, will share the information that they get with me. And I'm afraid we exist in a world where not too many people are willing to knock on somebody's door. I find that sad. They'll write me a letter, asking me what I have learned—but they won't, in turn, go and find out more themselves. And the reason that's such a crippling thing is because black people, as we know, have been leaving the South for years and years—going back to the 1880s. So the black people who know something about Robert Johnson have often gone north. So my leads book is full of what people told me, "Well, this person knew a lot but he's gone. He lives in Madison, Wisconsin," or "This fellow lives in Detroit." And I've gone to a lot of these places and located pertinent people and information. But every time I went anywhere in the South, I gathered many, many such leads—people saying "Go to Charleston—go to Sacramento." So when people ask me questions, I suggest they do some original work, and I offer to give them leads—particularly leads in locations nearby to them. But unfortunately it's not very often that people have come back and actually have done that.

There's another part to that work which is simply the process I went through in trying to locate him—and then there's a lot of interesting stories about people I *did* find and about people who claimed to be Robert Johnson—or about people I suspected. For example, there was a guy who called me from Oklahoma, repeatedly over some years, who said that it was his father who had made the records. And he had some very persuasive information—correspondence with the record company that he told me about on the phone. I was able to check some of it because he knew some details that generally would not be known. And I'm not sure that's not the right man—I can't say it is or it isn't. I spoke earlier about finding musicians and doing research for Orin Blackstone: Robert Johnson was one of those musicians. A death certificate was found with the name Robert Johnson on it. About the same time, I located a fellow by the name of Robert Johnson in Tunica County. There was a tendency by everybody to assume that they were the same person. One reason for thinking it was the same person is that the half-sister of the kid from Tunica County—the kid that I call Little Dusty—went to Tunica County to get a copy of that death certificate. Death certificates are sent to the state capitol—but this one was kicked back to the county registrar, who was asked to do an investigation. If you looked at the back of the death certificate, it said on there "No Doctor." So you have a guy who may have been a homicide or suicide. What happened to him? The head of the archives sent it back to a woman named Jordan and asked her to find out more about it. She wrote her report of her investigation on the backside of the death certificate. It says that he had come to play banjo at a country dance. Banjo—banjo? That doesn't fit—but then people said, "Well, she made a mistake." But I interviewed Mrs. Jordan—and it turned out she had an uncle—a white man—who played banjo in country dances himself. She was very interested in music; she went to ballroom dances at the Memphis Country Club. Walter Barnes had a noted jazz band that died in a fire at a dance in Natchez around 1940. A few days before the Walter Barnes band went to the job in Natchez, they were working their way south, and Mrs. Jordan went to a dance where the Walter Barnes band played. She was big on dancing. My point here is that there's no basis for saying she didn't know a banjo from a guitar. The only basis for saying that is to try and make that death certificate fit the well-known Robert Johnson.

Despite this contradiction in information, that death certificate was used to establish the estate. You're presenting this death certificate as the basis for the estate—yet the basis for the estate says he was a banjo player. I would urge people who like to believe the story that is prevalently printed, to sit down and say, "OK, what evidence do we have?" The first—and best—evidence are the records, the twenty-nine recorded sides. That's good evidence because it mentions some places where he obviously was—some of them are Mississippi River towns. He mentions Norfolk—which people, in order to get things simpler, decided to claim was a town in Arkansas. The assumptions run wild and they are generally bent so that they fit into one another.

I got a photograph from Carrie Thompson, of her half-brother, Little Dusty, the kid who grew up in Tunica County. I showed that photograph to people with the record company who had worked with him in the studios in Dallas and San Antonio.

Would that include Don Law?

Don Law was one of the sources—I saw him in Nashville—but by then he had become the biggest record producer in Nashville. He didn't like to talk about his Texas days; he wanted to tell you about Marty Robbins and Johnny Cash and people he was recording at that time. The ones that were most helpful—first was the widow of the salesman who had first found Robert Johnson and brought him to record. She had gone along on that road trip, so she spent three days in a car with him—and if you spend three days in car with anyone, you're going to get pretty well acquainted. And she had a good memory. And then there was the woman at the record company who paid the musicians just after they recorded. There was a shipping clerk who was assigned to make sure Robert Johnson and Black Boy Shine showed up when they were scheduled. This was a complicated operation—with engineers and equipment from New York. Record companies are always a little worried about people showing up on time—musicians in particular don't always have a good track record in this matter [laughs]. The shipping clerk was a source, but then best of all were other musicians who were around them during the time they were recording. For example—he recorded the same day as a Mexican group—and I found one of the Mexican musicians. Also, Robert was recorded the first day the Chuck Wagon Gang made any recordings. They were a family group who started in the days of the deep depression in Lubbock. Members of the Chuck Wagon Gang had the family name of Carter—of course they couldn't use that name on record because of the famous Carter Family, who were well established. The head of the group was Dad Carter. He and his children used to sit around and have family "sings" in the living room during the Dust Bowl days of the Depression. He and his family were desperate. Dad Carter went to a radio station and asked if they would give him five dollars a week to broadcast. They got that job and got by on that five dollars for a time. Then he thought, "Well, maybe we can do better in Ft. Worth." So he went down to Ft. Worth and went by a group of radio stations, and they immediately hired him. They immediately built up a huge audience—fan mail poured in. Don Law heard about this and invited them to come to San Antonio to record. They recorded what are called Heart Songs, and an Oklahoma blues and then a few religious songs. And then they did that again on their next session. It plainly became evident that their future was religious songs—usually original religious songs—and thereafter they never recorded anything but religious songs. They were enormously important to fans of Christian song—for years the Chuck Wagon Gang was among their favorite groups. The Chuck Wagon Gang made their first recordings the same week that Robert Johnson did—and some on the same day.

One of the daughters in the family, Anna Carter, later married Jimmie Davis, a noted recording star in his own right, the composer of the tune "You Are My Sunshine," and who later became the governor of Louisiana. I went to see Anna in Baton Rouge in a house very close to the executive mansion. She'd had a very striking experience. She was sixteen years old and hadn't, at that time, had much to do with boyfriends. While she was recording, all of a sudden there's this black face at the window—making eyes at her and paying attention to her. That was absolutely a first-time experience for her in several respects. There was never any particular contact between the two, but she saw enough of him to say—years later when she saw that picture—"No—that's not him." I showed her the photograph and she said, "No." So there's a lot of evidence against my early assumptions. This is the way I became disenchanted with the evidence I had gathered. So I became more interested in setting forth the information that came from people who definitely have been in contact with the man who made those records. There was no reason to assume that the name on the record label was the man's real name.

How did you track down Robert Johnson's half-sisters?

I was working for the Smithsonian at the time. I was based in Washington, D.C. I went all over the country but my office was in Washington, and I went to Washington once or twice a year. During fieldwork in Mississippi I located the place where a Robert Johnson—a guitarist—came from. I had located his neighbors—mostly his neighbors on the Letterman Plantation. I played some of the records for some of the neighbors and they said, "That was the guy who lived there." The neighbors' saying that it was Robert Johnson was not enough to confirm it—but it was enough to start looking into it. They told me his half-sisters had moved to the northeast somewhere around Washington or Baltimore. What's that—twenty million people? [laughs] So every time I was in Washington, the hotels all have phonebooks for the area, and I would leaf through the phonebooks and try to figure out how I could find them. All I had at that point was the last name for Bessie Hines and the reason the people back in Tunica County knew that was—their mother came up there after a while. So I kept looking in the phonebooks, zeroing in on the name Bessie Hines—who was a half-sister. I just started calling all the Hineses I could—which generated a hell of a phone bill at the hotel. And one day I got a woman on the phone and asked her if she knew anything about a musician named Johnson. See—I never gave too much information because if the person truly knew, then they could fill in the first name—or whatever. And the voice on the other end of the line said, "You mean my baby brother Robert?" [laughs] "Yes lady—that's the one." We talked a while but she was a fairly old woman, and I didn't want to tire her. I asked for her address, and her directions to her house were very distinctive. George Wallace had just recently been shot in a shopping center in Laurel, Maryland. She told me to find that shopping center and go around to the back of it—and that was the street she lived on. That's how she gave me directions to her place. I zipped right out there, and she talked for a long time. She told me a lot about her baby brother and she told me where her full sister, Carrie Thompson, lived—which was in Churchton, Maryland. She gave me a whole lot of different information from what Bessie had because each had known their half-brother during different periods. I bought photographs from them of lots of different things that were involved in his life and places they'd lived—he'd lived with each of them at different times. The photograph that's so well known today was among the photos I bought from them—the one which shows him in a suit, cradling a guitar with his legs crossed. I had nothing to do with the second photo, which shows a cigarette dangling from his mouth. If you recall, the US Postal Service issued a Robert Johnson stamp using that photo—but they removed the cigarette from his mouth.

Robert Lockwood startled me one day in a dressing-room conversation, saying his mother was still living—in fact, singing with a gospel choir then in St. Louis on a tour. So we called her to talk about the Robert Johnson who had once been her boarder. That didn't sort out his identity. Later, back in Houston, I did a stupid thing: I told people about the photograph. So people who visited me—there were usually one or two a month—wanted to see it. Peter Guralnick was one who came to see it—he came for other reasons, but he saw it. One guy came and wanted to see it and I showed it to him, and in the act of showing it to him, he saw where I kept it—in a wooden file cabinet. The following weekend Mary and I went to Galveston, and when we got back, we saw that somebody had been in our house. If you have a burglar, you figure they're going to look for the jar where you keep your money—or something to steal that they can sell. But this didn't seem to be an ordinary burglary because money was left behind in fairly easy places to find; but the next time I looked, that photograph was not there any longer. The other photos were filed in another place, and they were still there. The photograph was stolen from my house. I can't tell you who did it or anything regarding subsequent events. Except it was published and it was the starting point for getting Columbia to pay royalties if they could use the photograph. The estate was established in Greenwood, Mississippi, and a Mississippi attorney I know told me—twelve years ago—that the estate had generated fourteen million dollars—most of which went to the lawyers and agents. And if that's true, it's probably brought in a lot more money since. I don't know if that's true.

Approximately three months after our conversations I received the following extended email from Mack, elaborating his account of his Robert Johnson research and his latest thoughts on the subject:

It began not long after I heard his records for the first time. Penetrating, strange, not without fun, glowing in deep place, a profound artist. Early on, I learned [that] the story of his being poisoned after selling his soul to the Devil was circulating in two widely separated groups of people. It went around record collectors after his death by poison was told at a Carnegie Hall concert. Given as the reason he wouldn't appear as advertised. It was passed around in at least four states by the blues' primary audience. It was often mixed with other stories of deals with the Devil and souls being collected at the expired time. These were sincere beliefs, long told by priests and magicians. Folklore that Goethe knew. The idea came to me that Robert Johnson may have started the stories about himself to gain notice. He gave it vivid support in his song "Me and the Devil." Always allowing that [he] might have truly believed that his talent came from an encounter with the Devil. Blues singers often accepted the church teaching that singing blues is sinful and a certain path to damnation. They become tough-minded, brave, persisting with their style of life. Typical of legends, the death stories acquired variations as they passed among people. At first it was a woman who poisoned him. In one instance, I found witnesses who'd been present at a party house when a musician was murdered by poison obtained from a conjure woman. I gave out the information that it had been done by an angry husband. Soon the printed bio entries and books shifted from a woman to a man.

The Robert Johnson materials are mostly in files I took to Mexico to work on when I thought I had dependable answers. Doubts have rained down on them. Too many assumptions that soured on close inspection. I was unsettled when I went back to starting point. Why did I assume the man's real name was Robert Johnson? Why would I think a name on a record label trustworthy? The *Index* made clear how common nicknames were on blues records. The Yas Yas Girl, Memphis Minnie, Kokomo Arnold, Cow Cow Davenport. Collectors were discovering the same voice under two or more different names. They found Willie Kelly was actually Roosevelt Sykes, Ruth Day was Ruth Willis, Jim Foster was Sam Collins. "Straight" names were often pseudonyms—Maggie Jones, Charlie Lincoln, Peetie Wheatstraw, John Henry Barbee. Someone estimated only thirty to forty percent of what's on the labels are actual names. Blues singer are inclined to hide. I should have suspected a false name if only because of well-known examples in other parts of show business, where

John Wayne is Marion Morrison, Roy Rogers is Leonard Slye, Marilyn Monroe is Norma Jeane Baker. If you assume the person you want is named Robert Johnson, the person you find will be named Robert Johnson. In the early '50s I found one. A blues musician in New Orleans. I drove down Jackson Avenue looking for his street, gleefully thinking I was on the edge of taking the Robert Johnson back into a recording studio. Cosimo's probably. I found him a pleasant and helpful man, quick to tell me he wasn't the person I wanted. He described his shock when records appeared with his name on them. He'd learned to imitate the songs, told people they were his records, got some girls and made some money doing it. When I talked to him, he dismissed all that as youthful struggles for attention. We laughed about it and he told me his name was a very common name.

The census bureau says Robert Johnson is one of the ten most common names in their files. I'd climbed a tree in the wrong forest. Sloughing through this, it's useful to first identify the several blues musicians actually named Robert Johnson. A pond of muddy water. One was found by David Evans and by George Mitchell in Mississippi. Then there's the one I found in New Orleans in the '50s. Then another wrong man in Hot Springs, Arkansas. And didn't Gayle Wardlow find a piano player who'd been around Vicksburg? The 1938 death certificate names another possible. Then there's Claud Johnson's father, named on Claud's birth certificate as a musician named Robert Johnson living in Memphis in 1931. It was this document that eventually led to the probate court to decide Claud is the rightful heir to the estate. The court shunned the possibility the father might not be the one on the records. I don't know of any evidence that says so. They went forward assuming Claud's father was also the Little Dusty from Tunica County. Again, nothing shows that. Nothing shows either made the records, it's just easier that way.

A Mississippi lawyer formally advised the court of such identity problems in their accepting claims based on no more than a very common name. A name from an untrustworthy record label. He got back a snippy letter from a court-appointed lawyer whose busy hands were helping drain the estate. Typical of what happens to a rich, embattled estate—Claud vs. a half-sister. The bulk goes to paying fees, expenses, accountants among those favored by the court. More than muddy water, a swamp. The publicity over the estate battle made finding the right man hopeless. Not when a pot of gold is waiting to be collected. People came out of the woodwork saying daddy was Robert Johnson. My name in some articles led people to call asking support for their claim. Lawyers offered an honorarium for expert testimony. They went away when I told them the right man might be any of several musicians, or maybe none of them. I stayed out of it, put in an answering machine to screen calls. The world darkens when desperate people call for help, or even show up at the door. Most had deluded themselves, or gone to invention. One man wrote saying he still had the records his father brought home for him and enclosed a photograph of the 1961 album.

So who did make the records in San Antonio in 1936 and in Dallas in 1937? I'm still not certain. Yet I think there's a chance public records and untapped sources may sort out the matter. They should also try to find firsthand testimony. They say everyone is dead but it ain't so. The census bureau says there are 131,000 people a hundred or more years old. Some have a vivid memory of their young years. It's easier now. You can go to one nursing home and find a half-dozen of them. If they're from the same place, let them give you answers among the themselves. Three good candidates were actually named Robert Johnson. I learned of the first from Alan Lomax when he visited me—his brothers lived here—in 1959. Next year, based on what he said, I went to Bogalusa, Louisiana, and heard about a musician and lover murdered and thrown in the Pearl River. Poisoned by a woman he often stayed with. A couple who'd been neighbors described what happened. He'd go around the country playing music and come back smelling of other women.

In 1942 Willie Brown, in the course of recording for the Library of Congress, sent Alan to a Mary Johnson near the town of Lula [in Mississippi]. Alan recorded her as well. In the interview, which may be on the disc at the Library of Congress, she said her son Robert, a musician known as "Little Robert," had been given poison. She'd gone to the place, been present when he died. Son House added Little Robert made Bogalusa his main hang out. A jealous person put poison in his coffee. Alan was sure this was the right man. He goes into detail in his book *Land When the Blues Began*. Little Dusty, the boy who'd been partly raised on the Leatherman plantation, had been my first choice until problems came along. His stepfather was known as "Big Dusty" which made the boy "Little Dusty"—a name I use to distinguish among the candidates. Neighbors and friends described him and mentioned some songs he'd sung when growing up. He too must have been shocked when records with his name came out. I found his two half-sisters in Maryland, and a third in Chicago. He'd told them, at the time, he made the records. One believed him, another didn't have an opinion, the third said he exaggerated a lot. The largest problem is that his photograph couldn't be identified by the staff people who had worked in the Brunswick office in Dallas. People who'd dealt directly with the artists as they came to record. Vincent Liebler, at his home in Brooklyn—the engineer who did the San Antonio sessions—did not recognize the natty fellow in the picture. Vincent had spent time with him. The shipping clerk, Tony Garza, in town to help with the sessions, had taken both of them to a San Antonio cockfight. On two days they ate lunch together—joined by Buster Wharton and Black Boy Shine—around Alamo Plaza, buying hot tamales from the vendors.

To keep a simple story for the court, "Little Robert" and "Little Dusty" were turned into one person. The "Little" in both names had different meanings. One because of small stature, the other a nickname from his stepfather. Son House is the key informant about these two. At Newport in 1965 I listened closely as he answered endless questions about Robert Johnson. He talked about Little Dusty, his neighbor in the northern part of the county, when a question had to do [with] selling his soul. When the question concerned poisoning, he talked about Little Robert from Lula. Son House is not easy to understand, his interviews easily garbled by Yankee listeners. In print the Leatherman plantation became "Lottlemens." He is consistent, but the questions about Robert Johnson didn't fit what he knew. To interpret him, keep in mind he did not know Little Dusty's real name. To Son House he was Little Dusty or Robert Willis. Few people outside his family knew Little Dusty's real name. Others knew him as Little Dusty or Robert Spencer—both from stepfathers.

It would be helpful if someone would sort this out better. Son did a zillion interviews in the '60s, many on tape or on tape of radio programs. Going over these now, taking into account he was talking about different people, would produce a better grasp of what he knew. Although they lived twenty miles apart, the coincidence of two musicians named Robert Johnson in the same county worried me. I called in a statistician who ground the population numbers for Tunica County in 1930 and 1940, name frequency, and estimated the numbers of musicians in a rich place. She limited it to professional musicians—that is, those who made all or part of their income from playing in public. She said two were entirely possible. Which we already knew. One's mother was named Mary, the other Julia. After those three, there are three more chief possibilities.

To keep them straight, I think of the six as Claud's father, Little Robert, Little Dusty, San Antonio visitor, Oklahoma, a man called Slate. And a banjo player who I can't number in. Let's see if I can wade through. The fourth candidate is a blues singer remembered as "outstanding" whose family was certain he'd made records. They had two of the 78s. And postcards he'd sent home from San Antonio in November 1936. Not enough, but I don't dismiss him. The fifth: more impressive is the evidence described by a son who called from Oklahoma City but said he was in Fort Smith. Our phone conversations stretched over several years. In the second year he told me he was "on the bricks" because he'd run from a prison work gang. Every minute he was frightened he'd be caught and sent back. I told him the statute of limitations must have run out and offered to have a friendly lawyer write him. He didn't want to give his address. He said he had his father's correspondence with the Brunswick company in Dallas and read the letters to me. They were convincing, exactly the kind of letters that were sent to artists. One invited him to return to make more records. My caller offered to sell them to me. We set a price. It turned into the kind of pick up you'd use paying a ransom. At two in the morning I left the money at a stone marker when two lights flashed on a hillside. It was along on a lonely road through park land. As agreed, I drove on to the Arkansas border so he could go the other way. Nothing was delivered to my motel next day. Early on he'd said the letters were signed by Don Law—the sales manager in Dallas. I asked if there were initials below the signature. He'd said yes, DL, followed by two dots, one above the other, and two more initials in smaller type. The small letters fit the name of Don Law's secretary. Standard office style of the day. She married soon after and took on different initials. How could he have learned her initials in 1936? Unlikely, but not impossible. After all, if I had done it, someone else could, particularly someone after a pot of gold. That one is close to having my vote. The only prospect who claims to have clear evidence. In one call he accidently gave me a clue that might allow finding him, but I haven't followed it up. I probably should—or do I really not want to settle this?

To add confusion, the first candidate, Claud's father, the musician who'd loved Vergie Mae in Copiah County, has been rolled up as the same person as both of the ones from Tunica County. Three Robert Johnsons regarded as one. Nothing supports the idea, it's just easier that way. The sixth is the man murdered at a Mississippi party house. He sang "Terraplane Blues" and "Kind Hearted Woman." That's the kind of thing that tempted me into assumptions. Sounds like it has to be the right man. Until you consider how many imitators, some very good imitators, went about claiming to have made this or that record. Our modern imitators show how convincing a skilled person can be. This man was known only by the nickname "Slate," a pretty good barrier to learning who he really was. This murder did not produce a death certificate. He was buried quietly on the plantation. In any case the date—apparently 1942—doesn't fit anything else. Unless you want to question the 1938 date first offered by the unreliable John Hammond. It might be a good idea. Then of course there's the Robert Johnson named on a 1938 death certificate from Le Flore County. Gayle Wardlow found this official document. An electrifying stroke and everything seemed to fit. Then Gayle went back, asking to see the original piece of paper. The back side said the county registrar, Cornelia Jordan, had been asked to investigate further. The scrawl "No Doctor" in the space for medical details worried the director of Vital Records. Cornelia went out to the plantation. Her report said the dead man had come from Tunica County to play banjo at a country dance. Banjo? Suddenly the official document began to crumble. People she talked to thought he'd died of syphilis. No poison, but syphilis. No guitar, but a banjo. The bottom line—there's little or nothing to put any of them in a Texas studio. The stories and blur of names are in the maw of oral tradition. In Florida one can hear several reports of how Blind Blake died: most say he died in a street car accident in a Georgia town, but another has him poisoned by a jealous lover. The discouraging thought is the right man need not be any of the candidates. I'm not sure I succeed here in passing on the essentials of the quandary. It's difficult to communicate. It's overwhelmed me. If you want to know about Robert Johnson, go to the twenty-nine records he made. They tell all you need to know.

I'm retired and watching—or listening to—movies I treasure. I'm trying to catch up with Iris DeMent and Fountains of Wayne. Yet if an editor turns up, I'll put him or her to work saving manuscripts. Weekends we'll go to do unexpected things—a state park where well-fed alligators roam among the visitors, or the realm of Brick House Gully, Jeff McKissack's Orange Show, or John and Dominique de Menil's great collection of art. I like to visit one of the most peaceful places on earth, the Rothko Chapel, or the statue of Lightning in Centerville, Elvis Presley's first 78, or Blind Lemon's guitar, kept for years by his sister. I cherish my copy of the revised A to E of *Index*. A storefront church offering the best deal in town, the sign reading "Paz, Amor, Pesos y Tiempo"—peace, love, money, and time enough to enjoy them—Cervantes, I think, slightly modernized. I visit nearby shops that sell green cards to the needy. On every trip an Aztec statue sold to me as a statue of St. Peter at the Pyramid of the Sun has accompanied me, always facing the road ahead, on every trip. At the right time of year I travel to the great flyway where migrating birds funnel down the coast to Mexico, where the whooping cranes linger. To a restaurant with a delight of boiled red crawfish, another with Central American seafood inventions, a third that's collected regional versions of magnificent Tex-Mex. Take a trip on Interstate 10, the blues' most destructive freeway that swept away the Thomas family houses, the small house in Beaumont where Blind Willie Johnson lived and held church services, and Blind Blake's favorite corner in Jacksonville. My hazy eyes allow some writing. Using a voice-recognition program, it moves along. I've gone back to my first love, writing plays. "Zero at the Bone" concerns a fictional meeting of Emily Dickinson, Walt Whitman, and John Henry. I say with relief this one is polished and finished. Now I'm working on one about George Pettibone, a relative accused of killing an ex-governor of Idaho. The politician who'd gone into office promising not to wage war against striking miners in the silver and gold country, then sent the state militia to burn them out. One morning he walked out to get his newspaper, and the gate blew up in his face. They took George, Charles Moyer, and Big Bill Haywood—all leaders in the IWW—to Denver for trial. A mistake. Denver is a mining town where they were heroes. The jury said they were innocent. That's back story. The play is about George, the bomb maker, coming back to consider what needs to be done today.

My father became a factory representative for DuPont X-ray film. What he did was go around and teach doctors how to use X-ray machines properly. Doctors were quick to buy gadgets and not very quick to learn how to use them. In the 1930s and 1940s people knew about radiation but they didn't believe it—it took the atomic bomb to make people realize what radiation could do. So doctors, particularly doctors in small towns, were using X-rays without standing behind a lead partition, or wearing a lead apron. My father taught them to position the patient properly and then stand behind the lead partition—". . . otherwise, you're going to fry your balls!" So he saved the balls of a lot of people in West Texas and Central Texas and in all of the five states he traveled. The point of all this is that during the summers he would take me along with him on these long trips. At that point I'm still not quite sure that I like Texas—but I'm seeing a lot of it as well as a lot of Mississippi and Louisiana, also Oklahoma plus part of Kansas and part of New Mexico.

He'd take me along to far West Texas or Mississippi small towns where white doctors had a rear entrance for "colored." He was a fountain of lore about his territory. Told me about the Bad Boys of Bosque County, took me to Hymel's and other great Cajun restaurants along River Road [south of Baton Rouge], explained the newly rich people of Oklahoma City, where oil wells were springing up in both front and back yards. He knew the courting habits of the horned toad, the intermarried Indian and immigrant out-group living in a pocket of land where the Arkansas River joins the Mississippi. In Oklahoma he found a man to tell me the story of Pretty Boy Floyd. He was a beloved bank robber and hero who, before making his getaway, would pause to build a bonfire with the bank's farm mortgages. In Oklahoma one does not speak ill of Pretty Boy Floyd. All of this reflects his specialized love for his part of the world. Calling on doctors left him time to talk to patients in the waiting room, learning surprising things. Back in Dallas he'd pass this on to his beer-drinking buddies in his favorite tavern only a few feet from the taxi strip at Love Field. Our travels were full of the unexpected. I'd seen Jack Teagarden and his orchestra at a Dallas theater, then near Vernon in West Texas. Then one Sunday my father suddenly turned off the highway and drove a few miles to the edge of the Red River. A black baptism ceremony was in progress. Glorious singing, a triumphant sound while immersing white robed people in the brown water. My father told me he'd bought Jack Teagarden a drink, who then told him he first heard jazz at the river baptisms in Vernon.

And he said, "This is where Jack Teagarden first came and heard black people baptizing people in the river. And that's when he began to know black music." Now, this is not new information—it's just that he took me to that place. And he kept doing things like this—I think it was to enhance my interest. He was a person who loved Texas—in a peculiar way. He loved things about it that were not what people usually emphasized. He kept doing it—and I learned a lot. In the summer of 1936 my father took me to the San Antonio Zoo in Brackenridge Park. While we were there, we had lunch at the Japanese Tea Garden where a strolling musician walked among the tables, taking requests. When he stopped at our table my father asked for a song and gave him a dollar bill. I have a vague and untrustworthy memory of the guitar and his voice having a sweet sugary sound. Years later, when my father was dying, we talked about our trips, and I asked if he remembered the tea garden singer. He said, "It was Lonnie Johnson."

Years later, when I had begun doing fieldwork and photography, I had done some work for the Smithsonian, and on this particular trip my wife was with me. We went and found the last living ox driver in Texas, who worked oxen in a lumber camp. He got oxen, who are enormous animals, to move "an inch this way—a quarter of an inch that way"—we're talking four big oxen—to move this log into exactly the right position. Then he would switch them over to the other side of the wagon and move the chains to the log, and the oxen would pull that log on the opposite side up a ramp and load that log onto a wagon. It's an enormously fascinating thing—I don't know if anybody's ever filmed it. So I went there and photographed the process and talked to the people, particularly this guy, who was reputed to be the last such person—in Texas, at least. To this day I can't believe you could get such huge animals to move such a tiny distance by just talking to them softly. He had a special language he talked to the oxen. And when I left there, the guy said to me, "Well Mr. McCormick, I'm sure glad you came back." And I said, "What do you mean come back? This is the first time I've been here." And he said, "Oh no—you was here before—a long time ago, but I remember you." After a while I realized that was my father. Up until that time I had not previously understood how much my father had influenced, what became essentially my life's work. I thought I was doing all this on my own, but then I thought about all the different places we had stopped on those long trips, and the things he had shown me and talked about.

LIST OF INTERVIEWS

Ray Flerlage	Person-to-Person Interview	June 23, 2000
Bob Koester	Person-to-Person Interviews	April 2 and 9, 2003
Gayle Dean Wardlow	Person-to-Person Interview	May 29, 2003
Mike Rowe	Person-to-Person Interview	June 9, 2005
Paul Oliver	Phone Interview	April 25, 2006
Jim O'Neal	Phone Interview	July 28, 2006
Dick Waterman	Phone Interview	March 7, 2007
Pete Whelan	Phone Interview	December 4, 2007
John Broven	Phone Interview	December 15, 2007
Sam Charters	Phone Interview	March 12, 2008
Dick Spottswood	Phone Interview	July 14, 2009
Bob Dixon	Phone Interview	September 3, 2009
Chris Strachwitz	Phone Interview	May 11, 2010
Chris Barber	Phone Interview	September 9, 2010
David Evans	Phone Interviews	January 29, 2011, and February 5, 2011
Jacques Demêtre	Phone Interview	August 29, 2011
Phil Spiro	Series of Emails	November/December 2011
Paul Garon	Person-to-Person Interviews	February/March 2013 and March 8, 2016
Mack McCormick	Phone Interviews	December 2010 and January/March 2011

INDEX

For purposes of alphabetizing, nicknames are generally treated as part of the name.

Aagaard, Cecil, 380
ABC record label, 152
Abe Books, 380
Abner, Ewart, 248
Abrams, Jerry, 344
ACA Recording Studio, 383, 385, 387
Ace record label, 175, 178
Acuff, Roy, 82, 85, 86, 114, 120, 400, 407
Adams, Woodrow, 261, 311
Adelphi record label, 315
Adins, George, 370
Advent record label, 317
Afro-American Folk Music from Tate and Panola Counties, Mississippi, 314
Akers, Garfield, 73, 91
Aladdin record label, 32
Alamo Plaza, 416
Albert, Don, 378, 379
Albert, Irving, 135
Albert Wynn's Gutbucket Five, 125
Albold, Volker, 322
"Alcohol and Jake," 104
Alexander, Texas, 327, 328, 379, 380, 384
Alex Club, 157
Allen, Dick, 22
Allen, Hoss, 86
Allen, Pecan, 100
Alligator record label, 164, 212, 352
Allison, Luther, 79, 80, 158, 165, 221
Allman, Diane, 164, 352, 356
Almanac Record label, 390, 391
Altshuler, Bob, 234, 235
Amazon (internet service), 380
Ambrose, 3
American Federation of Musicians, 16, 285
American Folk Blues Festival, 162, 180, 184, 186, 336, 347, 350
American Forces Network (AFN), 271
American Guild of Variety Artists, 285
American Music record label, 149
American Skiffle Bands, 24
Ammons, Albert, 180
Ampex tape recorder, 237, 326, 342
Amsterdam News, 29
Anarchy Magazine 350, 372
Anderson, Eric, 69, 84
Anderson, Marion, 190, 198
Anderson, Pink, 38
Angola Prisoner Farm 395
Angola Prisoner Blues (LP), 343
Ann Arbor Blues Festival, 80, 217, 355
Anthology of the Blues, The (French CD set), 251
Apollo Theater, 291
ARC (American Record Company), 113, 124, 129
Archibald, 176
Archive of American Folk Song, 235, 236
Archive of Folk Culture, 236
Arhoolie Records, 8, 76, 317, 333, 342, 344, 346, 391
Armstrong, Lil Hardin, 278
Armstrong, Louis, 27, 28, 67, 86, 136, 159, 227, 230, 243, 273, 324, 378, 379
Armstrong Twins (Floyd and Lloyd), 324
Arnold, Billy Boy, 42, 154, 168, 196, 218, 369
Arnold, Eddie, 82
Arnold, James "Kokomo," 2, 245, 249, 250, 251, 351, 414
Artistic record label, 210
Arsenal (magazine), 370

ASCAP (American Society of Composers, Authors and Publishers), 318
Asch, Moses, 24, 27, 28, 30, 33, 34, 35, 36, 56, 257
Asch, Sholem, 36
Ashby, Harold, 159
Ashcraft's Law Firm, 152
Ash Grove Lounge, 160, 304
Association for Recorded Sound Collections (ARSC), 240
Atkins, Ace, 120
Atlantic record label, 148, 167, 236, 256, 258, 353
"Atomic Energy," 402
Atomic Mama's Wang Dang Doodle Blues Show (radio program), 216
Auld, Georgie, 377
Audiophile record label, 154
Audiophone Recording Studios, 345
Austin, Lovie, 50
Autobiography in Blues (Lightning Hopkins LP), 384
Autrey, Gene, 379, 380
Avalon Productions, 72
"Avalon's Blues," 72, 128, 229
Avon Paperback Books, 354
"Ay-Tete-Fee," 336

"Baby Please Don't Go," 403
"Backdoor Friend," 185
"Background of the Blues, The," 7
Bacova's Ceska Kapela 379
Baez, Joan, 38, 69, 72, 228
Balfour, Robert, 322
"Ball and Chain," 342
"Ball of Kierramuir, The," 404
Band, The, 397
Bankhead, Tommy, 32
Bankston, Dink, 312
Barbara's Bookstore, 353, 354, 373
Barbecue Bob (Robert Hicks), 5, 258
Barbee, John Henry, 162, 163, 414
Barber, Chris, 17, 121, 182, 283
Barefoot Bill, 383, 409
Barlow, Bruce, 80
Barnes, "Booba," 221, 222
Barnes, George, 141
Barnes, Walter, 411
Baron, Bob, 215
Barraza, Hermanas, 379
"Barrelhouse Dance," 125
Barretta, Scott, 225
Barrie and Rockliffe, 13
Barth, Bill, 115, 262
Bartholomew, Dave, 176
Basic Linguistic Theory, 133
Basie, William "Count," 243, 325, 377
Bass, Ralph, 221
Bastin, Bruce, 175, 236, 316, 317
Bates, Deacon L. J., 127
Bayou Boys, 239
BBC (British Broadcast Company), 8, 9, 13, 15, 20, 271, 275, 331
B. B. Junior, 156
B. B. King Treasures, 82
Bea & Baby record label, 219
Beale Street Jug Band, 321
Beasley Books, 353
Beatles, 268, 278
Beatty, Warren, 232
Bechet, Sidney, 17, 276
"Bedlam," 376, 377
Beehive Lounge, 154
Beggars Banquet, 232
"Begin a New Life on Christmas Day" (Parts One and Two), 125
Beiderbecke, Bix, 227
Belafonte, Harry, 193
Bell, Carey, 221
Bell, Lurrie, 221
Bell record label, 126
Benton, Buster, 160
Benwell, Trevor, 121, 123
Berkeley Folk Festival, 328
Berlin, Irving, 244
Berry, Chuck, 40, 167, 297, 325
"Between Midnight and Day," 83
Beverley Cavern, 325
Bigard, Barney, 324
Big Bama, 23
"Big Boss Man," 86
Big Dusty, 416
"Big Fat Mama," 103
Big John's (music club), 347
Big Maceo (Merriweather), 179, 196, 245, 249, 278, 369

Big Mama's Blues Show (radio program), 216
"Big Road Blues," 91, 103, 105, 107, 317
Big Road Blues (book), 301, 304
Big Tree (Houston), 388
Bikel, Theodore, 398
Billboard magazine, 145, 173
Bill Boyd's Cowboy Ramblers, 154
"Bird's Nest Bound," 91, 102
Birmingham Jubilee Singers, 127
Birmingham Quartet, 127
Bishop, Dickie, 278, 279, 284
Bishop Quiroga, 394
Bizor, Billy, 377
Black, Stu, 156, 159
Black Ace, 19, 329, 331, 332, 333, 346
Black and White Lounge, 185
Blackbirds of Paradise, 88
Black Boy Shine, 393, 411, 416
Black Chicago, 184
Black Lion record label, 342
Black Magic, 158
Black Metropolis, 184
Black Panther Party, 373
Black Patti record label, 58, 59
"Blacksnake Dream Blues," 127
"Blacksnake Moan," 110
Blackstone, Orin 378, 379, 380, 410
Blackstone Rangers (street gang), 42, 209
Blackwell Guide, 349
Blacks, Whites, and the Blues, 182
Blake, Blind (Arthur Phelps), 61, 67, 258, 279, 384, 418
Bland, Bobby, 189
Blind Log, 316
Blind Pig (piano club), 251, 345, 347, 348
Block, Rory, 73
Bloomfield, Mike, 159, 188, 196, 197, 200, 201, 204, 208, 361, 397
"Blueberry Hill," 167
Bluebird record label, 42, 117, 120, 124, 125, 141, 148, 245, 351, 379, 393
Blue Flame (blues club), 39, 41, 42
Bluegrass Unlimited magazine, 239
Blue Horizon record label, 317
Blue Lake record label, 151
Blue Note record label, 149
Blue Note Record Shop, 139, 142
B.L.U.E.S. Club, 215
Blues and Gospel Records, 1902–1943, 124, 128, 131, 132, 376, 393, 410
Blues & Rhythm magazine, 174
Blues and the Poetic Spirit, 351, 358, 359, 362, 363, 370, 373
Blues Appreciation Society, 169, 180
Blues Classics record label, 339, 343
Blues Fell This Morning, 7, 12, 123, 246, 360, 362
"Blues For Queen Elizabeth," 401
Blues Foundation, 77
Blues Hall of Fame, 77
"Blues in C," 377
Blues Legends, 189, 190
Blues Man record label, 318
Blue Smitty, 184
Blues of Tommy Johnson: A Study of Tradition, 311
Blues Piano Orgy, 159
Blues Recording Fund, 123
Blues Records, 1943–1966, 172
Blues Records, 1943–1970, 172, 174
Blues Review Quarterly, 290
Blue Sky Boys, 405
Bluesmen Book, The 363
"Blue Suede Shoes," 168
Blues Unlimited Books, 171
Blues Unlimited magazine, 88, 118, 167, 170–77, 182, 211, 212, 216, 295, 297, 305, 307, 311, 348, 355
Bluesville record label, 38, 303, 345
Blues World (internet site), 64
Blues World magazine, 311
Blumenthal, Dave, 152
BMI (Broadcast Music Incorporated), 318
Bokelman, Marina, 297, 299, 303, 305, 307, 308, 309, 311, 313
Bolden, Buddy, 26, 49, 50, 68
Bolic Sound Studios, 224
Bonner, Weldon "Jukeboy," 338
Bonnie and Clyde (movie), 232
Booker T. Washington Theater, 20, 137, 140, 141
Bookman magazine, 27
Boots and his Buddies 378, 379
Boots Pharmacy 350
Boots' Place (St. Louis blues club), 138
"Boppin' the Rock," 336

Boston Tea Party, 80
Bothwell, Johnny, 376
Bowden, Ron, 276, 278, 284
"Bo Weevil Blues," 102
Boy, Andy, 146, 379
Boyd, Billy 379
Boyd, Eddie, 17, 219, 249
Boyd, Joe, 151
Boyd, Warwick, 151
Bracken, Jimmy, 248
Bracey, Ishman, 73, 91, 94, 103–10, 113, 115–16, 307, 308–9
Bradfield, Bert, 245
Bradford, Alex, 248
Bradford, Perry, 29, 68
Bramlett, Bonnie and Delaney, 75
Bray, Jim, 276
Breaux Brothers, 379
Breidenbach, Paul, 146
Brenston, Jackie, 319
Breton, Andre, 371, 373
Brickskeller, 229
Bright, Cornelius, 301, 309
Brill Publishers, 133
"Bring It to Jerome," 168
Brister, Dink, 308
British Hot Blues Society, 273
Broadcasting the Blues, 13
Broadside of Boston magazine, 258, 260, 264–65, 267, 295
Brogger, Arne, 314
Broke and Hungry Blues, 153
Bromberg, Bruce, 319
Broonzy, Big Bill, 4–5, 16–17, 67, 76, 124, 129, 136, 141, 143, 162, 195, 198, 244, 245, 251, 278, 285, 288–89, 334, 350, 369, 409
Broven, John, 182
Brown, Gatemouth, 219, 409
Brown, Henry, 28, 139
Brown, Hosanna, 134
Brown, J. T., 157, 217
Brown, James, 158, 195
Brown, Joe, 186
Brown, Les, 376
Brown, Milton, 379
Brown, Pearly, 343
Brown, Peter Balfour, 155, 156
Brown, Richard "Rabbit," 27, 64
Brown, Ruth, 82
Brown, Sterling, 13
Brown, Willie, 58, 73, 77, 87, 91, 94, 96, 98, 100–101, 102–3, 112, 206, 234, 258, 265, 301, 305, 309, 416
Brownsville Blues, 153
Brunis, George, 155
Brunswick record label, 116, 124, 125, 127–28, 139, 237, 382, 416, 417
Bruynoghe, Yannick, 288
Bryant, Precious, 83
Buck, George, 343
Budapest String Quartet, 239
"Bull Doze Blues," 63, 406
Bulletin of the Hot Club of France, 245
"Bull Fiddle Rag," 125
Bunch, Sam, 356, 367
Bunn, Teddy, 291
Bureau of Ethnology, 235
Burleson, Hattie 379
Burley, Dan, 29, 279
Burnette, Ranie, 302, 313–15, 319
Burns, Eddie, 248
Burns, Ralph, 377
Burnside, R. L., 310, 313, 315, 319, 320
Burrell, Blind Pete, 314
Burse, Charlie, 24, 331
Burton, Buddy, 62
Busby, Buzz (Bayou Boys), 239
Bussard, Joe, 228, 234, 267
Butterfield, Paul, 159, 189, 197, 211, 349, 361

Cadillac, Bobbie, 388
Cadillac Baby, 219–21
Café Yana, 70, 259, 296, 300
Cage, Butch, 330
Cahn, Rolf, 255
"Cairo Blues," 32
"California Dreamin'," 297
Callicott, Joe, 313
Calt, Steve, 65–66, 77, 88–89, 92, 97, 101, 117, 366
Cambridge University Press, 133
Cameo record label, 378
Campbell, Little Milton, 82, 154
Candid record label, 336, 401
Canned Heat (blues/rock group), 63, 73, 115, 268, 299, 300, 305, 406

"Canned Heat Blues," 103–4
Cannon, Gus, 10, 38–39, 216, 312, 331
Cannon, Viola, 96
Cannon's Jug Stompers, 24, 38
Capitol record label, 82, 179, 382, 407
Carey, Dave, 15, 121, 132, 380
Carneal, Bob, 235
Carnegie Hall, 28, 40, 76, 414
Carr, Leroy, 51, 86, 110, 112, 137, 244, 355
Carter, Anna, 412
Carter, Bo, 94, 109–10, 233, 331, 351, 379
Carter, Dad, 412
Carter, George, 233
Carter, Mother Maybelle, 72, 82
Carter, Vivian, 248
Carter Family, 254, 379
Carter Family (Chuck Wagon Gang), 412
Cartwright Brothers, 379
Casey, Smith, 255
Cash, Johnny, 411
Cash Box magazine, 168–69, 173
Cat on a Hot Tin Roof (play), 286
Cavalier record label, 343
Cavern, the, 278
"C. C. Rider," 167. *See also* "See See Rider Blues"
Celestian, Papa, 377
Center for the Study of Southern Culture, 220
Cephas, John, 405
"Cha-Cha-Cha in Blues, 155
Champion record label, 51, 54, 56, 59, 86, 126, 139
Chance record label, 159, 223
Chapman, John, 145–46
Charles, Ray, 168, 392
Charters, Ann, 29, 30, 32, 34, 37, 41
Charters, Sam, 63–64, 80, 87, 254–55, 257, 269, 293–94, 327–28, 345, 351, 352, 360, 363, 380
Chasin' That Devil's Music, 88, 93
Chatman, Isaiah, 308
Chatmon, Sam, 331
Chauliac, Leo, 243
Chauvard, Marcel, 246–48, 250
Chavez, Cesar, 72
Checkerboard Lounge, 156, 217, 347
Checker record label, 177
Chenier, Clifton, 219, 336–38, 403
Chess, Leonard, 155
Chess, Phil, 204
Chess record label, 40, 42, 80, 165, 167, 177, 179–80, 185, 221, 223, 244, 286, 320
Chicago: The Blues Today, 29, 39–42, 80, 352
Chicago Blues as Seen from the Inside, 188
Chicago Breakdown, 174, 184, 359
Chicago Defender (newspaper), 368
Chicago Opera House, 198
Chicago Scene magazine, 188, 197, 203
Chicago Seed (newspaper), 213
Chief, The, 221
Chief Henry's Indian String Band, 379
Chief record label, 155
Chicago Theater, 401
Chilton Publishers, 13
China Lu, 92
Chisholm, Malcolm, 159
Chmura, Helen, 122, 124
Choice, Harriet 354
Choppin' Charlie, 395, 399, 406
Christian, Polite Frenchy, 55
Chrystal Springs Ramblers, 379
Chuck Wagon Gang 380, 412
Cima record label, 336
Cincinnati Post (newspaper), 190–91
Citizen South, Citizen North (film), 152
City Hall Records (distributor), 65
City Lights Publishing, 362, 365
C. J. record label, 210
Clapton, Eric, 75–76, 118–19, 208, 232, 291, 372
"Clarinet Marmalade," 378, 379
Clark, Charles, 210
Clark, Sanford, 168
Clarke, Kenny, 244
"Clarksdale Moan," 296
Clay, Francis, 290
Clay, Shirley, 68
Clayborn, Rev. Edward W., 127
Clearwater, Eddie, 221
Clooney, Betty, 376
Clooney, Rosemary, 376
Clovers, The, 325
Club 47, 255–56, 259, 293
Club Carib, 248
Club Hangover, 325
"Coal Black Mare," 313
Cobbs, Willie, 222–23

Cobra record label, 157, 159, 173, 210
Cole, Jessie, 233
Coleman, Bongo George, 403
Coleman, Jaybird, 59
Coller, Derek, 122, 128, 170, 401
Collins, Judy, 84
Collins, Lee, 154, 159
Collins, (Cryin') Sam, 52, 54, 58, 126, 414
Columbia College, 364
Columbia record label, 56, 59, 61, 63, 67, 71–72, 76–77, 91, 111–13, 122, 124, 127, 141, 146–48, 227, 237, 244, 256, 273, 303, 378, 380, 382, 414
Colyer, Ken, 121, 276–77, 282, 284
Combelle, Alix, 243
"Come On in My Kitchen," 76
Commander Cody and His Lost Planet Airmen, 80
Commodore record label, 144
Concert-Tone tape recorder, 145, 147
Condon, Eddie, 135, 280
Coney, Ira, 317
Connerly, L. V., 306
Conover, Willis, 271
Constantine, Larry, 289
Conte, Gerard, 245
Conversation With The Blues, 388, 390
Copacabana Club, 159
Cook, Ann, 67
Cooke, Sam, 81
"Cool Drink of Water," 103
Cooper, Harry, 243
Cooper, Rob, 378, 379
Cooprider, Jim, 112
Coral Record label, 383
Cosimo's Recording Studio, 415
Cotton, Elizabeth, 72, 266
Cotton, James, 40, 79–80, 198, 210, 249, 290
Country Blues, The (book), 25, 30, 35, 37, 63, 254, 293–94, 327, 345, 352, 360
Country Blues, The (record), 29, 32–33, 38, 63, 254
Country Blues (Lightning Hopkins LP), 384
Country Joe and the Fish, 43
Country Music Discography, 131–32
Country Music Hall of Fame, 328
Courlander, Harold, 24, 34
Cowdery, Charles K., 189–90
Cox, Ida, 50, 67, 228
Cream (rock group), 75–76, 118–19, 232
Crescent Press, 13
Crosley Radio, 190
Crown record label, 56
Cruddup, Arthur "Big Boy," 161–62, 165, 245
Crumb, R., 228
"Crying My Blues Away," 125
CTA (Chicago Transit Authority), 160
Cullom, Ann, 32
Curley's Blues Club, 41
Curtis, Peck, 311, 343
"Cut My Toenail," 155

Da Capo Press, 362, 365, 366
Dad (Blues pianist), 140
Daddy Hotcakes, 32
"Dad's Piece," 140
Dailey, Pappy, 337
Dale, Larry, 248
Dallas Athletic Club, 379
Dance, Stanley, 362
Dane, Barbara 361
Darby, Teddy, 356, 357
"Dark Was the Night, Cold Was the Ground," 23
Darling, Eric (Rooftop Singers), 38–39
Darrington Prison Farm, 395
Davenport, Charles "Cow-Cow," 128, 273, 414
Davenport, Lester, 168
David, Allyn, 376
David, Jack, 189
Davis, Angela, 365, 368
Davis, Blind John, 16, 211, 218, 244
Davis, Bobby, 209
Davis, Rev. Gary, 66, 69, 72–73, 81
Davis, Jimmie, 412
Davis, John, 134
Davis, Larry, 221
Davis, Maury, 153
Davis, Miles, 38, 82, 138
Davis, Walter, 10, 137, 140–42, 409
Davis Congress Shop, 152–53
Davis' Record Shop, 168
Dawkins, Jimmy, 165
Dawson, Sid, 145
Day, Lisa, 189–90, 202
Day, Ruth, 414

"Death Letter Blues," 77, 205
Death Upon a Spear, 134
Decca record label, 62, 120, 122, 124, 129, 141, 237, 245, 249–50, 273, 282–83, 317, 351, 357, 358, 382
Decca record label, British, 174
Deep Morgan, 137
Delauney, Charles, 132, 243–45, 378
Delius, Frederick, 377
Delmar, 137
Delmark record label, 76, 80, 137–38, 140, 144–45, 158–59, 165, 178, 208, 221, 293, 345, 346
Delta Big Four, 100
"Delta Murder" 394
Deluxe Music Shop, 20
Deluxe Record Shop, 140
Deluxe Restaurant, 140
Deluxe Taxi Cab Company, 140
Demetre, Jacques, 6, 19
Demond, Frank, 325–26
Denson, E. D. (Ed), 258
DeSanto, Sugar Pie, 162
Desusa, Bob, 342
Detroit Junior (Emory Williams), 156
Dexter, Al, 379
Dial record label, 144
Dickinson, Emily, 419
Diddley, Bo, 168, 256
Dillehay, M.S., 379
Dinwiddie Colored Quartet, 130
"Dirty Dozens," 145, 147
"Dirty Mutha Fuyer," 154
Discophile magazine, 16
Distler, Marion, 35, 37
Dixie Five, 146
Dixieland Jug Blowers, 24
Dixie Stompers, 141, 144–46, 148, 153
Dixon, Dorsey, 232, 235
Dixon, Robert M. W., 15, 123, 129, 163, 349, 376
Dixon, Willie, 17, 162–63, 211, 339
Dizz, Lefty, 209
Dobell, Doug 401
Dobell's Record Shop, 123
Dockery, Will, 92
Dockery's Plantation, 87, 91–92, 98–99, 120, 301, 309
Document Label, 67
Dodds, Johnny, 50
Domino, Fats Antoine, 167, 176, 207
Dominos, The, 325
Donegan, Anthony "Lonnie," 276, 278–79, 282, 284
"Doodle It Back," 128
Dorsey, Thomas (Georgia Tom), 19, 214, 218
Dorson, Richard, 303
Dotson, Sally, 308
Douglas, Ethel 366, 367, 368
Douglas, K. C., 326, 335
Dowling Street (Houston), 383
Down at Theresa's, 198
Downbeat record label, 342
Down Beat magazine, 158, 338
"Down on the Levee," 138
"Down the Dirt Road," 102
Drake, St. Clair, 184
Dr. Demento, 303
"Drew Tradition," 306
Driggs, Frank, 56, 63
Dr. Jazz, 24
Dr K's Boogie Disease, 182
"Dry Spell Blues," 91, 102
Duerson, Herve, 68
Dumaine, Louis, 67
Dunn, Emmanuel, 307
Dunn, Johnny, 29
Dunson, Johnnie Mae, 185, 219
DuShays, James (String Wizards), 142
"Dust My Broom," 162
Dupree, Champion Jack, 17, 244, 247–48, 251
Dylan, Bob (Robert Zimmerman), 36, 69, 72, 189, 397

Eagle, Bob 368, 370
Eaglin, Snooks, 343
East, Alfred Paul, 398
"Easy Winner," 233
Ebony magazine, 192
ECW Press, 189
Eddie and Sugar Lou's Hotel Tyler orchestra, 379
Edison Books, 183, 359
Edison record label, 237
Edwards, Bernice 379, 391, 392, 393
Edwards, David "Honeyboy," 97, 101, 119, 347

Edwards, John, 28, 303. *See also* John Edwards Memorial Foundation
Electric Factory, 80
Electric Flag, 208
Elektra record label, 78, 151
Ellington, Duke, 28, 67, 140, 142, 159, 240, 243, 273, 283
Ellis, Big Chief, 235
Ellis, Segar, 379, 380
Ellison, Ralph, 358
Elsewhere Blues Club, 215
Elwood, Phil, 325
Emerson, Billy "The Kid," 222
EMI, 283
Encounters, 407
English Musicians Union, 16
"Entertainer, The," 233
Eric Clapton: Nothing but the Blues (film), 189
Ernie's Record Shop, 86, 180
Ertegen Brothers, 56
Eskin, Sam, 335
Eskridge, Rosie, 119–20
Estes, Sam, 152–53
Estes, Sleepy John, 64, 73, 122, 148, 152–54, 156, 162, 179, 196, 205, 266, 273, 278, 293–95, 300, 321, 346
Ethnic Music on Records, 235, 237
Eureka Brass Band, 24, 30
Evans, David, 70, 175, 258–59, 265, 368, 415
Everly Brothers, 167
"Every Time I Feel the Spirit," 127
Ewell, Don, 145
Excello record label, 170–71, 308
Excelsior record label, 342
Expo '74, 399
Ezell, Will, 380

Facebook, 362
Fahey, John, 115, 258, 262, 267–68, 303–4
Falls, Mildred, 288
Fantasy record label, 152
Feel Like Going Home, 370
Ferlinghetti, Lawrence, 362
Ferris, Bill, 220, 303
Festival of Britain, 275
Fickle Pickle, The (music club), 345, 347
Fieldstones, The, 320
Fiester, Ron, 142
Fifth Ward (Houston) 380, 390, 391, 403
"Fifty Miles of Elbow Room," 56
Filmore East, 80
Filmore West, 80, 208, 341
"Fine and Dandy," 377
Fire record label, 248
Flatt (Lester) and Scruggs (Earl), 232, 239
"Flirty Gertie," 167
Floyd, Pretty Boy, 419
Floyd, Troy, 379
Flyright record label, 175, 236, 317, 332
"Foggy Bottom Breakdown," 238
"Foggy Mountain Breakdown," 232
Folklore Centers, 35
Folklyric record label, 330, 344
Folk Music in America (LP), 228, 235, 237, 404
Folk Song Society, 72
Folkways Records, 24–25, 32, 33–34, 36–38, 56, 63–64, 70, 194, 199, 293, 333, 339, 346, 360
"Fool, The," 168
Ford, Wheeler, 100
Ford, "T-Model," 223
Forest City Joe (Pugh), 217
Forrest, Jim, 151
Fort Worth Catastrophe, 393
Foster, Jim, 126, 414
Four Brothers record label, 156
"Four Moore Brothers," 386, 387
Four Star record label, 324
Fourth Ward (Houston) 380, 390, 391, 392
Fox, Harry, 36
"France Blues," 54
Frank Dailey's Meadowbrook, 376
Franklin, Minnie, 92
Fraher, James, 201–2
Frankau, Lady, 350
Frederico, Frank, 377
Freeland, Dick, 239
Freidlander, Bea, 366
"French Waltz," 338
Frenchtown (Houston), 403, 404
Frenchy's String Band, 55
"From a Foot Race to a Resting Place," 401–2
Fruchtman, Efrim, 305–6
Fuentes, Rumel, 344
Fugs, the, 293

Fuller, Blind Boy, 136, 245, 339, 409
Fuller, Jesse, 70, 72, 294, 326, 335, 343
Fuller, K. G., 248
Fulsom, Lowell, 328, 342
Fulson, Martin, 342
Funderberg, Anson, 214
Fury record label, 248
"Future Blues," 73

Gailbraith, John, 150
Garbo, Greta, 407
Garon, Beth, 354, 364, 365, 366, 367
Garon, Paul, 139, 151, 155, 211, 364, 372
Garza, Eva, 379
Garza, Tony, 416
Gates, Rev. J. M., 127, 215
Gatewood, Ernest, 159, 209
Gayten, Paul, 176
Geddins, Bob, 326, 332, 334, 336
Gennett (Electrobeam) record label, 51, 52, 54, 56, 58–59, 66, 94, 99, 110, 124, 126, 132, 145, 378
"Gentle on My Mind," 146
"Georgia on My Mind," 146
Gershwin, George, 244, 405
"Get Your Mind on It," 128
Gibson, Lacey, 222
Gifford, Walt, 146, 151
Gillespie, Dizzy, 144, 244
Gillis, Frank (Dixie Five), 146
Gillum, Jazz, 136, 194–96, 205, 326
Ginsberg, Allen, 362
Givens, Bill, 57, 62–64, 88, 231, 269
Glass, Paul, 155, 156
Glenn, John, 385
Glover, Henry, 248
Glover, Lillian (Memphis Ma Rainey), 258, 260, 294, 295
Godrich, John, 15, 16, 122–24, 129–30, 132, 170, 348, 349, 376
"Going Down Slow," 249
"Going Home," 277
"Goin' Up the Country" 305, 317
Golden Gate Quartet, 251
Gold Star recording studio, 329, 337
Gold Star record label, 329, 337–38, 380, 383
Goldstein, Ken, 35, 38, 303, 335
"Gone Dead Train," 117–18
Goodman, Benny, 51, 243, 377, 401
"Good Morning Blues," 179
"Good Morning Little School Girl," 31
Gordon, Lorraine, 230
Gordon, Max, 230
Gordon, Robert, 235
Gordy, Barry, 165
Gosden, Robin, 175
Graham, Bill, 75
Gramophone Company, 179
Grand Ballroom (Cedar Point, OH), 376
Grand Crossing, 406
Grant, Leola B. "Coot," 151
Granz, Norman, 283
Gray, Glen, 376
"Great Bloody Wheel, The," 404
Green, Archie, 153, 303
Green, Grant, 151
Green, Jesse, 209
Green, Peter, 291
Green Door Club, 154
Greenhill, Manny, 72
Green's Longe, 320
Greensmith, Bill, 174, 182
Greenwood Press, 380
Griffin, Sin-Killer, 255
Griswold, Emerson, 254, 256
Groom, Bob, 305
Grossman, Stephen, 73
Guitar Player magazine, 88, 354
Guralnick, Pete 370, 413
Guthrie, Woody, 254–55, 279, 284, 286, 293
Guy, Buddy, 39, 41–43, 74–75, 78–80, 155–58, 198, 249, 338, 348
Guy, Phil, 210

Hackett, Bobby, 376
Halcox, Pat, 276, 278
Haley, Bill, 167
Hall, Edmond, 145
Hamilton, Marybeth, 364
Hammond, John, Jr., 72, 81–82
Hammond, John, Sr., 76, 418
Hampton, Lionel, 243
Hancock, Hunter, 323, 325
Handy, W. C., 95–96

Hanover Books, 172
Hansen, Barry (Dr. Demento), 303–4
Harden, Tim, 69, 80, 84
"Hard Time Killing Floor Blues," 232
Hare, Pat, 205, 249, 290
Harlem Matinee (radio program), 323
Harpo, Slim, 171, 216–17
Hartford, John, 146
Harris, Marion, 23
Harris, Peppermint, 390, 391
Harris, Shakey Jake, 157–58
Harris, William, 58–59, 68, 89
Harris, Wynonie, 244
Harvard University, 366
"Hastings Street," 61
Hawes, Bess, 318–19
Hawkins, Coleman, 244
Haymes, Dick, 407
Haywood, Big Bill, 419
Hear Me Howlin', 341
"He Arose from the Dead," 127
"Heartbreak Hotel," 167
Heatwave (magazine), 372
Hegamin, Lucille, 29
Helfer, Erwin, 146, 354
Hemisphere, The, 399
Hemmingway, James, 140
Hemphill, Jesse Mae, 315, 319–21
Hemphill, Sid, 313
Hendrix, Jimi, 80–81, 196
Henderson, Fletcher, 68, 140
Henderson, Gary, 239
Henderson, Skip, 119
Henderson, Solomon, 252
Hentoff, Nat, 391, 401
Henry, Clarence "Frogman," 176
Henry, John, 419
Henry, Lawrence, 149
Herman, Woody 290, 376
"Homanaje a John F Kennedy," 405
Herwin record label, 58, 63, 112, 405
Herzhaft, Gerard, 320
Hezekiah and the House Rockers, 319–21
Hickerson, Joe, 235
Hifi Stereo (magazine), 391
Higgham, Stan, 2
Hightone record label, 319
"High Water Blues," 102
High Water Blues (LP), 317
High Water record label, 318–19
Hill, Bertha "Chippie," 67, 86
Hill, Jessie, 167
Hill, Raymond, 319
Hines, Bessie, 413
Hilltoppers, 167
Hi record label, 305
Hite, Bob, 299–300
HMV (His Master's Voice) company, 125, 179, 271–73
Hocott, George, 138
Hodeir, Andre, 245
Hodes, Art, 155
Hodges, Johnny, 137
Hoffman, Larry, 354
Hoffman, Steve, 351
Hogg, John, 329
Hogg, Smokey, 329, 342
Holiday, Billie, 67, 137, 142, 324, 394
Hollywood Palladium, 376
Hollywood Show Lounge, 159
Holmes, Jimmy, 302
Holmes, Joe, 117–18. *See also* King Solomon Hill
Holmes, Myrt, 308
Holts, Roosevelt, 301–2, 305–7, 314–15, 317–18
Holy Modal Rounders, 293
Homesick James [Williamson], 42, 80, 82, 186, 220, 249, 368
"Home Town Skiffle," 279
"Honey Bee," 244
"Hoochie Coochie Man," 287
Hoodoo Man, 79, 151, 153, 157, 158
Hooker, Earl, 209, 217, 338–39
Hooker, John Lee, 8–9, 81, 197, 200–201, 244, 248, 256, 258, 299
Hopkins, Sam "Lightning," 12, 30–31, 72–73, 79, 81, 162, 177, 299, 325–29, 331, 336, 339–40, 350–52, 360, 382–84, 386, 401, 404
Hopkins, Willie, 188
Horton, Big Walter, 41, 184, 224
Hoskins, Tom, 229, 259, 298
"Hot and Bothered," 28
"Hot Dogs," 127
Hot Fox record label, 322

House, Eddie "Son," 17, 50, 54–55, 58, 62, 66, 70–78, 81–83, 89, 91, 96, 100–102, 108, 114, 116, 205–6, 228, 256–64, 266–69, 294–99, 311, 355, 409, 416, 417
House Un-American Activities Committee, 37
Houston, Bee, 341
Houston, Joe, 325
Houston Chronicle, 385
Hovington, Frank, 230, 236
Howard, Eddie, 376
"How Come You Do Me Like You Do," 127
Howling Wolf (Chester Burnett), 17–18, 74, 79, 82, 86, 96–97, 101, 157, 162, 203–5, 207, 209, 211, 216–18, 249, 256, 258, 289, 299, 325–26, 341, 347
"Howling Wolf Blues," 393
"How Long, How Long," 110
Hubner, Charlie, 51
Hug, Armand, 377
Huggins, Cilla, 174, 221–22
Huggins, Mick, 221–22
Hughes, Howard, 375, 385
Hughes, Langston, 12–13, 34, 37
Hughes, Tom, 387
Humes, Helen, 324
Hundred Club, 185
"Hungry Spell," 313
Hunt, Prince Albert, 380
Hunt, Van "V", 320, 368
Hunter, Alberta, 67
Hunter, Jellyroll, 126
Hurley, Jack, 297
Hurricane of the Valley, The, 379
Hurt, Mississippi John, 25, 55, 66, 70, 72–75, 78–79, 81–83, 119, 128, 228–30, 232–34, 236, 259–60, 264, 266, 294–96, 298, 300, 406
Hutto, J. B., 39, 41, 79, 159–60, 165, 184, 230, 232–34, 236

"I Am a Linguist," 133
"I Believe I'll Make a Change," 129
"I Feel So Good," 147
"If I Had a Million Dollars," 146
"If You Haven't Any Hay," 66
Iglauer, Bruce, 164–65, 177, 211–13, 352, 353, 354
"I Got Rhythm" 377
"I'm a Man," 168
"I'm Gonna Let Him Ride," 324
"I'm Gonna Murder My Baby," 205
"I'm So Glad," 76, 232
Index To Jazz 378, 380, 414
"I Need a Hundred Dollars," 248
Interstate Appliance Supply, 142
Invisible Man, The, 358
Ish Kabibble, 145
I Spy, You Die, 134

"Jab Blues," 121
Jackovack, Nick, 144
Jackovack Bar, 144
Jackson, Bruce, 294, 297
Jackson, Dewey, 50, 145
Jackson, Franz, 154, 159
Jackson, Jim, 110
Jackson, Lee, 42, 224
Jackson, Lil' Son, 328, 330–33, 338, 346
Jackson, Mahalia, 244, 251, 288
Jackson, Papa Charlie, 50
Jackson Blues Boys, 94
Jagger, Mick, 231–32
"Jailhouse Blues," 126
Jam Session (radio program), 135
James, Clifton, 162
James, Elmore, 115, 175, 249, 347
James, Harry, 51, 376
James, Skip, 50, 54–55, 58, 66, 72, 74–79, 81–82, 89, 91, 94, 107, 109–10, 113–16, 229–30, 232–33, 258, 262, 264, 266, 294–97, 299, 301–2, 304, 307, 309, 355, 366
James (Jane's) Alley, 27
J & J Lounge, 320
Jaxon, Frankie "Half-Pint," 233
Jazz: A History of the New York Scene, 29, 35
Jazz: New Orleans, 1885–1957, 22, 24, 29
Jazz at Massy Hall, 144
Jazz Club (radio program), 275
Jazz Collector record label, 121
Jazz Discography, 121, 132, 380
Jazz Document record label, 244
Jazz Finder '49
Jazz Hot magazine, 244–46, 250–51
Jazz Information magazine, 279
Jazz Journal, 6, 163, 169, 180, 251
Jazzmen, 26, 49

Jazz Monthly, 15, 125
Jazz Purists Society, 3–4
Jazz Record Center, 52, 54, 56
Jazz Record Mart, 147, 151, 153, 158, 208, 212, 215, 345, 346, 347, 352
Jazz Records, A–Z, 1897–1931, 123, 131
Jazz Report magazine, 143
Jazz Selection record label, 245
Jazz Society record label, 244
"Jealous Hearted Blues," 121
Jefferson, Blind Lemon, 6, 26, 31, 77, 110, 127, 244, 279, 327, 388, 392, 393
Jenkins, Robert, 308
Jenkins, Snuffy, 343
Jim & Jesse (McReynolds), 238
Jimenez, Flaco, 344
Jiv-A-Tones, 167
JOB record label, 186
"Joe Kirby Blues," 103
Joe's Music record shop, 147
John Edwards Memorial Foundation, 303, 316. *See also* Edwards, John
"John Henry, The Steel Driving Man," 405
Johnny Pepper's, 41–42
John R (Richbourg), 86
Johnson, Bessie, 56
Johnson, Big Jack, 223
Johnson, Blind Willie, 23, 33, 255, 269, 380, 418
Johnson, Bob, 225
Johnson, Bunk, 161, 324
Johnson, Buster, 56
Johnson, Claud, 415, 417
Johnson, Daisy Douglas, 363, 366, 367, 368, 370
Johnson, Edith North, 10, 20, 28, 32, 139–40
Johnson, Evelyn, 82
Johnson, Guy B., 364
Johnson, James "Stump," 10, 141
Johnson, Jesse, 140
Johnson, Jimmy, 221
Johnson, LeDelle, 88, 103, 309, 312
Johnson, Lonnie, 5, 20, 28, 32, 149, 162, 217, 244, 275, 278, 339, 354, 420
Johnson, Louise, 100
Johnson, Mager, 305, 307–8, 310–11, 314–15
Johnson, Mary, 10, 20, 139–40, 148, 357, 416
Johnson, Merline (the "Yas Yas Girl"), 51, 409, 414
Johnson, Patti, 222, 226
Johnson, Pete, 2
Johnson, Robert, 6, 23, 33, 62–63, 65, 71, 73, 76, 87, 90–91, 94, 103, 107, 109, 113, 119–20, 136, 158, 175, 180, 206, 222, 228, 245, 256, 293–94, 310, 339, 345, 351, 354, 379, 380, 384, 393, 408–18
Johnson, Stovepipe, 218
Johnson, Tillie, 62
Johnson, Tommy, 50, 87–88, 91, 93–94, 103–10, 113–14, 257, 300, 302, 305, 307, 309–10, 312, 409
Johnson, Willie (guitarist), 224. *Cf.* Johnson, Blind Willie
"Jole Blon," 383
Jones, Carl, 210
Jones, Coley, 379
Jones, Compton, 315
Jones, Curtis, 17, 251, 348
Jones, Eddie "One-String," 313
Jones, Floyd, 184, 186
Jones, Leroi, 359
Jones, Letha, 221
Jones, Little Hat, 147, 379
Jones, Maggie, 414
Jones, Max, 7, 179
Jones, Monroe, 223
Jones, O. D., 308
Jones, Richard M., 86, 116
Joplin, Janis, 342
Joplin, Scott, 24, 233
Jordan, Charlie 357, 358
Jordan, Cornelia 41, 418
Jordan, Louis, 67, 145, 291
Joslyn, Fred, 163
Jug Stompers, (Gus) Cannon's, 24, 38
Jugstra, Doug, 139
Juke Blues magazine, 174–75, 182
"Just Like John," 127
Just the Blues (French CD set), 252
JVB record label, 248

Kabakian, 245
"Kansas City Blues," 110
Kaplan, Arnold, 152
Kaplan, Ben, 33
Kapp, Jack, 358
Katz, Fred, 302

Kay, Rick, 182
"Keep On Scratchin'," 338
Kellert, Leon, 155
Kelly, Jo Ann, 339, 361
Kelly, Willie 414
Kennedy, President, 405
Kent, Don, 155, 178, 182, 347, 348, 355, 360
Kenton, Stan, 376, 383
Keppard, Freddy, 50, 68, 228
Kerouac, Jack, 362
Kerr, Charles H. (publishers), 357, 358, 365
Key Largo Club, 161
Keynote record label, 144
"Key to the Highway," 154, 195, 326
KFVD (radio station), 323
KHOU (radio station), 390
Kimbrough, Junior, 319
"Kind Hearted Woman," 417
Kinebrew, Willis, 310
Kinnell, Bill, 128
Kinetic Playground, 80, 211
King, Albert, 154, 208, 211
King, B. B., 82–83, 201–2, 208, 211, 223, 249
King, Freddy, 81
King, Willie, 226, 371
King Biscuit Radio Program, 343
King Edward Hotel, 108
King of the Delta Blues Singers, 92
Kingsblood Royal (novel), 192
Kings of Rhythm, 319
King Solomon Hill (Joe Holmes), 85, 88, 117–18
King Solomon Hill Baptist Church, 117
Kingston Trio, 293
Kirkland, Eddie, 248
"Kitchen Man," 278
Kit Sales (mail-order record business), 142
Klatzko, Bernie, 55, 57–58, 60, 62–63, 87–88, 90, 92–93, 95, 114, 228, 260, 269, 299, 364, 405
Klauberg, Big Joe, 52, 54, 56, 68
Knight, Marie, 286
Knoxville World's Fair, 399
Koester, Bob, 79, 123, 141, 149, 178, 202, 205, 208, 211, 215, 334, 338, 346, 347, 348, 349, 352, 357, 361, 363
Komora, Ed, 88
Korner, Alex, 275, 278, 291
Korson, Rae, 235
Krupa, Gene, 376
KSAN (radio station), 335
Kunaal, 14
Kunstadt, Len, 29, 177
Kuykendall, Pete, 228–29, 232, 237, 239
KWBR (radio station), 325
Kweskin Jug Band, 72, 293, 300
KXYZ (radio station), 379
KXYZ Novelty Band, 379
Kyser, Kay, Orchestra, 145

Lacey, Rubin, 73, 108, 304
Ladnier, Tommy, 50, 68
"Lady Luck," 335
Laibly, Art, 100, 392
Laine, Frankie, 238
Land Where Blues Began (book), 416
Lane, Chester, 145
Langmeade, John, 179
Lanier, Buck, 317
LaRocca, James, 175–76
"Last Fair Deal Gone Down," 90
Lauderdale, Jack, 342
Laurie, Annie, 176
LaVere, Steve, 119, 223, 314, 354
Law, Don, 411,412, 417
Lawhorne, Sammy, 210
Lay, Sam, 80
Lazy Lester, 171
Leadbelly (Huddie Leadbetter), 163, 179–80, 248, 255, 279, 293–94, 300, 305, 330, 387
Leadbitter, Mike, 16, 88, 167–75, 177, 182, 338, 348, 372
Leake County Revelers, 113
"Leaves Is Fallin' on the Ground," 330
"Leaving Town Blues," 107
LeCigale (French show lounge), 243
Lee, Doug, 139
"Left Alone Blues," 108
Legacy of Tommy Johnson, The (LP), 305, 317
Legends (blues club), 217
Lenoir, J. B., 17–19, 215, 249
Lester, Julius, 78
Letterman Plantation, 412
Lewis, George, 23, 145–46, 256, 325, 330
Lewis, Johnny, 339
Lewis, Meade Lux, 2, 324

Lewis, Ramsey, 152
Lewis, Sinclair, 192
Lewis, Ted, 380
Lewis, Walter "Furry," 25, 30, 37–38, 255, 312
Library of Congress, 2, 13, 70, 130, 228, 235–36, 238–39, 255, 258, 262, 295–96, 311, 313, 317, 333, 366, 404, 416
Liebler, Vincent, 394, 416
Light Crust Dough Boys, 154, 375, 378
Lightning Slim, 171, 353
Lincoln, Charlie, 414
Lindeman, Bill, 157
Lippman, Horst, 17, 162, 336
Lipscomb, Mance, 10, 19, 72, 74, 79, 329–31, 333–34, 383, 385–87, 388, 390, 401, 404, 405
Lipscomb, Tee (T), 386
Liston, Virginia, 139
Little Ann, 248
Little Boy Blue, 343
"Little Brown Bird," 178
Little Dixie (Missouri), 400
Little Dusty 410, 411, 415–17
Little Hudson, 184
Littlejohn, Johnny, 338–39
Little Robert 416, 417
Little Sandy Review (magazine), 307
Little Son Joe (Ernest Lawler), 367, 369
Little Walter (Marion Jacobs), 10–11, 12, 42, 79, 154, 177, 202, 249
Living Blues Cookout, 215
Living Blues magazine, 164, 177, 183, 211–13, 215–17, 220, 222–23, 226, 351, 354, 356, 361, 370
Lloyd, A. L., 255
Lockwood, Robert, Jr., 82, 175, 224, 413
Loft, The (coffee house), 258
Lofton, Crippled Clarence, 179–80, 244
Logan Brothers, 354
Lomax, Alan, 2, 24, 70, 235–36, 256, 258, 307, 313, 318–19, 353, 408, 416
Lomax, John, 130, 235, 387, 395, 399
Lomax, John, Jr., 328, 408
London, Mel, 155
London American record label, 167
London record label, 168
Lonesome Sundown, 171, 308
Longhair, Professor, 176
Look Back in Anger (movie), 284
Look magazine, 189
Lopez, George, 400
Lord, Albert, 304
Lornell, Kip, 319
Los Conquistadores, 405
Los Pinguinos del Norte (Penguins of the North), 344
Lost & Found (CD set), 289, 291
Louis Armstrong and the Blues (LP), 151
"Louisiana Blues," 337
Louisiana Honeydrippers, 343
Louisiana World's Fair, 399
Love, Bill, 50
Love, Jasper, 10
Love, Willie, 10
Lovel, Jim, 216
"Lovin' Sam from Down in 'Bam," 128
Lowery, Pete, 175, 316
Luther Wade Plantation, 119–20
Lynn, Smilin' Smokey, 325
Lyttleton, Humphrey, 179, 273–74

MacColl, Ewan, 255
MacFarland, Barrelhouse Buck, 138
Macon, Uncle Dave, 113
Maddox Brothers and Rose, 324
Magic Sam, 78–82, 153, 157–58, 165, 213, 225
Magic Slim, 221
Magnacord tape recorder, 344
"Ma Grinder," 390
Mahal, Taj, 25, 78, 266
Mainer, Wade, 240
"Mama Blues," 376, 377
Man and the Blues, A (record), 42
M & O Blues, 73
Mandolin Blues, 153
"Man of Constant Sorrow, A," 400
Marable, Fate, 145
Ma Rainey and the Classic Blues Singers, 182
Marcus, Greil, 366
Marcy, Mary, 365
Margolin, Bob, 290
Mariposa Folk Festival, 72
Marquee Club, 285
Marsh, Orlando, 61
Marshall, Fred, 403
Marshmellow record label, 151

Marsh Studios, 99
Marvelous Freedom Vigilance of Desire Re-united (exhibition), 364
Mason, Ditty, 310
Mason, Norman, 145
Matassa, Cosimo, 176
Matchbox record label, 317
Mathus, Jimbo, 223
Martin, Fiddlin' Joe, 261, 310–11
Martin, Jake, 310
Maxwell Street, 184, 202, 346
Mayfield, Percy, 85
Mazzolini, Tom, 214
McCarthy, Albert, 15, 121, 132, 380
McCeney, George, 239
McClennen, Tommy, 179, 245, 347
McCormick, Mary, 413
McCormick, Robert "Mack," 10, 19, 30–31, 119, 182, 327–29, 331–35, 371, 387
McCoy, Charlie, 307
McCoy, Ethel, 370
McCoy, George, 370
McCoy, Kansas Joe, 148, 250, 366, 367
McCoy, Robert Lee, 141
McCoy, Willie, 376
McDowell, Fred, 72, 79, 81, 230, 236, 258, 266, 295, 297–98, 301–2, 304, 307, 310, 312, 315, 340
McGee, Rev. F. W., 56, 127
McGee, Dennis, 230
McGhee, Walter "Brownie," 12, 69, 72, 74, 81, 217, 245, 251, 278–79, 284, 286, 289–91, 294, 345, 346, 354, 360
McIntorsch, Lonnie, 56
McKinney's Cotton Pickers, 140
McKune, Jim, 54–57, 64, 228, 364
MCM record label, 221
McMullin, Hayes, 97–98
McMurry, Lillian, 104, 175, 342
McNeely, Big Jay, 325
McShann, Jay, 400
McTell, Blind Willie, 25, 32, 116, 258, 316–17
McTell, Kate, 316
McWilliams, Andy, 224
"Me and the Devil," 414
Melly, George, 121
Melodeon record label, 230, 232
Melody Maker magazine, 179
Melotone record label, 124
Melrose, Lester, 162, 195, 203, 358, 369
"Memphis Blues," 95
Memphis Blues and Jug Bands, 182
Memphis Blues Caravan, 314
Memphis Country Club 411
Memphis Jug Band, 10, 24, 31
Memphis Minnie, 112, 136, 216, 237, 339, 354, 358, 362, 363, 365, 366, 367, 368, 369, 370, 414
Memphis Slim, 162, 197, 199, 249, 251, 360, 369
Mercury record label, 156
Merritt record label, 125
Meteor record label, 248
Mezzrow, Mezz, 271
Miantinomi Avenue House (Newport), 266
"Midnight at the Oasis," 151
"Midnight Rounder," 125
Mielke, Bob, 325–26
Milestone record label, 304
"Milkcow Blues," 116, 379
Miller, Rev. Booker, 92–93, 96–97, 99, 101
Miller, Eddie, 138
Miller, Glenn, 136, 143, 273
Miller, J. D., 171
Miller, Punch, 54, 143
Miller-Freeman Publishers, 88
Millinder, Lucky, 286
Mills, Ken, 328–30, 335
Mingus, Charles, 144
Mississippi Blues Trail Project, 225
Mississippi River Publishing Company, 318
Mississippi Sheiks, 94, 105, 109, 379
Mitchell, George, 155, 310, 313–16, 415
Mitchell, Guy, 167
Mobile Four, 127
Mobile Strugglers, 24, 31
Modern Albums, 333
Modern Jazz Quartet, 286
Modern Music record shop, 142
Modern record label, 177, 324, 331
Mohr, Kurt, 177, 246, 248
Monk, Thelonius, 38
Monroe, Bill, 238, 353, 400, 407
Monroe, Charlie, 238
Montgomery, Eurreal "Little Brother," 17, 123, 128, 159, 182, 249
Montreal Festival 399

Monty Sunshine, 276–77
"Moon Goin' Down," 102
"Moon Is Rising," 141
Moore, Alice, 139
Moore Brothers 386
Moore, Elizabeth, 96
Moore, Jim, 119, 340
Moore, Scotty, 38
Moore, Tom, 329, 335, 344, 386, 387
Moore, Whistlin' Alex, 9, 331, 333, 388, 390
Moore, Williams, 258
Morante, Jose, 405
Morning Edition (radio program), 240
Morris School for Boys, 375
Morrison, Harry, 142
Morrison, Van, 287
Morton, Ferdinand "Jellyroll," 24, 143, 145, 154, 227, 272–73
Mosley, Will, 100
Moss, Buddy, 316
Mother Blues (music club), 347
"Motherless Children Have a Hard Time," 387
Motion Picture, Broadcasting, and Recorded Sound Division, 236
Motor City Reveille, 146
Motown record label, 164–65
Moyer, Charles, 419
"Mr. Charlie," 336
Mr. Lee's Lounge, 203
Muldaur, Geoff, 151, 255
Muldaur, Maria, 151
Muddy Waters (McKinley Morganfield), 8, 11, 17–18, 40–41, 74, 79, 82, 86, 99, 154–55, 157, 178, 180, 197–201, 203, 207–8, 210–11, 217, 244–45, 249, 256, 278, 286–87, 289–91, 299, 317, 325, 341, 347, 348
Mud Island Museum, 367
Mulligan, Gerry, 286
Mulligan, Mick, 121
Murphy, Matt, 222, 249
Murphy, Turk, 325
Music Mirror, 6
Music River Publishing Company, 318
Music While You Work (radio program), 271
"Muskrat Ramble Cha-Cha-Cha," 280
Musselwhite, Charlie, 159, 197, 214, 339, 347, 361
"My Black Mama," 103
"My Mother's Eyes," 28

Nagra tape recorder, 236, 311, 402
Napier, Simon, 16, 88, 167–72, 175, 178, 180, 182, 305, 348, 355
National Educational Radio, 239
National Endowment for the Arts, 318
National Federation of Jazz Organizations, 275, 286
National guitars, 113, 268
National Observer (newspaper), 264
National Park Service, 399
Nations, Opal, 176
Negro Worksongs and Calls, 333
Nelson, Dad, 379
Nelson, Dirty Red, 154, 249
Nelson, Stu, 268
"Nehi Blues," 118
Nessa, Chuck, 160
"Never Ending Song of Love," 75
Nevins, Rich, 60–62, 89
Newberry Library, 354
New Lost City Ramblers, 69
New Orleans (movie), 324
Newport Folk Festival, 39, 66, 72, 74, 77, 81, 229, 231, 259, 263–67, 395, 396, 399, 416
"New Stop and Listen Blues," 105
Newsweek Magazine, 116, 264–65
Nichols, Albert, 151
Nighthawk, Robert, 105, 141, 310, 343
Niles, Abbey, 27
"Ninth Street Stomp," 393
Nix, Rev. A.W., 125
Nix, Willie, 185, 223
Nixon, Hammie, 153, 162, 266, 293, 295, 320–21
Nketia, Kwabena, 14
Noah Lewis Jug Band, 320
Noble, Gene, 86
"Nobody Knows You When You're Down and Out," 121
Norman, Gene, 324
Northwestern University, 358
Nunn, E. D., 154, 346

Oberstein, Eli, 56, 393
Obrecht, Jas, 88
O'Brien, Charlie, 138–40, 143, 357

O Brother Where Art Thou, 232
Obsolete Music Hour (radio program), 240
Ochs, Phil, 69, 84
O'Day, Anita, 376
Odeon record label, 248
ODJB (Original Dixieland Jazz Band), 135
Odum, Howard, 364
Odyssey Coffee House, 267
Oertle, Ernie, 113
Ojeda, Fred, 344
Okeh record label, 51, 53, 59, 64, 67–68, 105, 112, 116–17, 122, 124, 127, 151, 179, 271, 303, 378, 406
"Oklahoma Hills," 324
OJL (Origin Jazz Library), 62–64, 70, 88, 91, 107, 231, 256–58, 261, 269, 294, 320, 339, 349, 360, 405
Old Timey record label, 339
Old Town (Chicago neighborhood), 347
Ole Miss (University of Mississippi), 89, 220
Oliver, King, 143, 227–28, 240, 278
Oliver, Paul, 123–24, 128, 132–33, 172, 178, 182, 214, 245–46, 305, 312, 329–32, 348, 349, 355, 360, 363, 364, 388, 389, 406, 407
Oliver, Valerie, 330–31, 349
Olsson, Bengt, 312
O'Neal, Jim, 164, 175, 177, 183, 310, 348, 352, 353, 364, 368
"One Mo' Time," 230
One-String Sam, 248
Only a Miner, 303
"Only You," 167
"Ooh-Poo-Pah-Doo," 168
Ory, Kid, 324
Oster, Harry, 307–8, 330, 343–44
Oswald, Bob, 138, 145–46
Oswald, Vivian, 138
"Outside Woman Blues," 118
Owen, Robert, 316
Owens, Eli, 314–15
Owens, Jack, 301–2, 309, 314–15, 317, 319
Owens, Willie Scarecrow, 54
Oxford English Dictionary, 404
Oxford, Jumpin' George, 325–26
Oxford University Press (OUP), 130–34

Pace Jubilee Singers, 130
PACE Trust, 366
Page, Jimmy, 291
Page, Patti, 238
Palmer, Robert, 306
Palmer, Singleton, 149
Panassie, Hugues, 177, 243–46, 378
Paramount record label, 50–51, 53–54, 58–59, 61–64, 66, 70, 90, 94, 99, 100, 104–5, 107, 110, 112, 117, 124–25, 127, 137, 143, 149, 151–52, 213, 258, 262, 279, 378, 392, 393
Parchman Prison Farm, 318, 395
Parker, Charlie, 137, 144, 244
Parker, Junior, 217
Parker, Knocky, 153–54
Parlophone Record Company, 179, 272
Parrot record label, 151
Parth, Johnny, 67, 215
Pastor, Tony Orch, 376
Paterson, Neil, 172
Patterson, Ottilie, 121, 283–84, 286, 290
Patton, Charley, 33, 50, 54, 56–57, 63–64, 70, 73, 77, 87, 89–90, 92–103, 105, 107–10, 112–13, 206, 213, 228, 231, 245, 257, 260, 294, 300–301, 305, 309–10, 312, 318, 355, 360, 393
Paxton, Tom, 228
Peabody Hotel, 331
"Peach Orchid Mama," 393
Peacock Jazz Club, 137
Peer, Ralph, 38, 105
Peetie's Buddy (Harmon Ray), 141
Peidmont record label, 115, 232
Pelltier, Paul, 174
People's Songs magazine, 192
Pepper, Johnny, 41
Pepper's Blues Lounge, 41–42, 154, 160, 198, 208
Perfect record label, 124, 279
Perin, Jacques, 251
Perkins, Carl, 168
Perkins, Pinetop, 83
Perls, Nick, 58, 60, 63, 70–71, 73, 88–89, 234, 259–60, 262, 267, 295, 299, 305, 311, 355
Perryman, Gus, 149
Petard, Gilles, 251
Peter, Paul, and Mary, 70, 228, 397
Peters, Nancy 362
"Petite Fleur," 276, 279, 284, 291
Pettibone, George, 419
Philadelphia Folk Festival, 79, 82

Phillips, Brewer, 368, 369
Phillips, Bruce, 131
Phillips, Dewey, 292
Phillips, John, 146
Pickens, Edward "Buster," 10, 327, 332, 389, 390
Pierce, Billie and Dede, 330
Piedmont record label, 229–30
Pine Tavern, 239
Piney Woods Blues, 145
Pinson, Bob, 328–29, 339
Pin-Up Lounge, 138, 145
"Pistol Packing Mama," 379
Pitchford, Lonnie, 223
Playback magazine, 380
Playboy magazine, 349
Playboy Paperback Books, 354
Plymouth Jazz Club, 179
Poetry of the Blues, The, 33
Pokempner, Marc, 198, 202
Polka Dot Inn (Blues club), 141
"Pony Blues," 94
Pope, Jim, 258
Pope, Wayne, 333
Porgy and Bess, 405
Porter, Bob, 82
Porter, Cole, 244
Postis, François, 244, 246
Powell, Bud, 144
Powell, Ginnie, 376
"Prairie Blues," 379
Pratches Brothers, 313
"Pratt City Blues," 121
"Preaching the Blues," 96, 102
Presenting the Country Blues, 305
Preservation Hall, 325, 330
Preservation Hall Jazz Band, 325
Presley, Elvis, 38, 162, 166–68, 207, 305, 318
Prestige Records label, 35, 37–40, 144, 149, 151, 198, 258, 303, 335, 360, 384, 385
Preston, Dennis, 283–84
"Pretty Thing," 168
Price, Sammy, 8, 246, 248
Primitive Piano, 140, 147
Prince Albert (piano player), 248
"Prodigal Son," 72, 231–32
Profile record label, 155
Proletariet Lives (book series), 358
"Promised Land," 297
Pruter, Robert, 368
Pullman Company, 192
Pullum, Joe, 379, 380
Pye record label, 283, 284

Quiet Knight (music club), 217
Quinn, Bill, 32, 337–38, 382, 383
Quinn, Herb, 309, 315
Quinn, Snoozer, 379

Rachell, James "Yank," 153, 347
Radcliff, Charles, 350, 351, 372
Radio Ghana, 14
Raeburn, Boyd, 376
Raglan record label, 404
"Railroadin' Some," 405
Raines, Embry, 316
Rainey, Gertrude "Ma," 22, 50–51, 121, 143, 151, 228, 349, 365
Raitt, Bonnie, 81
Raitt, John, 81
Ramos, Michel, 243
Ramsey, Frederic, 26–27, 32, 34, 49–50
Ramsey Prison Farm, 396
R & B Monthly, 174, 177
R & B Panorama, 177
Randolph, John, 153
Randy's Record Shop, 180
Rau, Fritz, 17, 162, 336
Ravel, Maurice, 377
RBF Record label, 33, 64, 256, 293
RCA Victor Records, 42, 124–25, 129, 136, 179, 245, 271. *See also* Victor record label
Real Blues forum, 362
Really the Blues (book), 271
Really the Country Blues, 33, 64, 70, 88, 91, 257, 360
Record Cellar (record shop), 180
Record Changer magazine, 5, 50, 52
Record Exchange magazine, 136
"Recording the Blues," 132
Record Makers and Breakers: Voices of Independent Rock 'n' Roll Pioneers, 178
Record Research Craft, 333
Record Research magazine, 55, 177
Record Shop, The, 135

Red Arrow Club, 154, 159
Redding, Otis, 80–81
Red Lick Records, 357
Red Lightning record label, 220
Red River Blues, 175
Reed, Jimmy, 74, 86, 177, 207, 219, 345
Reed, Levi, 219
Reed, Long Cleve, 54
Reed, Mama, 219
Reed, Willie, 379
Reese, Doc, 266
Reinhardt, Django, 243–44
"Remember Me," 324
Renard, Henry, 54, 56
Reno, Don, 353
Reprise record label, 333, 387,
Research Craft (pressing plant), 145
Rey, Alvino, 376, 377
Reynolds, Blind Joe, 88, 110, 118–19
Reynolds, George, 149
Rhodes, Ed, 25
Rhythm & Blues in New Orleans, 171
Rhythm & Blues magazine, 197, 200–202, 204
Rhythm and Blues Panorama, 246
Rice, Rev. D. C., 56
Rice Hotel (Houston), 379, 380
Rice University, 385
Rich, Buddy, 376
Richard, Seth, 233
Ricks, Jerry Philadelphia, 78, 223
Riding with the Blues, 225
Rinzler, Ralph, 37
"River Blues Parts 1 and 2," 342
Riverboat Enterprises, 151
Rivers, Boyd, 321
"Riverside Blues," 126
Riverside record label, 144, 149, 151, 255
Roach, Max, 144
Robbins, Marty, 411
Roberts tape recorder, 326, 342
Robeson, Paul, 192–93, 198
Robinson, Bobby, 248
Robinson, Fenton, 209
Robinson, Jim, 23, 377
Rocha, Pedro, 379
"Rock around the Clock," 167, 280
"Rocket 88," 319
Rockin' Lucky (radio host), 335
"Rock Island Line," 276, 279, 282–84
Rodgers, Jimmie, 85, 108, 146, 180, 379
Rogers, Ike, 139
Rogers, Jimmy, 177, 180, 185, 368, 369
Roland, Walter, 55
"Rolling Stone," 244
Rolling Stones, 72, 79, 207, 231–32
Rollins, Sonny, 38
Rooftop Singers, 38
Roosevelt Holts and Friends, 317
Roosevelt University, 373
Rooster Crowed in England, The, 401
"Rooster Crowed in England, The," 401
Rooster record label, 220–23, 225–26
Roots of the Blues (book), 47–48
Roots record label, 317
Rose, Pete, 402
Rosemont, Franklin 353, 357, 359, 360, 370–73
Rosemont, Penny 357, 370–73
Rose Record Store, 136, 345
Ross, Doctor (Isaiah), 340
Rooster record label, 371
Rotante, Anthony, 177
Rounder record label, 236, 313, 317
"Round Square Dance," 157
Routledge Press, 13
Rowe, Mike, 172, 174, 359
Roy, Harry, 3
Royal American Shows (traveling carnival), 143
Royal Festival Hall, 275, 283–84
RPM record label, 223
Rugolo, Pete, 377
Rural Electric Associates, 111
Rush, Otis, 39, 41, 43, 80, 157, 159, 209, 219, 225, 249, 348
Rush, Tom, 228, 293, 300
Russell, Bill, 49, 60, 89, 149, 154
Russell, Pete, 179
Russell, Tony, 131–32, 182, 184, 312, 359, 360
Rust, Brian, 15, 123, 125, 129, 131–32, 177, 401
Ryan, Marc, 296, 305, 307
Rye, Howard, 130–33
Ryland, Buddy, 383

Sabre record label, 223
Sacred Steel (group), 353

"Salty Dog," 50
Sanders Recording Studios, 63
"Sand Mountain Blues," 402
San Francisco Blues Festival, 214
"Saturday Blues," 106, 108
Saturday Review of Literature, 334, 403
Savage Joy, 407
Savannah Syncopators, 14
Savoy record label, 346
Savoy Record Shop, 51
Scarborough, Dorothy, 364
Schanechie Records, 89
Scheuning, Neala, 364
Schitzmeyer, Ken, 142
Schneider, Jake, 52–54, 56
Scholarly Press, 132
Schraeder, Bob, 145
Schroeder, Patty 351
Scobey, Bob, 325
Scott, Frank, 317
Scott, Hammond, 219
Screening the Blues, 360
Scruggs, Earl, 232, 238–39
SDS (Students for a Democratic Society), 373
"Search for Robert Johnson, The," 101
Searching for Aboriginal Languages: Memoir of a Field Worker, 134
Sebastian, John, 73
Second Fret (club), 82
Seeger, Mika, 398
Seeger, Mike, 238
Seeger, Peggy, 343
Seeger, Pete, 37, 188, 255, 293–94, 397, 398
"See See Rider Blues," 121. *See also* "C. C. Rider"
Segal, Joe, 151–53
Sehorn, Marshall, 176
Sellers, "Brother" John, 246, 285
"Selling the Jelly," 320
"Sentimental Blues," 379
"September in the Rain," 376
Seroff, Doug, 130
Session record label, 144
78 Quarterly, 49, 50, 55–56, 59, 64–65, 88–89, 117, 349
77 Label, 401
Seymour Schwartz, 150
Seymour's Record Shop, 150–51
Shade, Will, 10, 24–25, 312
"Shake 'em On Down," 313
"Shake Your Shimmy," 125
Sharpe, Jack, 380
Shaw, Eddie, 223
Shaw, Elijah, 139
Shaw, Robert, 389, 390, 400, 406
Shayne, Freddy, 139
Sheatsley, Paul, 177
Sheppard, Joe, 118
Sherwood, Betty, 376
Shields, Lonnie, 223
Shines, Johnny, 39, 87, 185–86, 304, 321, 369
Short Brothers (Jimmy & Leon), 383
Short, J. D., 32, 70, 147–49
Shurman, Richard, 211
Sid Dawson's Riverboat Ramblers, 145
Sidenberg, Sid, 82
Sierra Sound Studios, 342
Silvertone record label, 126
Simmons, Little Mac, 141, 154, 209
Sims, Diane, 239
Sims, Henry, 89, 99
Sinatra, Frank, 384, 407
Singer of Tales, A, 304
Singleton, Zutty, 324
Singleton Palmer's Dixieland Six, 149
Sing Out magazine, 78, 204
Sirens record label, 140
Six and Seven-Eights String Band, 24, 34
Sky Songs, 161
Slate, 417, 418
Slaven, Neil, 16, 174, 182
Slay, Emmitt, 248
"Sliding Delta Blues," 104
Sloan, Henry, 95
Slotnikoff, Joel, 64
Smilby, 349
Smith, Anthony, 13
Smith, Archie, 100
Smith, Bessie, 3, 22, 68, 121, 159, 179, 228, 244, 273, 278, 365, 393
Smith, Blyther, 210
Smith, Charles Edward, 26
Smith, Clarence "Pinetop," 3, 180
Smith, Francis Wilfred, 128, 348
Smith, Funny Paper, 393, 409

Smith, Harrison, 52
Smith, Harry, 32–34, 56, 64, 257
Smith, Huey "Piano," 176
Smith, Jabbo, 230
Smith, Joe, 68, 159
Smith, Mamie, 29
Smith, Robert Curtis, 10, 331
Smith, Tab, 137
Smith, Thunder, 338
Smith, Trixie, 151
Smithsonian Festival of American Folk Life, 399, 408
Smithsonian Institution, 37, 399, 400
Smitty's Corner (blues club), 154, 249, 290
"Snatch It Back and Hold It," 156
Solidarity Bookstore, 373
Solomon, Maynard, 38–39, 78
Solomon, Seymour, 38
Sonett record label, 43
Songs of Death and Tragedy, 401, 404
Songsters and Saints, 18
Sorrow Come Pass Me Around (LP), 317
Sortier, Ann, 141
Sosira, 14
Souchon, Edmond 388
Souffront, Andre, 214, 353
Soul Bag magazine, 251
Sound Machine (band), 319
Sounds Good (record store), 215
Sounds of the South, 236
South, Eddie, 244
"South Bound Train," 290
Southern Music Company, 38–39
South Texas Street Rambler, 406
South to New Orleans: The Music of the Cajun Bayou, 171
Spand, Charlie, 61, 140
Spann, Otis, 39–40, 43, 139, 157–59, 198–200, 217, 249, 287, 290
Spann, Pervis, 82
Spaulding, Henry, 32
Spear, Allan H., 184
Speckled Red, 128, 138–41, 145–49, 154
Speir, H. C., 94, 99, 103–7, 109–10, 112–13, 118, 309
Spence, Joseph, 35
Spencer, Robert, 416
Spindletop, 375
Spirit of Memphis Quartet, 244, 248
Spirituals to Swing concert, 76
Spires, Arthur "Big Boy," 309
Spires, Bud, 309
Spiro, Phil, 70–71, 73, 258, 294–95, 311
Spivey, Victoria, 10, 20, 29, 389, 392
"Spoonful," 102
Spottswood, Dick, 62, 64, 66, 115, 261, 404, 405
Spottswood, Louisa, 229–30, 233–34, 236–37, 261
Spruell, Papa Freddie, 116
Spruill, "Wild" Jimmy, 248
Stacey, Jess, 154
Stackhouse, Houston, 105, 214, 217, 223, 310, 312, 317, 343
Stackhouse (store), 221, 223
Stackhouse record label, 222
Stanchell, Jealous James, 402
Stanley Brothers, 239
Stanley, Ralph, 400
States record label, 141, 151
Stax record label, 305
Steel Pier (Atlantic City), 376
Stein and Day Publishers, 132, 355
Steiner, John, 60–61, 149, 151–52, 154, 339
Stella Guitars, 113
Sterns, Marshall, 295
Stewart-Baxter, Derek, 6, 182, 349
Stewart K., 182
Stewart, Rex, 377
Stidham, Arbee, 195
Stitt, Sonny, 291
"St. James Infirmary," 380
St. Louis Argus (newspaper), 141
"St. Louis Blues," 23, 95, 243
St. Louis Jazz Club, 137, 143–44
St. Louis Jimmy (James Oden), 18, 138, 249, 290
St. Louis Music Company, 112
St. Marie, Buffy, 84
Stockholm Slim (Per Notini), 158–59
Stokes, Frank, 18
Stoneman, Scott, 239
"Stones in My Passway," 23
"Stop and Listen," 105
Story of the Blues (book), 12,363
Story of the Blues (exhibition), 14
Story of the Blues (French CD set), 251

Storyville magazine, 129
Storyville record label, 163
Storyville Publications, 129–30
Storyville Stompers (band), 326
Stovall, Babe, 72, 296–97, 301–2, 306, 308
Stovall's Plantation, 286
Stover, Don, 239
Strachwitz, Chris, 8, 10, 18–19, 162, 182, 317, 345, 348, 363, 370
Strickland, Napoleon, 313–14, 316
String Wizards, 142
Stucky, Henry, 115
Studio Vista Publishers, 132, 182, 184, 355, 356, 357
Suggs, Doug, 138
Sullivan, Ira, 151
Sumlin, Hubert, 204, 341
Sunnyland Slim, 155, 162, 186, 199–200, 220, 249, 340, 400
Sun Ra, 144
Sun record label, 167, 179, 223
Sunset Boulevard 407
"Sun Song," 144
Sun Studios, 38
Super Chikan, 222–23
Superior record label, 59
Supertone record label, 126
Sutton, Ralph, 275
Sweet as the Showers of Rain, 47
"Sweet Home Chicago," 90, 158
Swing record label, 243–45
Swing Time record label, 342
Switched on Bach, 268
Sykes, Roosevelt, 17, 128, 137, 141, 159, 400, 401, 414
Sylvio's Lounge, 154, 203–4

"Tain't Nobody's Business," 291
Taj Mahal. *See* Mahal, Taj
Talent record label, 329
Tamony, Peter, 303
Tampa Red (Hudson Whittaker), 19, 128, 136, 162, 179, 211, 216–17, 245, 249, 369
Tarheel Slim, 248
Tate, Buddy, 377
Taylor, Billy, 151
Taylor, Danny "Run Joe," 248
Taylor, Eddie, 184–86, 249, 369
Taylor, Floyd, 248
Taylor, Hound Dog, 165, 209, 221
Taylor, Irene, 379
Taylor, Montana, 179–80
Teagarden, Jack 419
Telefunken tape recorder, 122
"Tell Me Baby," 117
Temple, Johnny, 103, 114, 116, 307, 309
Tempo record label, 121
Tennessee Valley Authority, 111
"Terraplane Blues," 76, 417
Terry, Sonny, 12, 70, 74, 81, 179, 245, 251, 278–79, 284, 286, 288, 290–91, 294, 345, 346
Testament record label, 304, 317–18
Texas Barrelhouse Piano, 390, 391, 401
Tharpe, Sister Rosetta, 136, 246, 286, 288
"That's No Way To Get Along," 72
Theard, Sam, 128
Theresa's Blues Lounge, 41, 155–56, 208, 210, 347
Theroux, Ed, 394
"Third Street's Goin' Down," 138
Third Ward (Houston), 383, 391
This Is Jazz (radio program), 135
"This Old World Is in a Terrible Condition," 402
Thomas, George, 388
Thomas, Henry "Ragtime Texas," 63, 91, 405, 406
Thomas, Hersal, 388
Thomas, Hocial, 388
Thomas, Lafayette, 248
Thomas, Rufus, 319
Thomas, Son, 321
Thomas, Willie, 330
Thomas Family, 388, 391, 392
Thompson, Carrie, 411, 413
Thompson, Charlie, 137, 149
Thompson, Cotton, 379
Thompson, Sonny, 249
Thornton, Big Mama, 340–41
"Three Miles South of Cash in Arkansas," 324
Thurber, Cheryl, 315–16
Tillman, Floyd, 379
Time magazine, 192
Tiny Topsy, 249
Tisdom, James, 406
"T-Model" Ford, 223

"To Each His Own," 376
"Tom Moore's Farm," 386, 402, 406
Tommy Johnson (book), 301, 305, 312, 317
Tonneau, Serge, 177, 246
"Toot Toot Tootsie Bound," 127
Toussaint, Allen, 176
Tower Record Store, 136
Townsend, Henry, 32, 82, 141, 174, 356, 357
Toy, Minnie, 92
Tradition record label, 384
Trails, Sinclair, 401
Transition record label, 144
Travis, Bob, 62
Treasury of Field Recordings (Vol I & II), 386, 401, 402, 403, 408
Trianon Ballroom, 189
"Trouble in Mind," 67
Trumpet around the Corner, A, 27
Trumpet record label, 104, 148, 151, 175, 330, 342
Tubb, Ernest, 339
Tucker, Sophie, 380
Turk's Head Café, 255
Turner, Bez, 174, 182
Turner, Big Joe, 342
Turner, Ike, 224–25, 319
Turner, Othar, 310, 313–15, 318
Turner, Tina, 224
Turner's Lounge, 42, 159–62, 184
Tuskegee Institute Singers, 130
Tyler, T-Texas, 324

Umphrey, Walley, 56
"Undertakers Blues," 56
Unexpurgated Folksongs of Men, The, 401
United Record Distributors, 151
United record label, 151
University of Connecticut, 351
University of Illinois Press, 130, 366
University of Kumasi, 14
University of Mississippi (Ole Miss), 89, 220
"Up in Heah," 156
USA record label, 155
US Postal Service, 413
Utopia, 393

Valdes, Bebo, 47
Vanguard Record label, 38–40, 43, 75, 77–78, 80, 156, 230, 398
Van Ronk, Dave, 35, 38, 73, 293
Van Singel, Amy, 164, 177, 208, 211, 216, 220, 222, 348, 353, 354, 370
Vaughan, Sarah, 82
VeeJay record label, 147, 248
Venson, Playboy, 186
Vergie Mae, 417
Verhanen, Kosti, 190
Vernon, Mike, 174, 317
Vestine, Henry, 115, 170, 262, 299
Victor record label, 32, 51, 53, 59, 64, 67–68, 104–5, 108, 111–12, 116, 124–25, 129, 137, 142, 237, 244, 309, 324. 379. *See also* RCA Victor Records
Victrola, 111
Village Vanguard, 230
Vincent, Johnny, 175
Vinson, Eddie "Cleanhead," 244
"Violent Love," 157
VJM (*Vintage Jazz Mart*) magazine, 56, 121–23
Vocalion record label, 53, 63–64, 110, 112, 120, 124, 127, 148, 163, 179, 237, 358, 377, 393
Vogue record label, 244, 320
Vollmer, Al, 230
Von Battle, Joe, 248
Von Schmidt, Eric, 255, 293
Vreede, Max, 170, 393

Wade, Luther, Plantation, 119–20
Wade, Tee Nincy, 96
Wald, Elijah, 339, 351, 364
Wald, Jerry, 376
"Walk Right In," 38
Walker, Aaron "T-Bone," 180
Walker, Jimmy, 186
Walker, Robert "Bilbo," 223
Walking a Blues Road, 36
Walking John (trombone player), 377
"Walking the Blues," 96
"Walking the Floor over You," 339
"Walking to Jerusalem," 127
Walking to New Orleans, 171, 176
Wallace, George, 413
Wallace, Sippi, 388, 389
Waller, Fats, 243
Walnut Street Record Shop, 51
Walton, Mercy Dee, 335

Walton, Wade, 10, 123, 330
WAMU (radio station), 239
Ward, Clara, 248
Wardlow, Gayle Dean, 57, 60, 65, 260, 269, 301, 307, 309, 312, 364, 415, 418
WARL (radio station), 238
Warner Brother records label, 82
Warren, Levi, 42
Washboard Sam, 136, 326, 369
Washington, Jackie, 293
"Washington D.C. Hospital Center Blues," 232
Waterman, Dick, 79, 128, 161–62, 229, 259–60, 262, 264–66, 269, 295, 311
Watson, Doc, 82
Watson, Loren, 110
Watters, Lu, 275
Wax Trax (record store), 215
"Way Back Down Home Blues," 116
Weary, Esau, 314
Weaver, Curley, 316
Weavers, The, 293
Webb, "Boogie" Bill, 176, 309, 317
Webb, George, 273–74
"Weeping Willow Blues," 121
Weinstock, Bob, 38
Weir, George, 74
Welding, Pete, 188, 197, 200, 204–5, 214, 304, 314, 317–18, 334, 338, 403
Weldon, Casey Bill, 370
Wells, Junior, 39, 41–42, 78–80, 151, 153–58, 209–11, 217, 221
West, Stan, 364
West Dallas Street (Houston), 390
"West End Blues," 378
West Side Soul, 80, 153, 158
WGAX (radio station), 238
Wharton, Buster, 416
"What'd I Say," 168
Wheatstraw, Peetie (William Bunch), 5, 86, 112, 129, 136–38, 355, 356, 357, 363, 365, 372, 409, 414
Wheeler Auditorium, 325
Whelan, Pete, 33, 57, 88, 90, 228, 231, 234, 269, 349, 364
"When the Levee Breaks," 368
"When Your Way Gets Dark," 102
Whitance, Jack, 56
White, Booker "Bukka," 3, 66, 70, 78, 97, 114, 161, 232, 256, 258, 260, 265, 267–68, 294–95, 297–99, 368
White, Josh, 17
Whiteman, Paul, 380
White Rose Club, 186
Whitman, Walt, 419
Whittaker, Hudson. *See* Tampa Red
Wilfong, Bob, 267
Wilgus, D. K., 303
Wilhoft, John, 144
Wilkins, Joe Willie, 223
Wilkins, Robert, 55, 66, 72, 109, 115–16, 229–3, 235–36, 261–62, 264, 266, 295, 368
Wilkinson, Ed, 153
Williams, Claude, 400
Williams, George Bullet, 59, 91
Williams, Big Joe, 17, 43, 145–9, 152, 156, 182, 196, 211, 218, 258, 293, 304, 334–35, 345, 346, 347, 357
Williams, Jabo, 121
Williams, John, 13
Williams, Rev. Johnny, 184
Williams, John "Piano Red," 261–62
Williams, L. C., 338
Williams, Mayo "Ink," 117, 249–50, 358
William Morrow Publishers, 359
Williams, R.G., 395, 396, 398
Williams, Robert Pete, 258, 266, 297–98, 307–8, 343
Williams, Winehead Willie, 220
Williamson, (John Lee Curtis) Sonny Boy I, 217
Williamson, ("Rice" Miller) Sonny Boy II, 79, 162, 175, 177, 223, 290, 312, 340–43, 350, 351
Willis, Chuck, 167
Willis, Little Sonny, 248
Willis, Mott, 305, 310, 314–15
Willis, Ruth, 414
Wills, Bob, 85, 240, 379, 393,
Wilmer, Valerie, 128
Wilson, Al (Alan), 70, 73, 256–59, 265, 267, 269, 293–96, 298–300, 303–4, 307, 309
Wilson, Jackie, 81, 189
Wilson, Teddy, 394, 400, 401
Windmere Club, 145
Windy City Six, 137, 138
Wiseman, Mac, 238

Witherspoon, Jimmy, 39, 342
WLAC (radio station), 86
WNIB (radio station), 216
WNUR (radio station), 216
Wolfe, Bernard, 271
Wolf record label, 310
Wollensak tape recorder, 326
Womack, Jimmy, 402
Woman with Guitar, 371
"Woman, Woman Blues," 91, 104
Woods, Big Boy, 126
Woods, Oscar "Buddy," 19
"Work House," 278
World Pacific record label, 161
World's Fair in Chicago (1893), 238
Wrencher, Big John, 142, 186
Wright, Richard, 7, 13
Wright Aeronautical Corporation, 191
WTAM (radio station), 376
WXFM (radio station), 216
Wyatt, Bill, 122, 128
Wyler, Michael, 125
Wynn, Albert, 125

XERB (radio station), 323–24
"X" record label, 32
X Vault record label, 150

Yacht Club, 148
Yamasaki, Paul, 362
"Yancey Special," 379
Yancy, Jimmy, 138
Yaqui Indians, 29
Yazoo record label, 58, 70, 89, 267
"Yellow Dog Blues," 95
YMCA (Young Man's Christian Association), 345, 346
Yonder Come the Blues, 133
"You Are My Sunshine," 412
"You Know You Didn't Want Me," 335
Young, Ed, 353
Young, Ernie, 170
Young, Johnny (mandolinist), 39, 338
Young, Johnny (pianist), 151
Young, Lester, 377
Young, Lonnie, 353
Young, Mighty Joe, 41, 154, 209
Youngblood, Arzo, 309, 317
Youngblood, Isaac, 309
Young Brothers, 313
"Young Woman's Blues," 68

Zanzibar Lounge, 154
"Zero at the Bone," 419
Zorn, Tim, 214, 353
Zydeco, 403
"Zydeco Sont Pas Sale," 338

STEVE CUSHING has hosted *Blues Before Sunrise* for more than thirty years. He is the author of *Blues Before Sunrise: The Radio Interviews.*

BARRY LEE PEARSON is a professor of English at the University of Maryland and the author of *Jook Right On: Blues Stores and Blues Storytellers.*

Music in American Life

Only a Miner: Studies in Recorded Coal-Mining Songs *Archie Green*
Great Day Coming: Folk Music and the American Left *R. Serge Denisoff*
John Philip Sousa: A Descriptive Catalog of His Works *Paul E. Bierley*
The Hell-Bound Train: A Cowboy Songbook *Glenn Ohrlin*
Oh, Didn't He Ramble: The Life Story of Lee Collins, as Told to Mary Collins *Edited by Frank J. Gillis and John W. Miner*
American Labor Songs of the Nineteenth Century *Philip S. Foner*
Stars of Country Music: Uncle Dave Macon to Johnny Rodriguez *Edited by Bill C. Malone and Judith McCulloh*
Git Along, Little Dogies: Songs and Songmakers of the American West *John I. White*
A Texas-Mexican *Cancionero*: Folksongs of the Lower Border *Américo Paredes*
San Antonio Rose: The Life and Music of Bob Wills *Charles R. Townsend*
Early Downhome Blues: A Musical and Cultural Analysis *Jeff Todd Titon*
An Ives Celebration: Papers and Panels of the Charles Ives Centennial Festival-Conference *Edited by H. Wiley Hitchcock and Vivian Perlis*
Sinful Tunes and Spirituals: Black Folk Music to the Civil War *Dena J. Epstein*
Joe Scott, the Woodsman-Songmaker *Edward D. Ives*
Jimmie Rodgers: The Life and Times of America's Blue Yodeler *Nolan Porterfield*
Early American Music Engraving and Printing: A History of Music Publishing in America from 1787 to 1825, with Commentary on Earlier and Later Practices *Richard J. Wolfe*
Sing a Sad Song: The Life of Hank Williams *Roger M. Williams*
Long Steel Rail: The Railroad in American Folksong *Norm Cohen*
Resources of American Music History: A Directory of Source Materials from Colonial Times to World War II *D. W. Krummel, Jean Geil, Doris J. Dyen, and Deane L. Root*
Tenement Songs: The Popular Music of the Jewish Immigrants *Mark Slobin*
Ozark Folksongs *Vance Randolph; edited and abridged by Norm Cohen*
Oscar Sonneck and American Music *Edited by William Lichtenwanger*
Bluegrass Breakdown: The Making of the Old Southern Sound *Robert Cantwell*
Bluegrass: A History *Neil V. Rosenberg*
Music at the White House: A History of the American Spirit *Elise K. Kirk*
Red River Blues: The Blues Tradition in the Southeast *Bruce Bastin*
Good Friends and Bad Enemies: Robert Winslow Gordon and the Study of American Folksong *Debora Kodish*
Fiddlin' Georgia Crazy: Fiddlin' John Carson, His Real World, and the World of His Songs *Gene Wiggins*
America's Music: From the Pilgrims to the Present (rev. 3d ed.) *Gilbert Chase*
Secular Music in Colonial Annapolis: The Tuesday Club, 1745–56 *John Barry Talley*
Bibliographical Handbook of American Music *D. W. Krummel*
Goin' to Kansas City *Nathan W. Pearson Jr.*
"Susanna," "Jeanie," and "The Old Folks at Home": The Songs of Stephen C. Foster from His Time to Ours (2d ed.) *William W. Austin*
Songprints: The Musical Experience of Five Shoshone Women *Judith Vander*
"Happy in the Service of the Lord": Afro-American Gospel Quartets in Memphis *Kip Lornell*
Paul Hindemith in the United States *Luther Noss*

"My Song Is My Weapon": People's Songs, American Communism, and the Politics of Culture, 1930–50 *Robbie Lieberman*
Chosen Voices: The Story of the American Cantorate *Mark Slobin*
Theodore Thomas: America's Conductor and Builder of Orchestras, 1835–1905 *Ezra Schabas*
"The Whorehouse Bells Were Ringing" and Other Songs Cowboys Sing *Collected and Edited by Guy Logsdon*
Crazeology: The Autobiography of a Chicago Jazzman *Bud Freeman, as Told to Robert Wolf*
Discoursing Sweet Music: Brass Bands and Community Life in Turn-of-the-Century Pennsylvania *Kenneth Kreitner*
Mormonism and Music: A History *Michael Hicks*
Voices of the Jazz Age: Profiles of Eight Vintage Jazzmen *Chip Deffaa*
Pickin' on Peachtree: A History of Country Music in Atlanta, Georgia *Wayne W. Daniel*
Bitter Music: Collected Journals, Essays, Introductions, and Librettos *Harry Partch; edited by Thomas McGeary*
Ethnic Music on Records: A Discography of Ethnic Recordings Produced in the United States, 1893 to 1942 *Richard K. Spottswood*
Downhome Blues Lyrics: An Anthology from the Post–World War II Era *Jeff Todd Titon*
Ellington: The Early Years *Mark Tucker*
Chicago Soul *Robert Pruter*
That Half-Barbaric Twang: The Banjo in American Popular Culture *Karen Linn*
Hot Man: The Life of Art Hodes *Art Hodes and Chadwick Hansen*
The Erotic Muse: American Bawdy Songs (2d ed.) *Ed Cray*
Barrio Rhythm: Mexican American Music in Los Angeles *Steven Loza*
The Creation of Jazz: Music, Race, and Culture in Urban America *Burton W. Peretti*
Charles Martin Loeffler: A Life Apart in Music *Ellen Knight*
Club Date Musicians: Playing the New York Party Circuit *Bruce A. MacLeod*
Opera on the Road: Traveling Opera Troupes in the United States, 1825–60 *Katherine K. Preston*
The Stonemans: An Appalachian Family and the Music That Shaped Their Lives *Ivan M. Tribe*
Transforming Tradition: Folk Music Revivals Examined *Edited by Neil V. Rosenberg*
The Crooked Stovepipe: Athapaskan Fiddle Music and Square Dancing in Northeast Alaska and Northwest Canada *Craig Mishler*
Traveling the High Way Home: Ralph Stanley and the World of Traditional Bluegrass Music *John Wright*
Carl Ruggles: Composer, Painter, and Storyteller *Marilyn Ziffrin*
Never without a Song: The Years and Songs of Jennie Devlin, 1865–1952 *Katharine D. Newman*
The Hank Snow Story *Hank Snow, with Jack Ownbey and Bob Burris*
Milton Brown and the Founding of Western Swing *Cary Ginell, with special assistance from Roy Lee Brown*
Santiago de Murcia's "Códice Saldívar No. 4": A Treasury of Secular Guitar Music from Baroque Mexico *Craig H. Russell*
The Sound of the Dove: Singing in Appalachian Primitive Baptist Churches *Beverly Bush Patterson*
Heartland Excursions: Ethnomusicological Reflections on Schools of Music *Bruno Nettl*
Doowop: The Chicago Scene *Robert Pruter*

Blue Rhythms: Six Lives in Rhythm and Blues *Chip Deffaa*
Shoshone Ghost Dance Religion: Poetry Songs and Great Basin Context *Judith Vander*
Go Cat Go! Rockabilly Music and Its Makers *Craig Morrison*
'Twas Only an Irishman's Dream: The Image of Ireland and the Irish in American Popular Song Lyrics, 1800–1920 *William H. A. Williams*
Democracy at the Opera: Music, Theater, and Culture in New York City, 1815–60 *Karen Ahlquist*
Fred Waring and the Pennsylvanians *Virginia Waring*
Woody, Cisco, and Me: Seamen Three in the Merchant Marine *Jim Longhi*
Behind the Burnt Cork Mask: Early Blackface Minstrelsy and Antebellum American Popular Culture *William J. Mahar*
Going to Cincinnati: A History of the Blues in the Queen City *Steven C. Tracy*
Pistol Packin' Mama: Aunt Molly Jackson and the Politics of Folksong *Shelly Romalis*
Sixties Rock: Garage, Psychedelic, and Other Satisfactions *Michael Hicks*
The Late Great Johnny Ace and the Transition from R&B to Rock 'n' Roll *James M. Salem*
Tito Puente and the Making of Latin Music *Steven Loza*
Juilliard: A History *Andrea Olmstead*
Understanding Charles Seeger, Pioneer in American Musicology *Edited by Bell Yung and Helen Rees*
Mountains of Music: West Virginia Traditional Music from *Goldenseal* *Edited by John Lilly*
Alice Tully: An Intimate Portrait *Albert Fuller*
A Blues Life *Henry Townsend, as told to Bill Greensmith*
Long Steel Rail: The Railroad in American Folksong (2d ed.) *Norm Cohen*
The Golden Age of Gospel *Text by Horace Clarence Boyer; photography by Lloyd Yearwood*
Aaron Copland: The Life and Work of an Uncommon Man *Howard Pollack*
Louis Moreau Gottschalk *S. Frederick Starr*
Race, Rock, and Elvis *Michael T. Bertrand*
Theremin: Ether Music and Espionage *Albert Glinsky*
Poetry and Violence: The Ballad Tradition of Mexico's Costa Chica *John H. McDowell*
The Bill Monroe Reader *Edited by Tom Ewing*
Music in Lubavitcher Life *Ellen Koskoff*
Zarzuela: Spanish Operetta, American Stage *Janet L. Sturman*
Bluegrass Odyssey: A Documentary in Pictures and Words, 1966–86 *Carl Fleischhauer and Neil V. Rosenberg*
That Old-Time Rock & Roll: A Chronicle of an Era, 1954–63 *Richard Aquila*
Labor's Troubadour *Joe Glazer*
American Opera *Elise K. Kirk*
Don't Get above Your Raisin': Country Music and the Southern Working Class *Bill C. Malone*
John Alden Carpenter: A Chicago Composer *Howard Pollack*
Heartbeat of the People: Music and Dance of the Northern Pow-wow *Tara Browner*
My Lord, What a Morning: An Autobiography *Marian Anderson*
Marian Anderson: A Singer's Journey *Allan Keiler*
Charles Ives Remembered: An Oral History *Vivian Perlis*
Henry Cowell, Bohemian *Michael Hicks*
Rap Music and Street Consciousness *Cheryl L. Keyes*
Louis Prima *Garry Boulard*

Marian McPartland's Jazz World: All in Good Time *Marian McPartland*
Robert Johnson: Lost and Found *Barry Lee Pearson and Bill McCulloch*
Bound for America: Three British Composers *Nicholas Temperley*
Lost Sounds: Blacks and the Birth of the Recording Industry, 1890–1919 *Tim Brooks*
Burn, Baby! BURN! The Autobiography of Magnificent Montague *Magnificent Montague with Bob Baker*
Way Up North in Dixie: A Black Family's Claim to the Confederate Anthem *Howard L. Sacks and Judith Rose Sacks*
The Bluegrass Reader *Edited by Thomas Goldsmith*
Colin McPhee: Composer in Two Worlds *Carol J. Oja*
Robert Johnson, Mythmaking, and Contemporary American Culture *Patricia R. Schroeder*
Composing a World: Lou Harrison, Musical Wayfarer *Leta E. Miller and Fredric Lieberman*
Fritz Reiner, Maestro and Martinet *Kenneth Morgan*
That Toddlin' Town: Chicago's White Dance Bands and Orchestras, 1900–1950 *Charles A. Sengstock Jr.*
Dewey and Elvis: The Life and Times of a Rock 'n' Roll Deejay *Louis Cantor*
Come Hither to Go Yonder: Playing Bluegrass with Bill Monroe *Bob Black*
Chicago Blues: Portraits and Stories *David Whiteis*
The Incredible Band of John Philip Sousa *Paul E. Bierley*
"Maximum Clarity" and Other Writings on Music *Ben Johnston, edited by Bob Gilmore*
Staging Tradition: John Lair and Sarah Gertrude Knott *Michael Ann Williams*
Homegrown Music: Discovering Bluegrass *Stephanie P. Ledgin*
Tales of a Theatrical Guru *Danny Newman*
The Music of Bill Monroe *Neil V. Rosenberg and Charles K. Wolfe*
Pressing On: The Roni Stoneman Story *Roni Stoneman, as told to Ellen Wright*
Together Let Us Sweetly Live *Jonathan C. David, with photographs by Richard Holloway*
Live Fast, Love Hard: The Faron Young Story *Diane Diekman*
Air Castle of the South: WSM Radio and the Making of Music City *Craig P. Havighurst*
Traveling Home: Sacred Harp Singing and American Pluralism *Kiri Miller*
Where Did Our Love Go? The Rise and Fall of the Motown Sound *Nelson George*
Lonesome Cowgirls and Honky-Tonk Angels: The Women of Barn Dance Radio *Kristine M. McCusker*
California Polyphony: Ethnic Voices, Musical Crossroads *Mina Yang*
The Never-Ending Revival: Rounder Records and the Folk Alliance *Michael F. Scully*
Sing It Pretty: A Memoir *Bess Lomax Hawes*
Working Girl Blues: The Life and Music of Hazel Dickens *Hazel Dickens and Bill C. Malone*
Charles Ives Reconsidered *Gayle Sherwood Magee*
The Hayloft Gang: The Story of the National Barn Dance *Edited by Chad Berry*
Country Music Humorists and Comedians *Loyal Jones*
Record Makers and Breakers: Voices of the Independent Rock 'n' Roll Pioneers *John Broven*
Music of the First Nations: Tradition and Innovation in Native North America *Edited by Tara Browner*
Cafe Society: The Wrong Place for the Right People *Barney Josephson, with Terry Trilling-Josephson*
George Gershwin: An Intimate Portrait *Walter Rimler*
Life Flows On in Endless Song: Folk Songs and American History *Robert V. Wells*

I Feel a Song Coming On: The Life of Jimmy McHugh *Alyn Shipton*
King of the Queen City: The Story of King Records *Jon Hartley Fox*
Long Lost Blues: Popular Blues in America, 1850–1920 *Peter C. Muir*
Hard Luck Blues: Roots Music Photographs from the Great Depression *Rich Remsberg*
Restless Giant: The Life and Times of Jean Aberbach and Hill and Range Songs *Bar Biszick-Lockwood*
Champagne Charlie and Pretty Jemima: Variety Theater in the Nineteenth Century *Gillian M. Rodger*
Sacred Steel: Inside an African American Steel Guitar Tradition *Robert L. Stone*
Gone to the Country: The New Lost City Ramblers and the Folk Music Revival *Ray Allen*
The Makers of the Sacred Harp *David Warren Steel with Richard H. Hulan*
Woody Guthrie, American Radical *Will Kaufman*
George Szell: A Life of Music *Michael Charry*
Bean Blossom: The Brown County Jamboree and Bill Monroe's Bluegrass Festivals *Thomas A. Adler*
Crowe on the Banjo: The Music Life of J. D. Crowe *Marty Godbey*
Twentieth Century Drifter: The Life of Marty Robbins *Diane Diekman*
Henry Mancini: Reinventing Film Music *John Caps*
The Beautiful Music All Around Us: Field Recordings and the American Experience *Stephen Wade*
Then Sings My Soul: The Culture of Southern Gospel Music *Douglas Harrison*
The Accordion in the Americas: Klezmer, Polka, Tango, Zydeco, and More! *Edited by Helena Simonett*
Bluegrass Bluesman: A Memoir *Josh Graves, edited by Fred Bartenstein*
One Woman in a Hundred: Edna Phillips and the Philadelphia Orchestra *Mary Sue Welsh*
The Great Orchestrator: Arthur Judson and American Arts Management *James M. Doering*
Charles Ives in the Mirror: American Histories of an Iconic Composer *David C. Paul*
Southern Soul-Blues *David Whiteis*
Sweet Air: Modernism, Regionalism, and American Popular Song *Edward P. Comentale*
Pretty Good for a Girl: Women in Bluegrass *Murphy Hicks Henry*
Sweet Dreams: The World of Patsy Cline *Warren R. Hofstra*
William Sidney Mount and the Creolization of American Culture *Christopher J. Smith*
Bird: The Life and Music of Charlie Parker *Chuck Haddix*
Making the March King: John Philip Sousa's Washington Years, 1854–1893 *Patrick Warfield*
In It for the Long Run *Jim Rooney*
Pioneers of the Blues Revival *Steve Cushing*
Roots of the Revival: American and British Folk Music in the 1950s *Ronald D. Cohen and Rachel Clare Donaldson*
Blues All Day Long: The Jimmy Rogers Story *Wayne Everett Goins*
Yankee Twang: Country and Western Music in New England *Clifford R. Murphy*
The Music of the Stanley Brothers *Gary B. Reid*
Hawaiian Music in Motion: Mariners, Missionaries, and Minstrels *James Revell Carr*
Sounds of the New Deal: The Federal Music Project in the West *Peter Gough*
The Mormon Tabernacle Choir: A Biography *Michael Hicks*

The Man That Got Away: The Life and Songs of Harold Arlen *Walter Rimler*
A City Called Heaven: Chicago and the Birth of Gospel Music *Robert M. Marovich*
Blues Unlimited: Essential Interviews from the Original Blues Magazine
Edited by Bill Greensmith, Mike Rowe, and Mark Camarigg
Hoedowns, Reels, and Frolics: Roots and Branches of Southern Appalachian Dance
Phil Jamison
Fannie Bloomfield-Zeisler: The Life and Times of a Piano Virtuoso *Beth Abelson Macleod*
Cybersonic Arts: Adventures in American New Music *Gordon Mumma, edited with commentary by Michelle Fillion*
The Magic of Beverly Sills *Nancy Guy*
Waiting for Buddy Guy *Alan Harper*
Harry T. Burleigh: From the Spiritual to the Harlem Renaissance *Jean E. Snyder*
Music in the Age of Anxiety: American Music in the Fifties *James Wierzbicki*
Jazzing: New York City's Unseen Scene *Thomas H. Greenland*
A Cole Porter Companion *Edited by Don M. Randel, Matthew Shaftel, and Susan Forscher Weiss*
Foggy Mountain Troubadour: The Life and Music of Curly Seckler *Penny Parsons*
Blue Rhythm Fantasy: Big Band Jazz Arranging in the Swing Era *John Wriggle*
Bill Clifton: America's Bluegrass Ambassador to the World *Bill C. Malone*
Chinatown Opera Theater in North America *Nancy Yunhwa Rao*
The Elocutionists: Women, Music, and the Spoken Word *Marian Wilson Kimber*
May Irwin: Singing, Shouting, and the Shadow of Minstrelsy *Sharon Ammen*
Peggy Seeger: A Life of Music, Love, and Politics *Jean R. Freedman*
Charles Ives's *Concord*: Essays after a Sonata *Kyle Gann*
Don't Give Your Heart to a Rambler: My Life with Jimmy Martin, the King of Bluegrass
Barbara Martin Stephens
Libby Larsen: Composing an American Life *Denise Von Glahn*
George Szell's Reign: Behind the Scenes with the Cleveland Orchestra *Marcia Hansen Kraus*
Just One of the Boys: Female-to-Male Cross-Dressing on the American Variety Stage
Gillian M. Rodger
Spirituals and the Birth of a Black Entertainment Industry *Sandra Jean Graham*
Right to the Juke Joint: A Personal History of American Music *Patrick B. Mullen*
Bluegrass Generation: A Memoir *Neil V. Rosenberg*
Pioneers of the Blues Revival, Expanded Second Edition *Steve Cushing*

The University of Illinois Press
is a founding member of the
Association of American University Presses.

University of Illinois Press
1325 South Oak Street
Champaign, IL 61820-6903
www.press.uillinois.edu